EVENTS

EVENTS

A CHRONICLE OF THE TWENTIETH CENTURY

Edited by

PHILIP L. COTTRELL

Oxford • New York

OXFORD UNIVERSITY PRESS

1992

Project editor Peter Furtado
Project art editor Ayala Kingsley
Volume editor Sue Martin
Art editor Frankie Wood
Assistant editor Elaine Welsh
Picture research manager Alison
  Renney
Picture researcher Suzanne
  Williams
Indexer Ann Barrett

AN EQUINOX BOOK

Planned and produced for
Andromeda Oxford Ltd

Copyright © 1992 Andromeda
Oxford Ltd

Published in the United States by
Oxford University Press, Inc.,
200 Madison Avenue,
New York, N.Y. 10016

Oxford is a registered trademark of
Oxford University Press

Library of Congress Cataloging-in
Publication data

Events in the twentieth century /
edited by Philip L. Cottrell.
       p.   cm.
  Includes index
  ISBN 0-19-520923-0
  1. Civilization, Modern–20th
  century–Chronology I. Cottrell,
P.L.
CB425.E85   1992
909.82–dc20
91-26833 CIP

Printed in Singapore
by CS Graphics

CONTRIBUTORS

Steven Chapman
Freelance writer, Oxford, UK

Ann Furtado
Freelance writer, Oxford UK

Neil Grant
Freelance writer, Twickenham, UK

Michael March
Freelance writer, Oxford, UK

Maria Quantrill
Freelance writer, Oxford, UK

CONTENTS

PREFACE

The 20th century has proved to be a turbulent period for humankind. The tempo of change has been unprecedented, while the interactions between the different parts of the world have risen sharply. At the turn of the century it was possible for a person with general interests to maintain an awareness of current affairs by keeping abreast of the political and cultural trends largely in Europe and North America. Today it has become essential for such a person to keep an eye on events across the globe, and across a much wider range: popular culture, technology, economic and business trends, for example, figure more prominently than a hundred years ago.

The ever-increasing pace of change and breadth of items of interest can be seen in the newspapers, magazines and broadcasting through which most people keep informed. Newspapers cannot report on everything, and they tend to focus on a story for only a few weeks or months, before moving on to the next. Few magazines or broadcasting networks now maintain permanent worldwide coverage, instead relying on information fed through agencies.

The present book seeks to capture the events of the headlines from every part of a "composite worldwide" newspaper or magazine. Here we find political stories from all corners of the globe, together with natural or human disasters, firsts of every kind, in sport, human endeavor, fashion, technology and the arts, and some key dates that throw light on some of the trends that have shaped the everyday life of the 20th century. It is global in its range and though it makes judgements about what should be included and what might be omitted, it attempts to avoid commentary, by focusing on the simple questions of who did what, when.

For the person who seeks a full understanding, the skills of the historian are required to complement those of the journalist or the chronicler. Events form the basis of history, in terms of what happened and when. In themselves, however, events are not history. History is concerned with why things have occurred, with interrelations and causation, so that particular outcomes can be explained, if not always totally understood. Consequently the present volume is not a history in itself, but it provides the building blocks of history. And the linking references between some of the entries themselves, and the connections made in the index, begin to chain some of the events together and provide outline patterns to particular developments as they unfold.

Inevitably a volume such as this gives rise to questions about the selection of material, and the stance of the selector. In this case, we have sought to include the most important events, as they occurred, for future developments in the history of the world, and at the same time to give the flavor of the year, in terms of what attracted interest at the time. The selection also encompasses the ephemeral – those things that may have been all-consuming at the time, but which made little or no impact on the experience of humanity. To this extent this volume is more than a concise global newspaper of record, as it draws attention to fads and fashions which are equally of importance to the understanding of the life of our century.

Philip Cottrell   University of Leicester

INTRODUCTION

The structure of this book is simple, far simpler than the events that it contains. Within the double-page spread that covers the events of each year, material has been distributed into four general strands: Politics, Society, Culture and Science. Where possible, individual entries are listed in date order, and the relevant countries (where the event happened, nationality of the protagonists) indicated. Most entries carry a single piece of information, though many refer to two or more events, closely related in date or theme. Throughout, information has been selected for its importance in building up an overall picture of the history of the world in the 20th century, or for expressing the flavor of the year, through interesting but essentially more trivial items.

The reader may wish to trace a complex story through several events, which may or may not occur in the same year. Sometimes stories spill over from one major strand into another. In such cases, cross-references are suggested at the end of the first entry. Where the cross-reference – which is indicated by the cross-reference symbol, followed by a date, thus (› 14 Apr) – refers to a day and month, without mention of a year, the cross-reference is to a story in the same strand, and in the same year, as the original entry. Where the cross-reference is to an event listed in another strand, the reference gives the new strand, followed by the date, thus (› Society, 3 Jan 1914).

POLITICS

This strand includes all main stories relating to international relations, military events, the internal political affairs of nations, and elections. Economic affairs and events such as strikes are included here where these have a strongly political dimension: thus a general strike, called explicitly to overthrow a government, may be included in this strand, whereas a strike for higher wages or improved working conditions may be included under Society. Such distinctions can never be cut and dried.

SOCIETY

This strand embraces national and international economic events, social trends and legislation, business events and other associated stories. It also includes disasters, both human and natural, and other "newsworthy" items that go to make up the flavor or character of the year. Such items may include records (biggest, highest, first) and general technological developments that change the character of everyday life (which usually means their widespread adoption or marketing, rather than the technical breakthrough itself). Also covered are sports meetings and records, and fashion. The Society strand also includes the winners of the Nobel Prizes for Peace and Economic Sciences.

CULTURE

As well as "high" art (painting, sculpture, architecture, music and opera productions, theater, literature and dance), this strand also covers broadcasting and film, and popular music. The Culture strand also carries the name of the winner of the Nobel Prize for Literature.

SCIENCE

This strand includes important conceptual and technical advances in the pure sciences, medicine and engineering, and the achievement of technological breakthroughs in many fields. Some of the more everyday technological developments very soon filter down into daily life, whereas others remain in the domain of the specialist. The Science strand also includes the Nobel Prizewinners for Physics, Chemistry and Physiology or Medicine.

1900-1909

No new epoch began in 1900. The Western imperial powers continued their colonial expansion across the globe under the impulse of the "new imperialism" that had begun in the 1880s, driven by the rivalry between the European Great Powers. This expansion was apparently welcomed by some, as in the Cook Islands, but fiercely resisted by others. Within Europe, nationalism continued to be a force, marked in 1900 by demonstrations for home rule in Dublin and the insistence of the Finns on keeping their language; in Asia too nationalism brought about the reinstatement of Shintoism in Japan and the Boxer rebellion in China. The World Exhibition in Paris, which drew over 50 million visitors in six months, revealed a world view that was still Eurocentric, but the life of Western urban dwellers was to be increasingly affected by developments in the New World, which in 1900 saw the sale of the first hamburger and the formation of the first jazz band.

▲ Hector Guimard, architect and furniture designer, created the Art Nouveau style entrances for the Paris Metro subway system for the 1900 Paris Exhibition. As a pointer to the art of the new century, they were misleading; but as relics of the age they are unsurpassed.

● **24 Jan**: French and Italian governments arrive at an arrangement establishing their respective territorial rights in the Red Sea littoral.

● **1 Feb**: After a 10-day battle, forts erected by Mat Salleh, the rebel leader in British North Borneo, are stormed by the British troops. Mat Salleh is killed and his troops taken prisoner.

● **6 Feb**: The USA, Britain and Germany exchange ratifications of the Samoa Treaty, agreed in 1899, dividing the administration of the islands between the three powers.

● **27 Feb**: The Labour Representation Committee (representing the Independent Labour party, Trades Union Congress and various socialist organizations) is formed with J. Ramsay MacDonald as secretary, becoming the Labour party in 1906 (UK).

● **28 Feb**: Gen. Sir Redvers Buller leads the relief of Ladysmith (SA), one of three British strongholds besieged by the Boers (Kimberley was relieved on 15 Feb and Mafeking on 17–18 May). The Boer War had broken out in October 1899 as a result of disagreements between Boers and British in South Africa. After initial gains by the Boers, the British invaded the Orange Free State and the Transvaal, finally claiming victory in Sep 1900. The Boers now adopt guerrilla tactics, countered by Gen. Herbert Kitchener by confining 120,000 Boer women and children into the first concentration camps, where over 20,000 die of disease and neglect.

● **15 Mar**: The British government raises a "Khaki loan" by public subscription to pay for the Boer War.

● **16 Mar**: The Social Democratic party is founded, becoming the Socialist party in 1901 (USA).

● **18 Mar**: A Russian attempt to secure a concession at Masampho, Korea, for a naval station, is blocked by Japanese opposition.

● **30 Mar**: Two agreements are signed between Russia and Korea: Korea grants a site for a coal depot and naval hospital at Masampho Harbor, and an agreement is made to exclude Russia and any other power from gaining similar advantages elsewhere in Korea.

● **20 Apr**: Ashantis around Coomassie attack the loyal tribe of Bekwais, causing a general rising of the disaffected tribes against the British government. On 6 Jun an attempt to relieve British forces at Coomassie is frustrated by the strongly fortified position of the Ashantis. On 15 Jul the garrison of Coomassie is relieved, after much fighting, and leading rebel chiefs surrender unconditionally on 7 Sep (W Afr).

● **30 Apr**: Hawaii becomes a US Territory, after a formal transfer of the islands to the USA on 12 Aug 1898.

● **19 May**: A British protectorate is established over Savage Island and Friendly Islands (Tonga), notwithstanding protest by the king, who claims sovereignty for himself and his descendants.

● **27 May**: First use of proportional representation, in a Belgian general election.

● **28 May**: Beginning of the Boxer Rebellion in China. The Boxers, or I-ho chu'an ("Righteous and Harmonious Fists"), a patriotic society hostile to foreigners and encouraged by an antiforeign clique at the Imperial Court, attack Fengtai railroad station after foreign diplomats in Beijing demand their suppression. Foreign legations are besieged, and over 230 foreigners, many of them missionaries, are killed in Shansi during Jun and Jul, along with many Chinese Christian converts. An international force is sent to attempt to put down the rebellion.

● **27 Jul**: Kaiser Wilhelm II, in a speech at Bremerhaven (Ger), exhorts the German part of the expedition to China to be ruthless in crushing the Boxer Rebellion.(›7 Sep 1901).

● **29 Jul**: Assassination of Italian King Umberto I by an anarchist; he is succeeded by the more liberal Victor Emmanuel III (until 1946).

● **2 Sep**: A large nationalist demonstration takes place in Phoenix Park, Dublin. Resolutions are passed adopting a program of the Irish Nationalist League, demanding Home Rule and the abolition of landlordism, and calling on the Irish party to hold aloof from all English parties.

● **Sep**: Fifth congress of the socialist Second International in Paris (Fr).

● **8 Oct**: Lord Ranfurley, governor of New Zealand, formally annexes the Cook Islands, at the unanimous request of the chiefs and people.

● **5 Nov**: In view of widespread disaffection in Spain, all Carlist (extreme right wingers who resort to armed rebellion) journals are suppressed and Carlist clubs closed. The constitution is suspended throughout the country, and numerous people are arrested, including priests and bishops.

● **6 Nov**: William McKinley is elected for a second term as US president.

● **13 Nov**: Ogaden Somalis, in British East Africa, rise against the British government.

● **14 Dec**: A Franco-Italian agreement gives France a free hand in Morocco, and Italy a free hand in Libya.

● The British government assumes direct control of the Royal Niger Company's territories. Land in the Niger delta and along the lower reaches of the river is added to the Niger Coast Protectorate (renamed Southern Nigeria) and northern territories become the Protectorate of Northern Nigeria.

SOCIETY

- **4 Jan**: An earthquake in the Caucasus kills over 1,000 and destroys many cattle and much property.

- **Jan**: Russia, via the Franco–Russian Banque d'Escompte de Perse, grants a loan of 22.5 million roubles, in order that Persia can liquidate an earlier British loan (1892) and require no other loan offers for 10 years. Russia also gains concessions for construction of railway lines in north Persia. Russia thus becomes the principal creditor of the Persian government.

- **Jan**: Thousands die in an influenza epidemic in the UK.

- **Feb**: Beginning of severe strikes in Vienna and Bohemia.

- **6 Mar**: A Roman amphitheater is discovered by excavation at St André-sur-Cailly, France.

- **14 Mar**: US dollar goes formally onto the gold standard, and a gold reserve of $150,000,000 is provided for.

- **19 Mar**: Arthur Evans discovers the Minoan civilization while excavating at Knossos, Crete.

- **Mar**: In India, more than 5 million people hit by drought and crop failures seek famine relief from the British colonial government. (›Aug).

- **2 Apr**: The "Southern Cross" expedition, led by M. Borchgrevink, arrives off Bluff, New Zealand, having determined the true magnetic position of the South Pole. The party had reached the farthest southward point ever attained.

- **14 Apr**: The World Exhibition in Paris opens; it has had over 50 million visitors by the time it closes in Nov.

- **26 Apr**: A 36-hour fire destroys the city of Hull on the north shore of Ottawa River, and a large portion of Ottawa City. 15,000 are left homeless, and £3,000,000 worth of damage is recorded (Can).

- **14 May–22 Jul**: The second modern Olympic Games are held in Paris. Women are allowed to compete for the first time.

- **4 Jun**: Four die and several are injured in an accident on the electric railroad between Budapest and Auwinkel. The crush of passengers released the brakes and the car was set in motion down a steep incline and turned over.

- **12 Jun**: A new German naval law allows for a 17-year program of shipbuilding in order to make the German navy one of the largest in the world.

- **16 Jun**: The German Emperor formally opens the Kiel Canal, connecting the North Sea and the Baltic.

- **4 Jul**: The Finnish senate refuses to promulgate an imperial manifesto declaring Russian to be the official language of Finland, since only 8,000 out of 2,700,000 speak that language.

- **Jul**: Opening of the Paris Metro, begun in 1898, for which Hector Guimard designed the Art Nouveau station entrances (Fr).

- **10 Aug**: Dwight F. Davis and Holcombe Ward win the first Davis Cup tennis tournament (USA).

- **Aug**: Famine in India worsens. Heavy rains fall, causing serious floods.

- **9 Sep**: A cyclone devastates the coast of Texas and a tidal wave destroys the town of Galveston. Over 4,000 are killed and $10,000,000 worth of damage done to property.

- **11 Sep**: 150,000 coalminers strike in Pennsylvania (USA).

- **16 Oct**: Anglo-German agreement regarding the Yangtze Basin provides for the continuation of the "open door" policy toward China and eschews territorial ambitions on the part of the Great Powers.

- **26 Oct**: Belgium adopts old age pensions though these are denounced as inadequate by the socialists.

- **16 Dec**: The National Civic Federation for the arbitration of labor disputes is formed in the USA.

- Shintoism is reinstated in Japan to counter Buddhist influences.

- Statesman Giovanni Giolitti begins financial and social reforms in Italy.

- Establishment of the Hokkaido Takushoko Ginko, a bank for financing the development of the northern island of Hokkaido in order to incorporate it more fully into the Empire (Jap).

- The American Federation of Labor (AFL) is formed from 216 trade unions (USA).

- The hamburger is first put on sale in New Haven, Connecticut (USA)

- William Muldoon becomes the first professional wrestling champion (USA).

- The first motor race with international competitors takes place, from Paris to Lyon (Fr).

- The Cake Walk becomes the most fashionable dance in the USA and Europe, having originated earlier among American black slaves, using the dance as a satire on elegant white ballroom dances.

CULTURE

- **14 Jan**: Giacomo Puccini's opera *Tosca* is premiered in Rome.

- **Jun**: An exhibition of sculptures by Auguste Rodin opens in Paris.

- **9 Dec**: First performance of *Nocturnes* by Claude Debussy, written in 1899.

- **14 Dec**: The Château de Bel Oeil, near Tournai, erected in 1394, is totally destroyed by fire, including all its priceless pictures and treasures (Bel).

- Gabriele D'Annunzio: *Il Fuoco* (The Flame of Life), novel strongly influenced by the ideas of German philosopher Friedrich Nietzsche (It).

- Carl Spitteler: *Olympian Spring*, novel (1900–05) (Swi).

- French poet and essayist Charles Péguy founds *Les Cahiers de la quinzaine*.

- Arthur Schnitzler's *Reigen*, a play in the form of ten dialogs, causes a scandal because of its sensational sexual content (Aust-Hung).

- Alfred Jarry: *Ubu enchaîné*, play, a sequel to *Ubu roi*; Jarry's work foreshadows the Theater of the Absurd (Fr).

- Leo Tolstoy: *The Resurrection*, novel (Russ).

- Anton Chekov's play *Uncle Vanya* receives its premiere at the Moscow Arts Theater, founded in 1898 by Konstantin Stanislavsky and Vladimir Nemirovich-Danchenko (Russ).

- Colette: *Claudine a l'école*, novel, the first in the Claudine series (Fr).

- Joseph Conrad: *Lord Jim*, novel (UK).

- Frank Wedekind: *Der Marquis von Keith*, play (Ger).

- Paul Gauguin: *Noa Noa*, account of the artist's travels in Tahiti (Fr).

- Friedrich Nietzsche: *Ecce Homo*, philosophy text (posth.) (Ger).

- Edmund Husserl: *Logische Untersuchungen* (Logical Investigations) (Ger).

- Jean Sibelius: *Finlandia*, tone-poem (revised version; original written 1899) (Fin).

- Gustav Mahler: Fourth Symphony, with a soprano setting of the poem "Das Himmlische Leben" (1892) from the folk-poem collection *Des Knaben Wunderhorn* (Aust-Hung).

- Edward Elgar: *The Dream of Gerontius*, oratorio (UK).

- First jazz band claimed by Buddy Bolden (USA).

- Gwen John: *Self-Portrait*, painting (UK).

- Auguste Renoir: *Nude in the Sun*, painting (Fr).

- Henri Toulouse-Lautrec: *La Modiste*, painting (Fr).

- Glassmaker and designer L.C. Tiffany opens Tiffany Studios, New York (USA).

- G. Méliès: *Cinderella*, film (Fr).

SCIENCE

- **28 May**: Total eclipse of the sun is observed along a line from Mexico to Portugal, Spain and Algiers.

- **2 Jul**: First flight of the airship *Graf Zeppelin* (Ger).

- **14 Dec**: German physicist Max Planck states that energy is emitted in discrete parcels, which he calls quanta, rather than continuously, thus laying the basis for the quantum theory.

- Introduction of the Box Brownie camera by Kodak (USA).

- J.E. Keeler discovers that certain nebulae have spiral structures (USA).

- Chemist M. Gomberg develops a carbon compound that has one valence location open, the first known radical (USA).

- F.E. Dorn discovers radon, a naturally occurring radioactive gas (Ger).

- P.U. Villard first observes gamma rays (Fr).

- Independent rediscovery by H. de Vries (Neth), K.F.J. Correns (Ger) and E.T. von Seysenegg (Aust-Hung) of Gregor Mendel's previously ignored 1865 work on heredity, after searching for confirmation of their own work.

- F.G. Hopkins discovers the first essential amino acid, tryptophan (UK).

- Walter Reed identifies the yellow fever virus and proves its link with mosquito bites – the disease had held up the completion of the Panama Canal.

- Sir Patrick Manson publishes a paper confirming that malaria is spread by mosquitoes.

- Work begins on the New York subway; the first section opens on 27 Oct 1904.

- Willem Einthoven first uses the electrocardiograph clinically (Neth).

- Italian inventor and physicist Guglielmo Marconi sets up his wireless telegraph company in the UK; his American company had been formed in 1899.

- R.A. Fessenden first transmits speech by wireless (USA).

- Sigmund Freud: *The Interpretation of Dreams*, psychology text, marks the beginning of psychoanalysis (Aust-Hung).

- The first escalator is demonstrated at the Paris World Exhibition (Fr).

- Kiyoshi Shiga prepares an antiserum against bacillary dysentery.

- The first offshore oil wells, fixed to piers, are drilled along the shore of the Caspian Sea and the west coast of the USA.

- The first fully automatic telephone exchange, accommodating 10,000 lines, is installed in New Bedford, Massachusetts.

1901

The death of Queen Victoria marked the end of an era, but "Victorian values" had been on the wane for some time. Attitudes continued to change, under the impact of works such as Sigmund Freud's "Psychopathology of Everyday Life" and Havelock Ellis's "Psychology of Sex." Everyday behavior was changed by the continued growth of the production of consumer durables. In the United States the success of the Box Brownie camera brought about the formation of Eastman Kodak, while mass production of automobiles began with Oldsmobile. The power of Western technology was also reflected in more brutal ways: white farmers obtained almost a million hectares (2 million acres) of land from the American Indians, while in China the Boxer uprising was mercilessly crushed by European troops. News of such events was to become almost immediate following Marconi's application of wireless telegraphy.

▲ The violent protests by Chinese nationalists against the bullying behavior of Western traders and governments broke into violence with the Boxer rising. Members of the "Society of the Harmonious Fists" carried out a number of atrocities, which were graphically reported in the West. A military expedition by several Western powers was mounted to put the rising down.

● **1 Jan**: The Commonwealth of Australia is created. The first cabinet is led by Edmund Barton. The Labor party, under John C. Watson, strongly influences policy from the outset.

● **22 Jan**: The death of Queen Victoria ends a period marked by the expansion of the British Empire towards its greatest extent, and Britain's peak as a world power. She is succeeded by Edward VII.

● **7 Feb**: The sultan of Turkey orders thousands of troops to the Bulgarian frontier because of unrest in Macedonia. (›5 Apr)

● **8 Feb**: Russian offers to evacuate Manchuria in return for Chinese concessions in Manchuria, Mongolia and Chinese Central Asia, are opposed by China, Japan and Britain. Further Anglo-Japanese protests (6 Apr) force Russia to drop the drafted convention with China.

● **4 Mar**: Inauguration of US president William McKinley and vice-president Theodore Roosevelt. (›14 Sep)

● **6 Mar**: An assassination attempt is made on Kaiser Wilhelm of Germany, but he escapes with minor wounds.

● **17 Mar**: An anti-czarist riot occurs in St Petersburg as students attack the Kazan Cathedral and hand out anti-czarist leaflets in the streets to try to stop a mass and as a protest against the excommunication of Leo Tolstoy. It is put down by Cossack troops. Similar riots take place in Moscow, Odessa, Kiev and Karkov (Russ).

● **23 Mar**: Rebel leader Emilio Aguinaldo is captured after a revolt against American hegemony in the Philippines.

● **5 Apr**: The leading members of the Macedonian Committee, a revolutionary group of Bulgarians agitating for the freedom of Macedonia from Turkey and its establishment as a separate state, are arrested.

● **25 May**: Limited franchise in local elections is granted to women in Norway.

● **29 May**: Lord Salisbury's memorandum defending Britain's policy of isolation brings an end to discussions regarding an Anglo-German alliance.

● **Jun**: Forces of the "Mad Mullah" sect in North Somaliland, hostile to Abyssinians on the frontier and British power in the North Somaliland Protectorate, are routed by a British expedition.

● **12 Jun**: Cuba becomes a US protectorate, as a condition of American withdrawal from the island after its occupation during the Spanish–American war of 1898.

● **4 Jul**: William H. Taft (USA) is installed as first civil governor of the Philippines.

● **9 Aug**: Colombian troops invade Venezuela. On 8 Sep forces from Venezuela, Ecuador and Nicaragua are reported to have invaded Colombia.

● **9 Sep**: Austrian emperor Franz Josef restores diplomatic relations with Mexico, broken off in 1867 when the Habsburg emperor Maximilian was executed.

● **7 Sep**: End of the Boxer Rebellion, when a peace protocol is finally signed by the 12 foreign powers and China, after Russian forces drive thousands of Chinese to their deaths in the Amur River and seize southern Manchuria (4 Sep–10 Oct) and German forces carry out further punitive missions. The protocol provides for heavy penalties against China: payment valued at US$738,820,707 over 40 years, a trade tariff revision, the fortification of the foreign legations, and punishment of 96 Chinese officials.

● **14 Sep**: US president William McKinley is assassinated by a Polish anarchist, and succeeded the same day by Theodore Roosevelt.

● **25 Sep**: Britain annexes the Ashanti kingdom, to form part of the Gold Coast (W Afr).

● **18 Nov**: The Hay–Pauncefote Treaty recognizes the sole right of the USA to build the Panama Canal. On 11 Dec, the USA announces that the Nicaraguan government has agreed to lease perpetually to the USA a strip of land 10 km (6 miles) wide, including the route of the proposed canal.

● **25 Nov–4 Dec**: During a visit to St Petersburg, Prince Ito of Japan drafts a Russo-Japanese agreement on Korea, but drops negotiations on 7 Dec in order to conclude an alliance with Britain.

● **26 Nov**: The UK and Italy sign an agreement fixing the frontier between Sudan and Eritrea (N Afr).

● The Social Revolutionary party, inspired by the earlier (founded 1876) populist movement, is organized in Russia; its aim is chiefly the nationalization of land and its methods are terrorism and assassination.

SOCIETY

- **3 Feb**: Six naptha springs at Baku catch fire. It spreads later to the neighboring petroleum magazines, containing over 15 million poods of petroleum, which are completely destroyed along with the surrounding buildings. Around 30 die and around 100 are seriously injured (Russ).

- **10 Feb**: Violent demonstrations against the Jesuits in Madrid, Granada, Seville and other parts of Spain. The several days of rioting are intensified by popular dislike of the marriage of the Princess of the Asturias to the Count de Caserta, grandson of Ferdinand VII of Naples. Gen. Azcarraga and his government resign on 26 Feb.

- **25 Feb**: Serious fire breaks out in Montreal, damaging $5,000,000 worth of property.

- **Feb**: Workers strike against the tax policy of the Catalonian government (Sp). (›10 Feb)

- **10 Mar**: Excommunication of Count Leo Tolstoy by the Holy Pan-Russian synod on account of his denial of the dogmas and sacraments of the Russian church.

- **11 Mar**: Phenomena of red snow and "blood" rain are reported from Sicily and later from the Austrian Tyrol. At Rome, it is accompanied by an unusual rise in temperature.

- **25 Apr**: Several cylinders of picric acid ignite, causing a series of explosions at Griesheim Elektron Factory near Frankfurt-on-Main. Over 100 die.

- **Apr**: First mass-produced gasoline-driven car, the Oldsmobile, is introduced (USA), the first car built at a rate of over 10 per week.

- **9 Jun**: Several days of sectarian riots break out in Belfast (UK).

- **29 Jun**: Passage of the Associations Bill (Fr), which requires all religious establishments for teaching and charitable aid founded since the mid-19th century to apply for authorization for their existence from parliament (›18 Mar 1903).

- **1–2 Jul**: Around 100 die in Greater New York as a result of excessive heat, when temperatures reach 37 degrees Celsius in the shade.

- **14 Jul**: Beginning of a steelworkers' strike in the USA, which does not end until 16 Sep.

- **22 Jul**: The House of Lords decides, in the case of the Taff Vale Company versus the Amalgamated Society of Railway Servants, that a trade union can be sued in its registered name as a corporate body, therefore confirming trade unions status as legal bodies but allowing them to be sued for strike damages. This is one factor leading to the formation of the Labour party in 1906 (UK).

- **21 Aug**: Foundation of the Cadillac automobile company in Detroit (USA).

- **Aug**: 800,000 ha (2,000,000 acres) of land in Oklahoma is bought from Red Indian tribes by white settlers (USA).

- **Sep**: The Congress of the International Association for the legal protection of workers agrees on a package of workers' legislation for all countries.

- **1 Oct**: Conference of officers of the Friendly Societies passes a unanimous resolution to approach the government with a scheme for state pensions (UK).

- **16 Oct**: President Roosevelt angers his opponents in the South when he invites black educationist and reformer Booker T. Washington to dinner at the White House. On 28 Oct race riots, sparked off by the meeting, leave 34 dead (USA)

- **18 Oct**: Sir William Henry Wills creates the Imperial Tobacco Company (UK).

- **24 Oct**: Incorporation of Eastman Kodak Company (USA), following the success of the Box Brownie camera.

- **Oct**: The Belgian parliament establishes a fund for the unemployed.

- **2 Dec**: The US Supreme Court decides that Puerto Ricans are not US citizens (under the terms of the peace treaty between the USA and Spain), and therefore are not entitled to the rights and privileges guaranteed to citizens of the states of the union by the US constitution.

- **Dec**: Demonstrations and riots by unemployed workers take place in Budapest (Aust-Hung).

- Foundation of the International Trade Union in Amsterdam.

- J.P. Morgan merges the Carnegie Steel Corporation and the Federal Steel Corporation to form the US Steel Corporation, the first billion-dollar corporation (USA). Arrangements are concluded on 7 Mar.

- William K. D'Arcy (NZ) secures a 60-year concession to exploit oil in Persia, in return for £20,000 and the same value in paid-up shares, as well as 16 percent of annual profits; no oil is discovered until 1908, at Masjid Sulaiman.

- The Banco Hispano Americano and Banco de Vizcaya are established (Sp).

- The Federal Immigration Restriction Act prohibits the permanent residence of non-whites in Australia because of the cheapness of their labor.

- Nobel Peace Prize won by Henri Dunant (Swiss) and Frédéric Passy (Fr).

CULTURE

- **27 Jan**: Death of Italian opera composer Giuseppe Verdi, born in 1813.

- **31 Mar**: Antonin Dvorak's opera *Rusalka* is premiered in Prague (Aust-Hung).

- **16 Jul**: A first folio edition of Shakespeare's plays is sold at Christie's auction rooms for £1,720.

- **9 Sep**: Death of French painter Henri de Toulouse-Lautrec at the age of 36.

- **26 Dec**: First performance of August Strindberg's play *The Dance of Death* (Swe).

- Poet Rabindranath Tagore founds his school at Santiniketan (Ind).

- The first Nobel Prize for Literature (Swe) is awarded to French poet René-François-Armand Sully-Prudhomme.

- Miles Franklin (pen-name of Stella Maria Sarah Miles Franklin) publishes her first novel, *My Brilliant Career*, at only 16 (Aus).

- Anton Chekhov: *Three Sisters*, play (Russ).

- Stefan Zweig: *Silberne Saiten*, poems (Aust-Hung).

- Frank Wedekind: *König Nicolò, oder So ist das Leben* (King Nicolò, or Such is Life), play (Ger).

- Samuel Butler: *Erewhon Revisited*, novel (USA).

- Rudyard Kipling: *Kim*, novel (UK).

- Friedrich Nietzsche: *Nietzsche contra Wagner*, philosophy text (posth.) (Ger).

- Thomas Mann: *Buddenbrooks*, novel (Ger).

- Akiko Yosano: *Tangled Hair*, poems (Jap).

- Sergei Rachmaninoff: Second Piano Concerto (Russ).

- Edward Elgar: Cockaigne Overture (UK).

- Maurice Ravel: *Jeux d'eau*, for orchestra (Fr).

- Bruno Walter becomes associate conductor to Gustav Mahler at the Vienna State Opera (Aust-Hung).

- Edvard Munch: *Girls on a Bridge*, painting (Nor).

- Beginning of Pablo Picasso's Blue Period (Fr).

- Paul Gauguin: *The Gold in Their Bodies*, painting (Tah).

- Societé des Artistes Décorateurs founded (Fr).

- Charles Rennie Mackintosh: Hill House, Helensburgh (1899–1901) (UK).

- Victor Horta: A L'Innovation department store, Brussels (Bel).

- J.M. Olbrich: Ernst Ludwig House, Darmstadt (Ger).

- Henry van de Velde is made head of the Weimar art schools (Ger).

- Georges Méliès: *The Indiarubber Head*, film (Fr).

SCIENCE

- **4 Apr**: Launch of the *Celtic* at Belfast, the largest ship in the world, 213 m (700 ft) long and 23 m (75 ft) wide.

- **22–28 July**: The International Tuberculosis Congress urges that "indiscriminate spitting should be suppressed".

- **2 Oct**: The British navy commissions its first submarine.

- **11 Dec**: The first transatlantic wireless telegraphy messages (radio telegrams) are transmitted by Marconi.

- **26 Dec**: First railroad reaches Lake Victoria from Mombasa and opens up the Ugandan interior (E Afr).

- **Dec**: The first Nobel Prizes for science are awarded to W.K. Roentgen (Physics, for his discovery of X-rays), J.H. van't Hoff (Chemistry) and E.A. von Behring (Physiology or Medicine), following Alfred Nobel's endowment of 1896 (Swe).

- Shellac 25 cm (10 in) diameter gramophone records with a spiral groove are introduced in the UK by the Gramophone and Typewriter Co Ltd.

- E. Rutherford and F. Soddy discover that thorium, left to itself, changes into another form, later discovered to be radium (UK).

- Discovery in Africa of the okapi, the last large land mammal to become known to science.

- Adrenalin extracted from animals by J. Takamine (Jap) is manufactured by Parke, Davis & Co (USA).

- Peter Cooper-Hewitt first produces the mercury vapor lamp, invented by Arons in 1892.

- P.V. de Camp attempts to prove that nearby stars have planetary systems (Neth).

- M.R. Hutchinson patents the first electric hearing aid (USA).

- E. Metchnikoff demonstrates how white blood cells fight disease (Russ).

- Publication of Max Planck's *Laws of Radiation* (Ger).

- K.C. Gillette announces that the safety razor will be on sale in December 1902 (USA).

- Wilhelm Maybach, technical director at the Daimler Works, constructs the first Mercedes car (named after his daughter) (Ger).

- Sigmund Freud: *The Psychopathology of Everyday Life*, psychology text, introduces the concept of the "Freudian slip" (Aust-Hung).

- Havelock Ellis: *The Psychology of Sex*, vol 1 (completed 1910) (UK).

- Hubert Booth invents the first practical vacuum cleaner (UK).

- Acetylene gas lamps replace candles and oil lamps on cars. These early models generate gas by dripping water on lumps of carbide.

1902

A record speed of 120km/h (74.5mph) put the motor car almost on a par with the average express train, while various early attempts at powered flight pointed the way to the achievement of a centuries-old dream. In reality, the further application of science was beginning to turn the urban commuter into a kind of troglodyte, as subway systems were opened in Berlin and London. Newsstands at subway stations carried placards that headlined the continuing divisions within Europe arising from the renewal of the Triple Alliance between Germany, Austria-Hungary and Italy and from the end of Britain's policy of "splendid isolation" after the signing of the Anglo-Japanese Treaty. European countries continued to jostle for influence abroad: the French government's plans to subsidize a railroad from Djibouti to Addis Ababa gave rise to protests from Italy and Britain, while Russia and Britain vied for influence in Persia. On the other hand, Britain, Germany and Italy acted in concert on behalf of their bondholders to force Venezuela to honor its debts.

▲ *A Voyage to the Moon* was one of the earliest exercises in harnessing the technology of the moving picture to the imagination. The film used elaborate moving sets and explored all kinds of illusions and visual tricks.

- **4 Jan**: Protests take place in Malta at new taxes and the substitution of English in place of Italian as the official language.
- **30 Jan**: The Anglo-Japanese Treaty is signed, safeguarding British and Japanese interests in China and Korea, and cementing a political alliance between the two countries in the event of war. The treaty, announced on 12 Feb, ends Britain's policy of "splendid isolation".
- **1 Feb**: Nearly 2,000 further troops leave the UK for South Africa.
- **8 Apr**: A Russo-Chinese accord provides for the Russian evacuation of Manchuria within 18 months.
- **10 May**: The German Kaiser grants some degree of self-government to Alsace-Lorraine.
- **30 May**: King Alfonso XIII suspends the Cortes amid growing labor unrest. Martial law is declared on 31 May.
- **31 May**: The Treaty of Vereeniging ends the South African (Anglo-Boer) War. The Boers accept British sovereignty, although representative institutions for the Boers are promised, as well as a grant of £3,000,000 to aid reconstruction of the destroyed Boer farms.
- **28 Jun**: The Triple Alliance (between Germany, Austria–Hungary and Italy) is renewed for 12 years from May 1903, though it may be canceled after six years.
- **12 Jul**: A.J. Balfour becomes British prime minister after the resignation of Lord Salisbury the previous day.
- **Jul**: In Australia, the Immigration Restriction Act makes possible exclusion of Orientals and even Europeans by means of a language test, to keep down the influx of settlers. Female suffrage is established for all federal elections.
- **14 Sep**: 20,000 demonstrate in Phoenix Park, Dublin, against the British government's strict measures to keep law and order.
- **22 Sep**: Finnish autonomy is abolished by Czar Nicholas II, and a Russian governor-general is appointed; Russian had been imposed as the official language in June.
- **1 Nov**: Signing of the Italo-French entente marks a low point in relations between the Triple Alliance powers. Italy will remain neutral if France is attacked by a third power.
- **1 Dec**: Austria and Russia agree to joint supervision of reforms in Macedonia.
- **9 Dec**: Britain and Germany seize the Venezuelan fleet (four ships) – the first open step resulting from the agreement between them to enforce their claims on Venezuela. Later in Dec, Britain, Germany and Italy blockade five Venezuelan ports to force the country to honor its debts; on 19 Dec the Venezuelan dictator Cipriano Castro agrees to submit European claims to the arbitration of the USA, and the blockade is lifted in Feb 1903.

- **16 Jan**: Germany obtains a license from Turkey to build a railroad from Konia to Baghdad (Mesopotamia).
- **17 Jan**: An earthquake in Mexico City kills 300.
- **20 Jan**: A spinning mill in Belfast collapses while in full operation: 12 women and girls are killed, and 20–30 injured (UK).
- **Jan**: Inaugural Rose Bowl game between leading college teams in American football (USA).
- **Jan**: Establishment of the first Labor Office (USA).
- **Jan–Feb**: Strikes of Mediterranean Railroad employees demanding recognition of their union, with the threat of a general strike; a settlement is reached in Jun (It).
- **1 Feb**: Economic, educational and military reforms begin in China with the return of the dowager empress and emperor to Beijing after the Boxer Rebellion; a revision of the legal code begins. Binding of women's feet and the ban on mixed Chinese-Manchu marriages are ended.
- **5 Feb**: The miners' working day is fixed at 9 hours. On 1 Apr the working day for women and children is cut from 11 to 10½ hours, but pay reduced accordingly (Fr).
- **6 Feb**: The French government agrees to subsidize the construction of the Djibouti to Addis Ababa railroad (built 1897–1918), provoking demands from Britain and Italy that the line be internationalized (Eth).
- **14 Feb**: Martial law is declared in Trieste as strikes for reduced working hours lead to clashes.
- **20 Feb**: A strike in Barcelona, beginning on 17 Feb, results in the death of 500 strikers. A state of siege is declared, and all business suspended. 80,000 are said to be involved (Sp).
- **Feb**: Strike of around 30,000 students in Russia after government measures directed against student organizations.
- **13 Mar**: Schools are shut in Poland as pupils refuse to sing the Russian imperial anthem.
- **26 Mar**: Death of Cecil Rhodes, British adventurer and founder of Rhodesia, at his home near Cape Town.
- **Mar**: Agreement is reached between the UK and Persia regarding the construction of a telegraph line between Europe and India.
- **7 Apr**: Texas Oil Company (Texaco) founded (USA).
- **9 Apr**: Incorporation of the Underground Electric Railway Company (UK).
- **13 Apr**: M. Serpollet sets a new automobile speed record of 120kph (74.5 mph) at Nice (Fr).
- **8 May**: The town of St Pierre in Martinique is destroyed with virtually all its inhabitants by a volcanic eruption of Mt Pelée (Fr W Ind).

CULTURE   SCIENCE

- **12 May–13 Oct**: Strike of anthracite coal miners demanding a 9-hour day, a wage increase and union recognition; they achieve the first two demands, but do not receive union recognition until 1916 (USA).

- **19 May**: A hurricane washes away 65 km (40 miles) of the Sind Railroad (Ind).

- **May**: International Congress of Miners demands nationalization of all mines.

- **29 Jun**: First Paris to Vienna automobile race is won by French car-maker Louis Renault.

- **25 Aug**: Harry de Windt successfully completes his 248-day trek from Paris to New York via Siberia.

- **3 Sep**: Violent disturbances at Agram, capital of Croatia, between Croatian and Serbian populations, result in many killed and wounded, and much damage done to property. Martial law is proclaimed.

- **5 Sep**: An Anglo-Chinese commercial treaty provides for a revision of the treaty system and internal reform in China, although it proves largely ineffective.

- **6 Oct**: Completion of the railroad between Bulawayo and Salisbury (Rhod).

- **Oct**: Strike of two-thirds of French miners.

- **13 Dec**: Persia, under pressure from Russia, introduces a tariff favorable to Russian goods but unfavorable to British goods. Russia also loans 10 million roubles to Persia, thus further increasing her influence there.

- **14 Dec**: Germany enforces a protectionist tariff, restoring higher duty on imported agricultural products.

- **18 Dec**: The Education Act places elementary and secondary education under local education authority control, with the result that the number of secondary schools doubles within five years (UK).

- Establishment of the Banco Español de Credito (Sp).

- Establishment of the Industry Bank (Jap).

- National Reclamation Act encourages family farms (USA).

- US president Theodore Roosevelt begins anti-trust legislation against corporations.

- Pepsi-Cola Company founded (USA).

- Federal tariff established in Australia, placing the country on the protectionist system.

- The rubber-cored golfball is invented (USA).

- The Nobel Peace Prize is won by Elie Ducommun (Swi) and Albert Gobat (Swi).

- **1 May**: *A Voyage to the Moon*, first science fiction film, released by Georges Méliès (Fr).

- Hugo von Hofmannsthal: *Ein Brief* (the "Lord Chandos letter"), essay (Ger).

- W.B. Yeats: First performance of *Cathleen na Houlihan* in Dublin (UK).

- Joseph Conrad: *The Heart of Darkness*, novel (UK).

- Arnold Bennett: *Anna of the Five Towns*, novel (UK).

- August Strindberg: *A Dream Play* (Swe).

- Arthur Conan Doyle: *The Hound of the Baskervilles*, Sherlock Holmes detective novel (UK).

- André Gide: *L'Immoraliste*, novel (Fr).

- Beatrix Potter: *The Tale of Peter Rabbit*, children's story (UK).

- Rudyard Kipling: *Just So Stories*, animal stories for children.

- Nobel prize for literature is won by Theodor Mommsen (Ger) for his historical writing, with special reference to his work *The History of Rome*.

- Harvard professor William James publishes his *Varieties of Religious Experience*, an attempt to reconcile science and religion (USA).

- Tenor Enrico Caruso makes his first recordings, singing into a wax disc recorder in a Milan hotel room. His recording of "Vesti la giubba" from *I Pagliacci* sells over a million copies (It).

- Carl Nielsen: Second Symphony (Den).

- Charles Ives: *The Celestial City*, cantata (USA).

- Jean Sibelius: Second Symphony (Fin).

- Claude Debussy: *Pelléas et Mélisande*, opera based on the story by Belgian Maurice Maeterlinck (Fr).

- Edward Elgar: *Coronation Ode*, choral work; (UK).

- F.T. Marinetti: *La Conquête des étioles*, painting (It).

- Claude Monet: *Waterloo Bridge*, painting (Fr).

- Norwegian artist Eduard Munch exhibits 22 paintings in his "Frieze of Life" series, including *The Kiss* and *The Scream*, in Berlin.

- Gustav Klimt: *Beethoven-frieze*, murals (Aust-Hung).

- Max Klinger: Bust of Friedrich Nietzsche (Ger) .

- Auguste Perret, architect: Apartments at 25 bis, Rue Franklin, Paris (Fr).

- Sir Giles Gilbert Scott designs Liverpool Cathedral.

- Turin International Exhibition (It).

- **15 Feb**: Berlin underground railroad opens (Ger).

- **22 Feb**: The Yellow Fever Commission announces its discovery that yellow fever is carried by mosquitoes (USA).

- **10 Apr**: A scheme for research into the origin and treatment of cancer is adopted by the Royal College of Physicians. A fund of £100,000 is to be raised, for equipping and maintaining laboratories devoted to cancer research (UK).

- **14 Aug**: G. Weisskopf attempts the first powered flight (Ger).

- **21 Aug**: Launch of *Cedric*, the largest vessel in the world, from Belfast. It has nine decks, and will take around 3,000 passengers with around 350 crew (UK).

- **10 Dec**: Completion of the first Aswan Dam after four years of construction (Egy).

- **17 Dec**: The first Cadillac automobile made in Detroit and sold in Buffalo, New York State.

- F.A. Krupp takes over the Germania shipbuilding yard at Kiel, and a great armaments business develops.

- R.A. Fessenden joins with two financiers to establish the National Electric Signalling Company to manufacture his inventions (USA).

- W. Bayliss and E. Starling discover the hormone secretin, initiating the science of endocrinology (UK).

- First use of the electric hearing aid, by Queen Alexandra at her coronation (UK).

- Disk brakes are first fitted to an automobile by F. Lanchester (UK).

- W. Pope develops optically active compounds based on sulfur, selenium and tin (UK).

- W. Normann patents a process for hardening liquid fats by means of hydrogenation, making available large supplies of solid fats for food and soap.

- H.W. Cushing begins a study of the pituitary body, the part of the brain central to the endocrine system (USA).

- E. Rutherford and F. Soddy announce their theory that radioactivity occurs when atoms disintegrate, releasing particles or energy in the form of radiation (UK).

- O. Heaviside (UK) and A.E. Kennelly (USA) discover the existence of an ionized atmospheric layer conducive to radio transmission, later known as the ionosphere or Heaviside layer.

- P. Lenard conducts his experiments into the properties of cathode rays (Ger).

- Herman Frasch develops a technique for extracting sulfur from deep deposits by pumping superheated steam and compressed air into the sulfur deposit (Ger).

- Sew-on press studs are invented (Fr).

- US vessels *Virginia* and *Connecticut* are the first ships to install radio telephones.

- First trans-Pacific cable laid, between Canada and New Zealand and Australia, halving the cost of a cablegram between the two continents.

- Belgian firm Dechamps offers the first automobile with an electric starter system fitted as standard.

- Louis Renault introduces the drum brake, soon to be developed for the majority of the world's vehicles (Fr).

- Wilhelm Ostwald patents the process for the conversion of ammonia into nitric acid.It will make possible the manufacture of the high explosive TNT (Ger).

- Carl von Linde discovers a way of "liquefying" air to produce pure oxygen and nitrogen, which become essential in many industrial processes.

- Swedish opthalmologist Allvar Gullstrand invents the slit lamp for use by eye doctors.

- Parisian physiologist Charles Richet describes anaphylaxis, an allergic reaction so acute as to cause collapse, disablement or even death.

- Nobel Prize for Chemistry is won by Emil Fischer in recognition of his special services in connection with his synthetic experiments in the sugar and purine groups of substances (Ger).

- Nobel Prize for Physics is won by Hendrick Lorentz (Neth) and Pieter Zeeman (Neth) for their research into the influence of magnetism upon radiation phenomena.

- Nobel Prize for Physiology or Medicine is won by Ronald Ross (UK) for his work on malaria.

If the 20th century began in any one year, an argument can be made for 1903, which saw the formation of the Bolshevik party led by V.I. Lenin, the design of the first teddy bear by Richard Steiff, and the first powered aircraft flight by the Wright brothers. Soon the sedative Phenobarbitone was discovered, the viscose method of producing artificial silk was developed, the first fully automated bottle-production plant went into production and the USA and Colombia signed the treaty that would permit the construction of the Panama Canal. However, in 1903 more attention was being paid to the progress of Scott's polar expedition and Maurice Garin's win in the first Tour de France cycle race. Newspapers – now being printed by electric-powered machines – featured such events alongside more disturbing news such as the reports of massacres of Jews in Russia, the murder of Alexander I and Queen Draga of Serbia and the introduction of severe immigration restrictions by the United States, which was a major cause for concern for many, especially in southern Europe.

▲ The future of powered flight was undreamt of in the early years of the century, except by a few men. In 1900 American air pioneers Wilbur and Orville Wright built their first glider, and over the next two years they tested over 200 models in a home-made wind tunnel, before making a new model onto which they eventually mounted two engines driving propellers. On 17 December 1903 they made four flights, the longest lasting 59 seconds.

● **1 Jan**: Edward VII (UK) is proclaimed king-emperor of India in a ceremony in Delhi.

● **22 Jan**: The USA and Colombia sign a treaty that will allow construction of the Panama Canal. On 18 Nov, USA and Panama sign a treaty to build the canal. (›3 Nov)

● **13 Feb**: Protocols of the agreements between the allies and Venezuela are signed in Washington. Orders are given on the following day for the raising of the blockade of Venezuelan ports.

● **23 Feb**: The sultan of Turkey accepts an Austro-Russian reform program for Macedonia, reorganizing the police and financial system, after its insurrection against Turkish rule in 1902. (›8 Sep)

● **Feb**: After the visit to South Africa of Joseph Chamberlain, Secretary for the Colonies, the British government accepts that a policy of British supremacy is unworkable and that Anglo-Dutch equality within the country would be a more sensible approach.

● **12 Mar**: The czar issues a manifesto concerning important reforms, including freedom of religion (Russ). (›16 Apr)

● **26 Mar**: A dictatorship is established in Finland under General Bobrikov (assassinated 23 Jun 1904).

● **16 Apr**: Massacre of Jews by peasants in Kishiniev, Bessarabia. Under Czar Nicholas II there has been persistent persecution of the Jews, believed to be responsible for organizing revolutionary terrorism (Russ).

● **Apr**: Crisis over the proposed German Baghdad Railroad from Konia to Basra which was to have been financed by France and Britain until the financiers of the project were scared off by a press campaign against it (Per).

● **10 Jun**: Alexander I and Queen Draga of Serbia are murdered by conspirators in the military, and Peter Karageorgevich is elected to the throne on 15 Jun as Peter I (until 1921).

● **12 Aug**: The Colombian senate refuses to ratify treaty with the USA on a canal through Panama.

● **12 Aug**: The Japanese send a memorandum to Russia after the failure of the latter to evacuate Manchuria. (›8 Feb 1904)

● **13 Aug**: Russia creates a special "Viceroy of the Far East" to keep order in Manchuria, and control the troops there. Having refused to evacuate the area under the terms of the Russo-Japanese Convention, due to have begun in April, Russia has now effectively annexed Manchuria.

● **8 Sep**: A report is received that Turkish troops have massacred thousands in Bulgaria. On 14 Sep the Bulgarian government asks the great powers to intervene in Macedonia, and on 25 Sep Britain says it will back Austro-Russian plans for settlement.

● **16 Sep**: Emperor Franz Josef declares his intention of maintaining a common and unified Austro–Hungarian army, despite Magyar demands for language and other concessions within the army; this raises a storm of protest in Hungary. (›Jul 1906).

● **14 Oct**: Britain and France sign an arbitration agreement, to refer judicial or treaty questions to the Hague Tribunal. On 25 Dec, France and Italy sign a similar agreement.

● **20 Oct**: USA/Canadian border dispute in Alaska is settled in favor of the USA.

● **2 Nov**: USA orders three warships to the Panama isthmus.

● **3 Nov**: Revolution in Panama. It proclaims its independence from Colombia, supported by the USA.

● **6 Nov**: USA recognizes the Republic of Panama after its declaration of independence from Colombia.

● **17 Nov**: Russian Social Democratic party splits at its London party congress into Mensheviks ("minority party", moderates, led by G. Plekhanov) and Bolsheviks ("majority party", extremists, led by V.I. Lenin).

● Founding of the Union of Liberation, consisting mostly of liberals, intellectuals and *zemstvo* (local council) workers, seeking a liberal constitution in Russia.

● Completion of the British conquest of northern Nigeria (since 1900), taking Kano on 3 Feb and Sokoto on 15 Mar. The protectorate does not come under a unified administration till Jan 1914.

● Wyndham's Act is passed, whereby Irish landlords are to be bought out, peasants to own their land, and repayment to be made over 68 ½ years. (›Society, 3 Jan)

● The Dutch Democratic Labor party is formed.

● Lord Curzon's tour of Persia reestablishes British supremacy there after approaches by Russia to build a railroad across the country to the Persian Gulf.

● **3 Jan**: Report of the Irish Land Conference suggests revision of rental payments as a means of dealing with the twin problems of land ownership and high farm rents (UK).

● **13 Jan**: A tidal wave in Polynesia kills thousands.

● **9 Feb**: Trade agreement between the UK and Persia.

● **14 Feb**: US Congress creates a Department of Commerce and Labor with its secretary in the cabinet.

● **Feb**: Anti-trust law in the USA is reinforced.

● **3 Mar**: Anti-immigration law is passed by US Congress to reduce immigration and keep out those considered "undesirable". This marks a shift in US immigration policy, which previously welcomed all comers. By 1900, the USA had already received over 35,000,000 immigrants.

● **18 Mar**: The French government refuses all applications to teach from religious orders, as part of its campaign to limit religious influence on education.

● **28 Mar**: News is received of the Antarctic Expedition under Captain Scott, who had reached the farthest southward point ever attained.

● **Mar**: Legislation for the regulation of children's labor is enforced in Germany.

● **13 Apr**: The National Strike Committee in the Netherlands, consisting of 40 unions, decides to abandon the week-long general strike, because of the government's use of the military. On 9 Apr, the government had passed a bill punishing civil service and rail strikes with imprisonment, thus prompting the strike.

● **21 May**: Joseph Chamberlain's campaign for an imperial tariff association results in the foundation of the Tariff League, promoting preferential trading within the Empire (UK).

● **28 May**: An earthquake in Constantinople kills 2,000.

● **16 Jun**: Foundation of Ford Motor Company by Henry Ford (USA).

● **19 Jul**: First Tour de France cycling race is won by Maurice Garin.

● **Jul**: An international monetary conference in Berlin demands a constant parity between countries of the gold and silver blocs.

● **10 Aug**: Fire in the Paris Metro kills 84 and injures many others.

● **11 Aug**: At least £1,000,000 worth of damage is caused when Jamaica is hit by a cyclone.

● **19 Aug**: At the Sixth Zionist Conference in Basel (Swi) Britain makes an offer of a Jewish homeland in Uganda, but delegates clash over the proposals.

● **10 Oct**: Emmeline Pankhurst founds the Women's Social and Political Union, a militant organization committed to achieving women's suffrage (UK).

● **13 Oct**: First World Series in baseball, won by the Boston Red Sox (USA).

● **21 Nov**: Launch of White Star SS *Baltic*, the largest vessel in the world.

● **29 Nov**: Clashes occur in Paris between gendarmes and working men demonstrating against the "exploitation" alleged to be practiced by labor agents.

● **Nov**: Strike of Spanish miners, demanding that their wages be paid weekly.

● **Nov**: Canada decides on a further increase of taxes on German imports.

● **30 Dec**: In a theater in Chicago, around 600, mostly women and children, die when fire breaks out on the stage.

● **Dec**: 50,000 Chinese coolies are imported into Transvaal (SA) after pressure from mining interests; the coolies prove so disorderly that they are eventually repatriated (1907).

● **Dec**: New trade agreement between Italy and Austria.

● Foundation of the Telefunken wireless telegraphy company (Ger).

● Beginning of legislation limiting the hours of labor of children; the 48-hour week for children in factories is finally established in 37 states by 1930 (USA).

● The Tata iron and steel empire founded in India; in 1907 it is incorporated and later becomes one of the world's largest steelworks.

● The Bankers Trust Company is established in New York.

● J.P. Morgan founds the International Mercantile and Marine Company, a shipping trust, in New York.

● A motor race from Paris to Madrid, starting on 23 May, and involving 250 entries, has to be stopped after several fatal accidents.

● Nobel Peace Prize is won by William Cremer (UK).

● "Typhoid Mary" (Mary Mallon) is discovered to be the carrier of the disease during an epidemic in New York. She was immune to the typhoid bacillus herself, and worked as a cook, fleeing from the authorities when she was discovered. This was the first of several outbreaks attributable to her.

● New Zealand provides for preferential treatment of British goods, and similar measures are passed in Australia.

● **Feb**: British newspaper *The Globe* announces that, for the first time, it is printed entirely by electricity.

● **21 Sep**: The first "Western" movie, *Kit Carson*, opens in the USA.

● August Strindberg: *Queen Christina*, play (Swe).

● Samuel Butler: *The Way of All Flesh*, a semi-autobiographical novel of middle-class life (posth.) (USA).

● Thomas Mann: *Tonio Kroger*, novel (Ger).

● George Bernard Shaw: *Man and Superman*, play (UK).

● Henry James: *The Ambassadors*, novel (USA).

● Guillaume Apollinaire: *Les Mamelles de Tiresias* (The Breasts of Tiresias), play (Fr).

● The Nobel Prize for Literature is won by Bjørnsterne Bjornson (Nor).

● Otto Weininger: *Sex and Character*, psycho-philosophical text; the author commits suicide aged 23 (Aust-Hung).

● G.E. Moore's *Principia Ethica* introduces a new era in British moral philosophy.

● First complete opera recording made, of Giuseppe Verdi's *Ernani*.

● Construction begins on Oscar Hammerstein's Manhattan Opera House, New York.

● Richard Strauss: *Elektra*, opera, with libretto by Hugo von Hofmannsthal (Ger).

● Arnold Schoenberg begins teaching composition in Vienna: among his pupils are Anton Webern and Alban Berg (Aust-Hung).

● Beginning of Gustav Mahler's collaboration with stage designer Alfred Roller at the Vienna State Opera (Aust-Hung).

● Foundation of the Salon d'Automne, an annual exhibition of painting (Fr).

● H.P. Berlage (architect): Exchange, Amsterdam (Neth).

● Founding of Letchworth, the first garden city in the UK, brainchild of Ebenezer Howard.

● The Wiener Werkstatte is founded as a craft cooperative (Aust-Hung).

● Alfred Stieglitz founds the periodical *Camera Work* (USA).

● Richard Steiff designs the first teddy bears (named after US president Theodore Roosevelt).

● **Mar**: A regular news service is started by radio between London and New York.

● **17 Dec**: The first heavier-than-air powered flight by the Wright brothers at Kitty Hawk, North Carolina, lasts 59 seconds (USA).

● Phenobarbitone, a long-acting sedative, is discovered.

● Edmond Fouché invents the oxyacetylene burner, capable of producing a flame of very high temperature (Fr).

● Williamsburg Bridge in New York opens, the first major suspension bridge to use steel rather than masonry towers.

● German surgeon Georg Perthes initiates radiation therapy for cancer when he finds that X-rays inhibit the growth of malignant tumors.

● Willem Einthoven invents the swing galvanometer, forerunner of the electrocardiograph (Neth).

● The first fully automatic bottle-making machine begins production, invented by M.J. Owens (USA).

● Newcastle upon Tyne Electric Supply Company installs the world's first alternator to have a rotating field magnet, a generator which produces alternating current, which is subsequently installed in power stations all over the world.

● Marie and Pierre Curie share the Nobel Prize for Physics with A-H. Becquerel, Becquerel for his discovery of natural radiation and the Curies for their later work on radioactivity.

● Nobel Prize for Physiology or Medicine is won by Danish physician Niels Ryberg Finsen for his success in killing the bacterium involved in the skin disease *lupus vulgaris*, brought on by the TB bacillus, by using ultra-violet light.

● W.H. Stearn and F. Topham develop the viscose method for producing artificial silk.

● W.S. Sutton and others argue that hereditary factors can be explained by the behaviour of the chromosomes (USA).

● R.A. Zsigmondy invents the ultramicroscope (Neth).

● W. Siemens develops an electric locomotive (Ger).

● E. Rutherford demonstrates that alpha particles are positively charged (UK).

● First three-color photography is developed by the Lumière brothers (Fr).

● First Harley-Davidson motorcycle is built (USA).

● Nobel Prize for Chemistry is won by Svante Arrhenius for his electrolytic theory of dissociation (Swe).

1904

Concepts of the superiority of Westerner or
"white" received a severe jolt as a result of the
successful Japanese attack on the Russian naval
base at Port Arthur. Russian blunderings were
subsequently confirmed by the shelling of British
trawlers in the North Sea after Russian naval
officers mistook them for Japanese torpedo vessels.
The Russo–Japanese War led to more widespread
tensions in international relations, between Britain
on the one hand and Russia and Germany on the
other, while the Japanese victories were celebrated
by Kokyo in his woodblock print "The Destruction
of Petropavlousk." Europe in general became much
more aware of the West's increasing contact with
the Orient, as evidenced by Puccini's opera
"Madame Butterfly." However, if Western
expansion was being rebuffed in East Asia, this
was counterbalanced by the recommencement of
the construction of the Panama Canal under
American direction. The world balance of power,
political and economic, was slowly altering. Within
Europe a further step toward the dividing lines of
1914 was taken with the signing of the Entente
cordiale between Britain and France, though its
initial effect was to resolve Anglo–French
differences elsewhere. In the United States,
president Roosevelt ramified the Monroe Doctrine
to support US intervention in South America and
forestall European expansion there.

▲ Japanese officers survey the remains of the Russian warships
sunk in Port Arthur harbor, after Japan launched a successful
preemptive strike on the harbor in a bid to curtail Russian
ambitions in the Far East.

- **Jan**: Beginning of uprising by Herrero tribesmen in German Southwest Africa, angry at the loss of their land to German settlers, with a massacre of over 100 German soldiers and settlers near the town of Okahandja. On 3 Oct, the chief declares war on Germany. The rebellion is not finally quelled until 1908.

- **6 Feb**: Maryland joins other southern states and disenfranchises black voters. Violence against blacks continues throughout the year (USA).

- **8 Feb**: Japan attacks the Russian naval base of Port Arthur, trapping the Russian fleet, after attempts at negotiation over Russia's Far Eastern policy; war is declared on 10 Feb. The Russian army suffers defeats at Yalu River and Liaoyang and retreats to Mukden. (›21 Oct; 2 Jan 1905)

- **13 Feb**: A treaty between Siam and France determines the border between Siam and French Indo-China.

- **13 Feb**: Turkish troops clash with 16,000 Albanian insurgents at Djakova. On 18 Feb Turks kill 800 rebels in Macedonia.

- **31 Mar**: British troops kill 300 Tibetans when they try to halt a British mission to Tibet (›3 Aug).

- **8 Apr**: Britain finally relinquishes all claims to Madagascar in an agreement with France.

- **8 Apr**: Signature of the Anglo-French entente – the "Entente cordiale" – after months of negotiation. The agreement resolves various longstanding differences, especially as regards the British occupation of Egypt and French interests in Morocco, and safeguards mutual interests such as the Suez Canal, Newfoundland, French Gambia, Siam, Madagascar and the New Hebrides.

- **27 Apr**: John C. Watson forms the first (minority) Labor cabinet in Australia, but this lasts only until 12 Aug.

- **15 Jun**: The UK and Brazil sign an arbitration convention to settle the disputed border of British Guiana.

- **12 Jul**: The UK signs a 5-year treaty with Germany to resolve disputes through arbitration, similar to that concluded between the UK and France.

- **28 Jul**: Assassination of Vyacheslav Plehve, Russian interior minister, provoked by his repressive policies and methods.

- **29 Jul**: France severs diplomatic links with the Vatican – the latest move in the battle between the increasingly anti-clerical government and the church.

- **3 Aug**: British forces take Lhasa, the capital of Tibet. (›9 Sep)

- **16 Aug**: The UK government officially protests to Russia over seizure and sinking of neutral merchant ships. (›21 Oct)

- **Aug**: Demonstrations in Crete demand union with Greece, but the Great Powers do not favor this.

- **7 Sep**: A treaty between Britain and Tibet, whereby the Dalai Lama agrees to forbid foreign intervention, halts the Russian advance in Tibet, and gives Britain trading posts.

- **19 Sep**: After pressure from the British government, Belgium appoints an international commission to investigate labor conditions and allegations of atrocities in the Congo Free State, the personal property of King Leopold II.

- **3 Oct**: A Franco-Spanish treaty publicly affirms the integrity and independence of Morocco, but secret clauses provide for eventual partition.

- **20 Oct**: A treaty between Bolivia and Chile formally ends the War of the Pacific (1879–1884), with a loss of Bolivian territory to Chile.

- **21 Oct**: Dogger Bank incident: the Russian fleet, passing through the North Sea on its way to the Far East, fires on British trawlers, sinking one of them with the loss of several lives. An international inquiry held in Paris blames Russia, and orders compensation to be paid. Anglo-Russian relations deteriorate markedly.

- **27 Oct–23 Nov**: Russo-German negotiations for an alliance against Britain, after British protests at the coaling of the Russian fleet by Germany, end in failure due to Russia's desire to consult its ally, France.

- **8 Nov**: Theodore Roosevelt wins the US presidential election.

- **19 Nov**: *Zemstvo* (local council) congress in St Petersburg demands the formation of a representative assembly and the granting of civil liberties (Russ).

- **2 Dec**: By the Roosevelt corollary to the Monroe Doctrine, the USA claims the right to act as an international policeman in the Western Hemisphere, in order to forestall European intervention and expansion in America.

- **10 Dec**: Nikola Pasic is first elected as Serbian premier, initiating a period of anti-Austrian nationalism.

- **26 Dec**: The czar issues a decree promising to improve conditions for the population, but warns that strikes and riots must stop.

SOCIETY

- **Jan**: Trade agreement between the USA and China.
- **22 Jan**: The town of Aalesund, on the west coast of Norway, is completely destroyed by fire, and over 10,000 left homeless.
- **25 Jan**: 200 miners are buried alive in a Pennsylvania mine.
- **22 Apr**: Nonviolent picketing during strikes is legalized in Britain.
- **23 Apr**: The USA buys the property of the French canal company in Panama for $40,000,000.
- **13 May**: Anglo-Chinese labor Convention is signed, permitting the introduction of "coolies" into the colonies. On 20 May the Chinese Labor Ordinance is declared at Pretoria (SA) to be operative.
- **28 Jun**: Over 700 Scandinavian emigrants die when the steamer *Norge* is wrecked off Ireland.
- **Jun**: Establishment of the German Employers' Association.
- **1 Jul–29 Aug**: Third modern Olympic Games takes place at St Louis, Missouri (USA).
- **Aug**: The International Miners' Congress calls for an 8-hour day and a minimum wage (Fr).
- **Aug**: End of disruption in the petrol industry at Boryslaw after the demand is met for a reduction in working hours (Aust-Hung).
- **27 Oct**: Opening of the New York subway. 150,000 people use it on the first day.
- Charles Rolls and Henry Royce go into partnership to manufacture cars. Rolls-Royce automobile company is founded in 1906 (UK).
- Establishment of the Banque de l'Union Parisienne (Fr).
- Foundation of the Daimler automobile plant near Stuttgart (Ger).
- Establishment of the Bank of the Ministry of Finance (China).
- Germany signs commercial treaties with Belgium, Russia, Switzerland, Italy, and Austria–Hungary.
- Establishment of the Bank of Italy by Peter Amadeo Giannini in San Francisco (USA).
- Foundation in Paris of the Fédération Internationale de Football Associations (FIFA).
- Cholera epidemic in Persia.
- Thomas Sullivan pioneers the teabag (USA).
- An electric machine that permanently waves hair is introduced (UK).
- Nobel Peace Prize is won by the Institute of International Law.

CULTURE

- **17 Jan**: Anton Chekhov's play *The Cherry Orchard* is first performed in Moscow. Chekhov dies on 15 Jul, aged 44, from tuberculosis (Russ).
- **1 Nov**: Premiere of George Bernard Shaw's *John Bull's Other Island*.
- W.B. Yeats: *On Baile's Strand*, play (UK).
- J.M. Barrie: *Peter Pan*, a children's classic play, is performed for the first time (UK).
- Joseph Conrad: *Nostromo*, novel of South American life (UK).
- Henry James: *The Golden Bowl*, novel (USA).
- J.M. Synge: *Riders to the Sea*, play, made into an opera by Ralph Vaughan Williams in 1931 (UK).
- Thomas Hardy: *The Dynasts* (Part I; Part II published 1906; Part III in 1908), a narrative in prose and verse about the Napoleonic wars (UK).
- The Nobel Prize for Literature is won by José Echegaray (Sp) and Frédéric Mistral (Fr).
- Rudolf Steiner: *Theosophy*, philosophy text (Ger).
- The Abbey Theater opens in Dublin, it becomes a focus for the Irish nationalist literary movement.
- Frank Wedekind: *Die Buchse der Pandora* (Pandora's Box), play; with *Erdgeist* (Earth Spirit), this forms the libretto of Alban Berg's (unfinished) opera *Lulu* (1935) (Ger).
- Frederick Delius: *Sea Drift*, for voices, chorus and orchestra (Fr).
- Gustav Mahler: *Sixth Symphony* (Aust-Hung).
- Leoš Janáček: *Jenufa*, opera (Aust-Hung).
- Béla Bartók (Hung) begins 15 years collecting and recording (on wax rolls) folk songs in Central Europe, Asia Minor and North Africa, often in collaboration with fellow-composer Zoltán Kodály.
- The first music radio transmission is made from Graz, Austria.
- Richard Strauss: *Sinfonia Domestica* (Ger).
- Giacomo Puccini: *Madame Butterfly*, opera (It).
- Henri Matisse has his first one-man show, in Paris.
- Henri Rousseau: *The Wedding*, painting (Fr).
- Kokyo: *The Destruction of the Petropavlousk* (Russo-Japanese war), woodblock print (Jap).
- Auguste Rodin, *Le penseur* (The Thinker), sculpture in bronze intended as the centerpiece of his *Gates of Hell* (Fr).
- Louis Sullivan: Schlesinger & Mayer (now Carson Pirie Scott) Store, Chicago (USA).
- Jean Jaurès founds the socialist (later Communist) periodical *L'Humanité* (Fr).

SCIENCE

- **4 May**: Work is resumed on the Panama Canal by the US.
- **21 Jul**: Completion of the Trans-Siberian railroad from Perm to Vladivostok – the longest continuous stretch of track in the world (Russ).
- Carl Duisberg merges the chemical plants Bayer, Agfa and Badische Anilin to form IG Farben (Ger).
- The caterpillar tractor is developed in California (USA).
- Development of the diode (two-electrode) thermionic valve by J.A. Fleming (UK).
- A. Glenny discovers the technique of diphtheria immunization (UK).
- J.P.T.L. Elster develops the photoelectric cell (Ger).
- C. Hulsmeier discovers the principle of radar, although the technology for practical radar is not developed until the late 1930s (Ger).
- The ultraviolet lamp is invented.
- Ronald Ross publishes his studies of the connection between the malaria parasite and the Anopheles mosquito (UK).
- A. Einhorn discovers the anesthetic procaine, first used intravenously in 1909, which has none of the side effects of cocaine.
- Neurologist S. Ramon y Cajal establishes the theory that the nervous system is composed only of nerve cells and their processes (Sp).
- R. Chittenden isolates glycogen, the form in which carbohydrates are stored in animal tissue (USA).
- Chemist F.S. Kipping discovers silicones (UK).
- Colgate Dental Cream is introduced in the USA.
- Glen Curtiss designs the first engine specifically intended for an aircraft (USA).
- The Thermos flask is introduced as a domestic item rather than in the laboratory, by Reinhold Burger (Ger).
- Henri Lebesque presents his theory of measure and the Lebesque integral, which extend the mathematical notions of integration and area to more general sets (Fr).
- Ernst Zermelo shows that every set can be well ordered, thus making possible the use of transfinite methods in mathematics (Ger).
- Marie Curie announces her discovery that pitchblende (uranium ore) contains two hitherto undiscovered radioactive elements, radium and polonium (Fr).
- F. Giesel discovers "actinium X", an isotope of radium.
- J.F. Hartmann first discovers interstellar matter: stationary calcium lines in the spectrum of the binary star Delta Orionis (Ger).

- J.J. Thomson puts forward the "plum pudding" model of the atom, arguing that negatively charged electrons are mixed up in positively charged atomic matter (UK).
- S.A. Arrhenius proposes a theory of immunochemistry (Swe).
- The offset lithography process becomes commercially available (USA).
- First answerphone is introduced, using a form of Poulsen's telegraphone (USA).
- The *Victorian* and the *Virginian* (UK) are the first transatlantic liners to be driven by steam turbines and the first with triple screws.
- Michelin introduce a pneumatic car tire whose raised, flat tread is stronger and provides better grip on the road than the smooth, round tread of existing tires (Fr).
- Frederic Simms invents the first car fender.
- The first metal alloy to be virtually unaffected by changes in temperature is discovered by Charles-Edouard Guillaume. "Invar" will be used for all precision instruments liable to be affected by temperature fluctuations (Swi).
- John Fleming develops a thermionic valve, which allows electricity to flow in one direction but not another. This invention changes the design of wireless (UK).
- Ivan Pavlov discovers the existence of conditioned reflexes and also wins the Nobel Prize for Physiology or Medicine for his work on digestion (Russ).
- Nobel Prize for Chemistry is won by William Ramsay (UK) for his work on the inert gases in air and determination of their place in the periodic system.
- Nobel Prize for Physics is won by John William Strutt (UK) for his work on the densities of gases and his discovery of argon.

Russia's defeats in its war with Japan led to internal revolution. It reached a climax on 22 January 1905 with the events of "Bloody Sunday". The czar responded with the introduction of an apparently more democratic form of government, the need for which was underlined by the mutiny of Russian sailors aboard the battleship Potemkin and by growing dissent in Poland. The continuing ineffectiveness of the autocratic czarist regime was made evident by the creation of the St Petersburg workers' soviet under Leon Trotsky, which could only be put down by bullets, and the subsequent failure of the Duma (parliament) elected by universal suffrage. Tension within Europe was heightened also by the Algeciras crisis, but this proved the strength of the newly formed Anglo–French entente. However, such political conflict went hand in hand with intellectual achievement: during 1905 the young physicist Albert Einstein began to recast human understanding of the physical laws governing the universe.

▲ "Bloody Sunday" in St Petersburg: troops fire on unarmed crowds who had gathered to see the priest Father Gapon present a political petition to the czar, causing about 200 deaths.

● **2 Jan**: Russians surrender Port Arthur to the Japanese after a 7-month siege. Japan inflicts a further disastrous defeat on Russian troops at Mukden on 10 Mar. (›27 May)

● **22 Jan** (9 Jan in Old Style): Bloody Sunday: after months of civil unrest, workers march on the czar's Winter Palace in St Petersburg and are fired upon by troops; 70 are killed and 240 wounded. Strikes and further unrest follow; in Warsaw strikers fire at troops. On 3 Mar Czar Nicholas II announces his intention to introduce a more liberal government (Russ). (›27 Jun)

● **Jan**: Gen. Louis Botha founds Het Volk, an organization seeking responsible government in the Transvaal, which is granted on 6 Dec 1906. Orangia Unie is founded along the same lines, for the Orange River Colony (SA).

● **11 Feb**: The US Senate adopts an amendment to each of the arbitration treaties concluded between the USA, Britain, Germany, France and the other powers at the end of 1904, whereby reference was to be made to The Hague. The amendment effectively nullifies the arbitration treaties, since it makes reference to The Hague more complicated, and prevents the automatic arbitration machinery being set in motion.

● **30 Mar**: Uprising in Crete after appeals for union with Greece are rejected by the Great Powers (1904).

● **31 Mar**: Kaiser Wilhelm II's visit to Tangier initiates the first Moroccan crisis: Germany's desire to maintain the open door policy in Morocco is perceived as a threat to French, British, Italian and Spanish interests; the Germans insist on a conference to discuss the matter, putting the Anglo-French entente to the test. French foreign minister Delcassé is forced to resign. (›28 Sep)

● **8 May**: Paul Miliukov forms the Union of Unions, calling for a parliament and universal suffrage in Russia.

● **27–29 May**: The 32-ship Russian fleet is totally destroyed by the Japanese in the battle of Tsushima Straits between Korea and Japan. The treaty of Portsmouth, mediated by US president Roosevelt, finally ends the war on 5 Sep.

● **7 Jun**: The Norwegian parliament declares dissolution of the union with Sweden, ratified by plebiscite on 13 Aug, and finally signed on 26 Oct. Prince Karl of Denmark ascends the Norwegian throne as Haakon VII, reigning until 1957.

● **27 Jun**: Mutiny on the battleship Potemkin while moored off Odessa in the Black Sea marks the culmination of a period of strikes and unrest, which leads Nicholas II to create a new Russian representative assembly called the Duma; however, its limited powers and the restricted franchise are insufficient to meet popular demand and unrest continues. (›20 Oct)

● **24 Jul**: Treaty of Bjorko renews attempts at a Russo-German alliance, but fails due to French refusal to join. (›28 Sep)

● **12 Aug**: Anglo-Japanese alliance is renewed for 10 years, and extended to include India.

● **28 Sep**: France and Germany agree on a conference on Morocco (Algeciras conference, 16 Jan–7 Apr 1906), and Germany tries again to win French accession to the Bjorko treaty.

● **16 Oct**: Partition of Bengal, detaching East Bengal and Assam from the remainder of the province, provokes nationalist opposition and the foundation of the All-India Muslim League on 30 Dec 1906, which demands separate communal representation in any future constitutional reforms (Ind).

● **26 Oct**: First workers' soviet (council) is formed in St Petersburg under Leon Trotsky to direct the Great General Strike (Russ). (›16 Dec)

● **30 Oct**: Nicholas II issues his October Manifesto in response to the strike action, granting Russia a constitution, and giving the Duma real legislative powers, with a more extended franchise and guaranteed civil liberties; the manifesto is rejected outright by the Social Democrats who, through the proliferating soviets, attempt to incite further strike action (Russ). (›10 May 1906)

● **28 Nov**: Universal suffrage is granted in Austria.

● **28 Nov**: The Sinn Fein party is founded in Dublin to work for Irish independence (UK).

● **16 Dec**: Members of the St Petersburg soviet are arrested, leading to an insurrection of workers in Moscow (22 Dec–1 Jan 1906), brutally suppressed by the army (Russ).

● **19 Dec**: Nicholas I of Montenegro grants a constitution, the government to be elected by universal suffrage.

● **Dec**: Beginning of the Persian Revolution, directed against the incompetent rule of Shah Muzaffar ud-Din and his corrupt minister Ayn ud-Dola. (›Jul 1906)

● Union of secret societies, the T'ung Meng Hui, is formed by Sun Yat-sen to expel the Manchus from China.

SOCIETY

- **1 Jan**: Belgian Henri Oedenkoven founds the world's first vegetarian organization (It).

- **21 Jan**: Protocol signed between the USA and San Domingo whereby the USA undertakes to adjust the Dominican debt, arrange the method of payment, and assume control of the Dominican Custom Houses, in order to repay the country's debts. It is officially denied that any protectorate is involved or intended.

- **Jan**: Strike of miners in the Ruhr and in Belgium, demanding a reduction of working hours (Ger/Bel).

- **Mar**: Introduction of the 8-hour day for miners under 18 (UK).

- **4 Apr**: A massive earthquake in Lahore claims over 10,000 lives (Ind).

- **1 May**: In clashes in Warsaw between workmen and troops during May Day demonstrations, 100 are killed and many injured.

- **May**: Meeting of the International Conference for the Protection of Laborers discusses night work for women.

- **29 Jun**: The Automobile Association is founded to protect the interests of motorists (UK).

- **8 Jul**: May Sutton (USA) becomes the first non-Briton to win a Wimbledon tennis title.

- **30 Jul**: Zionist Congress in Basel rejects offer by UK Prime Minister Balfour of a Jewish homeland in Uganda, made in 1903, and calls for one in Palestine.

- **21 Aug**: General strike begins in Poland in protest at the disregard for Polish rights in the manifesto creating the Russian Duma. A state of emergency is declared the next day. (›6 Nov)

- **9 Sep**: Thousands are feared dead in an earthquake in the Calabria region of Italy.

- **Sep**: The Trades Union Congress demands the introduction of an 8-hour day and free trade (UK).

- **Sep**: Worst famine since 1891 is reported in Russia.

- **14 Oct**: Suffragettes Christabel Pankhurst and Annie Kenney go to jail for assaulting police (UK).

- **20 Oct**: Nicholas II (Russ) permits the teaching of Polish in Polish schools for the first time in 15 years, but unrest in Poland grows. In November martial law is imposed.

- **23 Oct**: 550 die in Chile in workers' unrest.

- **6 Nov**: Riots break out in Warsaw in renewed calls for Polish autonomy.

- **8 Nov**: Peasants, policemen, army officers and government officials are involved in the massacre of over 1,000 Jews in Odessa (Russ).

- **Nov**: Famine spreads in Japan after failure of the rice crop.

- **4 Dec**: 125,000 Jews in New York march in sympathy with the plight of the Jews in Russia.

- **9 Dec**: A law promulgated by French premier Aristide Briand separates church and state, thus ending the mutual relationship established in the Napoleonic concordat of 1801 (Fr).

- A loan of $400,000,000 for Russia is agreed by France and Britain, on the condition that Russia supports France at the Algeciras conference on Morocco (Fr).

- Suffragettes in Britain step up their campaign for votes for women with hunger strikes and acts of violence.

- The H.J. Heinz Company of Pittsburgh (USA) puts Heinz Baked Beans on sale in Britain.

- Influx of Chinese students into Japan after Zhang Zhidong, an educational reformer, recommends the Japanese educational system.

- Chinese boycott US goods as a result of the exclusion of Chinese immigrants from the USA.

- Beginning of a tariff conflict, the "Pig War", between Austria and Serbia (until 1907).

- Foundation of the International Agricultural Institute in Rome (It).

- Max Weber's: *The Protestant Ethic and the Spirit of Capitalism* argues that Luther and Calvin are among the wellsprings of modern capitalism (Ger).

- Emile Jaques-Dalcroze first applies eurythmics to teaching schoolchildren; later he founds a eurythmics school at Hellerau (Ger) in 1911, and another in Geneva (Swi) in 1914.

- Opening of the first nickelodeon in Pittsburgh (USA).

- First illuminated track diagram is installed in a London railroad station signal box (UK).

- Elastic rubber replaces traditional whalebone and lacing in women's foundation garments.

- Nobel Prize for Peace won by Bertha von Suttner (Aut).

CULTURE

- George Bernard Shaw's plays *Major Barbara* and *Man and Superman* are both produced on the London stage (UK).

- E.M. Forster: *Where Angels Fear to Tread*, his first novel (UK).

- Heinrich Mann: *Professor Unrat*, novel (Ger).

- H.G. Wells : *Kipps*, novel (UK).

- Baroness Orczy: *The Scarlet Pimpernel*, a novel about the French Revolution (UK).

- Oscar Wilde: *De Profundis*, an essay of confession written in prison (posth.) (UK).

- Rainer Maria Rilke: *The Book of Hours*, poems (Ger).

- The Nobel Prize for Literature is won by Henryk Sienkiewicz (Pol).

- Franz Léhar: *The Merry Widow*, operetta (Aust-Hung).

- Gustav Mahler: *Kindertotenlieder*, a setting for soprano and orchestra of poems by Friedrich Rückert (Aust-Hung).

- Richard Strauss's *Salome*, an opera based on Wilde's play, creates a scandal but is highly successful (Ger).

- Claude Debussy's orchestral piece *La Mer* typifies Impressionism in music with its shimmering waves of sound (Fr).

- Frederick Delius: *A Mass of Life*, choral work on texts from Friedrich Nietzsche's *Also Sprach Zarathustra* (UK).

- Soprano Adelina Patti makes 14 records for the Gramophone Company at her Welsh castle, Craig-y-Nos, which are released on a special "Patti" label (UK).

- First exhibition of a group of young modernist painters, led by Henri Matisse, at the Salon d'Automne, Paris; they are dubbed *les Fauves* (The Wild Beasts) by critic Louis Vauxcelles for their startling use of color (Fr).

- Formation of the group of Expressionist painters known as *Die Brücke* (The Bridge): Ernst Kirchner, Erich Heckel, Karl Schmidt-Rottluff and Fritz Bleyl, later joined by Max Bechstein and Emil Nolde (Ger).

- Beginning of Pablo Picasso's Rose Period (Fr).

- Paul Cézanne: *Les Grandes Baigneuses* (Bathers), painting (Fr).

- Henri Matisse: *The Open Window, Collioure*, painting (Fr).

- Frank Lloyd Wright: Larkin Building, Buffalo (USA) .

- Franz Jourdain and Henri Sauvage, La Samaritaine department store, Paris.

- Alfred Stieglitz opens a gallery in New York to exhibit photography as a fine art (USA).

- Pathé Company of France automates the coloring of movie films.

SCIENCE

- First double-sided gramophone records released.

- J.A. Fleming's wavemeter is now used in all radio equipment determining the distance between successive wavefronts of equal phase along an electromagnetic wave (UK).

- Astronomer P. Lowell predicts the existence of a ninth planet beyond Neptune (USA).

- Physicist Albert Einstein publishes three papers that are crucial to the development of 20th-century science. In the first he puts forward the special theory of relativity, in which he argues from the absolute speed of light that energy and mass are equivalent. In the second he explains Brownian motion (the random movement of molecules in a liquid); and in the third he explains the photoelectric effect. The last two papers have a decisive effect on the development of quantum theory (Swi).

- Electrification of the London underground railroad system is completed.

- Clarence McClung discovers that female mammals have two X-shaped chromosomes whereas males have an X paired with a Y (USA).

- Artificial silk is made commercially through the viscose process by Courtaulds (UK).

- R. Willstatter begins his study of chlorophyll (Ger).

- G. Marconi invents the directional radio antenna (UK).

- J.B. Murphy pioneers arthroplasty – the creation of artificial joints (USA).

- Introduction of compressed air hammers in coalmining (Ger).

- Fouché and Picard invent oxyacetylene welding (Fr).

- A. Binet, V. Henri and B. Simon develop the intelligence test (Fr).

- G.W. Crile performs the first direct blood transfusion (USA).

- G. Voisin, E. Archdeacon and L. Blériot open the first aircraft factory in Billancourt, near Paris (Fr).

- Non-shatter safety glass is patented. By 1910, it is made under the name of Triplex.

- Nobel Prize for Chemistry is won by Adolf von Baeyer (Ger) for "the services he has rendered to the development of organic chemistry and the chemical industry through his work concerning organic dyes and hydrocarbon hydroaromatic compounds."

- Nobel Prize for Physics is won by Philippe von Lenard (Ger) for his work on cathode rays.

- Nobel Prize for Physiology or Medicine is won by Robert Koch (Ger) for his research into tuberculosis.

The rise of Western power since the early nineteenth century had been a consequence of industrialization, which after the 1870s had been increasingly supported by scientific and technological advances. None the less, humankind remained helpless in the face of natural forces, as was clearly shown by the massive San Francisco earthquake. The earthquake devastated the Pacific seaport and killed over 1,000 people. The financial consequences of the San Francisco quake severely affected the London insurance market, demonstrating how closely woven now was the fabric of Western capitalism. Claims on British companies amounted to £10 million after reinsurance, out of total claims of £225 million. In the realm of politics, potential enmity between the advanced countries was heightened by naval building programs, with the launch of the HMS Dreadnought, which rendered all other battleships obsolete, the German Naval Bill and Japan's decision to double its fleet within two years.

▲ **Devastated San Franciscans walk warily through the rubble of their city after the massive earthquake of 19 April. Thousands fled in ferries and trains as the business district and industrial areas were completely wiped out, causing more than $200 million worth of damage.**

● **10 Jan**: Beginning of discussions regarding an Anglo-French military treaty, creating a British obligation to France in the event of attack by Germany.

● **16 Jan**: Opening of the Algeciras conference on Morocco reaffirms Morocco's independence, but recognizes France's special position. Control of the country is divided between France and Spain, and a state bank instituted, under predominantly French control.

● **Jan**: Resignation of Japanese premier Katsura due to popular dissatisfaction with the outcome of the Treaty of Portsmouth (1905).

● **Jan**: Czar Nicholas II deploys troops to deal with unrest in the Baltic provinces.

● **3 Feb**: The Japanese government decides to almost double the size of its navy by 1908.

● **7 Feb**: At the UK general election, the Liberals under Henry Campbell-Bannerman come to power. The Labour Representation Committee, under James Keir Hardie, wins 29 seats, an increase of 27.

● **20 Feb**: British troops are sent to quell native revolt in northern Nigeria.

● **7 Mar**: In Finland, all male and female taxpayers over 24 are given the vote.

● **27 Apr**: Britain gains control of Tibet having signed a treaty with China whereby Britain is to control all roads into Tibet, and no foreign power may occupy, buy or lease territory in Tibet without British permission. The aim of the treaty is to prevent Russian expansionism.

● **3 May**: British ultimatum to Turkey to relinquish claims on the Sinai peninsula, which it had ruled since 1517.

● **10 May**: The first Russian Duma, elected by universal suffrage, meets; but the czar retains autocratic power. The Duma is boycotted by the more radical parties, and is dissolved on 21 Jul; on 31 Jul the deputies issue a manifesto urging civil disobedience before many flee to Finland. (›2 Nov)

● **May**: German Navy Bill, to increase the tonnage of battleships and to widen the Kiel Canal to allow larger battleships to pass through, accelerates the pace of the naval building race between Britain and Germany.

● **10 Jun**: Death of Richard ("King Dick") Seddon, prime minister of New Zealand since 1893. He had pursued an experimental state socialist program, including introducing female suffrage, in 1893 – the first country in the world to do so.

● **13 Jun**: Denshawi affair: the execution of natives who killed a British officer out on a pigeon-shooting party stirs up nationalist feeling in Egypt; more British troops are sent to Egypt in Jul.

● **4 Jul**: Tripartite Pact between Britain, France and Italy underwrites the integrity and independence of Ethiopia, and divides the country into spheres of influence.

● **20 Jul**: Peace treaty is signed between Guatemala, and El Salvador and Honduras, ending the war between them which had begun in May.

● **Jul**: Persian Revolution: after several thousand revolutionaries take refuge in the grounds of the British legation in Tehran, the shah is forced to dismiss minister Ayn ud-Dola and agrees (5 Aug) to the organization of a national assembly (*majlis*). This meets for the first time on 7 Oct to draw up a liberal constitution, signed by the shah on 30 Dec, the day before he dies. (›Aug 1906)

● **1 Sep**: British New Guinea is placed under Australian control and renamed Papua (the original Portuguese name).

● **28 Sep**: US War Secretary William Taft becomes provisional governor of Cuba in an attempt to restore peace between rebel and government forces. A power vacuum occurs on the resignation of president Palma.

● **Oct**: Hague tribunal settles disagreements between Canada and the USA over fishing rights.

● **2 Nov**: Bolshevik Leon Trotsky is exiled for life to Siberia for revolutionary activities (Russ).

● **6 Nov**: Reorganization of Chinese government ministries offers the possibility of constitutional government after a mission studies foreign states in 1905, but the ministries are placed under Manchu control.

● **12 Dec**: The Transvaal is granted local autonomy with white male suffrage (SA).

● **30 Dec**: Foundation of the All-India Muslim League (Ind).

● **Dec**: Parliamentary crisis in Germany as the Center party refuses to support a bill to reorganize the colonial office and provide funding for military action to quash the Hereros uprising in German Southwest Africa (since 1904). The Reichstag is dissolved and in fresh elections the Center and Socialist parties lose influence (Ger).

● **Dec**: The Indian Congress demands that the self-government system of other British colonies be extended to India.

SOCIETY

- **1 Jan**: The Aliens Act comes into force in the UK. Potential immigrants will now find themselves subject to extensive questioning on their financial position, and on their physical and mental health, before being admitted. Poor prospective immigrants from Russia and Central Europe are particularly affected.

- **22 Jan**: In Germany, "Red Monday" socialist reform rally attracts 250,000. Demands are made for suffrage reform.

- **27 Jan**: The River Thames catches fire as oil on the surface ignites (UK).

- **2 Feb**: 570 are injured in riots as government officials gather an inventory of church property. On 11 Feb Pope Pius X condemns the separation of church and state in France.

- **8 Feb**: A typhoon claims thousands of lives in Tahiti.

- **10 Feb**: Launch of HMS *Dreadnought*, the most powerful warship in the world, built in just four months.

- **16 Mar**: Bill passed in Japan for the nationalization of all railways.

- **20 Mar**: The island of Ustica in Sicily is devastated by a massive volcanic eruption.

- **22 Mar**: England wins the first rugby international, against France, in Paris, 35 points to 8.

- **Mar**: Beginning of a severe strike movement in Germany.

- **7 Apr**: Mount Vesuvius erupts, leaving hundreds dead and injured (It).

- **14 Apr**: In the USA, a mob burns two blacks to death in front of a cheering crowd of 3,000 in Ohio.

- **19 Apr**: Major earthquake in San Francisco destroys most of the city and kills at least 1,000 (USA).

- **22 Apr**: The "Interim Olympics" opens in Athens to celebrate the 10th anniversary of the modern era of the games.

- **1 May**: 3,000 workers are arrested in Paris during May Day demonstrations. On 20 May the leftist bloc is successful in parliamentary elections (Fr).

- **19 May**: Simplon tunnel between Switzerland and Italy opens – the longest in the world 20 km (12.5 miles) long.

- **May**: The US government prohibits any further expansion of the Rockefeller Oil Trust by passing the Sherman Act.

- **30 Jun**: The Pure Food and Drug Act prohibits mislabeling and otherwise tampering with foods (USA).

- **Jun**: First French Grand Prix motor race, near Le Mans is won by Hungarian Ferenc Seisz in a Renault (Fr).

- **Jun**: Hundreds of Jews are killed in planned anti-Jewish riots in Bialystok (Russ).

- **12 Jul**: A French court passes judgment rehabilitating the Jewish army officer Alfred Dreyfus after it is proved that the charges of treason brought against him in 1894 were false. On 21 Jul, Dreyfus is presented with the insignia of Chevalier of the Legion of Honor, and troops file past him (Fr).

- **18 Aug**: In Chile, the port city of Valparaiso is devastated by a massive earthquake.

- **30 Sep**: The first international hot air balloon race sets off from Paris.

- **17 Oct**: Photographs are sent over 1,600 km (1,000 miles) by telegraph (Ger).

- **24 Oct**: 11 Suffragettes are jailed in the UK for participating in riots during the Opening of Parliament.

- **26 Oct**: Pupils in German Poland strike against compulsory use of German for religious instruction.

- **Oct**: Segregation of Japanese schoolchildren in San Francisco leads to strained relations with Japan (USA).

- **11 Nov**: Two Italians make the first balloon crossing of the Alps.

- **15 Nov**: The Japanese launch the world's largest battleship, the *Satsuma*.

- Beginning of the drainage of the Zuider Zee (Neth).

- China pledges to suppress opium cultivation and consumption over 10 years after an agreement with Britain to cut the latter's imports of opium.

- Foundation of the Mercedes automobile company in Berlin (Ger).

- Katanga Mining Union is founded in the Belgian Congo.

- Night work by women is internationally forbidden.

- Norway adopts unemployment insurance.

- Lever Brothers introduce Lux soapflakes (UK).

- William Kellogg founds the Battle Creek Toasted Cornflake Company.

- American Jewish Commission is founded to protect the rights of Jews and fight injustice.

- J.J. Thomson demonstrates a new way of separating atoms, and wins the Nobel Prize for Physics for his discovery of the electron (UK).

- First Victorian Football League (Australian rules) final at Melbourne (Aus).

- Nobel Peace Prize is won by Theodore Roosevelt for his role in the signing of the Treaty of Portsmouth.

CULTURE

- **4 Jan**: Police in Berlin forbid "obscene" American dancer Isadora Duncan from dancing in public. Duncan's work consists of a simple, expressive movement to classical music.

- **Jan**: Gerhard Hauptmann's play *Und Pippa Tanzt* (Pippa Dances) first performed in Berlin (Ger).

- Joseph Conrad: *Mirror of the Sea*, memories and impressions (UK).

- John Galsworthy: *The Man of Property*, novel, the first of the Forsyte chronicles (UK).

- Robert Musil: *Die Verwirrungen des Zöglings Törless* (Young Törless), novel (Aust-Hung).

- Toson Shimazaki: *The Broken Commandment*, novel (Jap).

- The Nobel Prize for Literature is won by Giosuè Carducci, Italian poet.

- Albert Schweitzer: *The Quest for the Historical Jesus* (Ger).

- Arnold Schoenberg: First Chamber Symphony (Aust-Hung).

- Carl Nielsen's opera *Maskarade* is premiered in Copenhagen (Den).

- Edward Elgar: *The Kingdom*, oratorio (UK).

- Sergei Rachmaninoff: *Francesca da Rimini*, opera (Russ).

- Thaddeus Cahill demonstrates his Telharmonium, a prototype electric organ (Can).

- First Mozart Festival is held in Salzburg (Aust-Hung).

André Derain: *The Pool of London*, painting (Fr).

- Albert Marquet: *Le Havre, 14 juillet*, painting (Fr).

- Georges Braque: *The St Martin Canal*, painting (Fr).

- Otto Wagner: Post Office Savings Bank, Vienna (Aust-Hung).

- Frank Lloyd Wright: Unity Temple, Oak Park, Illinois (USA).

- First animated cartoon released by Vitagraph (USA).

- Legislation is put through on the minimum distance between cinemas, to curb proliferation (Russ).

- *The Story of the Kelly Gang*, the first full-length film, is released (USA).

SCIENCE

- **24 Aug**: Kidney transplants are performed on cats and dogs at a medical conference in Toronto (Can).

- Canadian-born R.A. Fessenden invents AM (Amplitude Modulation) radio and transmits voice and music (USA) via radio waves on Christmas Eve over a radius of over 161 km (100 miles).

- Lee de Forest invents the three-electrode vacuum tube (triode amplifier), a staple component of electronic equipment until the development of the transistor in 1948 (USA).

- F.G. Hopkins argues that "accessory food factors" (later called vitamins) are essential components of diet (UK).

- R.D. Oldham deduces the existence of the Earth's core (UK).

- Physicist W.H. Nernst postulates the third law of thermodynamics (Ger).

- Biologist T.H. Morgan uses the *drosophila* fruitfly to study heredity (USA).

- J. Bordet and O. Gengou cultivate the bacterium that causes whooping cough (Fr).

- August von Wasserman develops his test for syphilis (Ger).

- C. von Pirquet introduces the term "allergy".

- Charles Sherrington publishes *The Integrative Action of the Nervous System* (UK).

- A new typecasting machine allowing large display type for headlines and bills is invented by Washington I. Ludlow (USA).

- Wratton and Wainwright (UK) manufacture the first fully panchromatic plates for photography.

- Introduction of light bulbs with tungsten metal filaments, though they remain delicate and inefficient until a new method of preparing tungsten is devised in 1908.

- The first synthetic drug, Atoxyl, is developed in Germany by Paul Ehrlich. It kills the trypanosome that causes sleeping sickness.

- A. d'Arsonval and F. Bordas (Fr) invent freeze drying as a means of storing biological material for long periods.

- Nobel Prize for Chemistry is won by Henri Moissan (Fr) for his investigation and isolation of the element fluorine and "for the adoption in the services of science of the electric furnace called after him".

- Nobel Prize for Medicine or Physiology is won by Camillo Golgi and Santiago Ramón y Cajal for their work on the structure of the nervous system (It).

- J.J. Thomson wins the Nobel Prize for Physics for his discovery of the electron (UK).

The chain of events that led to World War I was furthered in 1907. The Triple Alliance between Germany, Austria-Hungary and Italy was renewed for another six years, while an entente was established between Britain and Russia. Diplomats from London and St Petersburg resolved differences regarding India and China. This new relationship between Britain and Russia worked in conjunction with the Entente Cordiale and with the Anglo-Japanese alliance. Concern over a possible outbreak in hostilities also brought about moves for peace: although the International Peace Conference at The Hague failed to restrict the pace of rearmament in Europe and the Pacific, it did establish an International Court of Justice and further developed an international system of rules for the conduct of war. Such political considerations did not, however, hold back developments in the arts: Pablo Picasso's painting "Les Demoiselles d'Avignon," heralded a new age of experimentalism, while in Italy composer Ferrucio Busoni was already outlining the possibility of electronic music.

▲ **Crowds in The Hague during the Peace Conference of 1907 demonstrated their hostility to war and their approval of disarmament proposals, but their placards declaring "Down with War!" were unable to influence the course of events. As was to be the case so often during the 20th century, nationalism remained a more potent force than pacificism.**

● **26 Jan**: Introduction of universal, equal and direct suffrage for parliamentary elections in Austria.

● **8 Feb**: The USA takes control of Dominican Republic customs for 50 years, and Dominican finances are rehabilitated after the economic bankruptcy of 1904.

● **11 Feb**: The Shah of Persia, Muhammad Ali Mirza, who was crowned on 19 Jan, recognizes constitutional government.

● **26 Feb**: First elections in the newly self-governing Transvaal: Louis Botha's Het Volk party wins 37 seats against 21 for the Progressive party, returning control of Transvaal to the Boers. Botha becomes premier on 4 Mar (SA).

● **5 Mar**: Second Russian Duma meets, more radical than the first, but the pressure of reactionary groups to return to the autocratic system forces its dissolution on 16 Jun, when a new electoral law in favor of the propertied classes, but to the detriment of the proletarian classes, is promulgated.

● **8 Mar**: Labour MP Keir Hardie's Women's Enfranchisement Bill is defeated. On 14 Feb, a record number of suffragettes, 57, appear in court after violent clashes with police (UK).

● **11 Mar**: Bulgarian prime minister Nicholas Petkov is assassinated by an anarchist.

● **15 Mar**: First women are elected to parliament, in Finland.

● **22 Mar**: Asiatic registration bill passed by the new Transvaal government restricts the immigration of Indians; it is opposed by Mohandas Gandhi, who, with the Indian population, begins a campaign of passive resistance (*satyagraha*) (SA).

● **26 Mar**: Martial law is declared in Romania as 4,000 peasants prepare to march on Bucharest. The insurrection is put down by the military.

● **8 Apr**: Anglo-French convention confirms the independence of Siam, establishing spheres of influence.

● **12 Apr**: A new army bill in Switzerland, due to increased international tension, creates a standing defense militia.

● **16 May**: The UK, France and Spain form a loose Triple Alliance, the Pact of Cartagena. It provides for the maintenance of the status quo in the Mediterranean, and is chiefly directed at the supposed German designs on the Balearic Islands and the Canaries.

● **May**: Riots break out in India, and troops are ordered in. On 6 Jun, the government declares that the UK will not withdraw from India under any circumstances. (›11 Oct)

● **10 Jun**: Franco-Japanese agreement provides for the integrity and independence of China; a similar Russo-Japanese agreement is secured on 30 Jul.

● **14 Jun**: Limited women's suffrage is introduced in Norway.

● **Jun**: Renewal of the Triple Alliance (Ger, Aust-Hung, It) for six years.

● **1 Jul**: Orange River Colony (SA), formerly the Orange Free State before coming under British military administration, is granted self-government by Britain, with a new constitution.

● **19 Jul**: Korean emperor Kojong (I T'aewang) abdicates under Japanese pressure, and the administration of Korea is placed under Japanese control on 25 Jul, provoking a popular uprising and war of independence. (22 Aug 1910)

● **30 Jul**: Russo-Japanese treaty provides for agreements over east and southern Manchurian railroads and spheres of influence in Manchuria.

● **30 Jul**: Election for the first assembly in the Philippines: Nationalists gain 32 seats, Independents gain 20 and Progressives gain 16.

● **31 Aug**: Finalization of the Anglo-Russian entente, aligning Russia with France and Britain against the Central Powers, as the Triple Entente. Persia is to be divided into Russian and British spheres of influence, with a neutral region between; Afghanistan to be removed from the Russian sphere of influence; recognition of Chinese control over Tibet and guarantee of the latter's integrity.

● **Aug**: Assassination of Persian minister Atabegi-Azam is a blow to the reactionary new shah Muhammad Ali Mirza, who attempts to circumvent the newly formed *majlis*; a liberal ministry is set up under Nasir ul-Mulk. (› 15 Dec)

● **8 Sep**: Establishment of the Guomindang (Kuomintang = KMT) nationalist party by Sun Yat-sen (Chi).

● **20 Sep**: French troops resume fighting with the rebels in Casablanca, Morocco, after the breakdown of peace talks.

● **26 Sep**: New Zealand becomes a dominion within the British Empire.

● **2 Nov**: The UK, France, Russia and Germany agree to guarantee Norway's independence.

● **14 Nov**: Third Duma meets (until 1912), with a conservative majority, although extensive social and economic reforms are carried out by new premier Pyotr Stolypin (Russ).

● **15 Dec**: Coup d'etat attempt by the Persian shah. Prime minister Nasir ul-Mulk is imprisoned, but the popular uprising this provokes forces the shah to yield.

● **Dec**: Subjugation of the Achinese by the Dutch completes their conquest of Sumatra.

● Parliamentary government and near-universal suffrage are introduced in Sweden.

SOCIETY

- **11 Jan**: People living in the German–Danish frontier zone are guaranteed citizenship of either country.

- **14 Jan**: A massive earthquake strikes Jamaica, killing hundreds and leaving thousands homeless.

- **22 Jan**: Around 1,500 are killed in a massive tidal wave in the Dutch East Indies.

- **Feb**: US Immigration Act limits entry of Japanese laborers after immigration peaks at 1,000,000.

- **Apr**: 20 million are reported to be starving in Russia in the worst famine on record.

- **14 Apr**: The first performance of Jozsef Nabodi's opera *Kossuth* in Budapest sparks off anti-Austrian demonstrations.

- **May**: French sailors in Marseille proclaim a general strike for better working conditions.

- **May**: First Isle of Man TT motorcycle race (UK).

- **9 Jun**: Start of first long-distance motor car rally, Paris to Beijing, won by Prince Borghese of Italy.

- **15 Jun–18 Oct**: Second Peace Conference at The Hague (Neth): arms limitations, suggested by Britain, are rejected by Germany, but conventions on debt collection, rules of war and neutrality are laid down. On 22 Aug a proposal to establish an International High Court of Justice is adopted. On 7 Sept, the conference adopts a rule that all powers must give notice of war.

- **Jun–Aug**: "Open door" agreements between Japan and France, Japan and Russia, on trading in China; China opens seven towns in Manchuria for international trade.

- **20 Jul**: 471 miners die in a Japanese mine disaster.

- **23 Jul**: The new port of Zeebrugge, near Bruges, is officially inaugurated by Leopold II of Belgium.

- **30 Aug**: In Vienna, women are allowed to be lecturers and assistants in universities and hospitals on the same terms as men.

- **8 Sep**: Pius X issues a papal encyclical condemning liberal modernist dogma (Vat).

- **13 Sep**: New Cunard liner *Lusitania* completes crossing of the Atlantic in a record five days (USA).

- **11 Oct**: Imposition of nationwide ban on public meetings of over 20 in India, against a background of serious riots.

- **15 Oct**: Town of Fontanet almost completely destroyed when a gunpowder factory explodes (USA).

- **21 Oct**: Financial crisis in the USA, with the collapse of 31 national banks and 212 state banks; J.P. Morgan organizes a fund by order of the US Treasury to support embarrassed companies during the economic crisis.

- **8 Nov**: Harvester decision of the Australian Arbitration Court establishes the concept of the basic wage.

- The Swiss National Bank is established as the central bank of Switzerland.

- Four million people in China starve in famine caused by heavy rains and crop failure.

- Formation of the Confédération Générale des Vignerons, an organization of vineyard workers, after a decline in wine prices (1906) causes an epidemic of strikes and unrest (Fr).

- Establishment of the Bank of the Ministry of Transport (China).

- Shell Oil Trust is founded (UK).

- The Lancia motor car goes into production in Turin (It).

- White miners in South Africa strike to preserve the job color bar, which prevents skilled jobs going to non-white workers.

- A ball bearing plant is founded in Goteborg (Swe).

- Lord Baden Powell founds the Boy Scout movement (UK)

- Foundation of the L'Oréal perfume and cosmetics empire (Fr).

- Nobel Peace Prize is won by Ernesto Moneta (It) and Louis Renault (Fr).

- First Rolls Royce Silver Ghost automobile is produced (UK).

- Persil washing powder is introduced, produced in Germany.

- London's *Daily Mirror* publishes the first front-page newspaper photograph transmitted by wire.

- William Harley and Arthur Davidson set up their motorcycle company, having been encouraged by the response to their first homemade motorcycle (1903) (USA).

CULTURE

- **10 May**: Premiere in Paris of Paul Dukas's opera *Ariàne et Barbe-Bleue*, after Maurice Maeterlinck's play (Fr).

- J.M. Synge's play *The Playboy of the Western World* causes riots when it opens at the Abbey Theater in Dublin, because of the way it appears to portray the Irish (UK).

- Hilaire Belloc: *Cautionary Tales for Children*, poems (UK).

- W.B. Yeats: *Dierdre*, play (UK).

- Stefan George: *The Seventh Ring*, poems (Ger).

- August Strindberg: *The Ghost Sonata*, play (Swe).

- The Nobel Prize for Literature is won by Rudyard Kipling (UK).

- Henri Bergson: *L'Evolution créatrice*, philosophy text (Fr).

- Mikhail Fokine: *Les Sylphides* (choreography of orchestrated Chopin piano pieces) (Russ).

- Igor Stravinsky: Symphony No. 1 (Russ).

- After resigning from the Vienna State Opera, Gustav Mahler is appointed to direct the Metropolitan Opera in New York (Aust-Hung/USA).

- Frederick Delius: *A Village Romeo and Juliet*, opera (Fr).

- Ferruccio Busoni: *Sketch of a New Esthetic of Music* (enlarged 1910), in which the author outlines the possibility of electronic music (It).

- Pablo Picasso: *Les Demoiselles d'Avignon*, painting. This work, which has been in progress for several years, is seen as the first Cubist painting (Fr).

- Paul Cézanne has a retrospective exhibition in Paris which inspires later development of Cubism (Fr).

- Paula Modersohn-Becker: *Self-Portrait with Camellia*, painting (Ger).

- Gustav Klimt: *Philosophy, Medicine and Jurisprudence*, fresco at Vienna University (destroyed by fire in 1945) (Aust-Hung).

- Adolf Loos: Kärntner Bar, Vienna (Aust-Hung).

- Foundation of the Deutscher Werkbund in Munich to promote industrial design (Ger).

- Peter Behrens joins AEG (General Electricity Company) as chief architect and designer, and is soon followed by Walter Gropius (Ger).

- Foundation of Hollywood, a suburb of Los Angeles, as a filmmaking center (USA).

- August Musger invents the slow-motion effect in film.

- First daily comic strip, "Mr Mutt" (later "Mutt and Jeff"), by Bud Fisher, appears in the *San Francisco Chronicle* (USA).

- First Ziegfeld Follies staged in New York by impresario Florenz Ziegfeld (USA).

SCIENCE

- **10 Apr**: French doctors announce the discovery of a new serum to cure dysentery.

- **Nov**: Maiden voyage of HMS *Mauretania*, largest and fastest ocean liner for 20 years and sister ship to the *Lusitania* (UK).

- R.G. Harrison announces a technique for culturing tissue cells outside of the body (USA).

- E. Fischer gives the name peptide to the simplest amino acid, and publishes his *Researches on the Chemistry of Proteins* (Ger).

- Potassium and rubidium are discovered to be radioactive.

- B.B. Boltwood discovers the use of uranium's radioactive decay to calculate the age of rocks (US).

- First regular radio broadcasts made by de Forest Radio Telephone Company (USA).

- Beginning of a wireless telegraph service between the USA and Ireland.

- P. Weiss develops the domain theory of ferromagnetism (Fr).

- Alfred Adler: *Study of Organ Inferiority and its Psychical Compensation*, psychology text (Ger).

- Pierre Cornu builds a prototype vertical takeoff helicopter, but it breaks up on landing (Fr).

- Georges Claude and Carl von Linde independently perfect the method of liquefying air and separating its component gases, making possible the first commercial production of the five inert gases found in air.

- Nobel Prize for Chemistry is won by Eduard Buchner (Ger) for his research into cell-free fermentation.

- Nobel Prize for Physics is won by Albert A. Michelson (USA) "for his optical precision instruments, and the spectroscopic and metrological investigations carried out with their aid".

- C.L.A. Laveran discovers the role of protozoans in causing diseases such as malaria, leishmanism and sleeping sickness. He wins the Nobel Prize for Physiology or Medicine for his work (Fr).

Although still a cause for excitement, the passage of automobiles along the roads of the advanced industrial nations was becoming a more frequent occurrence. The volume of motor traffic increased sharply from 1908, especially on American highways with the development of the Model T Ford, produced as a car for the people. The basic chassis of the Model T allowed the fitting of a variety of body types – salon, "buggy" or pickup truck. The United States' growing lead in the manufacture of automobiles was also indicated by the formation in 1908 of the General Motors Corporation by the merger of the Buick and Oldsmobile companies. The growing range of consumer durables made possible by mass production included mechanized gadgets to make housework easier, such as the Hoover vacuum cleaner. In Europe the use of such machines by the middle classes was in part an indication of rising labor costs, as domestic servants became more expensive. Controls on the exploitation of labor were increasing, and included the demand for a prohibition on children working at night.

▲ From 1 October 1908, the Model T Ford went into production at Henry Ford's Highland Park factory. Designed as a basic car for a wide market, it was particularly attractive to the dispersed rural communities of the American Mid-West, and by 1913 there was a Ford dealer in nearly every American town. By 1927, when production ceased, more than 15 million had been sold.

● **27 Jan**: Oklahoma becomes the 47th US state.

● **1 Feb**: Murder of King Carlos and the crown prince of Portugal in Lisbon results in the resignation of prime minister João Franco, who had instituted a dictatorship and a repressive regime; Manuel II succeeds and restores constitutional government.

● **12 Apr**: H. H. Asquith takes over as prime minister after the resignation of Campbell-Bannerman on grounds of health (UK).

● **14 Apr**: The Danish parliament adopts universal suffrage for taxpayers over 25.

● **30 Apr**: Two Englishwomen are killed by a terrorist bomb in Muzaffarpur, giving the Indian government a pretext to imprison the more prominent nationalist extremists (Ind).

● **Apr**: Signature of the Baltic Convention (Ger, Swe, Den, Russ) and North Sea Convention (Ger, Swe, Den, UK, Neth, Fr), providing for the maintenance of the status quo in the respective seas.

● **23 Jun**: Successful counter-revolution in Persia by Shah Muhammad Ali, with the support of Russian cossacks. The liberal constitution of 1906 is overthrown and many of the liberal leaders killed. Martial law is declared in Tehran, but in Tabriz a popular revolt seizes control, and attempts by the shah to regain control with the army leads to a deadlock. (› 26 Mar 1909)

● **5 Jul**: Insurrection by the "Young Turks", organized by Niazi Bey and supported by the Committee of Union of Progress and the Albanians, forces Sultan Abdul Hamid to restore the 1876 constitution (24 Jul); parliament convenes on 17 Dec with a large Young Turk majority (Tur). (› 26 Apr 1909)

● **11 Aug**: Kaiser Wilhelm II refuses to reduce the German naval program after discussions with King Edward VII (UK).

● **20 Aug**: King Leopold II of Belgium hands over the Congo State, formerly his private possession (since 1885), to the state; it is formally annexed on 15 Nov, becoming the Belgian Congo.

● **23 Aug**: Sultan Abd-el Aziz of Morocco flees after being defeated by Mulai Hafid, who declares himself sultan.

● **16 Sep**: Buchlau conference: Russia agrees to acquiesce in the Austrian annexation of Bosnia and Herzegovina. (›6 Oct)

● **25 Sep**: Casablanca incident: tension between France and Germany mounts after three German deserters from the French Foreign Legion are removed by force from the German consulate (Mor).

● **5 Oct**: Ferdinand I of Bulgaria declares independence from Turkey and assumes the title of czar; Turkey recognizes the secession on 19 Apr 1909.

● **6 Oct**: Annexation of Bosnia and Herzegovina by Austria angers Serbia and Montenegro, who had designs on the two provinces, and leads Russia to withdraw support and back Serbia against Austria–Hungary.

● **7 Oct**: Crete proclaims union with Greece; Greece officially takes over administration of Crete in Dec 1913, after withdrawal of Great Powers forces.

● **10 Oct**: Italy, France, and Russia put pressure on the Balkan states to hold a congress to settle the Balkan crisis. On 12 Oct, Russian minister Izvolski persuades UK to participate in a congress on the Balkan situation. From 9–14 Oct, Izvolski comes to London to try to secure UK support for his Straits program. However, UK makes its consent to the opening of the Straits conditional on obtaining Turkey's consent, and the scheme collapses. Negotiations to secure a conference continue throughout the autumn.

● **12 Oct** (until 3 Feb 1909): Constitutional convention to discuss the relationship between Cape Colony, Natal, Orange River Colony and Transvaal. The federal system is rejected and a Union of South Africa is proposed. A new parliamentary system is set up and both Dutch (Afrikaans) and English are established as official languages; the powers of the provincial governments are to be limited, subordinated to the Union government. (›31 May 1910)

● **3 Nov**: William Howard Taft (Republican) is elected president of the USA.

● **14–15 Nov**: Death of the dowager empress Cixi and the emperor Caitian ends the Guangxu period in China; succession of the boy emperor Pu Yi (until 1912).

● **4 Dec**: Naval conference in London, attended by 10 naval powers, agrees on various regulations of naval warfare, but this agreement is not ratified.

● Australia begins a 22-year program of construction of its first naval force. After a visit to the country by Lord Kitchener in 1909, a system of compulsory military training is introduced and an army is organized.

● Direct Dutch rule is established in Bali.

● Austria announces its intention to lay a railroad through the Sanjak of Novi Bazar toward Salonika, with the intention of dividing Montenegro and anti-Austrian Serbia.

● Suffragettes in Britain step up their campaign for the vote. On 21 June, 200,000 attend a rally in Hyde Park.

SOCIETY

- **8 Feb**: Britain's king and queen attend a Requiem Mass for the murdered king and crown prince of Portugal – the first English king to attend a Roman Catholic service in Britain since the Reformation.

- **11 Feb**: Patent rights over moving-picture camera are granted to Edison and major companies (USA).

- **18 Feb**: Plan for restriction of Japanese labor emigration to the USA is suggested by Japan, to settle disputes between the two countries.

- **Feb**: International shipping conference in London establishes passenger fares to end a price-cutting war.

- **Mar**: Meeting of employers in Berlin agrees on collective wage agreements (Ger).

- **4 Apr**: René Jeannel announces the discovery of prehistoric cave paintings at Louhans, France.

- **30 Apr**: Japanese cruiser *Matsushima* sinks off Pescadores Islands, after an explosion. Over 200 die.

- **May**: Movies are placed within the copyright laws (USA).

- **May**: Severe famine in Uganda.

- **Jul**: London hosts the fourth modern Olympic Games.

- **31 Jul**: Bush fires in British Columbia destroy around $7,000,000 worth of property and over 100 are killed. The town of Fernie is completely wiped out.

- **Sep**: International Conference for the Protection of Labor demands prohibition of night work for children.

- **1 Oct**: Ford Motor Co brings out the Model T Ford – the first mass market automobile, based on standard models with interchangeable parts. Ford goes on to develop the moving assembly line to speed up production. By 1913 there is a Ford dealer in every American city with a population over 2,000.

- **2 Oct**: Hundreds are reported dead in severe flooding in Hyderabad, India.

- **28 Oct**: Kaiser Wilhelm II creates international uproar by declaring, in an interview in the *Daily Telegraph*, that many Germans are anti-English, though he himself is friendly toward Britain. German chancellor Prince von Bülow is later forced to resign as a result of the interview.

- **12 Nov**: 360 miners die in a pit explosion in Hamm, Westphalia.

- **24 Dec**: World's first international aviation show is held in Paris.

- **26 Dec**: Jack Johnson (USA) becomes the first black world heavyweight boxing champion.

- **28 Dec**: Sicilian earthquake devastates the city of Messina. At least 200,000 die (It).

- Formation of the International Swimming Federation (FINA).

- USA remits half its share in the indemnities due to be paid by the Chinese government as a result of damage done during the Boxer rebellion. The funds go toward the founding of Tsing Hua College in 1911 and allow 1,100 Chinese graduates to study in the USA (1911–27).

- The Zeppelin airship company is established (Ger).

- Introduction of "use once and throw away" paper cups.

- Hoover company founded to market vacuum cleaner, which was invented in 1902 (UK).

- Appointment of the National Currency Commission to devise a new banking system (USA).

- General Motors Corporation formed in Detroit (USA) from the Buick and Oldsmobile firms.

- In USA, Federal Employers' Liability Act now covers industrial injury on interstate carriers.

- Creation of the Federal Bureau of Investigation (FBI) (USA).

- Old Age Pensions Act is passed by the British government. It comes into force 1 Jan 1909.

- Completion of the Hejaz Railroad (since 1900) from Turkey to the Holy Places of Islam in Arabia, built by popular subscription.

- Florence Lawrence becomes known as "The Biograph Girl", the first star to be created by the Hollywood publicity machine (USA).

- In London, *The Times* newspaper is acquired by Viscount Northcliffe, who also publishes the *London Daily Mail* and the *Daily Mirror*.

- **Aug–Oct**: Wilbur Wright makes a series of record-breaking flights in Europe.

- Nobel Prize for Peace won by Klas Arnoldson (Swe) and Frederik Bajer (Den).

CULTURE

- Rainer Maria Rilke: *Neue Gedichte II*, poems (Ger).

- Maxim Gorky: *The Confession* (Russ).

- First issues of Ford Madox (Ford) Hueffer's *English Review*, publishing the work of Thomas Hardy, Henry James, W.B. Yeats, John Galsworthy, Ezra Pound, Wyndham Lewis and others (UK).

- Foundation of the *New Age* review (until 1912) (UK).

- E.M. Forster: *A Room With a View*, novel (UK).

- The Nobel Prize for Literature is won by Rudolf Eucken (Ger).

- Arturo Toscanini takes over directorship from Gustav Mahler of the Metropolitan Opera in New York (USA).

- Anton Webern: *Passacaglia*, for orchestra, the composer's last tonal work (Aust-Hung).

- Arnold Schoenberg: Second String Quartet, the final movement of which (a soprano setting of a poem by Stefan George) is the first instance of 'atonal' music (Aust-Hung).

- Edward Elgar: First Symphony, (UK).

- Béla Bartók: First String Quartet (Aust-Hung).

- Aleksandr Skryabin: *Le Poème d'ecstase*, orchestral work (Russ).

- Benno Moiseiwitsch, pianist, makes his debut at Queen's Hall, London.

- Wassily Kandinsky: *Blue Mountain*, painting (Ger).

- Henri Matisse: *Harmony in Red*, painting (Fr).

- Symbolist artist Odilon Redon completes his *Ophelia among the Flowers* (1905–08) (Fr).

- Henri Matisse coins the term Cubism (Fr).

- Jack B. Yeats: *The Wake House*, woodcut (UK). Like his brother, the poet and dramatist W. B. Yeats, Jack Yeats was much concerned with Irish independence in cultural as well as political terms.

- Claude Monet destroys paintings valued at £20,000.

- Constantin Brancusi: *The Kiss*, sculpture (Fr).

- Jacob Epstein's Figures for the British Medical Association Building, the Strand, London, cause controversy (UK).

- Louis Sullivan: National Farmers' Bank, Minnesota (USA).

- Greene and Greene: The Gamble House, Pasadena, California (USA).

- Ludwig Mies van der Rohe joins AEG in Peter Behrens' office (Ger).

- Adolf Loos: *Ornament and Crime*, essay on architecture and design (Aust-Hung).

SCIENCE

- **14 Nov**: Albert Einstein presents his "quantum" theory of light (Swi).

- Hermann Minkowski formulates a four-dimensional geometry, in showing that the special theory of relativity is more complete if time is seen as a fourth dimension (Russ).

- I. Metchnikoff discovers the white blood cells (phagocytes) which devour bacteria (Russ).

- The international ampère is adopted by the International Conference on Electrical Units and Standards.

- A. Calmette and C. Guérin develop the first tuberculosis vaccine; after 15 years further development, it is used as BCG in the 1920s (Fr).

- British mathematician G.H. Hardy and German Physician W. Weinberg independently demonstrate the laws governing the frequency of occurrence of dominant hereditary traits.

- A.A. Campbell Swinton outlines a method of electronic scanning that forms the basis for the iconoscope, the prototype cathode-ray (TV) tube (UK).

- First international meeting of psychiatrists in Salzburg (Aust-Hung).

- Publication of A.E. Garrod's *Inborn Errors of Metabolism* (UK).

- The barium meal technique shows up a gastric ulcer for the first time through X-rays (Ger).

- C.F. Cross invents Cellophane.

- Invention of the tungsten filament by W.D. Coolidge (USA).

- F. Haber begins work on the Haber process for extracting nitrogen from the air to make ammonia for cheap fertilizer (Ger).

- H.K. Onnes liquifies helium (Neth).

- Giant and dwarf stellar systems described by E. Hertzsprung (Den).

- The gyro-compass by H. Anschütz-Kaempfe is patented (Ger).

- Hans Geiger (Ger) and Ernest Rutherford (UK) develop the Geiger counter to measure radioactivity.

- Two US chemists extract the whitest pigment (titanium oxide) from its natural sources, making possible a purer white for paper, textiles, etc.

- Nobel Prize for Chemistry is won by Ernest Rutherford (UK) "for his investigations into the disintegration of the elements and the chemistry of radioactive substances".

- Nobel Prize for Physics is won by Gabriel Lippmann (Fr), for his method of reproducing colors photographically based on the phenomenon of interference.

- Nobel Prize for Physiology or Medicine won by Paul Ehrlich (Ger) and Ilya Metchnikoff (Russ) for their work on the theory of immunity.

One of the features of the new century has been the ever-increasing pace of technological change, coupled with its application to the production of everyday items. The first successful powered flight had only taken place in 1903, but by 1909 Louis Blériot was able to fly across the English Channel in his monoplane, symbolizing the triumph of technology. Blériot's flight, however, also demonstrated that Britain could no longer be viewed as a European offshore group of islands that could be defended by superior naval power: within 10 years it was to be bombed by both airships and airplanes. But the British government continued to put its faith in its fleet, putting through a further naval bill in 1909, another move in the escalating warship-building race with Germany. When necessary, though, the Great Powers could still act in full concert, as was demonstrated by the enforced settlement of the crisis between Austria and Serbia provoked by the Austrian annexation of Bosnia-Herzegovina.

▲ Louis Blériot's flight across the English Channel on 25 July 1909 attracted wide publicity and led to a seven-day airshow in the French city of Reims. It was quickly realized that aircraft were not merely for sport, but a potential new form of transport, and one with military possibilities.

● **2 Jan**: The dismissal of Yuan Shihkai and the death of Chang Chidong, both liberals, dashes hopes for parliamentary elections in China, as power is passed to the Manchus. The meeting of the national assembly in 1910 demands the convocation of parliament, which is promised for 1913.

● **9 Jan**: Colombia signs a convention with the USA recognizing Panama. In 1914 a further treaty allows Colombia certain privileges in Panama, and the USA agrees to pay Colombia $25,000,000 for its recognition of Panamanian independence.

● **27 Jan**: The US governor leaves Cuba, and José Gomez is sworn in as president of the republic.

● **Jan**: Serious riots occur between Muslims and Hindus in India. (› 25 May)

● **8 Feb**: Franco-German agreement regarding Morocco reaffirms its integrity and independence, with recognition by Germany of France's interests in the country.

● **26 Feb**: Turkey recognizes the Austrian annexation of Bosnia-Herzegovina, and is paid compensation of 2.5 million Turkish pounds.

● **2 Mar**: War crisis between Austria and Serbia over the latter's refusal to relinquish its claims to Bosnia–Herzegovina is defused by the intervention of the Great Powers, who pressure Serbia to yield to Austria. (› 31 Mar)

● **12 Mar**: New British Navy Bill is passed due to fears regarding Germany's naval strength (› May).

● **26 Mar**: Russian troops invade northern Persia and occupy Tabriz, which is beseiged by the shah's army, in support of the shah.

● **31 Mar**: Serbia recognizes the annexation of Bosnia and Herzegovina and promises to curb anti-Austrian activities and improve relations with its northern neighbor.

● **19 Apr**: Turkey recognizes Bulgarian independence (proclaimed 5 Oct 1908). The Triple Alliance (Ger, Aust-Hung, It) recognizes its independence on 27 Apr.

● **26 Apr**: Sultan Abdul Hamid is deposed and exiled to Salonika after his support of an insurrection by the chiefly Albanian First Army Corps in Constantinople on 13 Apr, suppressed on 24 Apr; he is replaced by Muhammad V (Tur).

● **25 May**: Indian Councils Act enlarges the legislative councils and increases their power, granting separate electorates for Muslims and other minority groups, although this latter provision is condemned as divisive by moderate members of the Congress (Ind).

● **May**: An attempt by Baron Ferdinand von Stumm (Ger) to settle Anglo-German differences, in return for an agreement regarding naval affairs, is rebuffed by Britain since it threatens to weaken the entente with France and Russia.

● **Jun**: Ali Kuli Khan begins his march on Tehran to defend the liberal constitution regime, and captures the city on 12 Jul, deposing the shah on 16 Jul. The new shah is to be 12-year-old Sultan Ahmad (son of Muhammad Ali), who becomes a puppet of radical elements in the government (reigns until 1925) (Per).

● **14 Jul**: von Bülow resigns as German chancellor, and Kaiser Willhelm II replaces him with von Bethmann Hollweg.

● **21 July**: Georges Clemenceau and his government resign after a debate on the condition of the French navy. Aristide Briand takes over the French government.

● **26 Jul–26 Sep**: A revolutionary uprising in Catalonia, protesting at the inequality of military service arrangements, whereby the poorer classes have to render mandatory service, is suppressed (Sp).

● **16 Jul**: British prime minister A.J. Balfour tells MPs that giving equal rights to South Africa's blacks would threaten white civilization. 27 Jul: MPs give second reading to the South African Union Bill, but criticize the denial of the vote to blacks. 7 Dec: Royal Proclamation creating the self-governing Union of South Africa brings together the four colonies of the Cape of Good Hope, Natal, Transvaal, and the Orange River. Union had been promised by Britain at the end of the Boer War.

● **8 Aug**: The four protecting powers in Crete meet in Therapia to plan a settlement of the island's problems. An international fleet arrives in Crete on 17 Aug.

● **26 Oct**: Prince Ito (Jap) is assassinated by a Korean nationalist; he had resigned as governor-general of Korea after failing to reform the Korean administration.

● **28 Oct**: Belgian government announces major liberalizing reforms in the Congo.

● **4 Dec**: President José Zelaya of Nicaragua invites the USA, which backs the Nicaraguan revolutionaries, to see the conditions in the country. On 16 Dec, Zelaya resigns, under pressure from US marines. Dr José Madriz is elected to succeed Zelaya on 21 Dec.

● **19 Dec**: Juan Vicente Gomez declares himself president of Venezuela in the absence of President Cipriano Castro (until 1935).

● **Dec**: Civil war in Honduras between factions led by General Miguel Davila and President Bonila.

● Completion of the French conquest of Mauritania by General Henri Gouraud (since 1908).

SOCIETY

- **1 Jan**: US Motion Picture Patents Company is set up, licensing nine producers, including two French (USA).

- **11 Jan**: Public executions are resumed in France, after a long interval. Four members of the Pollet gang are guillotined for murder.

- **12 Jan**: 105 miners die in a pit explosion in West Virginia (USA).

- **18 Jan**: Brewers in New Zealand decide to abolish barmaids and women are mostly banned from buying alcohol in bars.

- **15 Mar**: US businessman H.G. Selfridge opens his department store on Oxford Street, London (UK).

- **23 Mar**: Ernest Shackleton arrives in New Zealand having led an expedition which came within 180 km (111 miles) of the South Pole, closer than any previous attempt.

- **6 Apr**: Robert Peary of the US Navy becomes the first person to reach the North Pole – his sixth attempt since 1902.

- **14 Apr**: The Anglo-Persian Oil Company is formed to operate the D'Arcy concession (1901) in Persia.

- **18 Apr**: Joan of Arc is beatified at a Vatican ceremony.

- **Apr–May**: Paris postal workers strike over demands to unionize and to affiliate with the Confédération Générale du Travail; over 200 employees are discharged and civil servants denied the right to strike (Fr).

- **22 May**: White firemen on the Georgia Railroad strike in protest at the employment of blacks. On 28 May, a mob attacks a black crew of a Georgia Railroad mail train as the strike by whites continues (USA).

- **Jul**: Agreement is reached between the USA and Germany on the use of patents.

- **19 Aug**: A decree imposes Hungarian as the official language of religious instruction in Romanian schools.

- **Aug**: A week of floods in Montarray, Mexico, kills around 1,500 and leaves 15,000 homeless.

- **Aug**: One-month general strike in Sweden over economic conditions.

- **2 Oct**: First railway built entirely by the Chinese opens, from Beijing to Kalgan.

- **6 Oct**: Payne–Aldrich tariff allows free importation of sugar, tobacco and hemp from the Philippines to the USA.

- **26 Oct**: Austria proposes a tax on bachelors to cope with the budget deficit caused by the annexation of Bosnia and Herzegovina.

- **14 Nov**: US president decides in favor of a naval station at Pearl Harbor in the Hawaiian Islands as a base to defend the USA from Japanese attack.

- **30 Nov**: Rejection by the House of Lords of UK prime minister David Lloyd George's "People's Budget" (passed by the Commons on 5 Nov), which proposed to shift the tax burden to the wealthy. (› Feb 1910)

- **Dec**: Complaint by the Standard Oil Company at the Supreme Court against the demanded suspension of its trust and against the anticartel legislation (USA).

- National Association for the Advancement of Colored People is formed by the merging of the Niagara Movement (young blacks led by W.E.B. Du Bois) and a group of concerned whites (USA).

- First kibbutz started at Degania Aleph (Pal).

- General Electric Company produces the first electric toaster.

- In Liberia, an American commission investigating the country's finances allocates aid until an international loan can be arranged.

- Federal old age pensions awarded to those over 65 and resident in Australia for over 25 years (Aus).

- German company Gelsenkirchener Bergwerks AG begins steel production in Luxembourg.

- Three-month strike by 20,000 garment workers in the USA.

- First permanent waves by London hairdressers (UK).

- Girl Guides are established in the UK, as a parallel organization to the Boy Scouts.

- Imperial (later International) Cricket Conference founded (UK).

- A telegraphic link over 11,000 km (7,000 miles) is established between the UK and India.

- *Vogue* magazine is bought by Condé Nast (USA).

- Nobel Peace Prize is won by Auguste Beernaert (Bel) and Paul d'Estairnelles de Constant (Fr).

CULTURE

- **9 Jan**: First performance of Maurice Ravel's piano triptych *Gaspard de la Nuit*, in Paris.

- **20 Feb**: Italian poet F.T. Marinetti issues his *Futurist Manifesto*, printed in *Le Figaro* (Fr).

- **18 May**: Debut in Paris of the *Ballets Russes* of Serge Diaghilev, with Mikhail Fokine as chief choreographer, Vaslav Nijinsky and Anna Pavlova as principal dancers, and sensational stage and costume designs by Leon Bakst and Alexandre Benois (Fr).

- **7 Oct**: Premiere in Moscow of Nikolay Rimsky-Korsakov's opera *Le Coq d'or* (The Golden Cockerel), choreographed by Fokine. It was prohibited in 1910 because of its satire on government (Russ).

- **28 Nov**: Sergei Rachmaninoff gives world premiere of his Third Piano Concerto.

- Robert Walser: *Jacob of Gunten: a Diary*, novel (Swi).

- First issue of the Acmeist periodical *Apollo* (until 1917) (Russ).

- Wladislaw Reymont: *Peasants* (4-vol novel, since 1902) (Russ).

- André Gide: *La Porte étroite* (trans. as Strait is the Gate, 1924), novel (Fr).

- Oskar Kokoschka: *Mörder, Hoffnung der Frauen* (Murderer, Hope of Women), prototype Expressionist play (Aust-Hung).

- J.M. Synge: *Deirdre of the Sorrows*, play (UK).

- Ezra Pound: *Exultations*, poems (UK).

- The Nobel Prize for Literature is won by Selma Lagerlöf (Swe).

- Gustav Mahler: *Das Lied von der Erde* (The Song of the Earth), a setting of Hans Bethge's 1907 translations of Chinese poems, for tenor, contralto and orchestra (Aust-Hung).

- Ralph Vaughan Williams: *Fantasia on a Theme by Thomas Tallis*, for double string orchestra and string quartet (UK).

- Richard Strauss: *Elektra*, opera, libretto by Hugo von Hofmannsthal (Ger).

- First transcription of blues – W.C. Handy's "Memphis Blues" (USA).

- Oskar Kokoschka: *Portrait of Adolf Loos* (Aust-Hung).

- Auguste Rodin: *Bust of Gustav Mahler* (Aust-Hung).

- Wassily Kandinsky founds the New Artists' Association (Ger).

- Peter Behrens: AEG Turbine Factory, Berlin (Ger).

- Daniel Burnham produces his plans for the improvement of Chicago (USA).

- Charles Rennie Mackintosh completes his School of Art, Glasgow (since 1897) (UK).

SCIENCE

- **24 Feb**: First color moving picture shown in Brighton (UK).

- **25 Jul**: French aviator Louis Blériot makes the first crossing of the English Channel by air, from Calais to Dover.

- K. Hofmann produces synthetic rubber from butadiene (Ger).

- E. Marsden determines if a thin gold foil is bombarded with alpha particles, some particles are heavily deflected or bounce back. Subsequent calculations by E. Rutherford result in the proposal that the bulk of an atom's mass is concentrated in a tiny, very dense nucleus (UK).

- A. Mohorovicic discovers discontinuity between the Earth's mantle and crust (Yug).

- S. Sorensen invents the pH scale of acidity (Den).

- Karl Bosch turns Haber's process for nitrogen synthesis into a commercial operation (Ger).

- W. Johannsen coins the terms "genes", "genotypes" and "phenotypes": key concepts for modern genetics (Den).

- The Meltzer–Auer tube is devised to assist breathing during mouth, throat or chest operations (USA).

- Publication of W. Bateson's *Mendel's Principles of Heredity: A Defense*, which applies Mendel's laws (based on a study of peas) to animals.

- E. Forlanini develops the hydrofoil ship.

- First commercially produced color films are made, after a process (Kinemacolor) developed by G.A. Smith the previous year (UK).

- H.W. Cushing discovers that acromegaly – the enlargement of the jaws, extremities and some organs – is due to overgrowth of the pituitary gland (USA).

- Leo H. Baekeland patents the process for making Bakelite, the first plastic to solidify on heating.

- Sigmund Freud lectures in the USA on psychoanalysis.

- First automatic telephone exchange is installed in Munich, Germany.

- C. Nicolle (Fr) shows typhus is spread by the body louse.

- Castrol introduce their first motor oil, designed specifically for automobile engines.

- Guglielmo Marconi (It) and Karl F. Braun (Ger) win the Nobel Prize for Physics for wireless telegraphy.

- W. Ostwald (Ger) wins the Nobel Prize for Chemistry for his work on catalysis.

- E.T. Kocher (Swi) wins the Nobel Prize for Physiology or Medicine for his work on the thyroid gland.

1910-1919

The death and state funeral of the king-emperor Edward VII marked a further development of "historic" pageantry and pomp in Britain, and was part of a process of transforming the monarchy into a constitutional figurehead. At this time the constitution was itself under challenge, as the House of Lords refused to pass David Lloyd George's "People's Budget", designed to fund social reform through more progressive systems of taxation. Generally across Europe, there was growing agitation for social reform. Dockers in both Britain and Germany struck for higher pay, while the parliament building in Berlin was besieged by 250,000 socialist demonstrators and a general strike was called in Spain. In France, a national rail strike disrupted rail traffic all over Europe. Such movements for change were mirrored in the arts. In Berlin the review Der Sturm, *a radical journal supporting Expressionism, began publication, while in Paris Pablo Picasso and Georges Braque were pushing out the boundaries of the visual arts with their development of Analytical Cubism. Technical developments made music available to a wider public: in January tenor Enrico Caruso broadcast opera on radio for the first time.*

▲ **Edward VII lying in state in Westminster Hall in London. Despite the ceremonial, Britain like many other European countries was in the process of moving toward a more purely constitutional monarchy – or none at all. Six months after Edward's death, revolution in Portugal forced the royal family to flee as the country was proclaimed a republic.**

● **13 Jan**: Five provinces in India are banned from holding "seditious" meetings in an attempt to halt unrest in the country. A new press censorship bill is announced on 4 Feb.

● **15 Jan**: France reorganizes the French Congo as French Equatorial Africa.

● **21 Feb**: Assassination of Egyptian premier, Butros Ghali, a Copt, by a nationalist fanatic. Further unrest follows after the execution of the assassin.

● **Feb**: General election in the UK ends with a dead heat for the Liberals and Conservatives. Asquith remains prime minister, and says the government will not reintroduce the budget (which the House of Lords rejected on 30 Nov 1909) until the House of Lords' veto has been abolished. (›18 Nov)

● **Feb**: Austro-Russian agreement to maintain the *status quo* in the Balkan peninsula reconciles the two countries.

● **27 Apr**: Louis Botha and James Hertzog found the South Africa party as a successor to Het Volk (Transvaal), Afrikaner Bond (Cape Colony) and Orangia Unie (Orange Free State, so renamed at the time of union), calling for independence and equality for the Boers (SA). (›31 May)

● **Apr**: The first majority Labor government in Australia under Andrew Fisher continues the program of heavy taxation on large and absentee-landlord properties, and resumes the system of allowing "desirable" white immigrants to settle in the Northern Territory.

● **Apr–Jun**: Insurrection in Albania over Albanian demands for autonomy is suppressed by the Turkish army.

● **6 May**: Death of Edward VII, succeeded by George V (UK).

● **24 May**: Starr Jameson founds the British-imperialist Unionist party (SA).

● **31 May**: Constitution of the Union of South Africa comes into effect. (›1 Jul)

● **May**: The Russian government orders thousands of Jews to leave Kiev. In Jun a delegation appeals to the US president for aid for Russian Jews, and on 12 Sep the Zionist Conference raises over 100,000 marks to establish a Jewish homeland in Palestine.

● **Jun**: The Russian Duma decides to abolish Finnish autonomy.

● **1 Jul**: The Union of South Africa becomes a dominion of the British Empire. (›15 Sep)

● **4 Jul**: A Russo-Japanese agreement provides for spheres of influence in Manchuria and mutual defense of interests. On 13 Jan they agree to the neutrality of the Manchurian railroad.

● **22 Aug**: After the Korean war of independence is suppressed, Korea is officially annexed to Japan and renamed Chosen.

● **28 Aug**: Montenegro declares full independence from the Ottoman Empire under King Nicholas I.

● **15 Sep**: First Union of South Africa elections, with 67 seats to the South African party against 37 to the Unionists; Louis Botha is the first prime minister.

● **3–5 Oct**: Revolution in Portugal: the Portuguese monarchy is overthrown and King Manuel II flees to England. The Portuguese Republic is proclaimed on 5 Oct, under a provisional government led by Dr Theophilo Braga, which institutes a fierce anticlerical policy.

● **7 Oct**: The Portuguese government orders the expulsion of all nuns and monks within 24 hours; this leads to the separation of church and state on 20 Apr 1911. On 17 Oct, the government banishes the royal family and abolishes the nobility.

● **18 Oct**: Eleutherios Venizelos becomes prime minister of Greece, beginning a program of financial, administrative and constitutional reform.

● **27 Oct**: British troops arrive at Lingah, Persia, to protect British interests amid local unrest.

● **4–5 Nov**: Tentative agreements between Germany and Russia allow Russia a free hand in northern Persia, in return for the end of Russian opposition to the Baghdad Railroad, for which a construction concession had been granted to a German company in 1899.

● **18 Nov**: Asquith announces that the king will dissolve parliament and that a second 1910 general election will be held in an attempt to resolve the constitutional crisis which had arisen when the House of Lords vetoed the 1909 "People's Budget". However, the general election held on 20 Dec makes little difference, with the Liberals winning only two more seats.(›15 May 1911)

● **14 Dec**: In Palestine, Turkish troops are sent to suppress an uprising of 20,000 Bedouin Arabs who are trying to free themselves from Turkish rule.

● The Northern Territory of Australia, formerly administered by South Australia, becomes a federal possession.

SOCIETY

● **Jan**: Serious floods occur in south, east, south-west and central France and Switzerland. (›May)

● **Jan**: The German government tells the USA it is ready for a tariff war.

● **Jan**: English miners strike for an eight-hour day; many miners and police are hurt in riots.

● **Feb**: Agreement is reached on the construction and management of a railroad through the St Gotthard pass between Germany, Italy and Switzerland.

● **Feb**: The first labor exchanges are opened in the UK.

● **10 Mar**: China abolishes slavery.

● **11 Mar**: 500 children are swept away when a dam bursts in the Rhondda Valley in Wales, though 494 are eventually rescued (UK).

● **10 Apr**: An antigovernment demonstration in Berlin is attended by 250,000 socialist supporters (Ger).

● **15 Apr**: Rioters in China burn buildings owned by foreigners.

● **Apr**: Measures are taken by the Russian government for the economic development of Siberia, including the construction of a railroad from Moscow to Irkutsk.

● **5 May**: An earthquake around Cartago, Nicaragua, kills 500.

● **May**: Halley's Comet comes within 13 million miles of Earth. It causes concern in France and Russia, and it is believed to be responsible for the bad weather. (› Jun)

● **2 Jun**: British explorers find pygmies in the Dutch New Guinea mountains.

● **11 Jun**: King Alfonso of Spain proclaims freedom of belief. On 9 Aug, the Vatican announces an imminent break with Spain over proposed controls on religious orders.

● **Jun**: Severe flooding affects central Europe.

● **16 Jul**: Rioting breaks out in Bilbao (Spain) as miners go on strike.

● **Jul**: Dr H. H. Crippen and his mistress Ethel Le Neve become the first criminal suspects to be caught via a radio link, when the captain of the SS *Montrose* radios his suspicions ashore (Can).

● **Jul**: A commercial treaty is agreed between Austria–Hungary and Serbia.

● **Aug**: Kinetophone, with moving picture and simultaneous sound – "talking pictures" – is demonstrated by T.A. Edison (USA).

● **Aug–Oct**: Dockers strike in Germany and in the UK for higher wages; in Spain, a general strike is called, and a nationwide rail strike in France disrupts railroads throughout Europe.

● **25 Oct**: Severe storms and a tidal wave in the Bay of Naples kill 1,000 (It).

● **5 Dec**: A barge convoy on the River Volga (Russ) sinks, and 300 workmen die.

● Establishment of the first industrial banks (USA).

● Nobel Peace Prize is won by the International Peace Bureau.

● The South American tango becomes a popular dance in the USA and Europe.

● Hairdresser Antoine creates "bobbed" hair in his Paris salon.

● Electrification of a section of the Magdeburg-Halle railroad (Ger).

● A note-issuing monopoly is given to the Swiss National Bank.

● Swiss railroads are nationalized.

● Arthur Evans completes the excavation of the ancient Minoan palace of Knossos, Crete (Gre).

● Father's Day is first celebrated in Spokane, Washington, DC (USA).

● Pathé Gazette processes the first film newsreel (USA/UK).

● Old age pensions are introduced in France.

● The first radio receivers in kit form go on sale to the public (USA).

CULTURE

● **1 Jan**: New York's Metropolitan Opera, with tenor Enrico Caruso, broadcasts opera on radio for the first time (USA).

● Charles Péguy: *The Mystery of the Charity of Joan of Arc*, poems (Fr).

● Rainer Maria Rilke: *The Notebook of Malte Laurids Brigge*, novel (Ger).

● E.M. Forster: *Howard's End*, novel (UK).

● Arnold Bennett: *Clayhanger*, novel (UK).

● Foundation in Berlin by Herwarth Walden of the review *Der Sturm*, a radical journal supporting Expressionism (Ger).

● The Nobel Prize for Literature is won by Paul Heyse (Ger).

● Gustav Mahler: Ninth Symphony, premiered posthumously under Bruno Walter in 1912 (Aust-Hung).

● Aleksandr Skryabin: *Prometheus*, in which the composer employs his imaginary "clavier lumières" ("light keyboard") that controls the production of colored light instead of sound (Russ).

● Edward Elgar: Violin Concerto (UK).

● First performance of Frederick Delius's opera *A Village Romeo and Juliet* at Covent Garden under Thomas Beecham (UK).

● Igor Stravinsky's ballet *The Firebird* for the *Ballets Russes*, based on a Russian fairytale and choreographed by Mikhail Fokine, is an outstanding success. Stravinsky wrote two more ballets for the *Ballets Russes*, *Petrushka* (1911) and *The Rite of Spring* (1913) (Fr).

● March band leader John Philip Sousa (USA) tours the world with his band.

● Alfred Stieglitz exhibits work by Gaston Lachaise, John Marin, Joseph Stella, Abraham Walkowitz, Max Weber, William Zorach and others at the 291 gallery in New York (USA).

● Henri Rousseau: *The Dream*, painting (Fr).

● Henri Matisse: *The Dance*, painting (Fr).

● Georges Braque: *Violin and Palette*, painting (Fr).

● Development of Analytical Cubism by Pablo Picasso and Georges Braque (Fr).

● Exhibition of Islamic art in Munich (Ger).

● Antonio Gaudí: Casa Mila, Barcelona (Sp).

● Adolf Loos: Steiner House, Vienna (Aust-Hung).

● First movie publicity stunt, with Gertrude Lawrence mobbed after reports of her death.

● Opening of the largest cinema yet built, the 5,000-seat Gaumont Palace in Paris (Fr).

● Biograph makes its first films in Hollywood (USA).

SCIENCE

● Alfred Wilm patents the process for producing duralumin, a lightweight, high-strength aluminum alloy, which later influences the evolution of the aircraft industry (Ger).

● Nobel Prize for Chemistry is won by Otto Wallach (Ger) "for his pioneer work in the field of alicyclic compounds".

● Nobel Prize for Physics is won by Johannes van der Waals, "for his work on the equation of state for gases and liquids", which had importance for modern refrigeration engineering (Neth).

● Nobel Prize for Physiology or Medicine is won by Albrecht Kossel (Ger) for "contributions to our knowledge of cell chemistry made through his work on proteins, including the nucleic substances."

● B. Ljundstrom constructs the high-pressure steam turbine (Nor).

● Prince Albert I of Monaco founds the Institute for Oceanography (Mon).

● J.J. Thomson, while measuring atomic masses of substances, provides the first confirmation that isotopes are possible (UK).

● R. Biffen breeds Little Jos, a wheat suitable for British climate and resistant to the yellow rust fungus (UK).

● Marie Curie's *Treatise on Radiography* is published (Fr). In 1910, she also succeeds in isolating a pure sample of radium.

● T.H. Morgan discovers that certain inherited characteristics are sex-linked (USA).

● F. Woodbury discovers the use of iodine as a disinfectant and antiseptic (USA).

● C. Parson's speed-reducing gear extends the use of geared turbines by improving the efficiency of the energy transfer between the steam turbine and the propeller (UK).

● G. Claude invents the fluorescent tube or "neon light" (Fr).

● The rotary intaglio printing process is developed by E. Mertens (Ger).

● L. Leuchs prepares the first antitoxic sera for botulism (Ger).

● Discovery of sickle-cell anemia by J. Herrick (USA).

● Establishment of the Rockefeller Foundation for the promotion of science (USA).

● F. Cottrell invents the electrostatic precipitator, which removes solid or liquid particles from gases. In doing so, it can clean ventilating air or reduce the emission of smoke from factory flues.

● Paul Ehrlich (Ger) uses Salvarsan as a drug to treat syphilis.

● Dr H. Frahm invents an anti-rolling device for ships.

The arrival of Norwegian explorer Roald Amundsen's expedition at the South Pole completed humankind's mastery of the outer limits of the globe. In Africa, once a center for exploration, the European Great Powers continued to vie for control. French, British and German interests clashed in Morocco, initiating a second crisis there. After its resolution by diplomatic discussions between Germany and France, the European colonization of Africa was almost complete; only Liberia and Ethiopia could now make any claim to independence. Germany established its own colonies in equatorial Africa, and Italy by force of arms annexed first the port of Tripoli and then Cyrenaica, Libya and Tripolitania, previously under Turkish rule – an action which involved the first military use of aircraft. Elsewhere in the world, popular revolutions were beginning to overthrow their oppressors. In Mexico, dictator Porfirio Diaz was forced to resign after 35 years in power, and in China revolutionary movements deposed the Manchu dynasty and established a provisional national assembly at Nanjing.

▲ Amundsen's expedition raised the Norwegian flag at the South Pole on 16 December 1911 after a long and arduous journey. The climate and terrain created challenges that produced amazing feats of courage and valor. Sometimes even this was not enough: Robert Scott's British expedition, reaching the South Pole soon after Amundsen, perished and never returned.

● **24 Feb**: The German Reichstag votes to increase the German standing army by 515,000.

● **1 Mar**: President Taft sends 30,000 US soldiers to the Mexican frontier in case of revolution. On 1 Apr, Mexican president Porfirio Diaz promises extensive reforms in the face of growing rebellion. On 15 Apr, US troops begin fighting the rebels, led by Francisco Madero, and on 20 Apr, the rebels refuse a ceasefire until president Diaz resigns. (›25 May)

● **23 Apr**: The French government decides to send more troops to Morocco to suppress the revolt there, ostensibly in response to an appeal from the sultan. The German press warn that a permanent French occupation would violate the 1906 Algeciras Conference agreement on Morocco's independence. (›21 May)

● **15 May**: 15-year-old Lij Yasu is proclaimed emperor of Ethiopia. In 1916, he is deposed after his conversion to Islam, since it is feared this will lead to closer links with Turkey and Germany.

● **15 May**: The Parliament Bill, restricting the power of the Lords, is passed in the House of Commons. It is finally passed by the House of Lords on 10 Aug after prime minister Asquith threatens to create as many peers as would be necessary to get the bill through the House (UK).

● **21 May**: French troops enter Fez (Mor) after anti-foreign unrest, and France is accused by Germany of violating the Algeciras agreement, initiating a second Moroccan crisis. (›20 Jun)

● **25 May**: Mexican dictator Porfirio Diaz is forced to resign by Francisco Madero, ending a 35-year rule. Diaz goes into exile in Paris, and Madero as president institutes a liberal regime (Mex).

● **26 May**: A constitution is granted to Alsace-Lorraine, with a two-chamber legislature and a substantial degree of autonomy (Ger).

● **20–21 Jun**: Franco-German discussions over the Moroccan crisis make little progress. Germany sends the gunboat *Panther* to Agadir on 1 Jul, supposedly to protect German companies, and the French request naval assistance from Britain (rejected on 4 Jul). (›21 Jul)

● **16 Jul**: Lord Kitchener (UK) becomes consul-general in Egypt, instituting a period of liberalization on one hand and suppression of agitation on the other.

● **21 Jul**: Chancellor of the Exchequer David Lloyd George's "Mansion House" speech makes clear Britain's refusal to be implicated in the Moroccan affair, causing recriminations between Britain and Germany. Britain begins to make preparations for war, but the crisis is defused by the agreement reached on 4 Nov.

● **17 Aug**: Northeastern and northwestern Rhodesia are united as Northern Rhodesia, administered by the South Africa Company.

● **20 Aug**: A liberal constitution is adopted by the Portuguese constituent assembly. Dr Manoel de Arriaga is elected first president of the republic on 24 Aug. (›1 Oct)

● **14 Sep**: Russian premier Pyotr Stolypin is assassinated by a revolutionary in Kiev.

● **29 Sep**: Beginning of the Tripolitan War between Italy and Turkey after an ultimatum to the Turks over peaceful entry into Tripoli is rejected. An Italian force lands at Tripoli on 5 Oct and occupies it and the other coastal towns soon after, proclaiming the annexation of Tripoli on 5 Nov. The Turks under Enver Bey continue opposition within Tripoli. (›Nov)

● **1 Oct**: Royalist peasants in north Portugal revolt, demanding the restoration of the monarchy (abolished in 1910). On 3 Oct, the Royalists are beaten by Republican troops in a battle at Oporto.

● **23 Oct**: The Cretan parliament votes for unification with Greece.

● **14 Oct–6 Dec**: Russia attempts to involve Turkey in a Balkan League in which the safeguarding of Turkish territory in Europe would be assured in return for allowing Russian warships through the Dardanelles.

● **Oct**: Beginning of the Chinese Revolution, which overthrows the Manchu dynasty after nearly 300 years. The revolutionary movements, aided by popular assent, spread almost bloodlessly throughout the south and west of China. (›4 Dec)

● **4 Nov**: Franco-German agreement is finally reached on Morocco, which becomes a French protectorate, while France cedes territory in the French Congo to Germany. In Africa, only Ethiopia and Liberia can now claim any independence.

● **5 and 29 Nov**: The Persian *majlis* (parliament) rejects two Russian ultimata to dismiss W. Morgan Shuster (›Society, 12 May), and Russia begins an invasion of northern Persia, creating tension in Anglo-Russian relations. (›Dec)

● **Nov**: Italy annexes Libya, Tripolitania and Cyrenaica.

● **4 Dec**: In China, premier Yuan Shikai signs a truce with rebel general Li Yuanhung. Revolutionary leader Sun Yat-sen is elected president of the United Provinces of China on 30 Dec by a revolutionary provisional assembly at Nanjing.

● **6 Dec**: Mongolia is declared a Russian protectorate.

● **Dec**: The Persian *majlis* is closed by a group of politicians who then form a directory, and Persia remains dominated by Russia until the outbreak of World War I.

- **3 Jan**: After a fierce gun battle with police and troops, a house in Sidney Street in London containing three anarchists burns to the ground. Two bodies are later found; one man is believed to have escaped.

- **Jan**: Rich oil strike in Borneo by Anglo-Saxon Petroleum Company.

- **Jan**: Miners go on strike in the Belgian coal district.

- **4 Feb**: Rolls Royce commission the "Spirit of Ecstasy" statuette to replace personal mascots on owners' cars.

- **Feb**: 100 people are reported to be dying daily in Manchuria from the plague.

- **26 Mar**: Welsh miners in the Rhondda Valley vote to continue their strike which began Sep 1910.

- **7 Apr**: Authors and musicians in the UK are granted copyright on their work for their lifetimes and for 50 years after their deaths.

- **13 Apr**: Rioting in the Epernay and Reims areas of France. Thousands of bottles of wine are smashed.

- **19 Apr**: The provisional government in Portugal separates church and state.

- **30 Apr**: A constitutional court establishes female suffrage in Portugal.

- **1 May**: Color "talkie" released, with sound on Biophon synchronized disk (Swe).

- **12 May**: At the invitation of the Persian government, W. Morgan Shuster (USA) is given powers to set in order the finances of Persia, but this is opposed by Russia (Per).

- **31 May**: Launch of the White Star liner *Titanic* at Belfast (UK). She and her sister SS *Olympic* are the largest vessels afloat.

- **May**: J. D. Rockefeller's Standard Oil Trust is dissolved by the US Supreme Court on the basis of antitrust legislation (USA).

- **May**: Inaugural Indianapolis 500 automobile race is won by Ray Harroun (USA).

- **7 Jun**: Over 100 are killed in an earthquake in Mexico City.

- **17 Jun**: In the UK, 40,000–60,000 supporters of the enfranchisement of women march through London.

- **1 Jul**: UK parliament passes the Shops Act, establishing a compulsory half-day holiday a week for shop workers.

- **Jul**: A heatwave in the USA kills 652 in one week.

- **3 Aug**: First military use of aircraft when Italians reconnoitre Turkish lines near Tripoli.

- **15 Aug**: 215,000 demonstrate in Brussels in favor of universal suffrage.

- **Aug**: Railmen and transport workers go on strike over low wages and rising prices, clashing with troops and bringing much of the UK to a standstill.

- **Aug**: A heatwave in London reportedly kills 2,500 children.

- **4 Sep**: It is reported that 100,000 have died in flooding along the Chang Jiang River, China.

- **6 Sep**: First successful swim across the English Channel for 36 years, by Thomas Burgess.

- **9 Sep**: Collapse at the Berlin stock exchange due to the Morocco crisis and German colonial policy.

- **18 Sep**: General strike is declared in Valencia, Spain, and martial law proclaimed (until 22 Oct).

- **11 Oct**: 700 die in an earthquake in southern California.

- **Nov**: Circulation of bank notes is fixed to 6.3 billion francs until 1925 (Fr).

- **16 Dec**: Roald Amundsen raises the Norwegian flag over the South Pole, two months ahead of Robert F. Scott's British expedition.

- **Dec**: Agreement between the UK, Russia and France prohibiting the capture of seals.

- **Dec**: National Insurance Act is passed, providing insurance against sickness or unemployment (UK).

- Nobel Peace Prize is won by Tobias Asser (Neth) and Alfred Fried (Aust).

- Olivetti Company is founded in Italy.

- Establishment of the Australian Central Bank.

- Famine reduces 30,000,000 Russians to starvation, but 13.7 million tonnes of grain are exported.

- A system of universal military training for 14 to 41-year-olds is established in New Zealand due to international tensions.

- Joseph Schumpeter publishes his *Theory of Economic Development* (Aust-Hung).

- Japanese commercial treaties are signed with the UK (3 Apr), France and Germany (28 Jun).

- First Monte Carlo automobile rally (Mon).

- Publication of F. Boas's *The Mind of Primitive Man* (USA).

- White line in the center of the road is first used in the USA.

- **26 Jan**: Richard Strauss's opera *Der Rosenkavalier* (The Knight of the Rose), libretto by Hugh von Hofmannsthal, is premiered in Dresden (Ger).

- Robert Musil: *Vereinigungen*, novel (Aust-Hung).

- Hugo von Hofmannsthal, *Jedermann*, play (Ger).

- D.H. Lawrence, *The White Peacock*, novel (UK).

- Joseph Conrad: *Under Western Eyes*, novel (UK).

- Ezra Pound: *Canzoni*, poems (UK). Born in the USA, Pound had moved to Europe in 1908. He champions the work of avant-garde writers such as James Joyce and T.S. Eliot.

- John Middleton Murry and others found the Modernist journal *Rhythm* (later *The Blue Review*) while Murry is still an undergraduate at Oxford (UK).

- The Nobel Prize for Literature is won by Maurice Maeterlinck (Bel).

- Béla Bartók: *Duke Bluebeard's Castle*, opera (first produced in Budapest 1918) (Aust-Hung).

- Arnold Schoenberg: *Harmonielehre*, a music theory teaching text, dedicated to Gustav Mahler (Aust-Hung).

- Jean Sibelius: Fourth Symphony (Fin).

- Irving Berlin: "Alexander's Ragtime Band", popular song (USA).

- Formation of *Der Blaue Reiter* (The Blue Rider) group of painters by Franz Marc and Wassily Kandinsky (until 1914). The name originates in the title of a Kandinsky painting, and is also the title of an almanac published by the group. Other members include August Macke and, for a time, Paul Klee (Ger).

- Composer Arnold Schoenberg exhibits his paintings with *Der Blaue Reiter* (Ger).

- Gustav Klimt: *Death and Life*, painting (Aust-Hung).

- Pablo Picasso: *Man Smoking a Pipe*, painting (Fr).

- Marc Chagall: *I and the Village*, painting (Fr).

- Leonardo da Vinci's *Mona Lisa* is stolen from the Musée du Louvre in Paris (found in Italy in 1913) (Fr).

- Jacob Epstein: tomb of Oscar Wilde, sculpture (UK).

- Josef Hoffmann, Art Nouveau architect: Palais Stoclet, Brussels (Bel).

- Walter Gropius and Adolf Meyer: The Fagus Factory, Alfeld-an-der-Leine (Ger).

- Atelier Martine (Fr) is founded by Paul Poiret as a design studio modeled on the Wiener Werkstatte (Fr).

- **Dec**: Marie Curie (Fr) wins an unprecedented second Nobel Prize for Chemistry, for her work on polonium and radium – but the Académie des Sciences in Paris refuses to admit her because she is a woman.

- Nobel Prize for Physics is won by Wilhelm Wien (Ger) "for his discoveries regarding the laws governing the radiation of heat".

- Nobel Prize for Physiology or Medicine is won by Allvar Gullstrand (Swe) "for his work on the dioptrics of the eye".

- Charles F. Kettering develops the first practical electric self-starter for automobiles (USA).

- T.H. Morgan suggests that certain hereditary traits are genetically linked on the chromosome, a discovery that leads to his plotting the first genetic map, of the positions of genes on the chromosomes of *Drosophila* fruit flies (USA).

- Building of the *Selandia*, the first ship with heavy oil engines (Den).

- Ferdinand Braun (Ger) and A.A. Campbell Swinton (UK) propose the use of a cathode ray in image-scanning, contributing to the development of television.

- Lewis machine-gun patented by I.N. Lewis.

- Ernest Rutherford and Frederick Soddy devise a scheme for the transmutation of elements (UK).

- C. Weizmann obtains acetone from bacteria involved in fermenting grain, providing an essential ingredient of cordite (UK).

- Thermal cracking technique for petroleum derivatives is developed by W. Burton (USA).

- P. Monnartz discovers the anticorrosive property of stainless steel (Ger).

- Ernest Rutherford deduces the nature of the atomic nucleus as a very small, dense core (UK).

- C.T.R. Wilson devises his cloud chamber, for observing the activity of electrons (UK).

- W. Hill develops the gastroscope for investigating abdominal illness (USA).

- H.K. Onnes discovers superconductivity at very low temperatures (Neth).

- T. Addis gives transfusions of normal plasma to hemophiliacs, therefore shortening their clotting time.

- Colt .45 automatic pistol is first used in the US Army after winning a government competition to find a heavy caliber weapon simple enough to be taken apart without tools, yet reliable under adverse conditions.

The "news story" of the year may have been the sinking of the passenger liner Titanic, but it was events in the Balkans that concerned the European Great Powers. A renewal of trouble had been under way since 1903, when a coup d'état in Serbia had put a strongly nationalist group in control and stimulated the drive for nationalism throughout the Balkans. Fears of Austrian expansion had proved justified when in 1908 it annexed the provinces of Bosnia and Herzegovina without warning, itself fearing Serbian territorial ambitions. In the same year, concern over new Turkish ambitions was aroused after its takeover by the "Young Turks". By October 1912, the highly volatile Balkan states of Serbia, Montenegro, Bulgaria and Greece were all at war with Turkey. Hostilities were ended by a peace conference in London in 1912/13, but quickly broke out again.

▲ Over half the passengers and crew of the *Titanic* died when the ship, claimed to be unsinkable because of its watertight bulkheads, collided with an iceberg on its maiden voyage across the Atlantic.

- **6 Jan**: New Mexico becomes the 47th US state.

- **10 Jan**: French cabinet resigns. Raymond Poincaré becomes prime minister of a coalition government on 13 Jan.

- **26 Jan**: Over 30,000 demonstrate in Ulster against British government proposals to give Ireland home rule.

- **Jan**: After elections, the socialists become the strongest party in the German Reichstag, largely due to the revisionism of Eduard Bernstein. On 16 Feb, chancellor Bethmann-Hollweg attacks the socialists and says the government does not intend to increase democracy, and on 18 Feb Kaiser Wilhelm refuses to give the customary audience to the socialist victors.

- **3 Feb**: A large-scale naval program is agreed in Japan, to build eight Dreadnoughts and eight armored cruisers, to take effect in 1913.

- **8 Feb**: UK Secretary for War Viscount Haldane undertakes a diplomatic mission to Berlin to try to achieve a naval agreement between Germany and Britain but it proves fruitless. (›8 Mar)

- **12 Feb**: Abdication of the boy emperor Pu Yi. Yuan Shikai is elected provisional president of the Chinese Republic on 15 Feb, following the resignation of Sun Yat-sen. A provisional constitution is promulgated on 10 Mar, and opposition parties are formed: the Progress party under Liang Qichao advocates a strong executive, and the Gu (Nationalist) party under Sun Yat-sen a parliamentary government. The elected parliament is convoked on 8 Apr 1913.

- **14 Feb**: Arizona becomes the 48th US state.

- **8 Mar**: A German naval bill provides for further enlargement of the navy, bringing to an end the Anglo-German discussions (since Nov 1910). Britain vows to retain naval superiority and in Jul recalls battleships from the Mediterranean for North Sea patrols.

- **13 Mar**: Alliance between Bulgaria and Serbia, joined by Greece on 29 May, ostensibly as a league against Turkey. (›1 Jun)

- **11 Apr**: Introduction of the third Home Rule Bill for Ireland, intended to provide for a bicameral parliament. The bill is criticized for unfairness to Protestant Ulster. Thousands protest against the bill in Belfast (UK).

- **17 Apr**: In Morocco, troops revolt against French rule.

- **18 Apr**: The Turks close the Dardanelles straits after bombardment by Italy, but they are reopened on 4 May after protests from Russia and other powers.

- **31 May**: US Marines land in Cuba to protect US interests there.

- **1 Jun**: Greece and Montenegro mobilize troops against Turkey. (›18 Sep)

- **1 Jul**: Morocco is declared a French protectorate by the Treaty of Fez.

- **30 Jul**: Death of the Meiji emperor Mutsuhito, succeeded by his son Yoshihito (until 1916), begins the Taisho era, largely a continuation of movements begun in the Meiji period (Jap).

- **Jul**: Beginning of civil war in Nicaragua, with intervention by the USA to protect the conservative government; Adolfo Diaz is elected president in Nov.

- **18 Sep**: War fever mounts in the Balkans as Bulgaria and Serbia make the decision to declare war on Turkey, using their demands for reforms in Macedonia as a pretext.

- **8 Oct**: First Balkan War: Montenegro, followed by Bulgaria, Serbia and Greece on 18 Oct, declares war on Turkey. As the Bulgarians advance toward Constantinople, the Russians warn (3–5 Nov) that any attempt to occupy the city will be resisted by the Russian fleet. On 24 Nov Austria announces opposition to Serbian access to the Adriatic Sea, and advocates an independent Albania. (› 28 Nov, 3 Dec)

- **18 Oct**: Treaty of Lausanne between Turkey and Italy ends the Tripolitan War: Italy promises withdrawal from the Aegean in return for Turkish withdrawal from Tripoli.

- **5 Nov**: Democrat Woodrow Wilson is elected US president.

- **7 Nov**: Treaty between Russia and Outer Mongolia secures the autonomy of the latter.

- **12 Nov**: Assassination of José Canalejos, liberal and anticlerical premier of Spain.

- **21–22 Nov**: Grey–Cambon correspondence between Paul Cambon, the French ambassador in the UK and Sir Edward Grey, the Foreign Secretary, strengthens the Anglo-French Entente by way of mutual consultations in the event of either country being militarily threatened.

- **27 Nov**: France and Spain sign a treaty outlining their respective spheres of influence in Morocco.

- **28 Nov**: Declaration of Albanian independence, with a provisional government under Ismail Kemal.

- **3 Dec**: Armistice between Turkey, Bulgaria and Serbia; Greece and Montenegro maintain offensives in Janina and Scutari respectively. (›17 Dec)

- **5 Dec**: Triple Alliance (Ger, Aust-Hung, It) renewed for six years from 1914.

- **17 Dec**: Opening of the London peace conference on the Balkan question, which breaks down on 6 Jan 1913 after the Turks refuse to relinquish Adrianople, Crete and the Aegean Islands; terms are finally accepted by Turkey on 22 Jan. (›9 Jan 1913)

SOCIETY   CULTURE   SCIENCE

SOCIETY

- **16 Jan**: Robert F. Scott (UK) reaches the South Pole, but he and his party perish in a blizzard on the return journey (c. 29 May).

- **Jan**: General strike in Lisbon over dissatisfaction with the new regime (1911); the city is placed under military rule (Port).

- **28 Feb**: Albert Berry (USA) makes the first parachute jump from a plane.

- **Feb**: Torrential rain causes severe flooding in Spain.

- **Feb**: Two percent of London's population are reported to be dying each week from the cold.

- **4 Mar**: 96 are arrested after a suffragette raid on the House of Commons. On 5 Mar, police raid the Women's Social and Political Union offices. On 28 Mar, the Women's Enfranchisement Bill is defeated in its second House of Commons reading.

- **7 Mar**: Henri Seimet becomes the first to fly nonstop from Paris to London, taking 3 hours 25 minutes.

- **29 Mar**: Minimum Wage Law is forced after a strike of 1,500,000 coal miners (26 Feb–6 April) (UK).

- **Mar**: A miners' strike in the Ruhr ends in failure (Ger).

- **Mar**: Girl Scouts of America founded.

- **15 Apr**: The SS *Titanic* (USA) sinks on her maiden voyage across the North Atlantic Ocean after collision with an iceberg, causing the deaths of 1,513 people.

- **Apr**: Gold miners' strike in Siberia is suppressed by the army (Russ).

- **9 May**: A Japanese protest over anti-alien land legislation in California (USA) is assuaged by assurances that it does not affect Japan's treaty rights of 1908 and 1911.

- **27 May**: A cinema fire in Valencia, Spain, kills 80.

- **May–15 Jun**: Transport strike in London triggers a sympathetic strike by 100,000 dockers (UK).

- **13 Jun**: In Austria, Frau Vikkunetska is elected the first woman MP, but Prince Thun of Bohemia refuses to sanction her election.

- **23 Jun**: Bridge over Niagara Falls collapses, killing 47.

- **28 Jun**: Suffragettes start a window-smashing campaign at Post Offices and Labour Exchanges (UK).

- **29 Jun**: Opening of the Olympic Games in Stockholm. An American of Red Indian descent, Jim Thorpe, wins both the pentathlon and decathlon (Swe).

- **1 Aug**: Airmail postal service opens between London and Paris.

- **8 Aug**: Over 120 die in a Westphalian pit disaster (Ger).

- **9 Sep**: Mass demonstrations in Athens demand liberation of all Greeks from Ottoman rule.

- **22 Sep**: A typhoon sweeps across Japan, killing hundreds.

- **Sep**: Formation of the Anglo-Chinese Bank.

- **Dec**: 245 miners are killed by an explosion in a coal mine in Hokkaido (Jap).

- The Nobel Peace Prize is won by Elihu Root (USA), but awarded in 1913, having been reserved.

- Russia adopts workmen's insurance.

- Benito Mussolini becomes chief editor of the Italian Socialist Party newspaper *Avanti*, until 1914, when he is sacked for supporting Italian intervention in World War I; he then forms his own newspaper, *Il Popolo d'Italia* (It).

- The state of Massachusetts institutes a minimum wage law for women and children (USA).

- A new newspaper, *Pravda* ("Truth"), begins to voice the ideas of Russia's underground Communist party in print (Russ).

- J.P. Morgan acquires the majority share in the Guarantee Trust Company and in the Bankers Trust Company (USA).

- Hellmann's Blue Ribbon Mayonnaise is introduced in New York.

- Sumitomo Bank and Yasuda Bank become joint stock companies (Jap).

- The Turkish Petroleum Company is founded to exploit reserves discovered in Mesopotamia.

- A textile workers' strike in Lawrence, Massachusetts, demonstrates the power of the International Workers of the World Union (USA).

- An SOS in Morse Code is adopted as the universal distress signal.

- The International Lawn Tennis Federation is founded in Paris (Fr).

- The fossil remains of the "Piltdown Man" are found. The bones are believed to be 50,000 years old but are proved to be a hoax in 1953 (UK).

- Secession of C.G. Jung (Swi) and A. Adler (Aust-Hung) from the psychoanalytic movement to form respectively the Analytical Psychology and Individual Psychology movements.

- First neon advertising sign in Paris, for Cinzano.

CULTURE

- **Mar**: Release of Sarah Bernhardt's second film, *La Dame aux caméllias* (Fr).

- **8 Jun**: Première of Maurice Ravel's ballet *Daphnis et Chloé* by the Ballets Russes, with choreography by Fokine (Fr).

- **Jun**: Universal Studios, one of Hollywood's largest companies, is founded by Carl Laemmle (USA).

- **Sep**: Keystone Company is founded by Mack Sennett, and the first "Keystone Cops" film is released (USA).

- Rabindranath Tagore: *Gitanjali*, poems (Ind).

- Thomas Mann; *Death in Venice*, novella (Ger).

- Viktor Khlebnikov and Vladimir Mayakovsky: *A Slap in the Face of Public Taste*, a Futurist literary manifesto (Russ).

- Franz Werfel: *Der Weltfreund*, a volume of lyrical poetry (Aust-Hung).

- Harriet Monroe founds *Poetry: A Magazine of Verse* in Chicago (USA).

- Gerhard Hauptmann (Ger) wins the Nobel Prize for Literature.

- Leopold Stokowski becomes conductor of the Philadelphia Symphony Orchestra (USA).

- Richard Strauss: *Ariadne auf Naxos*, opera, libretto by Hugo von Hofmannsthal (Ger).

- Frederick Delius: *Song of the High Hills*, choral work (Fr).

- Arnold Schoenberg: *Pierrot lunaire*, semi-staged work with a small ensemble and *sprechsgesang* soloist (Aust-Hung).

- Paul Dukas: *La Péri*, ballet (Fr).

- Vaslav Nijinsky presents his choreography of Debussy's *L'Après-midi d'un faune*, with the Ballets Russes; his portrayal of the Faun opens a new era in modern ballet (Fr).

- Dixieland Jazz Band opens at Reisenweber's Cabaret, New Orleans (USA).

- Franz Marc: *Tower of Blue Horses*, painting (Ger).

- Marcel Duchamp: *Nude Descending a Staircase*, painting (Fr).

- Wassily Kandinsky: *On the Spiritual in Art*, essay on painting (Ger).

- Giacomo Balla: *Dynamism of a Dog on a Leash*, Futurist painting (It).

- First of Pablo Picasso and Georges Braque's *papier collés*, leading to Synthetic Cubism (Fr).

- Umberto Boccioni: *Manifesto of Futurist Sculpture* (It).

- Guillaume Apollinaire: *The Cubist Painters*, collection of essays (Fr).

- Peter Behrens: AEG Factory Complex, Berlin (Ger).

- First film censor appointed in the UK.

- Fashion designer Coco Chanel opens her first salon, in Deauville (Fr).

SCIENCE

- **18 May**: Professor Mallada of the Royal Observatory at Mount Vesuvius becomes the first to descend to the bottom of a volcano's crater (It).

- Nobel Prize for Chemistry is won by Victor Grignard (Fr) for his discovery of the so-called Grignard reagent and by Paul Sabatier (Fr) in recognition of "his method of hydrogenating organic compounds in the presence of finely disintegrated metals", both of value in organic chemistry.

- Nobel Prize for Physics is won by Nils Dalen (Swe) "for his invention of automatic regulators for use in conjunction with gas accumulators for illuminating lighthouses and buoys."

- Nobel Prize for Physiology or Medicine is won by Alexis Carrel (Fr) "in recognition of his work on vascular structure and the transplantation of blood vessels and organs."

- Motor-driven movie cameras are introduced (USA).

- E.H. Armstrong devises the regenerative or "feedback" radio circuit (USA).

- R.A. Fessenden develops the heterodyne radio system (Can).

- J. Loeb attempts to explain the origins of life in terms of physics and chemistry (USA).

- Kasimir Funk coins the term "vitamin" (Russ).

- P.J.W. Debye propounds his theory of the specific heat of solids (Neth).

- V.F. Hess discovers cosmic radiation (USA).

- Albert Einstein formulates the law of photochemical equivalence (USA).

- C.T.R. Wilson's cloud chamber photographs lead to the detection of protons and electrons (UK).

- V. Kaplan begins development of a turbine for the exploitation of small waterfalls for hydroelectric power (Aust-Hung).

- Max von Laue discovers X-ray diffraction, a method for observing the atomic structure of crystals (Ger).

- Krupp company patents acid-resistant chrome-nickel steel (Ger).

- Cellophane, developed by J.E. Brandenburger in 1910, is manufactured for the first time by the French rayon company La Cellophane.

- R. Fischer patents a process of color photography using three light-sensitive layers on a single plate, which is universally adopted in the 1930s.

- Rufus Cole and Alphonse Duchez (USA) develop the first specific treatment for pneumonia, using a horse serum containing antibodies.

- Brothers Conrad and Marcel Schlumberger develop a technique for measuring the properties of subsurface rocks (Ger).

The vision behind both the Suez and the Panama Canals had initially been French, but the Suez Company became British-controlled, while the United States acquired the rights to the Panama Canal. The opening of the Panama Canal in 1913 did not have the same early impact on world transport as the completion of the Suez Canal had done half a century earlier, since the principal economic advantage of the new canal was the reduction of journey lengths between the east and west coasts of the United States. For routes from New York, the premier American port, to other destinations such as Hong Kong or Sydney, the reductions were not nearly so substantial. But if the opening of the Panama Canal underlined president Roosevelt's policy of US supremacy throughout the Americas, European influence made itself felt in quite a different way when European modern art hit America with the opening of the Armory Show exhibition in New York. The paintings took the American public by storm and encouraged American artists to move toward a new freedom of artistic expression, away from the shadow of war that was already darkening Europe.

▲ **US president Woodrow Wilson opened the Panama Canal on 10 October 1913 by pressing a button that detonated 40 tonnes of dynamite to open the last link between the Atlantic and Pacific Oceans. The canal cut the journey length between New York and San Francisco by two-thirds, but was mainly of importance for inter-American trade.**

● **9 Jan**: Turkey breaches the armistice in the Balkans by attacking the Bulgarians at Lake Derkos. (›23 Jan)

● **16 Jan**: Commons vote for, and Lords reject (30 Jan), home rule for Ireland; voted again 7 Jul, rejected by Lords on 15 Jul (UK). (›12 Jul)

● **17 Jan**: Raymond Poincaré is elected president of France.

● **23 Jan**: Coup d'etat by the Young Turks, angered by the concessions in the London peace treaty of 22 Jan. The new government refuses to hand Adrianople to Bulgaria. Muhammad Shevket Pasha becomes grand vizir; his assassination on 11 Jun leads to a period of repressive government by the Young Turks lasting until World War I (Tur). (›3 Feb)

● **3 Feb**: The First Balkan War is resumed. On 26 Mar the Bulgarians capture Adrianople, and on 16 Apr Bulgaria and Turkey conclude an armistice.

● **8 Feb**: Overthrow and execution (22 Feb) of Mexican president Francisco Madero by Victoriano Huerta. (›10 Oct)

● **4 Mar**: Woodrow Wilson is inaugurated as president of the USA.

● **5 Mar**: The French government decides to increase national service from two years to three.

● **18 Mar**: Prime minister of France, Aristide Briand, resigns when the senate rejects his proposals for electoral reform.

● **18 Mar**: King Giorgios I of Greece is assassinated; he is succeeded by Constantine I (until 1917).

● **8 Apr**: Opening of China's first parliament.

● **20 May**: The London peace conference reopens, leading to the signing of the Treaty of London, ending the First Balkan War. Turkey cedes much territory in the Balkan peninsula, including newly independent Albania, to deny Serbia access to the Adriatic, and abandons its claims to Crete. (›1 Jun)

● **31 May**: Seventeenth Amendment to the US constitution allows the popular election of senators.

● **1 Jun**: Signature of a Serbian-Greek military alliance against Bulgaria for ten years.

● **24 Jun**: Greece and Serbia break their former alliance with Bulgaria over the Macedonia and Thrace border dispute, initiating the Second Balkan War.

● **29 Jun**: An attack initiated on Serbian and Greek positions by Bulgarian commander Michael Savov (without the knowledge of the prime minister, Stojan Danev), gives Serbia and Greece the opportunity to attack Bulgaria, followed independently by Turkey and Romania. (›10 Aug)

● **30 Jun**: German Army Bill increases the peacetime army from 544,000 to 870,000, and in wartime a possible 5 million, at an estimated cost of one billion marks, the largest of the German army bills to date.

● **10 Jul**: "Second Revolution" in the southern provinces of China, after opposition fears that Yuan Shikai's loan from Britain, France, Japan and Russia will strengthen him in power. The movement is suppressed by Sep, and Yuan Shikai is elected president on 6 Oct. On 4 Nov he purges parliament of its Guomindang (Nationalist party) members, finally dissolving it on 10 Jan 1914.

● **12 Jul**: After a resolution signed in Belfast in Sep 1912, 150,000 Ulstermen pledge to resist home rule for Ireland, raising a 100,000-strong force of Ulster volunteers and threatening civil war (UK). (›4 Dec)

● **10 Aug**: Treaty of Bucharest ends one theater of the Second Balkan War, with substantial losses by Bulgaria to Romania (in the north, around the Danube) and to Serbia and Greece (in Macedonia), and the loss of much of the Aegean seaboard. (›23 Sep)

● **7 Sep**: Japan warns China that she will intervene in the unrest after Chinese troops kill Japanese civilians.

● **23 Sep**: Serbians invade Albania, but an Austrian ultimatum on 18 Oct forces them to evacuate.

● **29 Sep**: Treaty of Constantinople ends the Turco-Bulgarian theater of the Second Balkan War, with the Bulgarians losing Adrianople to the Turks. (›13 Dec)

● **10 Oct**: Mexican president Huerta arrests 110 members of the Mexican Congress. On 11 Oct, Huerta dissolves the Congress and declares himself dictator. (›3 Nov)

● **28 Oct**: German commander Liman von Sanders arrives in Turkey to reorganize the Turkish army and assume command of the First Army. France and Russia protest against his far-reaching powers, and as a result he gives up his command in Jan 1914.

● **3 Nov**: President Wilson gives president Huerta of Mexico an ultimatum to resign. On 15 Nov, rebel leader Pancho Villa takes Ciudad Juarez and announces plans to move on to Mexico City, and join up with other rebel forces to besiege Huerta.

● **5 Nov**: Recognition of the autonomy of Outer Mongolia by China.

● **Nov**: Mohandas K. Ghandi, leader of the Indian Passive Resistance Movement, is arrested and jailed in Natal, sparking off riots (SA).

● **4 Dec**: Royal proclamation bans the import of arms into Ulster; ports are to be watched.

● **13 Dec**: Division of southern Albania between Albania and Greece is agreed, with compensation to Greece in the Aegean Islands. A lingering dispute over the islands almost leads to a Turco-Greek war.

SOCIETY

- **2 Jan**: 300 Chinese troops are killed in a night raid by Tibetans.

- **13 Jan**: The pope bans films from churches and forbids films of a religious nature (It).

- **2 Feb**: Grand Central Station, the largest railway station in the world, opens, in New York.

- **19 Feb**: A suffragette bomb wrecks Chancellor of the Exchequer David Lloyd George's new house. After the government withdrew its Franchise Bill (28 Jan) because amendments had changed its nature too radically, suffragettes vowed to step up their militant strategy (UK).

- **25 Feb**: Federal income tax is introduced in the USA via the Sixteenth Amendment.

- **2 Mar**: Mobs attack suffragettes in Hyde Park and Wimbledon (UK).

- **28 Mar**: It is revealed that prohibition in the US is costing $2 million in decreased liquor revenues and by 1917 there are 26 states with prohibiting laws, of which 13 could be described as "bone dry".

- **14–24 Apr**: Strikes in Belgium demand a revision of the franchise laws, eventually achieved in May 1919.

- **Apr**: Suffragette leader Emmeline Pankhurst is sentenced to three years' imprisonment (UK).

- **29 Jun**: The Norwegian parliament grants women equal electoral rights with men.

- **30 Jun**: German Finance Law provides for a national defense tax (Wehrsteuer) to be levied once only on property and income.

- **3–5 Jul**: Widespread miners' strike in South Africa. Troops are sent in to control rioting.

- **1 Aug**: In Belgium, boxing is effectively outlawed by a new law requiring the attendance of magistrates at bouts.

- **Aug**: The USA declares an economic boycott against Mexico, after president Huerta orders expulsion of Americans.

- **1 Sep**: Louis Blériot performs the first loop-the-loop in an aircraft (Fr).

- **Sep**: A cholera epidemic spreads in the Balkans. By 11 Sep, 1,500 Romanian soldiers are already dead.

- **3 Oct**: The Underwood Tariff Act reduces duties on commodities where US goods control the market, or where previous protection has served its purpose (USA).

- **14 Oct**: 418 miners are lost when trapped after an explosion and fire in a coal mine in the Aber Valley (UK).

- **17 Oct**: In Germany, the world's biggest airship, Zeppelin L2, explodes with the loss of all 28 on board.

- **Oct**: The Panama Canal is opened, linking the Atlantic and Pacific oceans.

- **30 Nov**: Anglo-Turkish treaty gives Britain the concession to exploit all the oil in Arabia, Mesopotamia and Syria.

- **15 Dec**: Launch of HMS *Tiger*, the world's biggest battle cruiser (UK).

- **23 Dec**: Federal Reserve Bank Act divides the USA into 12 districts, each with its own federal reserve bank.

- **Dec**: "Zabern incident" in Alsace-Lorraine: Franco-German relations are damaged after a German officer wounds a lame cobbler with his sword and insults Alsatian recruits (Ger).

- Nobel Peace Prize is won by Henri La Fontaine (Bel).

- The USA is deluged with immigrants – over 6,000 arrive at Ellis Island in one day.

- A report by the chief Schools' Medical Officer states that one in 12 children at British state elementary schools is suffering from disease or the effects of malnutrition.

- United Federation of Labor and of the Social Democratic Party is founded in New Zealand, providing for the interests of industrial workers.

- Ivar Kreuger founds a match plant (Swe).

- Establishment of the National Credit Bank (Fr).

- Establishment of the Bank of China.

- The Department of Labor is created by president Wilson in response to American Federation of Labor pressure (USA).

- First crossword puzzle is published, in *New York World* (USA).

- First Far Eastern Games is held in Manila (Phi).

- Charter for the International Amateur Athletic Federation (IAAF) is drawn up in Berlin (Ger).

- Rudolf Steiner, founder of anthroposophy, builds the first Goetheanum, at Dornach (Swi), for the teaching of philosophy.

- The foxtrot comes into fashion.

- First electric refrigerator for home use is marketed (USA).

- Diesel-electric railway engines come into use in Sweden.

- Modern zipper fastener is developed by Gideon Sundbach (Swe), though it was first patented by W.L. Judson (USA) in 1893.

CULTURE

- **23 Feb**: First performance of Arnold Schoenberg's *Gurrelieder* (Songs of Gurra), in Vienna (Aust-Hung).

- Guillaume Apollinaire: *Alcools*, poems (Fr).

- Bengali poet Rabindranath Tagore is awarded the Nobel Prize for Literature (Ind).

- Maxim Gorky: *My Childhood* (Russ).

- Alain-Fournier: *Le Grand Meaulnes*, novel (Fr).

- Marcel Proust: *Du coté de chez Swann*, (Swann's Way) first volume of *A la recherche du temps perdu* (Remembrance of Things Past) (Fr).

- First Imagist manifesto appears in *Poetry*, Chicago (USA).

- Osip Mandelstam: *Stone*, poems (Russ).

- George Bernard Shaw's *Pygmalion*, play, first performed in Vienna.

- Georg Trakl: *Gedichte*, poems (Ger).

- D.H. Lawrence: *Sons and Lovers*, novel (UK).

- Edmund Husserl: *Phenomenology*, philosophy text (Ger).

- Igor Stravinsky's ballet *Le Sacre du printemps* (The Rite of Spring), for the *Ballets Russes*, is greeted with uproar (Fr).

- Claude Debussy: *Jeux*, for the *Ballets Russes* (Fr).

- Mikhail Matyushin: *Victory over the Sun*, first Futurist opera, designed by Kasimir Malevich (Russ).

- Futurist composer Luigi Russolo first demonstrates his "intonarumori" (noise intoners) (It).

- Bruno Walter becomes director at the Munich Opera (until 1922) (Ger).

- The Armory Show (exhibition) in New York first brings European modern art to the USA; among the paintings are works by Picasso and Duchamp (including his *Nude Descending a Staircase*) (USA).

- Man Ray: *Portrait of Alfred Stieglitz*, painting. Stieglitz, himself a photographer, exhibited the work of many avant-garde artists at his Gallery 291 in New York (USA).

- Robert Delaunay: *Circular Forms: Sun and Moon*, painting (Fr).

- F.T. Marinetti: *Zang tumb tumb*, Futurist peformance piece based on the siege of Adrianople (First Balkan War) (It).

- Jacob Epstein: *Rock Drill*, Vorticist sculpture (UK).

- Formation of the Schweizerischer Werkbund (Swi).

- Ezra Pound coins the term Vorticism to describe the breakaway movement instigated by Wyndham Lewis and other writers and artists.

- First films from Paramount Company are released (USA).

- Charlie Chaplin's first film for the Keystone Company is released (USA).

SCIENCE

- Nobel Prize for Chemistry is won by Alfred Werner (Swi) for his work on the linkage of atoms in molecules.

- Nobel Prize for Physics is won by Heike Kamerlingh Onnes (Neth) "for his investigations on the properties of matter at low temperatures which led, interalia, to the production of liquid helium".

- Nobel Prize for Physiology or Medicine is won by Charles Richet (Fr) for his work on anaphylaxis, an exaggerated allergic reaction to foreign proteins or antigens.

- R. Lorin states the basic principle of jet propulsion (Fr).

- E.A. Sperry invents the gyroscope stabilizer for aircraft (USA).

- W.D. Coolidge invents a hot-cathode X-ray tube (USA).

- H. Geiger invents a device for counting individual alpha rays known as the Geiger counter (Ger).

- Niels Bohr applies quantum theory to Rutherford's model of the atom, and formulates a new theory of atomic structure, with electrons in orbit in specific energy levels known as "shells" around the nucleus (Den).

- Diphtheria vaccine is produced by E.A. von Behring (Ger).

- J.B. Watson puts forward the behaviorist approach to psychology (USA).

- E. McCollum and M. Davis identify vitamins A and B in cow's milk.

- B. Schick develops the Schick test to determine immunity to diphtheria (USA).

- R.A. Millikan publishes his calculation of the charge of an electron (USA).

- Ford Motor Co introduces a moving assembly line that reduces assembly time from 12.5 to 1.5 hours per vehicle (USA).

- Harvard Classification of stars is adopted by the International Solar Union.

- Astronomers Ejnar Hertzsprung and H.N. Russell devise the Hertzsprung Russell (stellar magnitude) Diagram – a method of grouping stars by the relation between their absolute magnitudes and spectral types (USA).

- Composition of chlorophyll is discovered by R. Willstatter (Ger).

- F. Bergius develops coal high pressure hydrogenation, converting coal dust into oil (Ger).

- Publication of Bertrand Russell and A.N. Whitehead's *Principia Mathematica* (since 1910), which lays the foundation of calculus of propositions and modern symbolic logic (UK).

- A. Salomen (Ger) develops the technique of mammography, diagnosing breast tumors by X-ray.

Since 1789 the upsurge of nationalism had had a major impact upon the geopolitics of Europe, and in June 1914 it was to lead to the final undoing of the last major autocratic empires – Habsburg, Hohenzollen and Romanov. There had been almost continuous warfare in southeastern Europe since 1912 despite the Great Powers' efforts to settle the First and Second Balkan Wars by diplomacy. However, the assassination of Archduke Franz Ferdinand at Sarajevo, a Bosnian town, by a member of the Serbian "Black Hand" society, did not lead immediately to war. As with the other European "crises" which had repeatedly occurred since 1900, efforts were made toward a diplomatic settlement throughout July, although on this occasion they proved ultimately futile; indeed, some German historians have blamed the actual outbreak of hostilities upon the opaqueness of the stance taken by the British Foreign Office. Initially, as many expected, it looked as if the war would be short, with sweeping German advances in both the east and west. However, from the autumn the war in the west became rapidly bogged down in a gruelling and horrific conflict of attrition.

▲ On 28 June a 19-year old student named Gavrilo Princip shot the heir to the Austro-Hungarian throne, the Archduke Franz Ferdinand, in Sarajevo, thus precipitating World War I. After Serbia rejected a humiliating ultimatum from Austria, the latter, backed by Germany, declared war. In a bewilderingly fast chain of events, Russia, France and Britain joined forces against them.

● **21 Apr**: After several US Marines are arrested at Tampico (Mex), the US government demands satisfaction; the Americans occupy Vera Cruz after Mexican president Huerta rejects US demands.

● **26 May**: House of Commons pass the Irish Home Rule Bill for the third time, bypassing the House of Lords by way of the 1911 Parliament Act. The Act gives Ireland a unitary parliamentary system, but does not recognize a separate Protestant Ulster until a compromise is made by prime minister Herbert Asquith on 23 Jun, excluding Ulster from the bill. The bill receives royal assent on 18 Sep, but does not come into force until 1920 (UK).

● **15 Jun**: Denmark, Sweden and Switzerland form a defense league.

● **28 Jun**: Archduke Franz Ferdinand, heir to the Austrian throne, and his wife are murdered at Sarajevo (Bosnia) by Gavrilo Princip, a Bosnian activist for the anti-Austrian Serbian secret society Union of Death (The Black Hand). Austria correctly assumes the acquiescence of the Serbian government in the plot and sends a legal expert to Sarajevo to try to make out a case against Serbia.

● **5 Jul**: War crisis over the assassination of Franz Ferdinand: Germany pledges support for Austrian demands for justice; Hungary initially opposes war against Serbia, but later (14 Jul) agrees on condition that no Serbian territory will be annexed by Austria. Austria finally delivers its ultimatum to Serbia on 23 Jul, demanding an end to all anti-Austrian activities and a formal apology.

● **24 Jul**: Russia announces its intention to protect the integrity of Serbia. On 25 Jul Austria reassures Russia that no Serbian territory would be annexed in the event of war; France gives support to Russia. But Austria considers the Serbian response to the ultimatum unsatisfactory, and both the Austrians and the Serbians mobilize, despite attempts by Britain to call a conference to discuss the matter.

● **28 Jul**: Austria-Hungary declares war on Serbia, and bombards Belgrade on 29 Jul. German chancellor Bethmann unsuccessfully attempts to persuade Britain to remain neutral in the event of war against France and Belgium. Further attempts at negotiations between Russia and France on 30 Jul lead nowhere, and Russia mobilizes, despite German warnings.

●**31 Jul**: An ultimatum by Germany to Russia is left unanswered, and Germany declares war on Russia at 7.00 pm the same evening, after a day of Austrian, French and German mobilization.

● **2 Aug**: The British cabinet votes to support France (which is pledged to support Russia), and protect the French coast against German attack; meanwhile Germany begins its invasion of Luxembourg and delivers an ultimatum to Belgium, demanding free passage for its armies.

● **3 Aug**: Germany declares war on France on the pretext of frontier violations, knowing that France will support Russia, and begins the invasion of Belgium. As a result, Britain declares war on Germany on 4 Aug. Austria-Hungary's declaration of war on Russia on 6 Aug brings all of the main belligerents into the arena and thus begins World War I.

● **13 Aug**: The Austrians invade Serbia. At first they are repulsed, but on 2 Dec capture Belgrade; however, on 15 Dec the Serbs retake the city, driving the Austrians back across the border.

● **20 Aug**: The Germans take Brussels and advance into France.

● **23 Aug**: Japan declares war on Germany, and begins its takeover of German colonies in the Far East.

● **26 Aug**: The first of Germany's colonies, Togoland, is captured by an Anglo-French force. Other German colonies in Africa and elsewhere follow.

● **30 Aug**: First German air raid, on Paris.

● **3 Sep**: German forces are so close to Paris that the French government moves to Bordeaux.

● **5–12 Sep**: Allied counterattack at the battle of the Marne halts the German advance on Paris. German forces retreat to a line west of Verdun, from which the Allies try vainly to dislodge them in the battles of the Aisne (15–18 Sep), Picardy (22–26 Sep) and Artois (27 Sep–10 Oct). The Germans take Ghent and Lille.

● **Sep**: After initial gains, a Russian offensive into East Prussia is followed by German victories at the Battle of Tannenberg and the Battle of the Masurian Lakes; a total of 225,000 Russian prisoners of war are taken.

● **4 Oct**: Combined Austrian and German troops begin an attack on Poland, advancing as far as Warsaw and capturing Lodz.

● **29 Oct**: German cruisers, permitted by Turkey (though supposedly neutral) to pass the Dardanelles, are joined by Turkish warships, and together they bombard Odessa, Sevastopol and Thoedoria on the Russian Black Sea coast. On 2 Nov Russia declares war on Turkey, followed on 5 Nov by Britain and France.

● **30 Oct**: German troops in Belgium are halted at the First Battle of Ypres. An Allied offensive in December makes no headway, and both sides dig in for trench warfare on a line which does not vary by more than 16 km (10 miles) over the next three years.

● **8 Dec**: In the first major sea battle of the war, at the Falkland Islands in the South Atlantic, the British Royal Navy sinks four German ships.

● **18 Dec**: Egypt becomes a British protectorate.

● **24 Jan**: Building workers in the UK go on strike. On 30 Mar, 100,000 miners in Yorkshire begin a strike for a minimum wage. On 1 Apr, electricians strike for shorter hours. By 4 Jun, two million workers are on strike.

● **Jan**: Gen. Hertzog founds the Nationalist party, which becomes a platform for Boer separatism (SA).

● **Jan**: A general strike is initiated by South African gold and diamond miners and railmen (SA).

● **Jan**: Introduction of minimum wages and profit-sharing at Ford Motor Company to avoid threatened labor trouble (USA).

● **Jan**: 9 million are reported starving in northeast Japan.

● **1 Feb**: Opening of the Tanganyika railroad from Dar-es-Salaam to Lake Tanganyika (Ger E Afr).

● **Feb**: British explorer Captain Campbell Besley announces that his expedition to Peru has discovered the ruins of three Inca cities in the forests near Cuzco.

● **10 Mar**: Militant suffragette Mary Richardson slashes Velasquez's masterpiece, the *Rokeby Venus*, with a meat cleaver at the National Gallery, causing around £15,000 worth of damage.

● **8 May**: Smith-Levier Act provides for agricultural extension services by US Department of Agriculture country agents.

● **May**: Trade unions of miners, transport workers and railmen found a common committee for collective bargaining (UK).

● **15 Jun**: Anglo-German agreement over the Baghdad railroad, by which the Germans promise not to extend the railway south of Baghdad and recognize Britain's interests in Mesopotamia.

● **23–5 Jun**: The enlarged Kiel Canal is opened, improving access from the Baltic to the North Sea (Ger).

● **20 Jul**: Mohandas Gandhi departs for India after receiving assurances from Jan Smuts (colonial secretary of the South African government under Botha) that the 1913 Immigration Act will be enforced justly (SA).

● **31 Jul**: Socialist campaigner Jean Jaurès is murdered in Paris.

● **Jul**: Run on many central banks in Europe due to war crisis; the gold reserves of the Bank of England decrease from £38.6 to £28 billion (UK).

● **5 Aug**: Costa Rica and El Salvador protest against the Bryan Chamorro Treaty, which allows the USA to build a canal across Nicaragua. They take the issue to the Central American Court of Justice, which declares the treaty to be a violation of the treaties of 1907; but Nicaragua ignores the decision and thus destroys the authority of the court.

● **14 Aug**: Stock exchanges close and the convertibility of many currencies is suspended with the outbreak of World War I.

● **15 Aug**: The Panama Canal is opened to shipping, shortening the previous sea routes round the tip of South America by thousands of kilometers.

● **31 Aug**: St Petersburg is renamed Petrograd.

● **Aug**: All parties in the Reichstag agree on a large war credit to the government (Ger).

● **3 Oct**: 2,500 are feared dead in an earthquake in Turkey.

● **15 Oct**: Clayton Antitrust Act strengthens government stand against combination (USA).

● Cooperative societies claim nearly 4 million members (UK).

● A report shows that Britain's farmers produce less than a quarter of the nation's grain needs (UK).

● Ernest Shackleton's UK expedition to cross the South Pole from the Weddell to the Ross Sea is defeated by pack ice, though he discovers the world's largest known glacier. His ship *Endurance* is crushed by ice on 21 Nov 1915, and the party takes to boats, reaching Elephant Island on 14 Apr 1916; they are rescued on 30 Aug 1916.

● First electric traffic lights to control different streams of traffic are installed, at a crossroads in Cleveland, Ohio (USA).

● George Washington Carver reveals experiment results showing how peanuts and sweet potatoes can replenish soil fertility (USA).

● Nationalization of the Canadian Northern railroad after fears of a national credit collapse. The Grand Trunk railroad is nationalized in 1920, and the 23,000 miles of Canadian line become known as Canadian National Railways.

● The Bank of England is authorized by the government to issue banknotes in excess of the statutory limit because of the financial panic created by the war (UK).

● First brassiere patented, by Caresse Crosby (USA).

● Live models are used in US fashion shows for the first time.

● **Feb**: American Society of Composers, Authors and Publishers (ASCAP) is founded.

● **Jun**: Le Syndicat de Defense de la Grande Couture Française is founded, to protect copyright (Fr).

● **Jul**: The Performing Rights Society is formed (UK).

● Pär Lagerkvist: *Motifs*, novel (Swe).

● Heinrich Mann: *Der Untertan* (The Subject), novel satirizing life and institutions in Germany under the Kaiser (Ger).

● André Gide: *The Vatican Caves*, novel (Fr).

● Edgar Rice Burroughs: *Tarzan of the Apes*, the first Tarzan book (USA).

● James Joyce: *Dubliners*, a collection of sketches and short stories (UK).

● H.L. Mencken takes up editorship of *The Smart Set*, a literary magazine (until 1923) (USA).

● First issues of Wyndham Lewis's *Blast*, a Vorticist periodical (folds in 1915) (UK).

● First issues of *The Egoist* literary periodical, which starts as a feminist paper but goes on to publish articles on modern poetry and the arts. It serializes James Joyce's *Portrait of the Artist as a Young Man* in 1914–15 (UK).

● Paul Claudel: *The Hostage*, play (Fr).

● Charles Ives: *Three Places in New England*, for orchestra (USA).

● Aleksandr Borodin's opera *Prince Igor* (1890) is performed outside Russia for the first time, with the great bass Chaliapin (UK).

● Henry Cowell: *The Tides of Manaunaun*, for piano, an early use of pitch-clusters (USA).

● Ralph Vaughan Williams "Hugh the Drover" (opera) and "London Symphony".

● Egon Schiele: *Portrait of Friederike Maria Beer*, painting (Aust-Hung).

● Giorgio de Chirico: *The Philosopher's Conquest*, painting (Fr).

● Marcel Duchamp begins his series of "readymades" (Fr).

● Oskar Kokoschka: *The Tempest*, self-portrait with Alma Mahler (Aust-Hung).

● Antonio Sant'Elia produces his Futurist city designs (It).

● Giacomo Balla: *Macchina tipografica*, in which 12 performers together simulate a printing press with actions and onomatopoeic sounds (It).

● First major industrial exhibition by the Deutscher Werkbund, in Cologne, including Walter Gropius and Adolf Meyer's Model Factory and Henry Van de Velde's Werkbund Exhibition Theater (Ger).

● *The World, the Flesh and the Devil* – the first full-length color film (UK).

● **8 Jan**: In London, doctors successfully treat cancer with radium.

● Nobel Prize for Chemistry is won by Theodore W. Richards (USA) for his exact determinations of the atomic weights of a large number of chemical elements.

● Nobel Prize for Physics is won by Max von Laue (Ger) "for his discovery of the diffraction of X-rays by crystals", proving that these light waves have very small wavelengths, and also making it possible to determine the positions of atoms in crystals.

● Nobel Prize for Physiology or Medicine is won by Robert Bárány (Aust-Hung) for his work on the physiology and pathology of the vestibular apparatus, the organs of balance.

● Radio transmitter triode modulation is introduced.

● A cargo ship is built with a turboelectric engine (Swe).

● R.H. Goddard begins his rocketry experiments (USA).

● E.C. Kendall prepares pure thyroxin for the treatment of thyroid deficiencies (USA).

● A. Eddington shows that spiral nebulae are galaxies (UK).

● F.A. Lipmann demonstrates the role of ATP (adenosine triphosphate) in the release of energy in a cell (Russ).

● A. Carrel performs the first successful heart surgery on a dog, demonstrating his technique of suturing, the reconnection of blood vessels (Fr).

● R. Lewisohn discovers the anticoagulant properties of sodium citrate, making it easier to transport and store blood in large quantities for transfusion (USA).

● H.H. Dale proposes that acetylcholine is a compound involved in the transmission of nerve impulses (UK).

● J. Franck and G. Hertz confirm Bohr's atomic model by bombarding mercury vapor with electrons and measuring the frequencies of the emitted radiation (Ger).

● J.J. Abel isolate amino acids from blood (USA).

● E. Rutherford discovers the proton (UK).

● B. Gutenberg discovers the discontinuity between the Earth's mantle and core, an early contribution to the theory of continental drift (Ger).

● P. Duden and J. Hess synthesize acetic acid (vitamin C) (Ger).

● Tear gas shells are developed in Germany by Dr von Tappen.

● The world's first major sewage works to use bacteria in the decomposition of waste opens in Manchester (UK).

The unprecedented inception of total warfare, involving a struggle of industrial might on a scale never dreamed of before, forced the belligerent states to mobilize all the available forces of society. The German U-boats and the British naval blockade came to be seen as threats to everyday life, and like the futile Allied campaigns in Picardy had to be sustained by war production directly controlled by politicians and state bureaucrats. The burdens of war fell increasingly upon the hunched shoulders of common humanity, whether in the trenches, in the factories, or on the land. Taxes were increased, and women set to work in trade, industry and agriculture as their men died on the battlefield. In the end, the Allies won the war primarily because they were able to field their armies without starving their civilian populations. The lot of the common people was brilliantly reflected in the characterizations of Charlie Chaplin, which revealed the resignation of the born loser, whether in love or war, but as his career developed they were to produce biting satrical commentary on the tyranny of machine and dictator alike.

▲ Charlie Chaplin as the archetypal father in *The Kid*, with Jackie Coogan (1920). The public took Chaplin to its heart in the guise of the little man for whom nothing ever goes right.

● **9 Jan**: In Mexico, Pancho Villa signs a treaty ending the border conflict with the USA.

● **18 Jan**: Japan presents 21 secret demands to China including Japanese succession to German rights in Shandong, extension of leases in southern Manchuria, and further economic concessions. It is accepted by the Chinese government on 8 May.

● **19 Jan**: Germans first use Zeppelin airships to bomb Britain.

● **24 Jan**: British cruisers sink the *Blucher*, a German battle cruiser, on Dogger Bank.

● **28 Jan–14 May**: In Portugal, the pro-German dictatorship of General Pimenta de Castro is overthrown by a revolt of democratic forces.

● **4 Feb**: Germany announces a U-boat blockade of Britain. Britain in turn orders all goods bound for Germany to be seized.

● **4 Feb**: Winter battle in Masuria as Germans advance against the Russians in the north, capturing Memel; in Apr the Russian attempt to reach Hungary over the Carpathians is driven back.

● **10 Feb**: US president Woodrow Wilson warns Germany that attacks on US ships are a breach of US neutrality; he also protests to Britain for allowing ships to fly the US flag to dupe the Germans.

● **19 Feb**: Naval action against the Dardanelles begins, to divert the Turks from their Caucasian objectives. Under the brilliant leadership of Mustafa Kemal, the Turks repulse British and French ground forces at Suvla Bay (6 Aug) and Gallipoli (19 Dec–9 Jan 1916).

● **9 Mar**: The House of Lords gives a second reading to an emergency bill passing control of all factories not already producing armaments to the government for the duration.

● **6 Apr**: Italy demands South Tyrol, Trieste and Istria from Austria as the price of her neutrality. Neutrality talks with Austria break down on 18 Apr. (›29 Apr)

● **11–13 Apr**: British hold Basra against Turkish attack, but cannot reach Baghdad (Mesopotamia).

● **25 Apr**: Australian and New Zealand (ANZAC) forces, together with UK troops, land at Gallipoli.

● **22 Apr–18 May**: On the Western Front, the Germans first use chlorine gas during the Allied offensive of the Second Battle of Ypres.

● **29 Apr**: Italy, which had claimed neutral status at the outbreak of war, regarding Austria's offensive against Serbia as incompatible with the terms of the Triple Alliance, concludes a secret treaty (Treaty of London) with France, Russia and Britain and on 23 May declares war on Austria-Hungary.

● **7 May**: British passenger liner *Lusitania* is sunk by a German submarine off the Irish coast, with the loss of 1,198 lives, many of them American citizens. The USA protests and comes close to war with Germany. (Society › 6 Feb 1916)

● **13 May**: Gen. Botha, South African prime minister, captures German Southwest Africa.

● **22–25 May**: The British launch a spring offensive at Ypres. Heavy casualties are suffered both sides. The German army uses gas.

● **25 May**: The Asquith ministry becomes a coalition, and an inner circle of cabinet members, the War Committee, is formed to direct war operations. A Ministry of Munitions is established in Jul (UK).

● **1 Jul**: Joint Austro-German offensive into Poland captures Warsaw (4–7 Aug), Brest-Litovsk (25 Aug) and Vilna (19 Sep), and overruns all of Poland and Lithuania.

● **Jul**: Passage of National Registration Bill, for all those aged 15–65, though the government denies plans for forced labor and military conscription (UK).

● **9 Aug**: German and Austrian leaders propose a separate peace with Russia, which the czar rejects.

● **21 Aug**: Italy declares war on Turkey.

● **31 Aug**: Germany and Austria agree to partition Poland.

● **1 Sep**: Joseph Pilsudski launches a movement for a free Poland.

● **16 Sep**: Haiti becomes a US protectorate; US Marines remain in occupation.

● **21 Sep**: Bulgaria concludes an alliance with Germany, mobilizing against Serbia. Greece and Romania remain neutral, but Greece allows British and French troops to disembark at Salonika. They cannot, however, block the Bulgarian advance and, with Austrian help, Serbia and Montenegro are totally overrun by the end of the year.

● **22 Sep**: The Allies' "great offensive" begins with the Second Battle of Champagne and the Third Battle of Artois, intended to force the Germans out of northern France, but no significant result is achieved.

● **29 Oct**: Socialist Aristide Briand becomes prime minister of France for the fifth time after the resignation of René Viviani.

● **2 Dec**: Gen. Joseph Joffre is appointed commander-in-chief of the French army. On 15 Dec, Sir Douglas Haig replaces Sir John French as commander of the British forces on the Western Front.

● **7 Dec**: US president Wilson asks for a standing army of 142,000 with a reserve of 400,000.

● **7 Dec**: Turks begin a siege of the British at Kut-el-Amara (Mesopotamia) (until 29 Apr 1916).

- **7 Jan**: There are reports of Poles and Cossacks slaughtering Jews in eastern Europe.

- **13 Jan**: 29,000 die in a massive earthquake in central Italy.

- **Jan**: The German War Grain Association buys compulsorily all wheat, corn and flour stocks at fixed prices, and suspends private grain transactions as the British blockade begins.

- **Jan**: A distribution organization for the supply of food is established (Ger).

- **Jan**: Wimbledon tennis tournament is suspended for the duration of the war (UK).

- **Feb**: Opening of San Francisco World's Fair which includes exhibits from the warring European states (USA).

- **Feb**: The 1916 Berlin Olympic Games are canceled (Ger).

- **18 Mar**: The British government appeals to women to take up jobs in trade, industry and agriculture.

- **28 Mar**: International Socialist Women's Conference in Berne calls for peace.

- **8 Apr**: Buckingham Palace and other Royal Households abstain from alcohol, as George V leads campaign to cut down heavy drinking among armament workers, which is slowing production (UK).

- **24 May**: First Pan-American financial conference meets in Washington (USA).

- **May**: Beginning of artificial nitrate manufacture (Ger); it is used in explosives and fertilizers. Chile's nitrate trade suffers heavy losses due to the sea war and the manufacture of a substitute.

- **3 Jun**: Allied conference in Paris establishes the economic backbone of the war effort, leading to the introduction of the Shipping Control Commission (27 Jan 1916) and a Ministry of Blockade (23 Feb 1916).

- **3 Jul**: The British government estimates war costs at £3 million a day and by 18 Sep, the estimate has risen to £3.5 million (UK).

- **13 Jul**: A royal proclamation says all disputes must be reported to the Board of Trade before strike action is contemplated (UK).

- **Aug**: US banks grant a credit of $500 million to the UK and France.

- **Aug**: David Lloyd George, minister for munitions, demands that the economy become a war economy (UK).

- **Aug**: German industrialists demand the incorporation of Poland, Latvia, Lithuania, Estonia and the Ukraine into the German economic sphere.

- **15 Sep**: The Trades Union Congress decides to oppose conscription, but Lloyd George says "We cannot win without you" (UK).

- **31 Oct**: 1,500,000 Jews are reported to be starving in Russia.

- **14 Nov**: Thomas Masaryk, leader of the Czech nationalist movement, issues a manifesto, calling for the establishment of a Czechoslovak National Council and for a Czech legion to fight on the side of the Allies.

- **25 Nov**: William Joseph Simmons starts a new Ku Klux Klan (an anti-Jewish, anti-Catholic and white supremacist organization) in Georgia and attracts 100,000 members in six years (USA).

- **10 Dec**: The millionth Ford automobile leaves the assembly line (USA).

- **14 Dec**: Reports from west central Asia suggest that a million Armenians have been killed by Turks.

- Theosophist leader Annie Besant founds the Benares Hindu University and organizes the Home Rule League in India, and with Tilak (an Indian nationalist) agitates for home rule in 1917.

- US wheat crop tops 1 billion bushels.

- The sale of absinthe is outlawed in France. The liquor has caused blindness and death among heavy drinkers.

- First transcontinental telephone call is made, between New York and San Francisco, a record 7,640 km (4,750 miles).

- First armored vehicle with tracks built under the direction of an Admiralty Committee and named "Little Willie". A second model, "Big Willie" soon follows, and is accepted by the British Army, which orders 100 tanks of this type in Feb 1916 (UK).

- Kalman Kando builds the first electric locomotive to be powered by high frequency current, so that power can be drawn from the public electricity supply instead of from an independent generating station.

- The first motor scooter, the Auto-Ped, is marketed (USA).

- Motorized taxis appear (USA).

- The Sharp Company is founded to manufacture propeling pencils (Jap).

- Income tax in Britain reaches an unprecedented 15 percent.

- **8 Feb**: Release of D.W. Griffith's film *The Birth of a Nation*, an epic account of the history of the USA. Some cities ban showings, and there are widespread protests about its racialism (USA).

- Ezra Pound begins his poem sequence, *The Cantos* (the final book in the sequence, *Thrones*, is published 1959) (UK).

- John Buchan: *The 39 Steps*, novel (UK).

- William Somerset Maugham: *Of Human Bondage*, semi-autobiographical novel (UK).

- D.H. Lawrence: *The Rainbow*, novel, banned on publication on charges of obscenity (UK).

- Virginia Woolf: *The Voyage Out*, novel (UK).

- Ford Madox Ford: *The Good Soldier*, novel (UK).

- Death of British poet Rupert Brooke on active service.

- First issue of French satirical journal *Le Canard Enchaîné*.

- Franz Kafka, *Metamorphosis*, short story (written 1912) (Aust-Hung).

- Georg Trakl: *Sebastian in Traum*, poems (posth.) (Ger).

- Nobel Prize for Literature is won by Romain Rolland (Fr).

- Futurist Synthetic Theater manifesto, advocating the compression of space and events in performance works (It).

- F.T. Marinetti: *They're Coming*, a performance work in which the main characters are eight chairs (It).

- Charles Ives: *Concord* Sonata, honoring the writers of New England such as Emerson, Hawthorne and Thoreau (USA).

- Gustav Holst: *The Planets*, orchestral suite (UK).

- Maurice Ravel: *Piano Trio* (Fr).

- Richard Strauss: *Alpine Symphony* (Ger).

- Claude Debussy: *Etudes*, for piano (Fr).

- Hubert Parry: modern setting of the hymn "Jerusalem" to the words of William Blake (UK).

- Amedeo Modigliani: *Moise Kisling*, painting (It).

- Juan Gris: *Book, Pipe and Glasses*, painting (Fr).

- Pablo Picasso: *Harlequin*, painting (Fr).

- Kasimir Malevich exhibits Suprematist paintings in Petrograd.

- Vladimir Tatlin: *Counter Relief (corner)*, sculpture (Russ).

- Henri Gaudier-Brzeska: Bust of Ezra Pound (UK).

- Design and Industries Association is founded in UK, modeled on the Deutscher Werkbund.

- Charlie Chaplin stars in *Work*, based on a music-hall routine (USA).

- Nobel Prize for Chemistry is won by Richard Willstätter (Ger) for his work on chlorophyll and its constituent pigments.

- Nobel Prize for Physics is won by William Henry Bragg and his son William Lawrence Bragg (UK) "for their services in the analysis of crystal structure by means of X-rays".

- Einstein's general theory of relativity is published, incorporating gravitation into the special theory (1905). Among other things, Einstein predicts that space is curved; this is demonstrated when it is found that light rays that pass near the sun are bent (by Arthur Eddington, in 1919).

- Georg Cantor: *Contributions to the Founding of a Theory of Transfinite Numbers*, mathematical text (Russ).

- Hugo Junkers develops the first all-metal aircraft (Ger).

- Pyrex glass is developed by the Corning Glass Works (USA).

- First carcinogen identified by K. Yamagiwa and K. Ichikawa. They produce cancer in rabbits by exposing them for long periods to coal tar (Jap).

- J. Goldberger establishes that vitamin deficiency causes pellagra (USA).

- E.C. Kendall isolates the dysentery bacillus.

- F. Twort discovers bacteriophages – viruses that prey on bacteria (UK).

- M. and W. Lewis use time-lapse cinephotography to study cell growth.

- W.S. Adams discovers the first white dwarf star, Sirius B (Ger).

- Publication of Alfred Wegener's *Die Entstehung der Kontinente und Ozeane*, in which he expounds his theory of continental drift (Ger).

- Fokker airplanes become the first to be equipped with an interrupter gear allowing a machine gun to fire between the propeller blades (Ger).

- Manson Benedicks (USA) discovers that the germanium crystal can be used to convert alternating current (a.c.) into direct current (d.c.), laying the basis for the integrated circuit.

- P. Lanevin (Fr) invents the first ship's detector of icebergs and submarines – sound navigation and ranging (SONAR) – using quartz crystals to send out ultrasonic sound waves, which are reflected back.

- The structure of rocks beneath the Earth's surface is revealed by the torsion balance, which can detect minute differences in the gravity of rocks.

- Dr Ulrich reports on a new bromide compound, Sedobrol, which, when used in conjunction with a low-salt diet, is effective in the control of epilepsy (Swi).

- Morgan Parker (USA) patents the disposable scalpel.

The war of attrition on the Western Front had developed without any forethought – it was totally unplanned. But the resulting stalemate began to raise questions in the minds of politicians as to whether the hostilities would end with any clearcut conclusion in the field. German strategists decided to use attrition as a means of victory, whereby the armies of the Allies would be engaged and then put through a "meatmincer," with the aim that the consequent fatalities would be so horrific that victory would be secured. In the Battle of Verdun, the "meatmincer" took its toll for some 10 months, consuming the lives of nearly 700,000 troops from both sides, but without any army making a significant gain. As French troops bore the brunt at Verdun, the British launched a summer offensive on the Somme to provide relief. Here whole regiments were decimated on the first day of the attack. After more than four months, little ground had been gained.

▲ British troops go "over the top" during the Battle of the Somme. There had been some lack of confidence within the British General Staff about the good order of the common soldiers, so platoons of infantry were ordered to assault the German lines at the walk, rather than at the run, once the opening barrage had lifted and the mines had been detonated. This led to a loss of tactical advantage and no major advance.

● **11 Jan**: Russians and Turks begin offensive and counteroffensive in Armenia, lasting until Aug.

● **14 Jan**: Montenegro capitulates to the Austrian troops. On 20 Jan, it rejects the Austrian peace terms and resolves to continue fighting.

● **Jan**: Yaoundé, capital of the German colony Cameroons, in West Africa, falls to the Allies.

● **21 Feb**: After victory in the east, Germany concentrates on delivering a crushing blow to the Allies, beginning with the heavy bombardment of Verdun. French forces launch vigorous counterattacks in May. The war becomes a war of attrition: French losses at Verdun are estimated at 350,000, German only slightly less. The battle ends on 18 Dec.

● **21 Feb**: Germany warns the USA that the U-boat campaign extends to armed US merchantmen, but under US pressure agrees on 10 May to restrict submarine warfare. (›4 May)

● **22 Feb**: US president Woodrow Wilson announces his readiness to convene a peace conference, and lays out terms for mediation between the Allies and the Central Powers.

● **4 Mar**: Anglo-French agreement defines respective spheres of influence in the captured German colonies of Cameroons and Togoland, the former going to Britain and France, the latter ceded to France alone (effected 6 May 1919).

● **9 Mar**: Germany declares war on Portugal.

● **20 Apr**: Irish nationalist leader Sir Roger Casement disembarks on the Irish coast from a German U-boat; the Easter Rebellion, led by Padraic Pearse and the Irish Republican Brotherhood, begins on 24 Apr. The insurrection is suppressed on 1 May. Several of the rebel leaders are shot, and Casement is tried and executed on 3 Aug (UK).

● **29 Apr**: Mesopotamian town of Kut-el-Amara, besieged since 7 Dec 1915, falls to the Turks.

● **4 May**: German government averts a diplomatic breach with the USA by agreeing to scale down the submarine war, but insists that the USA oppose the UK naval blockade. (›3 Feb 1917)

● **9 May**: Sykes-Picot agreement between Britain and France, on the postwar partitioning of Turkey, which respects the Anglo-Russian-French agreement of 26 Apr on Russia's share of the spoils: Armenia, part of Kurdistan, western Anatolia and the Straits with Constantinople.

● **31 May**: Battle of Jutland (off Denmark) causes great damage to both the German and British fleets but proves inconclusive.

● **5 Jun**: Death of Field Marshal Lord Kitchener when the HMS *Hampshire*, on a secret mission to Russia, is sunk by a U-boat off the Orkneys. He is succeeded as Secretary of State for war by David Lloyd George on 7 Jul (UK).

● **Jun**: Russian troops gain some ground but fail to take Kovel when 15 divisions of Germans arrive from the Western Front; a million men are lost.

● **1 Jul-19 Nov** : New offensive on the Somme ends with appalling loss of lives and little ground gained, despite first ever use of tanks by the British. (›3 Dec)

● **3 Jul**: Russo-Japanese convention: Russia accepts the extension of Japanese influence in China, while Japan recognizes Russia's advance into Outer Mongolia.

● **27 Aug**: Romania declares war on Austria-Hungary, but by Dec is overrun and moves the government from Bucharest to Jassy just before the former is occupied.

● **27 Aug**: Gen. Erich von Falkenhayn is replaced as Chief of General Staff by Field Marshal Paul von Hindenburg.

● **29 Aug**: The Jones Act creates an elective senate of 24 members, providing greater powers for the Philippine government.

● **3 Sep**: New demands are made on China by Japan for further rights in South Manchuria and Inner Mongolia, granted by China in Feb 1917.

● **16 Sep**: The UK and France recognize the provisional government of "Czechoslovakia".

● **29 Oct**: Sherif Hussein of the Hejaz is proclaimed king of the Arabs, following the Arab Revolt begun in Jun; he is recognized by the Triple Entente powers on 6 Nov.

● **5 Nov**: Germany and Austria-Hungary proclaim an "independent" Polish kingdom.

● **11 Nov**: Wilson is reelected as US president in the closest race since 1888.

● **21 Nov**: Death of the Austrian emperor Franz Josef, succeeded by his grandnephew Karl (until 1918).

● **3 Dec**: Gen. Joffre is replaced by Gen. Robert Nivelle as head of the French forces on the Somme, following the failure of the offensive.

● **7–10 Dec**: Lloyd George becomes prime minister and forms a war cabinet (UK).

● **12 Dec**: Germany announces to the USA its preparedness to negotiate peace, but because all of the advantages at this stage lie with the Central Powers, the Allies reject this advance on 30 Dec.

● **18 Dec**: US president Wilson makes his peace proposals known to the belligerents, but the Allied reply (10 Jan 1917) is unpromising. The Germans continue negotiating. (›3 Feb 1917)

● **19 Dec**: Britain recognizes the provisional government of Eleutherios Venizelos, which had declared war on Germany and Bulgaria on 23 Nov (Gr).

● Belgian forces occupy Rwanda and Urundi, parts of German East Africa; these districts are assigned to Belgium on 30 May as a prospective mandate.

- **6 Jan:** Compulsory military service bill is passed by the UK parliament, against Labour opposition. On 25 April, a secret session of parliament decides to broaden the terms of conscription. (›13 Jun)

- **14 Jan:** In Holland, a breach of the Zuyder Zee dam at Katwoude in the worst storms for 90 years causes widespread devastation.

- **Jan:** In Germany, sugar prices increase rapidly, the tobacco tax is raised and butter rationing imposed. The potato blight contributes to starvation, which claims the lives of 700,000 people (Ger).

- **4 Feb:** National Bank of the Philippines is chartered as a public savings bank.

- **6 Feb:** Germany accepts full liability for the loss of US lives on the *Lusitania* in May 1915 and the right of the US to claim indemnity.

- **17 Feb:** The UK government appeals against the use of cars and motorcycles for pleasure.

- **Feb:** Riots occur in Berlin as a result of food shortages.

- **9 Mar:** Mexican rebel leader Pancho Villa leads a raid into New Mexico, killing 17 US citizens. On 10 Mar, a US posse of 5,000 is sent across the border to capture him. The rebel camp is routed on 31 Mar, and US troops depart on 5 Feb 1917.

- **8 April:** Women win the right to vote in national elections in Norway.

- **20 May:** The UK agrees to supply France with coal because most of the French mines are in the war zone.

- **21 May:** Start of British Summer Time, when the clocks are put forward an hour, a move expected to save hundreds of thousands of tonnes of coal.

- **May:** Provisional president of the Dominican Republic, Francisco Henriquez y Carvajal, refuses to sign a treaty handing financial control to the USA, and customs revenues are withheld by the USA.

- **13 Jun:** British miners vote overwhelmingly against conscription (UK).

- **1 Jul:** Alcohol is prohibited in Michigan, Montana, Nebraska and South Dakota, bringing the number of "dry" US states to 24.

- **2 July:** Race riots in East St Louis, Illinois; 39 are killed and hundreds injured (USA).

- **17 Jul:** Federal Farm Loan Bank Act establishes a federal land bank, farm loan associations and a federal farm loan bank to improve agricultural credit (USA).

- **23 Jul:** Independent Irish Nationalists hold a large meeting in Phoenix Park, Dublin, to protest at the government's Irish partition proposals.

- **Jul:** During the first seven months of the year there are more than 2,000 strikes by US workers.

- **4 Aug:** The USA pays $25 million for the Danish Virgin Islands.

- **Aug:** Further reports say that hundreds of thousands of Armenians are still being massacred by the Turks.

- **2 Sep:** US Senate passes a bill introducing an eight-hour working day.

- **7 Sep:** US Shipping Board is established to sell or charter merchant vessels to US citizens.

- **7 Sep:** Workmen's Compensation Act introduces protection for half a million federal employees (USA).

- **10 Oct:** Margaret Sanger and her sister Ethyl Bryne found the first birth control clinic in Brooklyn, New York, though it is raided by the police one month after opening.

- **7 Nov:** Jeanette Rankin becomes the first female member of Congress.

- **29 Nov:** The UK government announces it will take control of vacant agricultural land for food production.

- **7 Dec:** Germany is reported to have deported a million Poles for forced labor.

- **30 Dec:** The confidant and confessor of the Czarina, Grigory Rasputin, is assassinated by Prince Felix Yusupov and others, concerned by his excessive influence on affairs of state (Russ).

- General Motors Corporation becomes one of the world's leading automobile companies (USA).

- Switzerland becomes an international financial center with the issue of war loans.

- By the end of 1916, German U-boats are destroying 300,000 tonnes of shipping a month in their efforts to cut off British food supplies.

- Peter Nissen (Can) develops the Nissen hut, to provide temporary shelter for newly conscripted troops.

- Italian troops are issued with the first submachine gun, invented by Abiel Betel Revelli (It).

- France sets a new wheat price and controls on butter, cheese and oil.

- The first artificial silk (Rayon) knitwear is marketed (USA).

- Establishment of the South American championship in Association Football.

- Automobile windshield wipers are introduced (USA).

- **26 Jan:** Premiere of Enrique Granados's Spanish opera *Goyescas* at the Metropolitan Opera House. He had been invited to compose the opera after the performance in Paris in 1914 of his piano suite of the same name.

- Poet Robert Bridges edits *The Spirit of Man*, an anthology of prose and verse (UK).

- James Joyce: *Portrait of the Artist as a Young Man*, autobiographical novel (Ire).

- Edith and Osbert Sitwell: *20th Century Harlequinade*, poetry (UK).

- Henri Barbusse: *Feu* (Under Fire), novel (Fr).

- Soseki Natsume: *Light and Darkness*, novel (Jap).

- Nobel Prize for Literature won by Verner von Heidenstam (Swe).

- Carl Nielsen: Symphony No.4 (Den).

- Frederick Delius: *Requiem*, choral work (Fr).

- Edward Elgar: *The Spirit of England*, orchestral work (UK).

- Musical comedy *Chu Chin Chow* begins its run of 2,238 shows (USA).

- A group of painters, writers and musicians, including Jean (Hans) Arp, Tristan Tzara and Richard Huelsenbeck launch Dadaism at Hugo Ball's nightclub in Zürich, the Cabaret Voltaire. In 1917 they open a gallery and publish a journal (Swi).

- Jean (Hans) Arp: *Portrait of Tristan Tzara*, relief (Fr).

- Mark Gertler: *The Merry-Go-Round*, painting (UK).

- Otto Dix: *Wounded*, one of a series of lithographs inspired by Goya's series *The Horrors of War* (Ger).

- Georges Rouault begins his *Miserere et guerre* series of etchings (Fr).

- Tony Garnier: Olympic Stadium, Lyon (Fr).

- *Intolerance*, film by D.W. Griffith, an epic historical vision with a strong moral theme (USA).

- A.G. Bragaglia: *Perfido incanto*, Futurist film (It).

- Technicolor process first used in movies, in *The Gulf Between* (USA).

- Coco Chanel makes jersey, previously a fabric for underwear, chic (Fr).

- John Redfern (UK) designs the first women's uniform for the Red Cross.

- Erté (Russ) begins drawing covers for *Harper's Bazaar* (USA).

- The British edition of *Vogue* is launched.

- P. Langevin constructs an underwater ultrasonic source for submarine detection (Fr).

- Dodge Company produces the first all-steel bodywork for automobiles (USA).

- Treatment of war casualties leads to the development of plastic surgery.

- A. Sommerfeld amends Bohr's model of the atom, proposing an elliptical orbit for the electron (Ger).

- R.A. Millikan confirms Planck's constant (relating the quantum of energy to the frequency of radiation of an atom), using the photoelectric effect (USA).

- G.N. Lewis explains chemical bonding and valence of chemical elements by his theory of shared electrons, and shows that the number of electrons in compounds is nearly always even (USA).

- E.E. Barnard discovers what is later called Barnard's runaway star, with the largest proper motion of any known star (USA).

- Mass production of radio valves is started by Telefunken (Ger).

- Frederick A. Kolster (USA) develops the radio direction finder. Radio beacons are soon erected round coastlines, so that ships can take bearings in all weather.

- Pipes made from asbestos cement are produced commercially in Italy. They are light, free from corrosion and provide a smooth bore.

- Acetone is first prepared in significant quantities by the British Admiralty Powder Department. The high production rate is due to the use of a bacterium that makes acetone by fermenting grain.

- British electrical engineers Duddell and Mather develop the first industrial wattmeter for measuring directly and accurately electric power in high voltage cables.

- John Fisher (USA) develops the prototype of agitator washing machines.

- Vitamins A and B, identified in cow's milk in 1913, are declared essential for growth.

- Rudolph Matas teaches that no operation should be performed on a wounded patient until the effects of shock are reduced with adrenalin, intravenous saline and glucose.

- Edward Sharpey Schafer (UK) suggests that the islets of Langerhans in the pancreas secrete a substance which he calls insulin, which controls carbohydrate metabolism.

1917

The ever-escalating cost of the war, whether in economic or human terms, now made it essential for both sides to attempt to bring it successfully to a conclusion. The British tried to gain the advantage through the application of technological advance, developing the tank as a new weapon to combat the success of barbed wire and the machine gun as a means of defense; but its most advantageous use was not yet fully understood. In the event it was the entry of the United States into the war in April 1917 that turned the tide for the Allies. The Germans meanwhile looked for the cessation of warfare on the Eastern Front after the Russian Revolution of March 1917, permitting V. I. Lenin to return from Switzerland to Russia in a sealed railroad carriage in the correct expectation that the Bolsheviks would seize power and take Russia out of the war. But the arrival of American troops – well-fed, fresh and confident – in October changed the character of the Western Front, and Germany began to run out of manpower and matériel.

▲ British tanks, developed by the Admiralty, had first seen action during the Battle of the Somme in 1916, but it was not until the Battle of Cambrai in November 1917 that they began to achieve some measure of success; even then, a breakthrough was not established.

● **31 Jan**: A radical social constitution, the charter of the new Mexico, is adopted by the Mexican Congress, providing for, among other things, universal suffrage, restriction of church power, an eight-hour day and a minimum wage.

● **Jan**: UK prime minister Lloyd George launches an appeal for the entire nation to subscribe to a new War Loan: the cost of the war is estimated at over £5,700,000 a day.

● **3 Feb**: The beginning of unrestricted U-boat warfare causes the Americans to break off peace negotiations and sever relations with Germany. (›6 Apr)

● **Feb–Jun**: Secret peace negotiations between Emperor Karl of Austria and the French and British governments in Switzerland break down over Trieste (Aust-Hung).

● **2 Mar**: Puerto Rico becomes a US territory; Puerto Ricans are granted American citizenship, with compulsory voting.

● **8 Mar**: Strikes and unrest break out in Petrograd and a mutiny occurs there on 10 Mar. Next day the Duma refuses to obey an imperial decree that it be dissolved, and forms a provisional government headed by Prince Gyorgy Lvov (Russ).

● **9 Mar**: Capital of Russia moves from Petrograd to Moscow.

● **15 Mar**: Czar Nicholas II abdicates in favor of his brother Michael, who himself abdicates on 16 Mar in favor of the provisional government. The provisional government ushers in a period of civil liberties and other reforms: the independence of Finland (21 Mar), Poland (30 Mar) and Estonia (12 Apr) is recognized (Russ). The USA is the first country to recognize the new regime.

● **21 Mar**: The czar and czarina are arrested. In Sep they are sent to Siberia with their family "for protection against the Bolsheviks" (Russ).

● **6 Apr**: The USA declares war on Germany, after the discovery early in the year of the "Zimmermann note" which revealed German plans against the USA. (›7 Dec)

● **9 Apr**: First great Allied offensive of the year at Arras: Vimy Ridge is captured, and by 4 May British troops have advanced on the Somme to near St Quentin. Second offensive begins 16 Apr, but French troops are held back. In May/Jun mutiny breaks out in the French ranks.

● **16 Apr**: Vladimir Ilych Lenin and other leading Bolsheviks arrive in Petrograd after a journey from Switzerland across Germany in a sealed carriage, to direct the Petrograd Soviet. They demand a transfer of power to the Soviets, the unconditional end of the war on the Eastern Front, distribution of land to the peasants and control of industry by workers' committees (Russ).

● **28 Apr**: Gen. Philippe Pétain replaces Gen. Robert Nivelle as French commander.

● **10 May**: After the German U-boat devastation of British shipping reaches a peak in Apr, prime minister Lloyd George insists on the adoption of the convoy system.

● **May**: Crackdown by the French government on socialist and pacifist agitators, leading to the execution of 23 leaders.

● **7 Jun**: British troops launch a surprise attack on Messines Ridge, taking territory held by the Germans since 1915; on 31 Jun, the Third Battle of Ypres (Passchendaele) begins. In driving rain and Flanders mud, 400,000 soldiers give their lives to take 8km (5 miles) of territory. British troops are now as disaffected as the French.

● **12 Jun**: King Constantine of Greece abdicates at Allied insistence; Greece severs relations with the Central Powers and declares war on them on 27 Jun.

● **1 Jul**: Brief restoration of the Manchu dynasty in China until 12 Jul.

● **16–18 Jul**: After Aleksandr Kerensky, as minister of war, spurs on a final and failed offensive on the Eastern Front (29 Jun–7 Jul), the Bolsheviks attempt to seize power in Petrograd; but the coup fails, and many of the Bolshevik leaders (including Leon Trotsky) are arrested. Lenin escapes to Finland.

● **20 Jul**: Kerensky assumes the leadership of the provisional government (Russ).

● **20 Jul**: Pact of Corfu signed by Serbia, Montenegro, Croatia and Slovenia to form a single state under the Serbian dynasty.

● **Jul**: After initial losses, British fortunes are reversed by Col.T.E. Lawrence – "Lawrence of Arabia" – who begins a series of successful attacks, fighting with the Arab rebels on the Arabian peninsula, within the Turkish Empire.

● **20 Aug**: Second Battle of Verdun: Allies gain several key positions along the River Meuse, followed up by a further offensive.

● **3 Sep**: Germans capture Riga, followed by most of Latvia and the Baltic islands (11–20 Oct).

● **12 Sep**: Central Powers grant newly independent Poland a constitution, and appoint a regency council on 15 Oct.

● **9–14 Sep**: Counter-revolutionary coup by Gen. Lavr Kornilov, whose troops march on Petrograd, is unsuccessful (Russ).

● **25–27 Oct**: Sinn Fein convention in Dublin: a constitution for the Irish Republic is adopted and Eamon de Valera is elected president of Sinn Fein (UK).

● **Oct**: Italian forces suffer defeat at Caporetto. British and French troops are rushed in (3–5 Nov), and a line held on the Piave River.

SOCIETY CULTURE SCIENCE

SOCIETY

● **6 Nov** (24 Oct OS): Bolshevik Revolution: Bolshevik forces capture the government offices and the Winter Palace in Petrograd. They arrest members of the provisional government, but Kerensky escapes and goes into exile. On 7 Nov, the Second All-Russian Congress of Soviets hands over power to the Bolsheviks (Russ).

● **7 Nov**: Bolshevik government and the Council of People's Commissars is formed, headed by Lenin, with Trotsky as commissar for foreign affairs and Joseph Stalin as commissar for national minorities. On 20 Dec the council organizes the Extraordinary Commission to Combat Counter-revolution (Cheka) under Felix Dzerzhinsky (Russ).

● **20 Nov**: Proclamation of the Ukrainian People's Republic, recognized by the Bolsheviks by the Treaty of Brest-Litovsk (1918).

● **20 Nov**: Battle of Cambrai sees the first great tank raid: British troops nearly break through.

● **27 Nov**: Establishment of the Supreme War Council of leading Allied statesmen.

● **28 Nov**: Proclamation of Estonian independence; the Red Army invade to recapture the strategically important territory, but are blocked by the German occupation of the country in Dec.

● **3 Dec**: The Bolsheviks sue for peace with the Central Powers and an armistice is concluded on 15 Dec, ending all operations on the Eastern Front.

● **6 Dec**: Finland declares complete independence. The new Soviet government recognizes the Finnish terms of independence on 2 Jan 1918.

● **6 Dec**: Truce of Focsani ends hostilities between the Central Powers and Romania.

● **7 Dec**: The USA declares war on Austria-Hungary.

● **9 Dec**: After a new British offensive in Palestine, Jerusalem falls to Gen. Allenby's forces after heavy fighting.

● **23 Dec**: Formation of the Moldavian (Bessarabian) Republic, which proclaims its union with Romania on 9 Apr 1918.

● **4 Jan**: The UK and Germany agree to the exchange of all internees over 45.

● **29 Jan**: US Congress passes new immigration law requiring all immigrants over 16 to know 30–80 English words, and banning all Asians except Japanese.

● **3 Feb**: The German government introduces regulations on the use of coal as shortages occur.

● **10 Feb**: Zionist leader Chaim Weizmann meets government representatives to discuss the possibility of a Jewish colony in Palestine (Ger). (›2 Nov)

● **20 Mar**: Outrage is caused when a German submarine torpedoes a British hospital ship. The British government denies the German claim that such hospital ships carry munitions.

● **14 Apr**: Congress votes a $7 billion war loan (USA).

● **26 Jun**: George V orders members of the Royal Family to drop their German titles – Saxe-Coburg becomes Windsor and Battenberg becomes Mountbatten (UK).

● **Jun**: Second Liberty Act: fixing of the national debt at $45 billion (USA).

● **2 Jul**: Up to 75 blacks are murdered during race riots in East St Louis, Illinois (USA).

● **11 Jul**: Wilhelm II announces a system of equal, direct and secret suffrage in Prussia, and a three-class system of voting (Ger).

● **20 Aug**: Due to food shortages throughout Hungary, all prisoners serving less than two years in prison are released.

● **Aug**: Price freeze on food (USA).

● **2 Oct**: UK government declares a trade embargo on Sweden, Norway, Denmark and Holland, to stop supplies reaching Germans.

● **15 Oct**: Convicted spy and dancer Mata Hari (Neth) is executed in Paris.

● **Oct**: US government confiscates all German properties in the USA.

● **2 Nov**: Balfour Declaration of the British government in favor of Palestine becoming "a national home for the Jewish people".

● **Dec**: By the time hostilities end between the Central Powers and Romania, most of the important oil- and wheat-producing areas of Romania have been occupied.

● Until 1917 German U-boats sink British merchant ships faster than they can be built, and US ships are increasingly used. A shipbuilding campaign begins in the USA, doubling the size of the American fleet between 1916 and 1918.

● Nobel Peace Prize is won by the International Committee of the Red Cross.

CULTURE

● **12 June**: Premiere of Hans Pfitzner's opera *Palestrina* in Munich (Ger).

● Edward Thomas: *Poems* (posth.) (UK).

● Guillaume Apollinaire: *Calligrammes*, poems (Fr).

● Paul Valéry: *La Jeune Parque*, poems (Fr).

● Founding of the Hogarth Press by Virginia and Leonard Woolf (UK).

● Knut Hamsun: *Growth of the Soil*, novel (Nor).

● T.S. Eliot: *Prufrock and Other Observations*, poems (UK).

● Nobel Prize for Literature is won by Karl Kjellerup (Den) and Henrik Pontoppidan (Den).

● Luigi Pirandello: *Cosi è se vi pare* (Right You Are, If You Think You Are), play (It).

● Sergey Prokofiev: "Classical" Symphony (Russ).

● Alois Hába: *Suite for String Orchestra*, an early instance of the use of quarter-tones (Aust-Hung).

● Erik Satie: *Parade*, for the *Ballets Russes*, based on a story by Jean Cocteau, choreographed by Leonid Massine and with sets by Pablo Picasso. Picasso's designs for Diaghilev's production are described as "sur-réaliste" by Guillaume Apollinaire, the first use of the term (Fr).

● Feruccio Busoni: *Turandot*, opera (It), first performed in Zürich.

● Hugo von Hofmannsthal, Richard Strauss and Max Reinhardt initiate the Salzburg Festival (Aust-Hung).

● Béla Bartók: *The Wooden Prince*, ballet (Aust-Hung).

● First jazz record, *Dixieland Jazz Band One-Step*, issued by Victor (USA).

● George Grosz: *The Face of the Ruling Class*, lithograph (Ger).

● Piet Mondrian: *Composition in Black and White*, painting (Neth).

● Foundation of the De Stijl movement by Theo van Doesburg, Piet Mondrian and others (Neth).

● Gerrit Rietveld (Neth) designs his Red-Blue Chair, inspired by Mondrian's paintings.

● The Independents exhibition opens in New York, at which Marcel Duchamp's *Fountain*, a "ready-made" consisting of a urinal, is shown (USA).

● Tony Garnier publishes his plans for an Industrial City (first exhibited 1904) (Fr).

● H.P. Berlage: Revision of Master Plan for Amsterdam (Neth).

● Charlie Chaplin signs a contract with First National, worth $1 million annually. His films *The Immigrant* and *Easy Street* are released (USA).

SCIENCE

● **May**: F. Fischer produces coal paraffin and coal petrol (Ger).

● **Jun**: Helium is extracted from natural gas and used as a substitute for hydrogen in airships (USA).

● Carl Jung publishes his *Psychology of the Unconscious* (Swi).

● Clarence Birdseye develops his method of freezing as a way of preserving foods (USA).

● US Navy equips windproof flying jackets with "zippers".

● 100-inch reflecting telescope is installed at Mount Wilson (USA).

● K. Schwarzchild develops the equations that are later used to predict the existence of black holes from Einstein's relativity equations (Ger).

● J. Wagner von Jauregg treats syphilitic paralysis by injecting malaria (Aust-Hung).

● Rearrangement of chromosomes during meiosis known as "crossing over" is demonstrated.

● G. Lusk and R.J. Anderson discover the importance of calorie consumption in producing energy.

● E.C. Wente introduces the condenser microphone in the US, producing clearer and more uniform sound.

● Launch of the *Namsenfjord*, a sea-going vessel built of concrete.

● Completion of the trans-Australian railroad. The final 480km (300 miles) stretch is the longest straight stretch of track in the world.

● Nekal, an early commercial detergent, is produced in Germany, prompted by the shortage of soap during the war.

● French doctors identify the condition known as trench foot, caused by standing for long periods in water and in footwear which restricts the blood supply.

● J.D. Speid (UK) perfects the appendicectomy clamp, which enables the organ to be cut out with less risk of infection to surrounding tissues.

● Sigmund Freud completes *Introductory Lectures in Psychoanalysis* (Aust-Hung).

● The German Gotha is the first aircraft to be designed as a bomber, replacing the bomb-carrying Zeppelins.

● Nobel Prize for Physics is won by Charles G. Barkla (UK) "for his discovery of the characteristic Röntgen radiation of the elements".

World War I, despite its name, was essentially a European conflict, fought on European soil, a fact perhaps typified by the signing of an armistice with the German forces in the West in a railroad coach in the forest of Compiègne in France. And it was Europe that suffered the aftermath of war – political, economic and human. The Allies had not expected victory during 1918; such was the newly determined German spring offensive that for some months it seemed that the victory would go to the Central Powers. The closing year of the war was marked by social disturbance and revolution as well as by starvation and hardship, none of which were halted by the armistice. National revolutions developed in the Baltic states early in 1918, and the Habsburg Empire split apart in a welter of internal dissent. Bavaria attempted to secede from collapsing Germany, and Wilhelm II's abdication was followed by the Spartakist uprising in Berlin. Most worrying of all to liberal politicians was the potential threat of the spread of the Bolshevik revolution westward across industrial Europe.

▲ All hostilities ceased at 11 a.m. on 11 November 1918, after Marshal Foch accepted the German surrender on behalf of the Allies. The railroad carriage in which the signing took place was used again after the fall of France to German forces in 1940.

● **5 Jan**: British prime minister Lloyd George defines British war aims: self-determination for the East European and Balkan peoples after the breakup of the Austro-Hungarian Empire, and for the Middle Eastern peoples presently under Turkish domination (UK).

● **8 Jan**: US president Wilson outlines his Fourteen Points for peace, consisting of guarantees for national self-determination, the restoration of occupied Belgium, France and Russia, multilateral disarmament and the setting up of a League of Nations.

● **12 Jan**: Latvia proclaims its independence from Russia. Leon Trotsky, representing Russia at the peace conference in Brest-Litovsk, at first refuses to recognize the independence of the Baltic states without a plebiscite. (›18 Nov)

● **28 Jan**: Civil war in Finland as Finnish Communists seize Helsinki and overrun large parts of southern Finland. They are driven out of the country in Apr by a force of Whites supported by Germany.

● **9 Feb**: Treaty of peace signed between the Central Powers and the Ukraine.

● **10 Feb**: Trotsky declares the war on the Eastern Front ended, although a peace has not been made. But the Germans renew their advance and by early Mar are within 160km (100 miles) of Petrograd. Negotiations are resumed on 28 Feb (Russ).

● **16 Feb**: Formal declaration of Lithuanian independence. The Bolsheviks immediately invade, but are forced to withdraw and recognize Lithuanian independence under the conditions imposed by the Treaty of Brest-Litovsk (3 Mar). Lithuania allies itself with Germany on 14 May.

● **24 Feb**: Estonian independence proclaimed under German protection. By the Treaty of Brest-Litovsk, Soviet Russia has to recognize the sovereignty of Estonia. (›11 Nov)

● **3 Mar**: Treaty of Brest-Litovsk ends the war on the Eastern Front. Russia agrees to abandon Poland, the Baltic states, the Ukraine, Finland and Transcaucasia.

● **5 Mar**: Moscow becomes the permanent Russian capital, instead of Petrograd, and on 7 Mar, the Bolshevik party changes it name to the Russian Communist party.

● **21 Mar**: All-out German offensive on the Western Front pushes the line forwards by 65km (40 miles) before French reserves can check the advance. On 9 Apr there is a second great offensive south of Ypres, in which Armentières is captured. The Germans advance to within 40 miles of Paris.

● **5 Apr**: British and Japanese marines land at Vladivostok (Russ), and take command on 6 Jul.

● **22 Apr**: A report recommending limited self-government for India is denounced by the Indian Congress and the Muslim League as unsatisfactory.

● **Apr**: With the arrival of US air squadrons, Allied air superiority is complete.

● **7 May**: Treaty of Bucharest: Romania cedes Dobrudja to Bulgaria, and the Carpathian passes go to Austria-Hungary; the Germans take a 90-year lease of the Romanian oil wells.

● **15 Jun**: As the Habsburg monarchy crumbles, the Austrians make a last-ditch bid for victory, which fails; on 15 Sep the Austrian government appeals to US president Wilson for a peace conference, which is rejected.

● **10 Jul**: Promulgation of the Soviet Constitution, adopted by the Fifth All-Russian (later All-Union) Congress of Soviets, setting in place the "dictatorship of the proletariat" by the Communist party under V.I. Lenin.

● **15 Jul**: Allied counterattack aided by American forces pushes the Germans back across the River Marne; Soissons is recaptured on 2 Aug, and an Allied offensive follows, which forces the Germans back over the Hindenburg Line in early Sep.

● **16 Jul**: Czar Nicholas II, Czarina Alexandra and their children are murdered in Yekaterinburg (Russ).

● **30 Aug**: An attempt made on Lenin's life by a Social Revolutionary, initiates a reign of terror in which many bourgeois and intellectuals are murdered (Russ).

● **15–24 Sep**: A large Allied force begins a major offensive into Bulgaria. The Bulgarians sue for armistice, concluded on 30 Sep.

● **18 Sep**: Major British offensive in Palestine begins: with the aid of the Arabs, the Germans and Turks are driven back into Syria. Damascus, Beirut and Aleppo fall to the Allies. The Turks call for an armistice, signed on 30 Oct.

● **26 Sep**: The battles of the Argonne (until 15 Oct) and of Ypres (28 Sep–2 Oct) are sufficiently successful for the Allies to make the German government begin armistice and peace negotiations on 4 Oct.

● **14 Oct**: Czech national council in Paris forms a provisional Czech government, with Tomas Masaryk as president and Eduard Beneš as foreign minister, declaring an independent Czechoslovakia on 28 Oct. The Slovak national council votes for union with the Czechs on 30 Oct.

● **16 Oct**: Austrian emperor Karl proclaims a reorganization of the monarchy as a federal state, with complete self-government for each subject nationality. (›12 Nov)

● **17 Oct**: Hungary declares independence from Austria. A revolution follows on 31 Oct, and the national council proclaims the Hungarian Republic on 16 Nov.

● **24 Oct**: Italians attack the Austrian front from Trentino to the Adriatic Sea, completely routing the Austrian forces, and capture Trieste and Fiume.

SOCIETY

- **28 Oct**: Sailors' mutiny in Kiel, after orders that the German fleet attack the British, spreads to other seaports on 4–5 Nov.
- **29 Oct**: Kaiser Wilhelm II leaves Berlin for the army headquarters at Spa, alarmed at demands for his resignation in the Reichstag (Ger).
- **29 Oct**: Yugoslav National Council meeting in Zagreb proclaims Yugoslavian independence. (›7 Nov)
- **1 Nov**: Poland goes to war with the Ukraine to reconquer Galicia for the new Polish state. (›3 Nov)
- **3 Nov**: Armistice signed between the Allies and Austria-Hungary.
- **3 Nov**: Polish Republic proclaimed in Warsaw, led by Josef Pilsudski from 14 Nov; and on 27–28 Dec Polish troops occupy Posen.
- **7 Nov**: Yugoslav conference at Geneva votes for the union of Croatia and Slovenia with Serbia and Montenegro, proclaimed as the United Kingdom of the Serbs, Croats and Slovenes on 24 Nov, with King Peter of Serbia as ruler. (›26 Nov)
- **8 Nov**: Proclamation of the Bavarian Republic in Bavaria by Kurt Eisner, after a revolt in Munich the previous day.
- **9 Nov**: Abdication of Wilhelm II; he flees to Holland, to live there in retirement until his death in 1941. The German Republic is proclaimed, with a socialist majority government. A struggle for ascendence ensues between the Spartakists, led by Karl Liebknecht and Rosa Luxemburg, and the Social Democrats.
- **11 Nov**: Armistice signed on the Western Front. At 11 am, all hostilities cease.
- **11 Nov**: German troops begin their withdrawal from Estonia; once again (22 Nov) the Soviets invade but are driven out with help from the British fleet. Soviet Russia definitively recognizes Estonian sovereignty by the Treaty of Tartu on 2 Feb 1920. (›6 Jun 1919)
- **12 Nov**: Abdication of Austrian emperor Karl. The Austrian Republic is proclaimed the following day.
- **18 Nov**: Proclamation of Latvian independence, with Karlis Ulmanis as prime minister.
- **26 Nov**: Montenegro deposes King Nicholas and proclaims union with Serbia.
- **1 Dec**: British and American troops begin the occupation of Germany.
- **8 Dec**: Allied military administration of Turkey in place in Constantinople.
- **14 Dec**: A liberal government emerges in Romania under Ion Bratianu.
- **14 Dec**: "Khaki election" in Britain: coalition government under Lloyd George wins a large majority on a platform pledging punishment of Germany and demanding full reparations.

- **15 Jan**: General strikes take hold in Vienna, Prague and Budapest as workers' peace movements gather pace.
- **31 Jan**: Martial law is declared in Berlin after a series of strikes led by socialist Spartakists.
- **31 Jan**: The Gregorian calendar is introduced in Russia.
- **Jan**: Strikes occur in the German armaments industries.
- **Jan**: Agreement on mutual financial transactions and support is reached between Germany and Finland.
- **Jan**: A decision is made to plant 800,000 ha (2 million acres) of Britain with trees in a state-sponsored forestry scheme. A Forestry Commission is proposed, to ensure that in future Britain will have sufficient home timber for military and commercial needs.
- **3 Mar**: The entire male population of the Armenian town of Samsun is massacred by Muslims.
- **9 Mar**: A new Military Service Bill raises the maximum conscription age to 50, and introduces conscription to Ireland (UK). On 20 Jun, the government announces the abandonment of Irish conscription, and also the postponement of Home Rule, because of Irish protests.
- **5 Apr**: War Finance Commission is created with a reserve of $500 million for funding essential industries (USA).
- **10 Apr**: Webb-Pomerene Act encourages export trade by exempting associations from antitrust laws (USA).
- **Apr**: The Cunliffe Report recommends a return to the gold standard (UK).
- **Apr**: Corn and other agricultural products are delivered from the Ukraine to Germany and Austria.
- **19 Jun**: UK government announces the introduction of general rationing.
- **30 Jul**: Captain Sarret (Fr) makes the first ever parachute drop from a plane.
- **Jul**: Reichstag agrees upon a further 12 billion marks for financing the war (Ger).
- **Jul**: All industrial enterprises in Russia are nationalized.
- **Aug**: Agreement on economic cooperation between Romania, Germany and Austria.
- **22 Sep–8 Jan 1920**: Steel strike, defeated by the government despite popular sympathy (USA).
- Foundation of the Budokwai, Europe's first judo club, in London (UK).
- Invention of orienteering (Swe).
- Opening of the Venezuelan oilfields marks the beginning of the country's position as a leading oil producer.
- An influenza epidemic in India claims 5 million lives, and Spanish flu affects countries all over the world, killing more than the war in Europe.

CULTURE

- **14 Feb**: "Swanee", the first successful song by George Gershwin (USA).
- **Feb**: *New York Times* begins home delivery (USA)
- **25 Aug**: War Industries Board declares moving pictures an essential industry (USA).
- Aleksandr Blok: *The Twelve*, poem (Russ).
- Katherine Mansfield: *The Prelude*, novella (UK).
- First publication of the poetic works of Gerard Manley Hopkins (written 1884–89) (UK).
- Marcel Proust: *A l'ombre de jeunes filles en fleurs* (Within a Budding Grove), novel in the sequence *A la recherche du temps perdu* (Remembrance of Things Past) (Fr).
- Lytton Strachey: *Eminent Victorians*, biography (UK).
- Percy Wyndham Lewis: *Tarr*, novel (UK).
- James Joyce: *Exiles*, play (UK).
- John Drinkwater: *Abraham Lincoln*, play (USA).
- Igor Stravinsky: *A Soldier's Tale*, theater and ballet piece, is first performed in Lausanne (Swi).
- Arnold Schoenberg, aided by Alban Berg, Anton Webern and Eduard Steuermann, founds the Society for Private Musical Performances in Vienna (Aust-Hung).
- Alfred Denis Cortot, French pianist and conductor, founds the Ecole Normale de Musique in Paris.
- Tristan Tzara's *Dada Manifesto* represents the high-water mark of Dadaism's notoriety (Swi).
- Joseph Stella: *Brooklyn Bridge*, painting (USA).
- Paul Nash exhibits paintings of the Western Front battlefields, which he saw both on active service and as an official war artist (UK).
- Kasimir Malevich: *White Square on a White Background*, Suprematist painting (Russ).
- Christian Schad produces his first "schadographs", laying flat objects on photographic paper (Swi).
- *A Dog's Life*, starring Charlie Chaplin (USA).
- Formation of the Nihon Sosaku Hanga Kyokai (Japanese Creative Print Society) (Jap).
- National Design Organization is founded in Norway.
- First Tarzan film, *Tarzan of the Apes*, released (USA).

SCIENCE

- Nobel Prize for Chemistry is won by Fritz Haber (Ger) "for the synthesis of ammonia from its elements".
- Nobel Prize for Physics is won by Max Planck (Ger) for his discovery of energy quanta.
- E.H. Armstrong devises the superheterodyne circuit for radio (USA).
- The first three-color traffic lights are installed in New York.
- Radio crystal oscillator is introduced.
- First drill to have diamond cutting edges is introduced to Shell Oil Company by van der Gracht.
- Publication of A. Eddington's *Gravitation and the Principle of Relativity* (UK).
- E. Noether demonstrates that every symmetry in physics implies a conservation law and vice-versa (Ger).
- Publication of J.M. Coulter's *Plant Genetics*.
- British Army uses mixed antitoxin to combat tetanus and the gas gangrene bacilli.
- Harlow Shapley, after studying cepheid variable stars and the distribution of globular clusters, increases the estimated size of the Milky Way about ten times, and first proposes the modern structural model of the same (USA).
- ASDIC (Anti-Submarine Detection Investigation Committee) detectors replace passive microphones for detecting enemy submarines and mines (UK).
- HMS *Argus* is the first aircraft carrier to have a purpose-built flight deck allowing its squadron to take off and land on the same area.
- Development and manufacture of alkyd resins, which become essential components of paints, giving them improved drying performance, color characteristics and durability.
- Celucotton, a wood cellulose substitute for cotton, is developed to meet the urgent need for bandages and dressings.
- The USA announces a method of distilling alcohols, used in munition manufacture, from a cactus plant.

The Allied victory ushered in what proved to be a bitter peace – soon to be roundly attacked by the British economist J.M. Keynes. The peace conference was dominated by the "Big Three" – the heads of government of Britain, France and the United States. It was inevitable that the drafting of peace terms would be concerned with the pursuit of national interests, despite US president Woodrow Wilson's efforts for a "just peace". The terms of peace proved an elusive goal, and despite the signature of the Treaty of Versailles in June were not finally agreed until two years later. The enforcement of German reparations would have disastrous economic and political consequences until their payment was abandoned in 1932. Dissent was not only visible in relations between the victors and the vanquished; it was equally in evidence within the Allied camp. There were squabbles over access to Middle Eastern oil reserves, and even conflict over such Pacific islands as might be suitable to act as waystations for oceanic cable routes.

▲ The peace parades of July 1919 throughout the United Kingdom marked a moment of joy and relief after the years of suffering, as well as providing an opportunity to pay tribute to the memory of those who had given their lives in the war. In London, thousands marched down Whitehall past Sir Edwin Lutyens's new war memorial, the Cenotaph.

● **3 Jan**: Bolshevik army invades Latvia but is repulsed by German-Latvian forces backed by the Allies in Mar, and finally expelled; an armistice between Latvia and Soviet Russia is signed on 1 Feb 1920.

● **5–15 Jan**: Spartakist (Communist) revolt in Berlin, suppressed by the provisional majority Socialist government. Both Rosa Luxemburg and Karl Liebknecht are murdered while under arrest on 15 Jan (Ger).

● **10 Jan**: British troops occupy Baghdad, and the mandate for Iraq is later (25 Apr 1920) assigned to Britain, provoking an Arab insurrection against the British during Jul–Dec 1920, eventually suppressed.

● **17 Jan**: Ignace Paderewski forms a coalition cabinet in Poland, with Gen. Pilsudski as provisional president.

● **18 Jan**: Opening of the peace conference at Versailles to settle all claims against the Central Powers. On 23 Jan a resolution is adopted to create a League of Nations. (›11 Apr)

● **21 Jan**: Some 25 Sinn Fein MPs refuse to attend parliament in Westminster and organize their own parliament, the Dáil, and declare Irish independence. However, the Dáil is suppressed on 12 Sep, and a raid on Sinn Fein headquarters leads to the beginning of war (26 Nov), with Sinn Fein attacks on the police, and arson.

● **24 Jan**: Catalonian Union meets in Barcelona and drafts a home rule program for Catalonia (Sp).

● **Jan**: Czechs occupy the disputed area of Teschen on the Polish border; unrest continues until the territory is divided between Czechoslovakia and Poland on 28 Jul 1920.

● **Feb–Mar**: Communist insurrections in Berlin and other cities (Ger).

● **2 Mar**: Foundation of the Communist Third International, to propagate Communist doctrine and the notion of world revolution (Russ).

● **12 Mar**: After the Socialists gain 72 seats in the Austrian elections of 16 Feb, Karl Renner becomes chancellor.

● **21 Mar**: Formation of a socialist-Communist government in Hungary. A Communist dictatorship rapidly develops and Hungary begins to invade Slovakia on 28 May in order to reclaim it. On 10 Apr, Romanian troops begin an invasion of Hungary, to strengthen their claim to Transylvania. (› 4 Aug)

● **23 Mar**: Fascist party is formed by Benito Mussolini (It).

● **11 Apr**: Geneva is chosen as the seat of the League of Nations (Swi).

● **19 Apr**: Beginning of Vilna dispute (1919–22) between Poland and Lithuania. On 18 Apr 1922 the town is incorporated with Poland, but this is not recognized by Lithuania.

● **Apr**: Insurrection in Korea is severely suppressed by the Japanese.

● **Apr**: Gen. Hertzog of the South African Nationalist party requests recognition of complete independence for South Africa at the Paris peace conference, but his request is ignored.

● **7 May**: Mandate for German colonies south of the equator in the Pacific (except Nauru Island and Samoa, which go to New Zealand) is assigned to Australia; German East Africa is assigned to Britain, renamed Tanganyika, and the German settlers are repatriated to Germany; German Southwest Africa is assigned to South Africa.

● **9 May**: Franchise granted to certain women in Belgium.

● **15 May**: Greeks land at Smyrna to begin their attempted conquest of Turkey, with the political support of the Allies.

● **17 May**: Civil government is reestablished in Libya, which is then divided into Tripolitania and Cyrenaica.

● **19 May**: Turkish nationalist Mustafa Kemal lands at Samsun (Tur) and begins organizing resistance to the dismemberment of Turkey, secretly agreed to by the Allies. He is dismissed by the sultan on 8 Jul and finally outlawed (11 Jul).

● **May**: A delegation of prominent Filipinos arrives in the USA to press for Philippine independence.

● **1 Jun**: Proclamation of a Rhineland Republic, supported by France, which collapses after several months due to internal hostility to the separatist regime (Ger).

● **6 Jun**: Beginning of a Russo-Finnish war over Karelia; hostilities end with the Treaty of Tartu (14 Oct 1920), with a small territorial gain for Finland.

● **15 Jun**: Estonia adopts a democratic republican constitution, and passes a law (10 Oct) distributing land among the peasantry.

● **20 Jun**: The Scheidemann government (since 9 Nov) resigns in protest at Allied demands in the peace treaty; the treaty is signed on 23 Jun by a new cabinet under Gustav Bauer, to avert an Allied invasion (Ger).

● **21 Jun**: German fleet is scuttled at Scapa Flow by its own crews to prevent it from falling into the hands of the Allies.

● **28 Jun**: Treaty of Versailles: provides for the covenant of a League of Nations, and for territorial and economic cessions by Germany to the Allies, including the demilitarization of the Rhineland, the cession of Posen (Poznań) and West Prussia to Poland, the division of mandates for German colonies between the Allies, the destruction of the U-boat fleet and air force and severe restriction of naval tonnage and the armed forces. France regains Alsace-Lorraine. Controversially, Germany is to accept "war guilt" and make reparations, including payment for the war, the handover of ships and matériel.

SOCIETY

- **7 Jul**: The Treaty of Versailles is ratified by Germany, but not by the US Senate. The question of reparations is handed over to a Reparations Committee.

- **12 Jul**: Allied blockade of Germany lifted, but only after a large part of the country is reduced to near-starvation.

- **17 Jul**: Finland adopts a democratic constitution and Karl J. Stahlberg is elected president on 25 Jul.

- **29 Jul**: Italo-Greek treaty: Italy supports Greek claims in Thrace and Epirus in return for Greek support for an Italian protectorate over Albania and claims in Anatolia (Turk); the Dodecanese Islands to be ceded to Greece.

- **31 Jul**: Germany adopts the Weimar constitution, with a system of proportional representation and a powerful presidency. The government is forced to respect the integrity of Austria (22 Sep).

- **4 Aug–14 Nov**: Romanian troops occupy Budapest. They finally leave Hungary on 25 Feb 1920.

- **9 Aug**: By the Anglo-Persian agreement, Britain reaffirms the independence and integrity of Persia, though with a substantial degree of British ascendency. It is not, however, ratified by the Persian *majlis*.

- **9 Sep**: Declaration of Sivas after a nationalist congress (4 Sep) declares its opposition to Allied occupation and the creation of an Armenian state (Tur).

- **10 Sep**: Treaty of St-Germain between Austria and the wartime Allies ratifies the breakup of the monarchy into sovereign states and provides for reparations and military cuts.

- **12 Sep**: Gabriele d'Annunzio, Italian writer, war hero and nationalist, seizes Fiume and sets up a government.

- **16 Nov**: Mongolia is placed under Chinese suzerainty.

- **27 Nov**: Treaty of Neuilly between Bulgaria and the wartime Allies provides for reparations and military reductions, and deprives Bulgaria of its Aegean seaboard.

- **28 Nov**: Nancy Astor is elected Britain's first woman member of parliament.

- **23 Dec**: Government of India Act hands over administrative responsibility for certain areas to an Indian parliament (opens Feb 1921), but leaving key matters in the hands of the British governor. The Indian National Congress rejects the system but the National Liberal Federation cooperates, with some success.

- **2 Jan**: one and a half million Armenians are massacred by the Turks.

- **Jan**: Economic crisis in the USA due to the transformation of the war economy into a peacetime economy.

- **4 Feb**: French citizenship is extended to Algerians who have served in World War I, landowners and literates.

- **14 Feb**: Debate on universal suffrage in the Japanese Diet (at present limited to men over 25 with a good income) provokes demonstrations. The Diet is dissolved on 26 Feb.

- **1 Mar**: Martial law is declared in Spain after riots over food shortage.

- **18 Mar**: Rowlatt Acts passed, by which agitators can be interned without trial and tried without juries. Mohandas Gandhi proclaims a day of fasting and work stoppage in India; this leads to rioting in Amritsar, where five Englishmen are killed and an Englishwoman is beaten by the mob (Ind). (›13 Apr)

- **13 Apr**: Amritsar Massacre: on the orders of Gen. Reginald Dyer, Gurkha troops fire upon unarmed protestors, killing 379 people with 1,200 wounded. As a result Gandhi suspends his *satyagraha* (civil disobedience) program (Ind).

- **26 May**: Women are enfranchised in Sweden.

- **28 May**: Romanian Jews are emancipated and given rights of full citizenship, although antisemitism continues to be widespread.

- **May**: International Labor Organization is formed.

- **5 Jul**: 20-year-old Suzanne Lenglen (Fr) wins women's final at Wimbledon.

- **2 Sep**: Universal suffrage and proportional representation are introduced in Italy.

- **Sep**: International agreement prohibits the manufacture and importation of liquor into Africa.

- **Sep**: German finance minister Erzberger establishes a central tax office, thus strengthening Germany's financial sovereignty.

- **28 Oct**: National Prohibition Act (Volstead Act) is passed in the USA, severely restricting the manufacture and sale of alcohol.

- USA becomes the main creditor nation of the world.

- John Maynard Keynes's *The Economic Consequences of the Peace* sharply criticizes the Treaty of Versailles (UK).

- In Germany and Central Europe famine is now widespread.

- Introduction of the eight-hour day in France, the Netherlands and Spain.

- Jack Dempsey (USA) wins the world heavyweight boxing title for the first time.

- Nobel Peace Prize is won by US president Woodrow Wilson.

CULTURE

- **17 Apr**: United Artists Corporation founded by Charlie Chaplin, Mary Pickford, Douglas Fairbanks and D.W. Griffith (USA).

- **27 Apr**: National Association of the Motion Picture Industry agrees to submit films to censorship (USA).

- **10 Oct**: Richard Strauss's *Die Frau ohne Schatten* (The Woman without a Shadow), opera with libretto by Hugo von Hofmannsthal, is premiéred in Vienna (Aut).

- Louis Aragon and André Breton found the review *Littérature* (Fr).

- André Gide: *La Symphonie pastorale*, novel (Fr).

- Somerset Maugham: *The Moon and Sixpence*, novel (UK).

- G.B.Shaw: *Heartbreak House*, play (UK).

- Franz Kafka: *Ein Landarzt* (In the Penal Colony), novel (Cze).

- Virginia Woolf: *Night and Day*, novel (UK).

- Booth Tarkington's novel of the American Midwest, *The Magnificent Ambersons*, wins the Pulitzer Prize (USA).

- Harold Bauer, pianist, founds the Beethoven Association of New York.

- Béla Bartók: *The Miraculous Mandarin*, ballet (Hung).

- Edward Elgar: *Cello Concerto* (UK).

- Manuel de Falla: *The Three-Cornered Hat*, ballet for Diaghilev with choreography by Leonid Massine, designed by Pablo Picasso (Fr).

- The popularity of jazz spreads from the USA to Europe.

- Foundation of the Bauhaus in Weimar, directed by Walter Gropius, intended to bring together architecture, painting, design and other arts in a new relationship which would take advantage of new materials and techniques of the modern industrial age; teachers include Johannes Itten, Oskar Schlemmer, Paul Klee, Georg Muche, Theo van Doesburg, Lászlo Moholy-Nagy and Wassily Kandinsky (Ger).

- Lyonel Feininger: *Socialist Cathedral*, woodcut, cover of the first Bauhaus manifesto (Ger).

- Stanley Spencer: *Swan Upping at Cookham*, painting (UK).

- Max Bechmann's first exhibition, in Frankfurt (Ger).

- Vladimir Tatlin: Model of the *Monument to the Third International* (Russ).

- *The Cabinet of Dr Caligari*, film by Robert Wiene, takes Expressionism into the cinema (Ger).

- Abel Gance: *J'accuse*, an antiwar film using documentary sequences from World War I (Fr).

- Nobel Prize for Literature is won by Carl Spitteler (Swi).

SCIENCE

- **14–15 Jun**: J.W. Alcock and A. Whitten Brown make the first nonstop flight across the Atlantic Ocean from Newfoundland to Ireland in 16 hrs 27 mins.

- A. Eddington describes the bending of light by the Sun, after observations of a total eclipse on 29 May, as predicted by Einstein's general relativity theory (UK).

- J. Bjerknes discovers that cyclones originate as waves in the sloping frontal surfaces separating different air masses (Nor).

- F.W. Aston builds a mass-spectrograph and confirms the phenomena of isotopy (UK).

- Publication of T.H. Morgan's *The Physical Basis of Heredity* (USA).

- Ernest Rutherford first achieves artificial transmutation of an element, by bombarding nitrogen atoms with alpha particles, resulting in the disintegration of the nitrogen and the creation of hydrogen nuclei and an isotope of oxygen (UK).

- Edwin Hubble discovers cepheid variable stars in the Andromeda Nebula, which allows him to determine the distances between galaxies (US).

- First experiments with short wave radio takes place.

- The superheterodyne radio, developed by E.H. Armstrong, the first radio allowing uniform reception of a wide range of stations, goes into mass production (USA).

- Europe's first mass-produced car, the Citroen Type A, is launched (Fr).

- AT & T introduce the first dial telephones (USA).

- Eccles and Jordan (US) invent the flip-flop electronic switching circuit, which becomes a vital feature of future digital computers.

- The Italian Isotta-Fraschini Tipo 8 introduces the straight-eight engine to production cars. The engine soon becomes fashionable for higher-priced cars.

- Development of a new technique for probing rock structures beneath the Earth's surface using shock waves created by artificial explosions, which are then reflected back to a device at the surface.

- Georgiana Burke brackets organisms which cause botulism into two strains, each of which require a separate antitoxin.

- Nobel Prize for Physics is won by Johannes Stark (Ger) "for his discovery of the Doppler effect in canal rays and the splitting of spectral lines in electric fields".

- Nobel Prize for Physiology or Medicine is won by Jules Bordet (Bel) "for his discoveries relating to immunity".

1920-1929

In Europe especially, the advent of the 1920s was hailed as a new start, a period of rebuilding in which the newly formed League of Nations would prevent a recurrence of the horrors of war. For women in particular, the 1920s appeared to herald a new freedom. Their position in Western society had been changing since the 1880s, but change had been greatly accelerated by their contribution during World War I and by the struggle for enfranchisement. This was finally beginning to be won: in 1920 American women got the vote. The "new woman" was no longer only to be seen as a political protester or a munitions worker; like many of her male contemporaries, she threw herself into the business of unfettered enjoyment. With the onset of the Jazz Age, the pursuit of pleasure became all the rage; cabarets, nightclubs and dancing were the order of the day – an aspect of the 1920s immortalized in the novels of F. Scott Fitzgerald.

▲ New freedoms called for new fashions: French tennis star Suzanne Lenglen took Wimbledon by storm in daring short skirts, winning all three tennis titles.

● **10 Jan**: Official founding of the League of Nations, which meets for the first time on 15 Nov. The original members are those 32 Allied and Associative Powers that signed the peace treaties. 13 neutral states are also invited to join, and further nations join successively over the following 15 years.

● **23 Jan**: The Dutch government refuses to hand over former German emperor Wilhelm II (self-exiled in Holland since 1918), but agrees to intern him.

● **10 Feb, 14 Mar**: Plebiscites in Schleswig divide the province between Denmark and Germany.

● **29 Feb**: The new Czechoslovak constitution is modeled on that of France. The first elections follow on 18 Apr. (›27 May)

● **1 Mar**: Admiral Nikolaus Horthy is made regent and head of state of Hungary, and on 23 Mar proclaims the country a monarchy, with a vacant throne.

● **11 Mar**: Emir Faisal is proclaimed king of Syria, although both France and Britain refuse to recognize him. On 25 Jul the French capture Damascus, dethroning Emir Faisal, who flees the country.

● **13–17 Mar**: Kapp Putsch: an insurrection in Berlin, led by Dr Wolfgang Kapp. The government escapes to Stuttgart, but the movement collapses after a general strike.

● **16 Mar**: An allied force under Gen. Sir George Milne (UK) occupies Constantinople to maintain the straits and protect Armenia after a period of Turkish Nationalist agitation. The Nationalists are denounced and many exiled, and parliament is dissolved on 11 Apr (Tur). (›23 Apr)

● **19 Mar–3 Apr**: Spartakist uprising in the Ruhr is firmly suppressed by government troops, provoking French troops to occupy Frankfurt and some Ruhr towns in response (Ger).

● **9 Apr**: Beginning of a coup d'état in Mexico led by Adolfo de la Huerta, Alvaro Obregón and Plutarco Elias Calles. They capture Mexico City on 8 May, and president Venustiano Carranza is killed on 21 May. Obregón is elected president on 5 Sep.

● **23 Apr**: A provisional government is set up in Ankara by the Nationalists under Mustafa Kemal, which concludes a military agreement with Soviet Russia to secure necessary supplies (Tur).

● **25 Apr–12 Oct**: Russo-Polish War: the Poles attempt to capture the Ukraine from the Bolsheviks, taking Kiev on 7 May; a counterattack drives them back to the outskirts of Warsaw, where, aided by the French, the Poles defeat the Bolsheviks and in turn drive them back. The Treaty of Riga (18 Mar 1921) defines the Russo-Polish frontier, which remains until 1940.

● **25 Apr**: Syrian mandate is granted to France; Palestine and Transjordania become British mandates.

● **Apr**: The German Workers' party is renamed the National Socialist German Workers' party and plans to campaign against the Treaty of Versailles and against Jewish influence in Germany.

● **18 May**: Bolsheviks occupy Enzeli and Resht (Per) and set up a Soviet Republic of Gilan (until Oct 1921).

● **27 May**: Tomas Masaryk is elected first president of Czechoslovakia, with Eduard Beneš as foreign minister.

● **4 Jun**: Treaty of Trianon affirms the loss of former Hungarian territory to Czechoslovakia, Romania and Yugoslavia, and provides for Hungarian reparations and military reductions.

● **19–22 Jun**: Conferences of Hythe and Boulogne discuss the Near East and the reparations problem.

● **22 Jun**: Greeks begin their advance into Turkey, defeating the Turks at Alasheh, capturing Bursa (9 Jul) and Adrianople (25 Jul).

● **23 Jul**: British East Africa is renamed Kenya and becomes a crown colony.

● **Jul**: A special force of military police, known from their uniforms as "Black and Tans", are sent to Ireland to suppress the Sinn Fein uprising, beginning a period of bitter conflict that continues until 23 Dec, when the Government of Ireland Act is passed, providing for a parliament for each of southern and northern Ireland (UK).

● **10 Aug**: Treaty of Sèvres between Turkey and the wartime Allies: Greece gains Smyrna, eastern Thrace, Imbros, Tenedos and the Dodecanese (except Rhodes). The treaty is not recognized by the Turkish Nationalist government.

● **11 Aug**: By the Treaty of Riga, Soviet Russia recognizes Latvian sovereignty and relinquishes territorial rights.

● **14 Aug**: Treaty between Czechoslovakia and Yugoslavia forms the basis for the Little Entente, joined by Romania on 7 Jun 1921.

● **2 Sep**: Italians leave Albania after occupying most of the southern part of the country during World War I.

● **1 Oct**: New constitution for Austria on the Swiss federal model, with eight provinces.

● **28 Oct**: Romanian possession of Bessarabia is recognized by Britain, France, Italy and Japan.

● **9 Nov**: Danzig is proclaimed a free city under the mandate of the League of Nations (Ger).

● **3 Dec**: Turco-Armenian peace treaty ends mutual hostilities.

● **17 Dec**: Japan receives the former German islands of the Pacific – the Caroline, Marshall and Marianas archipelagoes – as mandates from the League of Nations.

● Beginning of a period of civil war in China between local leaders unable to find common cause after the death of former president Yuan Shikai (until 1926).

SOCIETY

- **5 Jan**: Boston Red Sox baseballer Babe Ruth is bought by the New York Yankees for a record $125,000.

- **Feb**: Food rationing begins in Italy. In Jun, riots follow government increases in the price of bread.

- **Feb**: Legislation on the establishment of works councils is enforced (Ger).

- **Feb**: Thousands are feared dead in a typhus epidemic in Poland.

- **1 Mar**: The US government returns the railroads, commandeered in the war, to their 230 owners.

- **Mar**: Beginning of a general strike, especially strong in the Ruhr (Ger).

- **21 Apr**: 140 are killed and hundreds injured in a tornado which sweeps across the southern states of the USA.

- **1 May**: A customs union is set up between Belgium and Luxembourg.

- **30 May**: Pope Benedict XV canonizes Joan of Arc.

- **5 Jun**: Merchant Marine Acts are passed, providing for the sale of wartime merchant vessels to private parties and the opening of new shipping routes (USA).

- **13 Jun**: Opening of the first International Feminist Conference, in Geneva.

- **5–16 Jul**: Spa Conference, at which Germany submits a reparations scheme to the Allies. Reparations are apportioned thus: France, 52 percent; British Empire, 22 percent; Italy, 10 percent; Belgium, 8 percent; the remainder goes to the smaller powers.

- **28 Jul**: A Native Affairs Commission is set up in South Africa to address the question of native reservations, which are considered inadequate.

- **Jul**: Suzanne Lenglen (Fr) becomes the first player to win all three Wimbledon tennis titles.

- **1 Aug**: Mohandas Gandhi begins a tour of India to enlist support for a noncooperation movement, boycotting foreign goods, courts, schools, official functions, legislature and overseas military service. The Indian Congress approves the program (4–9 Sep), and converts itself into an organization working for self-rule (*swaraj*).

- **28 Aug**: Women are enfranchised in the USA by the Nineteenth Amendment.

- **Aug**: Opening of the Antwerp Olympic Games, the first since the war (Bel).

- **6 Sep**: Transcontinental airmail service is established between San Francisco and New York (USA).

- **9 Sep**: Earthquakes in Italy kill some 500 and leave 20,000 homeless.

- **Sep**: International monetary conference in Brussels, during which stabilization of currencies and a return to the gold standard are discussed (Bel).

- **4 Nov**: Reports are received that the severe famine in China is leading some people to sell their children to buy food.

- **5 Dec**: Scotland votes against prohibition (UK).

- **15–22 Dec**: Brussels Conference: It is proposed that Germany pay 13,450 million gold marks in reparations over 42 years (Bel).

- The Australian high court grants the Commonwealth Conciliation and Arbitration Court authority to regulate labor conditions of state employees.

- Stock market collapse in London and New York.

- First ribknit elasticized onepiece bathing suit is made by the Jantzen Company (USA).

- German railways are nationalized.

- Unemployment insurance is introduced in Austria and extended more widely in Britain.

- Soviet Russia becomes the first country to legalize abortion.

- Development of "scientific management" to improve managerial techniques, after principles first laid down by Frederick W. Taylor (USA) in the 1880s.

- The Volstead Act (passed in 1919) becomes operative in the USA, enforcing Prohibition: the sale of intoxicating liquor becomes illegal (until 1933).

- Nicola Sacco and Bartolomeo Vanzetti, Italian-born anarchists, go on trial for murder in the USA. The trial become a *cause célèbre* among US liberals, who believe them to be victims of antibolshevist propaganda; but the men are sentenced to death in Jul 1921.

- President Obregón of Mexico appoints José Vasconcelas as minister of education; he enlists Mexico's artists – among them Diego Rivera, José Clemente Orozco and David Alfaro Siqueiros – to present the country's history as murals on public buildings.

- Nobel Peace Prize is won by Léon Bourgeois (Fr).

CULTURE

- **21 Feb**: Premiere in Paris of Darius Milhand and Jean Cocteau's "cabaret" ballet *Le Boeuf sur le toit* (The Ox on the Roof).

- **Feb**: *Futurist Aerial Theatre*, a manifesto text scattered from the sky by author/aviator Fedele Azari during an "aerial ballet" by Mario Scaparro titled *A Birth* (It).

- Paul Valéry: *Album des vers anciens*, poems (Fr).

- T.S. Eliot: *The Sacred Wood*, essays in literary criticism (UK).

- F. Scott Fitzgerald: *This Side of Paradise*, novel (USA).

- Wilfred Owen: *Poems*, published posthumously after his death in France just one week before the Armistice (UK).

- Katherine Mansfield: *Bliss and Other Stories* (UK).

- W.B. Yeats: *The Wild Swans at Coole*, poems (UK).

- Dmitri Temkin and Yuri Annenkov: *The Storming of the Winter Palace in Petrograd*, a restaging of this event during the Bolshevik Revolution (Russ).

- Igor Stravinsky: *Pulcinella*, ballet, a reworking of pieces originally attributed to Pergolesi (Fr).

- The group of composers known as *Les Six* – Louis Durey, Germaine Tailleferre, Darius Milhaud, Arthur Honegger, Francis Poulenc and Georges Auric – are temporarily united by their adherence to the antiromanticism set out in Jean Cocteau's 1918 manifesto *Le Coq et l'arlequin* (Fr).

- "Whispering/The Japanese Sandman", by Paul Whiteman, becomes the first record to sell one million copies, introducing jazz to a much wider audience in North America and Europe (USA).

- Piet Mondrian: *Composition I with Red, Black, Blue, Yellow and Grey*, painting (Fr).

- Charles Demuth: *Machinery*, painting (USA).

- Charles Sheeler: *American Landscape* (USA).

- The first Dada Fair, at the Burchard Gallery in Berlin (Ger), includes George Grosz's savage caricatures of greed and militarism; and a Dada Festival at the Salle Gaveau in Paris is attended by Tristan Tzara, André Breton, Paul Eluard and Louis Aragon.

- Kurt Schwitters begins his *Merz* series of collages made from garbage (Ger).

- Antonio Gaudí: Casa Mila, Barcelona (Sp).

- Avant-garde magazine *L'Esprit Nouveau* is founded by the architect Le Corbusier (Fr).

- Nobel Prize for Literature is won by Knut Hamsun (Nor) for his monumental work *Growth of the Soil*.

SCIENCE

- **Feb**: First public radio station is set up by Marconi (USA).

- **2 Nov**: Westinghouse Electrical Co makes the first general radio broadcast for the presidential election. The same company broadcast the first regular evening program on 31 Nov (USA).

- Nobel Prize for Chemistry is won by Walther Nermst (Ger) for his work on thermochemistry.

- Nobel Prize for Physics is won by Charles Guillaume (Switz) for his discoveries of the anomalies in nickel steel alloys.

- Nobel Prize for Physiology or Medicine is won by August Krogh (Den) "for his discovery of the capillary motor regulating mechanism".

- Building of the first all-welded ship in Birkenhead (UK).

- Handley Page Transport aircraft are fitted with radio detection finders (UK).

- J.T. Thompson invents the easily portable submachine gun (USA).

- K. Spiro and A. Stoll extract ergotamine for migraine treatment.

- Publication of A. Eddington's *Space, Time and Gravitation* (UK).

- F.W. Aston discovers that all atomic masses are integral multiples of the same number (UK).

- A.A. Michelson first measures the diameter of a distant star, Betelgeuse (USA).

- Hermann Staudinger demonstrates that small molecules polymerize to form plastics (Ger).

- M. Wolf shows the structure of the Milky Way (Ger).

- The Raschig process uses hydrogen chloride to chlorinate benzene (Ger).

- Disk autochanger for gramophones is first devised by HMV (UK).

- Commercially viable acetate fiber is made by British Celanese Ltd (UK).

- J.C. Shaw develops a sensing device for a milling machine, making it possible automatically to cut identical shapes from an original pattern.

1921

POLITICS

In terms of mass culture, the first half of the twentieth century was dominated by the cinema and in particularly by the products of Hollywood. The cinema offered escapism, first in the brittle world of the 1920s and then from the economic depression of the 1930s and the horrors of World War II. Rudolf Valentino, one of the major figures of the silent screen, let loose a whole series of undercurrents within the psyche of Western society with his film "The Sheik," which were thereafter played upon and commercially exploited. Interest in the "mysteries" of the desert had been heightened by the wartime exploits of T. E. Lawrence; but attempts to penetrate the almost closed Arabian world had been made from the mid-nineteenth century. During the 1920s film exploited this longing for romance and produced the mass adulation of the "star" — plus, of course, financial success at the box office. Yet many of Hollywood's silent stars proved ephemeral, as they were unable to make a successful transition to the "talkies."

▲ One of the great stars of the silent screen, Rudolf Valentino — seen here in *The Sheik* with Agnes Ayres — became the archetypal Latin Lover of the silent screen. His death in 1926, aged only 31, caused mass hysteria as thousands of female fans mourned him.

●**13–22 Jan**: The Italian Socialist party splits into moderates and radicals (Communists) (It).

● **19 Jan**: Pact of Union between Costa Rica, Honduras, Guatamala and El Salvador forms the Federation of Central America. An antifederalist revolution in Guatamala on 8 Dec causes it to be dissolved in 1922.

● **19 Feb**: Franco-Polish alliance gives Poland some necessary security, being surrounded by the hostile powers of Germany and Soviet Russia.

● **21 Feb**: Coup d'etat by Reza Khan in Persia establishes a new government. Reza Khan assumes the ministerial portfolio for war and becomes commander-in-chief of the armed forces.

● **23 Feb**: Mutiny of the navy at Kronstadt (on the Russian Baltic seaboard) is quelled with considerable bloodshed. The mutiny is the result of discontent due to the economic crisis in Russia and food shortages. (›Society, 17 Mar)

● **26 Feb**: Treaty between Persia and Soviet Russia secures the evacuation from Persia of the Bolsheviks, the cancellation of all debts owed by Persia to the former czarist regime and the surrender to Persia of all Russian property in the country.

● **27 Feb**: Fascist and Communist riots in Florence mark the beginning of a period of civil war between the two groups (It).

● **Feb**: At the London Conference the Allies attempt to reach an agreement between the Constantinople and Ankara governments in Turkey.

● **3 Mar**: Signature of an offensive and defensive treaty between Poland and Romania, against Russia.

● **8 Mar**: French troops occupy Dusseldorf, Duisburg and Ruhrort after an ultimatum to Germany regarding reparations is evaded. Germany is declared in default by the Reparations Commission on 24 Mar.

● **9 Mar**: By the Franklin-Bouillon agreement with Mustafa Kemal (Nationalist leader of the Ankara government), France agrees to evacuate Cilicia (Tur) in return for economic concessions. A similar agreement is signed between Kemal and Italy, providing for the latter's evacuation of Anatolia on 13 Mar.

● **16 Mar**: Kemal signs a treaty with Soviet Russia, returning Batum to the latter, in return for Russian recognition of the Turkish possession of Kars and Ardahan (Tur).

● **17 Mar**: Adoption of the Polish constitution, modeled closely on that of France.

● **23 Mar**: New Greek offensive in Turkey. In Aug-Sep the Greeks push towards Ankara, but are repulsed.

● **27 Mar**: King Karoly returns to Hungary to make a bid for the throne, but the opposition of neighboring states obliges him to return to Switzerland. (›21 Oct)

● **Mar–Aug**: World tour of the crown prince Hirohito: the first time a member of the Japanese imperial family has been abroad.

● **24 Apr, 29 May**: Plebiscites in the Tyrol and Salzburg give a majority vote for union with Germany.

● **13 May**: In elections in southern Ireland, Sinn Fein win 124 of the 128 seats. Parliament opens on 28 Jun, though with the complete abstention of the Sinn Fein delegates, who declare themselves the Dáil Eireann, rejecting the British settlement. (› 7 Jun)

● **28 May**: France resumes diplomatic relations with the Vatican (broken in 1904 after the separation of church and state in France).

● **7 Jun**: The new assembly for northern Ireland opens; Ulster Unionists have won 40 out of 52 seats. (›6 Dec)

● **21 Jul**: 20,000 Spaniards under Fernandez Silvestre are defeated in Morocco by the Riffians under Abd-el-Krim, with around 21,000 fatalities.

● **23 Aug**: Emir Faisal is proclaimed king of Iraq, after a plebiscite turns out 96 percent in his favor (until 1933).

● **12 Oct**: Partition of Upper Silesia between Poland and Germany, after a plebiscite on 20 Mar in favor of Germany.

● **21 Oct**: King Karoly marches on Budapest with an impromptu army, but, after the mobilization of Czechoslovakia and Yugoslavia, the Hungarian government is forced to turn him back and capture him, exiling him to Madeira. His rights to the throne are abrogated by the Hungarian parliament on 4 Nov.

● **12 Nov–6 Feb 1922**: Washington Conference (USA, UK, Fr, It, Bel, Neth, China, Jap, Port) meets to discuss naval armaments and Far Eastern questions. It has the following results: four-power (USA, UK, Fr, Jap) Pacific Treaty (13 Dec) regarding rights in the Pacific; Shandong Treaty (4 Feb) provides for the return by Japan to China of Kiaochow; two nine-power treaties (6 Feb) guarantee the integrity and independence of China and the "open door" policy; and the Naval Armaments Treaty (6 Feb) prohibits the building of large ships for ten years, by Britain, USA, Japan, France and Italy.

● **6 Dec**: Southern Ireland is granted dominion status within the British Commonwealth as the Irish Free State, a settlement denounced by Irish national leader Eamon De Valera but accepted by the Dáil Eireann on 7 Jan 1922.

● **24 Dec**: The Indian National Congress grants Mohandas Gandhi sole executive control.

● **Dec**: After a dispute between Austria and Hungary over Burgenland, a strip of territory assigned to Austria though occupied by Hungary, a plebiscite is held in favor of Austria, which receives most of the area.

SOCIETY

● **13 Jan**: General Confederation of Labor (CGT), the heart of the syndicalist movement (a movement advocating the abolition of the capitalist order and the establishment of a social order based on workers organized in production units), dissolved by court order (Fr).

● **18 Feb**: Aviator Etienne Oehmichen makes the first flight, as opposed to lift off, in a helicopter (Fr).

● **21 Feb–14 Mar**: The London Conference addresses the question of German reparations, for which schedules of payment are worked out (UK).(> 24 Mar)

● **Feb**: Unemployment in Britain exceeds the 1 million mark.

● **3 Mar**: 862 die when the steamer *Hong Moh* is shipwrecked in the South China Sea.

● **3 Mar**: Emergency Unemployment Act increases unemployment payments to 20s a week for men and 18s for women (UK).

● **17 Mar**: The collapse of the Russian economy as a result of the Allied blockade, civil war and the economic policies of the Bolshevik government leads Lenin to introduce the New Economic Policy (NEP). It is characterized by relative economic freedom after a period of enforced nationalization. Small-scale private industry and agriculture are encouraged, but this leads to criticism from within the party, which fears the growth of a wealthy peasant class (the kulaks) opposed to socialism.(> Aug)

● **24 Mar**: Reparation Recovery Act imposes 50 percent duties on German goods, reduced to 26 percent on 20 May.(> 27 Apr)

● **31 Mar–1 Jul**: Coal strike due to the rejection of nationalization proposals, but the miners accept a wage increase (UK).

● **Mar**: Trade relations are established between the UK and Soviet Russia.

● **20 Apr**: Colombian treaty grants $25 million and free access to the Panama Canal for Colombia in return for US possession of the canal.

● **27 Apr**: The Reparations Commission decides that Germany must pay 132,000 million gold marks.

● **29 Apr–5 May**: An ultimatum is sent to Germany demanding a payment of one billion gold marks by the end of the month on pain of occupation of the Ruhr. The money is raised by Germany by borrowing in London.

● **1–6 May**: Anti-Jewish riots by Arabs in Palestine, in protest at the increased influx of Jewish immigrants.

● **8 May**: Capital punishment is abolished in Sweden.

● **19 May**: Immigration Act restricts immigration by the percentage of the appropriate nationality already resident in the USA according to the 1910 census.

● **27 May**: Emergency Tariff Act raises duties on agricultural products, sugar and wool (USA).

● **May**: Trade relations are established between Germany and Soviet Russia.

● **21 Aug**: The Belgian government votes a credit of 300 million francs to develop the Belgian Congo by expanding its infrastructure.

● **Aug**: Great famine in Russia, with up to 18 million starving due to drought and the economic collapse during the war years.

● **19 Sep**: Completion of the first autobahn in Germany, the AVUS.

● **21 Sep**: An explosion at the BASF chemical works near Ludwigshafen kills 574 and injures over 1,000 (Ger).

● **Oct**: Establishment of Gosbank, the state bank (Russ).

● **23 Nov**: President Harding bans doctors from prescribing beer, closing a prohibition loophole (USA).

● **15 Dec**: Adoption of a higher tariff in Australia to protect the new industries that had been created during World War I.

● Gandhi's civil disobedience campaign in India reaches a new height this year. In spite of the movement being nonviolent, outbreaks of terrorist violence erupt frequently throughout the country, including clashes between Hindus and Muslims.

● Beginning of a wave of mergers among the smaller commercial banks (USA).

● Destruction by the boll weevil halves cotton production in Georgia and South Carolina (USA).

● Establishment of the Caisse Centrale des Banques Populaires (Fr).

● Venezuela begins to make its mark as an important oil-exporting country.

● Establishment of the Coal Council for organizing the distribution and supply of coal (Ger).

● First radio broadcast of a baseball game is made by Graham McNamce from the Polo Grounds in New York (USA).

● The game of table tennis is revived. When the name "table tennis" is formally adopted, the old "Ping Pong Association" founded in 1902 is revived.

● Opening of the first public record-lending library, in Detroit (USA).

● Charles Jourdan (Fr) sets up a shoe workshop.

● Coco Chanel (Fr) introduces her classic perfume, Chanel No 5.

● Nobel Peace Prize is won by Karl Branting (Swe) and Christian Lange (Nor).

CULTURE

● **13 May**: Dadaists enact the mock *Trial and Sentencing of M. Maurice Barrs by Dada* at the Salle des Sociétés Savantes in Paris (Fr).

● Anna Akhmatova: *Plantain*, poems (Russ)

● Karl Kraus: *The Last Days of Mankind*, play (Aut).

● Aldous Huxley: *Crome Yellow*, novel (UK).

● D.H. Lawrence: *Women in Love*, novel (UK).

● Eugene O'Neill: *Anna Christie*, play (USA).

● Luigi Pirandello: *Six Characters in Search of an Author*, play (It).

● Karel Čapek: *The Insect Play*, a satire on society and totalitarianism written in collaboration with his brother Josef, a painter and stage designer.

● Ludwig Wittgenstein: *Tractatus Logico-Philosophicus*, philosophy text (Aut).

● Foundation of the Donaueschingen Festival, devoted to contemporary music (until 1930) (Ger).

● Edgard Varèse: *Amériques*, for orchestra, which celebrates the composer's newly adopted country – he had emigrated from France to the USA in 1915.

● George Antheil: *Airplane Sonata* for piano – an example of the "machine age" art professed by the Italian Futurists.

● The redesigned Teatro alla Scala Milan opens under the directorship of Arturo Toscanini (It).

● Leoš Janáček: *Kátya Kabanová*, opera (Czech).

● Sergey Prokofiev: *The Love for Three Oranges*, opera (Fr).

● Paul Hindemith: *Morder, Hoffnung der Frauen*, opera, after Oskar Kokoschka's play of 1909 (Ger).

● Arthur Honegger: *Le Roi David*, oratorio (Fr).

● Man Ray produces his "rayographs" by laying opaque and translucent objects on photographic paper (Fr).

● Fernand Léger: *Le Grand Dejeuner* (Three Women), painting (Fr).

● Stuart Davis: *Lucky Strike* (USA).

● Wassily Kandinsky founds the Academy of Arts and Sciences of All the Russias in Moscow (USSR).

● George Grosz: *The Face of the Ruling Class*, engravings (Ger).

● M. Trucco: Fiat Works, Turin (It).

● Walter Gropius: Sommerfeld House, Berlin (Ger).

● First full-length feature talkie, *Dream Street* (D.W. Griffith) is produced by United Artists (USA).

● *The Sheik*, film with Rudolph Valentino (USA).

● Nobel Prize for Literature is won by Anatole France (Fr).

SCIENCE

● Nobel Prize for Chemistry is won by Frederick Soddy (UK) for his work on radioactive substances and isotopes.

● Nobel Prize for Physics is won by Albert Einstein (USA) "for his services to theoretical physics, and especially for his discovery of the law of the photoelectric effect".

● Hans Spemann postulates the existence of a chemical molecule that causes formative interaction between adjacent regions in an embryo, triggering them to develop, thus demonstrating that cells affect other cells near them (Ger).

● Thomas Midgeley develops tetraethyl lead, an additive to gasoline to prevent engine "knocking" (Ger).

● Edgar Dacque initiates phylogenetically oriented paleontology, the study of fossils with a view to finding out how different species evolved (USA).

● E.M. East and G.M. Shull perfect a hybrid corn (maize) strain that will greatly improve crop yields (USA).

● W.G. Cady discovers the stabilizing quality of the quartz crystal in radio signal reception, leading to the popularity of the crystal "cat's whisker" radio (USA).

● First medium-wave wireless broadcast (USA).

● Publication of Carl Jung's *Psychological Types* (Swi).

● J.N. Bronsted (Den) and G. von Hevesy (Swe) successfully separate isotopes.

● E. Rutherford and J. Chadwick disintegrate most of the elements (UK).

● Ear specialists use a microscope for the first time in ear operations.

● T.H. Morgan proposes that chromosomes are the carriers of hereditary information in a living cell (USA).

● O. Loewi proposes a chemical mechanism for the transmission of nerve impulses (USA).

● A. Calmette and C. Guérin refine and bring into use the BCG tuberculosis vaccine (Fr).

● F.G.Banting, C. Best, J. McLeod and J. Collip extract insulin from the human pancreas and begin a series of experiments on dogs to develop a treatment for diabetes (Can).

● H. Rorshach introduces his "inkblot" test for the study of personality in *Psychodiagnostics* (Swi).

Popular interest in Ancient Egypt had begun with Napoleon's Egyptian campaign at the turn of the 18th century, which led to the beginning of the major museum collection at the Louvre in Paris. The discovery of the tomb of the Egyptian pharaoh Tutankhamun by British archeologists Howard Carter and Lord Carnarvon in the Valley of the Kings at Luxor caught the imagination of the public in a similar way. The excavation revealed an almost complete collection of the funerary treasures of a pharaoh. When these were put on public display in the mid-1920s they made a major impression on Western sensibilities, influencing art and architecture as well as popular fashion. The event also reinforced popular misconceptions about the mysteries of past civilizations. In the cinema, a series of "mummy" films appeared. Tutankhamun's grave goods formed the first major world touring exhibition of its kind to be mounted in the 1970s, paving the way for subsequent similar global archeological expositions.

▲ The gorgeous gold and jewelled death mask of the young Egyptian pharaoh Tutankhamun.

● **8 Jan**: Plebiscite in Vilna shows a majority in favor of Poland, and the city and province are incorporated on 18 Apr, resulting in bitterness in relations between Poland and Lithuania.

● **9 Jan**: Due to his opposition to dominion status for Ireland, which was accepted by the Dáil Eireann, Eamon De Valera resigns and organizes a new Republican Society (15 Mar), engaging in terrorist warfare against the Dáil Eireann government (UK). (›25 Oct)

● **4 Feb**: An attack on the police station in Chauri Chaura by peasants and Indian nationalists causes the death of 22 policemen. Gandhi suspends the civil disobedience and noncooperation programs, but is arrested on 10 Mar and sentenced to six years' imprisonment (Ind).

● **12 Feb**: Succession of Pope Pius XI after the death of Benedict XV on 22 Jan.

● **28 Feb**: End of the British protectorate over Egypt. Egypt declares its independence, and Fuad I assumes the title of king on 15 Mar.

● **3 Mar**: Fascists under the leadership of Benito Mussolini overthrow the Fiume government, and the town is occupied by Fascist troops on 17 Mar. In May they drive the city government out of Bologna, and on 3–4 Aug seize Milan. (› 24 Oct)

● **13–17 Mar**: Conference between Poland and the Baltic States (Lat, Lith, Est) in Warsaw provides for a mutual defensive treaty in the event of attack by another power.

● **24 Mar**: Long-standing boundary dispute between Colombia and Venezuela is settled in favor of the former by a Swiss federal council.

● **25 Mar**: Military agreement between Iraq and Britain gives Britain a large degree of military control.

● **16 Apr**: Treaty of Rapallo between Soviet Russia and Germany establishes close economic and political ties between the two states. It is supplemented by further commercial (12 Oct 1925) and friendship/neutrality (Treaty of Berlin, 24 Apr 1926) treaties, which theoretically remain in effect until Hitler's invasion of the Soviet Union in 1941.

● **Apr**: Japan establishes civil government in the islands mandated by the League of Nations, and a large influx of Japanese immigrants follows.

● **1 May**: Latvian constitution of 1 May 1920 comes into effect, and elections on 8 Oct bring a victory for the Social Democrats.

● **22 May**: Italian general Pietro Badoglio begins an offensive against Libya, finally conquering the whole country in 1930.

● **18 Jun**: Insurrection of the Iraqi Kurds under Sheikh Mahmud, demanding autonomy or full independence, not suppressed until Jul 1924.

● **24 Jun**: Walther Rathenau, cabinet minister and Jewish industrialist, is assassinated by nationalists (Ger).

● **29 Jul**: Allies forbid the Greeks to occupy Constantinople. A Turkish counteroffensive against the Greeks beginning on 18 Aug is successful and is soon driving the Greek army before it. The Turks recapture the burning city of Smyrna on 9–11 Sep.

● **1 Aug**: Lithuania adopts a democratic republican constitution.

● **6–24 Sep**: Changchun conference with Russia fails, and Japan continues its occupation of the northern part of Sakhalin, an island between Russia and Japan that has been contested between them for many years.

● **16 Sep**: A British force under Gen. Sir Charles Harington arrives at Chanakkale in Turkey to defend the straits against the Turks. A conference on 3–11 Oct provides for the return of Eastern Thrace and Adrianople to the Turks, and the neutralization and internationalization of the straits.

● **22 Oct**: British prime minister David Lloyd George resigns, and is replaced by Andrew Bonar Law. He calls an election in November, at which the Conservative party wins a resounding victory.

● **24 Oct**: Fascist congress in Naples: Mussolini demands the formation of a Fascist government, but is refused by the Luigi Facta government of liberals and democrats. On 28 Oct Mussolini makes his March on Rome, provoking Facta to demand martial law, which the king refuses. Facta resigns, and the Fascists occupy Rome. (› 31 Oct)

● **25 Oct**: Adoption of a constitution by the Dáil Eireann, going into effect on 6 Dec, when the Irish Free State is officially proclaimed.

● **27 Oct**: Referendum in Southern Rhodesia votes against joining the Union of South Africa in spite of the tempting terms offered by South African prime minister Jan Smuts.

● **31 Oct**: King Victor Emmanuel III requests that Mussolini form a cabinet of Fascists and Nationalists, which he does on 31 Oct. On 25 Nov he is granted dictatorial powers (until 31 Dec 1923), and begins to seed the government apparatus with Fascist sympathizers (It).

● **1 Nov**: Mustafa Kemal abolishes the sultanate in Turkey, and Mohammad VI flees Constantinople. Abdul Mejid is proclaimed caliph on 18 Nov.

● **20 Nov**: Lausanne Conference concludes peace between Turkey and the Allies, leading to the Treaty of Lausanne. (› 24 Jul 1923)

● **30 Dec**: Proclamation of the Union of Soviet Socialist Republics (USSR), tying Russia, White Russia, the Ukraine and Transcaucasia together in a federal system, with its political control center in Moscow.

SOCIETY

- **1 Jan:** Flemish is placed on a par with French as official languages of Belgium.

- **1 Jan:** An estimated 33 million are now in danger of starvation in Russia.

- **4–13 Jan:** Conference of Cannes postpones German reparations payments. (› 31 May)

- **11 Feb:** Yap Treaty secures US foothold as regards the use of cable and wireless facilities in Yap (an island in the W. Pacific) and other Japanese mandates.

- **15 Feb:** Permanent Court of International Justice opens in The Hague (Neth).

- **Feb:** Strike of German railmen.

- **25 Mar:** Pope Pius XI urges a crusade against immodest women's fashions.

- **1 Apr–4 Sep:** Coalminers' strike over reduced wages and the system of deducting union fees from wages (USA).

- **10 Apr–19 May:** Genoa Conference, convened to discuss the economic problems of the world, breaks down after France insists that Russia recognizes the debts still outstanding from the its czarist period.

- **24 May:** A commercial treaty is signed between Italy and Soviet Russia.

- **31 May:** Reparations Commission grants Germany a moratorium on reparations payments until the end of the year, due to the collapse of the German mark. (› Jun)

- **May:** New law on the status of autonomy for the Reichsbank (Ger).

- **Jun:** International high finance comes out against a loan for commercializing the German reparations. (›7–14 Aug)

- **1 Jul:** Railway from Beira to the south bank of the Zambezi is opened, connecting Nyasaland with a port.

- **1 Jul–13 Sep:** Railroad shopmen's strike protesting at wage reductions (USA).

- **9 Jul:** Johnny Weissmuller, Austrian-born American immigrant, becomes the first man to swim 100m in less than one minute (USA).

- **7–14 Aug:** London Conference regarding conditions for a moratorium on German reparations: France's conditions for a moratorium – the seizure of some German goods – are rejected by Britain, and the policy of the two countries on this issue begins to diverge sharply. (› 9–11 Dec)

- **Aug:** Start of the hyper inflationary spiral of the German mark due to the reparations schedule. (›2–7 Nov)

- **Aug:** Unofficial women's Olympic Games are held in Paris (Fr).

- **10 Sep:** A commercial treaty is signed between Britain and Soviet Russia.

- **4 Oct:** The League of Nations guarantees an international loan to aid Austrian reconstruction, and establishes a commissioner to supervise finance (until 1926).

- **14 Oct:** Agrarian law in Finland distributes land among the peasantry.

- **Oct:** Foundation of the British Broadcasting Company Ltd (license granted 18 Jan 1923) (UK).

- **2–7 Nov:** A conference of experts on German currency crisis takes place in Berlin.

- **11 Nov:** 1,000 die in an earthquake in Chile.

- **Nov:** Archeologists Howard Carter and Lord Carnarvon find the tomb of Egyptian pharaoh Tutankhamun in the Valley of the Kings at Luxor, the richest collection of Egyptian treasures ever found.

- **9–11 Dec:** Second London Conference on German reparations: Britain offers to cancel Allied debts owed to itself, but France sticks to its earlier conditions, since the amount owed to France by Germany is greater than that owed to Britain by France.

- **26 Dec:** Reparations Commission declares "deliberate default" of Germany on payments, due to a delay in promised timber deliveries.

- **Empire Settlement Act:** Britain pledges to promote emigration to Australia and aid with emigrants' settlement on the land.

- **Mission of Dr Arthur C. Millspaugh (USA) to Russia to organize the country's finances (until 1927).

- Unemployed Glasgow workers undertake a hunger march to London (UK).

- Industrialists Hugo Stinnes (Ger) and de Lubersac (Fr) sign an agreement on the participation of German industrialists in the regulation of reparations.

- Establishment of the Open Market Committee in the USA.

- The UK imposes an import tax on all German products.

- The American cocktail becomes popular in Europe.

- Dance marathons – lasting for several days – become a craze in the USA.

- Nobel Peace Prize is won by Fridtjof Nansen (Nor).

- Jazz, typified by bands like King Oliver's Creole Jazz Band, creates excitement not just in the Deep South but in New York, Chicago and other northern cities (USA).

CULTURE

- T.S. Eliot's poem *The Waste Land* appears to critical acclaim (UK).

- James Joyce's novel *Ulysses* is published by Sylvia Beach in Paris; the book is banned from sale in the USA and Britain on grounds of immorality, and 500 copies are seized and burned by the US postal authorities upon arrival in the USA.

- Rainer Maria Rilke: *Duino Elegies* and *Sonnets to Orpheus*, poems (Swi).

- Virginia Woolf: *Jacob's Room*, novel (UK).

- E.E. Cummings: *The Enormous Room*, an account of three months spent in internment in France in 1917 (USA).

- Boris Pasternak: *Sister: My Life*, poems (USSR).

- Osip Mandelstam: *Tristia*, poems (USSR).

- Bertolt Brecht: *Drums in the Night and Baal*, plays (Ger).

- Sinclair Lewis, *Babbitt*, novel (USA).

- Hermann Hesse: *Siddhartha*, novel (Ger).

- Paul Valéry: *Charmes*, poems (Fr).

- Nobel Prize for Literature is won by Jacinto Benavente y Martinez (Sp).

- V. Margueritte's novel *La Garçonne* idealizes the androgynous gamine who was coming to represent the height of 1920s style (Fr).

- Founding of the PEN Club (an international association of writers in London by (Mrs) Dawson Scott.

- Oswald Spengler: *Decline of the West*, political philosophy (Ger).

- Karel Čapek: *RUR* (Rossum's Universal Robots), play using mirrors and film to create perspectival illusions – the first time film and live performance are combined.

- Wilhelm Furtwängler becomes director of the Berlin Philharmonic Orchestra (Ger).

- Alexander Zemlinsky: Lyric Symphony, setting of poems by Rabindranath Tagore (Aut).

- Carl Nielsen: Fifth Symphony (Den).

- Manifesto of the syndicate of workers, artisans, sculptors and painters is signed by David Alfaro Siqueiros, José Clemente Orozco and Diego Rivera (Mex).

- László Moholy-Nagy produces his first photograms, at the Bauhaus (Ger).

- Paul Klee: *The Twittering Machine*, painting (Ger).

- Erich Mendelsohn: Einstein Tower, Potsdam (Ger).

- Architect Le Corbusier exhibits his plans for a Contemporary City for Three Million Inhabitants (Fr).

- Constructivist version of Fernand Crommelynck's film *The Magnificent Cuckold*, directed by Vsevolod Meyerhold (USSR).

- F.W. Murnau: *Nosferatu*, an Expressionist film (Ger).

SCIENCE

- Nobel Prize for Chemistry is won by Francis W. Aston (UK), for his discovery of isotopes in a large number of non-reactive elements and for his enunciation of the whole-number rule.

- Nobel Prize for Physics is won by Niels Bohr (Den) for his work on the structure of atoms and their radiation.

- Nobel Prize for Physiology or Medicine is won by Archibald V. Hill (UK) for his work on the production of heat by muscles; and by Otto Meyerhoe (Ger-USA) "for his discovery of the fixed relationship between the consumption of oxygen and the metabolism of lactic acid in the body".

- H.T. Kalmus develops Technicolor, the first successful color process for films (USA).

- Insulin is isolated by F. Banting and C. Best (Can), and administered to diabetic patients.

- Development by R.A. Fessenden of the echo sounder for measuring submarine depths (USA).

- Jaroslav Heydrowsky introduces electrochemical analysis (polarography) (Czech).

- P.M.S. Blackett conducts experiments in transmutation of elements (UK).

- Publication of Niels Bohr's theory that electrons travel in concentric orbits around the atomic nucleus (Den).

- First use in children of the tuberculosis vaccine (Fr).

- H. Chick shows how rickets is curable by cod liver oil or sunlight, both of which are later shown to give the patient vitamin D (Aut).

- W.W. Coblentz obtains accurate measurements of the relative thermal intensities of star images (USA).

- Lee de Forest devises a way of recording sound and image on a single film (USA).

- The first US soybean processing plant opens in Illinois.

- The first underground train with automatic doors goes into service on London's Piccadilly Line.

- Completion of the largest hydroelectric power station in the world at Queenston, Ontario. It uses the cascade on the Canadian side of the Niagara Falls to drive its turbines and can generate enough electricity to supply the needs of over half a million people.

- The micropipette is demonstrated for the first time in London. It is capable of measuring minute quantities of liquid and is initially designed to deliver 0.02cc of liquid for the Schick tests for diptheria.

After World War I, the vanquished powers not only suffered the consequences of military defeat, but were also afflicted by economic instability. The economies of Austria, Germany and Hungary were all subjected to monetary madness as a result of inflation which developed into hyperinflation, destroying one of the basic measuring rods of capitalist society, as it became necessary to have basketfuls, and then barrow loads, of paper money just to complete the most basic transactions of daily life. The ultimate disastrous effects of hyperinflation became only too clear from 1921, beginning with the onset of the monetary whirlwind in Austria. This overall experience reinforced adhesion to monetary orthodoxy in other Western economies during the 1920s and was to have a lasting impact upon the subsequent conduct of German financial and monetary policy.

▲ A German housewife lights the stove for breakfast with several million marks – cheaper than buying kindling.

● **11 Jan**: French and Belgian forces occupy the Ruhr district of Germany after Germany's default on coal deliveries on 9 Jan. A Franco-Belgian commission takes over mines and railroads, and a policy of passive resistance is instigated by the German government (until 26 Sep). (> Society, Jan)

● **11 Jan**: Lithuanian-inspired uprising in Memel (under Allied control since 1918); the city is occupied by Lithuanian troops. An Allied commission grants Lithuania sovereignty of Memel on 16 Feb, and Memel is constituted as an autonomous region within the Lithuanian state, ratified by the Allies on 8 May 1924.

● **27 Jan**: The National Socialist party holds its first rally, in Munich (Ger).

● **9 Apr**: Promulgation of a new Afghan constitution, and reforms aimed at modernizing the country.

● **19 Apr**: Promulgation of the Egyptian constitution, with universal suffrage. The first elections on 27 Sep bring a great victory for the nationalist Wafd organization, and Saad Zaghul becomes premier on 28 Jan 1928.

● **26 May**: Transjordania is organized as an autonomous state (ruled since 1 Apr 1921 by Emir Abdullah ibn Hussein). The country becomes independent on 20 Feb 1928, but with military and some financial control by Britain.

● **9 Jun**: Bulgarian premier (since 6 Oct 1919) Stambolski is overthrown by a coup d'etat of officers, Macedonians and others, and shot on 14 Jun while attempting to escape. He is replaced by Alexander Zankov.

● **24 Jul**: Treaty of Lausanne: Turkey reliquishes all claims to non-Turkish territory lost during World War I, but recovers Eastern Thrace. The Bosporus straits are demilitarized and opened to all ships in peacetime, and to neutral and Turkish allied ships during wartime if Turkey is at war; if Turkey is neutral, all ships may pass through. (> 23 Aug)

● **3 Aug**: Calvin Coolidge is sworn in as US president after the sudden death of president Harding on 2 Aug.

● **23 Aug**: The Allies evacuate Constantinople, and the Turks take possession on 6 Oct. (> 14 Oct)

● **31 Aug**: Corfu Incident: Italian forces bombard and occupy Crete after an ultimatum to Greece (29 Aug) over the assassination on 27 Aug of five Italian diplomats during talks about the Greek–Albanian border. The Italian forces withdraw on 27 Sep after pressure from Britain and others.

● **1 Sep**: Southern Rhodesia becomes a British crown colony, with responsible government.

● **10 Sep**: The Irish Free State is admitted to the League of Nations.

● **12 Sep**: Mutiny at the garrison in Barcelona leads to the coup of Gen. Miguel Primo de Rivera the following day. Supported by the king, Alfonso XIII, he captures Barcelona and institutes martial law, suppressing all liberal opposition and dissolving the Cortes (parliament) (Sp). (>3 Dec 1925)

● **25 Sep**: Victory in the Indian National Congress for the Swaraj party (moderates), whose program is the achievement of home rule.

● **28 Sep**: Ethiopia joins the League of Nations, against British advice, supported by Italy and France.

● **1 Oct–8 Nov**: Imperial Conference allows dominions of the British Commonwealth the right to make treaties with foreign states (UK).

● **14 Oct**: Ankara becomes the capital of the Turkish Republic. (> 29 Oct)

● **21 Oct**: A Rhineland Republic, supported by Belgium and France, is declared at Aachen; it collapses on 31 Jan 1924 after the assassination on 9 Jan of the president of the separatist government (Ger).

● **28 Oct**: Reza Khan (minister of war and commander-in-chief since 1921) becomes premier of Persia. The shah, in the face of this near-dictatorship, exiles himself to Europe, where he dies in 1930.

● **29 Oct**: Turkish Republic proclaimed, with Mustafa Kemal as president and Ismet Pasha as prime minister. Kemal puts up many reforms: the caliphate is abolished (3 Mar 1924), polygamy outlawed (Aug 1925), religious orders suppressed (2 Sep 1925), and civil marriage is made compulsory (1 Sep 1926).

● **8–11 Nov**: Beer Hall Putsch: World War I general Erich von Ludendorff and National Socialist party leader Adolf Hitler make an unsuccessful attempt to overthrow the Bavarian government in Munich. Hitler is sentenced to five years' imprisonment. He is released after serving only one year, but during that time he dictates to co-conspirator Rudolf Hess his propagandist autobiography *Mein Kampf* (My Struggle) (Ger).

● Stanley Baldwin becomes UK prime minister after Andrew Bonar Law's resignation on grounds of ill health.

SOCIETY

- **Jan**: The German government inflates the mark yet further by printing excessive amounts of paper money to pay idle workers and compensate employers during the French occupation of the Ruhr. (> 26 Sep)

- **5 Mar**: Montana and Nevada introduce the first US old age pensions of $25 per month (USA).

- **29 Mar**: Death of French actress Sarah Bernhardt, aged 78.

- **Mar**: Daily weather forecast is first broadcast by the BBC (UK).

- **26 Apr**: Mexico recognizes oil concessions granted before the 1917 revolution.

- **23 May**: Belgian national airline Sabena is formed.

- **15 Jun**: Up to 20,000 are reported dead after an avalanche caused by an earthquake in Persia.

- **19 Jun**: Anglo-American war debt convention is signed by British prime minister Stanley Baldwin and US representative Andrew Mellon.

- **6 Jul**: Tennis champion Suzanne Lenglen (Fr) wins the Wimbledon Ladies' Singles for the fifth successive year.

- **1 Sep**: Tokyo is devastated by a great earthquake. There are widespread fires in Tokyo, Yokohama and nearby cities, with tidal waves and aftershocks; 200,000 people are killed by the disaster and property worth $1,000 million is lost (Jap).

- **26 Sep**: The disastrous devaluation of the German mark (now worth less than the paper on which it is printed) forces the end of the German policy of passive resistance to Franco-Belgian occupation of the Ruhr. The French franc too falls 25 percent, forcing the French to make direct agreement with mine operators to secure deliveries. (>Nov)

- **12 Oct**: National capital of Turkey is moved from Istanbul to Ankara.

- **6 Nov**: 1,000 shops in Berlin are looted during a spate of antisemitic rioting (Ger).

- **10 Nov**: The Reparations Recovery Act is suspended.

- **15 Nov**: In an effort to counter inflation, a new currency, the Rentenmark, is introduced, which will gradually replace the old inflated currency. It is secured by a mortgage on land and industry to the sum of 3,200,000,000 gold marks.

- **29 Nov**: The Reparations Commission appoints a committee of experts to examine German economic conditions, which results in the establishment of the Dawes Commission (USA) and the McKenna Commission (UK) to decide on the regulation of reparations. (> 9 Apr 1924)

- **Nov**: Micum Accords (Mission Interalli de Contrôle des Usines et des Mines, the Inter-Allied Control Commission for Factories and Mines), under which German industry in the Ruhr goes back to work.

- **18 Dec**: Commercial treaty between USA and Germany.

- **20 Dec–Jun 1926**: League of Nations-sponsored plan for the economic rehabilitation of Hungary, similar to that applied in Austria.

- Publication of two key economic texts, *A Tract on Monetary Reform* by J.M. Keynes and *Money, Credit and Commerce* by A. Marshall (UK).

- Antitrust legislation against the misuse of economic power (Ger).

- The USSR continues to export corn even in famine conditions.

- Founding of Aeroflot, the state airline, in the USSR.

- Sidney and Beatrice Webb: *The Decay of Capitalist Civilization*, political text (UK).

- Rise in popularity of the Charleston, a popular dance that comes to symbolize the age of the "flapper" (USA).

- Mother's Day, first celebrated in the USA in 1907, is first celebrated in Europe.

- First speedway race meeting is held, in New South Wales (Aus).

- Herbert Bayer of the Bauhaus designs the new one- and two-million mark banknotes for the Reichsbank (Ger).

- Yankee Stadium is opened in New York (USA).

- Wembley Stadium, the first national multisport center, opens in London (UK).

- Enrique Tiriboschi (Arg) swims the English Channel in a record 16 hrs 33 mins.

- First 24-hour Grand Prix motor race is held at Le Mans (Fr).

CULTURE

- **25 Oct**: Premier in Paris of Darius Milhaud's jazz ballet, *La Création des monde*, influenced African creation myth, with designs by Fernand Léger.

- Robert Frost: *New Hampshire*, poems (USA).

- Jean Cocteau: *Thomas l'imposteur*, novel (Fr).

- Italo Svevo: *Confessions of Zeno*, novel (It).

- Jaroslav Hašek: *Good Soldier Schweik*, novel (Czech).

- W.B. Yeats (Ire), poet, playwright and founder of the Irish National Theater in Dublin, is awarded the Nobel Prize for Literature.

- Leon Trotsky: *Literature and Revolution*, essay (USSR).

- William Walton: *Façade*, musical setting of texts by Edith Sitwell (UK).

- Zoltán Kodály: *Háry János*, suite (Hung).

- Arthur Honegger: *Pacific 231*, musical tone-painting of a moving locomotive, for orchestra (Fr).

- Arnold Schoenberg: Piano Suite, first fully 12-note work (Aut).

- Jean Sibelius: Sixth Symphony (Fin).

- Nikolai Foregger: *Mechanical Dances* (USSR).

- Igor Stravinsky: *Les Noces*, ballet based on a Russian folk tale (Fr).

- Béla Bartók: *The Miraculous Mandarin*, ballet (Hung).

- "King" Oliver and "Jelly Roll" Morton record New Orleans-style jazz, bringing jazz to a new wider audience.

- Ludwig Hirschfeld-Mack: *Reflected Light Composition*, moving light projections, scored to indicate color sequences, light sources, "dissolves", "fade-outs" etc, accompanied by a pianist (Ger).

- Alexander Rodchenko: photomontage illustrations for Vladimir Mayakovsky's *Pro Eto* ("About This"), a collection of poems (USSR).

- Formation of the Blue Blouse Group, whose repertoire consists of film, dance and "animated posters" with an overtly (Communist) political theme (USSR).

- Marcel Duchamp: *The Bride Stripped Bare by her Bachelors, Even*, sculpture (unfinished) (Fr).

- Max Beckmann: *Dance-Bar in Baden-Baden* (Ger).

- Auguste Perret: Notre-Dame, Le Raincy (Fr).

- Le Corbusier: *Vers une architecture*, text (Fr).

- First public exhibition of the Bauhaus, the Bauhaus Week, under the title "Art and Technology – A New Unity" (Ger).

- Cecil B. de Mille: *The Ten Commandments*, film (USA).

SCIENCE

- **15 Jul**: First regular air route between Moscow and Gorky is established (USSR).

- Nobel Prize for Chemistry is won by Fritz Pregl (Aut) "for his invention of the method of microanalysis of organic substances".

- Nobel Prize for Physics is won by Robert A. Millikan (USA) for his work on the elementary charge of electricity and the photoelectric effect.

- Nobel Prize for Physiology or Medicine is won by Frederick G. Banting (Can) and John J. R. Macleod (UK) for their discovery of insulin.

- First mill is developed for hot continuous wide strip rolling of steel after an idea of J.B. Tytus.

- German company Benz produces trucks with diesel engines.

- Robert H. Goddard invents the liquid fuel rocket, though the first successful launch is not until 1926 (USA).

- The bulldozer is introduced by LaPlante-Choate Company (USA).

- J. de la Cierva develops the basic principle of the autogiro (Sp).

- V. Zworykin invents the iconoscope, an early form of the cathode ray (TV) tube (USA).

- H. Souttar pioneers cardiac surgery by attempting to widen a constricted mitral valve (UK).

- Publication of A. Eddington's *Mathematical Theory of Relativity* (UK).

- G. Ramon develops a new tetanus vaccine (Fr).

- F. Lindemann investigates the size of meteors and the temperature of the upper atmosphere (UK).

- A.H. Crompton discovers that X-rays change in wavelength when scattered by matter (USA).

- O.H. Warburg develops a method for studying respiration – the breakdown of food molecules in the presence of oxygen to create energy – in thin slices of tissue (Ger).

- A theory of acids and bases – defined in terms of the availability or lack of hydrogen ions in a compound – is postulated by J.N. Bronsted (Den).

- P.J.W. Debye extends the Arrhenius theory of ionization of salt in solution to the crystalline solid state (Neth).

- L.A. Bauer analyzes the Earth's magnetic field.

- Sigmund Freud: *The Ego and the Id*, psychology text (Aut).

With the death of Lenin in January, the first stages of the Russian communist revolution came to an end. The experience of the civil war and its aftermath had been generally bitter. Recovery had only come with Lenin's introduction of the New Economic Policy, which sanctioned greater personal economic freedom, but by now against a background of the most severe famine and general economic collapse. The New Economic Policy continued to guide the fortunes of Soviet Russia until 1928, but some of its consequences added fuel to the power struggle within the Kremlin which raged during the mid-1920s between Trotsky and Stalin, who drew his support from those who favored a totally state-planned economy. Elsewhere in Europe, other forms of dictatorship took root. In Italy, fascism under Mussolini tightened its hold on power, while in Germany Adolf Hitler's jail sentence for his part in a failed coup gave him the chance to dictate his manifesto for Nazism, "Mein Kampf."

▲ Lenin lying in state in Moscow after his death on 21 January 1924. His death sparked off a power struggle between Leon Trotsky and Joseph Stalin, whose particular fitness for the highest state offices had always been doubted by Lenin. The struggle continued until Trotsky was finally exiled from the Soviet Union in January 1929.

● **21 Jan**: Death of V.I. Lenin begins a power struggle in the Kremlin between Joseph Stalin (at first supported by Leo Kamenev and Grigory Zinoviev) and Leon Trotsky (who later claims the allegiance of the latter two), which breaks out into open conflict in 1926. Before his death, Lenin had tried to check the rise of Stalin, believing him unfit for leadership.

● **21 Jan**: First Guomindang nationalist party (founded 1907) congress in Canton allows Communists to join the party, and accepts Russian military advisors; Jiang Jieshi heads German and Russian military instructors at the Whampoa Academy. The "Three Principles of the People" (Nationalism, Democracy and Social Progress) becomes a focus for Chinese loyalties (Chi).

● **22 Jan**: J. Ramsay MacDonald becomes the first British Labour prime minister, leading a minority government (until 4 Nov). During this period there is rapprochement between Britain and the USSR, recognized by Britain on 1 Feb, and a commercial treaty is signed on 8 Aug, giving Britain most-favored-nation status. (› 25 Oct)

● **25 Jan**: Treaty of alliance between France and Czechoslovakia.

● **27 Jan**: Treaty between Yugoslavia and Italy cedes the town of Fiume to Italy in return for Yugoslavia's gaining Porto Barros and facilities in Fiume.

● **4 Feb**: Mohandas Gandhi (arrested in 1922) is released from prison due to the deterioration in his health (Ind).

● **7 Feb**: Tangier becomes an international city, governed by representatives from Britain, France, Spain, Portugal, Italy, Belgium, Sweden, the Netherlands and later the USA.

● **6 Apr**: Fascists poll 65 percent of votes and are allocated 375 seats in the chamber in elections in Italy.(› 10 Jun)

● **Apr**: Russo-Romanian conference over Bessarabia fails after Romania refuses to hold a plebiscite in the disputed province.

● **1 May**: After King Giorgios II leaves Greece under pressure from the military junta led by Eleutherios Venizelos (18 Dec 1923), Greece is proclaimed a republic, with Admiral Paul Kondouriottis as provisional president.

● **31 May**: The USSR, in repudiation of czarist policy in China, relinquishes its concessions at Tianjin and Wuhan, as well as the remainder of the Boxer indemnity, which goes toward education; the Chinese Eastern Railroad is put under joint management.

● **10 Jun**: Giacomo Matteotti, socialist deputy and avowed antifascist, is assassinated by Fascist agents. Non-Fascist government members refuse to return to parliament until it is proved that the government is not responsible, but this enables Fascist leader Mussolini to squeeze out the opposition, finally forbidding their meeting on 3 Aug (It).

● **10 Jul**: Adoption of the Organic Law in Iraq introduces a liberal parliamentary constitution.

● **2 Oct**: Geneva Protocol put forward at the League of Nations by J. Ramsay MacDonald (UK), drafted by Eduard Beneš (Czech) and Nicholas Politis (Gre), provides for the compulsory arbitration of all disputes, defining the aggressor as the nation unwilling to submit to arbitration. It is rejected by Britain and the British dominions in Mar 1925 because of fears that Japan may use it to force Australia, Canada and New Zealand to reopen their ports to Japanese immigration.

● **3 Oct**: Sherif Hussein of the Hejaz is forced to abdicate after a military offensive by his political rival Abd al-Aziz Ibn Saud conquers much of Arabia (since May 1919). His son Ali succeeds, but after Ibn Saud takes Mecca (13 Oct) and the remainder of Arabia, he is forced to abdicate. (› 8 Jan 1926)

● **25 Oct**: In Britain a general election is provoked by the discovery of the "Zinoviev letter", inciting Britons to revolution; though the Soviet government claim it is a forgery, it is sufficient to topple the minority Labour government and produce a large Conservative majority at the polls.(› 21 Nov)

● **28 Oct**: Recognition of the USSR by France.

● **4 Nov**: Republican Calvin Coolidge wins a landslide victory in the US presidential elections.

● **20 Nov**: The assassination of Sir Lee Stack, sirdar of the Egyptian army and governor-general of the Sudan, provokes a British ultimatum on 22 Nov demanding satisfaction and the withdrawal of Egyptian troops from the Sudan; Egyptian premier Saad Zaghul refuses, and resigns in protest. His successor yields to the British on 24 Nov.

● **21 Nov**: Conservative prime minister Stanley Baldwin denounces the treaties made by Ramsay MacDonald with the USSR (UK).

● **1 Dec**: Communist uprising in Estonia, later suppressed.

● The Republican party is founded in Spain by Manuel Azana.

● **2 Jan**: The main railway stations in Paris are closed as the level of the Seine rises due to flooding (Fr).

● **10 Jan**: The submarine L-34 sinks off Weymouth, and all 43 on board are feared dead (UK).

● **26 Jan**: Petrograd is renamed Leningrad in honour of Lenin. His body is embalmed in Moscow for permanent public display (Russ).

● **Jan**: First Winter Olympic Games is held, at Chamonix (Fr). Competitors from 18 nations take part.

● **Feb**: Agreement between the UK and Germany reduces the reparation tax from 26 percent to 5 percent.

● **Feb**: Radio broadcasts are first used for educational purposes by Columbia University (USA).

● **9 Apr**: The Dawes Plan provides for a reorganization of the German Reichsbank under Allied auspices, with reparation payments of one billion gold marks per annum, increasing after five years to two billion gold marks per annum, and a loan to Germany of 800 million gold marks. This is accepted by Germany on 16 Apr, and on 16 Jul–16 Aug, a conference in London adopts the plan.

● **16 Apr**: Founding of MGM, when Metro Pictures, Goldwyn Pictures and the Louis B. Meyer Company amalgamate (USA).

● **Apr**: Plague spreads through the Punjab, where it has already claimed over 25,000 lives. Disinfection and inoculation programs are under way, and thousands of rats have been killed (Ind).

● **Apr**: Restrictive credit policy is adopted by the Reichsbank to defend the exchange rate of the mark (Ger).

● **Apr**: Opening of the British Empire Exhibition in London (UK).

● **21 May**: The USA remits $6 million of the Boxer indemnity, which is used (17 Sep) to found the China Foundation for the Promotion of Education and Culture, which makes annual grants for scientific education, and creates a large library.

● **26 May**: Immigration Bill limits further foreign immigration to the USA, and excludes totally the Japanese, bringing protest from Japan and creating ill feeling.

● **8 Jun**: Over 10,000 American Indians gather at Sand Springs, Oklahoma, to discuss their problems in the modern USA.

● **Jul**: American swimmer Johnny Weissmuller takes two gold medals at the Paris Olympic Games. 42 countries take part, but Germany does not compete.

● **Aug**: Legislation on the introduction of a new currency, the Reichsmark, intended to stabilize the economy, and a new set of regulations for the Reichsbank are put into force. The Reichsmark is introduced on 30 Aug (Ger).

● **Aug**: A financial agreement is made between China and Germany.

● **Aug**: Up to 50,000 are feared dead and 2 million homeless after severe floods in China.

● **12 Oct**: First Zeppelin flight across the Atlantic Ocean from Friederichshafen to New York (Ger/USA).

● **Oct**: Germany signs agreements on trade with France and the UK.

● **4 Nov**: Texas elects the first woman state governor, "Ma" Miriam Ferguson (USA).

● **Nov**: Captain Alfred Delingette and his wife make the first crossing of Africa from north to south by automobile, from Oran to Capetown.

● **Nov**: Strike of Austrian railmen.

● As motoring becomes ever more popular, the House of Lords discusses the introduction of driving tests to check the increasing number of road accidents (UK).

● **2 Dec**: It is revealed that comedian and film star Charlie Chaplin has married 16-year old Lita Grey (USA).

● Foundation of Imperial Airways (UK).

● Hairdresser Antoine creates a fashion for dying gray hair blue (UK).

● Foundation of the Deutsche Rohstahlgemeinschaft, the organization of steelworks (Ger).

● In the spring there is speculation in francs, but a sudden squeeze punishes the speculators (Fr).

● Slavery is officially abolished in Ethiopia.

● International Chess Federation (FIDE) is set up in Paris.

● Fashion designer Jean Patou opens sportswear shops in the French seaside resorts of Deauville and Biarritz.

● **4 May**: Opening of *Men*, a film with Pola Negri (USA).

● **May**: American Society of Composers, Authors and Publishers (ASCAP) denounces film and radio as "parasitic" (USA).

● **6 Nov**: Premiere in Brno of Leoš Janáček's opera *The Cunning Little Vixen* (Cze).

● Robert Musil: *Three Women*, short stories (Ger).

● George Bernard Shaw: *St Joan*, play (UK).

● Sean O'Casey: *Juno and the Paycock*, play (Ire).

● E.M. Forster: *A Passage to India*, novel (UK).

● Pablo Neruda: *Twenty Love Poems and a Song of Despair* (Chile).

● St John Perse: *Anabase*, poem (Fr).

● Thomas Mann: *The Magic Mountain*, novel (Ger).

● The Nobel Prize for Literature is won by Wladislaw Reymont (Pol).

● Erwin Piscator founds the Berlin Proletarian Theater (Ger).

● Rodolfo De Angelis forms his New Futurist Theater (It).

● Ferruccio Busoni: *Doktor Faust*, opera, premiered in Dresden in 1925 after Busoni's death (Ger).

● Giacomo Puccini: *Turandot*, opera left unfinished at the composer's death (premiered in 1926) (It).

● Arnold Schoenberg: *Erwartung* (Expectation), opera in one act with a single soprano role (composed 1909), is premiered in Prague (Cze).

● George Gershwin: *Rhapsody in Blue*, for piano and jazz orchestra, brings the influence of jazz into the concert hall (USA).

● Xanti Schawinsky: *Circus*, dance piece (Ger).

● Otto Dix: *War*, series of 50 engravings expressing the horrors of the trenches (Ger).

● Exhibition of the Blue Four, artists connected with the Bauhaus – Wassily Kandinsky, Paul Klee, Lyonel Feininger and Alexej von Jawlensky (Ger).

● Max Ernst: *Two Children are Menaced by a Nightingale*, painting (Fr).

● Official foundation of the Surrealist movement with the publication of André Breton's first Surrealist Manifesto, the first issue of *La Révolution surréaliste* and the first Surrealist exhibition, in Paris (Fr).

● Eugene Freyssinet: airship hangars at Orly, one of the earliest uses of prestressed concrete (Fr).

● Gerrit Rietveld: Schroeder House, Utrecht, a domestic house built in De Stijl style (Neth).

● Francis Picabia: *Entr'acte*, filmed by René Clair, is first shown in the interval during Picabia and Erik Satie's Dadaist ballet *Relâche* (Fr).

● Nobel Prize for Physics is won by Manne Siegbahn (Swe) for his work on X-ray spectroscopy.

● Nobel Prize for Physiology or Medicine won by Willhelm Einthoven (Neth) "for his discovery of the mechanism of the electrocardiogram".

● German scientists synthesize plasmochin, a quinine substitute, for the treatment of malaria.

● D. Keilin discovers cytochrome, an important cell respiratory enzyme (UK).

● H. Steenbock discovers that ultraviolet light increases the vitamin D content of food.

● W. Pauli introduces his exclusion principle, which helps to explain atomic structure statistically (Aut).

● Publication of L.V. de Broglie's study on the wave theory of matter (Fr).

● E.V. Appleton demonstrates that radio waves of sufficiently short wavelength will penetrate the Heaviside layer (UK).

● A. Eddington discovers that the luminosity of a star is approximately a function of its mass (UK).

● Mass production of the Leica camera begins. The first precision miniature camera commercially available (Ger).

● G. and G. Dick isolate the scarlet fever streptococcus (USA).

● Acetylene used as an anesthetic.

● S.G. Brown Ltd bring out their crystavox loudspeakers, improving sound quality in crystal radio sets (UK).

● Bell Laboratories, for research in physics, is founded jointly by American Telegraph Co (ATT) and General Electric Co (USA/UK).

● Publication of H. Oberth's *The Rocket into Interplanetary Space*, the first book to contain the notion of escape velocity.

In the early stages of the Russian communist revolution party discipline was increasingly enforced in political life, but in other spheres there was a high degree of freedom, creating an atmosphere in which social and cultural experimentation flourished. Modern art and architecture especially flowered during this period before being stifled from the late 1920s by the increasingly totalitarian regime of Stalin and the state imposition of "socialist realism" and functionalism. Architects such as the young El Lissitzky joined artists such as Vladimir Tatlin and Kasimir Malevich in exploring new forms and spatial concepts appropriate to a revolutionary society. Constructivist design appeared in the theater and on the streets as well as in architectural models, and spun off into posters, book wrappers and magazine covers. Maxim Gorky and the poet Vladimir Mayakovsky developed a dedicated revolutionary Bolshevik literature. In the world of Russian cinema this cultural liberation made itself seen in the works of directors such as Eisenstein and Pudovkin, perhaps best typified by Eisenstein's experimental film "The Battleship Potemkin."

▲ Photomontage became a popular technique, both for film and poster art. This photomontage poster advertises Sergey Eisenstein's film *The Battleship Potemkin*, based on the mutiny of the sailors on the *Potemkin* off Odessa in support of the 1905 revolution.

● **20 Jan**: Russo-Japanese convention heals the rift between the two countries, with Japan receiving oil and coal concessions in northern Sakhalin in return for the evacuation of Japanese troops.

● **21 Jan**: Proclamation of the Albanian Republic, with Ahmed Zog as first president; a constitution is promulgated on 2 Mar.

● **Jan**: Leon Trotsky is ousted as commissar for war, leaving power in the hands of Joseph Stalin backed by Grigory Zinoviev and Leo Kamenev (USSR).

● **Jan**: Benito Mussolini begins a purge on the opposition to his Fascist party (It).

● **9 Feb**: Germany suggests a Rhineland mutual guarantee pact, to replace the Geneva Protocol. It is accepted by Britain and France, on condition that Germany join the League of Nations.

● **Feb**: The Persian *majlis* grants premier Reza Khan dictatorial powers. (› 13 Dec)

● **Feb–Apr**: Uprising in Kurdistan against the religious policy of the Turkish government, is put down severely; the leaders are executed.

● **12 Mar**: Death of Chinese Nationalist leader Sun Yat-sen. He is succeeded as leader of the Guomindang (Nationalist) party by Jiang Jieshi.

● **16 Apr**: A bomb planted in Sofia Cathedral by Communists kills 123 people, provoking the government to ban the Communist party in Bulgaria (on 4 May).

● **18–19 Apr**: An attempted military coup against the democratic government in Portugal, accompanied by bloodshed in Lisbon, collapses quickly.

● **26 Apr**: Field Marshal Paul von Hindenburg is elected president of Germany.

● **Apr**: Foundation of the SS (Schutz Staffel, "protective echelon"). Originally a personal guard to Adolf Hitler, it later (1929–45) under Heinrich Himmler became the elite corps of the Nazi apparatus, divided into Allgemeine-SS (internal security) and Waffen-SS ("armed" SS, including Hitler's personal bodyguard and elite combat troops) (Ger).

● **1 May**: Cyprus (annexed 1914) becomes a crown colony of the British Empire.

● **12 May**: The Soviet constitution is revised to include Uzbekistan, Kazakhstan, Turkmenistan and other new republics.

● **30 May**: Student demonstrations at Shanghai and (23 Jun) at Guangzhou are dispersed by armed British troops, provoking a strike and boycott of British goods and shipping (until Oct 1926) (Chi).

● **17 Jun**: Arms traffic convention on the arms trade; a protocol prohibits the use of poison gas.

● **25 Jun**: Coup in Greece led by Gen. Theodoros Pangalos (Gr). (› 3 Jan 1926)

● **18 Jul–Jun 1927**: Uprising of the Druses (a political and religious sect) under Sultan Pasha in Syria, who are able to gain control of the countryside.

● **25 Aug**: The French leave Dusseldorf, Duisburg and Ruhrort (Ger).

● **Aug**: First national congress of the Ku Klux Klan, in Washington (USA).

● **9 Sep**: French and Spanish offensive under Marshal Henri Pétain, begins against the Riffians, led by Abd-el-Krim (N Afr).

● **22–23 Oct**: Greece invades Bulgaria in a border incident; the League of Nations fines Greece after a settlement on 14 Dec.

● **1 Dec**: Treaties after the Locarno Conference of 5–16 Oct provide for: mutual guarantee of Franco-German and Belgo-German borders; arbitration between Germany and Poland, Czechoslovakia, Belgium and France; Franco-Polish and Franco-Czechoslovak mutual assistance treaty in the event of German aggression.

● **3 Dec**: Due to popular discontent, Primo de Rivera reestablishes parliament, although of a predominantly military character, with himself as prime minister (Sp).

● **3 Dec**: Boundary between Northern Ireland and the Irish Free State is finally agreed.

● **13 Dec**: After declaring the self-exiled shah deposed on 31 Oct, Reza Khan is made shah (until 1941). He initiates a reform policy similar to that of Mustafa Kemal's in Turkey, with the exception of the antireligious policy (Per).

● **17 Dec**: Alliance between Turkey and the USSR provides for close economic and political ties.

● **28 Dec**: Prince Carol of Romania renounces his right of succession in order to live in exile with his mistress, Magda Lupescu. However, at the request of parliament, he returns with her on 6 Jun 1930 and replaces Michael, his son, as king (until 1940).

● Vietnamese Nationalist (1931, Indochinese Communist) party is founded by Nguyen Ai Quoc (Ho Chi Minh).

- **1 Jan**: Norway's capital, Christiania, is renamed Oslo.

- **7 Jan**: Launch of the *Emden*, the first German warship built since World War I.

- **24 Jan**: A total eclipse of the Sun is seen by 25 million people in the USA.

- **11, 19 Feb**: International opium conventions provide a more effective control over production and trade in opium.

- **2 Mar**: A new currency is introduced in Austria, the schilling.

- **23 Mar**: The state of Tennessee bans the teaching of the theory of evolution in schools (USA).

- **Mar**: Bill is passed granting universal male suffrage in Japan, with an increase of the electorate from 3 to 14 million.

- **Mar**: The International Motor Racing Federation decide to institute a world motor racing championship (Fr).

- **1 Apr**: The Hebrew University in Jerusalem is opened by Lord Balfour (Pal).

- **28 Apr**: In his budget speech, Chancellor of the Exchequer Winston Churchill announces that Britain will return to the gold standard. The gold standard is also restored in Germany, and the Gold Standard Act is enforced in the USA.

- **13 May**: The UK returns to the Gold Standard.

- **Jul**: A law is passed regarding the revaluations of loans and bonds, issued in marks, fixing liabilities after inflation (Ger).

- **Jul**: The British government grants miners special wages and establishes an arbitration committee to avoid a strike (Red Friday).

- **8 Aug**: Over 40,000 Ku Klux Klan members march through Washington (USA).

- **Aug**: Legislation on protection tariffs for industry and agriculture is enforced (Ger).

- **Aug**: Strike of tram and bus employees in Paris (Fr).

- **16 Sep**: The Liberian government and Firestone Rubber Plantation Co (USA) sign an agreement providing for the lease to Firestone of 1 million acres of land for 99 years and a loan to Liberia from Firestone of $5,000,000.

- **23 Sep**: New immigration restriction Act in Australia enables the governor-general to refuse entry to anyone of any class, race or occupation for any reason. Though never systematically applied, the Act makes possible the restriction of Italian immigration, which is resented, especially by unions and labor groups.

- **Sep**: Drought hits the southern and southwestern US states, and water is sold by the gallon.

- **Oct**: Germany signs agreements on trade with Italy and the USSR.

- **13 Nov**: South African prime minister Hertzog says his cabinet wants the segregation of blacks and more areas for their own use.

- **28 Dec**: Land law in Poland is passed to provide for the distribution of 200,000 hectares (500,000 acres) of land to the peasantry annually for 10 years.

- **Dec**: Party congress of the Communist party of the Soviet Union (CPSU) agrees on the need for the transformation of the USSR from an agrarian to an industrial country.

- Farmers in the USA, hard hit since the end of World War I by financial difficulties and world overproduction, leave the land at a rate of over half a million a year; the amount of land under production has fallen by five million hectares (12 million acres) since 1919 despite government assistance.

- Italy proposes cooperation with Britain regarding the exploitation of Ethiopia: Britain promises support for Italy in Ethiopia in return for Italian support for the British plan to build a dam at Lake Tana.

- Foundation of German chemicals combine IG Farben.

- Foundation of American automobile manufacturer Chrysler Corporation by Walter Chrysler.

- 170-day miners' strike takes place in the USA.

- The world's first motel, the Milestone Motel, opens in Monterey, California (USA).

- Nobel Peace Prize is won by J. Austin Chamberlain (UK) for his role in the Locarno negotiations, and Charles Dawes (USA) for his contribution to the Dawes Plan.

- Publication of Adolf Hitler's *Mein Kampf* (My Struggle) (2 vols, 1925–26), a manifesto for the Nazi party under the guise of pseudoautobiographical political philosophy.

- Fashion designer Madeleine Vionnet (Fr) begins to use the bias cut, and female curves are in vogue again.

- First issue of *New Yorker* magazine (USA).

- **21 Mar**: Premiere of Maurice Ravel's opera *L'Enfant et les sortilèges*, libretto by Colette, in Monte Carlo.

- Emily Dickinson: *Complete Poems* (posth., d.1886) (USA).

- John Dos Passos: *Manhattan Transfer*, novel (USA).

- Virginia Woolf: *Mrs Dalloway*, novel (UK).

- Eugenio Montale, *Ossi di seppia* (Cuttlefish Bones), poems (It).

- F. Scott Fitzgerald: *The Great Gatsby*, novel seen as typifying the Jazz Age (USA).

- Osip Mandelstam: *The Noise of Time*, autobiographical stories (USSR).

- Franz Kafka: *The Trial*, novel (not published until after his death in 1926) (Cze).

- Nobel Prize for Literature is won by George Bernard Shaw (UK).

- Jean Sibelius: *Tapiola*, tone poem (Fin).

- Alban Berg: *Wozzeck*, opera, libretto from Georg Büchner's play *Woyzeck* (Aut).

- Aaron Copland: *Music for the Theater*, orchestral work incorporating elements of jazz (USA).

- The Exposition des Arts Décoratifs in Paris, an international showcase of design and architecture, ushers in the new style named after it: Art Deco (Fr).

- G.F. Hartlaub's "Die Neue Sachlichkeit" (New Objectivity) exhibition opens in Mannheim, with paintings by Max Beckmann, Otto Dix and George Grosz (Ger).

- Constantin Brancusi: *Bird in Space*, sculpture (Fr).

- First of Max Ernst's "frottages", collages created from various rubbings (Ger).

- Publication of Paul Klee's *Pedagogical Sketchbook*, teaching text (Ger).

- The Bauhaus design school moves to Dessau, and reopens in Walter Gropius's specially designed new Bauhaus building (Ger).

- Joost Schmidt designs a mechanical stage for Bauhaus productions (consisting of four stages arranged telescopically, one of which is movable) (Ger).

- George Balanchine becomes principal choreographer of the *Ballets Russes* (Fr).

- Josephine Baker (USA/Fr), christened "a most beautiful panther" by the writer Colette, dances in *La Revue nègre* in Paris to great acclaim.

- Sergey Eisenstein: *The Battleship Potemkin*, film, notable for its revolutionary use of dramatic intercutting techniques (USSR).

- *The Gold Rush*, film starring Charlie Chaplin (USA).

- Nobel Prize for Chemistry is won by Richard Zsigmondy (Ger) for his work on colloid solutions.

- Nobel Prize for Physics is won by James Franck (Ger) and Gustav Hertz (Ger) "for their discovery of the laws governing the impact of an electron upon an atom".

- Hydrocarbon synthesis by F. Fischer and H. Tropsch leads to the development of synthetic gasoline for fuel, the so-called "Fischer-Tropsch reaction" (Ger).

- P.M.S. Blackett develops a technique for photographing the interaction of atomic particles (UK).

- E.V. Appleton measures the height of the ionosphere (UK).

- C. Bosch invents a process for preparing hydrogen on a manufacturing scale (Ger).

- L. Lazzarini experiments in bone transplants using rabbits (It).

- W.K. Heisenberg and N. Bohr develop quantum mechanics, the mathematical description of matter that takes into account the concept of matter as waveforms and the impossibility of defining exactly the position and velocity of any particle (Ger).

- First successful experiments in hydroponics – the soilless cultivation of plants fed only by nutrient-rich water (USA).

- The theory of gene centers is postulated by N.I. Vavilov (USSR).

- J. Collip obtains extract of the parathyroid gland for treating tetanus.

- First public demonstration of the photoelectric cell, in which light energy is converted into electricity (USA).

- Vannevar Bush develops the first analog computer, designed to solve differential equations (USA).

- R.A. Millikan discovers the presence of cosmic rays in the upper atmosphere (USA).

- Discovery of the Mid-Atlantic Ridge, a major undersea mountain range, by a German expedition using sonar.

- Wolfgang Pauli gives his exclusion principle, whereby in any atom no two electrons have identical sets of quantum numbers, a principle that leads to the determination of the electron structure of the heavier elements (Ger).

- Vladimir Zworykin files for a patent on a color television system; it is granted in 1928.

The general incidence of industrial disputes, measured by working days lost, had been declining in Britain since 1921. The General Strike of May 1926 marked an abrupt halt to this trend. The strike had its origins in industrial relations within the coalmining industry, which had become increasingly bitter since the end of World War I. Difficulties in 1925 had been assuaged by the government's providing a subsidy, for the second time, to maintain wages, but the subsequent attempt of the coalowners both to reduce wage rates and lengthen the working day produced deadlock in negotiations with the miners' leaders, which resulted in both a lockout and a strike. The labor movement as a whole backed the miners' case, because of the general fear of further wage cuts, following Britain's return to the Gold Standard at the prewar parity, which overvalued the pound sterling and thereby priced exports out of world markets. The General Strike was called off by the TUC after nine days, but various regional sections of the miners' union continued their struggle until the autumn.

▲ A burnt-out London bus, a casualty of the General Strike in Britain. The strike split the country, with many volunteers signing on to drive trains and buses and maintain supplies. It was called off on 20 May after only nine days, and in June 1927 the UK Trades Disputes Act outlawed general strike action.

● **3 Jan**: Theodoros Pangalos makes himself dictator of Greece after his coup d'etat of 25 Jun 1925, declaring void the republican constitution of 30 Sep 1925 (until 22 Aug).

● **8 Jan**: Abd al-Aziz ibn Saud is proclaimed king of the Hejaz, which he plans to rename Saudi Arabia.

● **Jan–Feb**: Turkey adopts new civil, criminal and law codes based respectively on the Swiss, Italian and German systems.

● **10 Feb**: Germany applies for admission to the League of Nations, and is admitted on 8 Sep (until the Nazi government withdraws Germany from the League in 1933).

● **12 Mar**: Danish parliament votes for near-total disarmament.

● **26 Mar**: Treaties of friendship between Romania and Poland (10 Jun), France and (16 Sep) Italy. The latter grants Romania a sizeable loan in return for oil.

● **7 Apr**: An assassination attempt on Fascist leader Benito Mussolini fails narrowly (It).

● **Apr**: Severe riots between Muslims and Hindus break out in Calcutta (Ind).

● **12–14 May**: Josef Pilsudski leads a military revolt against the government of Vincent Witos (since 10 May), and captures Warsaw, forcing Witos and president Wojciechowski to resign. Ignace Moscicki becomes president on 1 Jun, although Pilsudski holds the real power (Pol). (› 2 Oct)

● **18–26 May**: First meeting of the Preparatory Commission for a Disarmament Conference, appointed by the League of Nations in 1925.

● **28 May**: The democratic regime in Portugal is overthrown by a military coup led by Gen. Manuel Gomes da Costa, who is himself deposed by Gen. Antonio de Fragoso Carmona (elected president on 25 May 1928).

● **5 Jun**: A large part of the oil-rich Mosul area (formerly Turkish) is ceded to Iraq, providing settlement for a dispute dating from the Treaty of Lausanne (1923), when the question was left open.

● **10 Jun**: Spain leaves the League of Nations, but withdraws its resignation on 22 Mar 1928.

● **28 Jul**: Treaty between Panama and the USA, to protect the Panama Canal during wartime, and to allow maneuvers of US troops on Panamanian territory.

● **Jul–Oct**: Joseph Stalin triumphs over Leon Trotsky's leftist opposition faction, which has been promoting world revolution and the discontinuation of the New Economic Policy. Trotsky, Zinoviev, Radek and others are expelled from the Politburo and the Communist Party Central Committee (USSR). (›27 Dec 1927)

● **Jul–Oct**: In Jiang Jieshi's northern campaign, soldiers of the nationalist Guomindang, aided by the Russians, capture Hankou (6 Sep), Wuchang (10 Oct) and Nanjing (24 Mar 1927). A 40,000-strong international force is posted to protect Shanghai in 1927 (Chi).

● **7 Aug**: Treaty of friendship between Spain under Primo de Rivera and Italy under Mussolini, after mutual visits of leaders during 1924.

● **2 Oct**: Pilsudski becomes prime minister of Poland (until 1928), and initiates a period of dictatorship and repression, including dissolving the Sejm (lower house of the parliament) on 28 Nov 1927, although new elections make plain great opposition to the rule of the "colonels".

● **19 Oct–18 Nov**: Imperial Conference declares a British Commonwealth of autonomous, equal nations united by allegiance to the crown, enforced as the Statute of Westminster in Dec 1931.

● **2 Nov**: Attempted separatist coup in Catalonia (Sp) by insurgents based in France.

● **27 Nov**: Treaty of Tiranë between Italy and Albania provides for mutual assistance in maintaining the territorial status quo and Italy's nonintervention in Albanian affairs except by request.

● **Nov**: Communist revolt in the Dutch East Indies, not finally suppressed until Jun 1927.

● **17 Dec**: Antanas Smetona arrests the Lithuanian president and cabinet, making himself president, with Augustine Voldermaras as prime minister. He suspends the constitution, so becoming a dictator with the support of the Nationalist Union.

● **25 Dec**: Death of the Japanese emperor Yoshihito ends the Taisho period; succession by Hirohito begins the Shōwa period (until 1989).

● A conference of East African governors at Nairobi discusses the concept of an East African federation.

SOCIETY

- **21 Jan**: The Makwar Dam is completed on the Nile in Egypt, after concern that irrigation in the Sudan might deprive Egypt of enough water for its own crops.

- **29 Jan**: All students in Moscow are ordered to do compulsory military training.

- **3 Feb**: Czech becomes the official language in Czechoslovakia, but the rights of minority languages are guaranteed.

- **18 Feb**: It is announced that five cities built by the Maya civilization in the Yucatán peninsula have been discovered (Mex).

- **19 Feb**: 200 Mafia leaders are reported to have been arrested in Sicily (It).

- **13 Mar**: Pilot Alan Cobham (UK) completes the first air trip from London to Capetown and back, a journey lasting nearly three months. On 1 Oct, he completes the first round trip to Australia, a 45,000 km (28,000 mile) trip.

- **18 Mar**: 17 people are killed and 16 wounded in Beijing when troops fire on demonstrating students (Chi).

- **24 Mar**: Marion B. Skaggs establishes the Safeway chain of stores in Maryland (USA).

- **30 Apr**: Opening of a radio picture service transmitting pictures by radio between London and the *New York Times*.

- **1 May**: Coalminers go on strike, after threats to discontinue the government subsidy granted 1 Jul 1925 (UK).

- **3 May**: The Trades Union Congress calls for a general strike in sympathy with the miners. Some 2,500,000 trade union members take part. Volunteers, mainly from the upper classes, continue to provide essential services, and the general strike is called off on 12 May after the government promises to resume wage and hours negotiations. Later, the miners are forced to surrender unconditionally (UK).

- **9 May**: Richard Byrd and Floyd Bennett reach the North Pole in a Fokker monoplane, taking 15 hours to cover the 750 miles and return.

- **28 May**: 1,200 are reported killed by a cyclone and tidal wave in Burma.

- **15 Jul**: Financial crisis in France causes the fall of the Briand ministry: the French franc falls to the value of two US cents, and the budget remains unbalanced, aggravated by high public spending since World War I (⟩ 10 Aug).

- **31 Jul**: Mexican priests begin a strike (until 1929) after enforcement of anticlerical clauses of the 1917 constitution.

- **Jul**: The Belgian king is given dictatorial powers to solve a financial crisis, during which the Belgian franc is devalued and stabilized.

- **Jul**: New banking legislation is passed, fixing the amount of government borrowing at 400 million marks (Ger).

- **6 Aug**: Gertrude Ederle (USA) becomes the first woman to swim the English Channel.

- **10 Aug**: A sinking fund measure, to cover part of the national debt by way of inheritance taxes and income from the tobacco monopoly is introduced in France. (⟩Dec)

- **19 Sep**: 1,500 are reported dead and about 40,000 made homeless when a hurricane sweeps Florida (USA).

- **25 Sep**: An international slavery convention is signed by 20 states.

- **Dec**: Suspension of the Latin Currency Union as a result of French inflation.

- Imperial Chemicals Industries (ICI) is created as a counterweight to the German company IG Farben (UK).

- Foundation of Lufthansa airline (Ger).

- The Banca d'Italia obtains a note-issuing monopoly (It).

- Inflation in France is followed by stabilization of the franc at the devalued level.

- Quality control methods are developed in industry (UK).

- The Women's Cricket Association is formed (UK).

- First Central American and Caribbean Games is held, in Mexico City (Mex).

- Nobel Peace Prize is won by Aristide Briand (Fr) and Gustav Stresemann (Ger) for their roles in securing the Locarno Pact and establishing dialogue between France and Germany.

- Anthropometric survey results are used in Berlei Co's underwear designs (Aut).

CULTURE

- **19 Jun**: Premiere in Paris of George Antheil's *Ballet mécanique*, scored for, among other things, electric doorbells and two aircraft propellers.

- **23 Aug**: Death of film star Rudolph Valentino, aged 31 (USA).

- **Aug**: *Don Juan* "talkie" is released by Vitaphone, the film synchronized with the first 33.3 rpm phonograph record.

- André Gide: *Les Faux-Monnayeurs* (The Counterfeiters), novel (Fr).

- Ezra Pound: *Personae*, poems (USA).

- D.H. Lawrence: *The Plumed Serpent*, novel (UK).

- William Faulkner: *Soldiers' Pay*, novel (USA).

- Pär Lagerkvist: *Songs of the Heart*, novel (Swe).

- Franz Kafka: *The Castle*, novel (published posth. by Max Brod) (Cze).

- Sean O'Casey: *The Plough and the Stars*, play (Ire).

- T.E. Lawrence ("Lawrence of Arabia"): *The Seven Pillars of Wisdom*, a semi-autobiographical account of the Arab independence struggle against the Turks (UK).

- Alban Berg: Lyric Suite, for string quartet (Aut).

- Leoš Janáček: *The Makropoulos Affair*, opera based on Karel Čapek's novel (1923), is premiered in Brno (Cze).

- Oskar Schlemmer: *Gesture Dance*, Bauhaus dance piece for which Schlemmer devises a new notation system for the movements of the dancers (Ger).

- Opening of Anita Loos's musical *Gentlemen Prefer Blondes* on Broadway (USA).

- Pablo Picasso: *Guitar*, assemblage (Fr).

- Georgia O'Keeffe: *Black Iris*, painting (USA).

- Paul Klee: *Around the Fish*, painting (Ger).

- George Grosz: *Pillars of Society*, painting (Ger).

- Opening of a Surrealist gallery in Paris (Fr).

- Konstantin Melnikov: "Club Rusakov", Moscow (USSR).

- Antoni Gaudi : Cathedral of the Sagrada Familia, Barcelona. Begun in 1882, is it unfinished at Gaudi's death in 1926, though work continues later in the century (Sp).

- Adolf Loos: Maison Tristan Tzara, Paris.

- Fritz Lang: *Metropolis*, Expressionist film on a futuristic theme (USA).

- Jean Renoir: *Nana*, film (Fr).

- Release of *The General*, comedy film with Buster Keaton and Clyde Bruckman (USA).

- Nobel Prize for Literature is won by Grazia Deledda (It).

SCIENCE

- Nobel Prize for Chemistry is won by Theodor Svedberg (Swe) "for his work on disperse systems".

- Nobel Prize for Physics is won by Jean Perrin (Fr) "for his work on the discontinuous structure of matter, and especially for his discovery of sedimentation equilibrium".

- Nobel Prize for Physiology or Medicine is won by Johannes Fibiger (Den) for his discovery of the *spiroptera carcinoma*, which is important in the study of cancer.

- A wide range of synthetic colors for paint is launched by Du Pont (USA).

- Publication of T.H. Morgan's *The Theory of the Gene* (USA).

- H.J. Muller discovers that X-rays induce genetic mutations (USA).

- "Electrola", a new recording technique, is developed (USA).

- A.A. Michelson measures the speed of light using an apparatus of mirrors some 35 km (25 miles) apart (USA).

- H. Staudinger begins work on his polymer theory of plastics (USA).

- J.D. Bernal develops the "Bernal chart", for deducing the structure of crystals from photographs of X-ray diffraction patterns (UK).

- Liver extract is first used by W.P. Murphy and G. Minot, for treating pernicious anemia (USA).

- H. Gardiner-Hill and J.P. Smith use pituitary extract to treat lack of growth, lack of menstruation and sudden weight gain (UK).

- A liquid-fuel rocket is launched by R.H. Goddard at Auburn, Massachusetts (USA).

- E.P. Wigner introduces group theory into quantum mechanics (Hung).

- Erwin Schrödinger elucidates his Schrödinger wave equation (Aut).

- J.B. Sumner observes urease, an enzyme essential to the nitrogen cycle. This is the first time an enzyme has been crystallized, and proves them to be proteins (USA).

- ICI begins production of compound fertilizers, containing nitrogen, phosphorus and potassium (UK).

- Scottish engineer John Logie Baird demonstrates TV (UK).

- E.L. Thorndike's *The Measurement of Intelligence* describes how to use tests to develop numerical measures of intelligence (USA).

Commercial full-length films with soundtracks had been made in limited numbers since 1921, but in the public's mind the era of the "talkies" began with *The Jazz Singer. Its* outstanding success arose not only from the immediacy of the presentation, but also from the way in which it combined the past popularity of "minstrel" performances with the razzle-dazzle of jazz. The film caught the air of the times, both the continuing rise of prosperity within the United States and the "golden Twenties" in Europe. The problems of the immediate postwar period appeared now to have passed and a more settled world established, similar to the Indian Summer that Europe had experienced at the turn of the 19th century. It also marked a great change that was taking place, as trends and fashions from across the Atlantic increasingly dictated the nature of life not only in Europe, but all over the globe.

▲ Al Jolson's performance in *The Jazz Singer* lengthened cinema queues all over the Western world. The success of the film emphasized the new influence of the United States on social and cultural trends worldwide.

• **31 Jan**: End of Allied military control in Germany, which is passed over to the jurisdiction of the League of Nations.

• **3 Feb**: Revolt by a group of intellectuals grouped around Seara Nova against the military regime, in Oporto and (7 Feb) Lisbon, is defeated by 13 Feb after heavy fighting (Port).

• **21 Feb**: A conference between South African and Indian officials settles the question of aid for Indians willing to return to India.

• **9 Mar**: Self-government in Libya ends, and Tripoli and Cyrenaica are united under a single government on 24 Jan 1929.

• **5 Apr**: Treaty of friendship between Italy and Hungary, against France and the Little Entente countries, initiates close relations between the two countries, leading eventually to the Rome Protocols of 1934 between Italy, Hungary and Austria.

• **18 Apr**: Split in the Guomindang nationalist party between Jiang Jieshi and other conservatives, and the radicals in Wuhan; the former set up a new government in Nanjing. A purge of Russians and Communists from Wuhan appears to heal the split, in return for Jiang's temporary retirement from public life (8 Aug). Troops advancing on Beijing are partially blocked by Japanese protecting Jinan (Chi).

• **1 May**: After the Bavarian government lifts its ban on Adolf Hitler speaking in public, the Nazi party holds a meeting in Berlin (Ger).

• **3 May**: Riots between Sikhs and Muslims in Lahore leave 14 dead and 100 injured (Ind).

• **20 May**: Treaty between Abd al-Aziz ibn Saud and Britain, with the recognition by the latter of the independence of the kingdom of the Hejaz and Nejd (renamed Saudi Arabia on 22 Sep 1932).

• **May**: The UK severs diplomatic links with the USSR on grounds of espionage and subversion.

• **20 Jun–4 Aug**: Three-power naval conference in Geneva (UK, USA, Jap) fails to reach agreement regarding cruisers, destroyers and submarines.

• **Jun**: Indonesian Nationalist party (PNI) is founded.

• **1 Jul**: Administrative reforms in Czechoslovakia decentralize the government in order to satisfy Slovakia and Ruthenia, which both have pro-autonomy factions.

• **Jul–Oct**: Complaints by native chiefs in Samoa against the New Zealand-run administration lead to the repatriation of Germans, who had provoked the natives, and the takeover of their property.

• **12 Aug**: Eamon De Valera and other Irish Republican leaders agree to assume their seats in the Dáil Eireann and take the oath of loyalty to the British crown, after the Irish government passes legislation stipulating that elected members take up their seats or forfeit their rights.

• **22 Sep**: Slavery is abolished in Sierra Leone.

• **17 Oct**: Norway elects its first Labor government.

• **Oct**: Insurrection in Mexico after the government's nationalization of church property is suppressed by president Calles, and the leaders executed.

• **11 Nov**: Treaty of friendship between France and Yugoslavia, after the concern of the latter over Italian advances in the Balkans.

• **22 Nov**: Second Treaty of Tiranë between Italy and Albania in response to the Franco-Yugoslav treaty of 11 Nov, provides for a defensive alliance for 20 years and mutual economic concessions.

• **22 Nov**: Persia advances claims to the Bahrain Islands after discovery of oil there.

• **30 Nov–3 Dec**: Maxim Litvinov, Russian representative at the Preparatory Commission on Disarmament set up by the League of Nations, suggests complete and immediate disarmament, but this is rejected as a Communist ploy.

• **14 Dec**: Treaty between Iraq and Britain, by which Britain recognizes Iraq and military concessions are granted to Britain.

• **27 Dec**: Fifteenth All-Union Congress of the Communist party condemns all deviation from the party line as laid down by Joseph Stalin. Leon Trotsky and others are expelled from the party, and shortly afterwards exiled to the provinces (USSR).

• Beginning of the Communist organization of the districts of Jiangxi and Fujian. This becomes the core area of Communist control until 1934, when the Communists under Mao Zedong are dislodged from Nanjing by the Nationalists under Jiang Jieshi and begin the Long March (Chi).

SOCIETY

- **12 Feb**: 10 vessels collide and 3 sink in fog in the English Channel.

- **14 Feb**: An earthquake in Yugoslavia kills 600.

- **18 Feb**: 65,000 workers in Shanghai go on strike in protest at the presence of foreign troops in the city (Chi).

- **Feb**: Junkers Co (Ger) opens a regular air service to Tehran, Baku, Isfahan and Bushire in Persia (until 1932).

- **Feb**: Josef Pilsudski's government approves freedom of movement between Poland and the City of Danzig, administered by the League of Nations (Pol).

- **25 Mar**: First outside sports broadcast, of the Grand National, by the BBC (UK).

- **29 Mar**: Major Henry Segrave sets a new world land-speed record of 328.05 kph (203.841 mph) in his "Mystery" car, in Florida, taking the record from Malcolm Campbell (UK).

- **4–23 May**: International economic conference in Geneva (Swi).

- **13 May**: Collapse of the German stock market.

- **May**: Charles A. Lindbergh flies a solo nonstop flight from New York to Paris in *The Spirit of St Louis*, in 33 hrs 39 mins.

- **23 Jun**: UK Trades Disputes Act, outlawing general strikes and compulsory political levying by trade unions, is passed despite protests from Labour.

- **15 Jul**: General strike in Vienna after three Nationalists are acquitted of the murder of two Socialists (Aut). Riots break out as workers storm the Ministry of Justice and set it on fire. 89 people are thought to have died in the violence before order is restored.

- **17 Aug**: A hurricane destroys 22 Siberian villages, leaving 10,000 homeless (USSR).

- **Aug**: International congress of trade unions discusses the reduction of working hours.

- **Sep**: Babe Ruth hits his 60th home run of the baseball season, a record that stands for 34 years (USA).

- **Dec**: Decree by the Soviet government concerning a new organization of gold production (USSR).

- The Italian Fascist party introduces new labor legislation, the Labor Card.

- Nobel Peace Prize is won by Ferdinand Buisson (Fr) and Ludwig Quidde (Ger).

- Foundation of Vickers Armstrong aircraft company (UK).

- Opening of the motor racing circuit at Nürburgring (Ger).

- Golf: the first Ryder Cup is won by the USA under Walter Hagen.

- Shingled hair becomes all the rage for women and girls.

CULTURE

- **6 Feb**: 10-year-old violinist Yehudi Menuhin causes a sensation in Paris with his performance of Lalo's *Symphonie Espagnole*.

- **8 Apr**: First performance of Edgard Varèse's orchestral work *Arcana*, in Philadelphia, conducted by Leopold Stokowski (USA).

- **30 May**: Igor Stravinsky's opera-oratorio *Oedipus Rex*, with text by Jean Cocteau after Sophocles, is first given in a concert performance in Paris conducted by the composer; the first stage performance is in Vienna in 1928, conducted by Otto Klemperer (Fr).

- **14 Sep**: Death of dancer Isadora Duncan (USA) at the age of 49, when her scarf becomes entangled in the rear wheels of her car and strangles her (Fr).

- **Dec**: Broadway opening of Jerome Kern's musical *Showboat*, directed by Florenz Ziegfeld (USA).

- Nobel Prize for Literature won by Henri Bergson, French Philosopher.

- James Joyce: *Pomes Penyeach*, poems (UK).

- Ernest Hemingway: *Men Without Women*, novel (USA).

- D.H. Lawrence: *Mornings in Mexico*, travel literature (UK).

- Julien Benda: *La Trahison des clercs*, political commentary (Fr).

- Franz Kafka: *Amerika*, novel (posth., d. 1924) (Cze).

- Marcel Proust: *Le Temps retrouvé* (Time Regained), last volume of the seven-novel sequence *A la recherche du temps perdu*, begun in 1913 (posth., d. 1922) (Fr).

- Virginia Woolf: *To the Lighthouse*, novel (UK).

- William Faulkner: *Sartoris*, first of his novels to be set in the fictitious Yoknapatawpha County (published 1929) (USA).

- Hermann Hesse: *Der Steppenwolf*, novel (Ger).

- Sinclair Lewis: *Elmer Gantry*, novel (USA).

- Antonin Artaud: *Le Jet de sang* (The Jet of Blood), Surrealist play (Fr).

- Antonin Artaud and Roger Vitrac open the Théâtre Alfred Jarry, from which the "theater of cruelty" originates (Fr).

- Ernst Krenek's jazz-influenced opera *Jonny spielt auf* is premiered in Leipzig, and becomes a great success all over Europe (Ger).

- Kurt Weill's stage work *Royal Palace*, in a style much influenced by jazz and cabaret music, is premiered in Berlin (Ger).

- Henry Cowell founds his New Music Edition, publishing, among others, works by Carl Ruggles, Charles Ives, Anton Webern, Arnold Schoenberg and Edgard Varèse (USA).

- Leoš Janáček's *Glagolitic Mass* (completed 1926) receives its first performance (Cze).

- Arnold Schoenberg: String Quartet No 3 (Ger).

- Dmitri Shostakovich: Symphony No 2, "To October", with a chorus in the finale (USSR).

- Havergal Brian: Gothic Symphony (No.1) (since 1919) (UK).

- Duke Ellington, based at the Cotton Club in Harlem, New York, begins to make broadcasts of jazz numbers such as "Creole Love Call".

- Blues singers Ma Rainey and Bessie Smith begin to make recordings (USA).

- Cornet-player Louis Armstrong and his Hot Five record "St James Infirmary Blues" (USA).

- Martha Graham opens her school of Contemporary Dance in New York.

- The Surrealists align themselves politically with Communism (Fr).

- Stanley Spencer: *The Resurrection, Cookham*, mural painting (UK).

- Chaim Soutine: *Page Boy at Maxim's*, painting (Fr).

- Stuart Davis: *Egg-Beater No 2*, painting (USA).

- Architect Ludwig Mies van der Rohe organizes the first postwar Deutscher Werkbund exhibition, launching the International Style in architecture (Ger).

- Prototype factory-assembled house, the Dymaxion House, is designed by Buckminster Fuller (USA).

- Ludwig Mies van der Rohe designs the Weissenhofsiedlung, apartment building in the new International Style, Stuttgart (Ger).

- Karl Ehn: Karl Marx Hof, Vienna (Aut).

- J.J.P. Oud: Workers' Housing Estate, Hook of Holland (Neth).

- Abel Gance: *Napoléon*, epic historical film employing many experimental techniques, with music by Arthur Honegger (Fr).

- Fox's Movietone News, the first sound newsfilm, is released (USA).

- *They're Coming to Get Me*, first film with dialog, released (USA).

- Release of *The Jazz Singer*, starring Al Jolson, the first widely seen talkie (USA).

- Mae West is imprisoned for indecency in her Broadway show *Sex* (USA).

- Clara Bow achieves fame as the "It Girl", and becomes the symbol of the independent "free-spirited" young girl of the Jazz Age (USA).

SCIENCE

- Nobel Prize for Chemistry is won by Heinrich Wieland (Ger) for his work on the bile acids.

- Nobel Prize for Physics is won by Arthur Compton (USA) for his discovery of the Compton effect; and C.T.R. Wilson (UK) "for his method of making the paths of electrically charged particles visible by condensation of vapor".

- Nobel Prize for Physiology or Medicine is won by Julius Wagner von Jauregg "for his discovery of the therapeutic value of malaria inoculation in the treatment of dementia paralytica".

- George Lemaitre introduces the concept of the expanding universe, to explain the red shift in the spectra from distant galaxies, a theory that is eventually developed into the "Big Bang" theory (Bel).

- J.W. Anderson develops a hydraulic trace that makes possible the mechanical reproduction of complex patterns.

- Philo Farnsworth devises the dissector tube, contributing to the development of television (USA).

- W. Heitler and F. London provide bases for explaining the covalent bond using quantum mechanics (Ger).

- Niels Bohr states the notion of complementarity (Ger).

- Karl Landsteiner identifies blood groups M and N (Aut).

- W.K. Heisenberg propounds his "uncertainty principle" in quantum physics (Ger).

- Publication of T.H. Morgan's *Experimental Embryology* (USA).

- Publication of I.P. Pavlov's *Conditioned Reflexes* (USSR).

- G. Ramon and C. Zoellar are the first to immunize human beings against tetanus (Fr).

- H.S. Block introduces negative feedback in audio amplifiers to reduce distortion.

- Introduction of the pentode vacuum tube, providing an improved design for amplification, oscillation and pulse generation, and also for use in circuits for timing and counting.

- S. Junghans invents a process for continuous casting of nonferrous metals (Ger).

- First production of synthetic rubber (USA).

- Ford Motor Co introduces the Model A Ford, successor to the Model T (USA).

- Transatlantic telephone service begins between London and New York.

Medicine had been making increasing strides since the turn of the century in the battle against disease and infection. Insulin had been discovered, a new vaccine against tetanus had been developed, and the treatment of malaria had been furthered. Some of these achievements had arisen from systematic research, others were the result of accidental discovery. Penicillin the "wonder" antibiotic of the 1940s and 1950s, was the product of both. Alexander Fleming was working generally on molds and their medical application, but the discovery of penicillin came about through chance contamination. Initially the importance of this stray contamination was not realized, only later being followed up by scientists, Howard Florey and Ernst Chain. Even then the commercial production of the drug proved to be very difficult, and it was only fully developed because of the demands of World War II, when Anglo-American cooperation led to the mass production of penicillin to provide a treatment for the infection of battlefield wounds.

▲ Alexander Fleming, a bacteriologist at St Mary's Hospital, London, discovered penicillin through a chance contamination. It was to prove one of the most important medical discoveries of the century, saving millions of lives.

● **18 Jan**: Due to Norway's dependence on fishing and whaling, it annexes Bouvet Island, followed in 1929 by Peter Island (2 Feb) (both in the South Atlantic), Jan Mayen Island (8 May, in the Arctic) and finally (10 Jun 1931) a part of the East Greenland coast; the latter annexation is rejected by the Permanent Court of International Justice on 5 Apr 1933.

● **Jan**: Discovery by Austrian customs officials that Italy is supplying Hungary with arms provokes protests to the League of Nations by the Little Entente powers. A further discovery in Jan 1933 only confirms suspicions about the nature of the secret politics going on in Europe.

● **31 Mar**: Eleutherios Venizelos returns to Greece, and forms a cabinet on 4 Jul.

● **Mar**: The British colony of Malta becomes a dominion.

● **27 Apr**: Antonio de Oliveira Salazar becomes finance minister in Portugal, and reorganizes the battered Portuguese economy, eventually becoming premier on 5 Jul 1932, with dictatorial powers.

● **29 Apr**: British ultimatum to Egypt forces the latter to give up a bill that would have provided for freedom of public assembly, and on 19 Jul King Faud dissolves parliament until 1929.

● **3–11 May**: After Sino-Japanese clashes at Jinan, Japan temporarily seizes control of the Shandong railroads, provoking a Chinese boycott of Japan until 20 May 1929, when Japanese troops are withdrawn.

● **12 May**: Fascist Italy abandons universal suffrage and franchise is restricted to men over 21 paying syndicate rates or tax over 100 lire, reducing the electorate from 10 million to 3 million.

● **8 Jun**: Chinese Nationalist forces under Jiang Jieshi and other leaders occupy Beijing (renamed Beiping), and the capital is transferred to Nanjing. (› 10 Oct)

● **20 Jun**: Stephen Radich, Croatian Peasant party leader, is shot at in parliament by a Radical deputy. He dies on 8 Aug, and the Croat deputies withdraw from parliament (Yug).

● **1 Aug**: The Croats demand a federal system in Yugoslavia, and set up a separatist parliament in Zagreb in Oct, cutting ties with the Belgrade government. After efforts by the king to compromise, he proclaims a dictatorship on 5 Jan 1929, and all parties are dissolved on 21 Jan.

● **2 Aug**: Treaty of friendship is signed between Ethiopia and Italy for 20 years.

● **27 Aug**: Kellogg-Briand Pact is signed in Paris, providing for the universal renunciation of aggressive war, though no provision for sanctions against an aggressor is made. This is implemented by the League of Nations during a conference of 3–26 Sep, with the addition of compulsory arbitration, and accepted by 23 nations.

● **30 Aug**: After an all-parties conference in Lucknow adopts a resolution to press for dominion status, Jawaharlal Nehru, Subhas Chandra Bose and Srinivasa Iyengar organize the Independence of India League, with a program of complete independence (Ind).

● **23 Sep**: Treaty of friendship is signed between Greece and Italy, and a further one with Yugoslavia on 27 Mar 1929.

● **7 Oct**: Ras Tafari becomes king (*regus*) of Ethiopia, and initiates a policy of modernization.

● **10 Oct**: Temporary organic law in China provides for a council of state headed by a president. The Nanjing government is internationally recognized by treaties with 12 states (25 Jul–22 Dec). (›Nov)

● **6 Nov**: Republican Herbert Hoover is elected president of the USA.

● **Nov**: Hundreds of supporters of Leon Trotsky are arrested and exiled after demonstrations marking the anniversary of the 1917 revolution, as Stalin tightens his hold on power (USSR).

● **Nov**: After the assassination of Jhang Zuolin, military governor in Manchuria, by the Japanese on 4 Jun, his son Jhang Xueliang completes the unification of China by recognizing the government in Nanjing.

● Italian Communist party (founded 1921) leader, Antonio Gramsci is sentenced to 20 years' imprisonment. While there he writes his *Prison Notebooks*, in which he sets out his ideas for intellectual hegemony of the revolutionary movement.

● President Ahmed Zog of Albania declares himself king and is crowned in Tiranë.

- **11 Jan**: The Nakuru-Mbulamuti-Jinja railroad opens in Kenya.

- **19 Feb**: Briton Malcolm Campbell sets a land speed record of 475 km/h (206.35 mph) in "Bluebird" at Daytona (USA).

- **Feb**: Winter Olympics are held in St Moritz (Swi).

- **13 Mar**: 300 die and 700 are missing when a dam bursts near Los Angeles. (USA).

- **9 Apr**: Secularization of the Turkish constitution, since Islam is no longer considered the state religion. (> 3 Nov)

- **14 Apr**: In Bulgaria, an earthquake leaves 500 dead and 80,000 homeless. On 22 April, an earthquake in Corinth, Greece, leaves 50,000 homeless.

- **11 May**: The first scheduled television service begins, for 90 minutes three times a week (USA).

- **9 Jun**: Captain Charles Kingford-Smith arrives at Brisbane (Aus) after a trans-Pacific flight from California (USA).

- **18 Jun**: Amelia Earhart (USA) becomes the first woman to fly the Atlantic.

- **24 Jun**: Formal devaluation of the French franc from 19.3 US cents to 3.92 cents.

- **Jun**: US Agricultural Marketing Act encourages the establishment of cooperative farming associations.

- **Jun**: Official opening of a railroad from the Katanga Province to the Kassai River in the Belgian Congo, which provides communications between Leopoldville and the Katanga copper mines.

- **Jun**: Pan-American conference in Havana discusses the problems of trade between the American countries.

- **2 Jul**: Women are enfranchised on the same terms as men – universal suffrage over 21 (UK).

- **3 Jul**: The first commercially available television set, made by Daven Corporation, goes on sale (USA).

- **Jul**: The eighth modern Olympic Games opens in Amsterdam (Neth). Women's athletics are included in the Olympics for the first time.

- **15 Aug**: A railroad from Tabora (Tanganyika) to Mwanza (on the south shore of Lake Victoria) is opened.

- **16 Aug**: Compulsory military service is introduced in the USSR.

- **Aug**: Morris Motors launch the Morris Minor, a classic cheap family car (UK).

- **11 Sep**: Convention between Portugal and South Africa regarding transportation from the Transvaal to the coast, labor recruitment and other issues.

- **1 Oct**: Beginning of Joseph Stalin's first five-year plan in the USSR, designed to expand and develop heavy industry (mostly for defensive purposes) and collectivize farms, either into collective farms (*kolkhoz*) or state farms (*sovkhoz*). The kulaks, well-off middle-class farmers, are to be forced into the collective farms or executed. Stalin hopes to transform both industry and agriculture within ten years.

- **27 Oct**: Inauguration of the world's biggest reservoir, containing 36 km sq (14 square miles) of water, near Poona, India.

- **3 Nov**: The Roman alphabet is introduced in Turkey, first in newspapers and later in books; all Turks under 40 years of age are obliged to learn it.

- **20 Dec**: By treaty with China, Britain recognizes the Nanjing government and tariff autonomy; China agrees to abolish coast and interior duties.

- A wave of strikes by textile workers, railroad workers and others in Bombay is indicative of the rise in influence of the All-India Trade Union Congress (founded 1920) or the Communist party of India (founded 1923) (Ind).

- The Central Bank of China, established in 1924 in Canton, becomes the state bank.

- Record trading takes place on the New York Stock Exchange.

- J. Schick patents the electric razor which goes on sale in 1931 (USA).

- Umberto Nobile makes exploratory flights in the dirigible *Italia* from Spitsbergen over unexplored areas of the Arctic Ocean; on the return flight of his last trip, from Greenland, his airship crashes on the ice. Norwegian explorer Roald Amundsen dies during a rescue attempt in the Barents Sea.

- The Soviet government offers industrial concessions to foreign enterprises.

- Mrs Anastasia Chaikovsky, on a visit to New York, claims that she is the youngest daughter of the murdered czar of Russia.

- Federico García Lorca: *Romancero gitano*, a collection of gypsy ballads (Sp).

- Aldous Huxley: *Point Counter Point*, novel (UK).

- Radclyffe Hall's novel *The Well of Loneliness*, is banned because of its open treatment of lesbianism (republished 1949) (UK).

- Marina Tsvetayeva: *After Russia*, poem (Fr).

- André Breton: *Nadja*, novel (Fr).

- D.H. Lawrence's sexually explicit novel, *Lady Chatterley's Lover*, is published in Florence (It). It is not published in full in the UK until 1960, when Penguin Books are prosecuted for its publication under the Obscene Publications Act, but finally acquitted.

- Percy Wyndham Lewis: *The Childermass*, novel (UK).

- Evelyn Waugh: *Decline and Fall*, novel (UK).

- Martin Heidegger: *Being and Time*, existentialist philosophy text (Ger).

- Nobel Prize for Literature is won by Sigrid Undset (Nor).

- Leoš Janáček: *From the House of the Dead*, opera with text by the composer from Dostoyevski's novel, unfinished at the time of his death in Aug; it is first performed in 1930 (Cze).

- Kurt Weill: *Die Dreigroschenoper* (The Threepenny Opera), adapted from John Gay's *The Beggar's Opera* by Bertolt Brecht (Ger).

- Anton Webern: Symphony, for chamber orchestra (Aut).

- Charles Demuth: *I Saw the Figure 5 in Gold*, painting, inspired by William Carlos Williams's poem *The Great Figure* (USA).

- First meeting of the Congrès Internationaux de l'Architecture Moderne at La Sarraz (Swi).

- Ludwig Wittgenstein and Paul Engelmann: House for Gretl Wittgenstein, Vienna (Aut).

- Design magazine *Domus* founded, edited by Gio Ponti (It).

- Ecole de la Chambre Syndicale de la Couture is established to teach the craft of fashion (Fr).

- Designer Harley Earl (USA) is put in charge of General Motors' new Art and Color section.

- Columbia (EMI) takes over Pathé (UK).

- Release of the first full-length all-talking movie, with sound on film, *The Lights of New York* (USA).

- Luis Buñud and Salvador Dali, *Un Chier Andulou*, Surrealist film (Fr/Sp).

- Walt Disney creates his first Mickey Mouse cartoon, *Steamboat Willie* (USA).

- NBC organize a broadcasting link-up covering 48 states and dozens of well-known entertainers (USA).

- **8 Feb**: First international television tranmission from London to New York by John Logie Baird, who also demonstrates color television (UK).

- Nobel Prize for Chemistry is won by Adolf Windaus (Ger) for his research on the sterols and their connection with vitamins.

- Nobel Prize for Physics is won by Owen W. Richardson (UK) "for his work on the thermionic phenomenon".

- Nobel Prize for Physiology or Medicine is won by Charles Nicolle (Fr) "for the successful transmission of the exanthematous typhus fever to chimpanzees in the acute stages by the injection of a small amount of the body louse".

- Paul A. Dirac introduces a relativistic theory of the electron by combining quantum mechanics and relativity theory (UK).

- First working robot built by Rickards and A.H. Refell (UK).

- H. Geiger and W. Muller construct the "Geiger counter", an instrument for measuring radioactive radiation (Ger).

- Quartz clock, in which the oscillations of the quartz crystal control the clock's movement, is invented by J.W. Horton and W.A. Morrison (USA).

- H.N. Russell determines the abundance of elements in the solar atmosphere by studying the solar spectrum (USA).

- P.H. Diels and K. Adler develop a technique for combining atoms into molecules, useful in forming compounds such as synthetic rubber and plastics (Ger).

- G. Papanicolaou develops a technique for recognizing malignancy in cells taken from the vaginal wall, hence diagnosing uterine cancer (USA).

- F. Griffith discovers that genetic information is transmitted chemically (UK).

- Alexander Fleming (UK) discovers penicillin, when a chance mold appears on a Petri dish and destroys bacteria; but it is not until Howard Florey and Ernst Chain turn their attention to the discovery that its importance is recognized.

- C.V. Raman discovers the "Raman effect": a change in wavelength of light that is scattered by molecules (Ind).

- F. Boas's *Anthropology and Modern Life* refutes the fascist theory of the "master race".

- A. Szent-Györgyi discovers vitamin C (Hung/USA).

- F.A. Pareth founds radio chemistry (Ind).

- E.H. Land develops a polarizing filter (USA).

The crash of security prices on Wall Street, the New York stock exchange, in October 1929, has come to symbolize the beginning of the Great Depression, the crisis of the capitalist world economy during the 1930s, with its persistent high levels of unemployment and consequent social misery. However, the causes of the acute worldwide slump were complex and are still debated. The American economy, the dominant component of world capitalism since 1918, had already entered depression, with declines in both industrial production and the volume of building construction. Agriculture worldwide had been weak since the end of World War I and its difficulties had become even greater since 1927. Some manufacturing economies, such as Britain, had experienced severe structural problems throughout the 1920s, whereas other nations, like France, were hardly affected until the early 1930s. The slide into depression was marked by periods of limited recovery and in 1931 there were to be high hopes that the corner had been turned, which proved to be misplaced.

▲ Panic in New York followed the Stock Exchange crash of 24 October 1929. The crash began a vicious spiral of decline in industrial production resulting in high unemployment and mass impoverishment that reached out from the industrial center to affect developing and underdeveloped countries alike.

● **5 Jan**: General act of inter-American arbitration, similar to the League-endorsed Kellogg-Briand pact, is signed at the Pan-American conference in Washington (USA).

● **6 Jan**: The kingdom of the Serbs, Croats and Slovenes is renamed Yugoslavia, under a dictatorship established by King Alexander.

● **14 Jan**: Civil war begins in Afghanistan as King Amanullah is forced to abdicate. (‣ 8 Oct)

● **18 Jan**: Hilton-Young commission recommends a closer union of the British east African and central African colonies.

● **29 Jan**: Military insurgence in Ciudad Real, led by officers dissatisfied with the government of Primo de Rivera (Sp). (‣ 17 Mar).

● **Jan**: Leon Trotsky is expelled from the Soviet Union and takes refuge in Constantinople, and ultimately, via Norway, in Mexico. He continues to work, suggesting a Fourth International and writing a history of the Bolshevik Revolution, until his assassination in 1940 by a Stalinist agent. Many of his supporters are also arrested and exiled to Siberia. (‣ 17 Nov)

● **9 Feb**: Litvinov protocol, signed by Russia, Poland, Romania, Estonia and Latvia, provides for the renunciation of war.

● **11 Feb**: Lateran Treaties restore the temporal power of the pope over Vatican City with full sovereignty after more than 60 years, and the Italian government pays a total indemnity of 1,750,000,000 lire in a definitive settlement of its relations with the Papal States; but friction between the papacy and government continues.

● **17 Mar**: In Spain, agitation of intellectuals and students causes the government to close various universities to quell the unrest.

● **27 May**: The US Supreme Court upholds a decision denying citizenship to a Hungarian immigrant who is an avowed pacifist, even though Justice Oliver Wendell Holmes, opposing the decision, argues that the freedom to hold unpopular opinions is one of the most fundamental principles of the US constitution.

● **3 Jun**: Dispute between Peru and Chile over Tacna-Arica is resolved by US mediation: Chile receives Arica and Peru gains Tacna, with guarantees for a Peruvian port and transportation facilities at Arica.

● **5 Jun**: Second minority Labour government under J. Ramsay MacDonald, after an election on 30 May, resumes (1 Oct) diplomatic relations with the USSR broken off by the Baldwin ministry (UK).

● **21 Jun**: Another Mexican insurrection (Mar–Apr) leads to a compromise between state and church, modifying the state's anticlerical policies and easing the tension.

● **1 Jul**: The 1924 Immigration Act comes into force in the USA, in an attempt to maintain the country's ethnic composition of predominantly Northern European peoples.

● **4 Aug**: Serious attacks on Jews by Arabs in Palestine follow the Jewish demand for exclusive use of the Wailing Wall in Jerusalem.

● **11 Aug**: Zionist leader Chaim Weizmann forms the Jewish Agency in Zürich (Swi) to assist and encourage Jews worldwide to help develop and settle Israel.

● **Aug**: After the acceptance by Germany of the Young Plan, the Allied evacuation of the Rhineland begins (completed Jun 1930).

● **5–9 Sep**: French foreign minister Aristide Briand suggests a European federal union, but despite discussion by the League of Nations, the idea comes to nothing; it is not until after World War II that the concept is seriously considered.

● **22 Sep**: Confrontations take place between armed groups of Communists and Nazis in Berlin (Ger).

● **Sep**: The USA joins the International Court of Justice at The Hague (Neth).

● **8 Oct**: In a coup d'etat in Afghanistan by Gen. Muhammad Nadir Khan, he captures Kabul and is proclaimed (16 Oct) Muhammad Nadir Shah (until 1933). He continues the policy of modernization.

● **17 Nov**: Nikolai Bukharin and others of the rightist faction in the Politburo are expelled after advocating further concessions to peasants in the manner of Lenin's New Economic Policy. This leaves Joseph Stalin as unchallenged dictator (USSR).

● **18 Nov**: The USSR sends troops into Manchuria and over 200 Chinese are killed in the ensuing clashes.

● **Dec**: In the face of increasing violence between Muslims and Hindus, the All-India Congress again demands independence, threatening civil disobedience, and the Viceroy and Indian leaders discuss dominion status for the subcontinent.

● The Nazis are victorious in the Bavarian municipal elections.

SOCIETY

- **14 Feb**: St Valentine's Day massacre, when Chicago gangster Al Capone's mob kill six members of a rival gang. The gangs are involved in organized crime, especially the supply of illegal alcohol in the period of Prohibition.

- **11 Mar**: A new world land-speed record is set at 359 kph (223.2 mph) by Henry Segrave at Daytona Beach, Florida, in his streamlined car, "Golden Arrow" (USA).

- **16 May**: China regains tariff autonomy, when the powers grant her the right to fix her own tariff schedules.

- **7 Jun**: By the Young Plan (called after American banker Owen Young), Germany is to take responsibility for transferring payments from marks into foreign currency via the newly formed Bank for International Settlements in Basel. Germany is to pay a total annuity of 1,707,000,000 Reichsmarks until 1988, and Allied controls over the German economy will be removed. The plan is accepted during the Hague Conference of 3–6 Aug.

- **Jun**: Turkey introduces a high protective tariff to encourage industry.

- **Jul**: World congress of women's labor opens in Berlin.

- **Sep**: Collapse of the Allgemeine Osterreichische Bodencreditanstalt bank; it merges with the Osterreichische Creditanstalt (Aut).

- **24 Oct**: "Black Thursday": the great stock market crash on New York's Wall Street after the excesses of the Coolidge presidency (1925–29) precipitates the Great Depression (USA).

- **Dec**: Women in Turkey are given the vote.

- Unemployment in Germany reaches 3,200,000.

- Issue of the Kreuger loan of $125 million for 50 years (Ger) – a loan by Swedish financier Ivor Kreuger to the German government in return for industrial concessions.

- A total of 600 labor unions is reached in Japan, with a third of a million members; there are 576 labor disputes in 1929 in Japan.

- Foundation of Unilever (UK and the Netherlands).

- General Motors buys a quarter of the shares in the German AEG electricity company (USA/Ger).

- Beginning of tractor production in Stalingrad (USSR).

- The German airship *Graf Zeppelin* flies around the world, and Britain's new R101 makes its maiden voyage.

- Nobel Peace Prize is won by Frank Kellogg for his role in negotiating the Pact of Paris (USA).

- Clarence Birdseye markets his quick-freezing method for food, developed since 1917 (USA).

CULTURE

- **Jan**: Conductor Sir Thomas Beecham and the BBC agree to form a permanent symphony orchestra (UK).

- **14 Feb**: Dancer Josephine Baker is banned from performing in Munich for "indecency" (Ger).

- **29 Apr**: Sergey Prokofiev: *The Gambler*, opera based on Dostoyevski's novel of the same title, written during World War I and later revised, is first performed in Brussels.

- **19 Aug**: Death of Russian impresario Serge Diaghilev, whose activities with the *Ballets Russes* changed the course of classical ballet in the West, encouraging dancers such as Nijinsky and Pavlova and choreographers such as Fokine and Balanchine. He commissioned ballets from Stravinsky, Satie, Debussy, Ravel, Falla and many others, and sets from Russian stage designers such as Baks and Benois that changed the taste of a generation.

- Thomas Wolfe: *Look Homeward, Angel*, novel (USA).

- Robert Graves: *Goodbye to All That*, autobiographical account of the writer's life in the army during World War I (UK).

- Ernest Hemingway: *A Farewell to Arms*, novel of World War I (USA).

- Erich Maria Remarque, *All Quiet on the Western Front*, harrowing account of life on the German front in World War I (Ger).

- W.B. Yeats: *The Winding Stair*, poems (Ire).

- Federico García Lorca: *Poet in New York*, collection of Surrealist poems (published 1940) (USA).

- Jean Cocteau: *Les Enfants terribles*, novel (Fr).

- Tanizaki Jun-ichiro: *Some Prefer Nettle*, novel (Jap).

- Vladimir Mayakovsky: *The Bedbug*, play (USSR).

- Sean O'Casey's experimental antiwar play *The Silver Tassie* is rejected by W.B. Yeats and the Abbey Theatre in Dublin, confirming O'Casey's rift with Ireland.

- Virginia Woolf: *A Room of One's Own*, feminist essay (UK).

- Nobel Prize for Literature is won by Thomas Mann (Ger), principally for his novel *Buddenblooks*.

- Bruno Walter succeeds Wilhelm Furtwangler as conductor of the Leipzig Gewandhaus Orchestra (until 1933) (Ger).

- Paul Hindemith: *Neues vom Tage*, opera (Ger).

- William Walton: Viola Concerto (UK).

- Igor Stravinsky: *Capriccio*, for piano and orchestra (Fr).

- Salvador Dali (Sp) develops the "paranoiac-critical" technique of creating visual illusions in his paintings. Dali holds his first one-man show in Paris in Nov.

- Henry Moore: *Reclining Figure*, sculpture (UK).

- René Magritte: *The Use of Words I*, Surrealist painting (Fr).

- Max Ernst: *La Femme à 100 têtes*, engraving (Fr).

- Foundation of the Museum of Modern Art in New York, a symbol of the revolutionary significance of the work of avant-garde artists in the 20th century (USA).

- Diego Rivera: *Workers of the Revolution*, mural (Mex).

- Le Corbusier: Villa Savoye, Poissy, a domestic building in the International Style (Fr).

- Raymond Hood: McGraw-Hill Building, New York (USA).

- Ludvik Kysela: Bata Shop, Prague (Cze).

- Ludwig Mies van der Rohe: German Pavilion at the Barcelona Universal Exhibition, built of steel, concrete and glass (Sp).

- Oskar Schlemmer: *Glass Dance*, in which the dancer "wears" items of glassware (Ger).

- Raymond Loewy designs a streamlined duplicator for the Gestetner Co (USA).

- Opening of the film *Pandora's Box*, starring Louise Brooks, directed by G.W. Pabst (Ger).

- Alfred Hitchcock: *Blackmail* (USA).

- Opening of *Broadway Melody*, a film musical (USA).

- First Academy Awards ceremony (USA). The awards are given in recognition of outstanding work in the film industry in the previous year. Among the first winners are actress Janet Gaynor and director Frank Barzage.

- "Happy Days are Here Again" becomes a popular song (USA).

- The Decca company is launched by Edward Lewis.

- Tintin cartoon, drawn by Hergé, first appears in *The 20th Century* newspaper (Bel).

- American cartoonist Elzie Segar creates the spinach-eating, pipe-smoking sailor Popeye.

SCIENCE

- Nobel Prize for Chemistry is won by Hans von Euler-Chelpin (Ger-Swe) and Arthur Harden (UK) "for their investigations of the fermentation of sugar and fermentative enzymes".

- Nobel Prize for Physics is won by Louis de Broglie (Fr) "for his discovery of the wave nature of electrons".

- Nobel Prize for Physiology or Medicine is won by Christiaan Eijkman (Neth) and Frederick Gowland Hopkins (UK) "for their discovery of the growth-stimulating vitamins".

- P. Drinker invents the iron lung, an important life-support machine for polio victims (USA).

- Nuclear physicists Irène and Frédéric Joliot-Curie observe phenomena later identified by J. Chadwick as caused by the neutron (Fr).

- Construction begins on the Empire State Building (until 1931), which on completion becomes the tallest building in the world (USA).

- Werner Heisenberg and Wolfgang Pauli give their formulation of quantum field theory (Ger).

- G. Gamow proposes the "liquid drop" model of the atomic nucleus. This suggests that a large nucleus might be made to fission under impact (UK).

- Kodak develop a 16mm color film (USA).

- E.P. Hubble measures large red shifts in the spectra of extragalactic nebulae and shows that the speed of a galaxy's movement away is proportional to its distance from Earth, confirming the theory that the universe is expanding (UK).

- R. Goddard launches the first instrumental rocket, containing a barometer, a thermometer and a small camera (USA).

- Foam rubber is developed at Dunlop research laboratories by E. Murphy and W. Chapman (UK).

- E.D. Adrian, using an ultrasensitive galvanometer, is able to follow a single impulse in a single nerve fiber (USA).

- P. Levene discovers acids later known as DNA, the molecules transmitting genetic information in the nucleus of a living cell (USA).

- S. Levine is the first to make the connection between high blood pressure and fatal heart disease (USA).

- H. Berger publishes his paper on human electroencephalography based on experiments conducted since 1924 using primitive amplifiers (Ger).

- E. Doisy (USA) and A. Butenandt (Ger) independently isolate the female sex hormone estrone.

- Felix Wankel patents a rotary engine, though it does not become practical until 1951 (Ger).

- Publication of Albert Einstein's *Unitary Field Theory* (Ger).

1930-1939

Since the middle of the 19th century the skylines of the business centers of the major cities of the United States had come to be dominated by "skyscrapers". By 1910 in Chicago and New York there were 90 such buildings, each of more than 10 stories, and a decade later there were 450, including the splendid Chrysler building. However, this was not the tallest of these creations of the 1920s, for even as it reached completion it was being overshadowed by the erection of the Empire State Building, finished in 1931. The skyscraper came to symbolize the vigor of the New World, but this indicator of the rising tide of prosperity that the United States had enjoyed almost without interruption for the previous 40 years, became increasingly hollow after 1929. Economic confidence ebbed away during the depression experienced through the 1930s, despite initial attempts to ward this off with limited public works programs, and the imposition of the protectionist Hawley-Smoot tariff, were to no avail. The "good times" only fully returned with the mobilization of the American economy during World War II.

▲ **William Van Alen's Chrysler building in New York was a celebration of the Art Deco movement of the 1920s. It joined the growing cluster of skyscrapers which marked out Manhattan from the rest of New York.**

● **2 Jan**: All-India National Conference passes a resolution, proposed by Mahatma Gandhi, of complete independence from Britain and boycotts round-table conferences. (›14 Feb)

● **5 Jan**: Joseph Stalin gives orders for collectivization to be extended throughout the USSR, and for the kulaks (rich peasants) to be liquidated as a class, which may involve as many as 10 million people.

● **21 Jan**: An international naval conference meets in London between Britain, the USA, France, Italy and Japan to agree on ratios, sizes and schedules for their fleets. France and Japan block a move to abolish submarines. (›21 Apr)

● **28 Jan**: King Alfonso asks the dictator Primo de Rivera to resign and nominates Gen. Damaso Berenguer to restore the constitution of 1876 (Sp).

● **14 Feb**: Congress decides on a campaign of civil disobedience starting with a boycott of the salt tax (Ind). (›5 May)

● **23 Feb**: In the Dominican Republic, Rafael Leonidas Trujillo begins a 31-year dictatorship.

● **Feb**: Gen. Yen Hsi-shan, vice-commander-in-chief of the National Army, issues a challenge to the Nanjing government. On 5 Apr, the Nanjing government launches an expedition against Yen and his forces, finally re-establishing control in Oct (Chi).

● **28 Mar**: The new Nationalists change the name of Constantinople to Istanbul to rid it of its Greek associations (Tur).

● **30 Mar**: Agitation over financial problems leads to Heinrich Brüning replacing Hermann Muller's Socialist cabinet with a coalition of the right, but without a majority in the Reichstag (Ger).

● **31 Mar**: Revolt in Ethiopia leads to Ras Tafari becoming Emperor Haile Selassie of Abyssinia.

● **21 Apr**: London Naval Conference ends with the signing of a treaty limiting warships and aircraft carriers and regulating submarine warfare. However, France and Italy refuse to agree to the specific terms of the treaty.

● **1 May**: In Spain, calls to establish revolution by force lead to street fighting and rioting and a series of lightning strikes during the summer. (›12 Dec)

● **5 May**: Gandhi is arrested and taken to jail in Bombay, sparking off strikes, rioting and the burning of liquor shops. On 31 May, the viceroy announces new measures to deal with the campaign of civil disobedience (Ind). (›11 Oct)

● **22 May**: Syria is granted a constitution by France. It is to become a republic.

● **28 May**: Economic depression and social unrest in Bolivia lead to the fall of the regime of president Hernando Siles.

● **8 Jun**: The exiled Crown Prince Carol is elected king by the Romanian parliament.

● **21 Jun**: The Berlin chief of police bans the wearing of the swastika badge, which had been taken up by the National Socialists as a means of evading the German state authority prohibition against wearing uniform in public (Ger). (›13 Oct)

● **30 Jun**: Britain agrees to recognize the independence of Iraq upon Iraq's admission to the League of Nations, in 1932.

● **30 Jun**: The last French troops leave the Rhineland.

● **21 Jul**: Ismail Sidky Pasha becomes premier of Egypt, after the dismissal of nationalist premier Nahas Pasha.

● **5 Sep**: Revolution in Argentina is followed by the appointment of José Uriburu as president, supported by conservative groups.

● **14 Sep**: In German elections the Socialists win 143 seats and the Communists 77. The National Socialists increase their representation in the Reichstag from 12 to 107 seats (Ger).

● **11 Oct**: Pandit Jawaharlal Nehru, president of the Indian National Congress, is released from prison, but rearrested on 19 Oct (Ind). (›12 Nov)

● **13 Oct**: Nazi deputies arrive for the opening of the Reichstag in illegal uniform, causing uproar. Violent anti-Jewish demonstrations take place in the streets of Berlin (Ger).

● **16 Oct**: France announces its intention to build a line of defenses along the Franco-German border, which becomes known as the Maginot Line.

● **20 Oct**: The British government states its intention to allow a measure of self-government in Palestine whilst halting Jewish immigration and land purchase. Chaim Weizmann resigns as president of the Jewish Agency in protest.

● **26 Oct**: A revolutionary junta in Brazil seizes power and Dr Gertuilo Vargas is appointed as president.

● **30 Oct**: Turkey and Greece sign a treaty of friendship at Ankara.

● **4 Nov**: Franklin D. Roosevelt is reelected as governor of New York (USA).

● **9 Nov**: In the Austrian elections, a Christian Socialist government is elected; Nazis and Communists win no seats.

● **12 Nov**: In London, King George V opens a round-table conference on the future of India.

● **30 Nov**: National Socialists are victorious in municipal elections in Bremen (Ger).

● **12 Dec**: A mutiny at the garrison at Jaca in Spain, demanding a republic, is suppressed with difficulty. On 16 Dec a general strike is called in support of revolution.

SOCIETY

- **6 Jan**: The decision of Nova Scotia to end prohibition on sales of alcohol means that virtually the whole of Canada has some form of legal alcohol on sale.

- **18 Jan**: The Young Plan is signed by the German government. The amount of reparations (fixed at 38 billion marks) is payable in 59 annuities until 1988.

- **Jan–Mar**: Stalin seeks help from overseas to combat a threatened famine.

- **31 Mar**: Congress adopts the Public Building Act as a means of combating unemployment, and allocates $230 million to the program. On 4 Apr it allocates $300 million to a road building program (USA). (› 4 Nov)

- **24 Apr**: Amy Johnson, 27, becomes the first woman to fly solo from Britain to Australia.

- **30 Apr**: Workmen's Insurance Law passed: as a result 9 million workers are insured against sickness, old age and death (Fr).

- **2 May**: Dunning tariff imposes high duties but gives Britain preferential treatment (Can).

- **6 May**: Japan reluctantly consents to China's tariff autonomy; it is feared that Japan will lose a large market for her textile goods as a result.

- **7 May**: Bank for International Settlements (BIS) established in Basel (Swi) on capital of $500 million.

- **14 May**: The Hawley-Smoot Tariff Bill, raising duties on many items, is moving towards Congressional acceptance. A petition is signed by 1,028 economists protesting that such a law will have appalling national and international repercussions (USA).(›17 Jun)

- **17 May**: Issue of the international "Young" loan of 1.2 billion marks to commercialize the German reparations (USA).

- **19 May**: White women are enfranchised in South Africa.

- **26 May**: The International Olympic Committee recommends Berlin as host for the 1936 games.

- **May**: French minister of foreign affairs, Aristide Briand, publishes his memorandum for the establishment of a United Nations of Europe.

- **12 Jun**: Max Schmeling (Germany) beats Jack Sharkey (USA) for the world heavyweight boxing title (Ger).

- **13 Jun**: The Australian government announces its intention to place £1 million in next year's budget for the relief of unemployment.

- **14 Jun**: The British government says it will borrow £10 million to combat unemployment.

- **17 Jun**: President Hoover signs the Hawley-Smoot Tariff Bill. By the end of 1931, 25 countries will have taken retaliatory measures (USA).

- **12 Jul**: Cricketer Donald Bradman scores 334 runs for Australia in the Leeds Test Match (UK), and also the highest number of runs ever scored in one day of a Test Match – 309.

- **16 Jul**: President Hindenberg authorizes the budget by decree after the Reichstag refuses to pass it (Ger).

- **28 Jul**: British airship R101 begins its maiden flight across the Atlantic, arriving on 1 Aug after a flight of 77 hours 35 mins. On 5 Oct it explodes after crashing into a hillside in France; 44 people die.

- **30 Jul**: Uruguay wins the first football World Cup in Montevideo, beating Argentina 4–2.

- **7 Aug**: Unemployment figures in the UK reach 2 million, the highest total since 1921.

- **14 Aug**: The Church of England gives the go-ahead for the use of birth control where conception would be wrong and "if there is good moral reason why the way of abstinence should not be followed" (UK).

- **Aug**: The first British Empire (later Commonwealth) Games are held in Canada.

- **9 Sep**: The State Department issues an order prohibiting immigration because of mounting unemployment (USA).

- **8–12 Sep**: A special session of the Canadian parliament enacts emergency unemployment and tariff legislation.

- **29 Sep**: New York State Democrats adopt the abolition of prohibition as a policy (USA).

- **Sep**: Unemployment figures in Germany reach three million.

- **4 Oct**: The Commonwealth cabinet announces a plan to cut costs, including cuts in government and public service salaries (Aus).

- **5–12 Oct**: The first Balkan Conference is called at Athens in the hope of establishing better relations between the Balkan states and of improving the economic situation (Gr).

- **Oct**: Unemployment reaches 4.5 million in the USA. Hoover appoints a Committee on Unemployment Relief but aims to "preserve individual and local responsibility".

- **4 Nov**: Hoover asks Congress to appropriate up to $150 million for additional public works. Congress authorizes $116 million on 20 Dec (USA).

- **22 Dec**: Scandinavia, Holland, Belgium and Luxembourg sign the Oslo Agreement against raising tariffs without prior consultation.

- Wheat prices fall throughout the year as a result of increased production. By the end of the year, prices are at October 1894 levels.

- Turkestan-Siberian railroad is completed (USSR).

- Nobel Peace Prize is awarded to Nathan Söderblom (Swe).

CULTURE

- **9 Mar**: Premiere in Leipzig of Kurt Weill's opera *Rise and Fall of the City of Mahagonny*, with libretto by Bertolt Brecht (Ger).

- **1 Apr**: Josef von Sternberg's film *The Blue Angel* opens, starring Marlene Dietrich (Ger).

- **7 Dec**: Violinist Yehudi Menuhin, aged 13, plays to an audience of 7,500 at the Albert Hall, London.

- **11 Dec**: The film *All Quiet on the Western Front*, from Erich Maria Remarque's novel of 1929, directed by Lewis Milestone, is banned in Germany.

- Nobel Prize for Literature is awarded to Sinclair Lewis (USA).

- T.S. Eliot: *Ash Wednesday*, poem (UK).

- John Dos Passos: *The 42nd Parallel*, first volume in the trilogy USA (completed 1936) (USA).

- Hermann Hesse: *Narziss und Goldmund*, novel (Ger).

- Dashiel Hammett: *The Maltese Falcon*, detective fiction (USA).

- William Faulkner: *As I Lay Dying*, novel (USA).

- Hart Crane, *The Bridge*, poems that explore the myth of "America" (USA).

- W.H. Auden, *Poems 1930* (UK).

- The first issue of *Minotaure*, a primarily Surrealist journal (Fr).

- Igor Stravinsky: Symphony of Psalms, for chorus and orchestra (Fr).

- Leoš Janáček: *From the House of the Dead*, opera (Cze).

- Martha Graham: *Lamentation*, modern dance classic (USA).

- Thomas Hart Benton: *City Scenes*, painting (USA).

- Edward Hopper: *Early Sunday Morning*, painting (USA).

- Grant Wood: *American Gothic*, painting (USA).

- The Chrysler Building in New York City is completed. Designed by William Van Alen, it is the ultimate in Art Deco architecture.

- Le Corbusier completes his Villa Savoye at Poissy (Fr).

- Formation of the Tecton group of architects (UK).

- Moisei Ginzburg displays his "Green Moscow" city design project, an attempt to eliminate the distinction between urban and rural (USSR).

- *L'Age d'or*: Surrealist film by Luis Buñuel and Salvador Dali (Sp).

- Mervyn Le Roy: *Little Caesar* (starring Edward G. Robinson), the first in a remarkable cycle of gangster films (USA).

- *Anna Christie*, film based on Eugene O'Neill's play of 1921, Greta Garbo's first "talkie" and a great box-office success (USA).

SCIENCE

- **13 Mar**: Clyde Tombaugh, astronomer, announces the discovery of the planet Pluto (USA).

- **31 Mar**: The BBC broadcasts the first television talkie with perfectly synchronized sight and sound (UK).

- **6 Jun**: Frozen peas go on sale in Massachusetts. Produced by Clarence Birdseye, these are the first ever frozen vegetables to be marketed.

- **13 Jun**: O. Barton and W. Beebe make the first successful deep-sea dive in a bathysphere, off the coast of Bermuda.

- **30 Dec**: The first photograph of the Earth's curvature is exhibited in Cleveland, Ohio (USA).

- **Dec**: Du Pont announce the discovery of a new synthetic fiber material, Nylon, developed by Wallace Carrothers (USA).

- Frank Whittle, an aeronautical engineer, files a patent for a gas-turbine jet engine (UK).

- Hans Zinnsser develops an immunization against typhus (USA).

- M. Theiler develops a vaccine against yellow fever (SA).

- W. Pauli proposes a new particle (later known as the neutrino) to account for the apparent violation of the law of conservation of energy in beta decay (Ger).

- J.H. Northrop makes pepsin and trypsin in crystallized form, an important first step toward understanding the chemical nature of enzymes (USA).

- Introduction of the first tape recorder to use magnetized plastic instead of steel tape, allowing high quality sound and editing (Ger).

- Poly vinyl chloride (PVC), a flexible plastic substitute for rubber, is discovered by W.L. Semon (USA).

- Polystyrene, discovered in 1839, is commercially developed by IG Farbenindustrie (Ger).

- Hans Fischer wins the Nobel Prize for Chemistry for his work on chlorophyll (Ger).

- Karl Landsteiner wins the Nobel Prize for Physiology or Medicine for his definition of four human blood groups (USA).

- Chandrasekhara Raman wins the Nobel Prize for Physics for his laws of diffusion (Ind).

- A.E. Douglas determines the date of an American Indian site by using tree rings observed in artifacts, thus establishing the science of dendrochronology.

- V. Bush completes the differential analyser, an analog computer which can solve a variety of differential equations (USA).

- R. Drew invents Scotch tape (USA).

- The Bugatti Royale is launched, the largest production car ever built (It).

Spine-chilling horror movies such as "Frankenstein," starring Boris Karloff, and "Dracula" with Bela Lugosi in the title role, were box office successes at a time when escapism – for those who could afford it – was eminently desirable, for it was beginning to seem that capitalism itself was behaving like a monster out of control. By now the economic depression was well established throughout almost the entire Western world, and any hopes that trade would soon revive were dashed by a series of major bank failures. This financial crisis began in Austria, where remedial international action was prevented by French hostility toward a proposed customs union with Germany. In July the German banking system fell into disarray and in September a major international currency, the pound sterling, collapsed. This precipitated the almost complete disintegration of the international economic order so painstakingly built up during the years since the end of World War I. As the crisis grew, states generally rejected international solutions and turned inward to try to save themselves, initiating "beggar my neighbor" protectionist policies.

▲ James Whale directed the film of *Dracula*, starring Hungarian-born actor Bela Lugosi as the ever-fascinating Transylvanian vampire.

- **1 Jan**: Gen. Jorge Ubico makes himself president-dictator of Guatemala.

- **2 Jan**: President Florencio Harmodio Arosemena of Panama is forced to resign, and a military government is set up.

- **10 Jan**: Vyacheslav Molotov tells the Communist party Central Committee that half of Russian agriculture will be collectivized by the end of the year (USSR).

- **26 Jan**: Mahatma Gandhi is released from prison for discussions with the government (Ind). (› 4 Mar)

- **27 Jan**: Pierre Laval becomes premier after a cabinet defeat over the price of wheat (Fr).

- **8 Feb**: King Alfonso agrees the restoration of the constitution and fixed parliamentary elections for March. Following popular demand for a constituent assembly, Gen. Berenguer resigns (Sp). (›12 Apr)

- **16 Feb**: Pehr Svinhufvud becomes president of Finland, but his conservative leanings lead to fascist uprisings in 1932.

- **Feb**: Sir Oswald Mosley leaves the Labour party and organizes the fascist New party, precursor to the British Union of Fascists (UK).

- **Feb–Mar**: In Peru, a series of revolts obliges president Sanchez Cerro to give way to David Sanchez Ocampo. Fighting continues throughout the year. On 11 Oct elections result in a victory for Cerro with a majority of 50,000.

- **4 Mar**: The viceroy and Gandhi agree the Delhi Pact which allows Indians to make salt. The civil disobedience campaign is suspended and political prisoners are released (Ind).

- **8 Mar**: USSR-Turkish agreement on naval reductions in the Black Sea.

- **12 Apr**: Spanish municipal elections result in an overwhelming victory for the Republicans. Their leader, Alcala Zamora, calls for the abdication of the king. On 14 Apr King Alfonso leaves Spain without abdicating, and Zamora sets up a provisional government with himself as president (› 28 June).

- **22 Apr**: Treaty of friendship between Egypt and Iraq.

- **30 Apr**: Rebellion in Guangzhou. Forces under Gen. Zhan Zhaidong issue a declaration of independence for the provinces of Guangdong, Guizhou, Guanxi, Fujian and Hunan. On 5 May the People's National Convention in Nanjing adopts a provisional constitution that guarantees personal freedom and education (Chi). (›28 May)

- **13 May**: Paul Doumer is elected president of France.

- **28 May**: A new national government of China is inaugurated at Guangzhou by the rebels (Chi).

- **15 Jun**: Treaty of friendship and commerce between Poland and the USSR.

- **28 Jun**: Elections for the Spanish constituent assembly give the Republican-Socialist coalition a huge majority. On 9 Dec a Republican constitution is adopted with Alcala Zamora as president and Manuel Azana as premier.(› Society, 9 Dec)

- **10 Jul**: In a disagreement over fishing rights, Norway annexes East Greenland. Denmark protests and the matter is referred to the League of Nations (who ultimately find against Norway, in Apr 1933).

- **25 Jul**: Carlos Ibanez resigns as president of Chile because of general discontent with his economic measures; he is succeeded on 4 Oct by Juan Montero.

- **Jul**: Sino-Japanese crisis begins with violent anti-Chinese rioting in Korea. Japan refuses to compensate China for damage to property and China commences boycott of Japanese goods.

- **25 Aug**: After the Labour government resigns, a National Coalition government is formed with Ramsay MacDonald as prime minister (UK).(› 27 Oct)

- **3 Sep**: A new constitution is adopted in Yugoslavia, ending the royal dictatorship of King Alexander.

- **7 Sep**: Gandhi attends the second round-table conference on India in London, but it fails to reach agreement on representation of religious minorities. (› 28 Dec)

- **18 Sep**: Long-standing friction over Manchuria culminates in the Japanese invasion and siege of Mukden. On 24 Sep the Japanese government says it has no territorial designs on China but wants to protect Japanese nationals.

- **27 Oct**: In national elections in Britain, the National Coalition government wins 558 seats to the opposition's 56.

- **Oct**: A new public safety law is passed which declares the Republican Army illegal and sets up military tribunals to deal with sedition (Ire).

- **Nov**: Mao Zedong establishes the first Chinese Soviet Republic in the remote Jianxsi province.

- **2 Dec**: A coup d'etat enables Maximiliano H. Martinez to make himself president of Salvador.

- **11 Dec**: The Statute of Westminster defines the status of dominions of the British Commonwealth: they are allowed to have their own foreign policy and the option of exemption from British law.

- **19 Dec**: Fall of the Australian Labor government. The United Australia party forms a new government.

- **28 Dec**: Collapse of round-table conference: Britain is willing to grant India dominion status but Gandhi persists in demanding complete independence. Campaign of civil disobedience is resumed (Ind).

- **Introduction of universal suffrage in Ceylon.

SOCIETY

- **8 Jan**: Pope Pius XI issues an encyclical denouncing trial marriages and all forms of birth control and divorce.

- **Jan**: Unemployment in the USA is now 4.5 million and the Depression is spreading throughout the world.

- **Jan**: Bolivia defaults on foreign debt. Other Latin American countries follow suit, heralding the beginning of world financial collapse.

- **14 Feb**: $20 million drought aid bill becomes law, as drought claims the prairie lands of the southeastern USA.

- **3 Mar**: President Hoover signs a bill making Francis Scott Key's "Star Spangled Banner" the national anthem.

- **20 Mar**: Federal Council of Churches approves limited birth control.

- **21 Mar**: Plan is announced for a German-Austrian customs union. France, Italy and Czechoslovakia protest that this infringes Austrian sovereignty, and the plan is withdrawn.

- **25 Mar**: Nine young black youths are convicted of raping a white woman. The conviction is overturned by the US Supreme Court 1 Apr 1935, but the case becomes a *cause célèbre* for the nascent black rights movement.

- **4 Apr**: The first official air mail for Australia leaves England.

- **1 May**: The Empire State Building opens, the world's tallest structure (USA).

- **11 May**: Failure of Credit-Anstalt in Austria begins the financial collapse of Central Europe. (›16 Jun)

- **May**: A branch of Ford Motor Co opens in Cologne, Germany.

- **16 Jun**: Bank of England advances money to Austria but France withholds support. (›21 Jun)

- **20 Jun**: President Hoover proposes a one-year moratorium for reparations and war debts. French opposition causes delay, but on 6 Jul Hoover announces acceptance of moratorium by all creditor governments. (›11 Jul)

- **21 Jun**: Christian Socialist Karl Buresch forms a new coalition government between the Christian Socialists and Agrarians. The attempt to ward off total financial collapse lasts just under a year (Aut).

- **Jun**: An Italian loan spread over ten years is accepted by Albania. This subjects Albania to Italian economic control.

- **Jun**: Chancellor Heinrich Brüning declares German inability to continue payment of reparations.

- **1 Jul**: Opening of the Benguela-Katanga railroad completes the first trans-Africa railroad.

- **11 Jul**: Negotiations among the heads of the Reichsbank, Bank of England and Banque de France to counter the German financial crisis fail, leading to credit restrictions by the Reichsbank (Ger).

- **13 Jul**: Bankruptcy of German Danatbank leads to closure of all German banks until 5 Aug. Unemployment tops 6 million by the end of the year (Ger).

- **25 Jul**: May Committee reports an estimated budget deficit of £100,000 and proposes drastic economies, including reducing unemployment, which leads to a split in the cabinet (UK).

- **Jul**: Conference in London on German financial crisis.

- **3 Aug**: Massive floods on the Yangtze River kill 200,000 and inundate over 90,000 km sq (35,000 sq miles) (Chi).

- **19 Aug**: The Layton-Wiggin report calls for a six-month extension of foreign credit to Germany (UK).

- **24 Aug**: Chicago gangster Al Capone is sentenced to 11 years in prison for tax evasion (USA).

- **21 Sep**: Britain abandons the gold standard, followed by Sweden, Norway and Egypt. On 11 Dec Japan abandons the gold standard. By the end of the year only the USA, France, Switzerland, Belgium and Holland remain on the gold standard.

- **11 Oct**: Adolf Hitler wins the support of wealthy publisher Alfred Hugenberg and Ruhr industrialists Emil Kirdorf and Fritz Thyssen. The Nazi movement now has 800,000 members (Ger).

- **7 Dec**: Hundreds of hunger marchers descend on Washington, DC, demanding employment at minimum wages (USA).

- **9 Dec**: The new constitution in Spain proclaims complete religious freedom, separates church and state, secularizes education and dissolves the Jesuit Order.

- **Dec**: Conference in Jerusalem attended by 22 Muslim nations issues a warning against Zionism.

- Elijah Muhammad founds the Black Muslims in Detroit (USA).

- In Brazil, the National Coffee Department is established. It will supervise the destruction of large quantities of coffee in the hope of maintaining a good price in the world market.

- Alka Seltzer is introduced by Miles Laboratories of Indiana (USA).

- Nobel Peace Prize is awarded to Jane Addams (USA) and Nicholas Muarray Butler (USA).

CULTURE

- **Oct**: Moscow begins regular TV transmission (USSR).

- Erich Karlfeldt is posthumously awarded the Nobel Prize for Literature (Swe).

- Antoine de Saint Exupéry: *Vol de nuit* (Night Flight), novel written in the form of reportage (Fr).

- Pearl S. Buck: *The Good Earth*, novel set in China (USA).

- V. Sackville-West: *All Passion Spent*, novel (UK).

- Hermann Broch: *The Sleepwalkers*, novel (Ger).

- William Faulkner: *Sanctuary*, novel (USA).

- Virginia Woolf: *The Waves*, novel (UK).

- Eugene O'Neill: *Mourning Becomes Electra*, play (USA).

- First LP recording of Beethoven's 5th Symphony released by RCA-Victor.

- Sergei Rachmaninoff's music is condemned in USSR as decadent.

- Maurice Ravel writes his *Piano Concerto for the Left Hand* for the one-armed pianist, Paul Wittgenstein (Fr).

- William Walton: *Belshazzar's Feast*, oratorio (UK).

- Salvador Dali: *The Persistence of Memory*, sometimes described as the archetypal Surrealist painting (Sp).

- Pierre Bonnard: *The Breakfast Room*, painting (Fr).

- Otto Dix: *Girls*, painting (Ger).

- Henri Matisse: *The Dance*, murals at Barnes Foundation, Pennsylvania (USA).

- Foundation of the Abstraction-Creation association by Theo van Doesburg, Fernand Léger, Piet Mondrian, Kurt Schwitters, Wassily Kandinsky and others (Fr).

- Palace of the Soviets competition is won by Soviet architect B.M. Iofan (USSR).

- Martha Graham premieres her modern dance classic, *Primi-Mysteries* (USA).

- *City Lights*, film starring Charlie Chaplin – one of the last silent films (USA).

- *The Man Hunter*, film, the debut of Rin Tin Tin, also starring Charles Delaney (USA).

- *Animal Crackers*, film starring the Marx Brothers (USA).

- Fritz Lang: *M.*, film starring Peter Lorre (Aut).

- *Frankenstein*, film with Boris Karloff (USA).

- James Whale: *Dracula*, film with Bela Lugosi (USA).

- Walt Disney wins his first Academy Award with *Flowers and Trees*, first animated cartoon in Technicolor (USA).

SCIENCE

- **Jun**: Wiley Post and Harold Gatty circumnavigate the globe by air in 8 days, 15 hours and 51 minutes (USA).

- The Kinetic Chemical Corporation begins to commercially produce Freons – a non-flammable, non-toxic, low-boiling liquid refrigerant, later held responsible for deterioration of the ozone layer (USA).

- Chemist L.C. Pauling proposes that the phenomenon of resonance causes the stability of the benzene ring (USA).

- Electron microscope is developed by E. Ruska and R. Ruedenberg, working independently (Ger).

- The German Inland Ice expedition sets up metereological stations for winter observation in Greenland.

- The Antarctic Research Expedition, a British, Australian and New Zealand venture, explores the 4,000 km (2,500 mile) uncharted coastline and demonstrates that it is continuous.

- E. O. Lawrence and colleagues invent the cyclotron, a spiral atom-smasher that will prove essential in the study of the nuclear structure of atoms.

- Friedrich Bergins and Carl Bosch win the Nobel Prize for Chemistry for their work on high-pressure chemistry (Ger).

- O. H. Warburg wins the Nobel Prize for Physiology or Medicine for his discovery of respiratory enzymes (Ger).

- B. Rossi demonstrates that cosmic rays are powerful enough to penetrate a meter or more into solid lead.

- Marconi markets the micro-ray radio which uses ultra short waves. Pope Pius XI uses the system to link the Vatican to the papal summer residence at Castel Gandolfo (It).

- The first teleprinter exchange, prelude to the telex system, goes into operation in London (UK).

- E. Goodpasture uses live chick embryos to culture vaccinia virus, a breakthrough in technique for culturing viruses (UK).

- Paul Karrer isolates Vitamin A (Switz).

- Stereo sound recording is patented by A. Blumlein (USA).

- K. Goedel shows that the logical grounds for arithmetic are incomplete. This becomes accepted as Goedel's Proof, a landmark in modern mathematical logic (Aut).

- K.G. Jansky finds radio interference from the Milky Way, thus launching the modern discipline of radio astronomy (USA).

- A. Butenandt isolates the male sex hormone androsterone (Ger).

- Harold Urey and colleagues discover "heavy hydrogen", later named deuterium (USA).

1932

POLITICS

For many urban industrial workers the Depression had begun in 1929, but farmers all over the globe had felt the pinch of hard times for nearly a decade. By the early 1930s the world was hungry and overstocked with foodstuffs. World War I had increased European self-sufficiency, while the growth of demand for food was slowing with the decline in population expansion. The price of agricultural products such as cotton and wool was affected by the development of artificial fibers. While the growth in demand had slackened, agricultural prices fell because of a rise in supply. Farming was becoming increasingly mechanized and scientific. The consequent global pattern of agricultural poverty was not a simple one – a division between the advanced economies and the primary producers of the temperate world – for both the United States and Europe contained sizeable farming communities. Here, the presence of an agricultural crisis from the early 1920s had been partly masked by relative industrial prosperity. But in the 1930s there were no longer jobs in the towns for redundant agricultural workers, while the attempts of the industrial nations to protect their farming sectors worsened the position of food producers elsewhere.

▲ In the United States, the hardships of the agricultural depression of the 1930s were worsened by the onset of drought, which laid waste the prairie states, driving farmers from their homes in despair.

● **4 Jan**: The new viceroy, the Earl of Willington, refuses to discuss with Mahatma Gandhi ordinances imposed on Bengal, the northwest frontier and the United Provinces. Gandhi and the National Congress revive the campaign of civil disobedience.

● **7 Jan**: US Secretary of State Stimson protests against Japanese aggression in Manchuria and says that the USA will recognize no gains made through armed force – the Stimson Doctrine.

● **22 Jan**: Government troops crush a Communist uprising in northern Spain.

● **28 Jan**: Japanese occupy Shanghai, supposedly to "protect their nationals from banditry". The USA, Britain, France and Italy send forces to support the Chinese, who continue their boycott of Japanese goods. (› 18 Feb)

● **2 Feb**: 60 states including the USA and USSR attend a Geneva disarmament conference at which a French proposal for an international police force is opposed by Germany. Germany leaves the conference on 14 Sep. (› 11 Dec)

● **16 Feb**: In national elections the Republican (Fianna Fail) party, led by Eamon De Valera, is voted into office for the first time but with no overall majority. De Valera is elected president on 9 Mar (Ire).

● **18 Feb**: Japanese forces set up a puppet government in Manchuria and declare an independent country of Manzhouguo (Chi). (› 3 Mar)

● **21 Feb**: Discontent with financial policy forces Pierre Laval's government to resign; A. Tardieu forms a new government (Fr).

● **3 Mar**: After two months of fighting, during which the Japanese bomb Shanghai from the air, a truce is agreed. On 5 May China agrees a demilitarized zone with Japan and ends boycott of Japanese goods.(› 15 Sep)

● **13 Mar**: Field Marshal Paul von Hindenburg wins the national presidential election but fails to win overall majority. New election on 10 Apr reelects Hindenburg with 19 million votes to Hitler's 13 million and the Communists' 3 million (Ger).

● **24 Apr**: National Socialists gain election successes in Prussia, Bavaria, Württemberg and Hamburg (Ger).

● **15 May**: Murder of premier Ki Inukai ends party government in Japan. New government is organized under Viscount Makoto Saito.

● **31 May**: Chancellor Brüning resigns after disagreement with Hindenburg. New chancellor Franz von Papen organizes a "ministry of barons" excluding the National Socialists (Ger).

● **13 Jun**: Anglo-French pact of friendship signed at Lausanne.

● **29 Jun**: A long-standing border dispute between Bolivia and Paraguay over the Gran Chaco turns into open warfare.

● **5 Jul**: Antonio de Oliviera Salazar becomes premier with virtual dictatorial powers (until 1968) (Port).

● **18 Jul**: Turkey accepts an invitation to join the League of Nations.

● **20 Jul**: Chancellor von Papen removes the Social Democratic premier of Prussia by a show of force and brings Prussian autonomy to an end. Martial law is imposed on Berlin and Brandenburg, ostensibly because of civil disorder resulting from Nazi storm-troop activity (Ger).

● **25 Jul**: The USSR concludes nonaggression pacts with Poland, Estonia, Latvia and Finland, and on 29 Nov concludes a similar pact with France.

● **31 Jul**: Reichstag elections produce no overall majority for any party. National Socialists win 230 seats to Social Democrats' 133, Center's 97 and Communists' 89. On 13 Aug Adolf Hitler refuses Hindenburg's offer of vice-chancellorship (Ger).(› 17 Nov)

● **16 Aug**: Britain presents a plan for limited and separate representation for untouchables, renamed Harijans or "children of God" by Gandhi, but it is unacceptable to Gandhi who begins a "fast unto death". On 24 Aug the Poona Pact increases representation for untouchables and Gandhi ends his fast (Ind).

● **15 Sep**: The Japanese issue a protocol proclaiming Manzhouguo as a protectorate (Chi).

● **22 Sep**: Saudi Arabia takes its modern name.

● **24 Sep**: Per A. Hansson becomes premier of a socialist government in Sweden.

● **25 Sep**: Catalonia is granted autonomy, its own flag, language and parliament (Sp).

● **2 Oct**: Lytton Report to League of Nations recommends setting up of an independent government in Manzhouguo under Chinese sovereignty.

● **3 Oct**: Iraq joins the League of Nations and achieves full independence from UK.

● **4 Oct**: Count Stephan Bethlen resigns, Julius Gombos assumes power and allies with Fascist Italy (Hung).

● **8 Nov**: Franklin D. Roosevelt wins the presidential election in a Democrat landslide (USA).

● **17 Nov**: After further elections following the dissolution of the Reichstag on 12 Sep produce no majority again, von Papen resigns.

● **11 Dec**: No Force declaration of Britain, France, Germany and Italy. Signing of Geneva Protocol giving Germany equal rights with other nations.

● **19 Dec**: Third round-table conference on India begins in London. It ends on 24 Dec, and Britain announces the release of 28,000 prisoners including Gandhi.

SOCIETY

●**22 Jan**: The beginning of the second Soviet five-year plan to develop heavy industries. During 1932 famine devastates the country.

● **22 Jan**: In Guatemala, three towns are destroyed by the eruption of the volcano, Acatenango.

● **22 Jan**: Establishment of the Reconstruction Finance Corporation, an institution for financing the creation of work and encouraging business activity (USA).

● **4 Feb**: Winter Olympics open at Lake Placid (USA).

● **7 Feb**: The Scandinavian states join with Holland and Belgium in the Oslo Convention, a scheme to facilitate economic cooperation.

● **8 Feb**: Bulgaria renounces reparation payments.

● **24 Feb**: At Daytona Beach, Florida (USA), British racing driver Sir Malcolm Campbell sets a new land speed record of 408.721 kph (253.968 mph).

● **27 Feb**: Congress passes the Glass-Steagall Act authorizing the Federal Reserve Bank to expand credit and release government gold to business interests (USA).

● **29 Feb**: There is heated opposition to the Protective Tariffs Act which ends free trade (UK).

● **Feb**: Government assistance program for agriculture is announced (Fr).

● **2 Mar**: Aviator Charles Lindbergh's infant son is kidnapped. He is found murdered on 12 May; in September Bruno Hauptmann is arrested and convicted (USA).

● **Mar**: After the suicide of Kreuger, the Kreuger match company collapses with serious implications for the current financial crisis (Swe).

● **9 May**: Neon lights are used to illuminate the first flashing advertisements in the world at London's Piccadilly Circus (UK).

● **16 Jun**: At Lausanne, the Reparations Conference accepts proposal for a final reparations payment; but on 28 Dec US Congress refuses to accept proposal, and the Young Plan continues in effect.

● **18 Jun**: Enactment of new language regulations. French becomes the official language of Walloon provinces and Flemish that of Flanders (Bel).

● **19 Jul**: Conclusion of the Ouchy Convention between Belgium, Luxemburg and Holland, which aims to reduce economic barriers.

● **21 Jul**: Imperial economic conference between Great Britain, Australia, New Zealand, South Africa, Rhodesia, Ireland and Canada negotiates new trade tariffs and gives preferential status to dominion and British products.

● **30 Jul**: Summer Olympics opens in Los Angeles (USA).

● **Jul**: India competes in its first cricket Test Match.

● **Jul**: Japan imposes foreign exchange control.

● **Aug**: Von Papen announces an economic program for increasing business activity by the creation of work (Ger).

● **14 Sep**: The Belgian government is granted extraordinary powers to deal with an alarming budget deficit.

● **1 Nov**: London police repel a raid on Parliament by the jobless after a three-hour riot (UK).

● **10 Nov**: Britain and France ask the USA for debt relief. Greece defaults and Hungary announces that it cannot pay war debts.

● **21 Dec**: First Christmas broadcast by a reigning monarch, George V (UK).

● **26 Dec**: Earthquake in Gansu Province leaves 70,000 dead (Chi).

● **27 Dec**: South Africa leaves the gold standard.

● **27 Dec**: Radio City Music Hall opens in New York – the largest theater in the world devoted to cinema, it seats 6,000.

● France establishes the National Bank for Commerce and Industry as a successor to the National Credit Bank.

● Amelia Earhart becomes the first woman to make a solo flight across the Atlantic (from Newfoundland to Northern Ireland).

● Second Workers' Olympics takes place in Vienna, organized by the Workers' Sports Movement. It features over 100,000 competitors from 26 countries.

● Annual sales of radios soar to 4 million in the USA; over half of all homes have a set. In Britain, one and a half million sets are sold in the year.

● The first dishwasher is marketed (USA).

● The flexible rubber ice-tray is invented (USA).

CULTURE

● **Nov**: Walt Disney's Mickey Mouse and Silly Symphonies appear in color for the first time.

● Aldous Huxley: *Brave New World*, novel (UK).

● Louis-Ferdinand Céline: *Journey to the End of the Night*, novel (Fr).

● Boris Pasternak: *Second Birth*, poems (USSR).

● Ernest Hemingway: *Death in the Afternoon*, novel (USA).

● Damon Runyon: *Guys and Dolls*, short stories (USA).

● Nobel Prize for Literature is awarded to John Galsworthy (UK).

● Duke Ellington, creator of *Creole Rhapsody*, is recognized as the first composer of jazz and the first black musician of distinction (USA).

● Arnold Schoenberg: *Moses and Aaron*, opera (first two acts; the third was never completed) (Ger).

● Carl Ruggles: *Suntreader*, orchestral work (USA).

● *42nd Street*, musical with choreography by Busby Berkeley.

● Sir Thomas Beecham is appointed director of the new Royal Philharmonia Orchestra in London.

● George Gershwin: "I Got Rhythm", popular song (USA).

● Jay Gourlay: "Brother, can you spare a dime?", popular song (USA).

● Alexander Calder exhibits "stabiles" followed by "mobiles" (USA).

● Georgia O'Keeffe: *White Canadian Barn No. 2*, painting (USA).

● Stanley Spencer: *May Tree, Cookham*, painting (UK).

● Max Beckmann: *Seven Triptychs*, painting (Ger).

● Georges Rouault: *Christ Mocked by Soldiers*, painting (Fr).

● Ben Shahn completes his series of paintings of Sacco and Vanzetti, the two Italian anarchists executed in the USA in 1927 despite worldwide protests of their innocence (USA).

● Bauhaus design school is forced to move to Berlin, where it remains in an old warehouse until closed down by the Nazis in 1933.

● Industrial designer Norman Bel Geddes's book *Horizons* helps to spread Modernist ideas in design (USA).

● Fritz Lang: *The Testament of Dr Mabuse*, film (Ger).

● *Glad Rags to Riches*, film starring Shirley Temple, aged three (USA).

● *Night after Night* – film debut of Mae West (USA).

● Johnny Weissmuller, former Olympic swimming champion, makes his first Tarzan film, *The Ape Man* (USA).

● Opening of the first Venice Film Festival (It).

SCIENCE

● **19 Mar**: Sydney Harbor Bridge opens after seven years' construction (Aus).

● Nobel Prize for Chemistry is won by Irving Langmuir (USA) for his work in the field of surface chemistry.

● Nobel Prize for Physiology or Medicine is won by Edgar D. Adrian and Charles S. Sherrington (UK) for their work on the functions of neurons.

● Werner Heisenberg wins the Nobel Prize for Physics for his discovery of quantum mechanics (Ger).

● C.D. Anderson discovers the positron in cosmic rays and in 1933 succeeds in producing positions by gamma irradiation (USA).

● The use of vitallium, a non-corrosive metal, revolutionizes joint surgery (USA).

● K.G. Jansky establishes a foundation for the development of radio astronomy (USA).

● R. Kuhn isolates riboflavin, Vitamin B_2 (Ger).

● Adolf Windaus discovers the provitamin D_3, a sterol naturally produced in human and animal bodies.

● Laidlaw and Dunkin develop an inoculation against distemper in dogs (UK).

● Chemist W.H. Carothers synthesizes polyamide (USA).

● G. Domagk discovers the first sulfa drug, Prontosil, an important antibacterial agent (Ger).

● H. Weese uses the first intravenous anesthetic, hexobarbitone sodium (Ger).

● Zuider Zee drainage scheme completed, greatly increasing the land available for agriculture (Neth).

● C.G. King isolates vitamin C from lemon juice (USA).

● J. Cockcroft and E. Walton build the first particle accelerator and split the atom for the first time by bombarding lithium with protons (UK).

● D. Tietjens of the Westinghouse Electric Corporation discovers that streamlining can cut wind resistance in trains by over 60 percent (USA).

● R.S. Willows applies for a patent for his discovery of a crease-resistance process for fabric (UK).

● RCA demonstrates a television receiver with a cathode-ray picture tube (USA).

● J. Chadwick deduces the existence of the neutron, though its lack of electrical charge makes it impossible to detect directly (UK).

● Auguste Piccard enters the stratosphere in a sealed aluminum shell lifted by a balloon, and reaches 53,153 ft (16,201 m) the first venture by a human into the stratosphere.

The impact of the Depression upon German society led to political polarization and instability. With growing urban unemployment and heightened rural discontent, many shifted their allegiance to the outer extremes of the political spectrum. From the elections of 1930 the National Socialists gained substantially, harvesting the growing tide of despair and resentment that had been present since the immediate aftermath of the war. After the autumn of 1931 Hitler had the open support of sections of the German business community, overtly hostile to socialism since the early 1920s. The two national elections of 1932 produced no overall result. Hitler's victory at the ballot box in March 1933 was followed by suppression of civil liberties. The Nazi party became the only legal political body in Hitler's Germany and opposition in the elections of November 1933 could only be expressed by voters spoiling their ballot papers.

▲ Adolf Hitler came to power in March 1933. By 14 July the Nazi party had become the only legal party in Germany.

- **3 Jan**: Political tensions lead to premier De Valera dissolving the Dáil; in elections on 24 Jan, the Fianna Fail party gains a majority of one (Ire).

- **13 Jan**: US Congress passes the Howes Cutting Bill which proposes an independence plan for the Philippines while retaining US economic and military influence; the Philippine government rejects the plan in Oct.

- **28 Jan**: Kurt von Schleicher's ministry falls. Adolf Hitler is appointed chancellor by Hindenburg, but the Reichstag is dissolved for lack of a clear party majority, and new elections are set for 5 Mar (Ger).

- **31 Jan**: After a government crisis over the budget deficit Joseph Paul-Boncour resigns and Edouard Daladier becomes premier (Fr).

- **16 Feb**: The Little Entente countries (Cze, Rom, Yugo) hold a conference in Geneva and set up a permanent governing body in response to the rise of the Nazis in Germany.

- **27 Feb**: The Reichstag building is destroyed by fire. Hitler denounces the fire as a Communist plot; the Communist party is proscribed and Hindenburg suspends civil liberties and freedom of the press (Ger).

- **5 Mar**: Reichstag elections: the Nazis win 44 percent of the votes (288 seats), their allies the Nationalists 8 percent (52 seats); Socialists win 120 seats, Communists 81 and the Center 74 (Ger).

- **6 Mar**: Engelbert Dolfuss dissolves parliamentary government and bans parades and gatherings in response to Nazi rise to power in Germany (Aut).

- **12 Mar**: Hindenburg abandons the flag of the German republic and orders the Nazi swastika and the imperial flag to be flown side by side (Ger).

- **16 Mar**: Geneva Disarmament Conference: the British propose that European armies be reduced by half a million. Germany leaves the conference and the League after rejection of her rearmament plans.

- **16 Mar**: The victory of the National Socialists in Germany leads the Belgian government to take precautionary measures: 150 million francs are allocated to fortifications along the Meuse.

- **19 Mar**: Mussolini proposes a pact with Britain, France and Germany. The Four-Power Pact is signed on 15 Jul but proves to be of little importance.

- **20 Mar**: First concentration camp opened at Dachau for political prisoners (Ger).

- **23 Mar**: Enabling Act is passed by the Reichstag, allowing Hitler to rule by decree for four years. Hitler proceeds to effect a revolution in political, economic and social terms.

- **27 Mar**: League of Nations condemns Japanese military actions in Manchuria, and Japan leaves the League.

- **4 Apr**: Foreigners are barred from leaving Germany without a police permit.

- **2 May**: Hitler's police seize the headquarters of all the independent trade unions and place their leaders under arrest. On 17 May strikes and lockouts by workers are forbidden (Ger).

- **3 May**: Oath of allegiance to the British Crown is removed from the Irish constitution and Irish appeals to the Privy Council are made illegal.

- **4 May**: Finnish government forbids the military organization of political parties and groups.

- **26 May**: Australia claims one-third of the Antarctic continent, emphasizing its economic importance.

- **28 May**: In the city of Danzig, National Socialists win 39 out of 72 seats in the Senate; on 20 Jun the Nazi take over government and ally themselves with Nazi Germany.

- **31 May**: After several months of sporadic fighting the Japanese advance on Beijing. China and Japan agree a truce and a demilitarized zone.

- **14 Jul**: National Socialist party is declared the only legal party (Ger). (› 12 Nov)

- **15 Jul**: All-India Congress decides on a resumption of civil disobedience. On 1 Aug Gandhi is arrested and sentenced to one year in prison, but released after a few days on health grounds.

- **5 Aug**: Poland concludes an agreement with the city government of Danzig guaranteeing fair treatment of Polish inhabitants and assuring Danzig a share of Polish sea trade.

- **3 Sep**: Irish opposition parties of National Guard and Center form the United Ireland (Fine Gael) party under Eoin O'Duffy. William Cosgrave takes over as leader on 22 Sep.

- **11 Oct**: The nations of the Western Hemisphere sign a nonaggression and conciliation treaty in Rio de Janeiro.

- **12 Nov**: 92 percent of the votes in the Reichstag elections are for the Nazi list of candidates. There are no opposition candidates, but 3 million Germans express disapproval through invalid ballots (Ger).

- **16 Nov**: Syria and France sign a treaty committing themselves to a 25-year alliance and giving France control of foreign relations, army and finance.

- **16 Nov**: The USA resumes diplomatic relations and trade relations with the USSR (suspended since 1919).

- **19 Nov**: First official elections for the Cortes (parliament) result in parties of the right gaining 44 percent and the left 21 percent, which leads to a series of unstable governments (Sp).

- **29 Dec**: Ion Duca, Liberal premier of Romania, is murdered by the Iron Guard and succeeded by George Tartarescu.

- **14 Feb**: Closing of all banks in the state of Michigan gives warning of an impending banking crisis. Bank closures spread and reached a climax on 3 Mar (USA).

- **23 Feb**: British High Commissioner in Palestine rejects an Arab demand for restricted immigration and for making the sale of Arab lands illegal. Rejection of demands leads to an Arab policy of noncooperation and a boycott of British goods.

- **4 Mar**: Roosevelt persuades Congress to create a series of New Deal Agencies to provide welfare (USA).

- **4 Mar**: Federal Deposit Insurance Corporation is established to protect savers. (›27 May)

- **6 Mar**: US business virtually at a standstill; banks are closed for four days by presidential proclamation and an embargo placed on the export of gold so as to protect the gold reserve.

- **12 Mar**: Roosevelt inaugurates radio "fireside chats", showing the growing awareness of the power of mass communication (USA).

- **Mar**: Accession to power of the National Socialist party brings a reorganization of economic associations in a corporative pattern, and measures to create work (Ger).

- **1 Apr**: Persecution of the Jews begins with a national boycott of Jewish goods and professions (Ger).

- **8 Apr**: Emergency Relief Appropriation Act appropriates $4,000 million to be used, at the president's discretion, for relief and work relief and to increase employment (USA).

- **25 Apr**: Canada abandons the gold standard, and on 30 Apr USA follows.

- **26 Apr**: In the Netherlands a crisis cabinet is constructed in response to the serious financial situation and the growth of extremist movements on the right and left.

- **27 Apr**: Anglo-German trade agreement.

- **10 May**: Thousands of Berlin students stage a book-burning, destroying 20,000 books considered decadent, subversive or un-German by the Nazis (Ger).

- **12 May**: Agricultural Adjustment Act and Federal Emergency Relief Acts passed (USA). The former aims to eliminate surplus crops of basic commodities by curtailing production. In return for voluntarily reducing acreage or crops, farmers are given direct benefits or rental payments. The latter Act provides $250 million which is given as direct relief to the state, and a further $250 million which is allotted on the basis of $1 for every $3 of state and local funds spent on relief.

- **12 May**: Franco-Canadian trade agreement gives reciprocal tariff preferences.

- **17 May**: The Spanish government issues the Associations Law regulating the religious establishment: church schools are banned and church property nationalized.

- **22 May**: Automatic control of traffic begins in Piccadilly, London.

- **27 May**: Securities Act aims to protect investors through providing information on new security issues (USA).

- **May**: Agreements on trade relations between USSR and Italy and between France and Britain.

- **12 Jun**: World Economic Conference meets in London to seek a pact on international currency stabilization, but the conference is a failure.

- **16 Jun**: National Industrial Recovery Act creates a national recovery administration and Farm Credit Act creates administration to centralize all agricultural credit activities (USA).

- **25 Aug**: Canada, USA, USSR, Australia and Argentina sign a wheat agreement.

- **17 Oct**: US and Panama agree that Panama should be permitted all the commercial rights of a sovereign nation and that there should be no American economic enterprise detrimental to Panama in the Canal Zone.

- **28 Nov**: Opening of the Moroccan-Tunisian railroad uniting French possessions (N Afr).

- **5 Dec**: Prohibition ends when Utah becomes the 36th state to ratify the 21st Amendment (USA).

- **20 Dec**: Reports circulate that 400,000 Germans are to be sterilized for hereditary defects.

- **28 Dec**: Britain makes final payment to USA for war debts.

- The speaking clock of the Paris Observatory is put into operation.

- Albert Einstein leaves Germany and settles in USA at the Institute for Advanced Studies, Princeton.

- German Jews are banned from taking part in the 1936 Olympics.

- Nobel Peace Prize is won by Norman Angell (UK).

- Federico García Lorca: *Blood Wedding*, play (Sp).

- John Cowper Powys: *A Glastonbury Romance*, novel (UK).

- André Malraux: *La Condition humaine*, novel (Fr).

- George Orwell (Eric Arthur Blair): *Down and Out in Paris and London*, reportage (UK).

- Gertrude Stein: *The Autobiography of Alice B. Toklas*, memoir (USA/Fr).

- T.S. Eliot: *The Use of Poetry and the Use of Criticism*, literary criticism (UK).

- Vera Brittain: *Testament of Youth*, autobiography (UK).

- The ban on James Joyce's *Ulysses* is lifted by New York City judge John Woolsey.

- Nobel Prize for Literature won by Ivan Bunin (USSR).

- Kurt Weill: *The Seven Deadly Sins*, stage cantata, text by Bertolt Brecht.

- Richard Strauss: *Arabella*, opera (Ger).

- Aaron Copland: *The Short Symphony* (USA).

- Arturo Toscanini refuses to conduct at the Bayreuth Festival, in protest against the Nazis. Conductors Erich Kleiber and Otto Klemperer leave Germany.

- Balthus: *The Guitar Lesson*, painting (Fr).

- Alberto Giacometti: *The Palace at 4am*, sculpture (Swi).

- Jacob Epstein: *Ecce Homo*, sculpture (UK).

- The introduction of the Nazi policy condemning modern art decides many artists to leave Germany, including Wassily Kandinsky and Paul Klee.

- Triennale design exhibition held in Milan for the first time (It).

- The Bauhaus design school closes down; director Ludwig Mies van der Rohe leaves Germany.

- Russian-born choreographer George Balanchine moves to the USA, where in 1934 with Lincoln Kirstein he starts the School of American Ballet and becomes a major influence on modern ballet.

- Fashion designer Elsa Schiaparelli reintroduces broad shoulders to the female silhouette (Fr).

- M. Cooper: *King Kong*, film, noteworthy for its fine miniature work and special effects (USA).

- *The Power and the Glory*, directed by William Howard and starring Spencer Tracy, introduces a new narrative style in the cinema (USA).

- Leo McCarey: *Duck Soup*, starring the Marx Brothers (USA).

- Reuben Mamoulian: *Queen Christina*, starring Greta Garbo (USA).

- René Clair: *Quatorze juillet* (Fr).

- The Academy Award for Best Picture is won by *Cavalcade*.

- **15–22 Jun**: Wiley Post completes the first solo airplane flight around the world: 25,000 km (15,600 miles) in 7 days, 18 hours and 49 minutes.

- The world distance flying record is set by Maurice Rossi and Paul Codos who fly from New York to Syria, 9,100 km (5,657 miles) nonstop (USA).

- R.J. Van de Graaf develops a static electricity generator that can produce 7 million volts (USA).

- W. Meissner discovers that the magnetic field is excluded from the interior of a superconductor, the Meissner effect (Ger).

- Frequency modulation, which overcomes the problem of radio interference, is perfected by Edwin Armstrong (USA).

- A synthetic rubber, styrene/ butadiene rubber (SBR), is invented by IG Farbenindustrie (Ger); it revolutionizes the manufacture of automobile tires.

- P.A.M. Dirac (UK) and Erwin Schrödinger (Ger) win the Nobel Prize for Physics for their discovery of wave mechanics.

- T.H. Morgan receives the Nobel Prize for Physiology or Medicine for establishing that it is the chromosomes which carry hereditary traits (USA).

- W. Smith, C. Andrewes and P. Laidlaw succeed in isolating a virus from throat swabs of flu victims, a prelude to the development of influenza vaccines (UK).

- H.L. Marriott and A. Kekwick recommend a continuous drip technique for transfusing a large quantity of blood (UK).

- Evarts Graham performs the first successful pneumonectomy (lung removal) on a patient with lung cancer.

- Introduction of the Boeing 247, the first modern airliner; it cruises at 304 kph (189 mph).

- Discovery of the Steinheim skull leads to a rejection of the theory that Neanderthal man was in *Homo sapiens'* line of descent.

- The first rock paintings of prehistoric inhabitants of the Sahara Desert are found at Tassili (N Afr).

- The first commercially produced synthetic detergent is made by ICI (UK).

- Enrico Fermi proposes a theory of beta decay (USA).

- First all-metal wireless tube is made by Marconiphone Co (UK).

- T. Reichstein synthesizes pure vitamin C (Swi).

- E. Ruska devises a 12000x magnification transmission electron microscope (Ger).

China had been disintegrating since the 1890s as a result of increasing Western and Japanese penetration and a rising tide of internal opposition to Manchu rule. The republic formed in the 1910s was never consolidated. Japan took advantage of the mounting chaos and invaded Manchuria in 1931. In 1932 Japanese ascendency over Manchuria was achieved, and Pu Yi, who had abdicated as ruler of China in 1912, was installed as first regent, then emperor, of an independent kingdom named as Manzhouguo. Further Japanese encroachments upon China involved the aerial bombing of Shanghai in 1932 and a military advance upon Beijing in 1933. Mao Zedong had helped to form the Chinese Communist party in 1921 and 10 years later had established the first Chinese Soviet Republic in the remote province of Jiangxi in southeast China. The ferment within China during the early 1930s caused Mao to lead his followers on what became known as "the Long March" from Jiangxi to Yanan in the northwestern province of Shaanxi, where Mao established a Communist party power base.

▲ Mao Zedong's "Long March" across China to establish Communist party headquarters in Shaanxi province took him and his troops a full year. Travelling a distance of some 10,000 km (6,000 miles), Mao was able to make contact with considerable numbers of the Chinese peasantry, which supported him in his rise to power. The march became a symbol of Communist determination and dedication.

● **6 Jan**: The Chaco War between Paraguay and Bolivia recommences after the armistice called for by the League of Nations expires. (› 11 Dec)

● **10 Jan**: Marinus Van der Lubbe, a young Dutch Communist, is executed for supposedly starting the Reichstag fire of Feb 1933 (Ger).

● **14 Jan**: In elections in Catalonia the moderate left are victorious (Sp). (›7 Apr)

● **18 Jan**: A revolutionary movement led by the General Confederation of Labor and the Communists is fiercely suppressed (Port). (›16 Dec)

● **26 Jan**: Germany and Poland conclude a 10-year nonaggression pact.

● **30 Jan**: Suggestions of complicity in the Stavisky fraud affair force the resignation of premier Chautemps, and Edouard Daladier forms a new government. This is unacceptable to Republican groups, and violent street riots take place in Paris. Daladier resigns, and ex-president Gaston Doumergue forms a coalition cabinet of leaders from all parties except Socialists and Communists (Fr). (›8 Nov)

● **Jan**: Libya is formed by the union of Cyrenaica and Tripolitania with Fezia.

● **9 Feb**: Balkan Pact between Greece, Romania, Yugoslavia and Turkey.

● **11–15 Feb**: Following a decree banning all political parties, a Socialist uprising against chancellor Dollfuss's government is brutally crushed (Aut). (›30 Apr)

● **21 Feb–16 Mar**: French troops fight with Berbers in French Morocco. (›Nov)

● **1 Mar**: Japan consolidates her position in Manchuria by supporting Pu Yi, who assumes the title of Emperor of Manzhouguo (Chi).

● **17 Mar**: The Rome Protocols are signed by Austria, Hungary and Italy – a fascist counterpart to the Little Entente (Cze, Rom, Yugo).

● **24 Mar**: US Congress passes the Tydings-McDuffie Act which guarantees Philippine independence in 10 years' time.

● **7 Apr**: Socialists strike in Barcelona (Sp). (›6 Oct)

● **7 Apr**: Gandhi advises suspension of civil disobedience for home rule. On 6 Jun the government withdraws the majority of notifications regulating the illegality of the National Congress. (›25 Oct)

● **30 Apr**: The government declares the 72 Socialist seats annulled and the National Assembly endorses a new constitution establishing a dictatorship under Dollfuss (Aut).

● **3 May**: Hitler creates a People's Court as part of a judicial reorganization. The welfare of the state and Nazi goals become overriding legal principles. In future the court will hear all political cases *in camera*, and appeals can be made only to Hitler (Ger).

● **5 May**: The nonaggression pacts of Jul 1932 between the USSR and Poland and the Baltic States are extended into 10-year agreements.

● **19 May**: Coup in Bulgaria by army officers; Gen. Kimon Gueorguiev sets up a dictatorship for one year. On 12 Jun political parties are banned.

● **29 May**: The USA and Cuba sign a treaty releasing Cuba from its status as a US protectorate.

● **5 Jun**: The South African party led by Jan Smuts and the Nationalist party led by prime minister Hertzog join to form the United party (SA).

● **14–15 Jun**: Hitler visits Italian dictator Benito Mussolini in Venice to try to forge closer relations between the two countries.

● **23 Jun**: Saudi Arabia and the Yemen sign peace after a war of six weeks.

● **23 Jun**: Italy overcomes Albanian resistance to its policy of domination by sending a fleet to Durazzo.

● **30 Jun**: Night of the Long Knives: a great purge of the Nazi movement is carried out by Hitler and the SS. Hitler accuses the leaders of the Storm Troopers' Association (SA), or "Brownshirts", of plotting to overthrow him in a socialist-style revolution. The SA leadership is wiped out, with 77 persons summarily executed and the rank and file are effectively dismissed (Ger).

● **2 Jul**: Lázaro Cárdenas, one of the outstanding figures of the Mexican Revolution, is elected president of Mexico.

● **12 Jul**: In an attempt to control the growing fascist movement and the Labor Defense Militia, the Belgian government prohibits the wearing of uniforms and the formation of military units by political organizations.

● **25 Jul**: After six months of terrorist outrages a Nazi coup occurs during which chancellor Dollfuss is assassinated. The support of Italy and Yugoslavia and the action of Austrian Heimwehr troops prevents any German attempts at union, and on 30 Jul Kurt von Schuschnigg takes control of the government (Aut).

● **Jul**: Dr Gertuilo Vargas is elected president of Brazil under a new constitution.

● **2 Aug**: President Hindenburg dies, and under a new law the offices of chancellor and president are united. On 19 Aug a plebiscite is held; voters are harassed to vote for Hitler and 38.4 million out of 45.5 million do so. He takes the title of Führer.

● **12 Sep**: Latvia, Lithuania and Estonia sign the Baltic Pact aimed at defending their independence.

● **18 Sep**: National Socialist victories in Germany and German hostility to communism increasingly threaten the USSR, which joins the League of Nations and signs treaties with Czechoslovakia and Romania in an attempt to counteract German influence.

SOCIETY

● **6 Oct:** Socialists and separatists call a general strike against rising conservatism in Spain and mobilize for revolt. The government declares martial law and by 13 Oct the revolt is crushed, with many dead. At the same time a declaration of independence in Catalonia is crushed by government troops, and a revolt by miners in Asturias, where a Communist regime is declared, is similarly put down.

● **9 Oct:** King Alexander of Yugoslavia and French foreign minister Louis Barthou are assassinated in Marseille by a Macedonian revolutionary. Peter II ascends to the throne under a triple regency.

● **16 Oct:** Mao Zedong sets off from Jui-chin, in Jiangxi province, on the Long March to Shaanxi province where he makes contact with Communist forces in Oct 1935 (Chi).

● **25 Oct:** The annual general session of the National Congress reaffirms the goal of complete independence. Gandhi retires from leadership to devote himself to the welfare of the Harijans (untouchables) (Ind).

● **7 Nov:** United Australian party forms a coalition ministry with the Country party in Australia.

● **8 Nov:** Premier Doumergue resigns after a disagreement over financial measures; Pierre Flandin forms a coalition cabinet and pursues policies of economic liberty (Fr).

● **28 Nov:** Winston Churchill warns Parliament of the German air menace (UK).

● **30 Nov:** After political intrigue and rioting led by the Wafd party, the king suspends the constitution (Egy).

● **Nov:** A group of young Moroccans present a Plan of Moroccan Reforms which marks the birth of Moroccan nationalism.

● **1 Dec:** Serge Kirov, a close associate of Stalin, is assassinated. The Communist party purge of 1933 is renewed.

● **5 Dec:** Italian troops clash with Ethiopians at Ualual, a disputed point on the Ethiopia (Abyssinia)-Somaliland border. (›3 Sep 1935)

● **11 Dec:** The Bolivian government accepts the League of Nations recommendation for a neutral zone and demobilization but Paraguay rejects it and hostilities recommence. (›21 Dec)

● **16 Dec:** National Union party provides the only candidates in the general election (Port).

● **21 Dec:** After significant victories by Paraguayan forces, Daniel Salamanca, president of Bolivia, is overthrown in a military coup.

● **29 Dec:** Japan denounces the Washington Naval Treaty of 1922 and the London Naval Treaty of 1930 and says it will withdraw from both as from Dec 1936.

● Alfonso Lopez becomes president of Colombia and embarks on far-reaching social reforms.

● **30 Jan:** Gold price is raised from $20.67 to $35 per ounce after USA abandons the gold standard.

● **2 Feb:** President Roosevelt establishes the Export-Import Bank of Washington to encourage commerce with foreign nations (USA).

● **3 Feb:** The Nazis rewrite the Psalms to minimize references to the Jews (Ger).

● **5 Feb:** An Act is passed for the institution of 22 corporations governing agriculture, industry and commercial spheres. Mussolini says the Act will order, direct and guide economic life (It).

● **12–13 Feb:** A general strike is called to protest against the "fascist peril" (Fr).

● **15 Feb:** Civil Works Emergency Relief Act is passed (USA).

● **Mar:** End of tariff war between Germany and Poland.

● **Mar:** The French government reduces the salaries of officials and the pensions of ex-servicemen in an economy drive.

● **12 Apr:** The US Senate establishes a committee to investigate the manufacture and sale of munitions, especially the extent to which the munitions industry influenced and profited from World War I.

● **Apr:** Extension of import control over all industrial products (Ger).

● **10–11 May:** A severe dust storm lifts an estimated 300 million tons of topsoil from Texas, Oklahoma, Arkansas, Kansas and Colorado (USA).

● **23 May:** Bonnie Parker and Clyde Barrow – "Bonnie and Clyde" – are shot dead in Texas Rangers ambush after four years of robbery and killings (USA).

● **4 Jun:** "New Deal" legislation is enacted, giving farmers easier credit arrangements (Can).

● **14 Jun:** Reichsbank declares that in consequence of a lack of foreign currency Germany is unable to pay interest on long-term foreign loans.

● **Oct:** Unemployment reaches 10.8 million in the USA. In Germany unemployment has been reduced from 4 million in Jan to 2.6 million in Dec through conscription or compulsory work camps (Ger).

● **Dec:** US committee established to oversee boycott of German goods.

● The Traffic in Women Committee of the League of Nations is instructed to draft an international convention for the punishment of men living off immoral earnings.

● A woman gives birth to quins – the first recorded case of the birth of viable quintuplets (Can).

● First utility car allows passengers to travel in the front and carry goods or livestock in the rear (USA).

● Nobel Peace Prize is won by Arthur Henderson (UK).

CULTURE

● **Jan:** Premiere in Leningrad of Dmitri Shostakovich's opera *Lady Macbeth of Mtsensk* (*Katerina Ismailova*); it was denounced in *Pravda* as modernist and "confused", and not performed again in the USSR until after Stalin's death.

● F. Scott Fitzgerald: *Tender is the Night*, novel (USA).

● Robert Graves: *I, Claudius*, historical fiction (UK).

● Mikhail Sholokhov: *And Quiet Flows the Don*, novel (USSR).

● Henry Miller: *Tropic of Cancer*, autobiographical novel that is banned in the USA and UK (USA).

● William Saroyan: *The Daring Young Man on the Flying Trapeze*, short stories (USA).

● Federico García Lorca: *Yerma*, play (Sp).

● Nobel Prize for Literature is won by playwright Luigi Pirandello (It).

● The doctrine of "socialist realism" is propounded by Stalin's cultural spokesman A.A. Zhdanov at the Congress of Soviet Writers. It requires that the creative artist should serve the proletariat by producing realistic, optimistic and heroic works.

● Osip Mandelstam is imprisoned and exiled to the provinces for writing a poem denouncing Stalin (USSR).

● Paul Hindemith: *Mathis der Maler*, opera; its performance is banned in Germany.

● Sergei Rachmaninoff: *Rhapsody on a Theme of Paganini* (USA).

● Anton Webern: Concerto for Nine Instruments (Aut).

● Cole Porter: *Anything Goes*, musical (USA).

● Glyndebourne operatic festival is founded by John Christie (UK).

● Charles Sheeler: *American Interior*, painting (USA).

● John Piper: *Rye Harbour*, painting (UK).

● René Magritte: *The Rape*, painting (Fr).

● The stations provided for the new Moscow underground railroad (1934–38) are each in a different style but all reminiscent of a prerevolutionary splendor (USSR).

● René Clair's film *The Last Millionaire* is booed in Paris.

● Donald Duck makes his film debut in Walt Disney's short fillm *The Orphan's Benefit* (USA).

● *It Happened One Night* (USA), directed by Frank Capra and starring Clark Gable and Claudette Colbert, wins five Academy Awards.

● A mobile television unit is used daily for the first time to record sequences for an evening news program (Ger).

● A new look for the London Underground is advertised by E. McKnight Kauffer's posters (UK).

SCIENCE

● J.P. Lent develops Dicoumarol, a drug which reduces the level of clotting agents in the blood (USA).

● Physicist Frédéric Joliot-Curie and his wife Irène discover artificial radioactivity when they create radioactive phosphorus out of natural aluminum (Fr).

● Perspex is commercially produced by ICI (UK).

● The opening of the world's first commercial micro-ray radio service between airports at Lympne, Kent and St Inglevert, France, speeds transmission of weather and traffic information.

● Radar is successfully demonstrated at Kiel Harbor by R. Kuehnold (Ger).

● The first coiled-coil light bulb is introduced (USA).

● A. Butenandt isolates the female sex hormone, progesterone (Ger).

● I.I. Rabi begins his work on the atomic and molecular beam magnetic resonance method for observing spectra in the radio-frequency range (USA).

● A.O. Beckman develops the first pH meter.

● Protactinium is isolated in metallic form by A.V. Grosse (UK).

● John Bernal takes the first X-ray diffraction photograph of a protein crystal, pepsin (UK).

● Russian ecologist G.F. Gause is the first to state the principle that two similar species cannot occupy similar ecological niches for long periods of time.

● Chemist Robert Runnels extracts thiamin from rice polishings (USA).

● G.R. Minot and W.P. Murphy win the Nobel Prize for Physiology or Medicine for the discovery and development of liver treatment for anemia (USA).

● Nobel Prize for Chemistry is won by Harold C. Urey (USA) "for his discovery of heavy hydrogen".

● James Chadwick and Austrian-American physicist Maurice Goldhaber find the mass of a neutron to be greater than the mass of a proton plus an electron, suggesting that neutrons are truly elementary particles.

● Pavel Cherenkov discovers that when a particle travelling close to the speed of light passes through a liquid or transparent solid, it emits light: the "Cherenkov effect" (USSR).

● Werner von Braun develops a liquid-fuel rocket that achieves a height of 2.4 km (1.5 m) (Ger).

● M.L. Oliphant discovers tritium, the radioactive isotope of hydrogen (Aus).

● Wolfgang Pauli and Victor F. Weisskopf demonstrate that certain subatomic particles must have antiparticles (Aut).

The Japanese invasion of Manchuria in 1931 had dealt a severe blow to the postwar system of collective security established under the aegis of the League of Nations. The Italian invasion of Ethiopia (Abyssinia) proved even more damaging. From the early 1920s Mussolini had tried to cultivate domestic support through achievements in foreign policy, setting out to create an empire that would echo that of Ancient Rome. Italian designs on Ethiopia began to become clear from 1934 after a series of incidents on the ill-defined border dividing the African native empire and Italian Somaliland. During the early 1930s Fascist Italy had been regarded in both London and Paris as a useful counter to the rise of Nazi Germany, and Italy's general intentions in Africa were initially supported by France. But when in August 1935 both France and Britain offered terms allowing Italy to develop Ethiopia economically, these were refused and Mussolini's troops invaded on 3 October. League of Nations sanctions proved ineffectual, and the conquest was completed on 9 May 1936.

▲ Ethiopians salute a poster of "Il Duce" during the Italian invasion of Ethiopia. League of Nations sanctions were not tough enough to prevent the conquest being completed by May 1936, and French and British opposition resulted in the strengthening of links between Italy and Nazi Germany, cemented by the formation of the Berlin-Rome Axis in October 1936.

● **1 Jan**: President Mustafa Kemal takes the name Kemal Ataturk as part of a law requiring the use of family names (Tur).

● **7 Jan**: France and Italy conclude the Marseille Pact, by which the French make large concessions to Italy in Africa in an attempt to gain Italian support against Germany.

● **13 Jan**: League of Nations plebiscite in the Saar: 90 percent of voters vote for reunion with Germany. On 1 Mar it is returned to Germany.

● **15 Jan**: Stalin's purges of the Communist party continue in a series of show trials (USSR).

● **30 Jan**: The USSR doubles its army to 940,000.

● **1 Feb**: Anglo-German conference in London to discuss Germany's rearmament.

● **1 Feb**: After a border incident in which five Italians are killed, Italy sends troops into Ethiopia. (›16 Aug)

● **23 Feb**: Paraguay resigns from the League of Nations after 20 nations lift an embargo on arms in favor of Bolivia, its opponent in the Chaco War. (›14 Jun)

● **1–11 Mar**: Uprising led by Eleutherios Venizelos as a protest against royalism is suppressed (Gr). (›10 Oct)

● **2 Mar**: King Prajadhipok of Siam abdicates; Ananda Mahidol, aged 10, becomes king under a council of regency.

● **9 Mar**: Nikita Khrushchev is elected secretary of the Moscow Communist party (USSR).

● **9 Mar**: An informal public announcement that Germany has an air force marks the beginning of German rearmament in defiance of the Treaty of Versailles.

● **16 Mar**: Hitler publicly denounces the Treaty of Versailles, reinstates conscription, and upgrades the German army to 36 divisions.

● **20 Mar**: A labor ministry takes office, which will considerably extend social security legislation (Nor).

● **22 Mar**: By formal decree, Persia changes its name to Iran.

● **25 Mar**: Paul van Zeeland, an eminent financier, is given decree powers for a year to cope with Belgium's desperate financial situation.

● **Mar**: Communists defeat government troops to advance to within 50 miles of Guiyang, capital of Guizhou (Chi). (› Sep)

● **11 Apr**: France summons the Stresa Conference which attempts to work out a strategy in response to Germany's rearmament.

● **23 Apr**: Poland adopts a new constitution.

● **2 May**: France and USSR sign a treaty of mutual assistance for five years.

● **16 May**: USSR and Czechoslovakia conclude a mutual assistance pact.

● **19 May**: In general elections in Czechoslovakia the Sudeten party, many of whose members are Nazis, wins enough seats to become the second most powerful party.

● **4 Jun**: After economic disagreements and a run on French gold Pierre Laval takes over as premier (Fr).

● **7 Jun**: After the resignation of J. Ramsay MacDonald, Stanley Baldwin becomes prime minister of the continuing National Government.

● **9 Jun**: Japanese force the Chinese to submit to the Ho-Umezu Agreement which stipulates that any troops objected to by the Japanese must be removed from Hopei.

● **14 Jun**: After prolonged negotiations by a mediating committee comprised of representatives from the USA, Argentina, Brazil, Chile, Peru and Uruguay, the Chaco War between Paraguay and Bolivia is ended.

● **18 Jun**: UK and Germany conclude a naval agreement in which Germany agrees to limit her navy to not more than 35 percent of the British navy, signalling the UK's *de facto* acceptance of German rearmament.

● **27 Jun**: Peace Ballot results show that the public overwhelmingly supports peace efforts (UK).

● **25 Jul**: Third International agrees to cease opposition to military rearmament and to support democratic nations against their common enemies, the fascist states (USSR).

● **2 Aug**: Government of India Act separates Burma and Aden from India and sets out the new political structure of India. Indian National Congress objects.

● **16 Aug**: UK, France and Italy hold Paris Conference at which Italy is offered generous terms for economic development in Ethiopia (Abyssinia). Italy's refusal shows that Mussolini intends conquest of Ethiopia. (› 3 Oct)

● **20 Aug**: President Ibarra of Ecuador is overthrown by a military junta. On 16 Sep Federico Paez sets up a military dictatorship.

● **31 Aug**: President Roosevelt signs the Neutrality Act which forbids shipments of arms and munitions to belligerents once a state of war exists (USA).

● **3 Sep**: League of Nations arbitration tribunal reports on dispute over Ethiopia-Somaliland border area of Ualual: neither side is at fault since each considers the area within its realm.

● **10 Sep**: A "parliament" of white settlers meets and demands closer union of Kenya, Uganda and Tanganyika.

● **15 Sep**: German government proclaims the Nuremberg Laws, which legitimize persecution of the Jews and make the swastika the official flag of Germany.

- **Sep**: Revolutionary Marxist party, POUM, is formed from two communist groupings in Spain.

- **3 Oct**: Italians invade Ethiopia. On 7 Oct the League of Nations declares Italy the aggressor, and on 19 Oct imposes sanctions against Italy. (›18 Nov)

- **7 Oct**: Kurt Schuschnigg carries out a bloodless coup against Emil Fey, minister of the interior, and his Nazi allies (Aut).

- **10 Oct**: An army coup influences parliament to vote for restoration of the monarchy, and a plebiscite on 3 Nov is also in favor (Gr). (›25 Nov)

- **20 Oct**: End of Mao Zedong's Long March as Communists reach Yanan in north Shaanxi (Chi).

- **23 Oct**: Mackenzie King forms a Liberal ministry (Can).

- **3 Nov**: Socialist groups merge as Socialist and Republican Union under Léon Blum, and soon form close relations with Radical Socialists and Communists to found a Popular Front (Fr).

- **5 Nov**: Milan Hodza, Agrarian party, forms a ministry (Cze).

- **9 Nov**: Japanese troops invade Shanghai (Chi).

- **15 Nov**: Manuel Quezon y Malina, elected 17 Sep, is inaugurated as first president of the Philippines.

- **18 Nov**: League of Nations votes to apply economic sanctions against Italy, but excluding oil, which may be crucial. Italy severs economic ties with participating nations and institutes rationing. Italy and UK come close to open warfare.

- **19 Nov**: 2,000 are killed in Italian air raids on Ethiopia.

- **25 Nov**: King George II returns from exile and insists (1 Dec) on general amnesty (Gr).

- **25 Nov**: A law is enacted prohibiting the wearing of political uniforms or emblems (Ire).

- **29 Nov**: Michael Savage forms the first Labor ministry in New Zealand.

- **Nov**: A Communist revolt breaks out in Pernambuco and Rio de Janeiro. The government declares martial law and the president is granted almost dictatorial powers (Bra).

- **Nov**: Arab parties demand an end to Jewish immigration, which has increased from 30,000 in 1933 to 61,000 in 1935, the greatest number ever recorded (Pal).

- **12 Dec**: After a year's autocratic rule by the king the constitution of 1923 is restored and elections are planned (Egy).

- **13 Dec**: Eduard Beneš succeeds Tomas Masaryk as president of Czechoslovakia.

- **18 Dec**: Foreign Secretary Sir Samuel Hoare resigns over proposals of concessions to Italy in Ethiopia. Anthony Eden takes over (UK).

- **8 Jan**: Steel production is reputed to be up by 104 percent since Hitler's ascendance (Ger).

- **14 Jan**: Opening of oil pipeline from Iraq to Haifa on the Mediterranean coast (pipeline from Mosul to Tripoli had been opened Jul 1934). League of Nations attempts to settle a dispute between Iraq and Iran over the Shatt-al-Arab waterway, but it remains unsolved throughout the year.

- **Feb**: Mussolini places 3,000,000 gold francs at the disposal of the Albanian government as a token of friendship.

- **Feb**: German minister of finance is authorized to finance governmental creation of work without the consent of the Reichstag.

- **8 Apr**: US Congress adopts the Emergency Relief Appropriation Act authorizing $5 billion for immediate relief.

- **11 Apr**: Increasingly severe dust storms hit Kansas, Colorado, Wyoming, Texas and New Mexico (USA). Thousands of dollars' worth of crops and livestock are being lost and families flee the area.

- **23 Apr**: First section of Moscow subway is opened to the public.

- **Apr**: The first regular air services for passengers begin between the UK and Australia.

- **6 May**: The Works Progress Administration begins, planned to provide employment for millions in a series of public works programs. These include the Federal Arts Project whereby hundreds of artists are given work, providing much of the stunning photographic work recording the Depression period (USA).

- **27 May**: US Supreme Court declares National Industrial Recovery Act to be unconstitutional, thereby making the majority of the "New Deal" legislation illegal.

- **May**: The Yellow River floods, drowning 50,000 and covering hundreds of square miles of land (Chi).

- **13 Jul**: USSR and USA sign a trade pact.

- **27 Jul**: The French government is granted emergency financial powers.

- **14 Aug**: President Roosevelt signs the Social Security Act. On 30 Aug Wealth Tax increases surtax (USA).

- **Sep**: Roosevelt agrees to a "breathing spell" from government interference in business affairs (USA).

- **27 Nov**: Labor government enacts major program of social reform (NZ).

- **Nov**: First Pan-American economic conference demands an extension of international trade (USA).

- Jesse Owens breaks five athletic world records in one day (USA).

- Kodak launch Kodachrome, the first modern multilayer color camera film (USA).

- Nobel Peace Prize is won by Carl von Ossietzky (Ger).

- **30 Sep**: Premiere of George Gershwin's opera *Porgy and Bess* (USA).

- John Steinbeck: *Tortilla Flat*, novel (USA).

- Ivy Compton-Burnett: *A House and its Head*, novel (UK).

- Christopher Isherwood: *Mr Norris Changes Trains*, novel based on his experiences in Berlin (UK).

- André Malraux: *Le Temps du mépris*, (Fr).

- Allen Lane founds Penguin Books, producing the first cheap paperback editions and thereby initiating the paperback revolution (UK).

- T.S. Eliot: *Murder in the Cathedral*, play (UK).

- Clifford Odets: *Waiting for Lefty*, play (USA).

- Jean Giraudoux: *La Guerre de Troie n'aura pas lieu* (later trans. by Christopher Fry as *Tiger at the Gates*), play (Fr).

- John Gielgud's production of *Romeo and Juliet* in London stars Peggy Ashcroft as Juliet with Gielgud and Laurence Olivier alternating in the parts of Romeo and Mercutio.

- Dmitri Shostakovich: Fourth Symphony (USSR).

- William Walton: First Symphony (UK).

- Ivor Novello: *Glamorous Night*, first of a series of successful operettas (UK).

- Benny Goodman introduces "swing", which appeals strongly to young people and heralds the beginning of a "youth" movement.

- Jazz of Negro or Jewish origin is banned in Germany.

- Coleman Hawkins and Django Reinhardt hold a gig in Paris to celebrate the founding of the journal *Jazz Hot*.

- Fred Astaire and Ginger Rogers star in *Top Hat*, directed by Mark Sandrich, with lyrics by Irving Berlin (USA).

- Salvador Dali: *Giraffe on Fire*, painting (Sp).

- Max Ernst: *Lunar Asparagus*, painting (Fr).

- *Mutiny on the Bounty*, starring Charles Laughton and Clark Gable (USA), receives the Academy Award for Best Picture of the Year.

- *Becky Sharp*, directed by Reuben Mamoulian, is the first all-Technicolor talking film (USA).

- *Anna Karenina*, starring Greta Garbo and Fredric March is a great success (USA).

- *Toni*, film directed by Jean Renoir (Fr).

- Nobel Prize for Chemistry is won by Frédéric and Irène Joliot-Curie (Fr) "for their synthesis of new radioactive elements".

- Nobel Prize for Physics is won by James Chadwick (UK) "for his discovery of the neutron".

- Nobel Prize for Physiology or Medicine is won by Hans Spemann (Ger) "for his discovery of the organizer effect in embryonic development".

- R. Watson Watt builds the first practical aerial radar (UK).

- Fluorescent lighting is demonstrated by General Electric Co (USA).

- The sodium vapor street lamp is developed, giving an orange light.

- Hearing aids using a discrete battery and a small radio tube are invented.

- G. Domagk first uses the sulfa drug Prontosil for treating streptococcal infections in humans (Ger).

- A. Moniz pioneers lobotomy as a treatment for mental illness (Port).

- Konrad Lorenz describes imprinting in animal development (Aut).

- A.J. Dempster discovers the U-235 isotope of uranium (Can).

- H. Yukawa proposes that a new particle causes the attraction between particles in the nucleus (Jap).

- C.F. Richter devises the "Richter scale" of earthquake strength (USA).

- In Hong Kong, R. von Koenigswald finds the first evidence, fossil teeth, of *Gigantopithecus*, the largest primate known.

- Bengt Stromgren formulates his theory about the internal structure of stars (Den).

- Henrik Dam discovers vitamin K (Den).

- E. Calvin Kendall isolates a cortical hormone later known as cortisone.

- W. Ewing starts the seismic study of the sea bottom using refraction of waves caused by explosions (USA).

- John Gibbon and his wife develop the first prototype of the heart-lung machine (USA).

- Croatian-Swiss chemist Leopold Ruzicka finds the structure of testosterone, the male sex hormone (Swi).

- R. Shoenheimer uses isotopes of deuterium to trace fat storage and metabolism.

- Boeing introduce the B-17, the first 4-engined, all-metal, low-wing monoplane bomber, later known as the Flying Fortress (USA).

- The first artificial heart, a spirally coiled glass tube and pump, is used experimentally.

- The process of producing petrol from crude oil, pioneered by ICI in 1931, becomes fully commercial (UK).

Racism had been growing within Europe since before the turn of the century, fueled by nationalism, the perverted applications of ideas of Darwinian evolution and concepts of national efficiency. Before 1914 antisemitism was rife in czarist Russia, with pogroms leading to massive Jewish emigration to the United States. In the 1930s Hitler and the Nazis cultivated racism as a plank of popular support: the Jew in particular became a scapegoat for the problems that beset German society. German Jews were not permitted to compete in the Olympic Games held in Berlin in the summer of 1936. The wider implications of Nazi racial policy also became apparent through a program enforcing the sterilization of Germans with hereditary defects. The so-called Nuremberg Laws of 15 September 1935 led to all manner of restrictions, including the banning of performances of Negro or Jewish music. This pseudo-ideology received an unwelcome blow from black US athlete Jesse Owens's triumph at the Berlin Olympics.

▲ Undoubted hero of the Berlin Olympics was the black American athlete Jesse Owens, who won four gold medals in a remarkable display of brilliance almost equalling his success of the previous year, when he had established five new world records in one day. His victories also upset Hitler's notions of white superiority.

- **8 Feb**: Jawaharlal Nehru is elected president of the Indian National Congress.

- **16 Feb**: Leftwing (Popular Front) victory in the Spanish general election. Manuel Azaña organizes a new cabinet, proclaims a general amnesty, restores Catalan autonomy and institutes social reforms. Azaña becomes president on 10 May. (›17 Jul)

- **17 Feb**: A military revolt leads to the overthrow of president Ayala of Paraguay.

- **7 Mar**: Germany denounces the 1925 Locarno pacts and remilitarizes the Rhineland. UK, France, Belgium, Italy and League of Nations denounce treaty violation but take no action.

- **9 Mar**: New premier Koki Hirota organizes a cabinet dominated by the military and institutes a program of developing heavy industry (Jap).

- **23 Mar**: Italy, Austria and Hungary sign Rome Pact.

- **25 Mar**: USA, France and UK sign an agreement limiting naval expansion. Japan and Italy have withdrawn from the conference.

- **Mar**: Czechoslovakia begins to construct a series of fortifications along its border with Germany.

- **1 Apr**: Kurt von Schuschnigg reinstates military conscription in violation of 1919 Treaty of St Germaine (Aut).

- **2 Apr**: Conclusion of a treaty of nonaggression and Arab brotherhood between Saudi Arabia and Iraq. A series of pacts between Arab states follow, all of which are united in their stand on the Palestine question. (› Apr)

- **28 Apr**: Death of King Fuad I of Egypt, succeeded by King Farouk. In May elections the Nationalists make impressive advances; Nahas Pasha organizes a cabinet.

- **Apr**: Arab High Committee formed to unite Arabs against Jewish claims. Start of Arab rebellion in Palestine. Formation of secret Jewish force, Hagannah. (›12 Oct)

- **5 May**: Italians capture Addis Ababa; on 9 May Italy formally annexes Ethiopia (Abyssinia) and incorporates it into Italian East Africa, together with Eritrea and Italian Somaliland.

- **24 May**: In Belgian parliamentary elections the Rexists (fascists) win 21 seats. Paul van Zeeland introduces an extensive social improvement program (Bel). (›14 Oct)

- **2 Jun**: President Sacasa of Nicaragua is deposed by the National Guard led by Gen. Anastasio Somoza. In Dec Somoza becomes president and dictator (until 1956).

- **5 Jun**: As a result of Popular Front victory in 3 May elections, Léon Blum organizes the first Popular Front ministry and institutes a program of social reform (Fr).

- **4 Jul**: Emperor Haile Selassie of Ethiopia pleads for League of Nations assistance in expelling the Italians. However, the League votes to discontinue all sanctions against Italy.

- **11 Jul**: Germany and Austria conclude an agreement in which Germany promises to respect Austria's independence while Austria agrees to lead a course appropriate to a German state.

- **17 Jul**: Civil war begins as the Spanish army in Morocco proclaims a revolution against the left-wing Popular Front government in Madrid. The insurgents are supported by all parties of the right and most of the army and air force. (›24 Jul)

- **19 Jul**: Jiang Jieshi wins control of Guangdong and (6 Sep) of Guangxi. Regional Chinese leaders and Communists call for war against Japan. On 11 Aug Jiang Jieshi enters Guangzhou (Chi).

- **20 Jul**: Conference in Montreux votes to grant Turkey permission to refortify the Straits of the Bosphorus and the Dardanelles.

- **24 Jul**: Gen. Mola establishes a provisional rebel government in Burgos, the Junta of National Defense, under Gen. Miguel Cabanellas (Sp). (›6 Aug)

- **4 Aug**: Greek premier Metaxas makes himself dictator, proclaims martial law, suspends civil liberties and dissolves parliament.

- **6 Aug**: Insurgent leader Gen. Franco captures Badajoz and flies to Seville, receiving military assistance from Germany and Italy. The government is helped by the USSR and by many Western writers and intellectuals who form international brigades (Sp). (›4 Sep)

- **7 Aug**: US government issues proclamation of nonintervention in the Spanish Civil War.

- **19–23 Aug**: Communist leaders Grigory Zinoviev, Leon Kamenev and others are convicted and summarily executed as plotters against Stalin (USSR).

- **27 Aug**: Egypt concludes a treaty with UK under which British withdraw forces except for 10,000 men in Suez Canal zone. Egyptian troops may re-enter Sudan and there will be unrestricted Egyptian immigration into the Sudan.

- **29 Aug**: A move to the right and toward Germany is denoted by the enforced resignation of Romanian foreign minister Nicholas Titulescu.

- **4 Sep**: Rebel forces overrun Irun and San Sebastian while a new Popular Front government is organized in Madrid under Largo Caballero (Sp). (›1 Oct)

- **9 Sep**: France and Syria sign a treaty of friendship and alliance. It is agreed that the French mandate will end in three years' time and Syria will join the League of Nations. On 13 Nov France and the Lebanon conclude a treaty.

SOCIETY   CULTURE   SCIENCE

- **10 Sep**: Nazi campaign against Czechoslovakia denounces Czechs for playing host to Soviet military aircraft.

- **1 Oct**: Insurgents appoint Gen. Franco chief of state (Sp). (›8 Oct)

- **1 Oct**: Under threat of invasion, the Japanese demand various political and economic concessions from China. The Nanjing government refuses to acquiesce.

- **8 Oct**: Popular Front government promises home rule to Basque provinces (Sp). (›6 Nov)

- **10 Oct**: Von Schuschnigg removes all opposition and on 18 Oct declares himself Front Führer (Aut).

- **12 Oct**: Oswald Mosley, leader of the British Fascist party, heads an anti-Jewish march through London, causing furious rioting (UK).

- **12 Oct**: Arab general strike against Jewish claims ends as UK brings in troops and appoints Reed Commission to investigate Jewish demands for land purchases and increased immigration (Pal).

- **14 Oct**: Belgium secedes from military alliance with France, and on 22 Oct martial law is declared to curb the activities of the Rexists.

- **25 Oct**: The Berlin-Rome Axis is established through the new Italian foreign minister Count Galeazzo Ciano, Mussolini's son-in-law.

- **3 Nov**: The Dáil endorses a new constitution that reinstates the Senate and omits mention of Ireland's relation to the UK (Ire).

- **3 Nov**: Roosevelt wins a landslide victory in the presidential election; the Democrats retain majorities in the Senate and House (USA).

- **6 Nov**: Rebel forces begin a siege of Madrid, forcing the government to flee to Valencia (Sp).

- **18 Nov**: Italy and Germany issue proclamations recognizing the government of Gen. Franco in Spain. UK and France press for European nonintervention. Mussolini sends 75,000 Italian soldiers. (›16 Dec)

- **25 Nov**: The Anti-Comintern Pact is concluded by Germany and Japan; Italy joins later. Its aim is to threaten the USSR from east and west.

- **5 Dec**: Political structure is reorganized and a new "democratic" constitution is adopted promising universal suffrage, secret ballot and direct election to higher assemblies. The Communist party is the only political organization allowed (USSR).

- **8 Dec**: Peruvian president Oscar Benavides dissolves the constituent assembly and becomes virtual dictator.

- **10 Dec**: King Edward VIII abdicates in order to marry American-born divorcee Wallis Warfield Simpson. He is succeeded by his brother, King George VI (UK).

- **16 Dec**: Protocol signed in London for nonintervention in Spain.

- **29 Feb**: Second Neutrality Act extends 1935 Act to 1 May 1937 and prohibits the granting of loans to belligerents (USA).

- **3 Mar**: UK defense budget is increased.

- **7 Apr**: The Representation of Natives Act clarifies government policy towards blacks. Electoral registers of blacks are kept separately from whites, and blacks are allowed to elect three whites to represent them in the Union Parliament (SA).

- **Apr**: Trade agreement is signed between Germany and USSR.

- **23 May**: In Australia, new higher tariffs lead to considerable friction with Japan.

- **5 Jun**: French social reform program leads to sharp rise in production costs, flight of capital and inflation. (›2 Oct)

- **17 Jun**: Supreme Court nullifies most of "New Deal" legislation of R.B. Bennett's government in 1935 (Can).

- **Aug**: At Berlin Summer Olympics black American Jesse Owens wins four gold medals in track and field, discrediting Nazi theories of Aryan superiority.

- **9 Sep**: Tripartite Monetary Agreement signed to reorganize the international monetary system after the collapse of the gold bloc (USA/Fr/UK).

- **2 Oct**: French government devalues the franc in the face of uncontrollable inflation. On 5 Oct Italy devalues the lira.

- **19 Oct**: German four-year plan begins with Hermann Goering as economic minister.

- **Oct–Nov**: Hundreds of unemployed begin a protest march from Jarrow to London, but prime minister Baldwin refuses to see them (UK).

- **23 Nov**: Under new Mexican social and reform program, peasants receive expropriated lands. Expropriation Law permits government to seize private property, leading to 1937 nationalization of railroads and petroleum companies.

- Construction of Fort Knox, where half of the US gold stock is laid down.

- J.M. Keynes publishes his theories on tackling economic depression in *The General Theory of Employment, Interest and Money* (UK).

- Roll-on Roll-off (Ro-Ro) ferries operate between Britain and France for the first time.

- Fiat 500 is released as Italy's "people's car."

- British Broadcasting Corporation (BBC) starts regular television broadcasting from Alexandra Palace (UK).

- The first vitamin pill to come on the market is Vitamin Plus (USA).

- Nobel Peace Prize is won by Carlos Saavedra Lamas (Arg) "for his role as a peacemaker in the Chaco War between Bolivia and Paraguay".

- **4 Jan**: The first popular music chart based on sales is published by *The Billboard* in New York City.

- W.H. Auden: *Look, Stranger!*, poems (UK).

- Georges Bernanos: *Journal of a Country Priest*, novel (Fr/Bra).

- Aldous Huxley: *Eyeless in Gaza*, novel (UK).

- Margaret Mitchell: *Gone with the Wind*, best-selling historical novel (USA).

- Dylan Thomas: *Twenty-five Poems* (UK).

- Vladimir Nabokov: *Despair*, novel written while the author was living in Berlin; he left for Paris in 1937.

- Criticism of works of art, literature and music is forbidden in Germany.

- Terence Rattigan: *French without Tears*, play (UK).

- Federico García Lorca: *The House of Bernarda Alba*, Lorca's last play before his death in the same year in the Spanish Civil War.

- Nobel Prize for Literature is won by Eugene O'Neill (USA).

- Sergey Prokoviev: *Peter and the Wolf*, a story for narrator and orchestra intended to introduce children to the different orchestral instruments (USSR).

- Aaron Copland: *El Salón México*, for orchestra (USA).

- Samuel Barber: *Adagio for Strings* (USA).

- Benjamin Britten: *Our Hunting Fathers*, symphonic cycle for voice and orchestra to words by W.H. Auden (UK).

- Piet Mondrian: *Composition in Red and Blue*, painting (Neth).

- The International Surrealist Exhibition in London is opened by Salvador Dali, wearing a diving suit. Surrealism becomes more and more an international movement.

- Meret Oppenheim: *Tasse à thé en fourrure* (Fur Teacup), Surrealist object (Fr).

- Cubism and Abstract Art Exhibition at the Museum of Modern Art, New York, shows work by the group known as the American Abstract Artists.

- Marino Marini: *The Horseman*, sculpture (It).

- Frank Lloyd Wright begins building a house for the Kaufmann family at Bear Run, Pennsylvania; it is known as "Falling Water" (USA).

- Albert Speer builds the Congress Hall at Nuremberg as part of Hitler's grandiose architectural plans (Ger).

- *Modern Times*, Charlie Chaplin's last silent film (USA).

- *A Night at the Opera*, film starring the Marx Brothers (USA).

- Pinewood Film Studios open in England, with eight sound stages and seven acres of land.

- First diesel-electric vessel, the *Wupperthal*, is launched (Ger).

- Boulder (Hoover) Dam on Colorado River is completed, to hold the world's largest reservoir, Lake Mead (USA).

- First use of an oxygen tent (UK).

- D. Bovet discovers that sulfanilamide is the effective part of the "wonder drug" Prontosil (Swi).

- Alexis Carrel develops a form of artificial heart that is used during cardiac surgery (Fr).

- E.W. Mueller develops the field-emission microscope, the first device to show individual atoms (USA).

- F. Bloch suggests a method for polarizing neutrons by passing them through magnetized iron (USA).

- Catalytic cracking is developed for refining petroleum.

- Inge Lehmann proves the existence of the inner core of the Earth (Den).

- A. Belozersky isolates DNA in the pure state for the first time.

- John Meadville shows that a mouse's mother's milk can transmit cancer, the first significant evidence since 1911 that some cancers might be caused by viruses (USA).

- Sir Henry Dale (UK) and Otto Loewi (Aut) win the Nobel Prize for Physiology or Medicine for their work on the chemical transmission of nerve impulses.

- Nobel Prize for Physics is won by Carl D. Anderson (USA) for his discovery of the positron and Victor F. Hess (Aut) for his discovery of cosmic radiation.

- Nobel Prize for Chemistry is won by Peter Debye (Neth) for his work on dipoles and the diffraction of X-rays and electrons in gases.

- Tadeusz Reichstein isolates cortisone and finds its structure (Pol).

- R.R. Williams synthesizes vitamin B1 (thiamine) (USA).

- A. Church (USA) and A. Turing (UK) show independently that there is no single method for determining whether a statement in mathematics is provable or even true.

- Konrad Zuse builds a primitive form of digital computer using electromagnetic relays (Ger).

- The Ihagee Kine Exakta is the first single lens reflex camera to use 35 mm film.

- The Mercedes 260D is the first diesel-engined production car.

- The Supermarine Spitfire fighter aircraft makes its maiden flight (UK).

- Water injection, as a method of maintaining pressure in an oil well and so allowing controlled extraction, is developed at an East Texas oil field (USA).

- The Douglas DC-3 begins production (USA).

The 1930s saw the growth of passenger air travel. From 1926 Imperial Airways, a British company, began to develop an Empire-wide air service that by the late 1930s linked London directly with Karachi. An African service to Capetown was fully operational by 1932 and in December 1934 an Australian route was opened, covering nearly 20,000 km (12,000 miles). A commercial service across the Atlantic began in 1939. However, for intercontinental passenger-carrying services in the mid-1930s there were as yet few alternatives to the airship, though its dangers had been clear since the British R101 crashed in flames over France in October 1930. The commercial development of the airship ended after the explosion of the German airship "Hindenburg" in May 1937. Public horror was the greater for the newsreel film, originally intended to celebrate the aircraft's voyage, in which the horrific consequences were only too plain. Heavier-than-air aircraft came to be increasingly developed during the 1930s, especially in the United States with its large internal market. The Boeing 247, the first modern airliner, was introduced in 1933, while production of the Douglas DC-3 began in 1936.

▲ The giant airship *Hindenburg* exploded in a ball of flames as it came in to land in New Jersey on 6 May 1937 after a transatlantic flight, killing over 30 of its passengers and crew.

● **1 Jan**: Gen. Anastazio Garcia becomes president of Nicaragua, starting a family dictatorship.

● **7 Jan**: Poland signs an agreement with Danzig.

● **9 Jan**: Leon Trotsky arrives in Mexico, where he is given political asylum.

● **24 Jan**: Bulgaria and Yugoslavia sign a treaty of perpetual peace.

● **28 Jan**: The British Privy Council accords with the Canadian Supreme Court's earlier adjucation that most of the Bennett government's socialist legislation is unconstitutional (Can).

● **28 Jan**: The anti-Communist campaign ends as the Shaanxi (Communist) government and the Nanjing (Nationalist) government agree to cooperate against the Japanese under the leadership of Jiang Jieshi (Chi). (›7 Jul)

● **Jan–Feb**: Serious uprising in Honduras crushed by government.

● **19 Feb**: An attempt on the life of the Italian viceroy of Ethiopia (Abyssinia) leads to wholesale arrests and executions designed to intimidate the population.

● **1 Mar**: The Camp of National Unity is formed in support of the government and army. Workers and peasants react by forming a Workers, Peasants and Intellectuals Group. There is widespread unrest and peasant strikes (Pol).

● **18 Mar**: In the Spanish Civil War, the defeat of Italian legionaries at Briheuga checks the rebel threat to Madrid. (›26 Apr)

● **25 Mar**: Italy and Yugoslavia conclude a five-year nonaggression and neutrality pact, which strikes a blow at the Little Entente.

● **1 Apr**: The Government of India Act goes into effect. The All-India party, which won a majority in the elections, obtains an assurance from the British government that provincial governors will not pursue "detailed interference". All-India governments are set up in seven provinces and commence a program of social reform.

● **22 Apr**: Australian chancellor von Schuschnigg meets Mussolini in Venice. Mussolini advises him to pursue friendly relations with Hungary and the Nazis in Germany, but Von Schuschnigg tries to forge alliances with the Little Entente and France (Aut).

● **26 Apr**: The Basque village of Guernica is destroyed from the air by German bombers, arousing international horror (Sp). (›18 Jun)

● **1 May**: President Roosevelt signs a third Neutrality Act (USA).

● **17 May**: Popular Front government is supplanted by government led by Socialist Juan Negrin (Sp).

● **26 May**: Egypt joins the League of Nations.

● **28 May**: Neville Chamberlain becomes prime minister of Britain.

● **1 Jun**: Prince Konoye becomes premier of a National Union ministry (Jap).

● **12 Jun**: Beginning of purge of Soviet army generals. Up to 35,000 officers are arrested and executed in the following months.

● **18 Jun**: Rebels take Bilbao, followed by Santander on 26 Jun (Sp). (›28 Nov)

● **21 Jun**: Léon Blum resigns and Camille Chautemps forms a Radical-Socialist ministry with Blum as vice-premier. The new government began a campaign of financial reconstruction (Fr).

● **7 Jul**: Japanese troops on maneuvers clash with Chinese troops near Beijing, beginning the Sino-Japanese War. (›28 Jul)

● **8 Jul**: Peel Report issued in London recommending an end to the Palestine mandate and partitioning of the area into Arab and Jewish states is opposed by both Arabs and Jews. On 2 Aug World Zionist Congress votes to endorse the Peel Plan after revisions favouring the Jews. (›8 Sep)

● **28 Jul**: Japanese troops capture Beijing. They go on to take other Chinese cities. (›8 Aug)

● **Jul**: Kurdish insurrection in Syria demanding autonomy is put down by use of air forces.

● **8 Aug–8 Nov**: Shanghai Campaign, in which the Japanese ultimately triumph after heavy fighting. Merciless bombing of Chinese cities outrages world opinion. On 25 Aug Japan extends its naval blockade the entire length of the coast of South China. (›3 Nov)

● **15 Aug**: Prime minister Mackenzie King appoints a commission to study confederate relations and revise the British North America Act (Can).

● **15 Aug**: President Franco of Paraguay is forced to resign. Felix Pavia is elected constitutional president (11 Oct).

● **8 Sep**: At a Pan-Arab Conference in Syria, 400 representatives vote against the Peel Plan. They also decide to support financially the efforts of Palestinian Arabs and boycott Jewish goods and enterprises.

● **26 Sep**: British district commissioner in Palestine is murdered by Arabs. On 1 Oct members of the Arab High Committee are arrested and it is declared illegal. Pitched street battles lead to the British government setting up special military courts to deal with terrorists.

● **13 Oct**: Germany guarantees the inviolability of Belgium as long as Belgium refrains from military action against Germany.

● **16 Oct**: Fascist groups in Hungary form the National Socialist party.

SOCIETY   CULTURE   SCIENCE

- **17 Oct:** Following a call for autonomy of Germans within the borders of Czechoslovakia, riots take place and the government bans protest meetings and postpones the general elections. (›29 Nov)

- **22 Oct:** The dictator Paez is obliged to resign and Gen. Alberto Enriquez becomes provisional president of Ecuador with the support of the army. He begins a program of financial and legal reform.

- **3 Nov:** Brussels Conference meets to discuss Sino-Japanese War but Japan does not attend. (›20 Nov)

- **6 Nov:** Italy joins German-Japanese Anti-Comintern Pact. Italy leaves the League of Nations on 11 Dec.

- **10 Nov:** President Vargas proclaims a new constitution in Brazil, giving him dictatorial powers. Political parties are banned on 14 Dec.

- **17 Nov:** Lord Halifax (UK) visits Germany to attempt peaceful settlement of Sudeten (Czechoslovakia) problem – the beginning of the policy of appeasement.

- **20 Nov:** Chinese capital moved from Nanjing to Chongqing. On 12 Dec Japanese bombers attack American and British ships, producing acute international tensions. Nanjing falls on 13 Dec after heavy fighting and Japanese atrocities.

- **28 Nov:** Gen. Franco begins naval blockade of Spanish coast. On 5 Dec Loyalists begin a counteroffensive near Teruel.

- **29 Nov:** Sudeten Germans leave Czech parliament following ban on political meetings.

- **7 Dec:** Turkey denounces 1926 treaty of friendship with Syria. French send a military mission to Ankara.

- **28 Dec:** Elections in Romania lead to the fall of the Titulescu government. King Carol appoints Octavian Goga prime minister despite his National Christian party gaining only 10 percent of the electoral votes. Goga iniates a series of antisemitic laws.

- **29 Dec:** Irish Free State becomes Eire as a new constitution comes into force.

- **30 Dec:** Liberal Constitution party forms a ministry in Egypt.

- **1 Jan:** Public Order Act comes into force in UK, banning political uniforms and private armies.

- **Jan:** The Japanese yen is devalued.

- **Jan–Jun:** Widespread worker unrest as result of attempts to organize workers in the automobile and steel industries results in the large-scale unionization of the mass production industries (USA).

- **Mar:** New assistance plan for American agriculture, involving the support of prices by the regulation of supply.

- **6 May:** The German airship *Hindenburg* explodes in New Jersey (USA), killing 36 people and ending the development of the airship as a commercial proposition.

- **26 Jun:** Duke of Windsor (ex-King Edward VIII) marries Mrs Wallis Simpson in France (UK).

- **Jun:** International Labor Conference publishes a declaration on the introduction of the 40-hour week.

- **23 Jul:** Matrimonial Causes Bill facilitates divorce proceedings (UK).

- **Jul:** An economic committee for the promotion of trade is established between Germany, Belgium and Luxembourg.

- **24 Nov:** Walther Funk – considered to be more in accord with Nazi thinking – replaces Dr Hjalmar Schacht as minister of economics (Ger).

- **Nov:** Roosevelt introduces a program for increasing business activities, featuring an increase in house building and public activities (USA).

- The Super Kodak Six-20 camera is introduced – the first to have a fully automatic exposure control (USA).

- The Golden Gate Bridge opens to traffic across the entrance to San Francisco Bay (USA).

- G.W. Smedley develops a food freezing process after visiting the USA. Asparagus is the first packaged frozen food sold (UK).

- The first photocopier is demonstrated by Chester Carlson, a New York Law student (USA).

- AEG/Telefunken market the first magnetic tape recorder (Ger).

- Three Russian aviators fly nonstop over the North Pole from Moscow to Vancouver (Can), a distance of 8,500 km (5,288 miles).

- Aviator Amelia Earhart disappears during a flight over the Pacific Ocean. No trace of her is ever found.

- Romansch is recognized as the fourth Swiss national language.

- French railroads are nationalized, becoming the Société Nationale des Chemins de Fer (SNCF).

- Nobel Peace Prize is won by Robert Cecil (UK) for his efforts for the League of Nations.

- **8 Jun:** Hollywood's first "sex goddess", Jean Harlow, dies at the age of 26 (USA).

- **Jun:** Alban Berg's opera *Lulu* is premiered in Zürich.

- **11 Jul:** George Gershwin, whose compositions typified the 1920s in music as F. Scott Fitzgerald's did in fiction, dies aged 38.

- **Jul:** Adolf Hitler opens an exhibition of "Degenerate Art" in Munich featuring work by Jewish and "modern" artists such as Emil Nolde and Otto Dix, and denounces the decadence of German art under such influence.

- Christopher Caudwell: *Illusion and Reality*, Marxist literary criticism (UK). Caudwell was killed fighting in Spain with the International Brigade.

- John Steinbeck: *Of Mice and Men*, novel (USA).

- Ignazio Silone: *Pane e vino* (Bread and Wine), novel (It).

- J.R.R. Tolkien: *The Hobbit*, fantasy novel for children (UK).

- George Orwell: *The Road to Wigan Pier*, documentary of poverty and unemployment, published by the Left Book Club (UK).

- Karen Blixen (Isak Dinesen): *Out of Africa*, autobiography (Den).

- W.H. Auden and Louis MacNeice: *Letters from Iceland*, poems (UK).

- Nobel prize for Literature is won by Roger Martin du Gard (Fr)

- Dmitri Shostakovich: Fifth Symphony (USSR).

- Igor Stravinsky's ballet *Jeu de Cartes* is first performed (Fr).

- Carl Orff: *Carmina Burana*, settings of medieval poems, first performed in Frankfurt (Ger).

- John Cage: *The Future of Music*, manifesto on the use of noise in musical composition (USA).

- The musical *Pins and Needles* breaks box office records (USA).

- Paris World Fair features Joan Miró's murals and Raoul Dufy's décor, but the sensation is Pablo Picasso's *Guernica*, a nightmare image commemorating the German bombing of the Basque village on 26 Apr.

- B.M. Iofan: Soviet Pavilion at the Paris Exhibition.

- Walt Disney releases the first feature-length all-color, animated cartoon with sound, *Snow White and the Seven Dwarfs* (USA).

- Jean Renoir's *La Grande Illusion* becomes a classic antiwar film (Fr).

- *A Star is Born* directed by William Wellman, stars Janet Gaynor and Fredric March.

- Greta Garbo stars in *Camille* (USA).

- *Ecstasy* starring Hedy Lamarr creates a stir for its portrayal of a nude swimming sequence (USA).

- Nobel Prize for Physics is won by Clinton J. Davison (USA) and G.P. Thompson for their discovery of the diffraction of electrons by crystals.

- Nobel Prize for Physiology or Medicine is won by Albert Szent-Gyorgyi (Hun) for his research into the biological combustion processes with special reference to vitamin C.

- Nobel Prize for Chemistry is won by Walter N. Haworth (UK) and by Paul Karrer (Swi) for their work on vitamins.

- First rocket tests performed at Peenemünde by Werner von Braun and others (Ger).

- Frank Whittle builds the first jet engine (patented in 1930) (UK).

- C.D. Anderson discovers the mu meson (muon) in cosmic radiation (USA).

- Foundation of the Nobel Institute of Physics in Stockholm (Swe).

- M. Blau uses a photographic plate to examine cosmic radiation (Aut).

- First directional radio telescope built by G. Reber (USA).

- C.A. Elvehjem discovers Vitamin A.

- H.A. Krebs discovers the Krebs cycle – the chemical changes in a cell that convert oxygen and sugars to energy (respiration) (UK).

- Zinc protamine insulin is successfully used in cases of diabetes.

- Yellow fever vaccine is developed (USA).

- Pharmacologist Daniele Bovet discovers a prototype antihistamine (It).

- Scientists create the second sulfa drug, Sulfapyridine.

- William Cumming Rose establishes that only 10 of the 20 amino acids found in proteins are essential for rats; he later finds that eight are essential for humans.

- Building commences on a chain of defensive military radar stations reaching from the Solent to the Firth of Tay (UK).

- Latvian company Valsts Electrotechniska Fabrida produces the Minox, the first precision sub-miniature camera, marking the advent of tiny "spy" cameras.

- US biochemist Conrad Elvehjem identifies nicotinic acid as the substance effective in treating pellagra, a dietary deficiency disease. The substance, a part of the B complex of vitamins, is later renamed nicin.

- Italian doctors Ugo Cerletti and Lucio Bini pioneer electro-convulsive treatment (ECT) for the relief of symptoms in schizophrenia.

Hitler achieved a series of bloodless foreign policy coups during the 1930s, expanding German territory in keeping with his declared policy of creating a "Greater Germany" for the German people. In 1936 the Rhineland was remilitarized, and in 1938 Austria became a province of Germany with the Anschluss. His designs on Czechoslovakia were more worrying to the other European powers. From mid-1936 he had encouraged the demands of the "Sudeten" Germans, many of whom were Nazis, for autonomy. When in April the Prague government rejected these demands, rumors of German military mobilization spread, to which the Czechoslovak government responded in kind. It quickly became clear that Britain and France would continue their policy of appeasement. At Munich in September, in the absence of Czechoslovak representatives, the leaders of Britain, France, Germany and Italy began to carve up the Central European democracy. The Sudetenland was transferred to Germany, and six months later Bohemia, Moravia and Slovakia all became German "protectorates".

▲ **British prime minister Neville Chamberlain returns from the Munich Conference in September 1938, confident of having secured peace in Europe – but many MPs of all parties regard his policy of appeasement as a sellout to Hitler.**

● **4 Jan**: Britain postpones the Palestine partition scheme and appoints Woodhead Commission to investigate boundaries. Terrorist attacks by Arabs and Jews continue throughout the year, and Britain increases troop presence to 30,000. (›9 Nov)

● **10 Jan**: Japanese capture Qingdao after Chinese destruction of Japanese mills in the area, and on 6 Mar reach the Yellow River. However, Chinese guerrilla activity restricts the Japanese to the railroad and city areas. On 28 Mar the Japanese install a puppet government in Nanjing. (›10 May)

● **14 Jan**: Camille Chautemps revamps the French cabinet as a Radical Socialist ministry. (›13 Mar)

● **18 Jan**: King Carol of Romania dissolves parliament and (10 Feb) dismisses Octavian Goga, whose antisemitic policies have brought the country to the verge of economic collapse. The constitution is suspended and political parties suppressed.

● **4 Feb**: Adolf Hitler assumes leadership of the German ministry of war.

● **12 Feb**: Hitler bullies Austrian premier von Schuschnigg into agreeing an amnesty for imprisoned Austrian Nazis and allowing Nazis greater freedom of activity. (›24 Feb)

● **15 Feb**: Rebel leader Franco's forces recapture Teruel and begin a drive towards the Mediterranean. On 14 Apr they capture Vinaroz, cutting off government forces in Castile from Barcelona and Catalonia (Sp). (›23 Dec)

● **20 Feb**: Foreign Secretary Anthony Eden resigns in protest at prime minister Neville Chamberlain's policy toward an agreement with Italy prior to settlement in Spain. He is replaced by Lord Halifax (UK). (›16 Apr)

● **24 Feb**: Von Schuschnigg calls for a plebiscite on Austrian independence on 13 Mar. But on 11 Mar Hitler issues an ultimatum calling for von Schuschnigg's resignation; von Schuschnigg is replaced by Nazi Arthur Seyss-Inquart, who appeals to the German government to send troops to restore order. (›12 Mar)

● **2–15 Mar**: Purges continue in USSR with trial and execution of Nikolay Bukharin and others.

● **12 Mar**: The German army marches into Austria, meeting no resistance. On 13 Mar Austria is proclaimed a province of the German Reich. Persecution of Austrian Jews and anti-Nazis begins immediately. A plebiscite on 11 Apr reveals 99.75 percent in favour of union with Germany. The Anschluss is complete.

● **13 Mar**: Chautemps's government falls and Léon Blum forms a new Popular Front government. But like Chautemps, Blum faces opposition from the Senate and resigns. On 8 Apr Edouard Daladier takes over and is given decree powers until 31 Jul.

● **19 Mar**: Poland forces Lithuania to reopen its borders.

● **16 Apr**: UK and Italy conclude a pact in which the British recognize Italian sovereignty in Ethiopia and the Italians agree to withdraw troops from Spain at the end of the Civil War.

● **24 Apr**: The Sudeten Germans' demand for autonomy is rejected by the Prague government. (›19 May)

● **25 Apr**: Ireland agrees a pact with the UK setting aside the Ulster question, dissolving tariff barriers and returning coastal defences to Irish control. (›4 May)

● **30 Apr**: Switzerland applies to the League of Nations for recognition of its unconditional neutrality, which is accepted on 14 May.

● **3–9 May**: Hitler pays a state visit to Italian premier Mussolini in Rome which emphasizes the Rome-Berlin Axis.

● **4 May**: Under the new Irish constitution Dr Douglas Hyde – a Protestant and a leader of the Gaelic cultural revival – becomes first president.

● **10 May**: The Japanese resume their advance and take Xiamen, Suzhou, Kaifeng and Anking by 12 Jun. In Jul–Aug Russian and Japanese forces clash at Changkufeng Hill on the borders of Manzhouguo. (›22 Sep)

● **19–20 May**: Germans troops are rumoured to be on the Czechoslovak border. The Czechs mobilize; France and Britain warn Germany. (›7 Sep)

● **17 Jun**: Eamon De Valera's Fianna Fail party win 77 seats in national elections to the Opposition's 61 (Ire).

● **31 Jul**: Bulgaria signs a nonaggression pact with Greece which nevertheless permits rearmament.

● **3 Aug**: Mussolini begins a racist program against Italian Jews.

● **21–23 Aug**: The Little Entente recognizes the right of Hungary to rearm.

● **7 Sep**: Sudeten Germans break off relations with the Czech government. Street disturbances by extremists increase. France calls up reservists.

● **12 Sep**: Hitler demands the right of self-determination for the Sudeten Czechs. The Czech government proclaims martial law.

● **15 Sep**: British prime minister Neville Chamberlain meets with Hitler at Berchtesgaden. Britain and France press for Czech acceptance of German demands, while Hungary and Poland issue claims for Czech territory. Premier Hodza resigns and is replaced by Gen. Jan Sirovy. (›29 Sep)

● **22 Sep**: Japanese create a United Council for China at Beijing, clearly indicating their intention to turn China into a Japanese protectorate. They take Guangzhou with ease on 12 Oct, and Wuhan on 25 Oct. The Chinese government withdraws to Chongqing. USA, UK and other Western nations protest to no avail, although the League of Nations declares Japan the aggressor.

SOCIETY

● **29 Sep**: At the Munich Conference Hitler, Chamberlain, Mussolini and Daladier agree to transfer Sudetenland to Germany. The Czechs are not represented. France and the UK begin rearmament programs. Eduard Beneš, head of the Czech state, resigns and goes into voluntary exile in the USA, then the UK and France.

● **1–10 Oct**: Germany occupies Sudetenland, and Poland occupies Teschen.

● **4 Oct**: End of the Popular Front government as the Socialists and Communists abstain over a vote of confidence on the Munich agreements. Government now becomes much more rightwing (Fr).

● **6 Oct**: Slovakia is granted full autonomy; Ruthenia is granted autonomy on 8 Oct under the name of Carpatho-Ukraine. On 20 Oct the Communist party is outlawed and persecution of the Jews begins (Cze).

● **25 Oct**: Libya is declared part of Italy.

● **8 Nov**: In mid-term elections the Republicans make their first gains in 10 years, which is seen as a rebuff to Roosevelt (USA).

● **9 Nov**: Woodhead Commission reports that partition is unfeasible and calls for a conference of Jews and Arabs from Palestine and surrounding countries.

● **9–10 Nov**: The worst pogrom yet in Germany (Kristallnacht) takes place in response to the assassination of a Paris embassy official by a Jewish refugee. 100 Jews are killed; 20,000 are sent to concentration camps.

● **10 Nov**: Death of Kemal Ataturk, founder and president of the Turkish Republic. Ismet Inonu is elected as the new president.

● **22 Nov**: The government of Finland dissolves the Patriotic National Movement, a key fascist force.

● **26 Nov**: Poland and the USSR renew their nonaggression pact.

● **30 Nov**: There are calls in the Italian parliament and newspapers for the return of Corsica and Tunisia, currently under French control.

● **1 Dec**: A voluntary national register for war service is set up in the UK.

● **6 Dec**: France and Germany agree a friendship pact in which Germany expresses lack of interest in Alsace-Lorraine.

● **17 Dec**: Italy denounces its 1935 agreement with France.

● **23 Dec**: Franco begins his main offensive in Catalonia.

● **24 Dec**: At the Eighth American Conference in Peru, 21 American republics reaffirm the principle of mutual consultation and solidarity in the face of foreign intervention.

● **28 Dec**: Iraq severs relations with France.

● **Jan**: The German government urges the exclusion of non-Aryans from all positions in the private sector.

● **18 Mar**: In Mexico Lázaro Cárdenas's government takes over the properties of American and British oil companies valued at $450 million (the railroads had been nationalized in 1937). In Jul the US government proposes arbitration of claims against Mexico for expropriation of lands held by Americans, initially refused; compensation is agreed in Nov.

● **Mar**: The German reichsmark becomes legal tender in Austria and Austrian central banks are taken over by the Reichsbank.

● **Apr**: A work program is created at a cost of $4.5 billion (USA).

● **26 May**: A committee is set up to investigate un-American activities (USA).

● **May**: French premier Daladier publishes a national economic plan. (›12 Nov)

● **Jun**: Transformation of the Japanese economy into a war economy.

● **Jun**: Prime minister van Zeeland (Bel) publishes a plan for the enlargement of trade and reorganization of the world economy to counter protectionism.

● **5 Sep**: Mexico concludes barter agreements with Germany and Italy exchanging oil for manufactured goods previously imported from the USA.

● **24 Oct**: Wages and Hours Law provides for minimum wages and maximum weekly hours. It also prohibits child labor (USA).

● **12 Nov**: French government issues a large number of decrees aimed at improving the financial situation, which include a modification of the 40-hour week. This leads to an epidemic of strikes, culminating in a general 24-hour strike on 30 Nov. Government response is repressive.

● **17 Nov**: UK, Canada and USA conclude trade agreement involving sacrifices on all sides and indicating a growing spirit of cooperation between English-speaking nations.

● The Nobel Peace Prize is awarded to the Nansen International Office for Refugees, originally set up by Norwegian explorer Fridtjof Nansen in 1921 under League of Nations auspices, and the forerunner of the UN International Refugees Association.

● The Chinese divert the Yellow River southward to halt the Japanese invasion. 20,000 square miles are flooded and several hundred thousand people killed.

● New Zealand Social Security Act provides a state medical service.

● Italy wins World Cup football final against Hungary, retaining the cup they won four years ago.

● Cricketer Len Hutton scores 364 runs against Australia at the Oval Test Match, London.

CULTURE

● **16 Jan**: Benny Goodman gives the first jazz concert at New York's Carnegie Hall.

● **30 Oct**: Orson Welles's radio adaptation of H.G. Wells's novel *The War of the Worlds* is broadcast, causing widespread panic by its realism (USA).

● Jean-Paul Sartre: *La Nausée*, novel propounding existentialist theories (Fr).

● Samuel Beckett: *Murphy*, novel (Fr).

● Cyril Connolly: *Enemies of Promise*, essays with an autobiography (UK).

● William Faulkner: *The Unvanquished*, novel (USA).

● Graham Greene: *Brighton Rock*, novel (UK).

● Evelyn Waugh: *Scoop*, novel (UK).

● Christopher Isherwood: *Goodbye to Berlin*, novel (UK).

● George Orwell: *Homage to Catalonia*, based on the author's experiences in the Spanish Civil War (UK).

● Shiga Naoya: *A Dark Night's Passing*, novel (Jap).

● Nobel Prize for Literature is won by Pearl S. Buck (USA).

● Béla Bartók: *Violin Concerto* (Hung).

● Aaron Copland: *Billy the Kid*, ballet about the Wild West gunman William Bonney, first of a series of works based on American themes and material.

● Paul Hindemith: *Nobilissima Visione*, ballet choreographed by Leonid Massine. Hindemith's music is condemned by the Nazis and he leaves Germany in 1938.

● Conductor Arturo Toscanini withdraws from the Salzburg Festival in protest against the political situation in Austria.

● John Cage first creates his "prepared piano" (USA).

● Xanti Schawinsky: *Danse Macabre*, dance piece presented at Black Mountain College (USA).

● Crooner Frank Sinatra makes his radio debut (USA).

● Raoul Dufy: *Regatta*, painting (Fr).

● Pablo Picasso: *Woman in Easy Chair*, painting (Fr).

● Georges Rouault: *Ecce Homo*, painting (Fr).

● Salvador Dali is expelled from the Surrealist group by André Breton for his support for Hitler.

● International Surrealist exhibition opens in Paris.

● Frank Lloyd Wright builds Taliesin West, Phoenix, Arizona (USA).

● *Alexander Nevsky*, directed by Sergey Eisenstein with music by Prokofiev (USSR).

● Leni Riefenstahl: *Olympische Spiele 1936*, five-hour film of the 1936 Berlin Olympic Games (Ger).

● First issue of *Picture Post* appears (UK).

SCIENCE

● Nobel Prize for Physics is won by Enrico Fermi (It) "for his demonstrations of the existence of new radioactive elements produced by neutron irradiation, and for his related discovery of nuclear reactions brought about by slow neutrons".

● Nobel Prize for Physiology or Medicine is won by Corneille Heymans (Bel) "for his discovery of the role played by the sinus and aortic mechanisms in the regulation of respiration".

● R. Kuhn isolates vitamin B_6, and wins the Nobel Prize for Chemistry for his work on carotenoid and vitamin research (Ger).

● The radio altimeter, a gauge showing an aircraft's height above the ground, is developed at Bell Laboratories (USA).

● Ferdinand Porsche introduces the prototype of the Volkswagen "beetle" (Ger).

● Hungarian Lazslo Biró patents the ballpoint pen after being impressed by the quick-drying properties of printers' ink.

● H.H. Merritt and T.J. Putnam use a new anticonvulsant drug, Epanutin, as a treatment for epilepsy (USA).

● Julius Lempert introduces fenestration, cutting a window in overgrown layers of bone, to treat deafness (USA).

● C. Bridges produces a map of 1024 genes of the X chromosome of the Drosophila fruitfly (USA).

● H. Goosen catches a living coelacanth in the Indian Ocean. It had been presumed extinct for 60 million years.

● Otto Hahn is the first to split the uranium atom, opening up the possibility of atomic bombs (Ger).

● Paul Karrer synthesizes vitamin E (Switz).

● Harold Cox develops a vaccine for typhus (USA).

● Engineer T. Ross constructs the first machine able to "learn" from experience on the basis of feedback (USA).

● A new polymer from which Teflon non-stick pan coating will later be made is accidentally discovered by Roy Plunkett of Du Pont (USA).

● The manufacture of Nylon starts at the Du Pont de Nemours factory (USA). The first commercially produced product will be toothbrush bristles. Nylon yarn for stockings will be produced in Dec 1939.

● G.S. Callendar determines that human activities are causing an increase in the amount of carbon dioxide in the earth's atmosphere (UK).

● Philip Wiles develops the first total artificial hip replacement, using stainless steel (UK).

The film of Margaret Mitchell's novel "Gone with the Wind," a romantic portrayal of the bloody events of the American Civil War of the 1860s, reached the screen just as the second major conflict of the 20th century erupted in Europe. The Spanish Civil War of the late 1930s had already provided a chilling prelude. General Franco's victory was completed on 28 March, the same day that Hitler chose to denounce Germany's nonagression pact with Poland. Although diplomatic attempts were made to defuse the crisis, on 30 August his forces began to invade Poland. It was now clear that appeasement would not work; and by midday on 3 September France, Britain, Australia and New Zealand had declared war on Germany. Polish military resistance was soon crushed, for British and French forces were unable to intervene directly. The period that followed became known as the "phoney war", the lack of military activity contrasting strangely with the application of measures to protect civilians from bombing. School children were evacuated from London and Paris, gas masks issued and air raid shelters constructed.

▲ Clark Gable and Vivien Leigh starred in the film of *Gone with the Wind*, providing some much-needed escapism.

● **1–6 Jan**: France refuses to discuss Italian demands for cession of Algiers, Tunisia and Corsica, and premier Daladier visits North Africa where he is enthusiastically received.

● **17 Jan**: Norway, Sweden and Finland refuse a German bilateral nonaggression pact and insist on strict neutrality. However, Denmark, Estonia and Latvia enter into nonaggression pacts with Germany.

● **26 Jan**: With Italian assistance, Gen. Franco's rebel forces capture Barcelona. Over the next few weeks Franco secures Catalonia and 200,000 Loyalists flee to France (Sp). (›27 Feb)

● **29 Jan**: In the Indian Congressional elections, the radical leader Subhas Chandra Bose defeats Gandhi's candidate and becomes president for a second term. Congress delegates vote for Gandhi's program of complete independence and against Bose, who resigns on 29 Apr.

● **27 Feb**: UK and France unconditionally recognize the Franco regime as a legitimate government. Spanish president Azaña, based in Paris, resigns.

● **6 Mar**: Republican premier Negrin flies to France after a military coup; Gen. José Miaja forms the National Defense Council and vows to seek "peace with honor". However, conflict with the Communists continues and the National Defense Council is finally forced to accept unconditional surrender (Sp). (›28 Mar)

● **10–14 Mar**: The Prague government deposes premier Joseph Tiso for working for the separation of Slovakia. Tiso appeals to Hitler for support, and Hitler persuades president Hacha and foreign minister Chvalkovsky to place Czechoslovakia under his protection.

● **14 Mar**: Hungary invades and annexes Carpatho-Ukraine after heavy fighting.

● **15 Mar**: German troops occupy Bohemia-Moravia, which becomes a German protectorate, and Hitler enters Prague. On 16 Mar Tiso places Slovakia under German protection.

● **17 Mar**: The Palestine Conference in London attempts once more to settle the Jewish/Arab problem but ends without achieving a settlement. (›23 May)

● **20 Mar**: US ambassador is recalled from Berlin in protest at the invasion of Czechoslovakia; but the British and French claim that the guarantees they gave at Munich in 1938 applied to the whole of Czechoslovakia and the secession of Slovakia absolves them of responsibility.

● **23 Mar**: Germany annexes Memel (Lith), where the December elections had endorsed the National Socialist party.

● **28 Mar**: Civil war in Spain ends with the surrender of Madrid. Franco institutes the conviction of hundreds of Loyalists despite French and British protests. On 1 Apr the USA recognizes the new regime.

● **28 Mar**: Hitler denounces Germany's nonaggression pact with Poland of 1934. On 6 Apr France and the UK agree a mutual assistance pact with Poland. (›22 Aug)

● **2 Apr**: Japan and the USSR conclude a fishing rights treaty. In May the two nations begin fighting on the Manzhouguo-Outer Mongolia border.

● **7 Apr**: Italy invades Albania. King Zog flees to Greece and the Italian king Victor Emmanuel II assumes the crown.

● **7 Apr**: Spain joins Germany, Italy and Japan in the Anti-Comintern Pact.

● **11 Apr**: Under the influence of Germany, Hungary withdraws from the League of Nations; on 3 May Hungary institutes antisemitic laws.

● **15 Apr**: US President Roosevelt writes to Hitler and Mussolini asking them to guarantee peace in Europe and the Middle East but receives no answer.

● **27 Apr**: Hitler denounces the 1935 Anglo-German naval agreement.

● **22 May**: Hitler and Mussolini sign a 10-year political and military alliance which becomes known as the Pact of Steel.

● **23 May**: The UK government endorses a plan, opposed by Arabs and Jews, for an independent Palestinian state within 10 years. However, the matter never comes before the League of Nations due to the outbreak of war.

● **14 Jun**: The British refuse to give up four Chinese accused of terrorism and in response the Japanese blockade the British concession at Tianjin and demand withdrawal of British support for the Chinese Nationalist government.

● **23 Jun**: France and Turkey conclude a treaty of mutual aid. Turkey declares itself on the Allied side.

● **Jul**: UK announces suspension of the 1940 immigration quota for Jews as a result of large numbers of illegal immigrants entering Palestine.

● **22 Aug**: UK repeats its guarantee of protection for Poland and pleads for a conference on German territorial claims. (›25 Aug)

● **23 Aug**: Germany and the USSR sign a nonaggression pact and secretly define spheres of interest, shocking the other Western powers. The treaty invalidates the Anti-Comintern Pact.

● **25 Aug**: Hitler reiterates his demand for freedom to deal with Poland while both Germany and the UK increase military preparations.

● **30 Aug**: Poland begins partial mobilization while the German SS in Polish uniforms stage an attack on a German radio station at Gliewitz in a ploy to imply Polish aggression.

● **1 Sep**: Germany invades Poland and annexes Danzig.

SOCIETY

● **3 Sep**: The British ultimatum to Germany to withdraw from Poland expires at 11.00 hours and at 11.15 hours British prime minister Neville Chamberlain declares war. France, Australia and New Zealand also declare war while Mussolini announces neutrality.

● **5 Sep**: The USA declares neutrality in the European war.

● **5 Sep**: J.C. Smuts becomes premier of South Africa.

● **10 Sep**: The first units of the British Expeditionary Force begin to land in France.

● **16 Sep**: German troops surround Warsaw but the Poles refuse to surrender. Soviet troops invade from the east. On 19 Sep the Polish government withdraws to Romania.

● **27 Sep**: Poland surrenders. On 30 Sep a German/USSR treaty of friendship partitions Poland.

● **28 Sep**: USSR signs a mutual assistance pact with Estonia; on 5 Oct a similar pact with Latvia; and on 10 Oct a similar pact with Lithuania while ceding Vilna to Lithuania.

● **2 Oct**: Washington recognizes the Polish government-in-exile in Paris.

● **6 Oct**: Hitler attempts to make peace with Britain and France; his overtures are rejected.

● **19 Oct**: Hitler incorporates western Poland into the German Reich and establishes the first Jewish ghetto in Lublin.

● **4 Nov**: Roosevelt signs an amendment to the Neutrality Act which allows the USA to help the Allies by sale of arms.

● **8 Nov**: Hitler escapes death as a bomb explodes in a Munich beer hall 15 minutes after he has left.

● **18 Nov**: 60,000 tonnes of UK shipping are sunk in one week as a result of magnetic mines laid by German U-boats.

● **26 Nov**: After the Finnish government refuses Russian demands for military bases, the USSR renounces the 1932 Soviet-Finnish nonaggression pact; on 30 Nov the Russo-Finnish War begins as the Soviets invade. (›14 Dec)

● **13 Dec**: Three British warships pursue and corner the German *Graf Spee* in Montevideo harbour. The crew scuttle the ship rather than allow her to be captured.

● **14 Dec**: USSR is expelled from the League of Nations when it refuses to allow mediation in the war with Finland.

● **1 Jan**: IRA terrorist activities continue as a series of bomb blasts hits cities in the UK and in Northern Ireland.

● **12 Jan**: President Roosevelt requests an additional $525 million for defense.

● **Jan**: The Trans-Iranian Railroad is opened from the Caspian Sea to the Persian Gulf.

● **21 Mar**: UK and India sign a trade pact giving new concessions for Lancashire cotton goods being imported into India.

● **23 Mar**: Romania concludes an agreement with Germany giving the Nazis oil at privileged terms.

● **27 Apr**: Britain begins call-up of men aged 20–21.

● **30 Apr**: Opening of the New York World's Fair at which, for the first time, industrial design takes prominence over decorative art. The theme of the fair is "progress and peace".

● **Apr**: Germany establishes "Great German" tariff area.

● **20 May**: Pan American Airways begin regular commercial flights between the USA and Europe.

● **14 Jun**: USSR considers concealment of Mendel's genetic laws which are in conflict with Marxist dialectics.

● **24 Jun**: Brazil allows entry to 3,000 German Jewish refugees.

● **Jun**: The board of the Reichsbank protest after a law authorizing unlimited credits for the German government from the Reichsbank.

● **29 Jul**: Jenny Kammersgaad (Den) becomes the first person to swim the Baltic Sea.

● **23 Sep**: Sigmund Freud dies in London, whence he and his family had fled from Vienna early in 1938.

● **Sep**: Evacuation of school children from London and Paris begins. UK parliament discusses the building of air raid shelters for the general public.

● **Sep**: Control of foreign exchange, confiscations and reparations affect the international capital markets after the outbreak of World War II.

● **Sep**: USSR and Germany agree trade relations.

● **30 Oct**: A UK government white paper documents atrocities being committed in Nazi concentration camps.

● **12 Dec**: France and the UK agree on financial measures to ease the war burden.

● **27 Dec**: An earthquake in Turkey kills 11,000.

● Crisis in the citrus industry – Palestine's major industry – leads to almost half the working population being laid off by the end of the year.

● Ellison Brown wins the Boston Marathon in 2 hours, 28 minutes and 51.8 seconds (USA).

CULTURE

● James Joyce: *Finnegans Wake*, experimental novel (Fr).

● John Steinbeck: *The Grapes of Wrath*, epic novel of the American dustbowl disaster (USA).

● Nathanael West: *The Day of the Locust*, satire on Hollywood life (USA).

● Antoine de Saint-Exupéry: *Terre des hommes* (Wind, Sand and Stars), novel (Fr).

● Thomas Mann: *Lotte in Weimar*, novel based on a minor incident in the life of Goethe (USA).

● T.S. Eliot: *The Family Reunion*, play (UK).

● Nobel Prize for Literature is won by Frans Sillanpää (Fin)

● William Walton: Violin Concerto (UK).

● Béla Bartók completes his *Mikrocosmos*, a set of 153 piano teaching pieces (Hung).

● *Imaginary Landscape No. 1* – John Cage produces his first composed piece for elecrical reproduction apparatus (record turntables) (USA).

● Michael Tippett: Concerto for Double String Orchestra (UK).

● Arnold Schoenberg: *Kol Nidre*, for speaker, chorus and orchestra; partly based on a Jewish liturgical theme (USA).

● Ivor Novello: *The Dancing Years*, revue (UK).

● Jerome Kern: *The Last Time I Saw Paris*, musical (USA).

● "All or Nothing at All", sung by Frank Sinatra, sells a million copies.

● Pablo Picasso: *Night Fishing at Antibes*, painting (Fr).

● René Magritte: *Time Transfixed*, painting (Fr).

● Shiko Munakata: *The rakan subodai*, woodblock print (Jap).

● Stanley Spencer: *Christ in the Wilderness*, first in the series (UK).

● Joan Miró: *Seated Woman II*, painting (Sp).

● Ben Shahn: *Handball*, painting (USA).

● Jacob Epstein: *Adam*, sculpture (UK).

● Henry Moore: *Reclining Figure*, sculpture (UK).

● Frank Lloyd Wright: Johnson Wax Building (USA).

● Alvar Aalto: Villa Mairea, Noormarkku (Fin).

● Film of Margaret Mitchell's bestselling romantic novel *Gone with the Wind* stars Vivien Leigh as Scarlett O'Hara (USA).

● The film of *The Wizard of Oz* makes Judy Garland a star overnight.

● John Ford's classic Western, *Stagecoach*, starring John Wayne (USA).

● Jean Renoir: *La Règle du jeu* (The Rules of the Game) (Fr).

SCIENCE

● **Sep**: Igor Sikorsky constructs the first helicopter designed for mass production (USA).

● Nobel Prize for Physics is won by Ernest O. Lawrence (USA) for the invention and development of the cyclotron and for his results obtained with it with regard to artificial radioactive elements.

● Nobel Prize for Chemistry is won by Adolf Butenandt (Ger) "for his work on the mammalian sex hormones" and by Leopold Ružička (Swiss) "for his work on polymethylenes and higher terpines".

● Nobel Prize for Physiology or Medicine is won by Gerhard Domagk (Ger) "for his discovery of the antibacterial effects of Prontosil".

● Test flight of the first turbojet, the Heinkel He 178, designed by Pabst von Ohain (Ger).

● E.H. Armstrong builds the first FM radio broadcasting station (USA).

● A.N. Belozersky begins his experimental work to show that DNA and RNA are always present in bacteria.

● Austrian physicist Lise Meitner and her nephew Otto Frisch, who fled from Germany to Sweden to escape the Kristallnacht pogrom, explain the work of Hahn and Strassmann regarding the first artificially created nuclear fission.

● J.F. Joliot-Curie demonstrates the possibility of splitting uranium-235 (Fr).

● Because of fears that the Germans might be working on an atomic bomb, Albert Einstein is persuaded to write to president Roosevelt suggesting that uranium fission could be used to produce an atomic explosion. As a result the Manhattan Project is set up, which will in 1945 produce the first atomic bombs (USA).

● Niels Bohr proposes a liquid-drop model of the atomic nucleus (Den).

● ICI begins commercial production of polythene (UK).

● H. Dam and E.A. Doisy isolate pure Vitamin K (USA).

● J.R. Oppenheimer discovers the properties of what is later known as a "black hole" (USA).

● Paul Muller discovers that DDT is a potent insecticide.

● A new, rapidly spreading, disease of elm trees is identified (USA).

● John V. Atanasoff produces the first electronic computer (USA).

1940-1949

1940

POLITICS

During the spring of 1940 a series of lightning victories were achieved by German arms. Norway and Denmark were invaded on 9 April and a month later German troops attacked in the Low Countries. By mid-May French and British forces were in a hopeless position in northern France and on 14 June Paris was taken by German troops. Hitler's military triumph in the west was consolidated on 22 June by the armistice with France, which transferred the northern part of the country to German control. The map of Europe was also changing as a result of other conflicts. The Soviet Union acquired parts of Finland and then absorbed the Baltic republics. Italy invaded southern France and, subsequently, British colonial territories in Africa. The structure of the fascist forces was formalized by the drawing up of the German–Italian–Japanese pact in September, joined by Hungary and Romania in November. From the summer of 1940 the focus of the war in the west became the aerial battle between Britain and Germany, while on the ground the Balkans constituted the centre of conlfict.

▲ On 14 June 1940 Hitler's troops entered Paris. The French leaders made arrangements to seek an armistice, which was signed on 22 June, and the French government was relocated to Vichy under Marshal Pétain. General Charles de Gaulle promptly began to organize the French Resistance movement, supported by Winston Churchill's government in the UK.

● **1 Feb**: USSR begins a new offensive against Finland, attacking the Karelian Isthmus and Lake Kuhmo, followed up on 11 Feb by a continuous attack on the Mannerheim Line, breaking through near Summa.

● **Jan–Feb**: The Allies lose 400,000 tonnes of shipping to German U-boats in the Atlantic.

● **5 Mar**: Although the Finns cause heavy Soviet casualties, they are numerically overwhelmed and send a peace delegation to Moscow. On 13 Mar, an armistice is signed by which Finland cedes the Karelian Isthmus, the Rybachiy Peninsula and other territory to the USSR and leases the port of Hanko.

● **18 Mar**: German leader Hitler and Italian dictator Mussolini meet at the Brenner Pass in the Alps. Mussolini agrees to join Germany in the war against Britain and France. (›10 Jun)

● **20 Mar**: In a crisis over the lack of French aid to the Finns, premier Daladier is forced to resign and is succeeded by Paul Reynaud (Fr).

● **30 Mar**: The Japanese set up a puppet government in Nanjing (Chi).

● **9 Apr**: Germans invade neutral Norway and Denmark, advancing rapidly and causing the British to evacuate their forces from Norway by the end of Apr. The Norwegian royal family, government and gold reserves leave Oslo for Tromsö in the far north and a puppet government is set up under Vidkun Quisling. (›10 Jun)

● **9 May**: British prime minster Neville Chamberlain resigns and is succeeded by Winston Churchill, with a mandate to form an all-party coalition government. Labour leader Clement Attlee becomes deputy prime minister.

● **10 May**: Germany invades the Low Countries (Belgium, Luxembourg, the Netherlands) without warning and troops advance rapidly.

● **14 May**: Germans bomb Rotterdam after Dutch refusal of their surrender demand. The Dutch royal family goes into exile and the Dutch army is ordered to surrender.

● **16 May**: British and French forces begin to retreat in the face of advancing German Panzer Corps in Belgium. On 17 May German troops enter Brussels, forcing the government to move to Ostend. On 28 May King Leopold agrees to the surrender of the Belgian army without consulting the Belgian government or the Allies.

● **20 May**: Germans capture Amiens and Abbeville, cutting off the British and Belgian forces from the main French armies.

● **24 May**: German troops attack Boulogne and Calais while the British Royal Navy evacuates 5,000 men.

● **29 May–3 Jun**: Allied forces are evacuated from Dunkirk in an operation involving all available ships. 215,000 British and 120,000 French troops are rescued but almost all equipment has to be abandoned.

● **10 Jun**: Italy declares war on Britain and France.

● **10 Jun**: The Norwegian king and government leave Tromsö for Britain and order Norwegian forces to cease fighting.

● **12–22 Jun**: USSR issues ultimatums to Lithuania, Estonia and Latvia demanding territory and new government. They occupy Kaunas and Vilna and on 15 Jul annex the three states after a favorable plebiscite.

● **14 Jun**: Germans troops take Paris. The USA refuses French request for aid on 15 Jun, and on 16 Jun Marshal Philippe Pétain replaces Paul Reynaud as premier.

● **22 Jun**: France agrees to an armistice by which French forces are to be disarmed and northern and western France surrendered to German control; the remainder will nominally remain under French rule, with the French parliament based in Vichy. On 10 Jul the French parliament dissolves the Third Republic and transfers all state powers to Pétain.

● **27 Jun**: Romania refuses the Russian demand for the cession of Bessarabia and Bukovina, whereupon the Russians invade. On 9 Jul Romania places itself under German protection.

● **28 Jun**: Gen. Charles de Gaulle, French under-secretary of war before the armistice, is recognized by Britain as the "Leader of all Free Frenchmen" and begins to organize French resistance.

● **30 Jun**: German troops invade the Channel Islands.

● **3 Jul**: The British attack the French Navy in North Africa and off Plymouth and Portsmouth, intending to stop the French navy from falling into the hands of the Germans. The Vichy government breaks off diplomatic relations with Britain on 5 Jul.

● **10 Jul**: Hitler launches the aerial Battle of Britain with action over the Channel and a bombing raid on the South Wales docklands. (›18 Aug)

● **18 Jul**: The British close the Burma Road, thereby prohibiting the passage of supplies to Chinese Nationalists from the outside world.

● **Jul–Oct**: Peak period of German U-boat success against Allied shipping. In Sep Britain loses 160,000 tonnes of shipping.

● **3 Aug**: Italy invades British Somaliland (N Afr) from bases in Ethiopia, leading to a British withdrawal followed by a decision to send a large tank force to the area.

● **6 Aug**: Britain abandons its outposts in Shanghai and Tianjin province, leaving the area under Japanese contro (Chi).

● **18 Aug**: The Battle of Britain reaches its peak: 180 German bombers have been shot down since July, and the Luftwaffe now switches to urban targets in the south of England.

SOCIETY   CULTURE   SCIENCE

- **20 Aug**: Exiled Bolshevik leader Leon Trotsky is assassinated by a Stalinist agent, Ramón Mercador (Mex).

- **23 Aug**: An all-night bombing raid on London signals the beginning of the "Blitz". Raids on provincial British cities follow.

- **3 Sep**: USA agrees to send Britain 50 over-age destroyers in exchange for leased bases in Newfoundland and the Caribbean.

- **11 Sep**: UK parliament interprets the massing of German barges and merchant ships in northern French ports as preparation for invasion by the Germans.

- **13 Sep**: Italy begins an invasion of Egypt.

- **22 Sep**: Start of Japanese occupation of Indochina, which blocks aid to the Chinese.

- **27 Sep**: A German-Italian-Japanese pact is concluded providing a 10-year military mutual assistance and economic alliance.

- **Sep**: British RAF bombers begin raids on German cities.

- **10 Oct**: The Germans conduct a plebiscite in Luxembourg which shows that 97 percent of the population oppose their occupation. No plebiscites are conducted elsewhere.

- **18 Oct**: The Vichy government introduces antisemitic laws (Fr).

- **28 Oct**: The Italians begin to invade Greece and Albania, and British troops are sent to aid the Greeks. On 21 Nov the Greeks capture 2,000 Italians at Koritza and drive the Italian forces back into Albania.

- **Oct**: German and Italian forces enter Romania and occupy Bucharest. King Carol is made to abdicate in favor of his young son Michael.

- **5 Nov**: President Roosevelt decisively wins a record third-term election against Wendell Wilkie, the Republican candidate (USA).

- **11–12 Nov**: The British cripple the Italian fleet in the port of Taranto.

- **14 Nov**: The Luftwaffe devastate the industrial city of Coventry (UK). However, air attacks subsequently become more sporadic. The Germans have sustained heavy losses, 2,375 planes since Aug.

- **20 Nov**: The Stimson-Layton Agreement between the USA and UK provides for a partial standardization of military weapons and equipment and begins a policy of pooling technical knowledge, patents and formulas in armament production.

- **20 Nov**: Hungary joins the Berlin-Rome-Tokyo Pact; on 23 Nov Romania also joins.

- **9 Dec**: The British begin an offensive against the Italians. On 13 Dec they enter Libya.

- **3 Jan**: Roosevelt submits a budget of $8.4 million including $1.8 million for defense.

- **8 Jan**: Food rationing begins in the UK with restrictions on bacon, butter and sugar.

- **1 Feb**: British women are to receive the old age pension at 60.

- **1 Feb**: A record budget, of which half is allocated to military expenditure, is submitted to the Diet (Jap).

- **Feb**: Coronation of the five-year-old Dalai Lama in Tibet.

- **Mar**: US commercial airlines for the first time complete a year of operations without a single fatal accident.

- **12 May**: Churchill makes the first of his inspirational speeches, declaring: "I have nothing to offer you but blood, toil, tears and sweat", but stressing his determination to win (UK).

- **14 May**: Recruiting begins for a volunteer home defense force – the "Home Guard" – from men otherwise debarred from military service (UK).

- **May**: Labour Authorization Law is passed, by which all can be forced to work if needed (UK).

- **4 Jun**: Churchill broadcasts his most famous speech: "We shall fight on the beaches, we shall fight on the landing grounds, we shall fight in the fields and in the streets, we shall never surrender" (UK).

- **Jun**: The working day in the USSR is increased from seven to eight hours. In Jul agricultural reforms confiscate land from farmers and impose stricter discipline. In addition large price rises are introduced.

- **23 Jul**: Purchase tax is imposed (UK).

- **31 Jul**: UK production of fighter aircraft is found to be 50 percent above target. 1,200 planes have been manufactured since 1 May, enabling the RAF to catch up with Luftwaffe air power.

- **13 Sep**: The Selective Service Act initiates compulsory call-up for males aged 21–35 (USA). Canada and the USSR begin similar conscription programs.

- **26 Sep**: In an attempt to cut off Japanese supplies, President Roosevelt places an embargo on the export of scrap steel and iron outside the Western Hemisphere, except to Britain (USA).

- **1 Oct**: A solar eclipse in South Africa blots out daylight for 230 seconds and is reported as the most perfect eclipse ever seen.

- **26 Nov**: In Warsaw work begins on a Jewish ghetto, described by the Germans as a "health measure" (Pol).

- **Nov**: Prehistoric cave paintings are discovered in the Lascaux caves (Fr).

- **Graham Greene**: *The Power and the Glory*, novel (UK).

- **Ernest Hemingway**: *For Whom The Bell Tolls*, novel based on the author's experiences in the Spanish Civil War (USA).

- **Carson McCullers**: *The Heart is a Lonely Hunter*, novel (USA).

- **Dylan Thomas**: *Portrait of the Artist as a Young Dog*, short stories (UK).

- **Arthur Koestler**: *Darkness at Noon*, novel inspired by the trial of Bukharin during Stalin's purges (UK).

- **Lennox Berkeley**: First Symphony (UK).

- **Igor Stravinsky**: Symphony in C Major. During its composition (1938–40) Stravinsky moves from Paris to Los Angeles, where he spends the rest of his life.

- **Michael Tippett**: *A Child of our Time*, oratorio to the composer's words, for solo voices, choir and orchestra (UK).

- **Anton Webern**: *Orchestral Variations* (Aut).

- **Benjamin Britten**: *Sinfonia da Requiem*, written while Britten and tenor Peter Pears are in the USA.

- **Max Beckmann**: *Circus Caravan*, painting (Neth).

- **Wassily Kandinsky**: *Sky Blue*, painting (Fr).

- **Henri Matisse**: *Rumanian Blouse*, painting (Fr).

- **Paul Klee**: *Death and Fire*, painting.

- **Pablo Picasso**: *Woman Dressing Her Hair*, painting (Fr).

- **Grandma** (Anna Mary Robertson) **Moses**, American primitive painter, has her first one-woman show in New York at the age of 80 after being discovered by an art collector.

- **John Piper**: *St Mary le Port, Bristol* (UK).

- **Official British war artists** are appointed: Edward Ardizzone, Muirhead Bone, Henry Lamb, John and Paul Nash, Henry Moore and Eric Ravilious.

- **Albert Speer and Adolf Hitler**: plan for a New Berlin.

- **Raymond Hood and others**: Rockefeller Center, New York.

- **Designers Charles Eames and Eero Saarinen** (Fin) win a MOMA competition with their bent plywood chairs (USA).

- **Packaging for *Lucky Strike* cigarettes** is redesigned by Raymond Loewy (USA).

- *The Great Dictator*, starring, written and directed by Charlie Chaplin; it is also his first talkie (USA).

- *Rebecca*, directed by Alfred Hitchcock, wins the Academy Award for the Best Picture of the Year.

- Walt Disney's *Fantasia* is the first film recorded in multi-dimensional sound and broadcast in stereophonic sound (USA).

- **Nov**: The Jeep (from GP, general purpose), a four-wheel-drive military vehicle capable of operating over rough terrain, is introduced into the US forces.

- **Karl Landsteiner and A.S. Wiener** discover the Rhesus factor in blood, later linked to hemolytic disease in newborn babies (USA).

- As a fortuitous result of German requisitioning of all wheat and rye supplies, Dutch doctors recognize that celiac disease can be caused by sensitivity to gluten.

- **Vincent Du Vigneaud** identifies biotin, the compound previously known as vitamin H (USA).

- **Herbert M. Evans** uses radioactive iodine to prove that iodine is used by the thyroid gland.

- **Carl Jung**: *The Interpretation of Personality*, psychology text (Swi).

- **Howard Florey and Ernst Chain** develop penicillin as an antibiotic. E.P. Abraham and Chain discover germs which are resistant to penicillin, prompting a search for further antibiotics (UK).

- **Edward Cohn** separates albumin, globulin and fibrin fractions of blood plasma. Albumin will be used to treat shock, globulin to treat infection and fibrin to halt bleeding (USA).

- Uranium 235 is isolated from the heavier isotope uranium 238, making the first nuclear bomb possible (USA).

- Freeze drying is used for food preservation for the first time (USA).

- Cavity magnetron, a new tube making radar more sensitive, is invented (UK).

- A cyclotron is built at the University of California for producing mesotrons from atomic nuclei (USA).

- **M.D. Kamen** discovers carbon-14 (Can).

- The Plan Position Indicator is developed: it shows an aircraft, detected by radar echo, on a circular screen as a pattern of fast-moving dots against a cartographic background. The PPI is used for antisubmarine patrol and blind bombing (UK).

- The first gas-powered turbine in the world to generate electricity for public use begins operating at a power station in Neuchâtel (Swi).

- The collapse of the Tacoma Narrows suspension bridge within four months of its opening leads to an understanding of the need for aerodynamic stability in bridges and to the intensification of research into the effects of wind on large structures (USA).

- Mechanical cotton pickers are tested (USA).

1941

POLITICS

During 1941 the global nature of the hostilities became clear as military conflict spread out beyond the confines of Europe. German victories in the west during 1940 were now paralleled by equally rapid gains in the east, following the invasion of the Soviet Union on 6 July. This German onslaught was halted in November, by which time German troops were in sight of Moscow. The war in the Pacific began with the Japanese attack on 7 December on Pearl Harbor and other American and British bases, while on 11 December Germany and Italy declared war on the United States. Allied military gains during the year were limited and in North Africa were to prove to be only temporary. More important for the Allies were other developments. The inception of the American Lend-Lease program started the logistics for the ultimate Allied victory. The Atlantic Charter concluded by Roosevelt and Churchill gave the Western Allies a political program for rebuilding world order, so laying the foundations for the United Nations. Civilians around the world began to tighten their belts as rationing took hold, not only in the Allied countries affected by German U-boat attacks, but also in Russia and Japan.

▲ After the USA refused to enter negotiations with Japan, the Japanese launched a surprise attack on the US Pacific Fleet at anchor in Pearl Harbor, Hawaii, destroying 29 ships and numerous aircraft and personnel, thus bringing the USA into the war.

●3–5 Jan: British attack the Italians at Bardia in Libya, which they take two days later (N Afr).

● 10 Jan: Germans launch their first attack on Malta, which remains under siege until Nov 1942.

● 20 Jan: President Franklin D. Roosevelt is inaugurated for his third term as president.

● 22 Jan: Italians surrender Tobruk, a major Libyan port, to the British.

● 30 Jan: The Italians are driven from Kenya by the South African army.

● 6 Feb: The British take another major Libyan port, Benghazi, and the Italians take flight westwards. On 12 Feb German troops under Gen. Rommel arrive in Tripoli. (›30 Mar)

● 17 Feb: Turkey and Bulgaria sign friendship agreements with Germany. On 1 Mar Bulgaria joins the Tripartite Pact, and on 2 Mar German troops move into Bulgaria.

● 17 Feb: Emperor Haile Selassie joins Gen. Orde Wingate and his "Gideon Force" of guerrillas in an attempt to drive the Italians out of Ethiopia. On 6 Apr British and Ethiopian troops take Addis Ababa, forcing the Italians to retreat; and on 3 Jul the Italian troops surrender.

● 27 Mar: Following a secret meeting with German leader Adolf Hitler, Prince Paul, regent of Yugoslavia, announces that the nation will join the Tripartite Pact. Air force officers lead a coup to replace him by 17-year-old King Peter. (›6 Apr)

● 30 Mar: The German counteroffensive in North Africa begins. Benghazi is retaken on 4 Apr, Tobruk is isolated on 5 Apr, and on 25 Apr Rommel invades Egypt. (›18 Nov)

● 1 Apr: A coup is staged in Iraq by Rashid Ali and army officers in opposition to British presence. Britain lands troops to put down the coup and secure oil supplies (19 Apr). On 31 May Rashid Ali flees to Iran, and Iraq agrees to an armistice.

● 6 Apr: Hitler invades Yugoslavia; Greece is invaded as part of the same maneuver. On 12 Apr Belgrade surrenders to the Germans and two days later King Peter flees to Athens. On 17 Apr Yugoslavia signs an armistice with Germany.

● 13 Apr: USSR and Japan sign a five-year neutrality agreement which allows the Russian leader Joseph Stalin to switch forces from Siberia to the western front.

● 14–18 Apr: In Greece, Greek and British troops are forced back by advancing Germans. On 22 Apr the Greek army surrenders.

● 7 May: A German weather ship is captured off Iceland and is found to be carrying secret documents on the German's coding machine, Enigma. On 9 May a captured U-boat provides the cipher machine and code books.

● 10 May: In a major raid, German bombers heavily damage the House of Commons in London. Rudolf Hess, deputy leader of the Nazi party, flies alone to Scotland, claiming to bring peace proposals; he is captured and imprisoned.

● 15 May: President Roosevelt takes into "protective custody" all French ships in US ports.

● 20 May–1 Jun: The Germans invade and secure Crete with heavy losses on both sides.

● 21 May: An American merchant ship, the *Robin Moore*, is sunk by a German U-boat inside Roosevelt's defense line. American public opinion becomes increasingly hostile to the Germans.

● 23–27 May: In a major battle in the Atlantic the British Navy sinks the German battleship *Bismarck*.

● 8 Jun: British and Free French forces invade Syria to prevent German aircraft operating from Syrian bases. On 11 Jun Syria agrees to an armistice and will in future be administered by the Allies.

● 22 Jun: The Germans invade the USSR in an operation codenamed Barbarossa. The initial German advance is rapid. The Finns take advantage of the situation to invade Karelia.

● 6 Jul: Soviet troops abandon Poland and the Baltic states, and on 9 Jul the Germans cross the Dnieper and Dvina rivers and head for Smolensk, taking over 300,000 Soviet prisoners. On 16 Jul the Germans take Smolensk; on 27 Jul they enter the Ukraine. (›15 Sep)

● 12 Jul: The British and Russians sign an agreement of mutual assistance.

● 26 Jul: Following a Japanese ultimatum demanding military control of the French colonies of Indochina, Britain and the US freeze Japanese assets. On 27 Jul Japanese troops occupy Indochina.

● Jul: German U-boats are increasingly successful in their campaign against Allied shipping. On 1 Jul the US Navy starts antisubmarine patrols from Newfoundland.

● 9–12 Aug: UK prime minister Winston Churchill and US president Roosevelt meet secretly aboard a ship in the Atlantic and sign the Atlantic Charter, a statement of principles setting forth eight goals for the world. On 24 Sep 15 nations, including the USSR, endorse this charter, which will become the blueprint for the United Nations.

● 24 Aug–9 Sep: In a move to safeguard oil supplies, Britain and the USSR launch a joint invasion against Iran, which meets with little opposition. (›16 Sep)

● 4 Sep: The US destroyer *Greer* is attacked by a German U-boat while on convoy escort, leading Roosevelt to order that US warships and planes "shoot on sight" any Axis ship within the American Defense Zone.

SOCIETY

● **15 Sep**: Siege of Leningrad begins (›27 Jan 1944). On 19 Sep the Germans take Kiev; on 1 Oct the British and Americans issue a joint declaration of support and aid to the USSR; on 16 Oct, with the Germans only 95 km (60 miles) from Moscow, the government is transferred to Kuibishev. (›24 Oct)

● **16–17 Sep**: The shah of Iran fails to expel all Axis nationals, which leads to an Allied occupation of Tehran. The shah abdicates in favor of the crown prince, Muhammad Reza Pahlavi.

● **16 Oct**: Gen. Hideki Tojo, who favors war, becomes prime minister of Japan.

● **24 Oct**: Siege of Sevastopol begins (›2 Jul 1942). The first German offensive against Moscow is a failure; but by 23 Nov, the Germans approach to within 55 km (35 miles) of Moscow. (›27 Nov)

● **17 Nov**: The Japanese ambassador to the US, Kichisaburo Nomura, begins negotiations with the State Department in Washington. (›1 Dec)

● **18 Nov**: The British launch a new offensive to relieve Tobruk (N Afr). On 23 Nov British and German troops clash near Tobruk, Rommel's Afrika Korps suffering heavy losses. On 10 Dec the British reach and relieve Tobruk. Rommel retreats westward.

● **26 Nov**: Lebanon declares itself an independent state, taking advantage of French inability to respond.

● **27 Nov**: The Russians launch a counteroffensive, forcing the Germans to evacuate Rostov-on-Don. On 29 Nov a further counteroffensive is launched from Moscow, and on 5 Dec Hitler abandons Operation Barbarossa in face of freezing weather and heavy casualties. Britain declares war on Finland, Hungary and Romania for their refusal to cease war against the USSR.

● **28 Nov**: 20,000 Italian troops surrender as the Allies secure Ethiopia (Abyssinia).

● **1 Dec**: The Japanese government rejects the terms offered by the USA. On 6 Dec Roosevelt appeals to Emperor Hirohito to use his influence to avoid war.

● **7 Dec**: The Japanese attack the US Pacific Fleet at anchor in Pearl Harbor, Hawaii, sinking 29 ships, destroying 188 planes and killing 2,403 personnel. The Japanese also attack US bases in the Philippines, Guam and Midway and British bases in Malaya and Hong Kong.

● **8 Dec**: USA and Britain declare war on Japan.

● **10 Dec**: The Japanese capture the island of Guam and land on Luzon, the principal Philippine island.

● **11 Dec**: Germany and Italy declare war on the USA.

● **22–23 Dec**: The Japanese capture Wake Island. On 25 Dec the British surrender Hong Kong, and on 27 Dec Manila (Phil) is declared an open city by the USA as the Japanese advance.

● **26 Feb**: Italy and Germany agree that for the duration of the war, delivery of goods between their two countries will be effected without regard to trade balance or clearing. Italy also begins a program of transfer of Italian workers to Germany.

● **Feb**: The UK government imposes a trade blockade against Romania and Bulgaria.

● **11 Mar**: Roosevelt signs the Lend-Lease Act, which empowers the president to transfer ships, arms and war materials to any country vital to US interests and to defer their payments. Congress agrees to $7 billion as an initial budget allocation.

● **Mar**: The "Women for Victory" campaign is launched in Germany. UK minister for labor Ernest Bevin calls on Britain's women to fill vital jobs in factories and the auxiliary services.

● **Mar**: A law is passed for an extension of the war economy in the UK.

● **11 Apr**: Roosevelt establishes the Office of Price Administration to control prices and profits, an attempt to contain wartime inflation (USA).

● **Apr**: In Japan rice rationing begins.

● **23 May**: Joe Louis wins his 17th world heavyweight boxing title defense (USA).

● **14–16 Jun**: Roosevelt uses his emergency powers to freeze all German and Italian assets in the USA.

● **Jul**: Ration cards are introduced in Leningrad and Moscow. In Aug an Emergency War Plan for the economy is approved.

● **Jul**: The BBC (UK) begins broadcasts to Europe encouraging resistance movements, prefacing the broadcasts with the Morse Code signal for V and the slogan "V for Victory". V for victory becomes a symbol of Western European resistance.

● **Aug**: The USA imposes an embargo on petroleum and crude oil against Japan.

● **6 Sep**: Reinhard Heydrich, head of German security police, orders that all Jews aged six or over are to wear a distinguishing Star of David.

● **30 Oct**: Roosevelt offers $1 billion worth of supplies to the USSR under the lend-lease program (USA).

● **7 Nov**: USA agrees a lend-lease agreement with Cuba. On 11 Dec Cuba declares war on Japan, Germany and Italy.

● **9 Dec**: UK call-up is extended to single women aged 20–30.

● **15 Dec**: US Congress appropriates $10 billion for the defense of the USA and for lend-lease aid, and extends military service requirements.

● The American Red Cross Blood Donor Service is established.

● Clothes rationing begins in the UK and "utility" clothing and furnishings are promoted.

CULTURE

● **May**: Premiere in New York of the film *Citizen Kane*, written, directed, produced by and starring Orson Welles.

● **Oct**: Premiere of the film of Dashiell Hammett's *The Maltese Falcon*, directed by John Huston and starring Humphrey Bogart (USA).

● F.Scott Fitzgerald: *The Last Tycoon*, novel (USA).

● Franz Werfel's: *The Song of Bernadette* (USA), novel about St Bernadette of Lourdes, based largely on missions, is a worldwide success except in countries dominated by the National Socialists, where it is banned.

● Louis Aragon: *Le Crève-Coeur*, poems. Aragon, earlier involved with the Surrealist movement, becomes one of the most popular of the poets of the French Resistance.

● Ilya Ehrenburg: *The Fall of Paris*, novel (USSR).

● Henry Miller: *The Colossus of Maroussi* (USA).

● W.H. Auden: *New Year Letter*, poem (USA).

● Virginia Woolf: *Between the Acts*, novel (UK).

● Allen Curnow: *Island and Time*, poems (NZ).

● Bertolt Brecht: *Mother Courage and her Children* and *The Resistible Rise of Arturo Ui*, plays (USA).

● Noel Coward: *Blithe Spirit*, comedy (UK).

● Dmitri Shostakovich: Seventh (Leningrad) Symphony, written in Leningrad while the city is under siege (USSR).

● William Walton: Scapino Overture (UK).

● Olivier Messaien: *Quatuor pour la fin du temps*, for violin, clarinet, cello and piano, written while Messaien was a prisoner of war in Germany, and first performed in his prison camp.

● Paul Nash: *Bombers over Berlin*, painting (UK).

● Henry Moore makes a series of drawings in crayon of Londoners taking refuge from the Blitz in the subway stations; Feliks Topolski draws and paints British forces at the front and in naval engagements (UK).

● Stanley Spencer: *Shipbuilding in the Clyde*, painting (UK).

● Arshile Gorky: *Garden in Sochi*, painting (USA).

● Walter Gropius and Marcel Breuer design Workers' Housing in New Kensington, near Pittsburgh, USA.

● *How Green was My Valley*, directed by John Ford, wins the Academy Award for Best Picture of the Year (USA).

● Walt Disney's film *Dumbo* opens in New York.

SCIENCE

● **Dec**: Beginning of the Manhattan Project, a secret program of research leading to the development of the atomic bomb. Run by Gen. Leslie Groves and physicist Robert Oppenheimer, it is based in Oak Bridge, Tennessee, and Los Alamos, New Mexico (USA).

● Britain introduces the H2S aerial radar system, which allows identification of landmarks and urban areas in poor visibility or at night.

● Grand Coulee Dam, Washington, begins operation (USA).

● Konrad Zuse's Z2 computer is the first to use electromagnetic relays and a punched tape for data entry (Ger).

● In printing, the first plastic lithographic plates are produced, followed by presensitized plastic plates.

● C.B. Huggins shows that female sex hormones can be used to control prostate cancer (USA).

● S.A. Wakeman coins the term "antibiotic" to describe substances that kill bacteria without injuring other forms of life (USA).

● G.W. Beadle and E.L. Tatum develop the theory that genes control chemical reactions in cells, later known as the one-gene, one-enzyme hypothesis (USA).

● Norman Gregg suggests the first connection between German measles (*rubella*) in pregnancy and congenital abnormalities in infants (Aust).

● Albert Coons devises immunofluorescence to track down unidentified disease organisms (USA).

● G.N. Flerov discovers spontaneous fission of uranium (USSR).

● J D. Bernal investigates the physics of air raids (UK).

● J.R. Whinfield and J.T. Dickson develop the synthetic polyester fiber Terylene (UK) (called Dacron in the USA).

● IG Farbenindustrie begins to produce polyurethanes (Ger).

● E. McMillan and G.T. Seaborg discover the artificial element plutonium (USA).

Over the course of 1942 the tide of military advantage began to turn in favour of the Allies. The critical battle of the European war was that at Stalingrad, where Russian troops first halted the German advance, although at a terrible cost to the city, and then defeated the besieged German army. German retreat was also secured in North Africa, although Anglo-American forces were not yet in a position to open a second front on the European mainland. In the Pacific the Japanese advance was blunted, with the battles in the Coral Sea, at Midway and at Guadalcanal. These critical Allied victories were only achieved with the full mobilization of society and the coordination of national economic potentials. This involved civilian deprivation, with the state direction of all economic forces to ensure that only production essential for military victory was undertaken. Scientific and technological research were likewise directed toward a single goal: Alan Turing's all-electronic calculating device was dedicated to cracking German codes.

▲ **By the beginning of 1942, women had been pressed into service in munitions factories, on the land and in the auxiliary services. Freed from the shackles of social convention, they achieved a new sense of equality.**

● **1 Jan**: Representatives of 26 nations meet in Washington, DC, and issue a Declaration of the United Nations. This affirms their cooperation and agreement not to make separate peace treaties with Axis powers.

● **2 Jan**: The Japanese capture Manila (Phil). On 11 Jan they invade the Dutch East Indies, and also take Kuala Lumpur (Malaya). On 19 Jan they invade Burma. (›1 Feb)

● **15–28 Jan**: At the Rio de Janeiro Conference in Brazil, 21 American nations decide to break off relations with the Axis powers.

● **21 Jan**: Gen. Rommel launches a new offensive in the western desert. (›27 May)

● **29 Jan**: Britain and the USSR sign a treaty of alliance with Iran, which guarantees oil supplies for the Allies while recognizing the sovereignty and political independence of Iran.

● **1 Feb**: British forces in Malaya are forced to withdraw to Singapore. On 15 Feb the Japanese invade Singapore, forcing the British and Australians to surrender. On 19 Feb the Japanese bomb Darwin (Aus). (›8 Mar)

● **1 Feb**: The German commissar appoints Vidkun Quisling "minister president". Quisling abolishes the constitution and makes himself dictator (Nor).

● **26 Feb**: Japanese land in Java. On 7 Mar they land on New Guinea.

● **1 Mar**: The USSR begins a counteroffensive against German forces. (›2 Jul)

● **8 Mar**: Japanese take Rangoon (Burma) as the British evacuate their troops. (›9 Apr)

● **9 Apr**: Bataan (Phil) surrenders to the Japanese. On 29 Apr the Japanese enter Lashio, Burma, cutting off the overland route to China; on 30 Apr the British withdraw from Burma.

● **10 Apr**: The Indian Congress rejects the British proposal for postwar self-government, demanding immediate independence. Another campaign of mass civil disobedience begins. In Aug, after violence and riots in Bombay, Mahatma Gandhi and other Congress leaders are arrested.

● **4–7 May**: The Battle of the Coral Sea is fought beween the USA and Japan off southern New Guinea. The USA inflicts heavy losses on the Japanese and prevents them from invading Australia. (›3 Jun)

● **26 May**: An Anglo-Soviet agreement is signed in London promising 20 years of mutual aid.

● **27 May**: Rommel commences a powerful drive which recaptures Tobruk on 21 Jun. The Germans cross into Libya and the British retreat to El Alamein. (›30 Aug)

● **29 May**: Czech resistance fighters assassinate Gestapo leader Heydrich; in Jun the Germans obliterate the Czech village of Lidiče in reprisal.

● **3–7 Jun**: US and Japanese aircraft, submarines and carriers engage in a great battle off the island of Midway in the Pacific Ocean. The result is indecisive, and the Japanese lose the initiative in the Pacific naval war.

● **2 Jul**: The Germans begin a summer offensive, capturing the Black Sea port of Sevastopol after an eight-month siege and driving towards Rostov (captured 24 Jun) (USSR).

● **7 Aug**: US troops land on Guadalcanal in the Solomon Islands. In Nov US ships inflict heavy losses on the Japanese navy and a supply convoy under escort, emphasizing their control of the seas around Guadalcanal.

● **17 Aug**: Americans make the first of a series of bombing raids over Europe.

● **19 Aug**: Siege of Stalingrad, an important communications center, by the Germans begins (›10 Jan 1943). (›14 Sep)

● **19 Aug**: An Allied combined operations raid on the European continent tests the possibility of launching an invasion. British and Canadian troops spend nine hours ashore and destroy German outposts and radiolocation beacons.

● **22 Aug**: Brazil declares war on Germany and Italy after several Brazilian ships are sunk by German U-boats.

● **30 Aug**: Rommel launches a sustained attack but is driven back. On 23 Oct the British Eighth Army begins the third British offensive. Commanded by Gen. Montgomery, the British drive the Germans east out of Egypt, retaking Tobruk on 13 Nov. (›8 Nov)

● **14 Sep**: The Germans penetrate Stalingrad. Russian troops counterattack on 21 Sep. (›19 Nov)

● **9 Oct**: 100 US bombers escorted by 500 British fighters carry out the biggest daylight raid so far, destroying the railroad works at Lille (Fr).

● **8 Nov**: US general Dwight D. Eisenhower leads a combined Anglo-American invasion force in North Africa. On 10 Nov Oran falls to US troops and Admiral Darlan, Vichy France's commander, orders all French forces in North Africa to cease fighting. (›21 Dec)

● **11 Nov**: The Germans proceed to total occupation of France as Allied successes in North Africa encourage fears of an Allied invasion of the Mediterranean coast of France. (›27 Nov)

● **19 Nov**: Russian troops attack towards Kharkov (taken 16 Dec) while surrounding Stalingrad and the attacking German forces. On 12–13 Dec Gen. Manstein fails to relieve the German forces in Stalingrad.

● **27 Nov**: As German troops enter Toulon, French sailors scuttle the remainder of the French fleet which is at anchor in the harbor.

● **21 Dec**: The British Eighth Army reoccupies Benghazi.

SOCIETY

- **14 Jan**: President Roosevelt issues a proclamation ordering all aliens in the USA to register with the government. In Mar approximately 100,000 Japanese are interned.

- **20 Jan**: At the Wahnsee Conference in Berlin, Heydrich presents Hitler with plans for the "Final Solution" to the Jewish "problem": transportation to concentration camps and extermination. Hitler agrees and Adolf Eichmann directs the SS unit who will put the plan in action (Ger).

- **Jan**: The US automobile industry is transformed into an armament industry.

- **Jan**: First American GIs arrive in the UK.

- **Jan**: Establishment of the Central Bank for the Baltic states by the German government.

- **Feb**: UK and France agree to common execution of war economy and war production.

- **Feb**: International conference on social issues in Santiago (Chile).

- **11 Mar**: Brazil confiscates Axis property in reprisal for the sinking of Brazilian merchant ships.

- **4 Apr**: The War Production Board halts all nonessential building to conserve materials. The prices of every major item are frozen, affecting living costs (USA).

- **6 Apr**: White bread becomes no longer available in the UK.

- **21 Apr**: After reports of mass starvation in Greece as a result of German requisitioning of crops and stores, the Swedes announce their willingness to supply ships for transport of grain. The US and UK governments agree to supply monthly shipments of wheat to Greece.

- **Apr**: A central planning committee is formed to coordinate war production (Ger).

- **Apr**: Nonagricultural labor is conscripted for harvesting (USSR).

- **May**: US Congress creates the Women's Auxiliary Army Corps.

- **May**: Transportation of Jews from Holland begins. Dutch workers are also transported for forced labor in German factories.

- **Jun**: USA and USSR sign a lend-lease agreement providing reciprocal defense aid.

- **Jun**: The Germans decree that all Jews in the Occupied Zone of France over the age of six must wear the identifying yellow Star of David. On 14 Jul deportation of Jews begins. By 3 Aug the antisemitic campaign extends to the unoccupied zone.

- **1 Jul**: The Coal Commission takes over colliery leases in Britain.

- **29 Jul**: A combined British and American Production and Resources Board is established in London. This board will allocate material and industrial priorities.

- **30 Jul**: A bill introduces full conscription in Canada.

- **Jul**: Agreement on the delivery of war products and raw materials between the UK and USSR.

- **Jul**: US Congress creates the Women's Naval Reserves.

- **14 Sep**: The Vichy government establishes compulsory labor for men aged 18–65 and unmarried women 20–35 in response to German demands for labor collaboration.

- **Sep**: US bombers begin daily raids on France.

- **3 Oct**: A new price control law freezes wages, rents and farm prices (USA).

- **10 Oct**: Compulsory conscription of men and women for work in German factories is introduced in Belgium.

- **21 Oct**: US Congress passes the largest tax bill in US history. The allocation of $9 billion includes a Victory Tax of 5 percent on all incomes over $624.

- **23 Oct**: National Labor Service Act is introduced (USA).

- **Oct**: The Alaska Highway is opened.

- **Oct**: A cyclone and tidal wave devastate north-west Bengal, which exacerbates the acute shortage of food caused by the Japanese invasion of Burma.

- **Oct**: Neighborhood associations take over rationing at local level in Japan.

- **Nov**: Deportation of Jews from Norway begins.

- **1 Dec**: Gasoline rationing is extended throughout the USA. The Emergency Price Control Act allows ceilings on prices and rents.

- **1 Dec**: The Beveridge Report on Social Insurance is submitted to the House of Commons (UK). After the war this will form the foundation of the welfare state.

- **8 Dec**: UK conscription is further extended.

- **Dec**: The German government declares products of occupied regions (with the exception of the eastern areas) as free of duty.

- Gilbert Murray founds the Oxford Committee for Famine Relief (OXFAM). Initially aimed to aid starving women and children in Greece, Oxfam was to become one of the major relief agencies dealing with the refugee problem at the end of the war (UK).

- Establishment of the Wartime Finance Bank in Japan, for financing war factories.

- In Poland 50,000 Jews are killed as the SS "purge" ghettos.

CULTURE

- **29 May**: "White Christmas", written by Irving Berlin and recorded by Bing Crosby, becomes a best selling record (USA).

- Albert Camus: *L'Etranger* (The Outsider), existentialist novel (Fr).

- T.S. Eliot: *Little Gidding*, poem, completes the Four Quartets sequence, published separately between 1936 and 1942 (UK).

- Robert Frost: *A Witness Tree*, poems (USA).

- Jean Genet: *Nôtre dame des fleurs* (Our Lady of the Flowers), novel (Fr).

- Evelyn Waugh: *Put Out More Flags*, novel written while the author was serving in the Royal Marines (UK).

- Thornton Wilder: *The Skin of our Teeth*, play (USA).

- Sean O'Casey: *Red Roses for Me*, play (Ire).

- Mao Zedong redefines the didactic and utilitarian function of literature in his essay "Talks at the Yenan Forum on Art and Literature", in which he advocates a literature for the people in works of revolutionary political content and perfection of artistic form (Chi).

- Aaron Copland: music for Agnes de Mille's *Rodeo*, ballet, and *A Lincoln Portrait*, for speaker and orchestra (USA).

- Roy Harris: Fifth Symphony (USA).

- Gian Carlo Menotti: *The Island God*, opera, first produced at the Metropolitan Opera in New York.

- Igor Stravinsky: *Danse concertante* (USA).

- The first golden disk is awarded to Glenn Miller by RCA Victor for *Chattanooga Choo-Choo* (USA).

- Pablo Picasso: *Woman with an Artichoke*, painting (Fr).

- Georges Braque: *The Kitchen Table*, painting (Fr).

- Henri Matisse: *The Idol*, painting (Fr).

- Piet Mondrian: *New York City* and *Broadway Boogie-Woogie*, paintings (USA).

- Graham Sutherland: *Red Landscape*, painting (UK).

- Max Ernst: *Europe after the Rain*, painting (USA).

- Edward Hopper: *Nighthawks*, painting (USA).

- *Holiday Inn*, film starring Bing Crosby (USA).

- *Les Visiteurs du soir*, directed by Marcel Carné (Fr).

- Luchino Visconti: *Ossessione* (Obsession) (It).

- Part 1 of *Ivan the Terrible*, film directed by Sergei Eisenstein (USSR).

- Walt Disney: *Bambi* (USA).

- Cosmetics and perfume company Coty founds its American Fashion Critics Award (USA).

SCIENCE

- **May**: The portable rocket launcher nicknamed "Bazooka" is tested by the US army.

- **Jul**: First flight of the earliest jet fighter, the Messerschmidt Me262 (Ger).

- **Oct**: The XP-59, the USA's first jet plane, makes its maiden flight.

- **Dec**: In Chicago, nuclear physicist Enrico Fermi heads a team which creates the first controlled chain reaction in what is the first experimental nuclear reactor (USA).

- Wartime conditions focus attention on nutrition and progress is made in understanding the most efficient ways of processing, preserving, reducing, storing and transporting foods. Methods of conserving vitamins in processed foods are found (UK).

- Martin Camras invents an improved coating for magnetic tapes (USA).

- The nylon parachute is invented (Ger).

- The Germans test their first V-1 surface-to-surface missile.

- Grote Reber makes the first radio maps of the universe (USA).

- Vincent Du Vigneaud deduces the complex two-ring structure of biotin (USA).

- American chemist Louis Fieser develops napalm, used in incendiary bombs (USA).

- Frank Spedding produces two tonnes of extremely pure uranium for use in developing the nuclear bomb (USA).

- John Atanasoff and Clifford Berry complete the ABC or Atanasoff-Berry Computer, the prototype of all later electronic computer designs (US).

- H.R. Griffith and Enid Johnson introduce curare as a muscle relaxant during medical operations (Can).

- S.E. Luria obtains the first good electron photomicrographs of a bacteriophage (USA).

- S. Hertz and A. Roberts pioneer radiation treatment for hyperthyroidism.

The liquidation of Polish Jews had begun in 1942 when, it is estimated, Nazi SS forces killed 50,000 in ghetto "purges", while those who survived were transported to the death camps. Even this did not bring to an end the suffering of Warsaw. In August 1944 a further uprising in the city failed to receive the anticipated support from the Russian advance, and consequently the city was devastated in a series of German reprisals, with 200,000 of its inhabitants dying. As Warsaw suffered, the Allies began to achieve a rolling tide of victory on the field of battle. Axis forces in North Africa surrendered in mid-May 1943, while in July Soviet troops were triumphant in the great tank battle of Kursk and Allied forces landed in Sicily, with Italy invaded in September. American troops gained the advantage in the Pacific during November with landings at Bougainville. As the foundations for victory were clearly laid, so Western planning for the postwar world began in earnest, directed not only toward resolving immediate postwar problems of relief, but also to the erection of a new world economic institutional mechanism.

▲ Antisemitism had been endemic in Europe, especially Eastern Europe, for many years, and with the rise of the Nazi party in the 1930s many Jews fled from Germany and Austria. After the German invasion of Poland, Jews were rounded up and put into ghettos, which were then systematically "reduced"; the survivors were sent to the death camps.

● **10 Jan**: The Russians demand the surrender of Stalingrad by the occupying German forces. Field Marshal von Paulus refuses. On 30 Jan the Russians destroy the German army southwest of Stalingrad, and on 31 Jan Paulus surrenders, ending German ambitions in the USSR at a cost of 150,000 German troops and 50,000 Russians. (›8 Feb)

● **14–24 Jan**: US president Franklin D. Roosevelt and British prime minister Winston Churchill meet at Casablanca (Mor) to discuss policy. Agreement is reached on the invasion of Sicily and Italy, the continuous bombing of Germany and the maintenance of supplies to the USSR. The Allies will demand the unconditional surrender of Germany and Japan.

● **15 Jan**: The Japanese begin to withdraw from the strategic site of Guadalcanal in the Solomon Islands. The last Japanese troops leave on 9 Feb. On 21 Jan US and Australian troops gain the advantage in New Guinea. (›11 May)

● **23 Jan**: The Germans retreat from Tripoli, destroying many installations, and the British Eighth Army enters the city and takes over the port (Lib). (›10 Feb)

● **8 Feb**: Russian troops retake Kursk, site of a vital railroad junction, a year after it first fell to the Germans (USSR). (›14 Feb)

● **10 Feb**: The Eighth Army reaches the Tunisian frontier. After a series of fierce battles, Rommel's army is decisively beaten near Thala and the Germans prepare to evacuate Tunisia. On 21 Feb the Allied armies are placed under the supreme command of Gen. Dwight D. Eisenhower. (›29 Mar)

● **14 Feb**: The Russians retake Rostov and Kharkov. On 22 Feb Gen. Manstein begins a German counteroffensive, but lack of troops and supplies and the spring thaw thwart further German advance (USSR).

● **5 Mar**: The British begin the Battle of the Ruhr, an attempt to destroy German industrial plant. Although there are 43 major bombing raids between now and 12 Jul the Germans continue production. (›17 May)

● **29 Mar**: Gen. Montgomery's troops break through the Mareth Line into southern Tunisia. (›7 May)

● **Mar**: The Germans come close to defeating the convoy system, destroying 120 Allied ships. Meanwhile, the RAF drop 900 tonnes of bombs on the center of Berlin in a single half hour.

● **7–11 May**: Allied forces capture Tunis and Bizerta, giving the Allies control of Mediterranean shipping and exposing Italy to invasion attempts. On 12–13 May German and Italian forces surrender, ending Axis powers attempts at conquest of Africa.

● **11 May**: US troops retake Attu (Aleutian Islands), captured by the Japanese in June 1942.

● **17 May**: The RAF breach two huge dams in the Ruhr and Eder valleys, using specially designed bouncing bombs.

● **22 May**: Soviet authorities dissolve the Third Communist International in an attempt to reassure the Allies about its abandonment of expansionist aims.

● **22 May**: In the face of heavy losses, Admiral Doenitz orders all U-boats in the North Atlantic to cease operations against Allied convoys.

● **3 Jun**: The French Committee of National Liberation is formed under the joint presidency of generals de Gaulle and Giraud. By 1 Aug de Gaulle manages to reduce Giraud's role to that of military adviser.

● **5 Jun**: The regime of president Ramón Castillo of Argentina is overthrown in a military coup. Gen. Pedro Ramirez forms a new government with Juan Perón as minister of labor.

● **5 Jul**: The Japanese government announces cession to Thailand of six of the states of Malaya.

● **5–17 Jul**: The Russians, reinforced by US and UK armament shipments, gain the strategic advantage by holding off a massive German offensive. The Battle of Kursk features the largest tank offensive of the war (USSR).

● **10 Jul**: The invasion of Sicily begins with landings by Allied troops. Opposition is light but the island is not completely captured until the fall of Messina on 17 Aug.

● **19 Jul**: 500 US bombers carry out an air raid on Rome under orders to avoid sites of cultural significance. On 25 Jul King Victor Emmanuel forces the Fascist leader Mussolini to resign and places him under arrest. Antifascist Marshal Pietro Badoglio is asked to form a government and announces the dissolution of the Fascist party.

● **24 Jul–2 Aug**: British and US planes carry out a series of bombing raids on Hamburg (Ger), creating a fire storm which kills 50,000 civilians and makes 800,000 homeless.

● **1 Aug**: The Japanese have established a puppet government in Burma and now announce that the country is independent and at war with the USA and Britain.

● **13–24 Aug**: Roosevelt, Churchill and Canadian premier Mackenzie King meet in Quebec to discuss the invasion of France and the campaign in the Pacific. It is agreed that the supreme commander of the invasion will be American and that the Allies will continue to aid Jiang Jieshi in China.

● **26 Aug**: USA, Britain, Canada, Russia and China give limited recognition to the French Committee of National Liberation.

● **3 Sep**: British troops cross the Strait of Messina and begin the invasion of mainland Italy. Marshal Badoglio signs a secret armistice agreeing to surrender on 8 Sep. The Italian surrender is announced on this date.

SOCIETY   CULTURE   SCIENCE

SOCIETY

- **9 Sep**: Iran joins the UN and declares war on Germany. (›28 Nov)

- **10 Sep**: The Germans occupy Rome and Milan and begin to evacuate Sardinia. Some troops are sent to Corsica where the French rise against them. Free French forces liberate Corsica on 4 Oct.

- **12 Sep**: A German parachute regiment rescues Mussolini from house arrest. On 15 Sep he proclaims the establishment of a Republican party which becomes influential in German-occupied Italy.

- **13 Sep**: Jiang Jieshi is elected president of the Chinese Republic and announces that democratic government will be established when war ends.

- **25 Sep**: The Russians cross the River Dnieper, north of Kiev, and take Smolensk. Kiev is recaptured on 6 Nov.

- **27 Sep–1 Oct**: After three days of street fighting, the US Fifth Army takes Naples. On 12 Oct the Americans begin the assault toward Rome by attacking German forces on the Volturno River.

- **13 Oct**: Italy declares war on Germany.

- **19–30 Oct**: Foreign ministers of the USSR, UK and USA meet to discuss postwar treatment of the Axis powers, punishment of war criminals, and the creation of an international organization to work for peace.

- **1 Nov**: US forces land on Bougainville in the Solomon Islands (Pacific), beginning a campaign that will not be won until Mar 1944.

- **28 Nov–1 Dec**: Roosevelt, Churchill and Stalin meet in Tehran to agree war plans. They also pledge economic aid to Iran for the period of the war and after.

- **1 Dec**: In the Cairo Declaration Roosevelt, Churchill, Stalin and Jiang Jieshi announce their intention to force Japan to withdraw from Manchuria and surrender.

- **12 Dec**: Eduard Beneš, leader of the Czechoslovak government-in-exile, signs a treaty for postwar cooperation with the USSR.

- **24 Dec**: The Soviet winter campaign begins. It consists of three major offensives: in the Ukraine, in the Crimea and in the north.

- **26 Dec**: The last operational German capital ship, the *Scharnhorst*, is sunk by the British battleship *Duke of York*.

- A Croatian, Josip Broz, who uses the pseudonym of Tito, becomes leader of the pro-Russian resistance army in Yugoslavia. After the fall of Italy in Sep, the British give assistance, and on 29–30 Nov the Congress at Jajce announces the creation of a republic under Marshal Tito.

- **27 Jan**: At the beginning of 1943 there are estimated to be between 5 and 6 million deported or "forced" workers in Germany. However, the Reich is still short of labor and the Nazi government issues a decree for the mobilization of women between 17 and 45.

- **Jan**: Stock markets are placed under government control in Germany.

- **Jan**: Agreement on economic cooperation between Germany, Italy and Japan to facilitate exchange of military supplies.

- **10 Feb**: Roosevelt establishes a minimum 48-hour working week as a wartime measure (USA).

- **Feb**: All enterprises not needed for war production are closed (Ger).

- **Feb–Mar**: Mahatma Gandhi stages a 21-day fast in protest against his imprisonment in Poona (Ind).

- **12 Mar**: The lend-lease program is extended for a year (USA).

- **20 Apr**: An uprising in the Warsaw ghetto is brutally crushed by the Germans, who blow up the synagogue. At least 10,000 Jews are killed and the remainder transported to concentration camps (Pol).

- **28 Apr**: Wildcat strikes sweep the Pittsburgh coal mines (USA).

- **1 May**: Compulsory arbitration is enforced in the British coal industry.

- **18 May–3 Jun**: The United Nations hold a food conference at Hot Springs, Virginia, calling for a fairer postwar distribution of resources.

- **May**: The Germans give Dutch gentiles married to Jews the choice of deportation or sterilization. This provokes violent protest from the Catholic and Protestant churches.

- **26 Jul**: US Congress passes the Smith-Connally Anti-Strike bill which imposes a 30-day strike notice requirement and by which promotion of strikes becomes subject to criminal charges.

- **Aug**: After six months of successful Norwegian resistance to compulsory labor mobilization, the Germans place the country under martial law and begin to close down businesses and purge the police force of sympathizers.

- **5 Nov**: The Senate passes the Connally resolution for US involvement in an international postwar peace organization.

- **Dec**: Publication of a plan for the establishment of a worldwide Bank for Reconstruction and Development of the United Nations by J.H. Morgenthau (USA).

- The United Nations Relief and Rehabilitation Administration is established for the reconstruction of all countries subjugated by Axis powers in the course of the war.

- J.M. Keynes and H.D. White publish plans for the reorganization of international payments and currencies after the war.

CULTURE

- Hermann Hesse: *The Glass Bead Game*, his last novel (Swi).

- Thomas Mann: *Joseph and His Brothers*, novel sequence (USA).

- Henry Green: *Caught*, novel (UK).

- Ricardo Molinari: *Mundos de la Madrugada*, poems (Sp).

- Halldór Laxness: *The Bell of Iceland*, novel of Icelandic life (Ice).

- Jean-Paul Sartre: *L'Etre et le néant* (Being and Nothingness), existentialist philosophy (Fr).

- Mary McCarthy: *The Company She Keeps*, novel (USA).

- Jean-Paul Sartre: *Les Mouches* (The Flies), play (Fr).

- Bertolt Brecht: *The Life of Galileo* and *The Good Woman of Setzuan*, plays (USA).

- William Saroyan: *The Human Comedy*, play (USA).

- Lennox Berkeley: *Divertimento* (UK).

- Alan Bush: Cello Concerto (UK).

- Aram Khachaturian: *Ode to Stalin*, and *Gayane*, ballet (USSR).

- Ralph Vaughan Williams: Symphony no. 5 in D (UK).

- Carl Orff: *Catulli Carmina*, settings of Catullus' poems (Ger).

- Dmitri Shostakovitch: Eighth Symphony (USSR).

- Béla Bartók: *Concerto for Orchestra* (USA).

- Eduard Tubin: Sinfonia Lirica (No.4).

- The jitterbug dance craze strikes the USA.

- *Oklahoma*: Richard Rodgers and Oscar Hammerstein develop the American musical based on indigenous themes instead of show-business glitter. "Oh what a beautiful morning" becomes a big hit.

- Wilfredo Lam: *The Jungle*, painting (Cuba).

- Henry Moore: *Madonna and Child*, sculpture (UK).

- Pablo Picasso: *The Bull's Head*, sculpture (Fr).

- Jackson Pollock: *Pasiphae*, painting (USA).

- Film of Ernest Hemingway's novel *For Whom the Bell Tolls* stars Ingrid Bergman and Gary Cooper, directed and produced by Sam Wood (USA).

- Orson Welles directs and stars in the film of Charlotte Bronte's novel *Jane Eyre* (USA).

- *Casablanca*, starring Humphrey Bogart and Ingrid Bergman and directed by M. Curtiz, wins the Academy Award for the Best Picture.

- Crooner Frank Sinatra makes his film debut in *Higher and Higher*, delighting teenage fans (USA).

- *Sanshiro Sugata*, directed by Akira Kurosawa (Jap).

SCIENCE

- Gerard Kuiper discovers that Titan, the largest known satellite of Saturn, has its own atmosphere (USA).

- Henrik Dam of Denmark and Edward A. Doisy of the USA share the Nobel Prize for Physiology or Medicine for the discovery of, and discovery of the composition of, vitamin K.

- György Hevesy of Hungary wins the Nobel Prize for Chemistry for his use of isotopes as tracers.

- The Nobel Prize for Physics is won by Otto Stern (Ger) "for his contribution to the development of the molecular-ray method and his discovery of the magnetic moment of the proton".

- Chemist Albert Hofmann discovers that LSD is hallucinogenic (Swi).

- Wilhelm Kolff develops the first kidney dialysis machine (Neth).

- Selman A. Waksman discovers the antibiotic streptomycin (USA).

- George Papanicolaou publishes the *Diagnosis of Uterine Cancer by the Vaginal Smear*. His method of detecting cancerous cells becomes the Pap smear test in clinical use (USA).

- The world's first operational nuclear reactor is activated at Oak Ridge, Tennessee (USA).

- The Dow Corning Corporation begin to manufacture silicones, which are relatively neutral in contact with other substances or the human body, and come to be extensively used in "spare part" surgery (USA).

- Penicillin is first used to treat chronic illnesses.

- Jacques-Yves Cousteau and Emile Gagnan invent the Aqualung, a self-contained underwater breathing apparatus (SCUBA) that revolutionizes underwater exploration (Fr).

- S. Junghans develops continuous casting of steel (Ger).

- Alan Turing and others develop the first all-electronic calculating device, known as Colossus. At first it is dedicated to cracking German secret codes (UK).

- The insertion of telephone repeaters into telephone lines at regular intervals allows amplication of the signal and so improves clarity of sound.

- Plasticized PVC begins to be used in electrical insulation and vehicle tires in place of rubber.

- Chemists at the University of Stockholm produce xylocaine, a local anaesthetic which is safer than the cocaine-procaine group (Swe).

- P.O. McCallum and G.M. Findlay discover that hepatitis is actually two distinct diseases caused by different viruses.

- The "Big Inch" oil pipeline is opened, transporting oil 2,400 km (1,475 miles) from Texas to the eastern seaboard (USA).

Allied military successes involved the resolution of the problems of mounting effective seaborne landings. In Europe these were largely "set piece" events, beginning with French North Africa in 1942. In the Pacific theater it was a question of taking island chains, which involved decisions regarding which "links" could be ignored and which had to be secured. In all these operations, the availability of landing craft, together with supporting logistical vessels, was crucial to the seizing of the initiative in the early stages, and the maintenance of continuing supply involved the construction of artificial harbours, the laying of underwater fuel pipes and the building of temporary airstrips. Western grand strategy had given primacy to securing victory in Europe. Once accomplished, resources could be and were switched to the Pacific. As the possibility of victory became more certain, the Allies began to discuss postwar policy. In July delegates from 44 nations met at Bretton Woods in the USA to discuss economic and financial measures, while later in the year representatives of the USA, UK and China met at Dumbarton Oaks to discuss the promotion of peaceful solutions to international problems.

▲ Coastguard-manned carriers were among the first to drop their ramps at Manila after US forces had driven the Japanese from the capital city of the Philippines, unloading soldiers and supplies for the liberated city.

● **4 Jan**: Allied units launch an attack on the German Gustav Line between Naples and Rome. On 22 Jan Allied forces make a surprise landing at Anzio and Nettuno (It). (›2 Feb)

● **20 Jan**: British RAF drops 2,300 tonnes of bombs on Berlin.

● **27 Jan**: As part of the Soviet forces' northern offensive, Leningrad is relieved after a two-year siege.

● **29 Jan**: As part of the US offensive in the Pacific, the Marshall Islands are retaken, and also the Carolines and Marianas. Kwajalein Atoll falls after heavy fighting (1–7 Feb) and then Eniwetok (17–21 Feb). (›12 Mar)

● **Jan**: The Brazzaville Declaration outlines France's postwar colonial policy in Africa. It includes a rejection of autonomy and independence.

● **2 Feb**: The Allies temporarily lose the initiative in Italy as large German forces counterattack around Anzio. In mid-Mar the Allies launch a heavy bombing raid and tank assault on the Gustav Line. (›11 May)

● **20–27 Feb**: US Air Force conducts a series of massive raids on centers of the German aircraft industry.

● **6 Mar**: US bombers begin daylight raids on Berlin.

● **12 Mar**: The US offensive in the Pacific led by Gen. Douglas MacArthur continues along New Guinea, taking Holland and Aitape (22 Apr–5 Aug) and Sansapor (15 Jun).

● **2 Apr**: Soviet troops enter Romania.

● **8–10 Apr**: The liberation of the Crimea begins with the Russian capture of the port of Odessa. On 8–13 May Hitler gives permission for withdrawal of German troops from the Crimea, and on 12 May Sevastopol is recaptured.

● **9 Apr**: Gen. Charles de Gaulle becomes commander-in-chief of the Free French forces.

● **5 May**: Mahatma Gandhi is set free (Ind).

● **11–18 May**: The Allies finally break the Gustav Line across central Italy and force the Germans from the Cassino area. On 23 May Allied forces launch an offensive from Anzio and despite resistance they reach Rome on 4 Jun. (›19 Aug)

● **1 Jun**: The BBC broadcast the first coded message to the French Resistance that an Allied invasion is imminent.

● **6 Jun**: Operation Overlord (D-Day) begins just after midnight with the dispatch of two US airborne divisions followed by 4,000 invasion ships, 600 warships, 10,000 planes and 176,000 Allied troops. The Germans have failed to anticipate the invasion and are unsuccessful in countering it.

● **10 Jun**: German SS troops massacre the entire village of Oradour-sur-Glane near Limoges – 642 people – in reprisal for the capture of an SS officer (Fr).

● **10–15 Jun**: Soviet forces attack and break through Finnish positions. On 4 Sep a ceasefire is declared on the Finnish front, and on 19 Sep a Finnish armistice is signed.

● **13 Jun**: The first German V-1 flying bomb lands in London, killing six civilians.

● **15 Jun**: US forces capture Saipan island in the Pacific. On 18–20 Jun in the Battle of the Philippine Sea the Japanese lose at least 400 planes and three carriers.

● **22 Jun**: Resistance fighters in Denmark destroy the Dansk Industri-Syndicat, the largest Danish arms factory and the last of the Danish factories working for the Germans.

● **27 Jun**: US troops take the French port of Cherbourg, gaining a vital foothold. On 18–25 Jul US forces take St Lo and launch an attack to isolate German units in Brittany, which is accomplished by 10 Aug.

● **3 Jul**: Russian troops take Minsk, capturing 100,000 German soldiers.

● **18 Jul**: Gen. Tojo resigns as prime minister and chief of staff, indicating a growing desire amongst Japanese statesmen to end the war.

● **20 Jul**: In Germany, Klaus von Stauffenberg and others make an abortive attempt to assassinate Hitler at his Wolf's Lair headquarters in East Prussia. All those involved are executed.

● **23 Jul**: Russian troops cross the Curzon Line in Poland. On 28 Jul they take Brest-Litovsk and on 20 Aug launch an offensive in Bessarabia and Romania. On 30 Aug Soviet troops enter Bucharest. On 13 Sep an armistice is signed.

● **1 Aug**: The Warsaw rising begins as an attempt to establish an anti-Communist government in advance of the expected Russian arrival. However, the Russian advance halts and German reprisals leave 200,000 Poles dead.

● **15 Aug**: The Allies invade southern France between Cannes and Toulon and drive the Germans up the Rhône Valley.

● **19 Aug**: The British Eighth Army takes Florence, securing Allied control of Italy up to a line running from Livorno to Ancona.

● **24 Aug**: French Resistance forces take most of Paris; the German commandant, Gen. Choltitz, ignores Hitler's order to resist fiercely. On 25 Aug the US Fourth Armoured Division enters Paris and Choltitz surrenders. Gen. de Gaulle enters Paris in the wake of the Fourth Army and on 30 Aug the seat of provisional French government is relocated in Paris. On 28 Aug the last German forces in Toulon and Marseille surrender.

● **4 Sep**: Allied forces capture Antwerp (Bel) and the flying bomb sites in Pas de Calais (Fr). Brussels is liberated on 5 Sep.

- **11 Sep**: US troops cross the German frontier near Trier but stiff German resistance halts the advance. On 15 Sep the US Seventh and French First Armies sweep up the Rhône Valley and join the US Third Army at Dijon. American, British and French forces are then reorganized in liberated France for an assault on Germany. On 28 Sep Calais is liberated.

- **17 Sep**: British troops are dropped in Holland with the aim of capturing the Arnhem Bridge, key to control of the River Rhine. However, they meet with fierce resistance by German troops and are withdrawn after heavy casualties.

- **27 Sep**: Soviet forces invade Albania.

- **29 Sep**: Soviet forces invade Yugoslavia, liberating Belgrade on 20 Oct.

- **9–20 Oct**: British prime minister Churchill and foreign secretary Anthony Eden visit Moscow to discuss postwar spheres of influence with USSR premier Stalin. It is agreed that Poland, Bulgaria and Romania will come under Russian influence while Greece will retain links with Britain. Hungary and Yugoslavia will come under both nations' influence.

- **13 Oct**: Athens is occupied by Allied forces, and on 18 Oct the Greek government returns to Athens (›3 Dec).

- **14 Oct**: Gen. Rommel commits suicide on the instruction of two of Hitler's staff who inform him that he is suspected of complicity in the assassination attempt on Hitler.

- **23 Oct**: Gen. de Gaulle's government is recognized by the Allies (Fr).

- **23 Oct**: Soviet troops invade Hungary, and on 27 Dec surround Budapest.

- **23–26 Oct**: In the Battle of Leyte Gulf the Japanese fleet is destroyed by US forces, who have been fighting in the Philippines since Jul.

- **7 Nov**: President Roosevelt wins an unprecedented fourth presidential victory (USA).

- **3–29 Dec**: British forces help to put down a Communist-sponsored civil war in Athens and Piraeus. The Greeks announce that a regency will be established under Archbishop Damaskinos who replaces the ousted King George II.

- **16 Dec**: The Germans launch a major offensive in the Ardennes Forest, Belgium, which becomes known as the "Battle of the Bulge" because of the bulge it creates in the Allied line.

- **29 Jan**: Martin Borman, Hitler's private secretary and a leading antisemite, announces a state-financed plan to increase the number of "pure" Germanic children through a program of selective breeding.

- **29 Mar**: US Congress approves a joint resolution authorizing up to $1,350,000,000 for a United Nations Relief and Rehabilitation Agency.

- **3 Apr**: The US Supreme Court rules that Negroes cannot be barred from voting in primary elections.

- **May**: The Spanish government agrees to restrict shipment of minerals to Germany; in response the USA cancels its embargo on oil shipments for Spain.

- **22 Jun**: President Roosevelt signs the Servicemen's Readjustment Act which will provide financial aid to veterans. This Act, which is widely admired, becomes known as the GI Bill.

- **1–22 Jul**: Delegates from 44 nations meet at Bretton Woods, New Hampshire, to discuss economic and financial measures. They agree to set up an International Monetary Fund and an International Bank for Reconstruction and Development, later known as the "World Bank".

- **Jul**: Beginning of total war economy in Germany, and introduction of the 60-hour week in industry.

- **21 Aug–7 Oct**: Representatives of the USA, UK, USSR and China meet at Dumbarton Oaks, Washington DC, to discuss forming an international organization to promote peaceful solutions to international problems after the war ends.

- **29 Aug**: The Majdanek (Pol) concentration camp is found by Russian and Polish troops. This is the first concentration camp to be found and it is estimated that 1,500,000 people have died here.

- **5 Sep**: The exiled governments of Belgium, the Netherlands and Luxembourg agree to establish a customs union after the war (Benelux).

- **Sep**: The Preparatory Committee for an Arab Congress holds its first meeting in Alexandria (Egy). Economic cooperation between Arab countries is discussed and the issue of further Jewish immigration into Palestine.

- **Sep**: The Conference of Quebec discusses the Morgenthau plan for the deindustrialization of Germany after the war.

- **Nov**: Coal mines in the Nord and Pas de Calais departments are nationalized (Fr).

- The Belgian armaments industries are nationalized and the currency reformed.

- French citizenship is extended to certain Muslim categories in the North African colonies.

- Nobel Prize for Peace is won by the International Committee of the Red Cross.

- **16 Dec**: Bandleader Glenn Miller, creator of the "big band sound", is lost at sea.

- Jorge Luis Borges: *Ficciones* (Fictions), short stories (Arg).

- T.S. Eliot: *Four Quartets*, poem sequence, first published as a whole (UK).

- Ivy Compton-Burnett: *Elders and Betters*, novel (UK).

- Jean-Paul Sartre: *Huis Clos* (No Exit), play (Fr).

- Saul Bellow: *Dangling Man*, novel (USA).

- Pär Lagerkvist: *The Dwarf* (Swe).

- Jean Anouilh: *Antigone*, play (Fr).

- Tennessee Williams: *The Glass Menagerie*, play (published 1945) (USA).

- Nobel Prize for Literature is won by Johannes Jenson (Den).

- Béla Bartók: Sonata for Unaccompanied Violin, the last work Bartók completed before his death (USA).

- Paul Hindemith: *Herodias*, opera (USA).

- Dmitri Shostakovich: Eighth Symphony (USSR).

- Sergey Prokoviev: Fifth Symphony (USSR).

- Aaron Copland's *Appalachian Spring*, ballet choreographed by Martha Graham, is first performed in Washington, DC. Copland later produces an orchestral version which becomes enormously popular (USA).

- Leonard Bernstein: *On the Town*, musical, and *Fancy Free*, jazz-style ballet (USA).

- Francis Bacon's painting *Three Figures at the Base of a Crucifixion* makes him a controversial figure overnight (UK).

- Jackson Pollock: *Don Quixote*, painting (USA).

- Graham Sutherland: *Christ on the Cross*, painting (UK).

- Henri Matisse: *The White Dress*, painting (Fr).

- Pablo Picasso: *Seated Woman in Blue*, painting (Fr).

- Georges Rouault: *Homo Homini Lupus*, painting (Fr).

- *Frenzy*, film directed by Alf Sjoberg (Swe).

- Sergei Eisenstein: *Ivan the Terrible* part I, film. Part II is released in 1958 (USSR).

- *Going my Way* wins the Academy Award for the Best Picture.

- *National Velvet*, starring Mickey Rooney and Elizabeth Taylor (USA).

- Release of the film of Shakespeare's *Henry V* starring Laurence Olivier and with music by William Walton (UK).

- In Sep the Germans introduce the V-2 liquid-fuelled rocket-propelled bomb.

- The Me 163B-1 Komet rocket plane is introduced, but its habit of exploding spontaneously makes it unsuccessful as a weapon (Ger).

- Greenwich Royal Observatory (UK) installs a quartz clock. The crystal at the nucleus of the clock vibrates 100,000 times a second, giving an accuracy of a second gained or lost every two and a half years.

- B.M. Duggar discovers the antibiotic aureomycin, the first of the tetracyclines (USA).

- Alfred Blalock performs the first operation on a "blue baby", a condition caused by a congenital heart defect, correcting blood supply to the baby's lungs.

- DDT is used to spray the population of Naples (It) in the first successful halting of an epidemic of typhus – the first large-scale use of DDT for health purposes.

- O. Avery, C.M. Macleod and M. McCarty isolate deoxyribonucleic acid (DNA) and determine that it is the hereditary material for almost all living organisms (USA).

- R.B. Cowles and C.M. Bogert find that desert reptiles regulate their body temperature by specific behavior patterns.

- Second uranium pile is built at Clinton, Tennessee, for manufacturing plutonium for an atomic bomb (USA).

- New cyclotron at the Carnegie Institution in Washington is completed (USA).

- Paper chromatography is developed as a tool of chemical analysis by A.J.P. Martin and R.L.M. Synge (UK).

- Quinine is synthesized successfully for the first time after Japanese supplies of natural quinine are cut off.

- The first automatic general-purpose digital computer, the Mark 1, goes into operation at Harvard University. Designed by a team of engineers from IBM led by Howard Aitken, the computer contains 800 km (500 miles) of wiring and although fast, taking only three seconds to multiply large numbers, breaks down often (USA).

- The Delaware (USA) aqueduct is completed. It is the world's longest tunnel (168.9 km/105 miles), built to supply water to New York City.

- Nobel Prize for Chemistry is won by Otto Hahn (Ger) for his discovery of the fission of heavy nuclei.

- Nobel Prize for Physiology or Medicine is won by Joseph Erlanger (USA), and Herbert Gasser (USA) for their work on the multiple functional differences of specific nerve fibers.

- Nobel Prize for Physics is won by I.I. Rabi (USA) "for his resonance method for recording the magnetic properties of atomic nuclei".

Victory over Germany and Japan after the long years of war was greeted in 1945 with scenes of rejoicing. The Germans surrendered unconditionally. The Japanese held out until the United States dropped atomic bombs on Hiroshima and Nagasaki. This final destruction was only the last of a series of horrors: the fire-bombing of Dresden, Hamburg and Tokyo caused untold civilian deaths, while the liberation of the Nazi death camps by the Allied armies revealed shockingly the measures taken by the Nazis against the Jewish population of Europe. Bergen-Belsen, Auschwitz, Dachau, with their vast piles of corpses, thousands of living skeletons and storerooms full of confiscated jewelry, clothes and human hair, offered images of horror impossible to forget. All these events raised unprecedented questions of morality as humankind tried to come to terms with the seemingly limitless potential for destruction it now possessed. One of the results was the development of major grassroots movements within Western democracy against atomic and other weapons of mass destruction that took place during the course of the next decades.

▲ The Allied armies which liberated the concentration camps were appalled by what they discovered. The sheer scale of the Holocaust quickly became undeniable, despite last-minute German attempts at a cover-up. An estimated 6 million Jews, plus hundreds of thousands of others, had lost their lives.

● **3 Jan**: In Japanese-occupied Burma, the Allies capture Akyab; they go on to take Mandalay on 20 Mar and Rangoon on 3 May. (›27 Mar)

● **12 Jan**: The second Soviet offensive begins. Budapest falls to the Red Army on 13 Jan, followed by Warsaw (17 Jan) and later Vienna (13 Apr).

● **14 Jan**: Turkey opens the Dardanelles straits to the Allies but remains neutral until 23 Feb, when it declares war on Germany and Japan.

● **20 Jan**: Hungary concludes an armistice with the USSR and declares war on Germany.

● **27 Jan**: The Red Army liberates the Nazi concentration camp at Auschwitz.

● **29 Jan**: The retreating German army leaves Belgium to the advancing Allies, now under the command of Field Marshal Montgomery, Supreme Allied Commander north of the Ardennes.

● **2 Feb**: Ecuador becomes the first South American country to declare war on Germany. Paraguay, Peru, Chile, Venezuela and Uruguay follow suit, with Argentina the last (27 Mar).

● **4–11 Feb**: US president Roosevelt, USSR premier Joseph Stalin and British prime minister Winston Churchill meet at Yalta in the Soviet Crimea to discuss the postwar division of Germany. (›22 Jun)

● **13 Feb**: German SS leader Heinrich Himmler approaches neutral Sweden to act as an intermediary to open peace negotiations with the Western Allies.

● **13–14 Feb**: An Allied firebomb raid on the German city of Dresden, packed with refugees from the East, leaves 135,000 dead.

● **24 Feb**: US troops capture Manila from the Japanese and, after fierce fighting, take the strategically important Iwo Jima Islands, only 1,400 km (870 miles) from Tokyo. (›6 Apr)

● **3 Mar**: Finland declares war on Germany after Germans refuse to disarm on Finnish soil.

● **4 Mar**: The Allied armies in the west reach the River Rhine and take Cologne (7 Mar).

● **9 Mar**: Massive bombing by USA of Japanese cities begins.

● **10–11 Mar**: In Indochina, Vietnam and Cambodia declare their independence. On 25 Mar France grants autonomy to Indochina.

● **19 Mar**: From Berlin, Hitler orders the adoption of a "scorched earth" policy to forestall Allied advances.

● **22 Mar**: The Arab League, consisting of Egypt, Syria, Iraq, Lebanon, Saudi Arabia, Transjordan, Yemen and Arab Palestine, is inaugurated in Cairo.

● **27 Mar**: Gen. Aung Sang incites mutiny in the Burmese army and civilian revolt against Japanese occupation forces; the army joins the Allies. Britain promises (14 May) to confer dominion status on Burma later but refuses independence. (›2 Aug)

● **6–7 Apr**: The US Navy destroys the Japanese fleet at the battle of Okinawa.

● **12 Apr**: Death of US president Roosevelt; he is succeeded by Harry Truman.

● **16 Apr**: The Red Army launches an assault on Berlin. On 23 Apr the Western Allies reach the German capital.

● **25 Apr**: 48 nations attend a conference in San Francisco to negotiate the UN Charter, which is signed on 26 Jun.

● **28 Apr**: The ex-dictator of Italy, Fascist leader Benito Mussolini, and his mistress Clara Petacci are shot by Italian partisans. Their bodies are strung up and put on public display in Milan as the Allies take Milan and Venice.

● **30 Apr**: Hitler commits suicide in his bunker in Berlin, after appointing Admiral Doenitz his successor.

● **30 Apr**: US troops liberate the concentration camp at Dachau. The camps at Bergen-Belsen and Buchenwald have been liberated earlier in the month.

● **2 May**: The war in the Mediterranean ends as the German commander in Italy surrenders to the Allied commander, Field Marshal Alexander.

● **4 May**: Field Marshal Montgomery receives the surrender of the German forces in Holland, north Germany and Denmark. German troops in Norway surrender on 5 May, and on 9 May Vidkun Quisling, the pro-Nazi premier, gives himself up to the Norwegian police. He is later shot as a traitor.

● **8 May**: Germany accepts unconditional surrender.

● **27 May**: Chinese troops capture Nanjing from the Japanese.

● **May**: Thousands die in Algeria after police put down riots against French colonial occupation. Anti-French disturbances begin in Syria and Lebanon on 8 May. British troops occupy Lebanon and Syria after the breakdown of their negotiations with France on 19 May.

● **1 Jun**: The Japanese abandon the island of Okinawa to US forces after 82 days of fighting in which the USA lose 7,000 men and the Japanese 100,000, as well as 4,000 aircraft, many flown by kamikaze pilots.

● **11–15 Jun**: Postwar political parties emerge in Germany, including the KPD (Communists) and the SPD (Social Democrats, or German Workers Party).

● **22 Jun**: The USA, Britain, France and the USSR partition Germany into occupation zones.

● **25 Jun–14 Jul**: A conference at Simla, called by the British viceroy of India to discuss the future of the country breaks up over disagreement with the Muslim League, led by M.A. Jinnah.

SOCIETY

● **17 Jul–2 Aug**: At a meeting at Potsdam, near Berlin, the Allies call for the unconditional surrender of Japan and agree on its subsequent occupation, demilitarization and democratization by the victors.

● **23 Jul–14 Aug**: Marshal Pétain, leader of the Vichy government in France, is tried for treason and given a death sentence, later commuted to life imprisonment.

● **26 Jul**: The Labour party wins a landslide victory in the British general election: 393 seats to the Conservatives' 189. Clement Attlee takes over as the new prime minister with a mandate for public ownership and social reform.

● **2 Aug**: British troops liberate Burma from Japanese occupation. Civilian government is restored in Oct.

● **6 Aug**: US atomic bomb destroys the Japanese city of Hiroshima and kills 78,000. A second, still more powerful, bomb is dropped on Nagasaki on 9 Aug. On 14 Aug president Truman accepts Japan's unconditional surrender, including the removal from power of the emperor Hirohito. The formal surrender is signed on 2 Sep.

● **9 Aug**: The USSR declares war on Japan, in accordance with the Yalta agreement of February, and invades Manchuria. On 15 Aug Japanese troops surrender to Soviet troops in northern Korea and later to US troops in the south. The country is split along the 38th parallel (2 Sep), pending agreement between the occupying powers on Korea's unification and independence.

● **13 Aug**: The World Zionist Congress demands that a million Jews be admitted to Palestine.

● **17 Aug**: Ahmed Sukarno declares Indonesia a republic with himself as president. The republic lasts until Dec, when it is overthrown by the British and Dutch and colonial status is restored.

● **25 Aug**: Ho Chi Minh, head of the People's Liberation Committee, proclaims the Republic of Vietnam with a provisional government at Hanoi.

● **7 Oct**: Fighting for control of Manchuria between Chinese Nationalists and Chinese Communists breaks out.

● **21 Oct**: France holds elections and introduces a constitutional referendum. On 14 Nov Gen. de Gaulle is appointed head of the French government.

● **29 Nov**: Marshal Tito proclaims a Federal People's Republic of Yugoslavia.

● **Nov**: The trial of Nazi leaders and war criminals opens in Nuremberg.

● **Nov–Dec**: Britain sets up a military administration in Malaya.

● **15 Dec**: Gen. MacArthur, the Supreme Commander of Allied Forces in Japan, frees Japanese political prisoners.

● **16 Jan**: De Gaulle nationalizes the Renault factories, and later Air France (9 Apr).

● **30 Jan**: Food riots break out in hungry, war-torn Berlin.

● **6 Feb**: London hosts an international trade conference.

● **28 Feb**: France secures a lend-lease deal from the USA and (20 Mar) signs an economic pact with Belgium, Holland and Luxembourg.

● **25 Mar**: Field Marshal Montgomery forbids British troops from having social contact with German women. The ban is lifted on 14 Jul.

● **30 Apr**: Women go to the polls in France for the first time.

● **May**: With the end of the war, the German monetary and banking systems collapse.

● **May**: The Economic and Social Council of the UN (ECOSOC) is set up in New York.

● **May**: The European Coal Commission is established in London.

● **4 Jun**: Demobilized German troops are put to work on the land to help food production.

● **Jul**: The British government introduces austerity measures to ease the balance of payments crisis.

● **Jul**: The National Front government in Czechoslovakia nationalizes coal mines, major industries and banks.

● **24 Aug**: President Truman orders an end to lend-lease agreements with wartime allies, which have cost the US $48.5 billion (USA).

● **Sep**: Truman announces his Fair Deal program, a package of social and economic reforms (USA).

● **Sep**: The British government launches a five-year plan to increase iron and coal production and announces the future nationalization of mining and transportation.

● **19 Oct**: Martial law is declared throughout Hungary after civil disturbances.

● **Oct**: Jackie Roosevelt Robinson becomes the first black player to be signed by a US baseball team.

● **5 Dec**: The government nationalizes the Bank of New Zealand and introduces new welfare state legislation (NZ).

● **Dec**: The International Monetary Fund (IMF) and International Bank of Reconstruction and Development (World Bank) are set up as special agencies of the UN following the Bretton Woods agreement of 1944.

● **Dec**: France, Austria, the Netherlands and Czechoslovakia initiate currency reforms.

● The Nobel Peace Prize is won by Cordell Hull (USA), for his international trade agreements and for his efforts in establishing the United Nations.

CULTURE

● **12 Mar**: Anne Frank, the Jewish girl whose wartime diary documented the persecution of the Jews, dies in Bergen-Belsen concentration camp, aged 15.

● **Apr–May**: Art treasures looted by the Nazis, including works by Rembrandt, da Vinci, Titian and Michelangelo, are discovered in an Austrian mine.

● **7 Jun**: Benjamin Britten's opera, *Peter Grimes*, receives its first performance in London.

● **10 Jul**: In Paris, the Louvre museum reopens.

● **15 Sep**: The Austrian composer Anton Webern is shot dead by a US sentry after disobeying an order to stop (Aut).

● **Nov**: Charlie Parker, one of the founders of "modern" jazz, records for the first time with a band under his own name.

● Jean-Paul Sartre: *L'Age du raison* (The Age of Reason), the first novel in his trilogy *Les Chemins de la liberté* (The Roads to Freedom) (Fr).

● George Orwell: *Animal Farm*, a fantasy novel attacking totalitarianism (UK).

● Evelyn Waugh: *Brideshead Revisited*, novel (UK).

● Carlo Levi: *Christ Stopped at Eboli*, novel (It).

● Hermann Broch: *The Death of Virgil*, novel (USA).

● Nobel Prize for Literature is won by Gabriela Mistral (Chile).

● Austrian philosopher Karl Popper publishes his two-volume critique of Plato, Hegel and Marx, *The Open Society and its Enemies* (UK).

● Ezra Pound, arrested in Italy by the US Army for his wartime pro-fascist radio broadcasts, writes his *Pisan Cantos* in prison (published 1948).

● Arthur Honegger: *Sinfonie Liturgique* (Swi).

● Igor Stravinsky: *Symphony in Three Movements* (USA).

● Richard Strauss: *Metamorphosen*, for 23 strings, written in memory of the destroyed Dresden Opera House.

● Dmitri Shostakovich: Ninth Symphony (USSR).

● Rodgers and Hammerstein's musical *Carousel* opens on Broadway (USA).

● Stanley Spencer begins his series of *Resurrection* paintings (UK).

● Alexander Calder: *Red Pyramid*, mobile sculpture (USA).

● Henry Moore: *Family Group*, sculpture (UK) .

● Yves Tanguy: *The Rapidity of Sleep*, painting (Fr).

● Hans Richter: *Liberation of Paris*, collage (USA).

● Marcel Carné: *Les Enfants du paradis*, film (Fr).

SCIENCE

● **8 Mar**: The first air-to-air missile is tested in the USA as part of a project to develop air defense against high-speed, high-altitude bombers. In Aug, V-2 missile components are shipped to the USA for study with a view to recruiting German scientists to aid R & D programs.

● **16 Jul**: The world's first atomic explosion occurs when a device is detonated at Alamogordo Air Base, New Mexico, the result of over three years' work on the Manhattan Project (USA).

● A test site for US rocket research is established at White Sands, New Mexico (US).

● The first radar signals are reflected from the moon by the Hungarian astronomer Z. Bay.

● Arthur C. Clarke, a science fiction writer, proposes the idea of a geostationary satellite (orbiting above one spot on the earth), which later (from 1965) becomes the basis of intercontinental communications (USA).

● Chemist Melvin Calvin first uses carbon-14 in an investigation of photosynthesis (USA).

● Studies of the cell, conducted by the cytologist Albert Claude using an electron microscope, show for the first time details of structures such as the endoplasmic reticulum and mitochondria (USA).

● Britain establishes the Atomic Research Centre at Harwell, Oxfordshire.

● L. Janossy investigates cosmic radiation (Hung).

● Fluoridation of water to combat tooth decay is introduced in the USA.

● British scientists Sir Alexander Fleming, Sir Howard Florey and Ernst Chain win the Nobel Prize for Physiology or Medicine for the discovery of penicillin and research into its use against disease.

● Wolfgang Pauli wins the Nobel Prize for Physics for formulating his "exclusion principle" for subatomic particles (Aut).

● Artturi Virtanen wins the Nobel Prize for Chemistry for his fodder preservation technique (Fin).

● Vladimir Veksler of the USSR designs a new kind of particle accelerator, the synocyclotron.

● John von Neumann publishes his draft report on EDVAC (Electronic Discrete Variable Computer) (USA).

● John Presper Eckert and John W. Mauchly develop ENIAC (Electronic Numerical Integrator and Computer), acknowledged to be the first genuine electronic computer (USA).

● The herbicide 2,4-D is patented and introduced (USA).

1946

After the world war chickens started coming home to roost. The Chinese resumed their civil war. Colonies which had witnessed the temporary humiliation of their masters raised their demands for independence, which was finally promised to India by Britain. In general, the political pendulum favored the Left. France, like Britain the previous year, elected a socialist government, but Juan Perón's success in Argentina proved that not all forms of fascism were dead and buried. Monarchs too experienced mixed fortunes. The reign of King Umberto II of Italy lasted barely a month, but in Greece a referendum favored restoration of the monarchy – though the immediate result was civil war. The Japanese emperor Hirohito had to give up his claim to divinity and become a purely constitutional monarch. In the new postwar order, the supremacy of the United States in the Western world was underlined by the decision to site the headquarters of the International Monetary Fund and the World Bank in Washington DC, and that of the newly inaugurated United Nations in New York.

▲ Trials of Nazi leaders and war criminals had opened in Nuremberg in November 1945. During March 1946 Hermann Göring was in the witness box. Despite his denial of any knowledge of the so-called "Final Solution" to the Jewish "problem", he was condemned to death, but took his own life before the sentence could be carried out.

● **12 Jan**: Albania is declared a people's republic.

● **19 Jan**: The Belgian government rejects Leopold III's demand for a referendum on the monarchy, after asking him in Jul 1945 to abdicate.

● **20 Jan**: Charles de Gaulle resigns as president of France, declaring that he is retiring from politics.

● **29 Jan**: The UN council chooses Trygve Lie, a Norwegian diplomat, as its first Secretary-General at the inaugural session of the UN General Assembly.

● **Jan**: The Japanese emperor gives up any claim to semi-divine status and Shinto ceases to be the state religion of Japan. (˃ Oct)

● **1 Feb**: Hungary declares itself a republic.

● **21–22 Feb**: Violent protests against British rule take place in many Indian cities. In Bombay, 60 people die and the Indian navy mutinies. (˃24 Jun)

● **24 Feb**: Juan Perón becomes president of Argentina, with his wife "Evita" (Maria Eva Duente) effectively as minister of labor.

● **25 Feb**: Mao Zedong and Jiang Jieshi agree to found a National Army that will include both Nationalists and Communists (Chi). (˃5 May)

● **2 Mar**: Ho Chi Minh is elected president of the Democratic Republic of Vietnam. France recognizes it as an autonomous state within French Indochina, but dispatches troops to Hanoi. (˃28 Dec)

● **5 Mar**: Winston Churchill coins the phrase "iron curtain" to describe the divide between Communism and the West.

● **21 Mar**: Nazi leader Hermann Göring denies that he or Hitler knew of the so-called "final solution" to the Jewish "problem" (Ger) (˃30 Sep).

● **22 Mar**: Transjordan becomes independent of Britain as Jordan.

● **29 Mar**: The Gold Coast becomes the first British colony to achieve an African parliamentary majority, leading to a new constitution.

● **Mar–May**: The USSR withdraws troops from Iran in exchange for 51 percent control of Iranian oil for 25 years.

● **18 Apr**: The dissolution of the League of Nations (superseded by the United Nations) formally takes place.

● **Apr–Jul**: A preparatory peace conference of the Big Four (France, UK, USA, USSR) is held in Paris.

● **1 May**: The announcement of an Anglo-American plan to partition Palestine and allow increased quotas of Jewish immigrants angers both Arabs and Jews, and gives rise to a spate of terrorist attacks. (˃22 Jul)

● **5 May**: Civil war between Chinese Nationalists and Communists breaks out. On 19 Aug Mao Zedong formally declares war on Jiang Jieshi's Nationalists.

● **7 May**: Prime minister Clement Attlee announces the withdrawal of British troops from Egypt.

● **8 May**: Nationalist riots in Algeria follow France's decision to extend French citizenship to colonial peoples.

● **May–Jun**: The Italians vote to end the monarchy. Victor Emmanuel III abdicates on 9 May.

● **24 Jun**: The Congress party rejects Britain's plan for India's independence announced on 16 May. (˃29 Jul)

● **4 Jul**: The Philippines become independent of the USA and receive $600,000,000 for reconstruction in exchange for granting a 99-year lease on US military bases.

● **22 Jul**: In Jerusalem, Zionist terrorists of the Irgun movement bomb the King David Hotel (the British Palestine Army Command HQ), killing more than 40 people (Pal).

● **29 Jul**: The All-India Muslim League demands the creation of a totally separate sovereign Islamic state of Pakistan. On 15–19 Aug, in Calcutta, clashes between Hindus and Muslims claim thousands of lives. (˃6 Dec)

● **8 Sep**: Bulgaria rejects the monarchy and votes to become a republic.

● **30 Sep**: The war crimes tribunal in Nuremberg sentences 12 Nazis to death and five others to terms of imprisonment. Rudolf Hess is jailed for life. On 16 Oct Hermann Göring takes his own life (Ger).

● **Sep**: In Greece, civil war follows the referendum of 1 Sep favoring the restoration of the monarchy.

● **Sep**: Nationalist leader Jomo Kenyatta returns to Kenya after 15 years in exile.

● **13 Oct**: A popular referendum approves a new constitution of the Fourth Republic, with reduced presidential powers (Fr).

● **20 Oct**: Berliners vote in the first free elections held in the city since 1933 (Ger).

● **30 Oct**: In Vienna the Austrian parliament calls for an end to the Allied occupation of the country.

● **Oct**: A new Japanese constitution renounces war, abolishes all forms of feudalism and declares the emperor a constitutional monarch.

● **27 Nov**: The Big Four finally agree to resolve the problem of Trieste by creating it a city-state.

● **5 Dec**: New York becomes the official permanent headquarters of the UN.

● **6 Dec**: In London, talks between British and Indian leaders on the future of the Indian subcontinent collapse after only three days.

● **14 Dec**: The UN rejects South Africa's demand to annex Southwest Africa.

● **28 Dec**: France declares martial law throughout Indochina, after bombarding Hanoi and forcing Ho Chi Minh to flee the capital.

SOCIETY

- **1 Jan**: Heathrow Airport near London opens as Britain's intended major national airport.
- **4 Jan**: Riots over bread shortages break out in Paris and Rouen (Fr).
- **30 Jan**: A referendum in Poland supports wide-ranging nationalization plans.
- **Jan**: The European Coal Organization is established.
- **9 Feb**: Soviet leader Joseph Stalin announces the USSR's fourth five-year plan, to begin on 15 Mar.
- **12 Feb**: The USA accuses Argentina of harbouring Nazi war criminals.
- **1 Mar**: The Bank of England is nationalized (UK).
- **Mar**: 350 German enterprises in the Ruhr and 1,200 in the Soviet-controlled zone are dismantled by the Allies (Ger).
- **Mar**: Washington, DC, becomes the permanent headquarters of the IMF and the World Bank (USA).
- **19 Apr**: US president Truman promises to supply 1,000,000 tonnes of wheat a month to Europe and Asia.
- **8 May**: The US government takes over the railroads and coal mines, crippled by strikes.
- **27 May**: The Committee of Scientific Manpower warns of a shortfall of 26,000 scientists in Britain by 1955 unless the government acts.
- **3 Jun**: The US Supreme Court rules that segregation of blacks on buses is against the constitution.
- **13 Jul**: The USA approves a $937,000,000 loan to Britain.
- **Aug**: The UK assumes control over the German iron and steel industries and the British Steel Control Board is established.
- **5 Oct**: Spain signs a commercial agreement with Argentina following president Perón's visit to Gen. Franco.
- **4 Nov**: China and the USA sign a commercial and friendship treaty.
- **9 Nov**: President Truman lifts controls on everything except some foods and rents (USA).
- **18 Dec**: Railroads, road haulage and ports are nationalized (UK).
- **Dec**: The UK and USA sign an agreement on a united economic area comprising their respective occupation zones in Germany.
- Argentina launches a five-year plan for self-sufficiency and nationalizes the banks and telecommunications.
- Italy gives the vote to women.
- Nobel Peace Prize is won by Emily Greene Balch (USA) and John Mott (USA).

CULTURE

- **7 Jan**: The BBC resumes television broadcasting, to less than 12,000 viewers (UK).
- **8 Feb**: US scholars complete the "Revised Standard Version" of the Bible.
- **27 Feb**: New York premiere of the film *The Road to Utopia*, starring Bob Hope, Bing Crosby and Dorothy Lamour.
- **24 Mar**: The BBC begins radio broadcast transmissions in Russian to the USSR (UK).
- **12 Jul**: Premiere of Benjamin Britten's opera *The Rape of Lucretia* at Glyndebourne, with Kathleen Ferrier in the title role (UK).
- **2 Aug**: The Salzburg Festival reopens after the war (Aut).
- **20 Sep**: The Cannes Film Festival, first planned for Sep 1939, opens (Fr).
- **29 Sep**: The BBC introduces its new radio channel for classical music, the Third Programme (UK).
- **24 Oct**: Ralph Richardson opens in Edmond Rostand's play *Cyrano de Bergerac* (UK).
- **10 Dec**: Hermann Hesse (Swi) is awarded the Nobel Prize for Literature.
- Dylan Thomas: *Deaths and Entrances*, collection of poems which establishes him with a wide public (UK).
- William Carlos Williams: *Paterson*, poem cycle concerned with the industrial city (completed 1958) (USA).
- Keith Douglas: *Alamein to Zem Zem*, experimental narrative based on the poet's wartime experiences in North Africa, published posthumously (NZ).
- André Gide: *Journal 1939–1942*, part of an autobiographical sequence (Fr).
- Simone de Beauvoir: *Tous les hommes sont mortels* (All Men are Mortal), (Fr).
- Jean-Paul Sartre: *Mort sans sépulture*, (trans. as The Victors), play (Fr).
- Elias Canetti: *Auto da fé* , novel (UK).
- Nikos Kazantzakis: *Zorba the Greek*, novel (Gr).
- Philip Larkin: *Jill*, novel (UK).
- Eugene O'Neill: *The Iceman Cometh*, play (USA).
- Jean Cocteau: *L'Aigle a deux têtes*, play (Fr).
- Christopher Fry: *A Phoenix Too Frequent*, poetic drama (UK).
- Terence Rattigan: *The Winslow Boy*, play (UK).
- Alec Guinness stars in Jean-Paul Sartre's play *Huis clos* and in Shakespeare's *King Lear* (UK).
- Peter Brook directs Shakespeare's *Love's Labour's Lost* at Stratford-on-Avon (UK).

- Wolfgang Steinecke founds the Summer Courses of New Music at Darmstadt (Ger), which will become highly influential on younger composers. Teachers include René Leibowitz, Olivier Messiaen, Karlheinz Stockhausen, Pierre Boulez, Bruno Maderna among others.
- The Institute of Musical Art and the Julliard Graduate School merge to form the Julliard School of Music (USA).
- Sergey Prokoviev: *The Duenna*, opera, originally planned for production in 1941 but postponed because of the war, opens in New York. The first eight scenes of his opera *War and Peace* are performed at Leningrad, though he goes on revising it until 1955.
- Darius Milhaud: Second Symphony (USA).
- Gian Carlo Menotti: *The Medium*, opera (USA).
- Irving Berlin: *Annie Get Your Gun*, musical (USA).
- The craze for jukebox music begins in the USA and UK.
- Roberto Matta: *Being With*, painting (USA).
- Hans Hoffman: *Immolation*, painting (USA).
- Wols: *The Blue Pomegranate*, painting (USA).
- Mark Rothko: *Prehistoric Memories*, painting (USA).
- Willem De Kooning begins a series of black and white paintings that established him alongside Jackson Pollock as one of the leading Abstract Expressionists (USA).
- Pablo Picasso inaugurates the pottery at Vallauris (Fr).
- A conference entitled "Industrial Design as a New Profession" is held at New York's Museum of Modern Art (MOMA).
- C. d'Ascanio designs the Vespa motor scooter for the Paggio company (It).
- Sven Markelius: Markelius House, Stockholm (Swe).
- Ludwig Mies van der Rohe: Alumni Memorial Hall, Chicago (USA).
- Erich Mendelsohn: Synagogue, Cleveland, Ohio (USA) (completed 1952).
- Frank Capra: *It's a Wonderful World*, film (USA).
- Jean Cocteau: *La Belle et la bête*, film (Fr).
- The United Nations Educational, Scientific and Cultural Organization (UNESCO) is founded.
- Nobel Prize for Literature is won by Hermann Hesse (Ger).

SCIENCE

- **21 Jan**: The UN establishes the Atomic Energy Commission in London.
- **14 Feb**: ENIAC (Electronic Numerical Integrator and Computer) goes into operation at the University of Pennsylvania.
- **25 Jul**: The USA carries out first subsurface atomic explosion, on Bikini Atoll in the Pacific.
- **Jul**: American physicist Vincent Schaefer discovers by chance that supercooled water vapor in carbon dioxide turns to snow.
- **22 Nov**: The ballpoint pen, the invention of expatriate Hungarian Lazlo Biró, goes on sale.
- **24 Dec**: The first Soviet nuclear reactor goes into operation.
- A German V-2 rocket is used to study the sun, taking a spectrograph to a height of 55 km (34 miles).
- Edward Appelto and Donald Hay discover that sunspots emit radio waves.
- Chester Carlson invents xerography (USA).
- Martin Ryle identifies the radio source Cygnus A, the first known radio galaxy (UK).
- Working independently, Max Dellbruck (Ger) and Alfred Hershey (USA) discover that viruses can combine to form new types of virus.
- Hermann Muller (USA), wins the Nobel Prize for Physiology or Medicine for his discovery of X-ray mutation of genes.
- American scientists James Sumner, John Northrop and Wendell Stanley share the Nobel Prize for Chemistry for their respective work on enzyme crystallization of a virus.
- Percy Bridgman (USA) wins the Nobel Prize for Physics for discovering the laws of high-pressure physics.
- The University of California builds the first synchro-cyclotron, capable of producing high-energy alpha particles (USA).
- The term "lepton" is introduced by Abraham Pais and C. Moller to describe particles such as the electron, which are not subject to the strong nuclear force (USA).
- Willard Libby introduces a method of dating ancient objects, known as radiocarbon dating, using the radioactive isotope carbon-14 (USA).
- Linus Pauling suggests how enzymes act as catalysts in biochemical reactions (USA).
- F. Bloch (Swi) and E.W. Purcell (USA). independently develop nuclear magnetic resonance.
- U. von Euler isolates noradrenalin (Swe).
- The drug Benadryl is sold to relieve the symptoms of hay fever.

Postwar austerity reached its peak in 1947, with more food rationed in Britain than during the war. The British Board of Trade implored women not to waste material on clothes – all in vain – Christian Dior's feminine "New Look" was a relief after the severity of uniforms and the need to make do with hand-me-downs. The Marshall Plan, a generous offer by the United States to support Europe's postwar recovery was accepted by most Western nations, but rejected by the Soviet Union as constituting a threat to the Communist states. The European colonial powers now tacitly acknowledged their reduced role in the world by beginning to divest themselves of their imperial possessions, though this was not simple. The deadlock between Hindu and Muslim in India was resolved by partition, but thousands were killed in intercommunal violence and millions were made homeless both before and after the establishment of India and Pakistan in August 1947.

▲ Dior's "New Look" rapidly swept the Western world, the most dramatic change in women's fashion since the demise of the bustle.

● **1 Jan**: A new constitution in the British colony of Nigeria provides for a limited form of self-government.

● **16 Jan**: Vincent Auriol is elected president of the new Fourth Republic. Veteran statesman Leon Blum resigns as caretaker premier; on 22 Jan the Socialist Paul Ramadier forms a cabinet (Fr).

● **19 Jan**: After elections in Poland favor the Communists, US president Harry Truman complains that they were not free and fair and were therefore in breach of the Yalta agreement of 1945.

● **21 Jan**: Gen. Jan Smuts, the South African premier, refuses to put Southwest Africa under UN trusteeship.

● **31 Jan**: The evacuation of British women and children from Palestine begins in the wake of increasing attacks by Jewish terrorists demanding a separate Jewish state. Martial law is declared on 3 Mar. (›4 May)

● **10 Feb**: Italy agrees to pay reparations to the Western Allies and to give up its African colonies and the Dodecanese islands (ceded to Greece). Finland, Hungary and Romania are required by treaty to relinquish territory to the USSR.

● **20 Feb**: Britain announces its intention to quit India by June 1948. Lord Louis Mountbatten is appointed the last viceroy, responsible for the handover of power. (›23 May)

● **5 Mar**: The USSR rejects Western proposals for the international control of atomic research.

● **12 Mar**: President Truman enunciates the "Truman doctrine" to oppose Communism throughout the world (USA).

● **25 Mar**: The Netherlands recognizes Indonesian independence.

● **31 Mar**: In Moscow, US Secretary of State George Marshall rejects a Soviet demand for reparations payments in return for allowing German economic unity. The USA and UK are proposing that Germany should be administered as a single economic unit, but the USSR and France disagree. Talks end in failure on 24 Apr.

● **14 Apr**: Gen. Charles de Gaulle founds his own political party, the Rassemblement du Peuple Français (RPF) (Fr).

● **4 May**: Irgun terrorists in Palestine bomb the British prison at Acre and release 251 Jewish inmates.

● **7 May**: The Communist party is outlawed in Brazil.

● **19 May**: Vietminh troops from North Vietnam attack Saigon in the South.

● **23 May**: The British cabinet agrees to Mountbatten's proposal to partition India into two states, one Hindu, one Muslim. (›Jun)

● **5 Jun**: At Harvard, George Marshall outlines his economic proposals (Marshall Plan) to save Europe from the postwar slump and from Communism. UK Foreign Secretary Ernest Bevin is enthusiastic, but the USSR is hostile to "dollar enslavement". (›2 Jul)

● **5 Jun**: President Truman attacks the Soviet Union for tightening its hold on Hungary, Romania and Bulgaria.

● **10 Jun**: Truman arrives in Ottawa, marking the first-ever state visit by a US president to Canada.

● **21 Jun**: Truman suspends $15 million credit to Hungary because of alleged Soviet interference and the exile of president Nagy. In Budapest, the new premier Lajos Dinnyes promises free elections in the autumn. (›1 Sep)

● **Jun**: Pandit Nehru and Muhammad Ali Jinnah, the leaders of the two major Indian political parties, Congress and the Muslim League, endorse Britain's plan for the partition of India.

● **2 Jul**: In Paris, the USSR declines to participate in the Marshall Plan, which is accepted by Britain and France. (›12 Jul)

● **6 Jul**: Spain makes a constitutional change to allow the return of the monarchy after the death of Gen. Franco.

● **11 Jul**: Mr Jinnah is appointed governor-general of the future state of Pakistan, making him the first non-white to hold this office in a British dominion. Lord Mountbatten, at the invitation of the Congress party, is to occupy a similar position in India after partition. (›15 Aug)

● **12 Jul**: Foreign ministers of 16 European nations meet in Paris to discuss the Marshall Plan. It is accepted by all countries except Czechoslovakia, Poland and Finland.

● **19 Jul**: The Burmese president U Aung Sang and six of his ministers are shot dead by political opponents.

● **5 Aug**: South Africa establishes a Bureau of Race Relations.

● **15 Aug**: India and Pakistan proclaim their independence under prime ministers Pandit Jawaharlal Nehru (India) and Liaqat Ali Khan (Pakistan). Both countries become British dominions.

● **29 Aug**: The USA calls for Soviet participation in four-power talks on Korea.

● **Aug–Sep**: An estimated 10,000 people are killed in border clashes in the Punjab. At Amritsar, 1,200 die in one of the worst of many massacres of Muslim refugees on their way to Pakistan. India and Pakistan agree to halt all traffic through the Punjab.

● **1 Sep**: The Communists win the Hungarian elections, leading to claims of irregularities.

● **2 Sep**: At Rio de Janeiro, the USA signs an Inter-American Defense Pact with its southern neighbors (Bra).

SOCIETY

• **18 Sep**: In Czechoslovakia, 142 people are arrested and charged with the attempted murder of president Eduard Beneš.

• **23 Sep**: In Sofia, Nikolai Petkov, the head of the opposition Agrarian party, is executed (Bul).

• **9 Oct**: French troops in Indochina attack Tongkin, following Ho Chi Minh's refusal of French peace terms on 10 Sep.

• **17 Oct**: Britain announces in Rangoon that Burma will become independent from 1948.

• **27 Oct**: The maharajah of Kashmir, a predominantly Muslim state, elects to join India rather than Pakistan, but Pakistan opposes the move. India promises to hold a referendum in Kashmir to decide its future provided that Pakistan does not interfere. (›28 Dec)

• **10 Nov**: Britain and the USA agree that Britain's mandate in Palestine will end on 31 May 1948. The first British troops leave Palestine on 16 Nov.

• **19 Nov**: In Vienna, Communists are expelled from the government (Aut).

• **23 Nov**: Robert Schuman becomes French premier.

• **25 Nov**: A four-power meeting opens in London to resume discussions on Germany and Austria.

• **29 Nov**: The UN votes to partition Palestine to include a separate Jewish state. The announcement provokes violent protest demonstrations in Jerusalem (30 Nov) and fighting between Arabs and Jews.

• **19 Dec**: Yugoslavia and Romania sign a friendship pact in Belgrade. King Michael I of Romania abdicates and the state is declared a republic on 30 Dec.

• **22–23 Dec**: The last refugees from India cross into Pakistan. Partition is estimated to have displaced 8.5 million people, of whom some 400,000 lost their lives.

• **25–31 Dec**: Greek royalist troops and Communists rebels clash at Konitza. The Communist party is outlawed in Greece on 27 Dec.

• **28 Dec**: Muslim guerrillas fight with Indian troops in Kashmir. The Kashmir question is referred to the UN Security Council on 30 Dec.

• **30 Dec**: A conference opens in Montego Bay, Jamaica, to discuss the formation of a West Indies Federation.

• **Dec**: The Ceylon Independence Act makes Ceylon a self-governing dominion in the British Commonwealth. Elections in Ceylon (10 Dec) give the United National Party (UNP) a huge majority.

• The Central Intelligence Agency (CIA) is set up by president Truman (USA).

• **Cominform** (Communist Information Bureau) is established by Andrey Zhdanov to coordinate East European Communists (USSR).

• **1 Jan**: Britain's 1,500 collieries are nationalized. On 1 May heavy industries are nationalized.

• **Jan–Feb**: Fuel and food shortages, combined with a record harsh winter, plunge Britain into chaos.

• **3 Apr**: A private medical company called BUPA (British United Provident Association) is set up in face of the new National Health Service (UK).

• **1 May**: Skeletons of a herd of mammoths are discovered in Tucson, Arizona (USA).

• **9 May**: In Hamburg (Ger) 150,000 people demonstrate against food shortages.

• **25 May**: The government in Helsinki announces its intention to introduce collective farming on a trial basis (Fin).

• **29 May**: The Indian Constituent Assembly outlaws "untouchability" .

• **23 Jun**: The US Congress passes the antilabor union Taft-Hartley Act over Truman's veto. Its provisions include a ban on the use of union funds for political purposes and a ban on the closed shop.

• **30 Jun**: The UK government reduces milk rations and announces further austerity measures to combat the economic crisis caused by a dollar shortage.

• **Jun**: US Secretary of State Marshall announces the European Recovery Program (ERP, the Marshall Plan). It runs from 1948 until 1952, during which time it makes available over $13 billion to the European countries that participate, mostly in the form of food, raw materials and equipment, contributing greatly to European reconstruction and recovery.

• **5 Sep**: Britain and the USA agree on joint control of mines in the Ruhr (Ger).

• **20 Sep**: Denis Compton makes cricketing history by scoring 3,816 runs, including 18 centuries, in a single season (UK).

• **5 Oct**: President Truman appeals to Americans to go without meat on Tuesdays and poultry and eggs on Thursdays to aid Europe (USA).

• **29 Oct**: The Benelux Customs Union, comprising Belgium, the Netherlands and Luxembourg, is established.

• **30 Oct**: The General Agreement on Tariffs and Trade (GATT) is signed by 23 countries. It aims to expand international trade through the abolition of tariffs, quotas and trade barriers. By Jan 1952 the 34 contracting countries account for more than 80 percent of world trade.

• **27 Nov**: Australian banks are nationalized.

• **14 Dec**: The USSR devalues its currency and ends rationing.

• Nobel Peace Prize is won by the American Friends Service Committee, and the Friends Service Council.

CULTURE

• **3 Jun**: Christian Dior introduces the "New Look" into women's fashion clothes, an ultrafeminine full-skirted antithesis to wartime styles (Fr).

• **24 Aug**: Edinburgh launches its International Festival of Music and Drama (UK).

• **20 Oct**: A Congressional committee launches an investigation into Communism in Hollywood (USA).

• **25 Nov**: Leaders of the US film industry "black" 10 Hollywood writers and producers who are alleged by Congress to be Communist sympathizers.

• **4 Dec**: Marlon Brando opens on Broadway in Tennessee Williams's new drama *A Streetcar Named Desire* (USA).

• French writer André Gide is awarded the Nobel Prize for Literature.

• Albert Camus: *La Peste* (The Plague), novel (Fr).

• Thomas Mann: *Dr Faustus*, novel (USA).

• Malcolm Lowry: *Under the Volcano*, novel (Can).

• Arthur Miller: *All My Sons*, play (USA).

• Jean Anouilh: *L'Invitation au château* (trans. as Ring Round the Moon, 1950), play (Fr).

• Alberto Moravia: *La romana* (The Woman of Rome), novel (It).

• Primo Levi: *Se questo un uomo* (If This is a Man), novel based on the author's experiences in Auschwitz concentration camp (It).

• Benjamin Britten: *Albert Herring*, opera (UK).

• Arnold Schoenberg: *A Survivor from Warsaw*, for reciter, male chorus and orchestra (USA).

• Gottfried von Einem: *Danton's Tod* (The Death of Danton), opera, is first produced at the Salzburg Festival (Aut).

• Arshile Gorky: *Agony*, painting (USA).

• Willem de Kooning: *Pink Angels*, painting (USA).

• Marc Chagall: *Madonna of the Sleigh*, painting (Fr).

• Marino Marini: *Horseman*, sculpture (It).

• Henry Moore: *Three Standing Figures*, sculpture (UK).

• Alberto Giacometti: *The Pointing Man*, sculpture (Swi).

• Le Corbusier begins his Unité d'Habitation in Marseille (completed 1952).

• The "Dead Sea Scrolls", containing ancient religious texts, some antedating the earliest known Hebrew examples, are discovered in a cave near Khirbet Qumran (Jordan).

SCIENCE

• **29 Aug**: Scientists announce that plutonium fission is suitable for nuclear power generation (USA).

• **14 Oct**: Chuck Yeager, flying a Bell X-1 aircraft, becomes the first person to break the sound barrier, with a speed of over 960 km/h (600 mph) (USA).

• **11 Nov**: Reports suggest that the USSR has tested its first atomic device in Siberia.

• Viktor Ambartsuryan, a Soviet astronomer, shows that the Milky Way contains the hottest, oldest type of stars (O stars) as well as groups of young stars (USSR).

• Carl and Gerty Cori, Czech-American biologists who worked on the metabolism of glycogen, share the Nobel Prize for Physiology or Medicine with A. Houssay (Arg), who studied the pituitary gland.

• Sir Edward Appleton wins the Nobel Prize for Physics for his discovery of the ionic layer in the atmosphere (UK).

• Sir Robert Robinson wins the Nobel Prize for Chemistry for his work on plant alkaloids (UK).

• Britain's first nuclear reactor begins operation at Harwell, Oxfordshire.

• The powerful antibiotic chloramphenicol is discovered. Its use is later restricted because of its harmful side-effects.

• Willis Lamb finds a small but unexpected difference between two levels in the hydrogen spectrum. Known as the Lamb shift, this discovery lays the foundation for quantum electrodynamics (QED) (USA).

• Karl von Frisch discovers that bees use the polarization of light for orientation (Aut).

• F.A. Lipmann discovers the compound coenzyme A, which is involved in the control of the energy level in cells (Ger).

• A.R.Todd synthesizes both adenosine diphosphate (ADP) and adenosine triphosphate (ATP), the compounds used by cells to handle energy (UK).

• Hungarian-British physicist Dennis Gabor developes the basic concept of holography, although the technique does not become practical until after the invention of the laser.

• The first microwave cooker goes on sale in the USA.

• Goodyear introduce the tubeless tire (USA).

1948

The state of Israel came into existence in 1948 on the basis of a partition of Palestine into Arab and Jewish regions agreed by the United Nations (including the Soviet Union) the previous year, but opposed by the Arabs. Thousands of Palestinian Arabs went into the refugee camps which for many of them were to become their permanent home, and the neighboring Arab nations promptly attacked. This gave Israel an opportunity to readjust its borders greatly to its own advantage – strengthening the bitter hostility of its neighbors. Elsewhere Communist aggression appeared to justify American fears of Communist expansion. In Czechoslovakia, the government was replaced by a Communist government with a new Soviet-style constitution, while in Korea the Communist-held North claimed its independence as the People's Republic of Korea shortly after president Syngman Rhee had proclaimed Korea a republic. In Indonesia martial law was imposed after a Communist uprising.

▲ On 14 May David Ben-Gurion proclaimed the creation of the state of Israel in Tel Aviv as the British mandate ended. As British troops left, the Arab states immediately invaded and entered Jerusalem, in a conflict over the "promised land" that was to continue for many decades.

● **4 Jan**: Burma celebrates its independence from Britain.

● **17 Jan**: Indonesia and the Netherlands agree to an armistice.

● **19 Jan**: India and Pakistan accept UN mediation to settle their differences.

● **30 Jan**: Indian leader Mahatma Gandhi is assassinated by a Hindu extremist, Nathuram Godre, in New Delhi. The news of Gandhi's death sparks off widespread rioting.

● **4 Feb**: Ceylon receives its independence and dominion status.

● **16 Feb**: North Korea, with Soviet support, declares itself a people's republic.

● **16 Feb**: Britain sends a warship to the South Atlantic to warn off Argentina from pressing its claim to the Falkland Islands (Malvinas), but expresses its readiness to resolve the issue through an international court.

● **17 Feb**: The Imam Yahya is assassinated in British-controlled Yemen. He is succeeded (14 Mar) by the dictator Imam Ahmad.

● **18 Feb**: John Costello becomes prime minister of Eire, after Eamon De Valera, who has held the post for 16 years, is voted out of office.

● **25–27 Feb**: The Communists take over power in Czechoslovakia, under prime minister Klement Gottwald.

● **10 Mar**: Jan Masaryk, the Czech foreign minister and opponent of Communism, mysteriously falls to his death from a high window. The official verdict is suicide. (›7 Jun)

● **17 Mar**: A 50-year mutual defence and cooperation treaty between Britain, France and the Benelux countries is signed in Brussels (Bel).

● **20 Mar**: A walk-out by Soviet delegates to the Allied Central Council, the body officially governing Germany, follows accusations that the West is conspiring against the USSR.

● **21 Mar**: Chinese Communists launch an offensive against Nationalist forces in Nanjing.

● **30 Mar–30 Apr**: The Pan-American conference meeting at Bogotá (Col) draws up the Charter of the Organization of American States.

● **1 Apr**: In Berlin, the USSR imposes strict checks on traffic leaving the city from the Western zones (Ger). (›24 Jun)

● **6 Apr**: Finland and the USSR sign a 10-year mutual defence agreement in Helsinki (Fin).

● **22 Apr**: The Jews capture Haifa from the Arabs after a battle in which 400 die (Pal).

● **1 May**: Communist North Korea claims jurisdiction over the whole of Korea; so does South Korea on 31 May. Syngman Rhee, president of South Korea, asks US troops to remain. (›15 Aug)

● **14–15 May**: The state of Israel is proclaimed, with David Ben-Gurion as head of a provisional government. British troops withdraw as the British mandate in Palestine ends. Arab League nations invade. On 16 May Chaim Weizmann becomes Israel's first president.

● **17 May**: Jordanian troops capture the old city of Jerusalem. (›9 Jul)

● **20 May**: The Nationalist leader Jiang Jieshi is reelected president of China.

● **26 May**: Jan Smuts, South African prime minister since 1939, is defeated at the polls by the Nationalist Afrikaaner party campaigning on an apartheid platform; Dr Daniel Malan becomes prime minister on 3 Jun.

● **7 Jun**: After the implementation of a new Soviet-style constitution in May, president Eduard Beneš resigns and is replaced (14 Jun) by Klement Gottwald. Beneš dies on 3 Sep (Cze).

● **18 Jun**: A state of emergency is declared in Malaya, following murders of British planters. Communist insurgents are hunted down and killed and the Malay Communist party (MCP), the Malayan People's (anti-Japanese) Army and the Old Comrades' Association are banned.

● **24 Jun**: The USSR, under threat of a merger of Western occupation zones in Germany, blockades all surface traffic between Berlin and West Germany; in response the Western Allies begin to airlift food and supplies to the beleaguered Berliners. (›1 Aug)

● **9 Jul**: Egypt and Iraq resume hostilities against Israel following the end of the month's truce called by the UN. The UN Security Council calls for a further ceasefire on 15 Jul. (›17 Sep)

● **20 Jul**: In the USA, American Communist party leaders are arrested. On 2 Aug the Un-American Activities Committee opens its inquiries into alleged Communist infiltration in government. President Truman denounces the proceedings (USA).

● **30 Jul**: The president of Hungary, Zoltán Tildy, resigns over the proposed collectivization of agriculture.

● **1 Aug**: France, Britain and the USA merge their occupation zones in Germany. On 2–6 Aug Soviet leader Joseph Stalin and his foreign minister Vyacheslav Molotov meet with Western representatives in Moscow to discuss Germany and the Berlin crisis.

● **15 Aug**: In Seoul, Korea is proclaimed a republic with Syngman Rhee its president. (›9 Sep)

● **19 Aug**: In Berlin, Soviet troops fire on demonstrators protesting against Soviet occupation (Ger). (›18 Oct)

● **20 Aug**: Communist rebels in Greece suffer defeat by government troops.

● **26 Aug**: Britain refuses to join a European Assembly (Neth).

● **4 Sep**: Queen Wilhelmina of the Netherlands gives up the throne to her daughter Juliana.

SOCIETY

● **9 Sep**: North Korea claims its independence as the Democratic People's Republic of Korea, with its capital in Pyongyang, and its leader Kim Il Sung pledges to unite Korea.

● **11 Sep**: Muhammad Ali Jinnah, the first governor-general of Pakistan, dies of heart failure.

● **17 Sep**: The rebel state of Hyderabad, a largely Hindu state under its own Muslim ruler, concedes defeat to the Indian army after five days of fighting (Ind).

● **17 Sep**: Count Folke Bernadotte, a UN mediator, is murdered by Israeli terrorists. On 18 Sep 200 suspects are apprehended and the Stern Gang is outlawed. Irgun, another Jewish terrorist group, disbands after a government ultimatum on 21 Sep (Isr).

● **19 Sep**: Ahmed Sukarno imposes martial law in Indonesia after Communists rebel in Madiun, Java. (›29 Dec)

● **23 Sep**: The Somali people appeal to the UN for a united Somalia after Ethiopia takes control of Somalia's Reserved Areas.

● **26 Sep**: Chinese Communists capture Nan, the capital of Shandong (Chi). (›31 Oct)

● **18 Oct**: With unrest growing in Berlin's Soviet sector, the USSR arms the German police (Volkspolizei) (Ger).

● **22 Oct**: The British Commonwealth is renamed the Commonwealth of Nations.

● **26 Oct**: In Paris, the Western powers draw up guidelines for a North Atlantic defense pact.

● **31 Oct**: After capturing Manchuria from Jiang Jieshi's US-backed Nationalist army, Mao Zedong's Communist forces take the provincial capital Shenyang (Mukden) (Chi).

● **3 Nov**: President Truman defeats Thomas Dewey in the US presidential election.

● **10 Nov**: Britain and the USA return mines and steel plants in the Ruhr to German ownership.

● **12 Nov**: In Tokyo, Gen. Tojo, Japan's wartime prime minister, and seven others are sentenced to death for war crimes.

● **30 Nov**: German Communists set up a government in Berlin's Soviet sector.

● **6 Dec**: The Un-American Activities Committee accuses Alger Hiss, a US State Department official, of passing secrets to the Soviets. Hiss is indicted on charges of perjury on 15 Dec.

● **10 Dec**: The UN Assembly adopts a declaration of human rights.

● **29 Dec**: The Dutch occupy Jakarta and arrest the Indonesian government. By the end of the year they are in control of the country.

● **Dec**: The Mau Mau, a secret society pledged to expel white settlers from Kikuyu territory, is formed in Kenya.

● **1 Jan**: Britain nationalizes its railways and (from 1 Apr) electricity.

● **12 Jan**: The US Supreme Court orders the state of Oklahoma to allow a black woman student to enter law school (USA).

● **24 Jan**: France devalues the franc by 80 percent (Fr).

● **27 Mar**: The building of the Aswan Dam formally begins (Egy).

● **14 Apr**: British MPs vote by 245 to 222 to suspend capital punishment for a five-year trial period. The bill is rejected by the House of Lords (2 Jun) but later passed with modifications to retain hanging for certain crimes.

● **16 Apr**: The Organization for European and Economic Cooperation (OEEC) is established. Its original purpose is to draft the formal request for aid from the USA under the Marshall Plan, but it goes on to pursue other collective policies to speed recovery and liberalize trade.

● **18 Jun**: The Allies in west Germany announce that a new currency, the Deutschmark, will replace the old Reichsmark (Ger).

● **25 Jun**: Boxer Joe Louis retains his world heavyweight championship by knocking out the challenger Jersey Joe Walcott at New York's Madison Square Gardens (USA).

● **5 Jul**: The National Health Service, together with other welfare schemes for the old and unemployed, comes into effect (UK).

● **29 Jul**: The Olympic Games, held in London, are formally opened by King George VI. Germany, the USSR and Japan do not compete. After the Games several East European athletes decide not to return home.

● **22 Aug**: The World Council of Churches (WCC) is founded in Amsterdam, with representatives of 147 churches from 44 countries.

● **14 Sep**: Scientists in Washington warn that food supplies will not keep will pace with the world's growing population (USA).

● **18 Sep**: A total of 895 flights in 24 hours by Dakota, Globemaster and York aircraft carrying 7,000 tonnes of supplies to the city of Berlin in its third month of blockade, establishes a new record (Ger).

● **1–4 Nov**: The UK government relaxes its controls on foodstuffs such as cocoa and jam and in manufacturing.

● **3 Nov**: The state of Kansas lifts its prohibition laws after 68 years (USA).

● In the USA, Professor Alfred Kinsey publishes his study of sexual mores, *Sexual Behavior of the Human Male*, popularly known as the "Kinsey report".

● Margaret Mead's *Male and Female: A Study of the Sexes in a Changing World* claims that much of Western culture derives from Western child-rearing practices.

CULTURE

● **3 May**: Tennessee Williams is awarded a Pulitzer prize for his play *A Streetcar Named Desire* (USA).

● **6 May**: Norman Mailer's first novel, *The Naked and the Dead*, is published (USA).

● **4 Oct**: The first volume of wartime prime minister Winston Churchill's history of World War II, *The Gathering Storm*, is published (UK).

● **10 Dec**: T.S. Eliot, American-born but a naturalized Briton since 1927, is awarded the Nobel Prize for Literature.

● Alan Paton, a white South African, publishes his acclaimed novel *Cry the Beloved Country*, a plea for racial tolerance and understanding.

● William Faulkner: *Intruder in the Dust*, novel (USA).

● F.R. Leavis, *The Great Tradition*, radical literary criticism (UK).

● Graham Greene: *The Heart of the Matter*, novel (UK).

● Jean Genet: *Les Bonnes* (The Maids), play (Fr).

● Nikos Kazantzakis: *Christ Recrucified*, novel (Gr).

● Jean-Paul Sartre: *Les Mains sales* (Dirty Hands), play (Fr).

● Christopher Fry: *The Lady's not for Burning*, play (UK).

● Bertolt Brecht: *The Caucasian Chalk Circle*, play (USA).

● Eugene Ionesco: *La Cantatrice chauve* (The Bald Prima Donna), play that marks a new flowering of the Theater of the Absurd (Fr).

● In the USSR, Stalin's cultural spokesman Andrey Zhdanov introduces a new crackdown on cultural freedom. Dmitri Shostakovich attracts particular criticism for his Ninth Symphony (1945), written to mark the end of the war but insufficiently heroic for Stalin.

● Richard Strauss: Four Last Songs (Ger).

● Ralph Vaughan Williams: Sixth Symphony (UK).

● Olivier Messiaen: Turangalîla Symphony, in 10 movements (Fr).

● Composer Benjamin Britten and tenor Peter Pears found the Aldeburgh Festival (UK).

● Jackson Pollock exhibits his controversial "action painting" in New York for the first time.

● Robert Motherwell, William Baziotes, Barnett Newman and Mark Rothko found a school of art to encourage Abstract Expressionism (USA).

● Andrew Wyeth: *Christina's World*, painting in the American Realist style (USA).

● Pier Luigi Nervi: Exhibition Hall, Turin (It).

● Vittorio de Sica: *The Bicycle Thieves*, neorealist film (It).

SCIENCE

● **10 Jun**: The first heart surgery to clear a blocked valve is performed by R. C. Brock of Guy's Hospital, London.

● **6 Jul**: The Vickers Viscount, the world's first turbine-propeller aircraft, flies for the first time (UK).

● **29 Sep**: Contamination from the undersea atomic test on Bikini Atoll (25 Jul 1946) is claimed by David Bradley, a scientist who took part, to have been much worse than expected (USA).

● **15 Dec**: The first French nuclear reactor starts up at Fort de Châtillon (Fr).

● The transistor is invented by William Shockley, W.H. Brattain and John Bardeen at Bell Laboratories (USA) to replace the thermionic tube.

● Academician Trofim Denisovich Lysenko's antigenetics theories become the official orthodoxy in Soviet biology; those taking opposing views are purged (USSR).

● Hermann Bondi, Thomas Gold and Fred Hoyle advance the steady-state theory of the universe in which continual creation of matter powers expansion. It later loses support to the "Big Bang" theory (USA/UK).

● George Gamow, Ralph Alpher and Robert Herman develop the "Big Bang" theory of the origin of the universe (USA).

● Paul Müller (Swi) wins the Nobel Prize for Physiology for his discovery of the effect of DDT on insects.

● Arne Tiselius (Swe) wins the Nobel Prize for Chemistry for his work on serum proteins.

● Nobel Prize for Physics is won by P.M.S. Blackett (UK) "for his development of the Wilson Cloud-chamber method and his discoveries therewith in the fields of nuclear physics and cosmic radiation".

● Manchester University's Mark I prototype, a stored-program electronic computer, starts operation (UK).

● P.S. Hench discovers that cortisone can be used to treat rheumatoid arthritis (USA).

● At Merck & Co, researchers headed by K.A. Folkers discover that certain bacteria need vitamin B12 for growth, enabling them to isolate the pure vitamin (USA).

● Edwin Land develops a film system that develops pictures inside the camera in about one minute (USA).

● Hungarian-born P.M. Goldmark develops the first long-playing record (USA).

● Marie Goeppert-Mayer (USA) and J.H.D. Jensen (Ger) independently suggest that protons and neutrons in the atomic nucleus occupy "shells" similar to those occupied by electrons.

● Swiss engineer George deMestral invents the fastener Velcro.

George Orwell's "1984", a nightmarish novel of life in a totalitarian state, had enormous public impact. Though set in the future, it seemed relevant to what was happening in the Communist bloc already, and adherents of liberalism and democracy were further shaken by events in China, where the Communists finally won the civil war that had continued, off and on, for the previous 20 years. The Nationalists, having lost Beijing and Shanghai, tacitly acknowledged defeat by retreating to the island of Formosa (Taiwan) but still claimed to be the rightful government of China. They were supported by the United States, and as a result the Nationalists held China's seat in the United Nations until 1971, Mao's new "People's Republic" being excluded. A further worsening of relations between the Soviet Union and the West had come with the sudden denial of overland access to West Berlin by the Communist authorities in June 1948. The Western nations retaliated by sending in over two million tonnes of food and supplies by a massive airlift that continued until the blockade was finally called off in May 1949.

▲ **Dakota freighters like this were extensively used during the Berlin airlift. Blocks of aircraft were sent out from West Germany every two hours to Tempelhof airport in West Berlin; those arriving at night were unloaded by torchlight since the electricity had been cut off.**

● **1 Jan**: The war between India and Pakistan over the control of Kashmir, whose Hindu ruler wished to join India despite the majority of his subjects being Muslims, officially ends. The UN arrange a plebiscite.

● **12–14 Jan**: Race riots in which Africans clash with Asians leave 105 dead in Durban (SA).

● **22 Jan**: In the civil war in China, Beijing falls to the Communists. The Nationalist leader Jiang Jieshi unsuccessfully appeals for a ceasefire.

● **25 Jan**: The first Israeli elections are won by David Ben-Gurion's Labor party. Chaim Weizmann is elected president (16 Feb).

● **28 Jan**: The USA demands that the Dutch, who are occupying Java (since 1 Jan), withdraw immediately from Indonesia. (›29 Jun)

● **14 Feb**: A Budapest court finds Cardinal Mindszenty guilty of treason and racketeering and sentences him to life imprisonment. The USA protests at the verdict.

● **24 Feb**: Israel and Egypt agree to a ceasefire. Egypt retains the Gaza Strip and part of S Palestine; Israel keeps control of most of the Negev, captured in the fighting. Egypt still refuses to recognize Israel. (›23 Mar)

● **4 Mar**: Vyacheslav Molotov is replaced as Soviet foreign minister by Andrey Vishinsky, who presided over the notorious treason trials of the 1930s (USSR).

● **8 Mar**: France recognizes Bao Dai as head of a non-Communist Vietnam with its capital in Saigon.

● **23 Mar**: Israel declares an armistice with Lebanon, and later (11 Apr) with Jordan.

● **31 Mar**: Greek Communist rebels launch an offensive in Macedonia and Thrace.

● **4 Apr**: In Washington, 12 nations – Britain, France, the Benelux countries, Denmark, Iceland, Italy, Norway, Portugal, Canada and the USA – sign the North Atlantic treaty. The North Atlantic Treaty Organization (NATO) represents about 350 million people.

● **6 Apr**: President Truman declares his readiness to use the atomic bomb again if it proves necessary (USA).

● **15 Apr**: Pope Pius XII calls for the holy places of Jerusalem to be made international. On 9 Dec the UN votes to internationalize Jerusalem, and on 13 Dec the Israeli government moves its capital from Tel Aviv to Jerusalem.

● **18 Apr**: Eire leaves the Commonwealth and becomes the Republic of Ireland.

● **26 Apr**: The USSR calls for four-power talks to resolve the crisis over the Berlin blockade.

● **27 Apr**: King George VI (UK) takes the title Head of the Commonwealth. India declares itself a republic but chooses to remain in the Commonwealth.

● **4 May**: At the UN the Soviet Union agrees to lift the blockade on Berlin from 12 May and no longer opposes the creation of a separate West German state.

● **11 May**: Israel, recognized by the UK on 29 Jan, becomes a member of the UN.

● **11 May**: Siam is renamed Thailand.

● **23 May**: The Federal Republic of Germany is proclaimed in the new capital city of Bonn. The FRG consists of the US, British and French zones of Germany. (›13 Aug)

● **25 May**: The USA rejects Soviet reparations claims against Germany at talks held between the Big Four (USA, Britain, France and the USSR) in Paris.

● **26 May**: Communist troops capture Shanghai from the Nationalists after a month-long siege (Chi).

● **2 Jun**: Transjordan is renamed the Hashemite kingdom of Jordan, with territory west of the Jordan river acquired during the Arab-Israeli war of 1948.

● **13 Jun**: Gen. MacArthur, in Tokyo, accuses the Soviet Union of promoting civil unrest in Japan.

● **16 Jun**: Bishops in Prague complain of government persecution following the seizure of the residence of the archbishop of Prague by the police. The church in Slovakia is nationalized (Cze).

● **25 Jun**: The South African Citizenship Act withdraws automatic citizenship rights (after five years) from Commonwealth immigrants, and outlaws mixed marriages between whites and blacks or "coloreds", ie Asians (SA).

● **29 Jun**: Dutch forces leave Jakarta, on the island of Java. (›2 Nov)

● **Jun**: African leader Kwame Nkrumah forms the Convention People's party in the Gold Coast.

● **13 Jul**: Pope Pius XII issues the Apostolic Acta, threatening to excommunicate Roman Catholic supporters of Communism.

● **19 Jul**: Laos becomes a semi-autonomous state within French Indochina.

● **8 Aug**: The Council of Europe, an organization to promote closer cultural and political cooperation between West European states, is established in Strasbourg (Fr).

● **13–14 Aug**: The Federal Republic of Germany goes to the polls with a 70 percent turnout and elects a Christian Democrat government. Dr Konrad Adenauer becomes the new Chancellor, aged 73 (15 Sep).

● **14 Aug**: Communist rebels led by Gen. Markos are defeated by government troops in the Vitsi mountains (Gr). (›16 Oct)

SOCIETY   CULTURE   SCIENCE

SOCIETY

● **29–30 Aug:** President Tito of Yugoslavia, facing a Soviet economic blockade, appeals to the USA for a loan. On 8 Sep the USA lends $20 million to Yugoslavia.

● **21 Sep:** The Communists proclaim a People's Republic of China, under its elected chairman Mao Zedong. The USSR is the first to recognize the new regime. Zhou Enlai is elected premier and foreign minister (30 Sep). On 8 Dec Jiang Jieshi sets up a Nationalist Chinese government on the island of Formosa (Taiwan).

● **21 Sep:** The UN makes Somalia (Italian Somalia) a trusteeship under Italy for 10 years. On 21 Nov the UN declares that all former Italian colonies are independent.

● **23 Sep:** Britain and the USA announce that the USSR has exploded its first atomic bomb, but there is no confirmation from Moscow.

● **28 Sep–1 Oct:** The USSR, followed by Poland and Hungary, and then Romania and Bulgaria, renounce their friendship and mutual assistance pacts with Yugoslavia.

● **7 Oct:** The German Democratic Republic, formed of the Soviet-occupied zone of Germany, is proclaimed under president Wilhelm Pieck and prime minister Otto Grotewohl. The USA denounces the GDR as "illegal and unconstitutional".

● **16 Oct:** The civil war in Greece ends as Communist insurgents lay down their arms.

● **26 Oct:** Britain, with £300 million worth of investments in China, becomes the first major Western power to recognize the new Communist republic. The USA, Canada and Australia refuse to do so.

● **2 Nov:** At a conference in the Hague, the Dutch agree to recognize Indonesia's independence.

● **8 Nov:** Cambodia becomes a semi-autonomous state within the French Union.

● **11 Nov:** Britain launches a drive against Communist rebels in Malaya and across the Thai border.

● **16 Dec:** Ahmed Sukarno is elected the first president of Indonesia. He promises, in return for the withdrawal of Dutch troops from the islands, not to nationalize Dutch economic interests.

● **30 Dec:** France relinquishes power in Vietnam after a US mission to Saigon.

● **Jan:** The Council for Mutual Economic Assistance (COMECON) is set up in the Eastern bloc as a means of promoting economic cooperation and development among member states. These include the USSR and the countries of Eastern Europe.

● **1 Feb:** The UK government announces an end to clothes rationing, effective from 15 Mar. On 2 Apr, at the end of a 10-year ban, floodlights and neon signs are switched on for first time since before the war.

● **18 Feb:** The blockaded city of Berlin receives its millionth tonne of airlifted supplies.

● **28 Feb:** Stalin introduces wide-ranging reductions in the prices of food and clothing (USSR).

● **1 Mar:** Joe Louis, world heavyweight boxing champion with 25 successful defences to his credit, announces his retirement from the ring at the age of 35 (USA).

● **4 May:** Italy's national soccer team is killed in an air crash in Turin (It).

● **1 Jun:** The French government asks for foreign wheat (Fr).

● **11 Jul:** The Transport and General Workers Union, the biggest in Britain, bans Communists and fascists from holding office.

● **15 Jul:** The Czech tennis star and Wimbledon finalist Jaroslav Drobny asks for political asylum in Geneva.

● **30 Jul:** The mayor of Berlin's western sector appeals for Marshall aid (Ger).

● **18 Sep:** Britain devalues sterling by 30.5 percent; nine other countries – Australia, New Zealand, South Africa, India, the Irish Republic, Denmark, Norway, Egypt and Israel – also devalue their currencies. On 19–20 Sep France devalues the franc and proposes a West European monetary union.

● **6 Oct:** "Tokyo Rose", who was found guilty of treason for broadcasting on behalf of the Japanese during World War II, is jailed for 10 years and fined $10,000.

● **9 Oct:** In Geneva, some 30 countries agree to cut tariffs in a bid to foster greater international trade.

● **12 Nov:** The Czech government announces that from the new year it will no longer recognize church marriages.

● **15 Nov:** After nationalizing the gas industry in May, the British government shelves plans to nationalize iron and steel and proposes that insurance companies be mutualized rather than nationalized.

● **10 Dec:** Lord Boyd-Orr, a former director of the UN Food and Agricultural Organization (FAO) and inventor of a scheme to feed the world's poor, wins the Nobel Peace Prize.

● **21 Dec:** The USSR launches a Soviet Peace Prize, an annual award open to all nationalities.

CULTURE

● **5 Jan:** Wilhelm Furtwängler is dismissed as conductor of the Berlin Symphony Orchestra because of his past Nazi sympathies (Ger).

● **13 Feb:** A radio station in Quito, Peru, is burned down by an angry mob after a dramatization of H.G. Wells's novel *The War of the Worlds*, about a Martian invasion, causes panic.

● **19 Feb:** Ezra Pound, confined to a mental hospital in Washington and indicted for treason, wins the first Bollinger prize for poetry (USA).

● **25 Mar:** Sir Laurence Olivier wins an Oscar for his performance in the title role of the film *Hamlet*.

● **2 May:** Arthur Miller wins the Pulitzer Prize for his play *Death of a Salesman* (USA).

● **10 Dec:** American author William Faulkner wins the Nobel Prize for Literature.

● George Orwell denies that his new novel *Nineteen Eighty-Four*, a bleak tale of a totalitarian future, is an attack on socialism or the Labour party (UK).

● Simone de Beauvoir: *Le Deuxième sexe* (The Second Sex), feminist study (Fr).

● Octavio Paz: *On Parole*, poems (Mex).

● T.S. Eliot: *The Cocktail Party*, play (UK).

● Nancy Mitford: *Love in a Cold Climate*, novel (UK).

● Bertolt Brecht moves to East Germany and founds the Berliner Ensemble with his wife, actress Helene Weigel.

● Carl Orff: *Antigone*, opera based on Sophocles' play in Hölderlin's translation, is first given at the Salzburg Festival.

● Graham Sutherland: *Portrait of Somerset Maugham*, painting (UK).

● Victor Pasmore: *Spiral Motives*, painting (UK).

● Robert Motherwell: *At Five in the Afternoon*, painting (USA).

● Ludwig Mies van der Rohe: Apartments at Lakeshore Drive, Chicago (completed 1951) (USA).

● Philip Johnson: Glass House, New Canaan, Connecticut (USA).

● Frank Lloyd Wright: Laboratory Tower for S.C. Johnson & Son, Racine, Wisconsin (USA).

● The British government sets up a National Film Corporation with a £5 million grant, under the chairmanship of Lord Reith, to encourage the development of British cinema.

● Carol Reed's film *The Third Man*, scripted by Graham Greene and set in postwar Vienna and starring Orson Welles, wins universal acclaim (UK).

● *Jour de fête*, Jacques Tati's anarchic comedy (Fr).

● Gene Kelly and Stanley Donen star in the musical film *On the Town* (USA).

SCIENCE

● **10 Jan:** The first 7-inch (18 cm) microgroove records, produced by Columbia Records and RCA Victor, go on sale in the USA.

● **6 Mar:** Britain produces plutonium for the first time.

● **25 Jun:** Scientists in New York announce the discovery of neomycin, a drug to combat tuberculosis.

● **27 Jul:** The world's first jetliner, the de Havilland Comet, makes its maiden flight (UK).

● **7 Aug:** A Gloster Meteor sets the record for the longest flight by a jet aircraft, lasting 12 hr 3 mins.

● **23 Aug:** A US Bell X-1 aircraft attains a height of 19,000 m (63,000 ft), the greatest so far achieved by a piloted aircraft.

● **25 Aug:** In New York, RCA unveil a system for color television broadcasting.

● **26 Dec:** Albert Einstein publishes his *Generalized Theory of Gravitation*, an attempt to unify the four forces of nature: gravity, electromagnetism and the strong and weak nuclear forces.

● The most powerful cyclotron (particle accelerator) in Europe goes into operation at Harwell, Oxford (UK).

● A new theory of the workings of the immune system is advanced by Frank Macfarlane Burnet, an Australian biologist, to explain the body's rejection of foreign tissue in skin grafts.

● Linus Pauling traces the cause of sickle-cell anemia to minor molecular abnormalities in the hemoglobin of the blood (USA).

● A rocket testing ground is established at Cape Canaveral, Florida (USA).

● American scientists create the first rocket with more than one stage by adding a small rocket to the top of a German V-2 rocket. It is launched from White Sands, New Mexico, and reaches a height of 400 km (240 miles).

● English biochemist Dorothy C. Hodgkin is the first to use an electronic computer to work out the structure of an organic chemical, penicillin.

● W.R. Hess (Swi) and A.E. Moniz (Port) win the Nobel Prize for Physiology or Medicine, Hess for his study of middle brain function and Moniz for prefrontal lobotomy.

● W.F. Giauque wins the Nobel Prize for Chemistry for his study of low-temperature chemistry (USA).

● Hidei Yukawa (Jap) wins the Nobel Prize for Physics for his prediction of the pion.

● EDSAC (Electronic Delay Storage Automatic Computer), at Cambridge University (UK), and BINAC (Binary Automatic Computer), the first electronic stored program computer in the USA, go into operation.

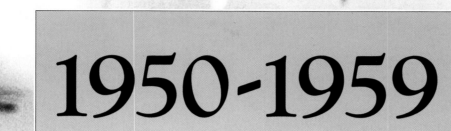

1950-1959

In 1950 it seemed a distinct possibility that the international hostilities that had brought about the Cold War would erupt in a third world war. When Communist North Korea invaded the South, which was still unofficially under UN auspices, the United States sent in troops to drive its forces back, causing a further rift with the USSR. Not content with repelling the invasion, General MacArthur in turn invaded the North, bringing Communist China – whose leader Mao Zedong had just signed a 30-year pact with the USSR – into the conflict. Chinese forces promptly repulsed the attack, and took the opportunity to invade Tibet as well. Meanwhile in the United States, the fear of Communism reached fever pitch as Senator Joe McCarthy launched a vitriolic personal crusade against Communists at home, claiming that they had massively infiltrated the federal government and demanding the introduction of new laws designed to halt "anti-American activities". Only in Europe was there a more hopeful attitude to the future, as French foreign minister Robert Schuman presented his plan for greater European economic integration.

▲ **The UN building in New York, symbol of unity – but in 1950 the UN denied entry to Communist China and sanctioned intervention in Korea.**

● **10 Jan**: The Soviet envoy to the UN Security Council walks out in protest at the continued presence of Nationalist China, despite their defeat by Mao Zedong's Communists. (›3 Aug)

● **12 Jan**: A state of emergency is declared in the Gold Coast after a wave of strikes against British colonial rule.

● **23 Jan**: Israel proclaims Jerusalem as its capital.

● **Jan**: Muhammad Ben Bella becomes leader of the "Organisation secrète", an anticolonial revolutionary movement in Algeria.

● **2 Feb**: France recognizes Laos and Cambodia as independent states.

● **7 Feb**: US and UK governments recognize the Vietnamese government of Bao Dai based in Saigon, although the USSR has recognized Ho Chi Minh's rival Communist regime centered on Hanoi.

● **14 Feb**: In Moscow, Mao Zedong and Joseph Stalin sign a 30-year mutual aid and friendship pact.

● **Feb**: In the USA, Senator Joseph McCarthy launches a campaign against alleged Communist infiltration of the federal government, but produces no proof. (›23 Sep)

● **1 Mar**: Klaus Fuchs, a top nuclear scientist, is found guilty of handing over atomic secrets to the USSR and sentenced to 14 years' imprisonment (UK).

● **1 Mar**: Jiang Jieshi is proclaimed president of Formosa (Taiwan) for a second time.

● **8 Mar**: German chancellor Konrad Adenauer proposes a Franco-German Union (FRG).

● **13 Apr**: Member states of the Arab League sign a mutual defense and cooperation agreement in Cairo (Egy).

● **14 Apr**: In Greece, the Venizelos government falls. Gen. Plastinas forms a new government.

● **24 Apr**: Jordan annexes Arab Palestine to include the West Bank in its territory.

● **1 May**: In Johannesburg, a demonstration against apartheid is put down by force, leaving 18 dead and 30 wounded (SA).

● **7 May**: In Nicaragua Gen. Somoza becomes provisional head of state.

● **11 May**: Christian Democratic Union party is founded by Konrad Adenauer (FRG).

● **25 May**: The Vietminh (Communist North Vietnamese forces) launch an offensive against French troops at Dong Khe. (›18 Sep)

● **22 Jun**: French foreign minister Robert Schuman pledges moves toward the future independence of Tunisia.

● **25 Jun**: North Korean troops cross the 38th parallel into South Korea. Three days later (28 Jun) the South Korean capital Seoul falls to the Communists.

● **26–27 Jun**: The UN decides to intervene in Korea, without the agreement of the USSR. On 1 July US troops land in Korea. (›26 Jul)

● **8 Jul**: In Belgium, half a million people demonstrate against the return of Leopold III; but parliament approves it and Leopold enters Brussels on 22 Jul after six years in exile. On 1 Aug 19-year-old son Prince Baudouin is appointed regent; he will become king at his majority.

● **25 Jul**: Walter Ulbricht is elected General Secretary of the Communist party of the GDR.

● **26–27 Jul**: Britain and France decide to send troops to Korea. On 1 Aug Australian prime minister Robert Menzies says an Australian fighting force will join them. (›25 Sep)

● **3 Aug**: UN Security Council denies Communist China entry to the UN.

● **18 Sep**: The Vietminh recapture Dong Khe from the French. On 10 Oct they overwhelm French troops to take Kaobang, and then force the French to evacuate the frontier zone with China.

● **23 Sep**: Voting against the president's veto, the US Senate supports Senator McCarthy's proposed laws to suppress anti-American activities.

● **25 Sep**: UN forces recapture Seoul after a surprise landing at Inchom on 16 Sep. On 28 Sep South Korean president Syngium Rhee returns to the South Korean capital. (›1 Oct)

● **26 Sep**: NATO votes in favor of including West Germany in a European defense force.

● **1 Oct**: South Korean forces cross the 38th parallel into North Korea. (›24 Oct)

● **21 Oct**: Chinese troops invade Tibet. The Dalai Lama, the Tibetan spiritual leader, is later reported to have fled.

● **24 Oct**: UN forces in Korea reach the Chinese frontier. On 26 Oct the North Korean capital Pyongyang falls to South Korean and UN troops.

● **1 Nov**: Soviet MIG 15 fighter planes make their first appearance in Korea. On 24–27 Nov Chinese forces drive out UN troops from the Manchurian border area of North Korea. (›5 Dec)

● **16 Nov**: King Farouk of Egypt calls for the evacuation of British troops from the Suez Canal zone and unification of Egypt with Sudan.

● **5 Dec**: UN forces are driven out of Pyongyang. On 16 Dec president Truman declares a national state of emergency in view of the reverses suffered by UN troops. (›24 Dec)

● **14 Dec**: The UN approves a proposal for a three-power commission to bring about a ceasefire in Korea.

● **19 Dec**: Gen. Dwight D. Eisenhower is named Supreme Commander of NATO forces.

● **24 Dec**: Chinese troops cross the 38th parallel into South Korea.

SOCIETY

- **12 Jan**: The USSR restores the death penalty.

- **16 Jan**: It is announced in Bonn that all food rationing except for sugar will end on 1 Mar (FRG).

- **27 Jan**: Gemstones and jewels worth 150 million French francs are stolen from the Aga Khan's wife and left outside a police station in Marseille (Fr).

- **8 Feb**: The French government passes a bill legalizing strikes and collective bargaining.

- **15 Feb**: German sources reveal that the FRG has over 2 million unemployed.

- **28 Feb**: In the USSR, the rouble is revalued and prices are cut by between 10 and 30 percent.

- **5 Mar**: A strike by miners lasting two months ends in a government-union agreement after failure to use troops as strike-breakers (Fr).

- **20 Mar**: The Polish government decides to confiscate church assets, but later (14 Apr) reaches accord with the church.

- **1 Apr**: Soviet leader Joseph Stalin's plan to increase the natural resources of the Urals, in particular to increase the forests by 30 percent in 12 years, is published.

- **8 Apr**: India and Pakistan sign a bill of rights for minorities in a bid to ease violence between Hindus and Muslims.

- **9 Apr**: Bolivia, facing political and economic crisis, devalues its currency by 43 percent and declares the Communist party illegal (11 Apr).

- **1 May**: China outlaws polygamy, infanticide and child marriages.

- **10 May**: The USSR halves the GDR's war reparations debt following representations by East German president Otto Grotewohl.

- **17 May**: The US Justice Department initiates antitrust suits against seven oil companies.

- **26 May**: Petrol rationing ends in the UK, but reaches its highest price for 30 years.

- **May**: French foreign minister Robert Schuman proposes that all French and West German coal and steel production be centralized under one authority (the Schuman Plan). The organization will be open to other European countries including the USSR, and aims to serve as a basis for closer European economic integration. (›20 Jun)

- **3 Jun**: French mountaineers reach the summit of Annapurna (8,078 m/ 26,000 ft) in the Himalayas, the highest mountain so far climbed (Nepal).

- **20 Jun**: Conference of the European Six (France, Germany, Italy, Belgium, the Netherlands, Luxembourg) on steel and coal opens in Paris. (›19 Nov 1951)

- **22 Jun**: Hungary and Czechoslovakia adopt Soviet-style penal codes.

- **28 Jun**: The government confiscates the church's property and land in Hungary. On 30 June university theology departments are closed.

- **28 Jun**: The England soccer team, co-favorites with host nation Brazil to win the football World Cup, are knocked out in the first round. The championship is eventually won by Uruguay.

- **27 Jul**: Italian cyclists withdraw from the Tour de France in protest at the allegedly insulting treatment they have received. The event is won by Ferdinand Kubler (6 Aug) (Fr).

- **5 Aug**: 150 French, British, Italian and German protesters tear down the Franco-German frontier in protest at the slowness of European union.

- **5 Aug**: US swimmer Florence Chadwick sets a new cross-Channel record of 13 h 23 mins (UK/Fr).

- **12 Aug**: Pope Pius XII publishes the encyclical *Humani generis*, warning against the accommodation of Roman Catholic theology to current intellectual trends.

- **22 Aug**: The European Assembly approves the Declaration of Human Rights.

- **3 Sep**: Giuseppe Farina of Italy becomes the world motor-racing champion.

- **29 Sep**: The GDR joins Comecon (Council for Mutual Economic Aid).

- **6 Oct**: The world's longest pipeline, linking US oilfields in the Gulf with the Lebanese port of Sidon on the Mediterranean – a distance of 1,700 km (1,050 miles) – is opened.

- **1 Nov**: Pope Pius XII declares the bodily Assumption of the Blessed Virgin Mary a dogma of the church (It).

- **22 Nov**: In Nicaragua 10,000 people are forced to leave their homes after the eruption of the volcano Cerro Negro.

- **22 Nov**: In Stuttgart, 61,000 soccer fans see the first postwar national German team defeat Switzerland 1-0.

- **1 Dec**: The number of drive-in cinemas in the US reaches 2,200, having doubled over the previous year.

- **13 Dec**: The USA ends Marshall aid to the UK though the policy continues until 1952.

- **25 Dec**: The ceremonial stone in the coronation throne in London's Westminster Abbey is stolen by Scottish nationalists who claim that it was wrongfully taken from Scotland in the 13th century. It is recovered on 11 Apr 1951.

- The Nobel Peace Prize is won by Ralph Bunche (USA).

- Diner's Club introduces the charge card, the first example of a credit card (USA).

CULTURE

- **14 Mar**: Doris Lessing's first novel *The Grass is Singing* is published (UK).

- **31 Mar**: Norwegian anthropologist Thor Heyerdahl publishes *The Kon-Tiki Expedition*, an account of his 8,000 km (5,000 miles) journey, lasting 101 days, across the Pacific on a raft.

- **1 May**: The musical *South Pacific* wins the Pulitzer Prize (USA).

- **11 Jun**: Henri Matisse receives the Grand Prix at the Venice 25th Bienniale (It).

- **17 Jun**: Premiere of Luis Buñuel's film *Los Olvidados* (Sp).

- **30 Jun**: Werner Egk's ballet *Französische Suite* opens in Munich (FRG).

- **4 Oct**: Bruno Walter becomes the first Jew to conduct an orchestra in Munich for 28 years (FRG).

- Bertrand Russell, mathematician, philosopher and campaigner against nuclear arms, is awarded the Nobel Prize for Literature for his *Marriage and Morals* (UK).

- Cesare Pavese: *La luna è il falò* (The Moon and the Bonfire), novel (It).

- Gilbert Ryle: *The Concept of Mind*, attack on philosophical dualism of mind and body (UK).

- Pablo Neruda: *Canto general*, a poetic history of South America (Chile).

- Tennessee Williams: *The Roman Spring of Mrs Stone*, novella (USA).

- London's Old Vic Theatre, damaged during an air raid in 1941, reopens with a production of Shakespeare's *Twelfth Night* (UK).

- Harry Partch: *Cloud Chamber Music* (USA).

- Luigi Dallapiccola's opera *Il prigioniero* (The Prisoner), premiered on radio in 1949, is first staged at the Teatro Comunale in Florence (It).

- Olivier Messiaen: *Mode des valeurs et d'intensités* (1949–50) (Fr).

- Jackson Pollock: *Lavender Mist*, painting (USA).

- Franz Kline: *Chief*, painting (USA).

- Henri Matisse: *Zulma*, painting (Fr).

- Jean Dubuffet: *Corps de dame*, painting (Fr).

- Barnett Newman: *Tundra*, painting (USA).

- Ceri Richards: *Cold Light. Deep Shadow*, painting (UK).

- Alberto Giacometti: *Four Women on a Base*, painted bronze (Swi).

- Le Corbusier begins work on the church of Notre-Dame-du-Haut at Ronchamp (completed 1955) (Fr).

- Jean Cocteau: *Orphée*, film (Fr).

- Michelangelo Antonioni produces his first feature film, *Cronaca d i un amore* (Chronicle of an Affair) (It).

- Akira Kurosawa: *Rashomon* (Jap).

- John Huston: *The Asphalt Jungle* (USA).

SCIENCE

- **21 Jan**: US scientists at Berkeley, California, discover the 97th element, which they call berkelium.

- **31 Jan**: American president Harry S. Truman orders the US Atomic Energy Commission to research and build the hydrogen bomb.

- **8 Mar**: Rover builds the first gas-turbine car (UK).

- **Apr**: John von Neumann, using the computer ENIAC, makes the first 24-hour computerized weather forecast (USA).

- **17 Jun**: R.H. Lawler, a Chicago surgeon, performs the first kidney transplant operation (USA).

- **7 Jul**: First transmission of color television in the USA.

- **9 Nov**: ICI announce that a new fabric, "Terylene", is to be manufactured at a factory to be built in the north of England (UK).

- Nobel Prize for Chemistry is won by Kurt Alder (Ger) and Otto Diels (Ger) for their discovery and synthesis of dienes.

- Cecil Powell (UK) wins the Nobel Prize for Physics for his photographic studies of atomic nuclei.

- Philip Hench, Edward Kendall (both USA) and Tadeusz Reichstein (Swi) win the Nobel Prize for Physiology or Medicine for the discovery of cortisone and other hormones in the adrenal cortex and their functions.

- Robert Wallace introduces the drug resperine, used in India in the form of snakeroot, to treat high blood pressure.

- Alfred Kastler, a Franco-German physicist, develops optical pumping, a forerunner of the laser, to show atomic structure.

- J.H. Oort proposes that comets are fragments from a distant cloud of matter (to become known as the Oort cloud) orbiting the Sun outside the planets.

- The US Atomic Energy Commission obtains plutonium from pitchblende.

- Studies of radio waves at New Physical Laboratory, Teddington, UK, and Stanford University, California, USA, give new calculations for the speed of light in a vacuum.

- A new element, element 98, is discovered by G.T. Seaborg of California University and called californium (USA).

- A jet-propelled pilotless aircraft is built in Australia.

- Danish scientists aboard the vessel *Galathea* investigate deep-sea marine life.

- Cyclamate is introduced as an artificial sweetener.

- The Vidicon, the first TV camera to use the principle of photoconductivity, is developed in the USA.

- Antihistamines become popular as cures for colds and allergies.

As British forces fought in Korea, Britain reelected its wartime prime minister Winston Churchill at the age of 77 and went on to celebrate the new decade in style: the Festival of Britain opened in London in May, aiming to provide something for everyone, from art and music through to big dippers and fireworks. It was a good year for the arts; the Royal Festival Hall was opened as part of the Festival of Britain celebrations, new operas by Britten and Stravinsky were premiered, and J.D. Salinger's novel "Catcher in the Rye" epitomized the definitive American teenager of the Fifties in its hero Holden Caulfield. But the most significant advance in people's enjoyment of music was technological – the long-playing record was introduced, bringing all kinds of music to a wider public. Outside Britain things were not so rosy. US president Truman sacked General MacArthur from his command for publicly contradicting the US policy of containment in Korea, while in Iran Dr Musaddiq shocked the West by nationalizing the British-owned Anglo-Iranian Oil Company.

▲ **A US soldier searches for Communist sympathizers in Korea as the war between North and South continues despite UN efforts to achieve a truce.**

● **3–4 Jan**: The South Koreans evacuate Seoul, which falls to the Communists next day.(›14 Mar)

● **24 Jan**: The Dutch government resigns following disagreements over the retention of Dutch sovereignty in West New Guinea.

● **31 Jan**: US authorities in West Germany commute the death sentences passed on 21 Nazi war criminals to life imprisonment.

● **31 Jan**: Getulio Vargas is inaugurated as president in Brazil.

● **1 Feb**: The UN votes by 44 to 7 to support a US resolution condemning Chinese intervention in Korea.

● **5 Feb**: The Gold Coast's first general election results in a victory for Kwame Nkrumah, who becomes chief minister.

● **14 Feb**: David Ben Gurion's government resigns after being defeated on religious education policies (Isr)

● **26 Feb**: The US Constitution is amended to limit presidents to two terms of office.

● **8 Mar**: The Iranian parliament votes to nationalize oil rather than share the profits with the UK through the long-established Anglo-Iranian Oil Co. (›15 Apr)

● **14 Mar**: After weeks of heavy fighting in various areas, UN and South Korean forces recapture Seoul. They cross the 38th parallel into North Korea on 26–7 Mar.

● **22 Mar**: Chinese forces in Korea launch a large-scale offensive, forcing a retreat by UN troops. (›11 Apr)

● **30 Mar**: The Group Areas Act comes into force in the Cape, Natal and Transvaal provinces (SA). (›14 May)

● **5 Apr**: In New York, Julius and Ethel Rosenberg are sentenced to death for selling atomic secrets to the USSR. (›19 Jun 1953)

● **11 Apr**: President Truman dismisses Gen. MacArthur as commander of UN forces in Korea for making public statements contrary to US policy; MacArthur's stated wish to extend the war into China is directly opposed to the USA's policy of containment. Gen. Matthew Ridgway is chosen as MacArthur's successor (USA).

● **15 Apr**: The Abadan oil refinery is closed and the region comes under martial law. On 28 Apr premier Hussein Ala resigns and Dr Muhammed Musaddiq is appointed to replace him (Iran).(›22 May)

● **5 May**: Iceland signs an agreement with the USA permitting NATO bases on its soil.

● **14 May**: The Afrikaner Nationalist government votes to disenfranchise the "Colored" (mixed race) population, who have held voting rights since the 19th century (SA).

● **18 May**: The UN passes a resolution banning the shipment of strategic materials to China.

● **22 May**: Premier Mussadiq of Iran orders the Anglo-Iranian Oil Co to leave Abadan in six days. The UK appeals to the International Court of Justice, but on 26 May Iran seizes the AIOC installations. (›5 Jul)

● **23 May**: In Beijing, China grant Tibet religious freedom in exchange for severing its ties with the West. (›9 Sep)

● **May**: President Arnulfo Arias revokes the Panamanian constitution on 6 May, giving himself absolute power. Protest riots follow and Arias is impeached and banned from holding public office.

● **1 Jun**: The Fianna Fáil party win the Irish elections. Eamon De Valera returns as premier (13 Jun).

● **7 Jun**: Guy Burgess and Donald Maclean, two senior British Foreign Office officials, disappear from London in suspicious circumstances that suggest they are Soviet agents.

● **13 Jun**: In Korea, UN forces again capture Pyongyang, the North Korean capital. The Soviet delegate to the UN calls unexpectedly for a ceasefire on 23 Jun. (›8 Oct)

● **17 Jun**: In the French elections, the Gaullists win most seats even though they poll 900,000 fewer votes than the Communists, who finish in third place behind the Socialists.

● **28 Jun**: In Budapest, Archbishop Jozsef Groesz is imprisoned for 15 years after being convicted of conspiracy against the government (Hung).

● **5 Jul**: The International Court finds in the UK's favor in its dispute with Iran over the nationalization of the Anglo-Iranian Oil Co. Iran appeals to the UN. (›27 Sep)

● **8 Jul**: UN and Communist representatives meet at Kaesong to discuss terms for an armistice in the Korean War. (›28 Nov)

● **16 Jul**: Leopold III abdicates and his son Baudouin I assumes the throne (Bel).

● **20 Jul**: Abdullah ibn Hussein, who has ruled Jordan for 30 years, is shot dead in Jerusalem. His son, Emir Naif, is proclaimed regent.

● **31 Jul**: The governor of South Vietnam and the French Commissioner are both assassinated. (›14 Nov)

● **12 Aug**: In East Berlin more than 1 million participants in the Communist Youth Rally demonstrate against the USA (GDR).

● **23 Aug**: The USA signs a treaty of friendship with Israel. On 30 Aug a mutual defence treaty with the Philippines is agreed.

● **24 Aug**: Police in Nairobi express concern at the rapid growth of the Mau Mau, a secret society pledged to drive the whites out of Kenya.

● **1 Sep**: A mutual defense treaty for the security of the Pacific is signed between Australia, New Zealand and the USA (the ANZUS pact).

SOCIETY   CULTURE   SCIENCE

- **8 Sep**: In San Francisco, 48 countries formally conclude a peace treaty with Japan. Japan loses most of its empire and is forbidden to rearm. US forces are to be stationed in Japan.

- **9 Sep**: Chinese troops enter the Tibetan capital, Lhasa.

- **20 Sep**: The NATO Council, meeting in Ottawa, invites Greece and Turkey to join the alliance (Can).

- **27 Sep**: Iranian troops take over the Anglo-Iranian Oil Co's refinery at Abadan. (›22 Jul 1952)

- **8 Oct**: Egypt denounces its 1936 treaty with the UK, and on 15 Oct rejects a four-power invitation to participate in a Middle East Defence Command, under which Britain would give up its rights in the Suez Canal. King Farouk is proclaimed king of Sudan on 15 Oct. (›19 Oct)

- **16 Oct**: Pakistani premier Ali Khan is assassinated by a Muslim extremist in New Delhi (Ind).

- **19 Oct**: British troops occupy the Suez Canal Zone. More troops are flown into the Canal Zone in a massive airlift. (›9 Nov)

- **25 Oct**: The Conservative party narrowly defeats Labour in a general election. Winston Churchill, at 77, becomes prime minister (UK).

- **8 Nov**: Following disarmament proposals put to the UN by the USA, the UK and France, the USSR counters with a proposal for a five-power peace pact.

- **9 Nov**: Egypt protests at the airlift of British troops into the Suez Canal Zone. (›4 Dec)

- **11 Nov**: Juan Perón is comfortably reelected president of Argentina.

- **14 Nov**: French and South Vietnamese troops capture the town of Hao Binh from the Vietminh.

- **16 Nov**: Egypt proposes that Sudan's future be decided by a UN-supervised plebiscite.

- **28 Nov**: After lengthy negotiations a truce line, corresponding roughly to the 38th parallel (the North-South Korea divide) is agreed between UN and Communist forces. (›21 Dec)

- **4 Dec**: A state of emergency is declared in Egypt following fierce fighting between British troops and Egyptian guerrillas. Egypt recalls its ambassador from Britain on 13 Dec.

- **6 Dec**: East and West Germany agree to send delegates to the UN to discuss holding free elections throughout Germany. The plan is opposed by the USSR.

- **21 Dec**: Gen. Ridgway demands that the Red Cross be allowed to inspect Communist POW camps. A UN delegation (23 Dec) accuses the Communists of failing to account for some 50,000 prisoners. Failure to reach agreement over the exchange of prisoners causes breakdown of talks.

- **24 Dec**: Libya, a former Italian colony, proclaims its independence.

- **2 Jan**: The Arabian-American Oil Co in Saudi Arabia agrees to share the profits with the Saudis.

- **9 Jan**: The UK government drops its East African groundnuts scheme, writing off debts of over £35 million.

- **20 Jan**: The shah of Iran authorizes the sale of his land to the peasants.

- **22 Jan**: China announces that all Japanese property in Manchuria held by the USSR will be transferred to China.

- **15 Feb**: Greece and Yugoslavia reestablish a rail link connecting the two countries after restoring mutual diplomatic relations (27 Jan).

- **18 Feb**: A national dock strike begins in New Zealand which lasts until mid-June.

- **4 Mar**: The first Asian Games open in New Delhi (Ind).

- **9 Mar**: UK parliament passes a bill to permit divorce after seven years' separation.

- **19 Mar**: In Paris, France, the FRG, Italy and the Benelux countries sign a 50-year agreement creating a European Coal and Steel Community.

- **28 Apr**: Census figures for India show a population of 356.9 million.

- **1 May**: Radio Free Europe, set up in Munich as a Western propaganda station, begins broadcasting to the Eastern bloc (FRG).

- **3 May**: The Festival of Britain and the Royal Festival Hall on London's South Bank are opened by King George VI (UK).

- **3 Jun**: In the Indian capital Delhi, the Socialist party stages a huge demonstration against the government's food and housing policies.

- **1 Jul**: The Colombo plan, whereby the richer Commonwealth member states assist the poorer ones, comes into effect. Later, it also includes aid from the USA to South and Southeast Asian countries outside the Commonwealth.

- **10 Jul**: In London, British middleweight boxer Randolph Turpin outpoints the reigning champion Sugar Ray Robinson to win the world title. Two months later, Robinson defeats Turpin to regain the title.

- **5 Sep**: Maureen ("Little Mo") Connolly, aged 16, becomes the youngest-ever winner of the ladies US tennis championship (USA).

- **24 Nov**: In the UK, Austin and Morris motor manufacturers announce plans to merge, making the new company the fourth largest in the world, after the US giants General Motors, Chrysler and Ford (UK).

- **17 Dec**: Foreign exchange trading is resumed in London after 12 years.

- The Nobel Peace Prize is won by Léon Jouhaux (Fr).

- **9 Jul**: Novelist Dashiell Hammett is jailed for six months for contempt of court after refusing to testify before the McCarthy Commission on un-American activities (USA).

- **10 Sep**: At the Venice Film Festival, Vivien Leigh is awarded the Best Actress prize for her role as Blanche Dubois in the film of Tennessee Williams's play *A Streetcar Named Desire*.

- **1 Dec**: Premiere of Benjamin Britten's opera *Billy Budd* in London.

- **10 Dec**: Pär Lagerkvist of Sweden wins the Nobel Prize for Literature.

- Eugene Ionesco: *The Chairs*, play (Fr).

- J.D. Salinger: *The Catcher in the Rye*, novel (USA).

- William Faulkner: *Requiem for a Nun*, an experimental work, part play and part prose narrative (USA).

- Carson McCullers: *The Ballad of the Sad Café*, novel (USA).

- Anthony Powell: *A Question of Uprising*, first in the 12-volume sequence *A Dance to the Music of Time* (completed 1975) (UK).

- Czeslaw Milosz: *The Captive Mind*, an apologia for leaving Poland by the Polish poet, writer and Resistance fighter who finally emigrated to the USA.

- Gian Carlo Menotti: *Amahl and the Night Visitors*, opera for television (USA).

- Paul Hindemith: *Die Harmonie der Welt*, symphony later extended to form an opera (USA).

- Igor Stravinsky: *The Rake's Progress*, opera to a text by W.H. Auden and Chester Kallman (USA).

- John Cage: *Imaginary Landscape No.4*, using radio receivers, and *Music of Changes*, for which decisions were made by tossing a coin.

- Elliott Carter: First String Quartet (USA).

- Salvador Dali: *Crucifixion*, painting (USA).

- Pablo Picasso: *Massacre in Korea*, painting (Fr).

- David Smith: *Hudson River Landscape*, sculpture (USA).

- Kenneth Armitage: *People in a Wind*, sculpture (UK).

- Henry Moore: *Reclining Figure*, sculpture commissioned by the Arts Council for the Festival of Britain (UK).

- Robert Motherwell publishes *The Dada Painters and Poets* (USA).

- Robert H. Matthew and J.L. Martin: The Festival Hall, London (UK).

- Alvar Aalto: Town Hall, Saynatsalo, Finland.

- Ludwig Mies van der Rohe: Lake Shore Drive Apartments, Chicago (USA).

- Carol Reed: *The Third Man*, film (USA).

- **31 Aug**: Deutsche Grammophon markets the first 33 rpm long-play record.

- **29 Dec**: The US Atomic Energy Commission produces nuclear-generated electricity at Arcon, Idaho (USA).

- Dirk Brouwer, a Dutch-American astronomer, first uses a computer to predict planetary orbits up to the year 2060, based on data going back to 1653.

- Shin Hirayama suggests that asteroids exist in family groups.

- The first visible objects in space related to a known radio source are identified by Walter Baade (Ger).

- Jan Oort, C.A. Muller and Hendrik Van de Hulst plot a map of the Milky Way.

- Fritz Lipmann discovers acetyl co-enzyme A, used by the body to break down fats and carbohydrates and produce energy for the cells (USA).

- Nikolaas Tinbergen publishes his work on animal behavior, *The Study of Instinct* (Neth).

- Robert Woodward synthesizes the steroids cortisone and cholesterol (USA).

- The drug methotexate is first used for the treatment of cancer of the uterus.

- The drug Antabuse is introduced to combat alcoholism.

- F.M. Burnet proposes clonal selection theory in immunology (Aus).

- Max Theiler (SA) wins the Nobel Prize for Physiology or Medicine for developing his yellow fever vaccine.

- Edwin McMillan and Glenn Seaborg (both USA) win the Nobel Prize for Chemistry for their discovery of plutonium and research into other transuranic elements.

- Sir John Cockcroft (UK) and Ernest Walton (UK) win the Nobel Prize for Physics for their discovery of transmutation of atomic nuclei (changing from one element to another) in particle accelerators.

- An experimental fast-breeder nuclear reactor designed by Walter Zinn, a Canadian-American, is built at Idaho Falls, Indiana (USA).

- Movies that are three-dimensional when viewed through polarized glasses are shown for the first time.

- Chrysler pioneers power steering in some of its motor vehicles (USA).

- UNIVAC, the first computer to store data on magnetic tape, designed by John Mauchly and John Eckert, becomes commercially available.

- A joint Dutch-Norwegian atomic research establishment opens at Hjeller, near Oslo (Nor).

In the year that US physicists exploded the biggest atomic bomb yet, watched on television by millions of viewers, and developed the first hydrogen bomb, many other more welcome – if sometimes controversial – scientific advances were being made. Various medical breakthroughs began to be put into general use. Following on the first kidney transplant in the previous year, an artificial heart was used to keep a Pennsylvania steelworker alive for 80 mintes while doctors strove (vainly, as it turned out) to correct an arterial block. A viable anti-polio vaccine was developed, and a harmless tranquilizer and an oral contraceptive were pioneered. The first sex-change operation took place in a blaze of publicity. Other researchers were concerned with the remote past rather than the immediate future. Michael Ventris deciphered Linear B, the oldest known form of Greek script, dating from around 1500–1200 BC; but another archaeological mystery, "Piltdown Man", supposed to be the remains of a proto-human from the Pleistocene era, proved to be a fraud.

▲ The first hydrogen bomb was exploded by the United States off Eniwetok Atoll in the South Pacific on 31 October. In 1950 the USSR had claimed to have its own atom bomb, and it seemed that the Cold War was heating up fast.

● **10 Jan**: In Washington, British prime minister Winston Churchill agrees to permit US bases on British soil.

● **14 Jan**: The UN Security Council refuses Tunisia's appeal to present its case for autonomy, sparking off nationalist risings. (›30 Mar)

● **20 Jan**: Iranian premier Muhammad Musaddiq revokes Iran's treaty of friendship with Britain made in 1857. (›22 Jul)

● **25 Jan**: Anti-British riots in the Suez Canal Zone early in the month culminate in the death of 46 Egyptians when British troops seize the police HQ at Ismailia.

● **18 Feb**: Greece and Turkey are admitted to NATO.

● **1 Mar**: Pandit Nehru's Congress party wins 364 of the 489 National Assembly seats in India's first national elections.

● **7 Mar**: China accuses the USA of using germ warfare in Manchurian Korea.

● **10 Mar**: Gen. Fulgencio Batista seizes power in Cuba.

● **10 Mar**: The USSR proposes a four-power conference on the unification and rearmament of Germany. In reply the UK, France and the USA stipulate the need for free elections throughout Germany. The USSR opposes UN supervision of elections. (›16 Jun)

● **21 Mar**: Dr Kwame Nkrumah becomes the first African prime minister south of the Sahara (Gold Coast).

● **30 Mar**: After large-scale civil unrest in Tunisia, anti-French riots also break out in Tangier, Morocco. (›18 Nov)

● **16 Apr**: NATO opens its new HQ, at the Palais de Chaillot, Paris.

● **22 Apr**: The biggest atomic bomb yet is exploded in the Nevada desert, watched by a television audience of some 35 million (USA).

● **23 Apr**: The Sudanese parliament adopts a draft constitution after the UK's offer to Sudan of limited self-rule.

● **23 Apr**: Prime minister Daniel Malan publishes the South African Government Bill, making parliament a high court, in order to prevent the Supreme Court from blocking racist legislation (SA). (›26 Jun)

● **25 Apr**: 6,000 French troops attack the Vietminh strategic base at Tay Ninh, northwest of Saigon. (›19 Nov)

● **28 Apr**: US occupation of Japan ends. Japan becomes self-governing after signing a peace treaty in Washington (15 Apr) marking the official end of World War II in the Pacific.

● **28 Apr**: Gen. Dwight D. ("Ike") Eisenhower steps down as NATO military chief and is replaced by Gen. Matthew Ridgway. (›11 Jul)

● **1 Jun**: The general election in Ceylon is won by the United People's party, led by Dudley Senenyake.

● **16 Jun**: The GDR announces the recruitment of a new "people's army". By December, some 100,000 East Germans are under arms, equipped with Soviet weapons.

● **26 Jun**: 150 are arrested as non-white races demonstrate peacefully against apartheid (SA). (›28 Nov)

● **11 Jul**: Eisenhower wins the nomination as Republican candidate in the presidential elections. (›5 Nov)

● **22 Jul**: The International Court of Justice at the Hague rules that it has no jurisdiction to intervene in the dispute between the Iranian government and the Anglo-Iranian Oil Co. (›22 Oct)

● **22 Jul**: Poland adopts a new constitution that provides some rights to private property and inheritance.

● **23 Jul**: Gen. Muhammad Neguib seizes power in Egypt. King Farouk abdicates in favor of his 9-month-old son Fuad II on 26 Jul.

● **5 Aug**: Japan and Nationalist China (Formosa/Taiwan) resume diplomatic relations.

● **11 Aug**: Prince Hussein, still a schoolboy, is proclaimed King of Jordan.

● **29 Aug**: UN aircraft attack Pyongyang, North Korea.

● **11 Sep**: Eritrea, a former Italian colony in North Africa administered by the UK, is federated with Ethiopia.

● **24 Sep**: Romania adopts a new constitution and new electoral laws.

● **3 Oct**: The UK explodes its first atomic bomb, on Monte Bello island, off the northwest coast of Australia.

● **19 Oct**: British troops are dispatched to Kenya following Mau Mau disturbances. A state of emergency is declared (20 Oct) and Jomo Kenyatta is arrested and charged with being the head of the Mau Mau. (›25 Nov)

● **22 Oct**: Iran breaks off diplomatic relations with the UK after failing to reach an agreement over the future of the country's oil.

● **31 Oct**: The USA explodes its first hydrogen bomb, at Eniwetok Atoll in the Pacific.

● **5 Nov**: Dwight D. Eisenhower, Republican, easily wins the US presidential election.

● **10 Nov**: In New York, Trygve Lie resigns as Secretary-General to the UN.

● **18 Nov**: The sultan of Morocco calls for restoration of sovereignty. Rioting against French rule breaks out in Dec.

● **19 Nov**: The Vietminh launch an all-out offensive against the French in Vietnam and (21 Nov) Laos.

● **25 Nov**: 2,000 members of the Kikuyu tribe are arrested as the Mau Mau begin an open revolt against British rule (Ken).

● **28 Nov**: After riots in which 14 are killed and 39 injured, the South African government bans meetings of more than 10 blacks.

SOCIETY

- **5 Jan**: The USA makes a five-year loan to India.
- **29–31 Jan**: The UK government announces a new austerity program.
- **8 Mar**: The Australian government imposes restrictions on all imports.
- **8 Apr**: President Truman orders an emergency takeover of the steel industry to preempt a strike (USA).
- **1 May**: The US airline TWA is the first to introduce a "tourist class" passenger service.
- **2 May**: The world's first jet airliner service opens with a flight by the BOAC (British Overseas Airways Corporation) Comet from London (UK) to Johannesburg (SA).
- **16 May**: Parliament supports a bill for equal pay for women (UK).
- **15 Jun**: The diary of Anne Frank, young Jewish victim of the Nazis, is published.
- **25–27 Jun**: President Truman vetoes the McCarran-Walter bill to restrict immigration, but is overridden by Congress (USA).
- **7 Jul**: The US liner *United States* wins the Blue Riband for crossing the Atlantic in a record time of 10 h 40 mins.
- **14 Jul**: On the island of Jamaica, 700 are arrested for trafficking in marijuana (W Ind).
- **15 Jul**: At 17, the American Maureen Connolly becomes the youngest player in the 20th century to win the Wimbledon ladies singles' title (UK).
- **19 Jul**: The Olympic Games are opened in Helsinki. The Czech Emil Zatopek wins three gold medals, at the same time breaking three Olympic records (Fin).
- **10 Sep**: West Germany agrees to pay Israel compensation for Nazi war crimes.
- **18 Sep**: Finland completes its reparations payments to the USSR.
- **19 Sep**: Film comedian Charlie Chaplin is the subject of an investigation in Washington after being suspected as a "subversive" (USA).
- **20 Sep**: Democrat presidential candidate Adlai Stevenson promises that if he becomes president he will guarantee equal employment rights for blacks (USA).
- **21 Nov**: High-grade uranium deposits are found in Australia.
- French theologian, organist and missionary surgeon Albert Schweitzer wins the Nobel Peace Prize for teaching "reverence for life".
- The treaty establishing the European Coal and Steel Community (ECSC) is ratified, setting up the administrative agency designed to integrate the coal and steel industries of France, West Germany, Italy, Belgium, the Netherlands and Luxembourg.
- A polio epidemic in the USA strikes some 47,500 people.

CULTURE

- **17 Feb**: Premiere in Hanover of Hans Werner Henze's first opera, *Boulevard Solitude* (FRG).
- **16 Oct**: Premiere of Charlie Chaplin's film *Limelight* (USA).
- **8 Nov**: Greek soprano Maria Callas takes London by storm in Bellini's opera *Norma* (UK).
- **24 Nov**: Agatha Christie's latest "whodunnit" play *The Mousetrap* opens in London.
- Samuel Beckett's play *En attendant Godot* (trans. as *Waiting for Godot*, 1955), is first published (Fr).
- Ernest Hemingway: *The Old Man and the Sea*, a parable about man's struggle with nature (USA).
- Dylan Thomas: *Collected Poems 1934–52* (UK).
- Amos Tutuola: *The Palm Wine Drinkard*, novel (Nig).
- Evelyn Waugh: *Men at Arms*, novel, first volume of the trilogy *Sword of Honour* (UK).
- Karlheinz Stockhausen's *Kreuzspiel* (Crossplay) establishes his reputation when it is played at the International Summer School of New Music at Darmstadt (FRG).
- Doris Lessing: *Martha Quest*, first novel in the five-volume sequence *Children of Violence* (UK).
- François Mauriac (Fr) wins the Nobel Prize for Literature.
- Dmitri Shostakovich: *Twenty-Four Preludes and Fugues* (USSR).
- Pierre Boulez: *Structures*, for two pianos, which lays the foundation for a new and influential musical language (Fr).
- John Cage: *4' 33"*, a work that consists of the chance elements that the audience may hear around them: no sound is played (USA).
- Merce Cunningham: *Suite by Chance*, ballet (USA)
- Henri Matisse: *Seated Blue Nude III*, cut paper (Fr).
- Helen Frankenthaler: *Mountains and Sea*, painting (USA).
- Willem de Kooning: *Woman I*, painting (1950-52) (USA).
- Sidney Nolan, known for his series of paintings of the Australian folk-hero Ned Kelly, exhibits his paintings of Central Australia made during the severe drought of 1952.
- Isamu Noguchi: *Even the Centipede*, sculpture.
- Gordon Bunshaft (Skidmore, Owings and Merrill): Lever House, New York.
- Elia Kazan's film *Viva Zapata!* stars Marlon Brando (USA).
- Gene Kelly directs, acts and sings in *Singin' in the Rain*, making its title song the hit of the year (USA).
- Humphrey Bogart is awarded the Oscar for Best Actor for his role in *The African Queen*, directed by John Huston.

SCIENCE

- **8 Mar**: An artificial heart is used for the first time in a Pennsylvania hospital, prolonging a patient's life by 80 minutes (USA).
- **14 Jun**: The launching of the world's first atomic submarine is attended by president Truman (USA).
- **26 Aug**: A Canberra jet bomber makes the first ever nonstop transatlantic crossing both ways, completing the round trip in under 8 hours, at an average speed of 850 km/h (530 mph) (UK).
- **30 Aug**: The Avro Vulcan, the world's first four-engine jet bomber, makes its maiden flight (UK).
- **Nov**: Kenneth Oakely announces that tests on the jawbone of the "Piltdown man" reveal that it is a fake. The fossil remains discovered in England in 1912 had been said to have belonged to a species of prehistoric man.
- Walter Baade discovers an error in the Cepheid luminosity scale, such that the galaxies are twice as far away as had been believed (Ger).
- Michael Ventris deciphers Linear B, the oldest known form of Greek, dating from c1500-1200 BC, roughly the period of the Homeric epics.
- Adriaan Blaauw, by showing that the expansion of the zeta-Persei star cluster is 1.3 million years old, proves that stars are being created all the time in the Milky Way galaxy.
- P.W. Merrill discovers technetium (a radioactive element with a short halflife) in S-type supergiants, proving that they have formed recently (USA).
- Martin Schwarzschild studies the evolution of stars by means of graphs of star clusters (Ger).
- A calf is born that was conceived using frozen semen (artificial insemination).
- Alan Hodgkin and Andrew Huxley (both UK) develop the theory of nerve excitation, caused by the passage of sodium and potassium in the nerve cells.
- Joshua Lederberg discovers that viruses can transmit genetic material between bacteria – an important step in the development of genetic engineering (USA).
- Eugene Asterinsky discovers rapid eye-movement (REM) in sleep, which is later associated with vivid dreams.
- British scientists Archer Martin and Richard Synge win the Nobel Prize for Chemistry for their discovery of paper chromatography as a method of separating elements.
- Selman Waksman (USA) wins the Nobel Prize for Physiology or Medicine for his discovery of streptomycin, a powerful antibiotic.
- Felix Bloch and Edward Purcell (both USA) win the Nobel Prize for Physics for their development of new methods for nuclear magnetic precision measurement.

- Glenn Seaborg discovers an artificial element, atomic number 99, left after the first hydrogen bomb test. It is called einsteinium.
- James van Allen (USA) develops the "rockoon" (balloon-launched rocket) to study the physics of the upper atmosphere.
- Douglas Bevis (UK) develops amniocentesis - drawing off amniotic fluid from the womb to test for abnormality of the fetus.
- Jean Dausset observes that subjects of repeated blood transfusions develop antibodies to the transfused blood. This discovery later proves useful in typing tissue for organ transplantations (Fr).
- The world's first sex-change operation is carried out by K. Hamburger, in Denmark, on George Jorgenson, afterward known as Christine.
- Jonas Salk produces a killed-virus vaccine against polio, which is used in mass vaccination programs from 1954. Salk's vaccine is later superseded by a live-virus one developed by Albert Sabin (USA).
- Robert Wilkins discovers the first tranquilizer, reserpine, previously used to treat high blood pressure.
- Sir Charles Frank predicts the formation of icosahedral symmetry in liquids cooled below their freezing point. Later research shows that rapidly cooled metals can have the structure of glasses, called metallic glasses.
- Donald Glaser discovers cosmic ray tracks in a bubble chamber (USA).
- Edward Teller, a Hungarian-American, leads the team that develops the hydrogen bomb, the world's first thermonuclear device (USA).
- The first pocket-sized transistor radio is marketed by Sony (Jap).
- A new antitubercular drug, isoniazid, is discovered (USA).
- A.D. Hershey and M. Chase prove that DNA is the genetic information carrier (USA).
- A rapid extension of use of radioisotopes in scientific research, medicine and industry takes place.
- "Acrilan", an acrylic fiber, is manufactured in the USA.
- A contraceptive pill of hesperidin is developed.
- A hearing aid using transistors instead of vacuum tubes is introduced.

1953

1953 proved to be a decisive year in a whole number of areas. In the USSR, the death of Joseph Stalin and Nikita Krushchev's rapid rise to power signaled the beginning of the end of years of repression. In Korea, an armistice finally brought to an end a war that had cost over 2 million lives. In North Africa, General Neguib finally disposed of the Egyptian monarchy and proclaimed a republic with himself as president and Colonel Gamel Abdul Nasser as his deputy. Edmund Hillary and Sherpa Tenzing Norgay reached the summit of the highest mountain in the world, in a British-led expedition whose success coincided with the coronation of the young Elizabeth II. And Francis Crick and James Watson discovered the structure of DNA, the "blueprint for life". The colonial struggle for independence continued: in Kenya, Jomo Kenyatta's conviction for organizing Mau Mau terrorism did not stop the drive against white domination, while in Southeast Asia the Vietminh forces continued their fight against the French.

▲ British scientist Francis Crick and his American colleague James Watson demonstrate the structure of DNA (dioxyribonucleic acid), the means whereby heredity is transmitted in living organisms. Their discovery paved the way for a better understanding of genetically inherited illness and for the development of genetic engineering.

- **12 Jan**: Yugoslavia adopts a new constitution, and Marshal Josip Tito is elected as the republic's first president (14 Jan).

- **18 Jan**: the Mau Mau steps up its attacks on white settlers in Kenya. (›8 Apr)

- **13 Feb**: The Catholic Church in Poland comes under state control. In Oct demonstrations against the move are put down by force.

- **16 Feb**: The SA government in Johannesburg gives itself emergency powers under the Public Safety Bill.

- **5 Mar**: Joseph Stalin dies of a cerebral hemorrhage, aged 73. He is succeeded as premier and First Secretary of the Central Committee of the Communist Party by Georgiy Malenkov. (›12 Sep)

- **5 Mar**: King Norodom Sihanouk proclaims independence for Cambodia.

- **31 Mar**: Dag Hammarskjold of Sweden is chosen to succeed Trygve Lie as Secretary-General of the UN.

- **8 Apr**: Jomo Kenyatta and five others are sentenced to seven years' hard labor for running the Mau Mau secret society.

- **11 Apr**: UN and Communist delegates in Panmunjom, Korea, agree terms for an exchange of sick and wounded POWs. (›18 Jun)

- **11 Apr**: France announces that the Vietminh forces have invaded Laos. By 28 Apr, the royal capital, Pakseng, has fallen. (›31 May)

- **15 Apr**: Nationalists secure a clear majority in South African elections.

- **17 Apr**: Following months of unrest and food shortages, the governor-general of Pakistan dismisses the government. The following day, a new government is formed under Muhammad Ali.

- **21 May**: Following the electoral victory of the Liberals, the Diet (Japanese parliament) nominates Yoshida Shigeru as premier (Jap).

- **31 May**: US Secretary of State John Foster Dulles warns of the possible "domino effect" (other states falling to Communism) in Southeast Asia if the French are defeated by the Vietminh.

- **17 Jun–12 Jul**: Martial law is imposed in East Berlin following an anti-Soviet uprising by workers (GDR).

- **18 Jun**: Gen. Neguib deposes the infant King Fuad II and proclaims a republic with himself as president. Col. Gamal Abdel Nasser is named as his deputy (Egy).

- **18 Jun**: The South Korean government releases 26,000 North Korean non-Communist prisoners. (›27 Jul)

- **24 Jun**: The UK parliament passes the Rhodesia and Nyasaland Federation bill, intended to join predominantly white, rich Southern Rhodesia to Northern Rhodesia and Nyasaland. (›20 Aug)

- **5 Jul**: Following the resignation of the Hungarian government on 2 Jul, Imre Nagy forms a ministry and promises to increase cultural and economic freedoms.

- **10 Jul**: The Soviet government announces the dismissal of Lavrentiy Beria, head of internal security. He is later tried and executed (USSR).

- **26 Jul**: Fidel Castro leads an abortive coup against president Batista of Cuba.

- **27 Jul**: An armistice brings an end to the Korean war, which has cost over 2 million lives.

- **14 Aug**: The USSR announces that it has tested its first hydrogen bomb.

- **20 Aug**: Premier Musaddiq of Iran is deposed by a royalist coup and arrested. The shah, who fled to Baghdad after the failure of an earlier coup (16 Aug), returns to resume power (22 Aug) and appeals to the world for financial aid.

- **20 Aug**: Demonstrations organized by the Nyasaland National Congress party against the country's federation with Rhodesia erupt into violence.

- **6 Sep**: The Christian Democratic Union (CDU) wins the West German election, with Konrad Adenauer returned as chancellor (9 Oct) (FRG).

- **12 Sep**: Nikita Khrushchev is appointed First Secretary of the Central Committee of the Communist party of the Soviet Union.

- **26 Sep**: Spain agrees to accept US military bases on its soil in exchange for economic aid.

- **8 Oct**: A decision by the USA and UK to hand over part of Trieste to the Italians (who lay claim to the whole region) angers the Yugoslavs. They protest that Trieste should become independent under UN auspices.

- **30 Oct**: In Austria, a general strike is called and there are widespread demonstrations against the country's continued occupation by Allied forces.

- **2 Nov**: Pakistan is declared an Islamic republic but elects to remain in the Commonwealth.

- **24 Nov**: Anti-Communist senator Joseph McCarthy accuses ex-president Truman of aiding suspected Communists (USA).

- **29 Nov**: French paratroopers capture the strategic plateau of Dien Bien Phu from the Vietminh. Ho Chi Minh, the Vietminh leader, offers an armistice (Vietnam). (›14 Mar 1954)

- **7 Dec**: David Ben Gurion resigns as Israel's prime minister. He is succeeded (9 Dec) by Moshe Sharett.

- **23 Dec**: Robert Oppenheimer, the "father" of the atomic bomb, has his security permit withdrawn by Eisenhower after being accused of associating with Communists and holding up the development of the hydrogen bomb (USA).

- **24 Dec**: Julius Nyerere is elected president of the Tanganyika African Association (Tan).

SOCIETY

- **1 Jan**: China implements its five-year economic plan.

- **3 Feb**: Burst dykes and widespread flooding claim more than 1,000 lives in the Netherlands.

- **27 Mar**: Following Stalin's death, the Soviet government declares an amnesty, releasing many prisoners or halving their sentences (USSR).

- **1 Apr**: The Soviet government announces a reduction in the prices of essential foodstuffs and consumer goods of between 10 and 50 percent.

- **4 May**: More than 2,000 East Germans pour into West Berlin following acute food shortages in the Communist zone. (›27 Jul)

- **29 May**: New Zealander Edmund Hillary and Sherpa Tenzing Norgay conquer Mount Everest, the highest mountain in the world. The expedition is a triumph for them and for the expedition's leader, Col. John Hunt.

- **30 May**: Czechoslovakia announces currency reforms and an end to food rationing.

- **2 Jun**: The coronation of Queen Elizabeth II takes place in London. The ceremony is seen on television by millions across the world (UK).

- **19 Jun**: After many unsuccessful appeals and much public support, Julius and Ethel Rosenberg, the convicted atom spies, go to the electric chair (USA).

- **8 Jul**: Argentina signs an agreement of economic unity with Chile and (14 Aug) a treaty with Paraguay aimed at forging closer economic ties between the two countries.

- **27 Jul**: The USA distributes food parcels to Germans in the Soviet sector of Berlin and in East Germany.

- **6 Aug**: Public service strikes begun by postal and railroad workers in France eventually involve more than 2 million state employees. At the end of the month the government agrees to cost-of-living increases and other concessions.

- **23 Aug**: The Soviet and East German governments sign a protocol canceling war reparations to the USSR with effect from 1 Jan 1954.

- **5 Sep**: President Eisenhower gives the new pro-USA government of Iran a $45 million grant.

- **Nov**: Smog masks are made available on the National Health Service for those in polluted areas or with respiratory diseases (UK).

- **4 Dec**: A large oilfield is struck in northwest Australia.

- **George Marshall** (USA), author of the Marshall Plan, wins the Nobel Peace Prize.

- **The Rev. Chad Varah**, of St Stephen's church, London, founds the Samaritans (UK), an organization to assist depressed or suicidal people.

- The disease myxomatosis spreads across Western Europe, killing millions of rabbits.

CULTURE

- **12 Jan**: Samuel Beckett's play *En attendant Godot* (Waiting for Godot) receives its premiere in Paris.

- **1 Feb**: 20th Century Fox Film Corporation announces the introduction of Cinemascope and stereophonic sound (USA).

- **17 Apr**: Charlie Chaplin, accused of Communism in the USA, his home for 40 years, decides to settle in Switzerland.

- **4 May**: In New York, Ernest Hemingway wins the Pulitzer Prize for his novel *The Old Man and the Sea* (1952).

- **8 Jun**: The Royal Opera House, Covent Garden, hosts the premiere of Benjamin Britten's opera *Gloriana* as part of a gala connected with the coronation of Queen Elizabeth II (UK).

- **15 Jul**: The film *Gentlemen prefer Blondes*, starring Marilyn Monroe and Jane Russell, is first shown in New York.

- **8 Oct**: The contralto Kathleen Ferrier dies from cancer at the early age of 41.

- **10 Dec**: In Stockholm, Winston Churchill (UK) is awarded the Nobel Prize for Literature for his historical works.

- **Richard Burton** gives a distinguished perfomance as *Hamlet* at London's Old Vic Theater.

- **James Baldwin**: *Go Tell it on the Mountain*, novel set in Harlem that deals with the situation of American blacks (USA).

- **Alain Robbe-Grillet**: *Les Gommes* (The Erasers), novel (Fr).

- **Jorge Luís Borges'** *Labyrinthes*, a collection of stories that establishes his international reputation, appears in a French edition; it is not published in English until 1962 (Arg).

- **Arthur Miller**: *The Crucible*, play based on the trials of the so-called witches of Salem in 1692 (USA).

- **Tennessee Williams**: *Camino Real*, play (USA).

- **Ian Fleming**: *Casino Royale*, the first of the James Bond stories (UK).

- **Saul Bellow**: *The Adventures of Augie March*, novel (USA).

- **Charles Olson**: *The Maximus Poems, 1–10*. As rector of Black Mountain College, an experimental liberal arts college, in the early 1950s, Olsen publishes work by Allen Ginsberg and Jack Kerouac, as well as that of the group known as the Black Mountain poets, in the *Black Mountain Review* (USA).

- **Nadine Gordimer**: *The Soft Voice of the Serpent*, collection of stories (SA).

- **John Wain**: *Hurry On Down*, novel (UK).

- **Dmitri Shostakovitch**: Tenth Symphony (USSR).

- **Ralph Vaughan Williams**: *Sinfonia Antartica* (UK).

- **Olivier Messiaen**: *Le Reveil des oiseaux*, for piano and orchestra, in which the composer's long-standing interest in birdsong begins to influence his music.

- **Carlos Chávez**: Symphony No.4, *Sinfonia Romantica* (Mex).

- **Earle Brown**: *Twenty-Five Pages*, an example of "mobile form", in which composed sections of music can be played in any sequence determined by chance or choice (USA).

- **Luigi Dallpiccola**: *Goethe Lieder*, for mezzo-soprano and three clarinets (It).

- **Luigi Nono**: *Epitaffio per Federico García Lorca*, choral work (It).

- **Henri Matisse**: *L'Escargot*, cut paper (Fr).

- **Josef Albers**: *Homage to the Square, "Ascending"*: one of a series of paintings begun in 1950 (USA).

- **Max Ernst**: *Cry of the Seagull*, painting (Fr).

- **Mark Tobey**: *Edge of August*, painting (USA).

- **Jackson Pollock**: *Blue Poles*, painting (USA).

- **Francis Bacon**: *Pope Innocent X, after Velasquez*, painting (UK).

- **Reg Butler**: monument to *The Unknown Political Prisoner* (UK).

- **Henry Moore**: *King and Queen*, sculpture (UK).

- **Jean Tinguely** exhibits his "spatial constructions", some of which are driven by a small motor, at the Galérie Arnaud in Paris.

- **Ossip Zadkine**: *To a Destroyed City*, monumental bronze for the entry to the port of Rotterdam (Neth).

- **Pier Luigi Nervi**: UNESCO Conference Hall in Paris (completed 1957) (Fr).

- *Monsieur Hulot's Holiday*, film comedy directed by and starring Jacques Tati (Fr).

- **David Bradley's** film of Shakespeare's *Julius Caesar*, with John Gielgud and James Mason, and Marlon Brando as Mark Antony, is released (USA).

- **Fritz Lang**: *The Big Heat*, film with Glenn Ford (USA).

- **Teinsuke Kinosuga**: *Gate of Hell*, film (Jap).

- **Federico Fellini**: *I Vitelloni*, film (It).

- **Kenzi Misoguchi**: *Ugetsu Monagarati* (Tales of the Pale Moon after Rain), film (Jap).

SCIENCE

- **25 Apr**: Francis Crick (UK) and James Watson (USA) discover the structure of DNA (dioxyribonucleic acid), the blueprint for life. They go on to develop the double-helix model for DNA to explain how heredity is transmitted in living organisms.

- **11 Nov**: Scientists identify the polio virus (USA).

- **Neymann** and **Scott** discover superclusters of galaxies.

- **Mabel** and **Lowell Hokin** (USA) discover that acetylcholine causes pancreas cells to increase their uptake of phosphorus groups into the cell membrane – a step toward discovering how cells communicate with each other.

- **Alfred C. Kinsey** and others produce a startling report (the "Kinsey report") on the sexual behavior of American women, concluding among other things that about a quarter of married women are unfaithful to their husbands (USA).

- **Fritz Lipmann** (USA) shares the Nobel Prize for Physiology or Medicine with Hans Krebs (UK) for their respective discoveries of coenzyme A and the citric acid cycle.

- **Hermann Staudinger** (FRG) wins the Nobel Prize for Chemistry for his study of polymers.

- **Fritz Zernike** (Neth) wins the Nobel Prize for Physics for his phase-contrast microscope.

- **Max Perutz**, an Austrian-British biochemist, discovers that X-ray diffraction of an organic molecule can be improved by the addition of a heavy element such as gold.

- **Karl Ziegler** (FRG) develops the first catalyst that combines monomers into a polymer in such a way as to produce an improved polyethylene. Giulio Natta (It) employs Ziegler's discovery to develop polypropylene, a new plastic which is cheaper than nylon but equal in quality.

- **Evarts Graham** and **Ernest Wydner** show that tars from tobacco smoke can cause mice to develop cancer.

- **Frederick Sanger** (UK) determines the structure of the protein insulin.

- **Donald Glaser** publishes the first bubble-chamber pictures of subatomic interactions (USA).

- **Michelin** (Fr) and **Pirelli** (It) introduce radial-ply tires.

- American physicist **Charles Townes** develops the maser (microwave amplification by the stimulated emission of radiation), forerunner of the laser.

- **Drs R.G. Bunge** and **J.K. Sherman** of the University of Iowa School of Medicine for the first time impregnate a woman using frozen sperm (USA).

- **J. Gibbon** performs the first open-heart surgery with a heart-lung machine (USA).

1954

POLITICS

Teenage fashions were due for a change, and the beginning of the Rock and Roll age, signaled by Elvis Presley's first single and Bill Haley's "Rock Around the Clock", coincided with the release of "The Wild One," in which Marlon Brando's leather jacket convinced the Teddy Boys to put aside their drape jackets and drainpipes. Another sign of changing times in the United States was the censure by the Senate of Joseph McCarthy's attacks on the army. The French army was in worse trouble, as it was compelled to fight a colonial rearguard action on two continents. After a long and ferocious siege, the Communist Vietminh forces finally overran the fortress at Dien Bien Phu, where General de Castries had ordered his artillery to fire on his own command post if the enemy broke through. The entire garrison of 16,000 was killed or captured in the worst blow to French prestige since their defeat by the Germans in 1940. France was also faced by nationalist unrest in Morocco and Tunisia, while by the end of the year more troops were being hastily transported to Algeria.

▲ 25-year-old British medical student Roger Bannister became the first man to run a mile in under four minutes. His time of 3 minutes 59.4 seconds set a new world record, and foreshadowed the astonishing progress in sport that was to take place during the second half of the century.

● **25 Jan**: The foreign ministers of France, the UK, USA and USSR meet in West Berlin to discuss the German and Austrian peace treaties and arms reduction. The USSR rejects proposals for a reunification of Germany.

● **26 Jan**: The USA ratifies a mutual security treaty with South Korea.

● **25 Feb**: President and premier Neguib is forced to resign by Col. Gamal Abdel Nasser, vice-president and founder of the revolutionary movement, but after popular demonstrations Neguib is restored to the presidency. (›18 Apr)

● **8 Mar**: USA and Japan conclude a mutual defense agreement.

● **14 Mar**: Between now and 7 May four separate offensives by the Vietminh wear down French defenses. (›21 Apr)

● **1 Apr**: Bomb attacks begin four years of terrorism by pro-Enosis (union with Greece) EOKA guerrillas, led by George Grivas (Cyprus).

● **18 Apr**: Col. Nasser again ousts Neguib as president and prime minister, though Neguib is restored to a nominal presidency (Egy). (›17 Nov)

● **21 Apr**: The US air force flies a French battalion to Indochina to defend Dien Bien Phu. On 26 Apr a conference begins in Geneva to negotiate a peace between France and the Vietnamese revolutionaries.(›27 May)

● **25 Apr**: Juan Perón is reelected president of Argentina and promptly arrests four opposition leaders.

● **Apr**: The US Senate begins an enquiry into Senator Joseph McCarthy's accusations of Communist infiltration within the US Army. (› Jun)

● **Apr**: The British begin a major operation against the nationalist Mau Mau movement (Ken). (›26 May)

● **7 May**: The fortress at Dien Bien Phu falls to the revolutionaries after a 55-day siege. On 10 May, at the Geneva conference, the Vietminh reject France's call for a truce and demand freedom for Vietnam, Laos and Cambodia. (›20 Jul)

● **13 May–22 Jun**: A five-power subcommittee of the UN disarmament commission meets to discuss the construction of an inspection system and the possibility of a ban on nuclear testing, but little real progress is made.

● **29 May**: Thailand compains to the UN Security Council that Communists in Indochina threaten her security. (› 8 Sep)

● **12 Jun**: The French government is defeated in the National Assembly. On 18 Jun Pierre Mendès-France becomes premier.

● **29 Jun**: The Potomac Charter, a six-point declaration of Western policy, is issued following a meeting in Washington between president Eisenhower and British prime minister Winston Churchill (USA).

● **Jun**: Senator Joseph McCarthy alleges Communist infiltration of the CIA and nuclear weapons plants. President Eisenhower says he will stop senator McCarthy from investigating the CIA (USA). (›2 Dec)

● **20 Jul**: An armistice is signed which arbitrarily divides Vietnam along the 17th parallel, though neither the USA nor the South Vietnamese delegation sign. A Communist regime will rule in the north and a nationalist government in the south, supported by the French. (›8 Oct)

● **7 Aug**: 11 die in riots in Morocco as nationalists demand independence and the return of the deposed sultan, Sidi Muhammad Ben Youssef. The French send in the Foreign Legion.

● **10 Aug**: Holland and Indonesia sever their last links.

● **12 Aug**: The UN Command officially withdraws from Korea, a year after the ceasefire was signed.

● **17 Aug**: President Eisenhower commits the USA to stop China invading Formosa (Taiwan) after Chinese Nationalists sink eight Communist Chinese gunboats off the island. On 5 Sep Chinese Communists attack Nationalist targets on the island of Quemoy. (›1 Dec)

● **8 Sep**: Fearing that the collapse of Indochina will be followed by that of other Asian states, US Secretary of State Dulles takes the initiative and facilitates the creation of SEATO, the Southeast Asia Treaty Organization, which is formed as a defensive alliance by the USA, UK, France, Australia, New Zealand, the Philippines, Pakistan and Thailand.

● **1 Oct**: A federal constitution takes effect in Nigeria.

● **5 Oct**: Italy, the USA, Yugoslavia and Britain sign a treaty to end the Allied occupation of Trieste.

● **8 Oct**: Communist soldiers occupy Hanoi as the French withdraw. Ho Chi Minh returns to lead the government in North Vietnam.

● **19 Oct**: An Anglo-Egyptian agreement is reached whereby British troops will leave the Suez Canal Zone by the end of 1956. Egypt agrees freedom of canal navigation.

● **23 Oct**: After a nine-power conference, an agreement is signed in Paris providing for West German sovereignty and permitting West Germany to rearm and enter NATO.

● **1 Nov**: Terrorist raids mark the beginning of the war of independence in Algeria. On 20 Dec France sends 20,000 troops to Algeria.

● **1 Dec**: The USA and the Chinese Nationalist government sign a pact of mutual security.

● **2 Dec**: Senator Joseph McCarthy is censured by the Senate for his behavior toward Senate members and army officials in his investigations into Communist subversion (USA).

SOCIETY

- **12 Jan**: The Burmese government and three oil companies form Burmah Oil.

- **Jan**: The South African Labor party backs a universal franchise.

- **Feb**: The frozen food industry in the USA exceeds $1 billion in sales.

- **22 Mar**: The London gold market reopens for the first time since 1939.

- **25 Mar**: RCA begins mass production of color televisions with a 12-inch screen, retailing for under $1,000 (USA).

- **30 Mar**: Canada's first subway line opens in Toronto.

- **15 Apr**: Margaret Sanger, American birth control campaigner, declares before the Japanese Diet that birth control would solve the problem of over-population in Japan.

- **6 May**: Roger Bannister becomes the first man to run the mile in under four minutes (UK).

- **13 May**: President Eisenhower signs the St Lawrence Seaway Bill, which authorizes construction of the seaway that will improve navigation between the Atlantic and the Great Lakes (USA/Can).

- **17 May**: The US Supreme Court declares racial segregation in American public schools to be unconstitutional.

- **Jun**: Consultations take place regarding a European Monetary Agreement.

- **1 Jul**: Sweden, Norway, Denmark and Finland agree a common labor market giving equal employment opportunities in each country to nationals of any of the others. (›Nov)

- **20 Jul**: After the armistice agreement dividing Vietnam into North and South Vietnam, refugees from the Communist regime in the north begin to move south.

- **Jul**: The first nuclear power plant in the Soviet Union starts production.

- **27 Aug**: The Communist party is outlawed in the USA. The new law imposes legal, political and economic penalties on party members.

- **Nov**: A plan is published for a common Scandinavian market.

- **17 Dec**: The British Petroleum Co is created, owning 40 percent of the new National Iranian Oil Co.

- The UK lifts restrictions on the export of rubber and other nonstrategic materials to the USSR.

- An international convention is agreed for prevention of pollution of the sea by oil.

- "Teddy Boys" appear on the streets of Britain, but the Home Secretary says they are not a problem.

- Nobel Peace Prize is won by the Office of the United Nations High Commissioner for Refugees.

- The first transistor radio, the Regency, is launched (USA).

CULTURE

- **25 Jan**: Dylan Thomas's radio drama *Under Milk Wood* is first broadcast by the BBC, with Richard Burton (UK).

- **12 Mar**: Premiere in a concert performance in Hamburg (FRG) of Arnold Schoenberg's opera *Moses and Aaron*, the first two acts of which were written in 1931–32.

- **Jun**: Victor market the first prerecorded tapes (USA).

- **18 Jul**: The first Newport Jazz Festival takes place (USA).

- **Jul**: Elvis Presley releases his first single, "That's All Right Mama" (USA).

- **14 Sep**: Benjamin Britten's opera *The Turn of the Screw* is first performed by the English Opera Group at the Venice Festival, conducted by the composer.

- **22 Sep**: Lennox Berkeley's opera *Nelson* is premiered at Sadler's Wells theater in London (UK).

- **30 Nov**: Graham Sutherland's unflattering portrait of Winston Churchill meets with a cool reception. It is later destroyed (UK).

- Simone de Beauvoir: *Les Mandarins*, novel (Fr).

- William Golding: *Lord of the Flies*, a powerful novel about human reversion to savagery (UK).

- John Betjeman: *A Few Late Chrysanthemums*, poems (UK).

- Max Frisch: *I'm not Stiller*, novel (Swi).

- Thomas Mann: *Confessions of Felix Krull*, novel (FRG).

- Iris Murdoch: *Under the Net*, novel (UK).

- Kingsley Amis: *Lucky Jim*, novel (UK).

- Raymond Chandler: *The Long Goodbye*, crime novel featuring his detective narrator Philip Marlowe (USA).

- Françoise Sagan's novel *Bonjour Tristesse* becomes an overnight success (Fr).

- Aldous Huxley: *The Doors of Perception*, which (together with *Heaven and Hell*, 1956) records the author's experiments with the drugs mescalin and LSD (UK).

- J.R.R. Tolkien: *The Lord of the Rings* (Parts I and II), fantasy novel (UK).

- Nicanor Parra: *Poemas y antipoemas* ("Poems and Antipoems") (Chile).

- Louis MacNeice: *Autumn Sequel*, poem sequence (UK).

- John van Druten: *I am a Camera*, highly successful dramatization of part of Christopher Isherwood's novel *Goodbye to Berlin*, about cabaret artist Sally Bowles in early 1930s Berlin (USA).

- Christopher Fry: *The Dark is Light Enough*, play (UK).

- T.S. Eliot: *The Confidential Clerk*, verse play (UK).

- The Nobel Prize for Literature is won by Ernest Hemingway (USA).

- Igor Stravinsky: *In Memoriam Dylan Thomas*, septet for the poet Dylan Thomas, who died in New York in 1953.

- Rolf Liebermann: *Concerto for Jazz Band and Symphony Orchestra* (Swi).

- Edgard Varèse: *Déserts*, for orchestra and tape recorder (USA).

- Karlheinz Stockhausen: *Studien*, electronic works composed at the newly founded Westdeutscher Rundfunk studio for electronic music (FRG).

- Luigi Nono: *La Victoire de Guernica*, for voices and orchestra (It).

- Iannis Xenakis: *Metastasis*, for orchestra (Fr).

- Aaron Copland: *The Tender Land*, opera (USA).

- Gian Carlo Menotti: *The Saint of Bleecker Street*, opera (USA).

- Dmitri Shostakovich is awarded the title of "People's Artist of the USSR".

- Sandy Wilson: *The Boy Friend*, musical (UK).

- Julian Slade: *Salad Days*, musical (UK).

- "Rock around the Clock" is recorded by Bill Haley and the Comets (USA).

- The Crew Cuts' "Sh-Boom" is the first rock n'roll hit in the USA.

- John Bratby: *Dustbins*, painting (UK).

- Pablo Picasso: *Sylvette*, painting (Fr).

- Jean Dubuffet: *Vagabonds*, painting (Fr).

- Balthus: *The Bedroom*, painting (Fr).

- Kenneth Armitage: *Seated Group Listening to Music*, sculpture (UK).

- Barbara Hepworth: *Two Figures, Menhirs*, sculpture (UK).

- "Design in Scandinavia" exhibition begins touring the USA.

- Italy launches the Compasso d'Oro awards for product design.

- Federico Fellini: *La strada*, starring Giulietta Massina (It).

- Elia Kazan: *On the Waterfront*, starring Marlon Brando (USA).

- Alfred Hitchcock: *Rear Window* (UK).

- Andrzej Wajda: *A Generation*, first film in his World War II trilogy (followed by *Kanal* and *Ashes and Diamonds*) (Pol).

- Akira Kurosawa: *The Seven Samurai*, one of the first Japanese films to make a big impact on the West (Jap).

- Eurovision, the European TV community, begins experimental transmissions linking Belgium, Denmark, France, West Germany, Italy, the Netherlands, Switzerland and Britain.

- Marlon Brando wears denim jeans and a leather jacket in Laslo Benedek's film, *The Wild One*, setting a new fashion.

SCIENCE

- **Jan**: The first nuclear-powered vessel – the submarine *Nautilus* – is launched.

- **Mar**: The Japanese begin investigation of radiation levels around Bikini Atoll, where the USA have exploded a hydrogen bomb.

- **Jul**: The prototype of the Boeing 707 makes its maiden flight (USA).

- **Jul**: After six years of research, the cause of the eye-burning smog of the Los Angeles area is identified as being the chemical action of sunlight on auto exhaust fumes and industrial emissions (USA).

- **29 Sep**: The Centre Européen de Recherche Nucléaire (CERN) is founded at Geneva.

- Texas Instruments develop the use of silicon in transistors in place of germanium (USA).

- Scientists working for the Bell Telephone Co (USA) develop the first solar-powered battery.

- Vincent du Vigneaud synthesizes two pituitary hormones – vasopressin which raises blood pressure and stimulates the kidney to retain water, and oxytocin which causes uterine muscles to contract in childbirth (USA).

- Max Born (UK) and Walther Bothe (FRG) share the Nobel Prize for Physics, for their work in quantum mechanics and cosmic radiation respectively.

- Nobel Prize for Chemistry is won by Linus C. Pauling (USA), for his research into the nature of the chemical bond and its application to the structure of complex substances.

- J. Enders, T. Weller and F. Robbins (USA) receive the Nobel Prize for Physiology or Medicine for work on culturing polio viruses. The anti-polio vaccine developed by Jonas Salk in 1952 is utilized in the first mass vaccination program of schoolchildren in Pittsburgh, Pennsylvania.

- E. R. Sears demonstrates that chromosomes in wheat can be substituted, allowing the development of hybrid wheats which are more resistant to disease and drought.

- Surgeons in Boston (USA) make the first successful organ transplant (of a kidney) between identical twins.

- The first suggestion is made of a connection between smoking and lung cancer.

- G.G. Pincus introduces the oral contraceptive pill after field trials in Haiti and Puerto Rico (USA).

- J. Hin Tijo and A. Lean demonstrate that humans have 46 chromosomes rather than 48.

- ICI develops the insecticide Paraquat (UK).

- Chlorpromazine (Thorazine) is developed for the treatment of mental disorders.

Ministers of defense were diplomatically active in 1955. The Soviet Union with its satellites formed the Warsaw Pact in response to West Germany's inclusion in NATO, giving the Soviet Union the right to station its troops in other member-countries. The first SEATO conference met in Bangkok to express concern regarding international Communism, while Britain, with Iraq, Turkey, and later Pakistan and Iran, formed the Baghdad Pact against Soviet expansionism in the Middle East. On a different note, the voice of the Third World was heard at the Bandung Conference, demanding an end to colonialism. South Africa, where apartheid was by now firmly entrenched, came in for criticism, and later withdrew from the UN on the grounds that the constant criticism contravened the UN charter, which forswore interference in internal affairs. The death of teenage idol James Dean received greater coverage in popular media than the death of the century's greatest scientist, Albert Einstein. Disneyland opened in California and Mary Quant's boutique opened in Chelsea — signs of the approaching Sixties.

▲ Marilyn Monroe became the great movie success of the 1950s, with *The Seven Year Itch* (1955), *Bus Stop* (1956) and *Some Like It Hot* (1959).

● **4 Jan**: The USA agrees to pay Japan $2,000,000 in damages for radioactive contamination caused by their atomic tests of March 1954.

● **12 Jan**: US Secretary of State John Foster Dulles inaugurates a defense policy of "massive retaliation": in future the USA will "depend primarily upon a great capacity to retaliate instantly by means and at places of our choosing".

● **17 Jan**: The USSR announces that it will share nuclear materials and scientific knowledge with Communist China, Czechoslovakia, Poland, East Germany and Romania.

● **18 Jan**: British forces continue their action against the Mau Mau in Kenya.

● **25 Jan**: The USSR issues a decree ending the state of war with Germany.

● **25 Jan**: Jacques Soustelle is appointed governor-general of Algeria in an attempt to restore order after pro-independence strife. (›5 Feb)

● **28 Jan**: President Eisenhower is granted emergency powers by the US Congress to permit US forces to protect Formosa (Taiwan) from Communist Chinese forces who are massing for an apparent invasion.

● **5 Feb**: Pierre Mendès-France resigns after a vote of no confidence regarding his handling of Algerian independence, and on 23 Feb Edgar Faure forms a ministry (Fr). (›21 Aug)

● **8 Feb**: Georgiy Malenkov is replaced by Marshal Nikolai Bulganin as premier (USSR).

● **23 Feb**: Foreign ministers of SEATO countries meet in Bangkok for the first time and agree to help one another combat international Communism.

● **24 Feb**: Turkey and Iraq sign a treaty of alliance, the Baghdad Pact, a mutual security organization intended to counter the threat of USSR expansion in the Middle East oil-producing regions. Pakistan, Iran and the UK also join.

● **2 Mar**: Egypt and Syria sign a defensive agreement.

● **24 Mar**: A new constitution comes into force in Tanganyika.

● **5 Apr**: Winston Churchill, 80, resigns as prime minister and is succeeded by Anthony Eden (UK).

● **18–27 Apr**: At the Bandung Conference in Indonesia, delegates from 29 African and Asian countries meet and call for an end to colonialism and for independence and UN membership for all.

● **5 May**: West Germany (FRG) becomes a sovereign state as president Eisenhower signs an order ending US occupation.

● **7 May**: In retaliation for ratification of the Paris agreement that permits West Germany to join NATO, the USSR annuls agreements with Britain and France.

● **14 May**: The USSR, Albania, Bulgaria, Czechoslovakia, Hungary, Poland, Romania and East Germany sign the Warsaw Pact, a 20-year mutual defense agreement.

● **15 May**: Austrian sovereignty is restored by a treaty signed by the UK, USA, France and USSR, which restores Austria's pre-1938 borders and prohibits economic union with Germany.

● **26 May**: Soviet premier Bulganin and First Secretary Khrushchev visit Yugoslavia and sign a treaty of friendship, which recognizes the possibility of the coexistence of different forms of socialism and is a major step toward Yugoslavian independence.

● **18 Jun**: President Perón uses the army to put down an uprising inspired by his plan to deprive the Catholic Church of its tax exemption; the Pope excommunicates Perón. (›16 Sep)

● **18 Jul**: Geneva summit begins, the first conference since 1945 involving the USA, USSR, UK and France. The aim of easing tension between the four powers is stated, but a further conference of the four powers (27 Oct–16 Nov) fails to implement the July directives.

● **21 Aug**: After rioting and violence in Morocco and Algeria, French premier Faure meets with Moroccan leaders to negotiate a peace settlement. It is agreed that the pro-French sultan and the resident general will resign. The sultan refuses to abdicate but eventually capitulates on 30 Oct.

● **29 Aug**: A conference opens in London between the UK, Turkey and Greece to discuss the position of Cyprus. (›26 Nov)

● **16 Sep**: Gen. Eduardo Lonardi leads a revolt which ousts President Perón of Argentina. Perón goes into exile (until 1971), and on 23 Sep Lonardi becomes provisional president. On 13 Nov Gen. Pedro Aramburu ousts Lonardi in a bloodless coup.

● **11 Oct**: President Eisenhower presents proposals for arms inspection to Soviet premier Bulganin, the prelude to agreements over armament control (USA).

● **23 Oct**: After a referendum in South Vietnam, emperor Bao Dai is deposed and a republic is proclaimed under Ngo Dinh Diem.

● **Oct**: Constantine Karamanlis is elected prime minister of Greece.

● **2 Nov**: David Ben Gurion forms a ministry in Israel.

● **9 Nov**: South Africa withdraws from the UN after UN refusal to discontinue consideration of 1952 Cruz Report on apartheid.

● **21 Nov**: The defense alliance of Turkey, Iraq, Iran, Pakistan and the UK holds its first meeting. Iraq pledges aid to any Arab state threatened by Israel.

● **26 Nov**: A state of emergency is proclaimed in Cyprus.

SOCIETY

- **31 Jan**: The South African government's plans to forcibly move 60,000 black Africans from Johannesburg to a new town outside the city provoke a 13-day peaceful protest. The move begins on 9 Feb.
- **Feb**: The USSR and India agree on the construction of an iron and steel works in India.
- **2 Mar**: The Soviet government introduces a decentralized system of agricultural planning to encourage initiative and independence amongst farmers.
- **Mar**: Currency reform takes place in China.
- **Mar**: Floods in Australia leave 44,000 people homeless; 300,000 sheep die in New South Wales.
- **3 May**: The USA and Turkey sign the first atoms-for-peace pact, leasing enriched uranium to Turkey for a research reactor and permitting the exchange of information and of radioactive isotopes for use in medicine, industry and agriculture.
- **May**: In India, the first five-year plan for economic development begins.
- **11 Jun**: Eisenhower proposes financial and technical aid to all non-Communist countries to develop atomic energy (USA).
- **Jun**: Conference of Messina prepares the way for the establishment of the European Economic Community.
- **1 Jul**: The USA gives $216 million in aid to South Vietnam.
- **Jul**: Disneyland opens at Anaheim, California.
- **Jul**: British driver Stirling Moss beats world champion Juan Fangio (Arg) in the British Grand Prix.
- **Aug**: The European Monetary Agreement is signed.
- **Sep**: Ninth session of GATT agrees upon revision of the GATT treaty, involving limitation of government subsidy and fixing of capital investment for developing countries.
- **Sep**: The Universal Copyright Convention comes into force.
- **Oct**: The USSR offers industrial, agricultural and technical help to any undeveloped Arab or Asian nation.
- **1 Dec**: A local segregation law in Montgomery, Alabama, is defied by a black woman, Rosa Parks. A boycott led by Martin Luther King ends eventually in a Supreme Court decision that the ordinance is unconstitutional.
- West Germany announces the implementation of the Hallstein doctrine, breaking off relations with states acknowledging East Germany.
- After the USA tightening of immigration controls in 1954, many West Indian immigrants go to the UK instead.
- The Wimpy Hamburger chain brings the hamburger to Europe from the USA.

CULTURE

- **27 Jan**: Premiere in London of Michael Tippett's opera The Midsummer Marriage, with Joan Sutherland (UK).
- **12 Mar**: Jazz saxophonist Charlie Parker, originator of bebop, dies aged 34.
- **30 Sep**: After great success starring in East of Eden (directed by Elia Kazan) and Rebel without a Cause (directed by Nicholas Ray), actor James Dean dies in an automobile accident at the age of 24 and becomes a cult hero (USA).
- **Sep**: Commercial television begins in the UK.
- Samuel Beckett's play Waiting for Godot has its London premiere.
- Arthur Miller: A View from the Bridge, play (USA).
- Vladimir Nabokov: Lolita, novel (USA).
- Jorge Luís Borges: Extraordinary Tales (Arg).
- Patrick White: The Tree of Man, Australian epic novel (Aus).
- Gabriel García Marquez: Leaf Storm and Other Stories, stories in which Marquez's mythical community of Macondo first appears (Col).
- Dylan Thomas: Quite Early One Morning, prose pieces (posth.) (UK).
- Alain Robbe-Grillet: The Voyeur, novel (Fr).
- Iris Murdoch: The Flight from the Enchanter, novel (UK).
- Philip Larkin: The Less Deceived, his first major collection of poems (UK).
- Evelyn Waugh: Officers and Gentlemen, second novel in the Sword of Honour trilogy (UK).
- Graham Greene: The Quiet American, novel set in Vietnam (UK).
- Pierre Boulez: Le Marteau sans maître, for contralto and six instruments, based around three poems by René Char (Fr).
- Karlheinz Stockhausen: Gesang der Junglinge (FRG).
- Luigi Nono: Incontri (It).
- Hans Werner Henze: König Hirsch, opera (It).
- Peter Maxwell Davies: Trumpet Sonata (UK).
- Carlisle Floyd: Susannah, opera (USA).
- RCA demonstrate a "synthesizer".
- Elvis Presley signs with Victor (USA).
- Salvador Dali: The Lord's Supper, painting (Sp/USA).
- Pietro Annigoni: H.M. The Queen, portrait of Elizabeth II (UK) which caused attendances at the Royal Academy's Summer Exhibition in London to break all records (It).
- John Bratby: Still Life with Chip-Fryer, painting (UK).
- Bernard Buffet: Circus, painting (Fr).

- Oskar Kokoschka: Thermopylae, triptych for the University of Hamburg (FRG).
- Australian artist Sidney Nolan paints a second series of Ned Kelly paintings (UK).
- Lynn Chadwick: Winged Figures, sculpture (UK).
- H.G. Adam: Concrete sculpture for Le Havre Museum forecourt (Neth).
- Larry Rivers: Double Portrait of Birdie, painting (USA).
- Robert Rauschenberg: Bed, painting (USA).
- Jasper Johns: Flags, Targets and Numbers, series of paintings completed between 1954 and 1955. Johns and Rauschenberg begin the movement toward Pop Art in the USA.
- Le Corbusier: La Tourette, Eveaux-sur-l'Arbresle, Lyon (Fr).
- Kenzo Tange: Hiroshima Peace Memorial (Jap).
- Eero Saarinen, General Motors Technical Center, Michigan (USA).
- Frank Lloyd Wright: Price Tower, Bartlesville, Oklahoma (USA).
- Viljo Revell: Kueneule Textile Works, Hanko (Fin).
- José Luis Sert: US Embassy, Baghdad (completed 1963) (Iran).
- Hochschule für Gestaltung (College of Design) is founded in Ulm (FRG).
- Furniture company Knoll International begins to bring classic prewar Modernist designs back into production (USA).
- Marty, produced by Harold Hecht and Burt Lancaster, directed by Delbert Mann and starring Ernest Borgnine and Betsy Blair, wins the Academy Award for the Best Picture (USA).
- Billy Wilder: The Seven Year Itch, starring Marilyn Monroe (USA).
- Juan Bardem: Death of a Cyclist.
- Ingmar Bergman: Smiles of a Summer Night (Swe).
- René Clair: Les Grandes Manoeuvres (Fr).
- Satyajit Ray: Pather Panchali, Ray's first film and the first in the Apu trilogy (Ind).
- Halldór Laxness (Iceland) wins the Nobel Prize for Literature.
- Alain Resnais: Nuit et brouillard (Night and Fog) (Fr).
- Michelangelo Antonioni: Le amiche (The Girlfriends) (It).
- Fashion designer Mary Quant opens her shop Bazaar on London's King's Road.
- Japanese fashion designer Hanae Mori's first shop opens on Tokyo's Ginza Street.

SCIENCES

- **18 Jul**: First use of atomically generated power in the USA at Schenectady.
- Andouin Dolfus ascends 7.25 km (4.5 miles) above the earth to make photoelectric observations of Mars.
- B.B. Burk discovers that Jupiter emits radio waves.
- Radiophysicists at Massachusetts Institute of Technology develop use of Ultra High-Frequency (UHF) waves (USA).
- Dorothy Hodgkin discovers the composition of Vitamin B_{12}, which becomes useful in treating pernicious anemia (UK).
- F. Sanger establishes the structure of the molecule of insulin (UK).
- Christopher Cockerell develops the first viable hovercraft which rides across water on a cushion of air (UK).
- An artificial diamond is used in cutting tools and drills for the first time at GEC in New York. Graphite is subjected to ultra-high pressure to change the atoms into a configuration that characterizes the diamond (USA).
- The congenital condition of hydrocephalus, in which an infant's head becomes progressively enlarged by a fluid build-up in the brain, is ameliorated by the Holtzer Shunt. The Shunt is implanted in the head to drain off the extra fluid.
- Owen Chamberlain and Emilio Segrè discover the antiproton, a negatively charged proton. This reinforces the theory that every elementary particle has an opposite counterpart (USA).
- First optical fibers are produced by Narinder Kapary (UK).
- S. Ochoa isolates an enzyme, from the bacterium Aztobacter vinelandii, capable of catalyzing the formation of RNA from nucleotides (USA/Sp).
- Albert Einstein pleads on radio for a halt to the arms race, shortly before his death at 76 on 18 Apr (USA).
- M.B. Hoagland, working with protein synthesis, establishes that transfer RNA combines with specific amino acids; these are later combined by messenger RNA, following instructions from DNA (USA).
- Clyde Cowan and Frederick Reines (USA) observe neutrinos for the first time, as predicted by Wolfgang Pauli.
- Hugo Theorell (Swe) wins the Nobel Prize for Physiology or Medicine for his work on oxidation enzymes.
- Nobel Prize for Physics is shared by Polykarp Kusch (USA), for his precision determination of the magnetic movement of the electron, and by Willis E. Lamb Jr (USA) for his discoveries concerning the fine structure of the hydrogen spectrum.
- Vincent du Vigneaud (USA) wins the Nobel Prize for Chemistry for his work on sulfur compounds, and for the first synthesis of a polypeptide hormone.

Less than eight months after Nikita Khrushchev's six-hour speech to the 20th Party Congress in which he denounced Stalin as a murderous criminal, the Soviet Union suppressed the Hungarian uprising with unbridled brutality. A running commentary was received in the West from a reporter in Budapest, firing from his office window as he operated the teleprinter. However, Western condemnation of Soviet aggression rang hollow since a few weeks earlier France and Britain, acting in secret collusion with Israel, had launched an attack on Egypt in response to Col. Nasser's nationalization of the Suez Canal. An ignominious withdrawal swiftly became necessary in view of US disapproval and a plummeting pound. The Suez crisis finished prime minister Anthony Eden's hitherto distinguished career, and blackened Britain's reputation in colonial and post-colonial countries.

▲ **The Hungarians were allowed only a brief moment of freedom before Soviet tanks rolled in to crush their bid for independence. After the clampdown, thousands of refugees fled across the Austrian border.**

- **1 Jan**: Sudan is proclaimed an independent democratic republic and on 19 Jan joins the Arab League.

- **13 Jan**: In response to the Dec 1955 Israeli attack on Syrian positions along the Sea of Galilee, Syria and Lebanon sign a mutual defense pact. On 24 Jan Jordan and Israel accept UN truce proposals. (›10 May)

- **1 Feb**: President Eisenhower (USA) and prime minister Anthony Eden (UK) issue the Declaration of Washington, which warns the peoples of Asia and Africa against seeking economic or political aid from the USSR.

- **14–20 Feb**: At the 20th congress of the Soviet Communist party in Moscow, Soviet premier Nikita Khrushchev denounces Stalin's policies and announces his desire to see the inauguration of a new peaceful image of the USSR.

- **2 Mar**: Morocco achieves independence from France. French and Spanish Morocco is united under Sultan Muhammad V.

- **9 Mar**: In Cyprus, Archbishop Makarios is arrested as a terrorist by the British and deported to the Seychelles Islands.

- **20 Mar**: Tunisia gains independence from France. Habib Bourguiba becomes the country's first president.

- **23 Mar**: Pakistan becomes the world's first Islamic republic but remains in the Commonwealth.

- **21 Apr**: Egypt, Saudi Arabia and the Yemen sign a military alliance at Jedda.

- **22 Apr**: China appoints the Dalai Lama chairman of a committee intended to prepare Tibet for regional autonomy within the auspices of the Chinese People's Republic.

- **10 May**: Dag Hammarskjold, UN Secretary-General, arranges an unconditional ceasefire between Israel, Egypt, Jordan, Syria and Lebanon.

- **13 Jun**: British forces evacuate the Suez Canal Zone (Egy).

- **28 Jun**: The biggest anti-Communist uprising since 1953 takes place when workers in Poland riot at an industrial fair in Poznań, calling for bread and freedom. Over 100 are killed. (›19 Oct)

- **19 Jul**: The USA and UK announce that they cannot participate in financing the Aswan High Dam project because of Egyptian connections with the USSR. On 26 Jul president Nasser seizes the Suez Canal under a nationalization decree, intending to use Canal revenues to build the dam.

- **1–2 Aug**: Britain, France and the USA hold talks in London on Suez while British and French forces are deployed in the area, raising the expectation of war.

- **19 Sep**: Second London conference on Suez meets and establishes Canal Users' Association. On 23 Sep Britain and France refer the Suez dispute to the UN Security Council. (›24 Oct)

- **Sep**: President Anastasio Somoza of Nicaragua is assassinated and succeeded by his son, Luis.

- **19–21 Oct**: Wladyslaw Gomulka, recently released from prison, is elected premier in the face of Kremlin disapproval (Pol). (›18 Nov)

- **23 Oct**: Hungarian uprising: a surge of nationalist feeling and an uprising by students demanding freedom coincides with unrest resulting from a poor harvest and fuel shortages, leading to a revolt in Budapest against Soviet occupation. (›31 Oct)

- **24 Oct**: It is announced that the armed forces of Egypt, Jordan and Syria will come under the command of the Egyptian minister of defence. Israel is alarmed, and on 29 Oct, after the Egyptians blockade the Israeli port of Eilat, Israel invades Egypt's Sinai peninsula.

- **30 Oct**: Egypt rejects the ultimatum issued by the UK and France for a ceasefire and partial withdrawal. The UK and France bomb Egyptian airfields and land forces on 5–6 Nov. This action is condemned by the UN and by the USA, and also by public opinion in both countries. (›7 Nov)

- **31 Oct**: In Hungary, the Russians appoint a new premier and First Secretary, Imre Nagy and János Kadar. Nagy announces that Hungary will leave the Warsaw Pact and seek neutral status.

- **4 Nov**: The USSR sends in tanks to shell Budapest and crush the rebellion. Nagy and other prominent figures are later executed, and several hundred thousand refugees flee to the West (Hung).

- **6 Nov**: In the US presidential election, Dwight D. Eisenhower, Republican, is reelected by 457 votes to 74, but the Democrats win a majority in both houses.

- **7 Nov**: The UN demands a ceasefire in the Middle East, which is accepted by the UK, France, Egypt and Israel, but the Canal is now blocked by sunken ships and destroyed bridges. (›5 Dec)

- **12 Nov**: The Sudan, Morocco and Tunisia are elected to UN membership.

- **18 Nov**: Gomulka signs an agreement with the USSR which confers a greater measure of economic and political freedom, but Russian troops stay in Poland.

- **2 Dec**: Fidel Castro lands on Cuba with a band of 82 exiles in an attempt to raise a revolt against Fulgencio Batista's regime. Most of his group are captured or killed, but Castro begins a campaign of guerrilla action.

- **5 Dec**: Following the arrival of the UN emergency forces in Egypt in mid-November, Anglo-French forces begin to withdraw. The last troops leave by 22 Dec. On 29 Dec UN salvage crews begin clearing the Suez Canal of debris, but the Canal does not reopen to maritime traffic until 7 Mar 1957.

- **18 Dec**: Japan is admitted to the UN.

SOCIETY

• **16 Jan**: Egypt makes Islam the state religion.

• **29 Feb**: A US federal court rules that the University of Alabama must admit Autherine Lucy, their first Negro student, who has been suspended after campus riots; on 1 Mar, in defiance of the ruling, the university permanently expels Miss Lucy. On 5 Mar the US Supreme Court rules that segregation is illegal in tax-supported colleges as well as public (state-run) schools.

• **Apr**: The US Supreme Court rules that racial segregation in public transportation is unconstitutional. Black leader Martin Luther King says that bus boycotting will continue in Alabama until Negro bus drivers are employed for predominantly Negro routes.

• **Apr**: World heavyweight boxing champion Rocky Marciano retires, having won all 49 bouts of his career (USA).

• **11 May**: The European Coal and Steel Community adopts resolutions on a European common market and an organization for the regulation of atomic power (Euratom).

• **May**: The second five-year economic plan is inaugurated in India. Far-reaching nationalization of industry is agreed.

• **Jul**: The OEEC agrees on a 90 percent liberalization of trade amongst its members.

• **16 Aug**: Protesters march from Aldermaston, the site of an atomic weapons research establishment, to London in protest against nuclear arms and the dangers of radiation (UK).

• **Sep**: Premier Zhou Enlai announces a plan to increase national income by 50 percent as part of the second five-year plan (Chi).

• **22 Nov**: The Summer Olympics open in Melbourne (Aus). The USSR wins more medals than any other nation.

• **29 Nov**: Gasoline rationing is introduced in France as a result of the Suez crisis; the UK follows on 17 Dec.

• The first commercial nuclear reactor in the UK is built at Calder Hall.

• West Germany becomes integrated into the world capital market.

• Automated banking begins at the Bank of America, where a computer is set up to handle 32,000 accounts.

• St Thomas's Hospital, London, becomes the first in the world to institute a system of radio paging for doctors (UK).

• Wilkinson Sword begin to market long-life stainless steel razor blades (UK).

• The first mass trial of birth control pills, directed by John Rock and Gregory Pincus, takes place in Puerto Rico.

• Prince Rainier of Monaco marries film star Grace Kelly.

CULTURE

• **15 Mar**: *My Fair Lady* opens on Broadway (USA).

• **24 May**: The Eurovision Song Contest is first televised.

• **29 Jun**: Playwright Arthur Miller marries Marilyn Monroe (USA).

• The London premiere of John Osborne's play *Look Back in Anger* marks the beginning of what becomes known as "Kitchen Sink Drama", shifting the emphasis from middle-class drawing-room comedies to the realities of ordinary life (UK).

• Eugene O'Neill's play *Long Day's Journey into Night*, written in 1940–41, is first seen on stage (USA).

• Brendan Behan's play *The Quare Fellow* opens in London at the Theater Workshop in Stratford East, directed by Joan Littlewood (UK).

• Jean Genet: *The Balcony*, play (Fr).

• Jean Anouilh: *Pauvre Bitos*, play based on the life of Robespierre (Fr).

• Friedrich Dürrenmatt: *The Visit*, black comedy (Swi).

• Albert Camus: *La Chute* (The Fall), appears in French; trans. into English 1957 (Fr).

• Allen Ginsberg's long experimental poem *Howl*, described as an elegy for the American Dream, typifies the American Beat generation.

• Yukio Mishima: *The Temple of the Golden Pavilion*, novel (Jap).

• James Baldwin: *Giovanni's Room*, novel (USA).

• John Berryman: *Homage to Mistress Bradstreet*, autobiographical poem (USA).

• Vladimir Dudintsev: *Not by Bread Alone*, novel (USSR).

• Colin Wilson's *The Outsider*, an existentialist work, enjoys a considerable success (UK).

• Olivier Messiaen: *Oiseaux exotiques*, for piano, wind and percussion (Fr).

• William Walton: Cello Concerto (It).

• Hans Werner Henze: *Song-cycle Expression K* (Kafka) (It).

• Igor Stravinsky: *Canticum sacrum ad honorem Sancti Marci nominis* (USA).

• Frank Martin: *The Tempest*, opera completed in 1955, is first performed in Vienna.

• Karlheinz Stockhausen: *Klavierstuck XI* (FRG).

• Malcolm Arnold: *Birthday Offering*, ballet, choreography by Frederick Ashton (UK).

• Humphrey Searle: *Noctambules*, ballet (UK).

• The Bolshoi Ballet visits London; Galina Ulanova is the star attraction.

• Lonnie Donegan's skiffle single "Rock Island Line" is an instant hit (UK).

• "Heartbreak Hotel" tops the charts and Elvis Presley emerges as a teen idol (USA).

• Barbara Hepworth: *Orpheus*, sculpture (UK).

• Lynn Chadwick: *Teddy Boy and Girl*, sculpture (UK). This year Chadwick wins the International Prize at the Venice Biennale, where a retrospective exhibition of his work is shown.

• Philip Guston: *The Clock*, painting (USA).

• Georges Braque: *Studio IX*, painting (Fr).

• Richard Hamilton's collage *Just What is it makes Today's Homes so Different, so Appealing?*, often regarded as the first recognizable Pop Art object, is exhibited at the Whitechapel Gallery in London in a show called "This Is Tomorrow" (UK).

• Construction begins on Brazil's new capital, Brasilia, on barren ground in east central Brazil. It becomes one of the world's major examples of large-scale city planning.

• Jørn Utzon's Opera House is begun in Sydney, Australia. Its construction poses many problems, and it does not open until 1973.

• Buckminster Fuller: Auditorium, Honolulu.

• Pier Luigi Nervi and Annibale Vitelozzi: Palazzo dello Sport, Rome.

• Michael Todd produces *Around the World in Eighty Days*, film based on the story by Jules Verne, directed by Michael Anderson and starring David Niven; it wins a clutch of Academy Awards and breaks box office records (USA).

• Cecil B. De Mille: *The Ten Commandments*, starring Charlton Heston (USA).

• The musical film *High Society* is directed by Charles Walters and stars Bing Crosby, Grace Kelly and Frank Sinatra (USA).

• Walter Lang directs *The King and I*, starring Yul Brynner and Deborah Kerr (USA).

• Ingmar Bergman: *The Seventh Seal* (Swe).

• Tennessee Williams writes the script for Elia Kazan's *Baby Doll* (USA).

• Kon Ichikawa: *The Burmese Harp* (Jap).

• Robert Bresson: *Un Condamne' mort s'est echappé*, film.

• *And God Created Woman*, directed by Roger Vadim, introduces Brigitte Bardot (Fr).

• The Design Centre opens in London, and the Associazione per il Disegno Industriale is founded in Milan. Belgium launches its Signe d'Or design awards.

• Couturier Cristobal Balenciaga creates his loose chemise dress, the "Sac".

• Nobel Prize for Literature is won by Juan Jiménez (Sp).

SCIENCE

• **17 Mar**: Physicist Irène Joliot-Curie, daughter of Pierre and Marie Curie, dies in Paris of leukemia, probably caused by working with radioactive materials.

• **25 Sep**: The first transatlantic telephone cable comes into use.

• FORTRAN, the first computer programming language, is developed (USA).

• The Bell Telephone Co develops a "visual telephone" capable of transmitting pictures simultaneously with sound (USA).

• Jacques Cousteau takes photographs of the ocean down to depths of 7.25km (4.5 miles). These are obtained from his research ship *Calypso*, which is anchored over the 7,772m (25,500ft) deep Romanche trench in the Atlantic.

• M. Shiner perfects a biopsy capsule to collect tissue from the intestine as an aid to diagnosis of intestinal disease (UK).

• US physicians pioneer hemodialysis – cleansing the blood on an artificial kidney machine.

• A. Kornberg isolates an enzyme, from the bacterium *Escherichia Coli*, capable of catalyzing the formation of DNA from nucleotides (USA).

• Romanian physiologist George Palade discovers that ribosomes are mostly ribonucleic acid (RNA) (USA).

• B. Cook, O. Piccioni, G.R. Lambertson and W.A. Wentzel discover the antineutron (USA).

• Choh Hao Li and colleagues isolate the human growth hormone.

• H. Friedman announces that solar flares are a source of X-rays (USA).

• John McCarthy develops Lisp ("List Processor"), the computer language of artificial intelligence (USA).

• B.C. Heezen (USA) and M. Ewing (USA) discover the Mid-Oceanic Ridge.

• E.W. Mueller develops the field ion microscope, the first instrument to picture individual atoms (USA).

• Alexander Poniatoff demonstrates the Ampex video tape-recorder in Chicago and introduces the video era.

• Cyril Hinshelwood (UK) and Nikolay Semenov win the Nobel Prize for Chemistry for their research into the mechanics of chemical reactions.

• Nobel Prize for Physiology or Medicine is won by André Cournand (Fr), Werner Forssmann (Ger) and Dickinson Richards (USA), for their discoveries concerning heart catheterization and pathological changes in the circulatory system.

• John Bardeen (USA), Walter Brattain (USA) and William Shockley (USA) win the Nobel Prize for Physics for their research on semi-conductors and the discovery of the transistor effect.

Probably the best-known creature of 1957 was a dog, Laika, which, a month after the Soviet Union had launched the first artificial satellite, was rocketed out of the atmosphere in "Sputnik II", demonstrating that space flight held no hidden threats to human life. Sudden fame, or notoriety, was also acquired by the town of Little Rock, Arkansas, where troops with fixed bayonets enforced a federal court order requiring desegregation of an all-white high school. There was no segregation at Wimbledon, where Althea Gibson became the first black ladies' champion, though there was in a restaurant in Delaware, where a Ghanaian government minister was refused service. Ghana itself, under the charismatic leadership of Kwame Nkrumah, became the first of the black African colonies of Britain to gain total independence. Britain, although shedding its empire, was not yet prepared to join the new European Economic Community.

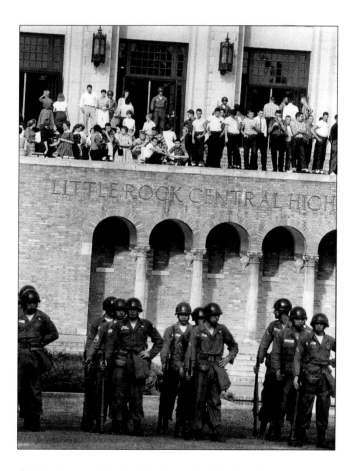

▲ Federal troops outside the Little Rock Central High School in Arkansas enforce desegregation.

- **10 Jan**: Harold Macmillan is appointed prime minister following the resignation of Anthony Eden (UK).

- **19 Jan**: Jordan is promised an economic subsidy by the Arab League to replace Britain's financial support, whereupon the Anglo-Jordanian treaty of 1948 is terminated (13 Mar).

- **30 Jan**: The UN General Assembly calls on South Africa to reconsider its apartheid policies.

- **31 Jan**: After a year of terrorist activities by the ALN (Armée de Libération Nationale) in pursuit of Algerian independence, the French send in the military. Their use of systematic torture turns French and world public opinion against French colonial policy.

- **4 Feb**: Luis Somoza is elected to his own term of office as president of Nicaragua.

- **15 Feb**: Andrey Gromyko, regarded as a hardliner toward the West, is appointed foreign minister (USSR).

- **5 Mar**: President Nasser of Egypt announces that he will deny Israel use of the Suez Canal; Saudi Arabia makes a similar declaration regarding the Gulf of Aqaba.

- **6 Mar**: Ghana, made up of the former British colonies of the Gold Coast and Togoland (W Afr), becomes an independent nation under Dr Kwame Nkrumah.

- **6 Mar**: Israeli forces complete withdrawal from Egyptian territory, and UN forces take over.

- **8 Mar**: The USA promises military aid to Saudi Arabia in exchange for use of the air base at Dhahran.

- **9 Mar**: Congress approves president Eisenhower's doctrine by which US forces will use military force to resist Communist aggression in the Middle East. (›3 Jun)

- **14 Mar**: In Cyprus, EOKA offers to suspend terrorist activities if Archbishop Makarios (held in exile by the British since 9 Mar 1955) is released. On 28 Mar he is released but is forbidden to return to Cyprus.

- **20 Mar**: Eisenhower and Macmillan meet at the Bermuda Conference to re-establish the "special relationship" between the USA and UK, which has been damaged by the Suez crisis.

- **25 Mar**: Representatives from "the Six" – France, West Germany, Italy, Belgium, the Netherlands and Luxembourg – sign the Treaty of Rome to bring the European Economic Community into existence.

- **14 Apr**: Pro-Egyptian elements in the Jordanian army rebel but the rebellion is put down by King Hussein, supported by the USA.

- **15 May**: Despite Russian appeals to the USA and UK to cease nuclear tests, the UK explodes its first hydrogen bomb in the Christmas Islands in the Central Pacific. Further tests are carried out on 31 May and 19 Jun and from 14 Sep–9 Oct in Australia.

- **3 Jun**: The USA joins the Baghdad Pact and affirms its determination to aid member nations in the fight against Communist aggression.

- **10 Jun**: The Liberal party loses to the Conservatives for the first time in 22 years. John Diefenbaker becomes prime minister on 17 Jun (Can).

- **4 Jul**: In a major shakeup of the Soviet leadership, Nikita Krushchev has three members of the Central Committee of the Soviet Communist Party expelled – Malenkov, Molotov and Kaganovich – and foils a challenge to his leadership supremacy (USSR). (›26 Oct)

- **29 Jul**: The Western powers and West Germany issue a declaration on German reunification and call for free elections.

- **26 Aug**: The USSR announces the successful testing of an intercontinental ballistic missile.

- **30 Aug**: The All African Federal Executive Council is formed in Nigeria.

- **31 Aug**: Malaya gains its independence after 170 years of British rule and becomes a member of the Commonwealth under Sir Tengku Abdul Rahman.

- **5 Sep**: Fidel Castro leads an uprising in Cuba, in which members of the Cuban army take part. However, Cuban dictator Fulgencio Batista's forces crush the revolt. On 29 Oct Batista suspends the constitution.

- **15 Sep**: In West German national elections, the Christian Democratic Union (CDU) led by Konrad Adenauer sweeps to victory.

- **21 Sep**: On the death of King Haakon of Norway, Olaf V succeeds to the throne.

- **22 Sep**: The military junta which has ruled Haiti for the last three months, elects François Duvalier ("Papa Doc") as president.

- **10 Oct**: After Syria and Turkey clash over border disagreements, president Nasser tells the UN that Egypt will not permit a violation of Syria's integrity and sends troops to Syria. On 16 Oct the USA threatens military action if Turkey is attacked. The Arab League affirms its support of Syria on 31 Oct, and the crisis gradually settles.

- **26 Oct**: Marshal Georgiy Zhukov, prominent military hero, is relieved of his duties as minister of defense, allegedly for promoting his own "cult of personality" (USSR).

- **16–19 Dec**: NATO heads of government reach an agreement on the establishment of a NATO nuclear missile force in Europe that is to remain under the putative control of the USA.

- **26 Dec**: The Afro-Asian Peoples Solidarity Conference, attended by delegates from 40 states, adopts resolutions backing Soviet appeals for peaceful coexistence and attacks the Eisenhower doctrine.

SOCIETY

- **15 Jan**: Egypt nationalizes French and British banks.

- **31 Jan**: The trans-Iranian pipeline from Abadan to Tehran is completed.

- **18 Feb**: A US grand jury indicts playwright Arthur Miller for contempt in HUAC (House Un-American Activities Committee) inquiry.

- **27 Mar**: France forms a company to exploit the mineral resources of the Sahara.

- **12 Apr**: West German nuclear physicists refuse to cooperate in the production or testing of nuclear weapons.

- **22 Apr**: US Army Air Defense Command announces that New York and other large US cities will soon be defended by missiles with atomic warheads.

- **23 Apr**: Albert Schweitzer (who won the Nobel Peace Prize in 1952) writes to the Norwegian Nobel Commmittee urging mobilization of world opinion against nuclear tests.

- **7 May**: Khrushchev announces a plan to decentralize the Soviet economy.

- **6 Jul**: Althea Gibson of the USA becomes the first black player to win a Wimbledon tennis title.

- **20 Jul**: Prime minister Harold Macmillan tells the British people that most of them "have never had it so good".

- **4 Sep**: In Little Rock, Arkansas, Governor Orval Faubus orders state national guardsmen to bar nine black students from the all-white high school. After a federal court order the students enter the school on 23 Sep and on the following day president Eisenhower orders federal troops to enforce desegregation in the town.

- **4 Sep**: The Wolfenden Report on homosexual offenses and prostitution recommends that homosexual acts between consenting adults should no longer be a criminal offense (UK).

- **4 Sep**: Egypt and Syria form an economic union.

- **10 Oct**: Ghana's finance minister, Komla Agbeli Gbdemah, is refused service in a Delaware restaurant and receives a personal apology from president Eisenhower (USA).

- **5 Nov**: Prime minister Macmillan announces that he will introduce legislation permitting women to sit and vote in the House of Lords (UK).

- **Dec**: The first nuclear power plant in East Germany begins operation near Dresden.

- **Dec**: The French government institutes control of prices and wages to counter inflation.

- The HMCS *Labrador* discovers a new northwest passage across the far reaches of Arctic Canada.

- Nobel Peace Prize is won by Lester Pearson (Can) for his role in resolving the Suez crisis.

CULTURE

- **26 Jan**: Francis Poulenc's opera *Dialogues des Carmélites* has its premiere at La Scala, Milan (It), followed in the same year by performances in Paris, Cologne and San Francisco.

- **11 Apr**: John Osborne's play *The Entertainer*, starring Laurence Olivier as the third-rate music hall comic Archie Rice, opens at the Royal Court Theatre in London.

- **4 May**: First prime time rock music TV network special (USA).

- Albert Camus (Fr) wins the Nobel Prize for Literature.

- Jack Kerouac: *On the Road*, semi-autobiographical novel by the man who coined the expression "the Beat generation" (USA).

- Max Frisch: *Homo Faber*, novel (Swi).

- Patrick White: *Voss*, novel (Aus).

- Vladimir Nabokov: *Pnin*, novel (USA).

- John Braine: *Room at the Top*, novel which later became a successful film (UK).

- Iris Murdoch: *The Sandcastle*, novel (UK).

- Ted Hughes: *The Hawk in the Rain*, first collection of poems (UK).

- Samuel Beckett's play *Fin de partie* (Endgame) is produced in French at the Royal Court Theatre in London; it appears in English the following year.

- Harold Pinter: *The Dumb Waiter*, play (UK).

- Lawrence Durrell: *Justine*, the first novel of the Alexandria Quartet (followed by *Balthazar* and *Mountolive* in 1958 and *Clea* in 1960) (UK).

- V.S. Naipaul: *The Mystic Masseur*, his first novel (UK).

- Leonard Bernstein: *West Side Story*, musical (USA).

- Carlos Chávez: *The Visitors*, opera with libretto by Chester Kallman (Mex).

- Malcolm Arnold: Third Symphony (UK).

- Elliott Carter: *Variations for Orchestra* (USA).

- Jean Françaix: *King Midas*, opera (Fr).

- John Gardner's opera *The Moon and Sixpence* opens at Sadler's Wells Theatre, London.

- Paul Hindemith: *Die Harmonie der Welt* (The Harmony of the World), opera (Swi).

- Igor Stravinsky: *Agon*, ballet (USA).

- Benjamin Britten: *The Prince of the Pagodas*, ballet (UK).

- Samuel Barber: *Vanessa*, opera with libretto by Gian Carlo Menotti (USA).

- Dmitri Shostakovich: Eleventh Symphony; Second Piano Concerto (USSR).

- Buddy Holly and the Crickets release their first single: "That'll be the Day" (USA).

- Bill Haley and the Comets make their first visit to Britain, to a rapturous welcome.

- The first stereo disks are marketed in the USA.

- Francis Bacon: *Screaming Nurse*, painting (UK).

- Graham Sutherland: *Princess Gourielli*, painting (Fr).

- William Baziotes: *White Bird*, painting (USA).

- Victor Vasarely: *Vega*, painting (Fr).

- Mark Rothko: *Violet Bar*, painting (USA).

- Jacob Epstein: *Christ in Majesty*, sculpture for Llandaff Cathedral, Wales (UK).

- H.G. Adam: *Phare des morts* (Beacon of the Dead), a monument for Auschwitz (Fr).

- The first Design Centre award scheme is launched in the UK.

- Japan's Good Design awards, the G-Mark, are established.

- Furniture designer Eero Saarinen (Fin/USA) creates his elegant plastic and aluminum "tulip chair".

- The Lotus Elite is shown by its designer, Colin Chapman. The new sports car is unique in having a glass-fibre body and in being available in kit form to be built by amateurs (UK).

- Ingmar Bergman: *Wild Strawberries* (Swe).

- Charlie Chaplin: *A King in New York* (USA).

- Mikhail Kalatozov: *The Cranes are Flying*.

- David Lean's film: *The Bridge on the River Kwai*, starring Alec Guinness, wins eight Academy Awards (UK).

- *The Three Faces of Eve* stars Joanne Woodward, directed by Nunnally Johnson (USA).

- Laurence Olivier acts in and directs the film *The Prince and the Showgirl*, costarring Marilyn Monroe (USA).

- Elvis Presley stars in *Jailhouse Rock* (USA).

- Otto Preminger films Françoise Sagan's novel *Bonjour Tristesse* (1954) (USA).

- Fashion designer John Stephen opens his first menswear shop in London's Carnaby Street.

SCIENCE

- **Feb**: Researchers in Cambridge, Massachusetts, report a new cryotron device to revolutionize computers – so small that 100 would fit in a thimble (USA).

- **1 Jul**: International Geophysical Year begins with scientists concentrating on Antarctic exploration, oceanographic and meteorological research and the launching of satellites into space.

- The first European particle accelerator opens in Geneva (Swi).

- Giberellin, a growth-producing hormone, is isolated.

- Alick Isaacs and Jean Lindenmann discover interferons, natural substances produced by the body that fight viruses (UK).

- A lightweight, high-speed dental drill is developed (USA).

- Albert B. Sabin of the Children's Hospital in Cincinnati produces a safe, live polio vaccine (USA).

- Czech chemist Frank Berger discovers the tranquilizer meprobamate (USA).

- Gordon Gould (USA) has the idea that will eventually translate into the laser, but he does not apply for a patent until 1959 and, because others have by then also started work on lasers, his patent is not accepted until after 1986.

- After workers manufacturing the herbicide 2,4,5-T develop skin disease, it is recognized that dioxin frequently contaminates such herbicides (FRG).

- Element number 102 is discovered and named nobelium (Swe).

- The accidental overheating of a type of glass, Fotoform, leads to the discovery of ovenproof pyro-ceram domestic cooking ware.

- Eric Linklater's novel *Private Angelo* is the first book to be entirely phototypeset – a revolution in printing technology after 400 years of typesetting from metal type (UK).

- G.E. Hutchinson defines the ecological niche as a region occurring in both space and the behavior of the organism concerned (USA).

- **4 Oct**: The USSR launches *Sputnik I*, the first man-made satellite. On 3 Nov *Sputnik II* is launched with a dog, Laika, on board, and instruments monitor her body's reactions.

- Daniel Povet (Swiss) wins the Nobel Prize for Physiology or Medicine for his work on synthetic compounds which inhibit the action of certain body substances.

- Alexander Todd (UK) wins the Nobel Prize for Chemistry for his work on nucleotides and nucleotide coenzymes.

- Nobel Prize for Physics is won by Tsung Dao Lee (Chi) and Chen Ning Yang (Chi) for their investigation of the so-called parity laws which led to discoveries regarding the elementary particles.

Throughout the world, colonial empires were crumbling. By the end of the year, most of the countries of French West and Equatorial Africa had become independent republics, though they retained close links with France. Algeria was a different matter; even the return, first as premier and then as president, of wartime hero Charles de Gaulle made no difference to the savage conflict that threatened to erupt into fullscale civil war in France itself. Elsewhere the Cold War continued to divide the nations of the world by their adherence to West or East. In Cuba, Fidel Castro finally overthrew the Batista regime, introducing Communism to the Americas. After the Suez crisis, Col. Nasser moved Egypt into the Soviet Camp, while the assassination of King Faisal brought an anti-Western regime to power in Iraq, which promptly aligned itself with Egypt. The United States meanwhile forged ahead in the space race, establishing NASA to assume direction of its burgeoning space research program.

▲ **No draft-dodging for the King of Rock and Roll – Elvis Presley answered his call-up papers, joining the US Army despite the hysterical protests of his millions of teenage fans.**

● **3 Jan**: The West Indian Federation (Barbados, Jamaica, Trinidad, the Leeward Islands less the Virgin Islands, and the Windward Islands), comes into being.

● **13 Jan**: 9,000 scientists from 43 countries present a petition to the UN urging an immediate international agreement to halt tests of nuclear bombs.

● **20 Jan**: The USSR warns Baghdad Pact nations against any attempt to introduce nuclear weapons and missile bases into their territories.

● **1 Feb**: Egypt and Syria declare an alliance, the United Arab Republic (UAR). On 8 Mar they are joined by Yemen, but meanwhile on 14 Feb Jordan and Iraq counter by merging as the Arab Union.

● **8 Feb**: In reprisal for alleged destruction of a French aircraft, the French bomb a Tunisian village on the Algerian border. The Tunisians blockade French military bases and demand the withdrawal of all 15,000 French troops based in the country.

● **22 Feb**: Following a vote by the constituent assembly to restore the 1853 constitution, Arturo Frondizi is elected president of Argentina – the first president to be elected in 12 years.

● **27 Mar**: Nikita Khrushchev succeeds Nikolai Bulganin as premier while retaining the position of First Secretary of the Communist party, thereby taking full control of the USSR in the first return to one-man rule since Stalin's death in 1953.

● **5 Apr**: Fidel Castro proclaims "total war" against the Batista regime in Cuba. (› Dec)

● **14 Apr**: Premier Gomulka announces that Polish workers' councils must give way to larger groups more susceptible to Communist party control. Strikes become illegal (Pol).

● **1 May**: On a visit to Moscow, president Nasser of Egypt signs an agreement committing Egypt to support of Soviet foreign policy, while the USSR agrees to promote liberation of all Asian and African peoples.

● **19 May**: The joint North American Air Defense Command (NORAD) is formed with headquarters at Colorado Springs (Can/USA).

● **1 Jun**: After gaining the military advantage in Algeria, the French generals suspect that the government will negotiate with the rebel FLN ("National Liberation Front") and accordingly seize power. With France on the verge of civil war over Algeria, the National Assembly approves the recall of Charles de Gaulle as premier of a "government of national safety" with power to revise the constitution (Aug).

● **14 Jul**: King Faisal of Iraq, his heir and premier Nuri-es-Said are assassinated. Brig. Gen. Abdul Karim el-Kassem becomes premier of the new government which aligns itself with Egypt's anti-Western, pan-Arab policies.

● **15 Jul**: South Africa resumes full membership of the UN.

● **31 Jul**: "Papa Doc" Duvalier defeats an attempted coup and the Haitian Congress grant his request to rule by decree for six months, making him a virtual dictator.

● **23 Aug**: Communist China begins a bombardment of the contested Quemoy and Little Quemoy Islands in the Taiwan Straits. On 27 Aug the USA dispatches an aircraft carrier and four destroyers to help defend the islands, and on 7 Sep the US fleet escorts a convoy of Nationalist Chinese ships carrying arms to Quemoy. (›17 Oct)

● **Aug**: During a tour of French Africa, de Gaulle announces that France will not stand in the way of colonies striving for independence.

● **28 Sep**: The French people approve a constitution for the Fifth Republic by referendum. The constitution, which gives the president extended powers, is approved and de Gaulle is elected president on 21 Dec with 78 percent of the popular vote. (›Oct)

● **2 Oct**: Following a popular referendum, Guinea becomes the only French African colony to decline de Gaulle's invitation to become a member of the French community. It becomes an independent republic with Sekou Touré as president.

● **7 Oct**: President Mirza proclaims martial law in Pakistan. On 24 Oct Ayub Khan forms a cabinet.

● **17 Oct**: Chinese Nationalist leader Jiang Jieshi asserts his determination to keep the Quemoy islands, and on 20 Oct the Communists recommence shelling; but the action dwindles over the next few months.

● **Oct**: De Gaulle announces a five-year plan for the industrialization of Algeria and promises additional military support. The FLN responds by forming the Provisional Government of the Republic of Algeria (GPRA) and appealing to the Communist world for support. The terrorist campaign is extended into mainland France.

● **23 Nov**: Ghana and Guinea announce that they will form the nucleus of a union of West African states.

● **27 Nov**: The USSR demands the creation of West Berlin as a demilitarized free city, but on 16 Dec the NATO council rejects the proposals.

● **28 Nov**: Mali, Mauritania, Senegal, Chad, Gabon and Congo-Brazzaville proclaim themselves republics. In Dec Central Africa, Niger, the Upper Volta, the Ivory Coast and Dahomey proclaim themselves republics.

● **Dec**: After six months of advance by Castro's guerrilla forces, Cuban dictator Batista rallies his forces for a last stand. In a series of actions, Castro's forces are victorious and Batista flees the country.

● **Dec**: Romulo Betancourt is elected president of Venezuela.

SOCIETY

- **3 Jan**: Edmund Hillary reaches the South Pole with a New Zealand expedition, beating a rival British group led by Vivian Fuchs by 17 days.

- **Jan**: The first commercial nuclear power plant in the USA comes into use.

- **3 Feb**: Belgium, the Netherlands and Luxembourg establish the Benelux Economic Union. This provides for free movement of persons, goods, services and capital.

- **6 Feb**: Many of the highly successful Manchester United football team – the "Busby Babes" – are killed in an air crash in Belgrade (Yug).

- **17 Feb**: The Campaign for Nuclear Disarmament (CND) is formed.

- **16 Apr**: The Brussels World Fair opens in Belgium.

- **21–23 May**: Comecon agrees upon increased economic cooperation. Communist China, North Korea, North Vietnam and Mongolia agree to integrate their economies with Comecon.

- **20 Jun**: Indonesia bans operations of the Royal Dutch Shell Oil group. On 3 Dec Dutch businesses in Indonesia are nationalized.

- **Jun**: Brazilian soccer player Pelé becomes a star after his team win the World Cup for the first time.

- **14 Aug**: Britain, France and other NATO countries announce relaxation for trade with the Soviet bloc and Communist China.

- **23 Aug**: Racial tensions erupt in violence when hundreds of black and white youths battle in Nottingham. Further race riots erupt on 31 Aug during the Notting Hill Carnival (UK).

- **27 Aug**: Establishment of the US National Aeronautics and Space Administration (NASA), which assumes the direction of US space exploration.

- **4 Oct**: BOAC begins a New York–London service. On 26 Oct Pan-American World Airways begin a regular transatlantic jet airliner service.

- **9 Oct**: Pope Pius XII dies and is succeeded by Cardinal Angelo Giuseppe Roncalli, who is elected on 28 Oct, taking the name Pope John XXIII.

- **23 Oct**: The USSR offers to lend Egypt $100 million toward the construction of the Aswan High Dam on the River Nile.

- **27 Dec**: The European Monetary Agreement is enforced; 11 European countries declare their currencies as freely convertible.

- Beginning of the Great Leap Forward (until 1960), a period of radical change in China intended to accelerate modernization, but which proves economically disastrous.

- Nobel Peace Prize is won by George Pire (Bel).

CULTURE

- **24 Mar**: Elvis Presley enters the army for two years' national service.

- **18 Jun**: The first performance of Benjamin Britten's opera *Noye's Fludde*, based on the Chester mystery play, is given at the Aldeburgh Festival (UK).

- T.S. Eliot: *The Elder Statesman*, play (UK).

- Brendan Behan: *The Hostage*, play (Ire).

- Peter Shaffer: *Five Finger Exercise*, play (UK).

- Arnold Wesker: *Chicken Soup with Barley*, play (UK).

- Harold Pinter: *The Birthday Party*, play (UK).

- Jean Genet: *The Blacks*, play (Fr).

- Max Frisch: *The Fire-Raisers*, play (Swi).

- Samuel Beckett: *Malone Dies*, novel (first published in French, *Malone meurt*, in 1951, and translated into English by the author).

- Elaine Dundy: *The Dud Avocado*, autobiography (USA).

- Graham Greene: *Our Man in Havana*, novel (UK).

- T.H. White: *The Once and Future King*, stories based on the Arthurian legend (UK).

- Boris Pasternak: *Dr Zhivago*, novel, first published in translation in Italy since the Soviet authorities refused to allow its publication in the USSR.

- Alan Sillitoe: *Saturday Night and Sunday Morning*, novel (UK).

- Truman Capote: *Breakfast at Tiffany's*, novel (USA).

- Giuseppe di Lampedusa: *The Leopard*, novel (It).

- Carlos Fuente: *Where the Air is Clear* ("La región más transparente"), novel (Mex).

- John Betjeman: *Collected Poems* (UK).

- Chinua Achebe: *Things Fall Apart*, first novel of four that reflect the current changes in Africa (Nig).

- Nobel Prize for Literature is won by Boris Pasternak (USSR).

- Ralph Vaughan Williams: Symphony No. 9 in E minor (UK).

- Van Cliburn (USA) wins the Tchaikovsky pianoforte competition in Moscow.

- Luciano Berio: *Thema (Omaggio a Joyce)*, electronic work (It).

- Jeunesses Musicales meet in Brussels (Bel).

- Witold Lutostawski: *Funeral Music*, for strings, in memory of Béla Bartók (Pol).

- Igor Stravinsky: *Threni* (USA).

- Olivier Messiaen: *Catalogue d'oiseaux* (Fr).

- Martha Graham: *Clytemnestra*, ballet (USA)

- Hans Werner Henze: *Ondine*, ballet choreographed by Frederick Ashton (It).

- Edgard Varèse: *Poème électronique* (Fr).

- John Cage: *Concert for Piano and Orchestra* (USA).

- Cliff Richard releases "Move It".

- The "Beatnik" movement, originating among young poets of California, spreads to Europe. The distinctive look of the Beat generation is epitomized by the black outfits and long hair of folksinger Juliette Greco.

- Phil Spector makes his first public performance, as part of a group called the Teddy Bears.

- Connie Francis becomes an overnight star with "Who's Sorry Now".

- Max Ernst: *Après moi le sommeil*, painting (Fr).

- Sidney Nolan: *Gallipoli*, painting (Aus).

- Karel Appel: *Women and Birds*, painting (Fr).

- Alexander Calder: *Monumental Mobile* and *The Dog* (stabile) (USA).

- Henry Moore: *Reclining Figure* for the UNESCO building, Paris.

- Barbara Hepworth: *Sea Form (Porthmeor)*, bronze (UK).

- Seagram Building, New York, designed by Ludwig Mies van der Rohe and Philip Johnson.

- Oscar Niemeyer: The President's Palace, Brasilia (Bra).

- Pier Luigi Nervi and Gio Ponti: Pirelli Building, Milan (It).

- Eero Saarinen: Yale Hockey Rink at Yale University (USA).

- Mathias Goeritz: Square of the Five Towers, Satellite City, Mexico City.

- Andrej Wajda: *Ashes and Diamonds*, last film in his World War II trilogy (Pol).

- Jacques Tati: *Mon Oncle*, film (Fr).

- Alfred Hitchcock: *Vertigo*, film (UK).

- Luis Bunuel: *Nazarin*, film (Sp).

- Claude Chabrol: *Le Beau Serge*, film (Fr).

- The film of Tennessee Williams's play *Cat on a Hot Tin Roof*, directed by Richard Brooks, stars Elizabeth Taylor.

- *Gigi*, directed by Vincente Minnelli, stars Leslie Caron and Maurice Chevalier (USA).

- Fred Zinneman's *The Nun's Story* stars Peter Finch and Audrey Hepburn (USA).

SCIENCE

- **31 Jan**: The USA launches the satellite Explorer to study cosmic rays. The *Vanguard* rocket follows on 17 Mar, to test solar cells, and *Atlas* is launched on 18 Dec to investigate radio relay. The data collected by Explorer leads to the discovery of the Van Allen belts – girdles of radiation from solar wind, trapped above the atmosphere by the Earth's magnetic field.

- A link is detected between the drug thalidomide, prescribed for morning sickness, and severe neonatal birth defects.

- The USSR launch the nuclear-powered icebreaker, *Lenin*.

- I. Donald pioneers the use of high-frequency sound waves (ultrasound) to examine unborn fetuses (UK).

- J. Enders prepares an effective vaccine against measles (USA).

- I. Darevsky discovers in Armenia an all-female lizard species that reproduces parthenogenetically (without male fertilization) (USSR).

- J. Dausset discovers the human histocompatibility system (Fr).

- Du Pont markets Lycra, an artificial elastic, the first of a succession of Spandex fibres that are stronger and last longer than rubber (USA).

- The first bifocal contact lenses appear on the market.

- The French design diesel locomotives specially for the new Trans-Europ-Express network, capable of cruising speeds of up to 140 kmh (90 mph).

- Mark Gregoire begins manufacturing nonstick frying pans coated with PTFE (polytetrafluoroethylene) under the brand name of Tefal (Fr).

- President Eisenhower's Christmas message to the nation is broadcast from a rocket circling the earth – a prelude to satellite communications (USA).

- The steady state theory of the universe is formulated by H. Bondi, T. Gold and F. Hoyle (UK).

- Arthur Schawlow and Charles Townes of Bell Laboratories apply for a patent on a laser (USA).

- The submarine USS *Nautilus* makes an undersea passage of the North Pole in a journey lasting 96 hours.

- George Beadle (USA) and Edward Tatum (USA) win the Nobel Prize for Physiology or Medicine "for their discovery that genes act by regulating definite chemical events". They share it with Joshua Lederberg (USA), who is cited for his discoveries regarding the genetic material of bacteria.

- Nobel Prize for Physics is won by Pavel Cherenkov (USSR), Ilya Frank (USSR) and Igor Tamm (USSR) for the discovery of the "Cherenkov effect".

- Frederick Sanger (UK) wins the Nobel Prize for Chemistry for his work on the structure of proteins, especially that of insulin.

1959

The last year of the decade was already looking forward to the coming Sixties, in architecture and design as well as politics and science. Frank Lloyd Wright's astonishing Guggenheim Museum in New York provided a truly modern home for its collection, and Oscar Niemeyer's Square of Three Powers in Brasilia formed a focal point for the newly built capital of Brazil, a symbol of the new technology that people were beginning to sense would shape their future. The United States continued the program of space trips that would culminate in manned flight by sending two monkeys up in a Jupiter rocket, while on Earth the new portable transistorized television set marketed by Sony of Japan equally showed the shape of things to come. Alec Issigonis's Mini broke all the rules to become one of the success stories of the Sixties. There was a new optimism in other areas, too. The Cyprus question was at last resolved, and Archbishop Makarios returned from exile as president of the new republic. In Kenya, the state of emergency was terminated after ten years of Mau Mau terrorism.

▲ Another triumph of new technology – the hovercraft SRN-1 made her maiden flight on 25 July, though there would not be a regular hovercraft service between Britain and France until 1968.

● **1 Jan**: Alaska becomes the 49th state of the USA.

● **2 Jan**: After Cuban dictator Batista flees, Fidel Castro takes control. Dr Manuel Urrutia is proclaimed head of a provisional government with Castro as commander-in-chief of the armed forces. (›2 Feb)

● **8 Jan**: Gen. de Gaulle is inaugurated as president of the Fifth Republic. Michel Debré becomes premier. Under the new constitution, de Gaulle has more power than any French leader since Napoleon III.

● **17 Jan**: The Federal State of Mali is formed by the union of the republics of Senegal and French Sudan.

● **27–28 Jan**: The 21st Congress of the Soviet Communist party ends with an agreement for common opposition to the revisionist movement led by Marshal Tito of Yugoslavia.

● **2 Feb**: Castro becomes premier of Cuba. On 15 Apr he undertakes an unofficial 11-day tour of the USA and Canada, who supported his insurrection.

● **2 Feb**: Mrs Indira Gandhi, only daughter of Indian prime minister Jawaharlal Nehru, is elected president of the ruling Congress party (Ind).

● **19 Feb**: Greece, Turkey and the UK sign an agreement establishing Cyprus as a republic, to come into force on 16 Aug 1960. The UK will retain two military bases on the island. On 1 Mar Archbishop Makarios returns to an ecstatic welcome and in Dec he becomes president.

● **20 Feb**: Political disturbances in Nyasaland (E Afr) lead to the arrest of Dr Hastings Banda and other leaders of the Nyasaland African Congress.

● **28 Feb**: An Anglo-Egyptian agreement is reached on the settlement of claims arising from the Suez crisis.

● **13–27 Mar**: In Tibet, widespread resistance to Chinese rule erupts into a revolt. Chinese forces crush the rebellion and the Dalai Lama flees to India, where he is granted asylum.

● **14 Mar**: De Gaulle refuses to put one-third of France's naval forces under NATO command and so begins French withdrawal from NATO. The USA transfers 200 aircraft from France to UK and West German air bases.

● **24 Mar**: Iraq withdraws from the Baghdad Pact and the Anglo-Iraqi agreement of 1956 lapses. (›30 May)

● **4 Apr–30 May**: The Ivory Coast signs a series of agreements with Niger, Haute Volta and Dahomey to form the Sahel-Benin Union.

● **20 Apr**: The United Federal Party win the Northern Rhodesian elections and the African National Congress is suppressed.

● **11 May–5 Aug**: At the Foreign Ministers' Conference in Geneva, the USA, UK, France and the USSR attempt to agree a plan for German reunification. No agreement is reached and the conference goes into recess.

● **30 May**: Iraq terminates its agreement with the USA, under which it receives military assistance, on the basis that there is a conflict with Iraq's policy of neutrality. (›21 Aug)

● **3 Jun**: Singapore becomes a self-governing state within the Commonwealth. On 5 Jun Lee Kuan Yew becomes the first prime minister.

● **4 Jun**: Jamaica is granted internal self-government within the West Indies Federation.

● **17 Jun**: Eamon de Valera, now 76, resigns as premier and becomes president of Eire.

● **23 Jul**: US vice-president Richard Nixon flies to Moscow to open the American National Exhibition there. The visit becomes a major diplomatic event.

● **Jul**: US troops are sent to Lebanon at the request of the Lebanese government.

● **4 Aug**: Laos declares a state of emergency as Communist-led guerrillas, the Pathet Lao, attack army posts in the north. Backed by the Chinese and North Vietnamese, they are seeking to win back the northern provinces they occupied two years ago. The USA sends economic aid but refuses military aid in the hope that the UN will resolve the problem.

● **21 Aug**: The Baghdad Pact changes its name to Central Treaty Organization (CENTO). At its first meeting, in Oct, the members reaffirm their pledge of mutual defense and economic development. The increasing involvement of Iran with Communism is seen as a threat.

● **21 Aug**: Hawaii becomes the 50th state of the USA.

● **29 Aug**: The Indian parliament discusses a number of recent border incidents in which Chinese troops have crossed into Indian territory. Indian troops are dispatched to the border areas.

● **Aug**: The anti-apartheid Progressive party is set up in South Africa.

● **Sep**: The prime minister of Ceylon, Solomon Bandaranaike, is assassinated by a Buddhist monk.

● **Sep**: Despite a year of military campaigns, which prove effective in dispersing the pro-independence ALN, French president de Gaulle speaks of a policy of self-determination for Algeria. Military leaders and political extremists organize themselves for a coup against the French government.

● **10 Oct**: The state of emergency in Kenya is ended after a period of 10 years.

● **9 Dec**: The UK and UAR resume diplomatic relations for the first time since 1956.

● **19 Dec**: At a meeting of the Western powers in Paris, it is decided to invite Soviet premier Nikita Khrushchev to attend a summit conference in Apr 1960.

SOCIETY

- **7 Feb**: The USSR agrees to aid Chinese industry, and also to participate in Iraq's economic development on a "vast scale".
- **11 Feb**: The shah of Iran rejects a Soviet offer of economic and technical aid in favor of a similar US offer.
- **23 Feb**: The European Court of Human Rights meets for the first time in Strasbourg (Fr).
- **Mar**: The Inter-American Development Bank is established by 19 American countries.
- **Mar**: The World Bank establishes the International Development Association (IDA).
- **10 Apr**: Akihito, the heir to the throne, becomes the first crown prince to marry a commoner in the history of the Japanese royal family.
- **16 Apr**: The first oil conference is held by Arab nations.
- **25 Apr**: The 650 km (400 mile long) St Lawrence Seaway opens (Can).
- **15 May**: Scientists warn of the need to prohibit catches of blue whales, whose numbers have been severely reduced by hunting for oil.
- **25 May**: Two monkeys survive a space trip that takes them to a height of 580 km (360 miles) above the earth in the nose cone of a Jupiter rocket – a prelude to the first manned space flight, expected within two years.
- **May**: The World Bank warns that the "poverty gap" between rich and poor countries is a greater danger than the Cold War.
- **4 Jun**: US-owned sugar mills and plantations in Cuba are expropriated.
- **5 Jun**: Ghana boycotts South African goods.
- **22 Jun**: Over 50,000 black South Africans riot in protest at plans to move them to a new township.
- **Jun**: Ingemaar Johansson defeats Floyd Patterson to become Sweden's first world heavyweight boxing champion.
- **Aug**: As Arkansas refuses once again to allow integration in its schools, police are sent to quell protests and ensure that blacks can enter (USA).
- **Oct**: The Stockholm Convention is signed between Austria, Denmark, the UK, Norway, Portugal, Sweden and Switzerland to form the European Free Trade Association (EFTA). It becomes operative in May 1960.
- **8 Nov**: The UAR and Sudan agree to share the Nile waters after construction of the Aswan High Dam.
- **10 Nov**: The UN General Assembly condemns apartheid in South Africa and racial discrimination anywhere in the world.
- **12 Dec**: The UN adopts a resolution drafted by the US and USSR promoting the peaceful use of outer space.
- Nobel Peace Prize is won by Philip Noel-Baker (UK).

CULTURE

- **3 Feb**: Singer and teen idol Buddy Holly dies in a plane crash shortly after releasing his first solo record "It doesn't matter any more". He was only 22 (USA).
- **6 Feb**: Premiere at the Opéra Comique in Paris of Francis Poulenc's one-act opera La Voix Humaine (Fr).
- **17 Jul**: Billie Holliday, one of the greatest ever blues singers, dies aged 44.
- Eugene Ionesco: Rhinoceros, play (Fr).
- Arnold Wesker: Roots, play (UK).
- John Arden: Serjeant Musgrave's Dance, play (UK).
- Shelagh Delaney's play A Taste of Honey opens at Joan Littlewood's Stratford East Theatre Workshop (UK).
- Jean-Paul Sartre: Les Sequestrés d'Altona (trans. as Loser Wins, 1960, and as The Condemned of Altona, 1961), play (Fr).
- Edward Albee: Zoo Story, play (USA).
- William Burroughs: The Naked Lunch, an account of life as a drug addict (USA).
- Heinrich Böll: Billiards at Half-Past Nine, novel (FRG).
- Muriel Spark: Memento Mori, novel (UK).
- Günter Grass: Die Blechtrommel (The Tin Drum), novel (FRG).
- Saul Bellow: Henderson the Rain King, novel (USA).
- Colin MacInnes: Absolute Beginners, novel that takes as its subject matter the new teenage and black immigrant lifestyle in London's Notting Hill area (UK).
- Robert Lowell: Life Studies, collection of poems (USA).
- Norman Mailer: Advertisements for Myself, experimental mix of fiction and nonfiction (USA).
- V.S. Naipaul: Miguel Street, short stories set in his birthplace, Trinidad (UK).
- William Faulkner: The Mansion, novel (USA).
- Uwe Johnson: Speculations about Jakob ("Mutmassungen Über Jakob"), novel (Ger).
- Charles Olson: Projective Verse, a manifesto against the domination of form (USA).
- Teilhard de Chardin: The Phenomenon of Man, combining a mystical Catholicism with modern scientific knowledge (Fr).
- Peter Maxwell Davies: Prolation, orchestral work (UK).
- Karlheinz Stockhausen: Zyklus, for percussion (FRG).
- Henri Pousseur: Rhymes from Various Sonorous Sources (employs electronic music and two orchestras) (Bel).

- Henri Dutilleux: Symphony No.2 (Fr).
- Karl-Birger Blomdahl's opera Aniara, set in a space ship and including passages of electronic music, receives its premiere in Stockholm.
- Bobby Darin's recording of "Mack the Knife" is top of the US charts for nine weeks.
- In the UK a revival of New Orleans-style "trad" jazz gets under way, with bands led by players such as Humphrey Lyttelton, Ken Colyer, Acker Bilk and Chris Barber.
- Stuart Davis: The Paris Bit, painting (USA).
- Morris Louis: Saraband, painting (USA).
- Jasper Johns: Numbers in Color, painting (USA).
- Franz Kline: Black, White and Gray (USA).
- Jean Tinguely: Baluba No.3, constructed of wood, metal, electric light and motor (Swi).
- Salvador Dali: Discovery of America by Christopher Columbus, painting (Sp).
- "The Americans": photographs by Robert Frank.
- Frank Lloyd Wright: Guggenheim Museum, New York City.
- Paul Rudolph: Art and Architecture Building, Yale University (USA).
- Oscar Niemeyer: The Square of the Three Powers, Brasilia.
- Arne Jacobsen: Royal Hotel, Copenhagen.
- Alain Resnais: Hiroshima mon amour, a nouvelle vague film with script by Marguerite Duras (Fr).
- Billy Wilder: Some Like It Hot, starring Marilyn Monroe (USA).
- François Truffaut: Les Quatre cent coups, one of the leading films of the French "new wave" seeking to escape the conventions of Hollywood (Fr).
- Satyajit Ray: Apur Sansai (The World of Apu), the last film in the Apu trilogy (Ind).
- Federico Fellini: La dolce vita (It).
- Robert Bresson: Pickpocket (Fr).
- Jean Cocteau: Le Testament d'Orphée (Fr).
- Carol Reed: Our Man in Havana, film of Graham Greene's novel published the previous year (UK).
- Tony Richardson: Look Back in Anger, film of John Osborne's controversial play of 1957 (UK).
- Sergey Eisenstein's Notes of a Film Director is published.
- William Wyler: Ben Hur, epic film starring Charlton Heston (USA).
- In France, fashion designer Pierre Cardin showed his first prêt-à-porter collection.
- Nobel Prize for Literature is won by Salvatore Quasimodo (It).

SCIENCE

- **2 Jan**: The USSR launches Lunik 1, which flies past the Moon and on to orbit the Sun. It carries instruments to measure the Moon's magnetic field, cosmic radiation and interplanetary space. Lunik II crashes on the Moon on 14 Sep, and Lunik III (launched 4 Oct) photographs the far side of the Moon for the first time ever.
- **Jan**: NASA selects 110 candidates for the first US manned space flight.
- **1 Apr**: The US Tiros becomes the first weather observation satellite.
- **Aug**: Alec Issigonis designs the Mini for the British Motor Corporation.
- **1 Dec**: The Antarctic Treaty is signed by 12 countries; the signatories agree to keep the continent free from military activities and to use it for scientific research.
- The first commercial Xerox copier is introduced.
- Grace Murray Hopper invents the computer language COBOL (USA).
- A new antibiotic is isolated, Cephalosporin C, which is effective against penicillin-resistant bacteria (UK).
- G.E. Hutchinson notes that two different species cannot occupy the same ecological niche (USA).
- The Vienna Cancer Institute creates the world's first bone-marrow bank after a group of Yugoslav scientists are successfully treated for radiation overdose with bone-marrow cells (Aut).
- C.E. Ford devises a method of making human chromosomes visible and sorting them into pairs. This enables him to show that congenital conditions, such as Down's Syndrome, can be traced to errors in chromosome make-up (UK).
- L.W. Alvarez and colleagues complete a bubble-chamber for detecting particles produced by the Cosmotron accelerator (USA).
- L.W. Alvarez discovers the neutral xi-particle (USA).
- The world's first geothermal power station is installed in New Zealand.
- Large reserves of natural gas are discovered offshore at Slochteren (Neth).
- Sony market the first portable transistorized television (Jap).
- Arthur Kornberg (USA) and Severo Ochoa (Sp) win the Nobel Prize for Physiology or Medicine for their discovery of the mechanism for the synthesis of ribonucleic acid and deoxyribonucleic acid.
- Jaroslav Heyrovský (Cze) wins the Nobel Prize for Chemistry for his development of the polargraphic methods of analysis.
- Nobel Prize for Physics is won by Owen Chamberlain (USA) and Emilio Segrè (It) for their discovery of the antiproton.

1960-1969

The beginning of the 1960s saw a further increase in the speed of decolonialization in both British and French Africa, with Nigeria, Somaliland, Mauritania and Mali all gaining independence. Cyprus too gained full independence, and by the end of the year president de Gaulle had reached the conclusion that the only solution to the Algerian problem was to permit self-determination. Only the white-dominated nations of southern Africa stood out against black majority rule. In his famous "wind of change" speech in Capetown, British prime minister Harold Macmillan signaled the end of colonialism and urged South Africa to abandon its policy of apartheid and follow principles of racial equality. The South African government responded with the violent massacre of black civilians at Sharpeville, which mobilized world opinion against it. Cuba strengthened its ties with the USSR; anti-American propaganda was given a helping hand when a U2 spy plane was shot down over the USSR, and the pilot parachuted to safety and a spectacular trial in Moscow.

▲ **After President Eisenhower's refusal to apologize to Moscow for the U2 spy plane affair, and the consequent accentuation of Cold War tensions, the election of the youthful and charismatic John F. Kennedy as president promised a welcome fresh approach to world problems.**

● **1 Jan**: French Cameroons trusteeship ends and independent Republic of Cameroons is declared.

● **6 Jan**: Cuba expropriates property belonging to the US-owned Manati Sugar Company. (›27 May)

● **14 Jan**: Soviet premier Khrushchev announces the reduction of Soviet armed forces by 1,200,000 from the existing total of 3,623,000 men.

● **Jan**: Japan signs a 10-year security pact with USA, renewing that of 1951. Mass demonstrations against the new treaty break out in Tokyo on 26 May.

● **3 Feb**: British prime minister Harold Macmillan makes his "wind of change" speech in Capetown, declaring that "whether we like it or not, this growth of national consciousness is a political fact" and urging South Africa to follow principles of racial equality.

● **15–16 Mar**: Elections in South Korea: Syngman Rhee is elected president for the fourth time. After protests on 18 Apr against rigged elections Rhee declares martial law, and police shoot dead 30 protestors. On 27 Apr Rhee resigns after a week of rioting in Seoul.

● **21 Apr**: Brasilia replaces Rio de Janeiro as the capital of Brazil.

● **27 Apr**: Togoland Trust Territory becomes independent as the Republic of Togo, Africa's smallest free nation.

● **28 Apr**: The Turkish government proclaims martial law in Ankara and Istanbul following student demonstrations. On 27 May premier Adnan Menderes is ousted in a bloodless military coup.

● **5 May**: The USSR announces it has shot down a US U2 aircraft on 1 May, flown by Francis Gary Powers, claiming it was on a spying mission. The USA claims it had strayed off course while doing weather research. US president Eisenhower refuses to apologize for the episode.

● **8 May**: Cuba renews diplomatic relations with the USSR.

● **8 May**: Leonid Brezhnev becomes president of the USSR.

● **14–17 May**: Big Four Summit in Paris fails: Khrushchev demands an apology for the spy plane affair and a promise that such an intrusion of Soviet air space will not recur. On 19 Aug a Soviet court sentences Powers to 10 years of detention after he pleads guilty to spying charges.

● **27 May**: US State Department announces the termination of aid to Cuba. (›12 Jul)

● **May**: Belgian authority in the Congo collapses. On 30 Jun the Belgian Congo becomes independent as the Republic of the Congo with Patrice Lumumba as premier and Joseph Kasavubu as president. (›6 Jul)

● **20 Jun**: Mali Federation (Senegal and Soudan) becomes independent within the French community.

● **26 Jun**: British Somaliland proclaims independence. On 1 Jul Somaliland and UN-run former Italian Somaliland are united as Republic of Somalia.

● **26 Jun**: Madagascar becomes independent within the French community, becoming the Malagasy Republic.

● **1 Jul**: Ghana becomes a republic within the Commonwealth with Dr Kwame Nkrumah as head of state and head of government.

● **6 Jul**: The Congolese army mutinies against Lumumba's government and European settlers. On 11 Jul the province of Katanga declares its independence under Moise Tshombe. Belgian and later UN troops are flown in.

● **12 Jul**: Krushchev vows to back Cuba in any effort to expel the USA from its naval base in Guatanama Bay. On 1 Nov Eisenhower states US determination to defend its base. (›7 Aug)

● **12 Jul**: France signs agreements with Chad, Central African Republic and Republic of the Congo providing for their independence within the French community. On 15 July a similar agreement is reached with Gabon.

● **21 Jul**: Mrs Sirimavo Bandaranaike becomes the first woman prime minister in the Commonwealth and in Asian history (Ceylon).

● **7 Aug**: Castro nationalizes all US-owned property in retaliation for "US economic aggression". (›19 Oct)

● **16 Aug**: Cyprus gains independence with Archbishop Makarios as president.

● **8 Sep**: East Germany imposes restrictions whereby West Germans need a permit for entry to East Berlin.

● **23 Sep**: At the UN General Assembly in New York, Khrushchev demands Dag Hammarskjold's removal as UN Secretary-General because of his leadership of the UN action in the Belgian Congo, and the removal of UN headquarters from the USA.

● **1 Oct**: Nigeria achieves independence within the Commonwealth.

● **5 Oct**: The entirely white electorate in South Africa vote in favor of a republic, although premier Verwoerd indicates his continued desire to remain in the Commonwealth.

● **19 Oct**: The USA imposes an embargo on shipment of most commodities to Cuba; on 20 Oct the US ambassador is recalled.

● **9 Nov**: In the US presidential election John F. Kennedy, Democrat, beats Richard Nixon, becoming the youngest man to win the US presidency.

● **28 Nov**: Mauritania gains its independence and becomes the Islamic Republic of Mauritania.

● **8–13 Dec**: French president de Gaulle visits Algeria and concludes that the only solution is self-determination.

SOCIETY

- **18 Jan**: Argentina, Brazil, Mexico, Paraguay, Peru and Uruguay establish the Latin American Free Trade Association (LAFTA).

- **29 Feb**: The seaport of Agadir in Morocco is destroyed by earthquake and tidal wave, followed by widespread fire, killing about 12,000.

- **9 Mar**: US civil rights campaigner Martin Luther King urges president Eisenhower to intervene to defuse racial tension in Montgomery, Alabama.

- **21 Mar**: Start of a campaign of civil disobedience against the pass laws (which require blacks to carry identity cards) begins in South Africa. A crowd converges on a police station at Sharpeville and the police open fire, killing 67 blacks. On 25 Mar all black political organizations in South Africa are outlawed.

- **1 Apr**: The UN Security Council calls on the South African government to initiate measures to bring about racial harmony.

- **10 and 21 Apr**: The US Civil Rights Bill gives authority to courts to appoint federal referees to safeguard Negro voting rights.

- **15–19 Apr**: Over 5,000 East Germans apply to be recognized as refugees and cross to West Berlin, the largest influx of refugees since 1953.

- **15 Jul**: West Germany and France sign an agreement providing for 400 million DM to compensate victims of Nazi persecution. Agreements are also signed with Belgium, Denmark, Greece, Luxembourg, the Netherlands and Norway.

- **29 Jul**: Ghana announces a complete boycott of South African goods and a ban on the entry or transit through Ghana of South Africans, except those who have declared their opposition to apartheid.

- **25 Aug**: The Olympic Games open in Rome. During the Games, Danish cyclist Knut Jenson collapses, hits his head and dies in the heat. A post mortem shows that he had taken a stimulant drug before the race.

- **10–24 Sep**: Iraq, Kuwait, Persia, Saudi Arabia and Venezuela decide to set up the Organization of Petroleum Exporting Countries (OPEC).

- **1 Nov**: The Benelux Economic Union (signed 3 Feb 1958) comes into force.

- **14 Dec**: Agreement is reached on the establishment of the Organization for Economic Cooperation and Development (OECD) as a successor to the Organization for European Economic Cooperation (OEEC), with 18 members.

- US National Association for the Advancement of Colored People boycotts retail stores which practice segregation at lunch counters.

- Nobel Peace Prize is won by Albert Luthuli (SA)

- Bobby Fischer, aged 16, successfully defends the US chess title.

CULTURE

- **5 Apr**: The film *Ben Hur*, directed by William Wyler and starring Charlton Heston, wins a record 10 Oscars (USA).

- **11 Jun**: First performance of the opera *A Midsummer Night's Dream* by Benjamin Britten (UK).

- **6 Jul**: An exhibition of Picasso's works opens at the Tate Gallery, London; it is seen by over 450,000 people before it closes on 18 Sep.

- **8 Sep**: British publisher Penguin Books is brought to trial for planning to publish D.H Lawrence's banned novel *Lady Chatterley's Lover* (1928). On 2 Nov the jury decides that the book is not obscene, and on 10 Nov Penguin's first print run of 200,000 copies sells out on the first day of publication.

- **16 Nov**: Death of US film star Clark Gable, aged 59, while making *The Misfits* with Marilyn Monroe.

- Randall Jarrell: *The Woman at the Washington Zoo*, poems (USA).

- Sylvia Plath: *The Colossus*, first collection of poems (UK).

- Harold Pinter: *The Caretaker*, play (UK).

- Arnold Wesker: *I'm talking about Jerusalem*, final play in the trilogy begun with *Chicken Soup with Barley* (1958) and continued in *Roots* (1959) (UK).

- Nobel Prize for Literature is won by French poet Saint-Jean Perse.

- First performance of Polish composer Krzysztof Penderecki's *Threnody to the Victims of Hiroshima*, for orchestra.

- Karlheinz Stockhausen: *Kontakte*, electronic music, consisting entirely of transitions of tone color, calculated by two scientific assistants in a laboratory (FRG).

- *Oliver*, Lionel Bart's version of Dicken's *Oliver Twist*, brings new life to the British musical.

- Japanese artist Sadao Watanabe, *Listening*, stencil print.

- Completion of US abstract painter Robert Motherwell's huge sequence of paintings under the title *Elegy to the Spanish Republic* (begun 1955).

- Swiss artist and sculptor Jean Tinguely produces *Homage to New York*, a mechanical sculpture.

- Alexander Calder: *Antennae with Red and Blue Dots*, mobile (USA).

- Marcel Breuer: IBM Research Center, La Gaude, near Nice (completed 1962) (Fr).

- Italian director Federico Fellini's film *La dolce vita* wins the Grand Prix at the Cannes Film Festival.

- Alfred Hitchcock: *Psycho*, starring Anthony Perkins and Janet Leigh (USA).

- Jean-Luc Godard's *A Bout de souffle* stars Jean Seberg and Jean-Paul Belmondo (Fr).

- Michelangelo Antonioni: *L'avventura* (It).

SCIENCE

- **23 Jan**: US Navy bathyscape *Trieste* dives to the bottom of Challenger Deep in the West Pacific, reaching a depth of 10,900 m (35,800 ft) and discovers that life exists at these depths. Since oxygen must therefore be exchanged by currents from higher levels, this casts doubt on the safety of disposing of radioactive wastes in deep sea troughs of this kind.

- **13 Feb**: France explodes its first atomic bomb in the Sahara, despite US and UN opposition.

- **11 Mar**: Launch of US spaceprobe *Pioneer V*, which later made important discoveries about the Earth's magnetic field.

- **1 Apr**: First weather satellite Tiros I is launched by the USA to transmit television images of cloud cover around the Earth.

- **16 Jun**: European Center for Nuclear Research (CERN) announces an agreement to exchange scientists with the Nuclear Research Center at Dubna near Moscow.

- **12 Aug**: Launch of US communications satellite Echo I, consisting of a balloon 30 m (100 ft) in diameter, which is able to transmit a two-way conversation on microwaves reflected off its aluminum surface.

- **19 Aug**: A Soviet spacecraft carrying two dogs is launched as a trial run for putting a man in space. The dogs are retrieved safely when the spacecraft returns after 17 orbits on 22 Aug.

- **24 Sep**: Launch of USS *Enterprise*, the first atomic-powered aircraft carrier.

- **4 Oct**: The communications satellite Courier IB is launched by the USA, the first of a network of active communications satellites providing the US Defense Dept with an international communications system.

- R. Minkowsky of Mount Palomar Observatory photographs two colliding galaxies 6,000 million light years away.

- The British vertical take-off aircraft, Hawker P1127, makes its first flight, using an engine with swiveling nozzles to change from vertical to horizontal flight.

- A group of surgeons from Birmingham, UK, develop the first pacemaker for patients with acute heart disease.

- The Nobel Prize for Medicine or Physiology is won by Sir M. F. Burnet (Australia) and Peter Medawar (UK) for the independent discovery of acquired immunity against foreign tissue.

- The Nobel Prize for Chemistry is won by the US chemist W. F. Libby for his work on archeological dating techniques using the radioactive isotope carbon-14 (radio carbon dating).

- The Nobel Prize for Physics is won by D. A. Glaser for his invention of the bubble chamber for the study of subatomic particles.

- The US nuclear submarine *Triton* completes its first circumnavigation of the globe underwater, traveling 66,800 km (41,519 miles) in 84 days.

- K. H. Hofmann synthesizes the pituitary hormone ACTH at the University of Pittsburgh, USA.

- Chlorophyll is independently synthesized by M. Strell (FRG) and R. B. Woodward (USA).

- The first optical maser or "laser" is developed by US physicist T. H. Maiman.

- S. Moore and W. H. Stein determine the sequence of all 124 amino acids in ribonuclease.

- The West German astronomer R. L. Mossbauer develops gamma rays of accurately defined wavelength; this technique is used to detect gravitational red shift.

- Astronomers T.A. Matthews and A.R. Sandage deduce the existence of qasars (USA).

- US geologist H. H. Hess develops the theory of sea-floor spreading, an important element in the theory of plate tectonics.

- The internationally accepted standard meter is redefined in terms of the wavelength of the krypton spectrum.

- The US Heart Association issues a report attributing higher death rates among middle-aged men to heavy cigarette smoking.

1961

The new US president, John F. Kennedy, began his term of office with great élan, creating the Peace Corps and promising a "New Frontier"; but before long his image was tarnished by the disastrous Bay of Pigs affair, when an anti-Castro force of Cuban exiles, backed by the CIA, attempted an invasion of Soviet-backed Cuba. Escalating fears of open conflict were only defused when the invasion failed miserably. Kennedy went on to increase the US defense budget and numbers of armed forces, and his decision to send two US Army helicopters companies with 400 troops as military advisers to South Vietnam, however well-intentioned, was to have appalling consequences throughout the 1960s. US fears of Communist expansion were fueled by the USSR's open determination to prevent the continual drain of refugees to the West: in July thousands of East Germans fled to West Berlin in anticipation of a Communist crackdown, which came with the building of the Berlin Wall in August. Among the refugees from the Eastern bloc was one of the USSR's most gifted artists, dancer Rudolf Nureyev.

▲ The rivalry between West and East was as fierce in space as on Earth. In the end it was the Soviet Union that put the first man into space, when Yuri Gagarin in *Vostok 1* orbited the Earth in April 1961, in a flight lasting 108 minutes. Less than a month later, US astronaut Alan Shepherd also achieved space flight.

● **3 Jan**: The USA severs diplomatic relations with Cuba.

● **20 Jan**: John F. Kennedy is inaugurated as the 35th president of the United States.

● **22 Jan**: Captain Henrique Galvao proclaims the first stage of a revolution to overthrow the near-dictator Portuguese premier, Dr Salazar.

● **25 Jan**: A bloodless military coup in El Salvador overthrows the left-of-center junta.

● **30 Jan**: A campaign of civil disobedience begins in Ceylon, organized by opposition groups to harry the government, and culminating in the declaration of a state of emergency on 17 Apr.

● **21 Feb**: Sir Roy Welensky, prime minster of the Central African Federation, rejects a British proposal for increased African representation in the Northern Rhodesian Legislature.

● **Feb**: Patrice Lumumba, deposed premier of the newly independent Congo, is murdered in suspicious circumstances in Katanga.

● **8–12 Mar**: At the Tananarive Conference, Congolese leaders make a tentative agreement to form a confederation. On 24 Jun Moise Tshombe agrees to reunite Katanga with the rest of the Congo, but he later repudiates this. (›13 Sep)

● **9 Mar**: The Dalai Lama, in exile in India, appeals to the UN to persuade Communist China to cease aggression in Tibet and restore its independence.

● **17 Apr**: An anti-Castro force of Cuban exiles, backed by the CIA, attempts an invasion of Cuba at the Bay of Pigs. International tension rises as Soviet premier Nikita Krushchev promises support to Cuba and criticizes the USA, but on 20 Apr Castro announces "total victory".

● **21 Apr**: A rightwing military rebellion in Algeria is suppressed after president de Gaulle takes dictatorial powers.

● **27 Apr**: Sierra Leone becomes independent within the Commonwealth.

● **Apr**: Guerrilla war breaks out in northern Angola between the Portuguese and Angolans seeking independence.

● **31 May**: The Union of South Africa becomes an independent republic and withdraws from the Commonwealth.

● **19 Jun**: Britain's protectorate over oil-rich Kuwait ends. On 25 Jun Iraq claims Kuwait. British troops land in Kuwait on 1 Jul, provoking a call from the UAR, backed by the USSR, for their withdrawal.

● **20–22 Jul**: Fighting breaks out between French and Tunisians over the French refusal to withdraw from the naval base at Bizerta. Armed deadlock continues until September, when French president de Gaulle declares his willingness to negotiate on its use.

● **26 Jul**: US president Kennedy proposes to increase US armed forces and raise the defense budget for 1961. (›11 Dec)

● **31 Jul**: British prime minister Harold Macmillan announces that the UK will try to join the European Common Market (EEC). Formal application is made on 10 Aug.

● **Jul**: East Berlin authorities issue an order demanding permits for East Berliners working in West Berlin. Thousands of East Germans flee to West Berlin in anticipation of a Communist crackdown. On 31 Jul the East Berlin authorities tighten controls on refugee routes.

● **13 Aug**: The border between East and West Berlin is closed by East Germany and blocked with barbed wire, and on 17–18 Aug the construction of the Berlin Wall begins against a background of Western protests.

● **21 Aug**: The last restrictions on the movements of Jomo Kenyatta, Kenya's veteran nationalist leader are lifted.

● **31 Aug**: The USSR announces its decision to resume test explosions of nuclear weapons.

● **1–6 Sep**: The Non-Aligned Nations Conference at Belgrade calls for complete disarmament and prohibition of nuclear tests, but on 5 Sep Kennedy announces US resumption of underground and laboratory tests.

● **13 Sep**: An attempt by UN forces to overthrow Moise Tshombe's secessionist regime in Katanga leads to heavy fighting. On 21 Dec Tshombe finally agrees to end Katanga's secession, and Katanganese MPs later take seats in the Congolese central parliament.

● **18 Sep**: UN Secretary-General Dag Hammarskjöld is killed in an air crash in Northern Rhodesia. On 3 Nov U Thant of Burma is elected Acting Secretary-General.

● **28 Sep**: A successful coup d'état in Syria enables it to secede from the UAR and restore Syrian independence as the Syrian Arab Republic.

● **24 Nov**: The UN General Assembly adopts a resolution that Africa should be respected as a denuclearized zone.

● **Nov**: Krushchev's de-Stalinization policy is stepped up: in Moscow, Stalin's body is removed from Lenin's mausoleum; Stalingrad is renamed Volgograd.

● **9 Dec**: Tanganyika becomes independent within the Commonwealth under prime minister Julius Nyerere.

● **9 Dec**: The USSR breaks off relation with Albania, and Albania is expelled from Comecon.

● **11 Dec**: Following US president Kennedy's decision to make a massive increase in the number of US military advisers in South Vietnam, two US Army helicopter companies with 400 troops arrive in Saigon.

- **3–7 Jan**: Morocco, Ghana, Guinea, Mali, the UAR, Libya, Ceylon and Algeria attend the Casablanca Conference and announce an "African Charter", binding them to a policy of closer association.

- **5 Jan**: General Arrangements to Borrow (GAB) among the 10 major industrial countries are decided by the IMF. The 10 countries agree to make resources amounting to $6,000 million available to each other in case of need.

- **21 Jan**: The Organization of Petroleum Exporting Countries (OPEC) is formally established at Caracas.

- **24 Jan**: Ethiopia imposes a boycott on South African goods.

- **Jan**: The USSR makes a 60 million rouble credit available to Poland to aid the construction of the Comecon oil pipeline.

- **1 Mar**: US president Kennedy sets up a Peace Corps of young men and women to serve overseas to bring progress to underdeveloped areas.

- **7 Apr**: The UN votes unanimously to censure South Africa's apartheid policy and calls for a UN committee to visit the country; but on 10 May the South African government refuses the UN a permit to enter.

- **11 Apr**: Nigeria imposes a total boycott on trade with South Africa.

- **11 Apr**: The trial of Nazi Adolf Eichmann begins in Jerusalem. On 15 Dec he is convicted of "crimes against the Jewish people, crimes against humanity, a war crime, and membership of hostile organizations", and sentenced to be hanged.

- **29 Jun**: An ILO conference calls for withdrawal of South Africa because of its apartheid policies.

- **9 Jul**: EEC representatives and Greece agree on Greek associate membership of the EEC.

- **16 Aug**: Members of the Inter-American Economic and Social Council agree to establish an Alliance for Progress for the social and economic development of Latin America.

- **17 Sep**: In London, the biggest yet "ban-the-bomb" demonstration ends in violent clashes and nearly 1,000 arrests as protesters demand an end to the current round of nuclear arms testing.

- **22 Sep**: Segregation on interstate buses ends after "Freedom Riders" campaign in the southern USA.

- **10 Oct**: The central volcanic mountain on the British island of Tristan da Cunha in the South Atlantic, thought to be extinct, erupts; 262 inhabitants of the island are evacuated.

- **1 Nov**: The UK government imposes new immigration controls.

- Nobel Peace Prize is won by Dag Hammarskjöld (Swe), the only time the award has been awarded posthumously.

- **14 Mar**: The New Testament is published as the first part of the New English Bible, inspired by a concern that the work of the Church is being hindered by the archaic language of the Bible. By the end of 1961, world sales are over 3 million copies.

- **20 May**: Premiere of Hans Werner Henze's opera *Elegy for Young Lovers* (FRG).

- **9 Jun**: Premiere in Zürich of Czech composer Bohuslav Martinu's opera *The Greek Passion*.

- **16 Jun**: Rudolf Nureyev, the leading male dancer with the Kirov Ballet, defects during a tour of Western cities and is granted political asylum in France.

- **2 Jul**: US novelist Ernest Hemingway is found shot through the head by his own gun.

- **12 Aug**: Eight paintings by Cézanne worth around £730,000 are stolen from a museum at Aix-en-Provence, France.

- **21 Aug**: Goya's portrait of the Duke of Wellington is stolen from the National Gallery, London.

- **28 Sep**: Folk and protest singer Bob Dylan causes a stir playing and singing his own songs in Greenwich Village (USA).

- **Sep**: Chubby Checker's pop single "The Twist" starts a dance craze.

- The La Mama Experimental Theater Club is founded in New York.

- John Osborne: *Luther*, play based on the life of the life of Martin Luther (UK).

- John Whiting: *The Devils*, play (UK).

- Samuel Beckett: *Happy Days*, play (Fr).

- Max Frisch: *Andorra*, play (Swi).

- Carl Zuckmayer: *Die Uhr schlägt eins*, play (FRG).

- Dissident Soviet writer Yevgeny Yevtushenko's anti-Stalinist poem *Babi Yar*, on the extermination of the Jews, is published; in 1962 it is set by Dmitri Shostakovich in his Thirteenth Symphony.

- Louis MacNeice: *Solstices*, poems (UK).

- Muriel Spark: *The Prime of Miss Jean Brodie*, novel later adapted for both stage and film (UK).

- Patrick White: *Riders in the Chariot*, novel (Aus).

- Evelyn Waugh: *Unconditional Surrender*, last novel in the *Sword of Honour* trilogy (UK).

- Joseph Heller's brilliant satirical novel *Catch-22* reflects a sharply cynical attitude to war (USA).

- The British satirical revue *Beyond the Fringe* opens, written and performed by Dudley Moore, Peter Cook, Alan Bennett and Jonathan Miller.

- Italian composer Luciano Berio completes *Epifanie*, a vocal work for the singer Cathy Berberian.

- Luigi Nono's opera *Intolleranza 1960* is premiered in Venice (It).

- Alexander Goehr: *Sutter's Gold*, cantata (UK).

- György Ligeti: *Atmosphères*, orchestral work (FRG).

- Witold Lutoslawski: *Venetian Games* (Pol).

- Elliott Carter: Double Concerto, for harpsichord and piano, with two chamber orchestras (USA).

- Italian conceptual artist Piero Manzoni creates his "Living Sculpture" in which the artist signs various individuals' bodies, then gives them a "certificate of authenticity" as a work of art.

- The Museum of Modern Art in New York mounts "The Art of Assemblage" exhibition, which marks a change in the approach to art from Abstract Expressionism toward Pop Art, Happenings, Earth Art and other new movements.

- Bulgarian-born Christo began by wrapping small objects, but they gradually increased in size through trees and automobiles to architectural monuments such as "Dockside Packages" (1961), in Cologne, West Germany.

- Peter Phillips: *For men only, starring MM and BB*, British Pop Art at its most chauvinist.

- Larry Rivers: *Parts of the Face (The Vocabulary Lesson)*, painting (USA).

- César: *The Yellow Buick*, compressed automobile (Fr).

- Italian architect Pier Luigi Nervi's Palazzo del Lavoro, Turin, is completed.

- British architects Peter Cook, Warren Chalk, Ron Herron, Dennis Crompton, Michael Webb and David Greene, found the Archigram group, whose initial pamphlet, *Archigram I*, advocates space capsules, a throwaway environment and mass consumer imagery in architecture.

- Stanley Kramer's feature film *Judgment at Nuremberg* is released (USA).

- Release of the film *The Misfits*, written by Arthur Miller for Marilyn Monroe and also starring Clark Gable, directed by John Huston (USA).

- Alain Resnais's *nouvelle vague* film *Last Year in Marienbad* (Fr) wins the Golden Lion at the Venice Film Festival.

- Luis Buñuel: *Viridiana* (Sp).

- Michelangelo Antonioni: *La notte* (It).

- Pier Paolo Pasolini: *Accatone* (It).

- Walt Disney: *101 Dalmatians*, cartoon feature (USA).

- The first haute couture miniskirts are presented by Marc Bohan at Dior and André Courrèges.

- Nobel Prize for Literature is won by Ivo Andrić (Yug).

- **12 Apr**: Cosmonaut Yuri Gagarin, in his Soviet spacecraft *Vostok I*, becomes the first man to orbit the Earth.

- **30 Apr**: Excavations at Pompeii uncover the calcified bodies of eight people enveloped by hot ashes from erupting Vesuvius, in AD 79.

- **5 May**: US astronaut Alan Shepard achieves space flight, going up through the atmosphere and down again, but does not go into orbit.

- **12 Jul**: The US satellite Midas III is placed in a near-polar orbit; it is designed to detect Soviet missiles on launching by infrared radiation.

- **Nov**: West German scientists discover a connection between the congenital malformation of the limbs in babies and the use of the drug thalidomide by their mothers in the early months of pregnancy.

- The Nobel Prize for Physiology or Medicine is won by Hungarian-American physicist G. von Békésy for his study of auditory mechanisms.

- R. Hofstadter (USA) and R.L. Mossbauer (FRG) share the Nobel Prize for Physics, Hofstadter for his work on the measurement of nucleons and Mossbauer for his on gamma rays.

- US chemist Melvin Calvin wins the Nobel Prize for Chemistry for his work on photosynthesis.

- Biochemist M.W. Nirenberg discovers the first known "letter" of the genetic code when he shows that three uridylic acid bases in a row in RNA form the code for a particular amino acid (USA).

- British astronomer Martin Ryle concludes from radioastronomical observations that the universe changes with time, challenging the "steady state" theory.

- J. Lippes develops an inert plastic intra-uterine device (IUD) as a contraceptive.

- Robert Hofstadter discovers the structure of protons and neutrons: a central positive core and two shells of mesons (USA).

- US physicists M. Gell-Mann and Y. Ne'eman independently develop a scheme for classifying elementary particles, which forms the beginning of the quark theory.

- Texas Instruments patents the silicon chip (USA).

- F.L. Horsfall announces that all forms of cancer are caused by mutations in the DNA of cells.

- US scientists under Severo Ochoa discover how the instructions on a DNA molecule are actually translated into the manufacture of protein, using RNA and ribosomes.

- British biochemists F. Crick and S. Brenner demonstrate that the genetic code of DNA consists of a string of nonoverlapping base triplets.

Nuclear war had never seemed more imminent than in the tense few days of the Cuban Missile crisis, when US warships blockaded the offending island and the world waited to see if Khrushchev and Kennedy would collide. The one person who was apparently not consulted was Cuban leader Fidel Castro. China made preparations for a border war with India, but like the Soviet Union, held back from a more serious conflict. In Algeria, the long and hideous civil war drew to a close, and Amnesty International was founded in an effort to record and publicize the kind of inhuman treatment of political opponents of which the Algerian war had provided many examples. Pop culture blossomed in the West. Claes Oldenburg produced his huge canvas hamburger, Warhol his silkscreen of Marilyn Monroe. Bob Dylan raced to the top of the charts with "Blowing in the Wind"; the Beatles sang "Love Me Do". James Bond (President Kennedy's favourite fictional hero) was metamorphosed on film as Sean Connery, and the guru of the Sixties, Marshall McLuhan, summed up the communications revolution with his famous description of "the global village".

▲ Conflict broke out in the Congo as Moise Thshombe again prevaricated over Katanga's incorporation, and the UN sent in troops to enforce cooperation.

● **1 Jan**: Western Samoa becomes the first independent sovereign Polynesian state.

● **3 Jan**: President Sukarno of Indonesia proclaims West New Guinea, belonging to the Netherlands, an Indonesian province. On 15 Jan Indonesian and Dutch naval units clash off the West New Guinea coast. (›15 Aug)

● **4 Jan**: The US and South Vietnamese governments issue a joint statement outlining an economic program for South Vietnam, which is condemned by the USSR as US interference.

● **2 Feb**: In Italy, the Socialists return into mainstream politics after years of isolation due to their links with the Communists, as Signor Fanfani forms a center-left government.

● **8 Feb**: The US Defense Department creates the Military Assistance Command (MAC) in South Vietnam; China protests.

● **8 Feb**: 8 people are killed and over 260 injured in anti-OAS (Organisation de l'Armée Secrète) demonstrations in Paris, after an OAS terrorist campaign in France. The rightwing fanatics are opposed to president de Gaulle's plan to grant Algeria self-determination.(›7 Mar)

● **15 Feb**: UK, US and French governments lodge protests in Moscow over recent incidents when aircraft have been "buzzed" in air corridors to Berlin.

● **26 Feb**: The IRA (Irish Republican Army) issue a statement announcing the suspension of a campaign of violence begun in 1956 against the Northern Ireland government, though still pledging resistance to "British forces of occupation in Ireland".

● **1 Mar**: Pakistan's new constitution establishes a presidential system of government. In Jun Ayub Khan is sworn in as president.

● **3 Mar**: The state of Malta comes into being, with Dr Borg Olivier as premier and former governor Sir Guy Grantham as head of state.

● **7–18 Mar**: Negotiations take place at Evian (Fr) to end the longstanding conflict between France and the pro-independence FLN in Algeria. On 19 Mar a ceasefire is agreed and a FLN Provisional Government is established. De Gaulle launches a French offensive to crush the OAS extremists.

● **14 Mar**: A 17-nation Disarmament Conference at foreign minister level opens in Geneva, but France declines to participate.

● **16 Mar**: Israeli forces raid Syrian positions as reprisals for Syrian attacks during Feb and Mar. The UN Security Council condemns Israel's action. In Dec Syria again attacks border villages, leading to the intervention of UN truce supervisor, Gen. Carl von Horn.

● **25 Apr**: The USA resumes nuclear tests in the atmosphere in response to the USSR's series of over 50 tests during fall 1961.

● **Apr**: Michel Debré resigns as French premier after 3 ¼ years, and is succeeded by Georges Pompidou.

● **6 May**: Nam Tha (Laos) falls to the Pathet Lao, prompting the sending of US and other forces to Thailand to counter the Communist threat in Laos. On 23 Jul, 13 states at the Geneva Conference sign a declaration guaranteeing Laotian neutrality.

● **10 Jun**: Socialist Haya de la Torre is elected president of Peru, but the elections are annulled and the army takes over government.

● **28 Jun**: The UN General Assembly demands a new constitution in Southern Rhodesia, including universal franchise.

● **1 Jul**: The Ruanda-Urundi Trust Territory achieves independence as the separate Republic of Rwanda and Kingdom of Burundi.

● **7 Jul**: The UK and Egypt sign an agreement on compensation for British subjects whose property was seized after the Suez crisis in 1958, in return for a UK loan of £3,570,000.

● **6 Aug**: Jamaica becomes independent within the Commonwealth.

● **15 Aug**: After talks organized by the UN, an agreement is signed by Indonesia and the Netherlands for a UN Temporary Executive Authority to administer West New Guinea until May 1963, when all or part of the administration will pass to Indonesia.

● **31 Aug**: Trinidad and Tobago becomes independent within the Commonwealth.

● **2 Sep**: The USSR agrees to deliver arms to Cuba to help it meet "threats from aggressive imperialist elements". (›22 Oct)

● **24 Sep**: Soviet president Leonid Brezhnev visits Yugoslavia. In Dec the Yugoslavian premier Marshal Tito makes a return visit, marking an improvement in relations between the two countries.

● **9 Oct**: Uganda gains independence within the Commonwealth under Dr Milton Obote.

● **10 Oct**: The West German magazine *Der Spiegel* publishes an article on a NATO exercise, suggesting that the Bundeswehr and Civil Defence are inadequate. (›26 Oct)

● **20 Oct**: The Chinese invade India as part of a continuing border dispute. On 24 Oct China proposes that both sides withdraw, but on 26 Oct India rejects this proposal and prime minister Nehru declares a state of emergency.(›21 Nov)

● **22 Oct**: US president Kennedy reveals that Soviet missiles have been based in Cuba, and on 24 Oct imposes a naval quarantine on Cuba to stop ships carrying offensive weapons, though letting essential civilian supplies through. The Organization of American States unanimously supports his policy. International tension mounts over the affair.

SOCIETY CULTURE SCIENCE

● **26 Oct**: Soviet premier Khrushchev sends a message to Kennedy offering to withdraw offensive weapons from Cuba only if US missiles are removed from Turkey.(›27 Oct)

● **26 Oct**: The offices of *Der Spiegel* are occupied and publisher and defense expert arrested. A storm of protest follows against the methods used and alleged infringement of the freedom of the press. (›5 Nov)

● **27 Oct**: Fears of military action grow as Kennedy insists that work on Cuban bases must stop as a preliminary to any proposals; once this condition is fulfilled, the dispute could be settled if the USSR will remove weapons systems from Cuba under UN supervision. The USA would call off the quarantine and give assurances against the invasion of Cuba.

● **28 Oct**: After secret exchanges between Washington and Moscow, the situation is defused as Khrushchev announces that he has ordered the weapons to be dismantled and returned to the USSR.

● **30 Oct**: The UN General Assembly again rejects a Soviet resolution to admit Communist China.

● **5 Nov**: The UN General Assembly adopts a resolution condemning all nuclear weapons tests and urges that they should cease by Jan 1963.

● **5 Nov**: The West German defense minister Dr Walter Strauss is relieved of his post. On 7 Nov the Bundestag debate on the *Der Spiegel* case begins. On 19 Nov, five Free Democrat ministers resign.

● **6 Nov**: The UN General Assembly adopts a resolution condemning South Africa for its apartheid policy and recommends member states to break off diplomatic relations and apply economic sanctions.

● **14 Nov**: Eritrea votes to become a provincial unit within Ethiopia, thus losing the autonomous status arranged by the UN with Ethiopia.

● **21 Nov**: After a major offensive in the border dispute with India, Chinese troops halt in a very strong position. Peking announces that it will withdraw troops to the McMahon Line and cease fighting if India accepts this front.

● **30 Nov**: U Thant is unanimously elected Secretary-General of the UN.

● **9 Dec**: Tanganyika becomes a republic within the Commonwealth under Julius Nyerere.

● **14 Dec**: Moise Tshombe again delays over Katangan incorporation into the Congo, and UN Secretary-General U Thant calls for an embargo on Katanganese copper and cobalt exports. On 29 Dec UN forces occupy Elisabethville, the provincial capital.

● **18–21 Dec**: President Kennedy meets with British prime minister Harold Macmillan in Nassau; they agree that the USA should provide the UK with Polaris nuclear missiles.

● **1 Jan**: The second stage of integration of the EEC is officially inaugurated. On 14 Jan a Common Agricultural Policy (CAP) is approved.

● **9 Jan**: A trade pact is set up between the USSR and Cuba involving the exchange of goods valued at over $70,000,000 during the year.

● **18 Jan**: Ireland requests membership of the EEC, followed by Portugal on 4 Jun. On 25 Jul Turkey begins negotiations for associate membership.

● **5 Apr**: The Great St Bernard Tunnel between Italy and Switzerland is completed, and on 14 Aug construction is also completed of the Mont Blanc Tunnel between France and Italy.

● **Apr**: The UK Colonial Secretary announces that controls on illegal entry to Hong Kong from China will be strictly enforced, as the swollen population is putting a strain on the economy.

● **7 Jun**: The Mongolian People's Republic joins Comecon.

● **17 Jun**: The African common market is established, comprising Morocco, Ghana, Guinea, Mali and the UAR.

● **20 Jun**: Farmers in Brittany dump artichokes in the streets in protest at low agricultural prices (Fr).

● **1 Jul**: Part I of the Commonwealth Immigrants Act comes into force, making provision for controlling immigration of Commonwealth citizens into the UK and authorizing deportation of certain Commonwealth citizens.

● **Jul**: Dawn Fraser (Aus) becomes the first woman to swim 100 m in under one minute.

● **19 Sep**: The Commonwealth Prime Ministers' Conference approves Britain's application to join the EEC.

● **30 Sep**: There are riots at Mississippi University as black student James Meredith attempts to register, escorted by 300 US marshals: 2 die and 70 are injured.

● **11 Oct**: The 21st Ecumenical Council is opened by Pope John XXIII in Rome. It is the largest ever gathering of the Roman Catholic hierarchy.

● **15 Oct**: Amnesty International, an organization that aims to improve the treatment of political prisoners worldwide, is established in London.

● **1 Nov**: Greece becomes an associate member of the EEC.

● **19 Nov**: Soviet premier Khrushchev demands a basic reorganization of the economic structure of the USSR to enhance Communist party control over the economy.

● The Trade Expansion Act gives the US government wide scope for trade bargaining, aimed at the reduction or complete elimination of tariffs between the USA and Europe.

● The Nobel Peace Prize is won by Linus C. Pauling, for his campaigning against nuclear testing and weapons.

● **30 May**: Benny Goodman, the prewar "king of swing", plays in Moscow to a audience that includes Soviet premier Nikita Khrushchev.

● **5 Aug**: Film star Marilyn Monroe is found dead of a drugs overdose in her Los Angeles home.

● Tennessee Williams: *The Night of the Iguana*, play (USA).

● Friedrich Dürrenmatt: *The Physicists*, play (Swi).

● Anthony Burgess: *A Clockwork Orange*, novel (UK).

● Anna Akhmatova completes her *Poem without a Hero* (since 1940) (USSR).

● Doris Lessing: *The Golden Notebook*, experimental feminist novel (UK).

● Alexander Solzhenitsyn: *One Day in the Life of Ivan Denisovitch*, novel based on life in the Soviet labor camps (USSR).

● Vladimir Nabokov: *Pale Fire*, novel (Swi).

● R.K. Narayan: *The Maneater of Malgudi*, novel (Ind).

● Nobel Prize for Literature is won by John Steinbeck (USA).

● Marshall McLuhan in *The Gutenberg Galaxy* coins the expression "the global village" with reference to electronic communications.

● Igor Stravinsky: *The Flood*, a musical play written for television.

● Benjamin Britten: *War Requiem*, which sets poems by World War I poet Wilfred Owen (UK).

● Dmitri Shostakovich: Symphony No. 13 (USSR).

● Peter Maxwell Davies: *Sinfonia*, for chamber orchestra, written in the USA.

● Olivier Messiaen: *Sept haikai*, for piano and small orchestra (Fr).

● Bob Dylan releases "Blowin' in the Wind" (USA).

● The Beatles sign with EMI and release "Love Me Do" (UK).

● Robert Rauschenberg: *Barge*, painting (USA).

● Andy Warhol: *Marilyn Monroe*, silkscreen, and *Green Coca Cola Bottles*, painting (USA).

● Jim Dine: *Six Big Saws*, oil, saw and nails on canvas (USA).

● Claes Oldenburg: *Giant Hamburger*, soft sculpture (USA).

● Alexander Calder: *The Four Elements*, mobile for the Stockholm Museum of Modern Art.

● Release of the film of Leonard Bernstein's successful musical *West Side Story*.

● François Truffaut: *Jules et Jim*, film starring Jeanne Moreau (Fr).

● *Dr No*, the first James Bond film, stars Sean Connery (UK).

● Roman Polanski: *Knife in the Water* (Pol).

● **23 Apr**: The US *Ranger* spacecraft is launched, and on 26 Apr hits the Moon.

● **26 Apr**: The USA launch the UK's first satellite, Ariel, at Cape Canaveral.

● **10 Jul**: The first active communications satellite, Telstar, allows TV transmission between Europe and the USA.

● **27 Aug**: The USA launch Venus spaceprobe *Mariner 2*.

● **Aug**: Two Soviet astronauts orbit the Earth together in closely matched orbits in *Vostok III* and *Vostok IV* as a rehearsal of a rendezvous in space.

● **Dec**: The UK and France announce a joint agreement to build a supersonic civil airliner, Concorde.

● Alex Moulton makes the first real change in bicycle design for 60 years, producing a bike which has tiny wheels, no crossbar, and resilient rubber suspension (UK).

● The Dounreay nuclear reactor in the north of Scotland runs successfully at high power using a "fast breeder reactor", an important step in the production of cheaper nuclear power.

● Three US astronauts orbit the Earth: John Glenn (Feb), Scott Carpenter (May) and Walter Schirra (Oct).

● US scientist John Lilly, after research with dolphins, announces that they are quicker to learn than any other animal used in such experiments and are able to mimic noises.

● General Motors install the first industrial robot (USA).

● The Nobel Prize for Chemistry is won by M.F. Perutz and J.C. Kendrew (UK) for their use of X-ray diffraction techniques to determine the structure of the protein molecule myoglobin.

● The Nobel Prize for Physiology or Medicine is awarded to J. D. Watson (USA) and F.H.C. Crick and M. Wilkins (UK) for their determination of the molecular structure of DNA.

● L.D. Landau (USSR) wins the Nobel Prize for Physics for his work on superfluidity in liquid helium.

● L. Harrington develops an operation for the correction of scoliosis (curvature of the spine) (USA).

● T.H. Weller develops a vaccine against rubella (USA).

● G. Daley and colleagues establish that there are two types of neutrino (USA).

● Lasers are first used in eye surgery.

● The publication of Rachel Carson's *Silent Spring* alerts the general public to the dangers of the introduction of chemicals into the ecosystem.

● N. Bartlett makes the first noble gas compounds by preparing xenon platinum hexafluoride (USA).

● B.D. Josephson discovers tunnelling between superconductors (UK).

1963

POLITICS

The "dream" that Martin Luther King described in his famous speech in Washington in August 1963 came a step nearer reality as the civil rights movement in the United States gained new strength under his leadership, backed by president Kennedy's promise to put continued pressure on Congress to pass the Civil Rights Bill. Governor George Wallace of Alabama earned a small niche in history for his refusal to comply with a court order to allow blacks into the university, and National Guardsmen were sent in to enforce the law. Kennedy was also received enthusiastically by the audience in West Berlin that heard his vigorous attack on Communism in June. This was the year of the Profumo scandal in Britain, when a young callgirl was found to have been sharing her favors between a cabinet minister and the Soviet naval attaché, and of the terrible earthquake that obliterated the Yugoslavian town of Skopje. But the event that would stick longest in the mind, one of those moments of shock so intense that everyone can remember for years afterward exactly what they were doing at the time, was the assassination of president Kennedy in Dallas, Texas – an event that to many marked the end of an era of hope.

▲ Civil rights activist Martin Luther King waves to the huge crowd at the Lincoln Memorial at the end of the march on Washington in August.

● **15 Jan**: Moise Tshombe of Katanga finally agrees to the UN plan to end the 30-month secession of Katanga from the Congo.

● **22 Jan**: France and West Germany sign a treaty in Paris pledging cooperation on foreign policy, defense and cultural affairs.

● **1 Feb**: Nyasaland becomes self-governing, with Dr Hastings Banda as its first prime minister. (›31 Dec)

● **8 Feb**: Premier Abdul Kassem Karim is overthrown and killed in a military coup in Iraq; he is succeeded by Col. Abdas Salām Arif. (›18 Nov)

● **9 Feb**: Leading member of the Zimbabwe African People's Union (ZAPU) Joshua Nkomo is arrested in a government crackdown (S Rho).

● **14 Feb**: After the unexpected death of Labour party leader Hugh Gaitskell, Harold Wilson is elected to lead the party (UK).

● **Feb–Mar**: An exchange of diplomatic notes between China and the USSR leads to arrangements to hold talks concerning their ideological differences; but the talks, held in Moscow 5–20 Jul, reach no agreement.

● **8 Mar**: The Syrian government is overthrown and a National Council of the Revolution established.

● **10 Mar**: Iraq proposes a military union of the five "liberated" Arab countries: Iraq, Syria, Algeria, Egypt and Yemen. On 8 Oct military union takes place between Syria and Iraq, followed by preparatory steps toward economic and political union.

● **17 and 27 Mar**: A group of Cuban exiles in Miami is alleged to have organized a hit-and-run raid on shipping in a Cuban port. A retaliatory incident by Cuba on 28 Mar is followed on 29 Mar by a Soviet note complaining to the USA of encouragement of such raids by exiles; the USA promises to take steps to avert them.

● **21 Mar**: The Chinese vice-minister of foreign trade arrives in London for discussions, the first Chinese minister to travel to the UK.

● **31 Mar**: An army coup in Guatemala overthrows president Miguel Fuentes.

● **Mar**: The British government withdraws its support for the Central African Federation and announces than Northern Rhodesia will be allowed to secede. White settlers in Southern Rhodesia claim they are being betrayed. (›13 Sep)

● **20 Apr**: The execution takes place of Julian Grimaldi, Spanish Communist leader during the Civil War, despite international appeals for clemency.

● **3 May**: The South African government takes discretionary powers against subversion. People thought to have information relating to acts of subversion can be held indefinitely for interrogation for successive periods of 90 days. (›7 Aug)

● **20 May**: President Sukarno of Indonesia is appointed president for life.

● **21 May**: The USSR proposes that there should be a nuclear-free zone in the Mediterranean.

● **22–26 May**: At a meeting of 30 African heads of state at Addis Ababa, Ethiopia, the Organization for African Unity (OAU) is formed to maintain solidarity and abolish colonialism.

● **28 May**: President Kekkonen of Finland proposes a Scandinavian nuclear-free zone, but the proposal is rejected by Denmark, Norway and Sweden.

● **May**: After protests against his rule, president "Papa Doc" Duvalier of Haiti declares martial law.

● **10 Jun**: The Arabs in Iraq resume civil war against the Kurds.

● **26 Jun**: US president Kennedy makes a vigorous attack against communism during a visit to West Berlin, telling his enthusiastic audience "Ich bin ein Berliner", in a declaration of solidarity with "all free men".

● **Jun**: Disruption returns to Greece after 10 years of relative stability, as the parliamentary opposition under George Papandreou refuse to recognize the 1961 general election as legitimate. On 11 Jun prime minister Constantine Karamanlis resigns.

● **5 Aug**: A nuclear test ban treaty is signed in Moscow by the UK, USA and USSR, agreeing a permanent ban on nuclear testing in the atmosphere, outer space or underwater. It is to come into force on 10 Oct, by which time about 100 states, but not France or China, have signed.

● **7 Aug**: The UN Security Council adopts a resolution calling on all states to cease the sale or shipment of arms to South Africa.

● **30 Aug**: A "hotline" telephone link is established between the US and USSR presidents.

● **3 Sep**: South African premier Verwoerd offers to guide the administrations of Bechuanaland, Basutoland and Swaziland so that they can eventually become self-governing Bantustans (black national states).

● **13 Sep**: The UK uses its veto for the first time since 1956 in the UN Security Council, on a resolution on Southern Rhodesia calling for universal suffrage and early independence.

● **16 Sep**: Malaysia is created from the Federation of Malaya, Singapore, Sarawak and North Borneo.

● **25 Sep**: The Dominican army overthrows the Bosch government and suspends the constitution.

● **1 Oct**: Nigeria becomes an independent republic with Dr Nnamdi Azikiwe as president.

● **1 Oct**: Newly appointed president of Algeria Ahmed Ben Bella announces the nationalization of all land owned by French settlers.

SOCIETY

- **10 Oct**: The scandal over security provoked by the involvement of UK Secretary of State for War John Profumo with model girl Christine Keeler brings about the resignation of Harold Macmillan as British prime minister. He is succeeded by Lord Hume, who renounces his title to become Sir Alec Douglas-Home.

- **15 Oct**: West German chancellor Konrad Adenauer resigns, aged 87, having held the position since 1949. Dr Ludwig Erhard succeeds him.

- **22–25 Oct**: Operation "Big Lift": an entire armored division of 16,000 US army and air force troops plus equipment is flown from Fort Hood, Texas, to West Germany as a demonstration of US strategic mobility.

- **Oct**: Border fighting breaks out between Algerian and Moroccan troops, but a ceasefire comes into force on 2 Nov.

- **1–2 Nov**: Ngo Dinh Diem, the increasingly unpopular president of South Vietnam, is killed in a US-supported military coup.

- **12 Nov**: Prince Sihanouk asks for the withdrawal of all US aid to Cambodia and later proposes a 14-nation conference to guarantee Cambodian neutrality. On 20 Nov China proclaims its support for Cambodia's "struggle against imperialism".

- **18 Nov**: The army overthrows the government in Iraq on behalf of the president. On 22 Nov the All-Military Revolutionary Council becomes the new government under president Aref.

- **22 Nov**: John F. Kennedy, president of the USA, is assassinated during a visit to Dallas, Texas, by Lee Harvey Oswald. TV cameras record the event. The vice-president, Lyndon B. Johnson, is immediately sworn in as the next president.

- **24 Nov**: Lee Harvey Oswald is shot dead at Dallas police headquarters by Jack Ruby, who is indicted for the murder two days later.

- **3 Dec**: Black nationalist leader Nelson Mandela is brought from jail to stand trial for treason in South Africa.

- **10 Dec**: Zanzibar becomes an independent state within the Commonwealth.

- **12 Dec**: Kenya becomes an independent state within the Commonwealth.

- **17 Dec**: The GDR and the West Berlin senate sign an agreement allowing West Berliners to be issued with passes to visit relatives in East Berlin over Christmas and the New Year.

- **21–25 Dec**: Fighting breaks out between Greek and Turkish Cypriots at Nicosia, Cyprus. British troops are sent in on 26 Dec, and on 30 Dec a neutral zone is established in Nicosia.

- **31 Dec**: The Central African Federation (Rhodesia and Nyasaland) is dissolved.

- **29 Jan**: Discussions on UK entry to the EEC collapse due to French opposition.

- **3 Apr**: Negro leaders in Birmingham, Alabama, launch a campaign against segregation. On 12 Apr Martin Luther King is arrested for leading a civil rights march in Alabama. (›5 May)

- **8 Apr**: Romania clashes with the USSR over Comecon integration plans.(›Dec)

- **11 Apr**: Pope John XXIII publishes the encyclical "Pacem in Terris", calling for end to the arms race and negotiations to end disputes. (›3 Jun)

- **5 May**: 1,000 are arrested on a civil rights march in Birmingham, Alabama. On 11 May segregationists bomb the homes of Negro leaders, and Kennedy sends in federal troops. (›1 Jun)

- **21 May**: The GATT Conference at Geneva agrees to launch multilateral trade negotiation for the "Kennedy Round" of tariff cuts, May 1964.

- **May**: The South Vietnamese government under Roman Catholic president Diem begins to persecute Buddhists. Martial law is declared on 21 Aug, and hundreds of Buddhist monks, nuns and students arrested.

- **1 Jun**: Governor George Wallace of Alabama says he will defy a court order to allow blacks into the University of Alabama, and US national guards are detailed to protect two black students as they enroll on 11 Jun. On 18 Aug James Meredith, the first Negro student at the University of Mississippi, receives his diploma.

- **3 Jun**: Pope John XXIII dies at the age of 81. On 30 Jun Cardinal Montini is enthroned as Paul VI.

- **20 Jul**: The EEC signs an association convention with 18 independent African countries at Yaoundé, Cameroon.

- **26 Jul**: A massive earthquake destroys the city of Skopje, Yugoslavia.

- **28 Aug**: Large-scale civil rights demonstrations take place in Washington. Martin Luther King has this message: "I have a dream… that the sons of former slaves and the sons of former slave owners would sit together at the table of brotherhood."

- **10 Sep**: American Express launches its credit card in the UK, five years' after its introduction in the USA.

- **12 Sep**: Turkey becomes an associate member of the EEC.

- **23 Oct**: The Bhakra dam in the Punjab, intended eventually to irrigate 4 million hectares (10 million acres), is completed after 15 years' work (Ind).

- **Dec**: The first Comecon plan for common scientific and technological development is enforced.

- Nobel Peace Prize is won by the International Committee of the Red Cross and the League of Red Cross Societies.

CULTURE

- **Jan–Feb**: The *Mona Lisa* is shown in Washington and New York, lent by the Louvre in Paris. Nearly two million people go to see it.

- **20 Feb**: First performance of Rolf Hochhuth's controversial play *Der Stellvertreter* (The Representative), which accuses Pope Pius XII of having failed to condemn the Nazi massacre of the Jews (FRG).

- **11 Oct**: Edith Piaf, French *diseuse*, dies at the age of 47.

- Günter Grass: *Hundejahre* (Dog Years), novel (FRG).

- John Le Carré: *The Spy Who Came in from the Cold*, Cold War thriller (UK).

- Anna Akhmatova: "Requiem", poem (USSR).

- Sylvia Plath: *The Bell Jar*, novel (UK).

- Louis MacNeice: *The Burning Perch*, poems (UK).

- Yukio Mishima: *The Sailor Who Fell from Grace with the Sea*, novel (Jap).

- John Arden: *The Workhouse Donkey*, play (UK).

- Michael Tippett: Concerto for Orchestra (UK).

- Benjamin Britten: Cello Symphony (UK).

- Leonard Bernstein: Symphony No.3, the "Kaddish" (USA).

- Hans Werner Henze: Symphony No.5 (It).

- The Beatles' song "I Want to Hold Your Hand" sells a million copies before release and goes straight to number 1 in the UK charts. They release their first LP, *Please Please Me*, and in Dec have five hits simultaneously in the Top Twenty.

- The Rolling Stones issue their first record, "Come On" (UK).

- Roy Lichtenstein: *Whaam!*, acrylic painting based on war action strip cartoon (USA).

- Heinz Mack: *Light Dynamo*, kinetic light picture (FRG).

- Antonio Tapiés: Black with two Lozenges painting (Sp).

- Bridget Riley: *Fall*, Op Art painting (UK).

- Eduardo Chillada: *Modulation of Space*, sculpture (Sp).

- Le Corbusier: Carpenter Center for the Visual Arts, Cambridge (USA).

- Alison and Peter Smithson: The Economist Building, London.

- Federico Fellini's autobiographical film *Eight and a half* (referring to the number of films he has made), is released (It).

- Joseph Losey: *The Servant*, starring Dirk Bogarde (UK).

- Alfred Hitchcock: *The Birds* (USA).

- Pierre Cardin produces his first ready-to-wear collection (Fr).

- Nobel Prize for Literature is won by George Seferis (Gr).

SCIENCE

- **2 Apr**: The USSR launch the unmanned rocket *Lunik IV* toward the Moon, but it misses by 8,500 km (5,300 miles).

- **10 Apr**: The US nuclear-powered submarine *Thresher* does not resurface after deep-diving trials in the North Atlantic, and her crew of 129 is lost.

- **12 May**: The US astronaut Gordon Cooper is launched from Cape Canaveral in a Mercury capsule, and makes 22 orbits of the Earth.

- **14 Jun**: Soviet astronaut Valery Bykovsky makes 82 orbits of the Earth.

- **16 Jun**: The USSR launch the world's first female astronaut, Valentina Tereshkova, into space.

- NASA news satellite Relay 1 transmits news exchanges between newspaper offices in the UK, USA and Brazil.

- Two theological scholars, using a computer for analysis, suggest that St Paul wrote only 4 of the 14 epistles in the New Testament.

- Friction welding is invented in the USSR.

- The Nobel Prize for Physiology or Medicine is won by Alan Hodgkin and Andrew Huxley of the UK and Sir John Eccles (Aus) for their work on the transmission of nervous impulses.

- Maria Goeppert-Mayer (USA), E. P. Wigner (USA) and J. Hans D. Jensen (FRG) share the Nobel Prize for Physics.

- The Nobel Prize for Chemistry is won by G. Natta (It) and K. Ziegler (FRG) for their synthesis of polymers for plastics.

- Anti-xi-zero, a fundamental atomic particle of antimatter, is discovered.

- M. De Bakey uses an artificial heart during cardiac surgery (USA).

- J.D. Hardy performs the first human lung transplant.

- F.D. Moore and T.E. Starzl perform first liver transplant.

- Carbon fiber is developed in the UK.

- A joint Canadian-American scheme is announced to build a dam across Passamaquoddy Bay and use tidal power to produce over 1 million kW per day of cheap electricity.

- A commercial vaccine for measles is developed after five years' research.

- Scientists in Cambridge, UK, develop a process for preserving food using radiation. They stress that it does not make the food radioactive.

The paradox of changing relations between black and white in postimperial Africa was exemplified by the installation as heads of government of politicians who had once been jailed by the very same authority that now handed over power to them with every appearance of approval. Jomo Kenyatta in Kenya, Kenneth Kaunda in Uganda and Hastings Banda in Malawi followed Julius Nyerere of Tanzania in making the transition from persecuted opponents to trusted and respected equals. In India, the death of Jawaharlal Nehru was a reminder that a similar transition – from political internee to world statesman – had taken place there too not so long ago. In southern Africa, though, the trend was reversed as Ian Smith took power in Southern Rhodesia and threatened a unilateral declaration of independence from Britain, while Nelson Mandela was sentenced to life imprisonment in South Africa. The notorious Gulf of Tonkin resolution opened the floodgates to military escalation in Vietnam.

▲ **No amount of concern over South Africa, Vietnam or Cyprus could stop the runaway success of the Beatles. Their first film,** *A Hard Day's Night,* **released in July, was soon showing simultaneously in more countries than any other film ever.**

● **9 Jan**: In Panama clashes erupt over disputed rights in the Panama Canal. Anti-US rioting breaks out, and on 10 Jan diplomatic relations with the USA are broken off. On 4 Apr relations are restored.

● **13–17 Jan**: Arab League "summit" conference of 13 states meets to discuss counter-measures against Israel's plans to divert the River Jordan. They agree to set up a unified military command.

● **20 Jan**: At the disarmament conference in Geneva, the USA and USSR agree to reduce production of enriched uranium and plutonium in the next few years.

● **27 Jan**: France establishes diplomatic relations with Communist China; on 10 Feb Nationalist China breaks off diplomatic relations with France.

● **30 Jan**: A military coup ousts the South Vietnamese government.

● **3 Feb**: Ghana becomes a one-party state after a referendum on 24 Jan.

● **Feb**: Tension between the Greek and Turkish communities grows after Turkish prime minister Ilonu walks out of talks held in London in Jan, requesting UN intervention to secure the rights of Turkish Cypriots. (›Apr)

● **11 Mar**: The UK and US embassies in Phnom Penh are attacked by mobs after the Western powers' failure to agree to Prince Sihanouk's appeal of Nov 1963, for a 14-power conference to guarantee Cambodian neutrality and territorial integrity.

● **31 Mar**: A military revolution in Brazil overthrows president Goulart. On 11 Apr Marshal Castello Branco is elected president by Congress.

● **13 Apr**: Ian Smith is elected prime minister of Southern Rhodesia.

● **26 Apr**: Zanzibar merges with Tanganyika to form the United Republic of Tanganyika and Zanzibar, with Julius Nyerere as president. On 29 Oct the republic is renamed Tanzania.

● **Apr**: A UN peacekeeping force is sent to Cyprus. On 10 Aug Turkey and Cyprus accept a UN ceasefire, ending the threat of war in the Mediterranean.

● **27 May**: Jawaharlal Nehru, prime minister of India for 17 years, dies aged 76. He is succeeded by Lal Bahadur Shastri, elected on 2 Jun.

● **3 Jun**: President Park Chung Hee of South Korea imposes martial law following riots against his repressive rule.

● **12 Jun**: In South Africa, Nelson Mandela and seven other African nationalists receive life sentences for "sabotage" and are flown to jail on Robben Island.

● **26 Jun**: Møise Tshombe, ex-president of the secessionist state of Katanga, is called out of exile to help form a new Congolese government. On 30 Jun the last UN forces leave the Congo, but rebel unrest continues. Tshombe is sworn in as premier on 10 Jul.

● **Jun**: The Palestinian Liberation Organization (PLO) is founded in Jerusalem (Isr).

● **6 Jul**: Nyasaland becomes the independent state of Malawi, with Hastings Banda its first prime minister.

● **2 Aug**: Three torpedo boats attack a US destroyer in international waters off the North Vietnamese coast; next day, two US destroyers are attacked in the Gulf of Tonkin.

● **7 Aug**: The US Congress passes the Gulf of Tonkin resolution after North Vietnamese patrol boats reportedly fire on another US destroyer. This in effect gives president Johnson formal authority to commit large forces to fullscale US intervention in North Vietnam. (›Nov)

● **3 Sep**: A state of emergency is declared in Malaysia after a series of warlike acts by Indonesia. On 4 Sep the UK, Australia and New Zealand agree to give assistance to Malaysia to expand its security forces.

● **21 Sep**: Malta becomes an independent state within the Commonwealth.

● **4–11 Oct**: An international conference of 58 non-aligned states meets in Cairo. It calls on all countries not to produce or acquire nuclear weapons.

● **15 Oct**: In a Kremlin coup, Nikita Khrushchev, now aged 70, is replaced as Communist party leader by Leonid Brezhnev and as premier by Aleksey Kosygin (USSR).

● **15 Oct**: A Labour government comes to power in the UK after 13 years of Conservative rule, with Harold Wilson as prime minister.

● **21–26 Oct**: An *indaba* ("meeting") of about 600 tribal chiefs and headmen in Southern Rhodesia supports the government in its demand for independence.

● **24 Oct**: Northern Rhodesia, renamed Zambia, becomes an independent republic within the Commonwealth, with Kenneth Kaunda as its first president.

● **25 Oct**: Prime minister Wilson warns Southern Rhodesia that any unilateral declaration of independence would result in the severance of trade and financial relations with the UK and the Commonwealth.

● **2 Nov**: At the behest of the royal family and religious leaders, King Saud of Saudi Arabia is deposed and crown prince Faisal becomes king.

● **3 Nov**: Democrat Lyndon Johnson wins a sweeping victory in the US presidential elections.

● **10 Nov**: Kenya becomes an independent republic within the Commonwealth with Jomo Kenyatta as its president.

● **Nov**: The Vietcong launch a major attack on the US base at Bien Hoa, following up with a series of guerrilla strikes (Viet).

SOCIETY

- **6 Feb:** The British and French governments agree to build a Channel Tunnel.

- **18 Feb:** The USA announces the ending of some of its military and economic aid to the UK, France and Yugoslavia.

- **25 Feb:** Cassius Clay beats Sonny Liston at Miami Beach to become heavyweight champion of the world (USA).

- **11 Mar:** South Africa withdraws from the ILO.

- **19 Mar:** Reports of atrocities against Hindus in east Pakistan lead to anti-Muslim demonstrations in India, and over 125,000 Hindu refugees leave east Pakistan.

- **23 Mar–16 Jun:** The UN Conference on Trade and Development (UNCTAD) is held in Geneva. It recommends economic cooperation among all nations, regardless of their social and economic systems and levels of development, and enlargement of the UN role in international trade.

- **4 May:** The "Kennedy Round" of GATT talks opens with a working hypothesis of making 50 percent across-the-board reductions.

- **Jun:** Romania opposes the establishment of a Soviet/ Bulgarian/Romanian economic complex in the Danube area, seeing it as a scheme to reduce Romanian autonomy.

- **2 Jul:** The US Civil Rights Act, granting legal recognition of the justice of Negro demands for equal treatment in voting, education, hiring, and use of public accommodations, is signed by president Johnson; but later in the month violent race riots break out in the New York districts of Harlem and Rochester.

- **22–26 Jul:** OAS foreign ministers meet in Washington and agree to impose economic sanctions on Cuba.

- **5 Oct:** 57 people crawl through an underground tunnel to escape from East Berlin.

- **5 Oct:** The UK government imposes a 15 percent import tax on a wide range of manufactured and semi-manufactured goods, to improve the balance of payments.

- **10–24 Oct:** The 18th Olympic Games are held in Tokyo.

- **26–29 Nov:** Indonesia places British firms under Indonesian control.

- **1 Dec:** The GATT secretariat publishes an economic agreement under which 64 of its members pledge to increase imports from less developed states.

- **21 Dec:** The House of Commons vote by a majority of 185 to abolish the death penalty for murder (UK).

- In Australia, Donald Campbell sets new land speed and water speed records.

- Nobel Peace Prize is won by Martin Luther King (USA).

CULTURE

- **15 Jan:** The world's first discotheque, the "Whisky-a-Go-Go", is opened in Los Angeles (USA).

- **8 Feb:** The Beatles arrive in New York to an ecstatic welcome, and "Beatlemania" sweeps the USA.

- **28 Mar:** Radio Caroline, the first pirate radio station operating from the North Sea, begins broadcasting.

- **12 Jun:** Premiere at the Aldeburgh Festival of Benjamin Britten's opera *Curlew River* (UK).

- **6 Jul:** Premiere in London of the Beatles' first film, *A Hard Day's Night*, directed by Richard Lester.

- **28 Sep:** Harpo Marx, the silent one of the famous Marx Brothers, dies at 70 (USA).

- **Oct:** Jean-Paul Sartre refuses the Nobel Prize for Literature on the grounds that writers should act on their readers only through their words, not through the kind of influence that publicized prizes produce (Fr).

- **9 Dec:** First performance takes place in Brussels of Karlheinz Stockhausen's *Mikrophonie I*, which uses electronics in live performance.

- John Osborne's new play *Inadmissible Evidence* opens at the Royal Court Theater in London, starring Nicol Williamson.

- As part of the Shakespeare quatercentenary celebrations, Laurence Olivier plays Othello for the first time in his career at the National Theater, London.

- Joe Orton: *Entertaining Mr Sloane*, black comedy (UK).

- Robert Lowell: *For the Union Dead*, poems (USA).

- Marianne Moore: *The Arctic Ox*, poems (USA).

- William Golding: *The Spire*, novel (UK).

- Philip Larkin: *The Whitsun Weddings*, poems (UK).

- James Baldwin: *Blues for Mr Charlie*, play (USA).

- Peter Weiss: *The Marat/Sade*, full title *The Persecution and Assassination of Jean-Paul Marat as Performed by the Inmates of the Asylum of Charenton under the Direction of the Marquis de Sade*, play (UK).

- Peter Shaffer: *The Royal Hunt of the Sun*, play (UK).

- John Arden: *Armstrong's Last Goodnight*, play (UK).

- Olivier Messiaen: *Couleurs de la cité céleste* for piano, wind instruments and percussion. (Fr).

- Roger Sessions's opera *Montezuma* has its first performance (USA).

- Igor Stravinsky: *Elegy for JFK* (USA).

- Peter Maxwell Davies: *Second Taverner Fantasia*, written while he was in the USA and had begun work on his opera *Taverner*.

- Iannis Xenakis: *Eonta*, for piano and brass, in which calculations of musical parameters are made by an IBM 7090 computer.

- Marc Chagall's decorated ceiling at the Paris Opéra, commissioned by the French Minister of Culture André Malraux, is unveiled.

- R.B. Kitaj: *London by Night*, painting (UK).

- Andy Warhol: *Orange Disaster*, painting (USA).

- Bridget Riley: *Crest*, Op Art painting (UK).

- Marisol: *Women and Dog*, fur, leather, plaster, synthetic polymer and wood construction (USA).

- Frank Stella: *Ifafa II*, shaped monochrome typical of the work of those artists associated with Post Painterly Abstraction (USA).

- Enrico Baj: *Lady Fabricia Trollopp*, collage (It).

- Carolee Schneemann: *Meat Joy*, in which performers cover themselves with the blood of meat carcases and wrestle on a black canvas laid on the floor (USA).

- David Smith: *Cubi XVIII*, one in a series of sculptures in metal (USA).

- Henry Moore: *Locking-piece*, sculpture (UK).

- James Stirling and James Gowan: Department of Engineering, University of Leicester (UK).

- Kenzo Tange: Main gymnasium and sports arenas for the Tokyo Olympics (Jap).

- Walt Disney releases *Mary Poppins*, directed by Robert Stevenson, with Julie Andrews.

- Peter Sellers plays three roles in the film *Dr Strangelove; or How I Learned to Stop Worrying and Love the Bomb*, directed by Stanley Kubrick (USA).

- The film of the musical *My Fair Lady*, directed by George Cukor, stars Audrey Hepburn and Rex Harrison (USA).

- Sidney Poitier becomes the first black actor to win the Oscar for Best Actor, for his performance in *Lilies of the Field* (USA).

- Jacques Demy: *Les Parapluies de Cherbourg* (Fr).

- Hiroshi Teshigahara: *Woman in the Dunes* (Jap).

- Michelangelo Antonioni: *The Red Desert*, his first colour film (It).

- Luis Buñuel: *Diary of a Chambermaid* (Sp).

- Britain's Mary Quant says that Paris fashion is out of date, and sells her modern, inexpensive clothes from new "boutiques" like her own shop, Bazaar.

- Vidal Sassoon changes the face of modern hairdressing with his superb short cut, epitome of the "Swinging Sixties".

SCIENCE

- **27 Mar:** The UK's second satellite, Ariel II, is launched from Wallops Island, Virginia (USA).

- **31 Jul:** US spaceprobe *Ranger 7* hits the Moon, after sending back 4,316 close-up shots of the Moon's surface.

- **17 Sep:** The UK is the first nation bordering on the North Sea to grant licenses for a full-scale search for oil and gas on the continental shelf.

- **13 Oct:** The three-man Soviet spacecraft *Voskhod* returns after having made 16 orbits of the Earth.

- **16 Oct:** China carries out its first successful nuclear test, and then calls for a world summit meeting to ban nuclear weapons and destroy stockpiles.

- **Nov:** *Mariner 4* (USA) and *Zond 2* (USSR) are launched with equipment for photographing Mars.

- The Aswan Dam on the River Nile is completed, but many unforeseen ecological changes result, including the increased erosion of the Nile Delta and a drop in numbers of sardines in the Mediterranean.

- CAT scanning (Computerised Axial Tomography) is developed by A.M. Cormack and G.N. Hounsfield (USA).

- The fundamental particle omega-minus is discovered by Murray Gell-Mann (USA), using the "Nimrod" cyclotron.

- The Nobel Prize for Physiology or Medicine is won by K.E. Bloch (USA) and F. Lynen (FRG) for their work on cholesterol and fatty acid metabolism.

- Dorothy Hodgkin (UK) wins the Nobel Prize for Chemistry for her analysis of the structure of vitamin B_{12}.

- The Nobel Prize for Physics is won by C.H. Townes (USA), N.G. Basov (USSR) and A.M. Prokhorov (USSR) for the development of maser and laser principles in quantum mechanics.

- The International Rice Research Institute at Los Paños, Philippines, starts the "Green Revolution" with the introduction of improved strains of rice that will give much greater yields.

- A.A. Penzias and R.W. Wilson detect cosmic radiation, providing decisive evidence for the "Big Bang" theory (USA).

- Murray Gell-Mann and G. Zweig independently propose the existence of quarks as the "building blocks" of protons and neutrons (USA).

- The US Surgeon-General's report *Smoking and Health* links lung cancer with smoking.

- Home kidney dialysis is introduced in the UK and USA.

- The first word processor is introduced by IBM in the USA and Europe.

- The introduction of container ships much simplifies international trade.

In 1965 US involvement in the Vietnamese war increased dramatically, with intensive bombing of the North, despite growing protests at home. It was a year for "strong" leadership, with Ian Smith declaring Southern Rhodesia's independence from Britain, the hard-headed Colonel Boumédienne taking power in Algeria, Hassan asserting the divine right of kings in Morocco, Ceauşescu inheriting the top job in Romania, and Indira Gandhi on the verge of electoral success in India. The race for the Moon began in earnest as an unmanned spacecraft landed to send back the first close-up photographs and astronauts rehearsed some of the procedures necessary for a "Moonshot". Meanwhile, the ambiguous nature of the pop revolution, part burgeoning industry and export drive, part youthful revolt, was reflected in the furore provoked in Britain when the queen bestowed upon the Beatles an honor usually reserved for distinguished servants of the state. A man universally recognised as a distinguished servant of the state, wartime prime minister Sir Winston Churchill, died at the age of 91.

▲ The state funeral of ex-prime minister Winston Churchill called forth all the trappings of British tradition. Thousands lined the streets of London to watch his funeral cortège pass on its way to Westminster Abbey.

● **2 Jan**: Indonesia withdraws from the UN following Malaysia's election to a seat on the Security Council.

● **14 Jan**: The prime ministers of Northern Ireland and the Republic of Ireland meet for the first time since the partition of 1921, in Belfast.

● **20 Jan**: Lyndon B. Johnson is inaugurated as US president for his first elected term of office.

● **24 Jan**: Sir Winston Churchill, wartime British prime minister, dies aged 91.

● **27 Jan**: South Vietnamese generals withdraw support for Tran Van Huong's government and seize power. On 16 Feb Phan Huy Quat forms a new government. On 19 Jun a new provisional constitution and military directorate is announced, and Nguyen Cao Ky becomes premier. (›7 Feb)

● **4 Feb**: In a press conference, French president Charles de Gaulle calls for discussion of the reform of the UN, a return to the gold standard and reunification of Germany.

● **7 Feb**: After Vietcong attacks on US areas in South Vietnam, US aircraft begin bombing raids on North Vietnam in retaliation. On 2 Mar the USA declares its combatant status. In the first attacks that are not a direct reprisal for Vietcong activities, over 160 US and South Vietnamese planes bomb a North Vietnamese naval base and munitions depot. (›22 Mar)

● **18 Feb**: Gambia becomes an independent state within the Commonwealth.

● **24 Feb**: After news in Jan that West Germany is giving arms worth $80 million to Israel, the UAR formally breaks off diplomatic relations with the FRG. The FRG halts all economic aid to the UAR. (›12 May. ›Society, 1 Mar)

● **26 Feb**: The Indonesian government seizes US-owned rubber plantations in Sumatra, and on 19 Mar takes over three foreign oil companies. On 24 Apr the state takes over all foreign companies.

● **19 Mar**: On the death of Romanian leader Gheorghiu Dej, Nicolae Ceauşescu becomes First Secretary of the Romanian Communist party.

● **22 Mar**: The US revelation that non-lethal gas is being used against Vietcong forces meets with critical world reaction. (›1 Apr)

● **29 Mar**: Congolese government troops, aided by white mercenaries, capture Watsa, the last important rebel stronghold in the northeast Congo.

● **1 Apr**: 17 non-aligned states petition the USA to hold talks to find a peaceful solution to Vietnam conflict. (›18 Apr)

● **9 Apr**: Indian and Pakistani troops clash in the Rann of Kutch border area over rival claims to Kashmir. A ceasefire is agreed on 1 Jul (›1 Sep).

● **29 Apr**: France and the USSR, in a joint statement, call for an end to foreign intervention in Vietnam.

● **29 Apr**: Australia announces that an 800-man battalion is being sent to Vietnam, causing controversy at home. On 27 May New Zealand announces that an artillery battery will be sent to Vietnam, causing further concern. (›28 Jul)

● **12 May**: The FRG establishes diplomatic relations with Israel, while 10 Arab states cut off relations with Bonn.

● **7 Jun**: King Hassan II of Morocco assumes absolute powers after the failure of attempts to form a government of national union.

● **19 Jun**: Algerian president Ahmed Ben Bella is deposed in a bloodless coup by army-supported socialist nationalists under Col. Houari Boumédienne, who later forms a new government.

● **22 Jun**: Japan and South Korea sign a treaty to restore full diplomatic relations after a lapse of 55 years.

● **13 Jul**: India extends diplomatic recognition to the 13 member countries of the Arab League, becoming the first nation to do so.

● **28 Jul**: President Johnson announces an almost immediate increase in US strength in Vietnam, from 75,000 to 125,000, and that draft calls will gradually be doubled. (›20 Sep)

● **1 Sep**: Pakistani forces cross the ceasefire line with India, and on 6 Sep Indian forces invade west Pakistan. On 20 Sep the UN Security Council calls for a ceasefire.

● **20 Sep**: The US House of Representatives approve the use of force by any American nation to prevent a Communist takeover.

● **15–18 Oct**: Mass antiwar demonstrations are held in the USA. (›5 Dec)

● **16 Oct**: Singapore becomes the 22nd member of the Commonwealth.

● **27 Oct**: Brazilian president Humberto Castello Branco dissolves all political parties due to rightwing military pressure, and decrees that his successor will be chosen by a majority of Congress, not a direct popular vote.

● **11 Nov**: Rhodesia, Britain's last colony in Africa, makes an illegal Unilateral Declaration of Independence (UDI) from Britain. Britain and the UN impose economic sanctions (›Dec).

● **17 Nov**: The UN General Assembly votes against the admission of Communist China.

● **5 Dec**: De Gaulle gains only 44 percent of the votes in the French presidential elections, failing to gain a clear majority. In a second ballot on 19 Dec he gains 55 percent to defeat his Socialist rival François Mitterand.

● **5 Dec**: China enters the Vietnam conflict to support North Vietnam.

● **Dec**: Nine African states break off relations with the UK because of its failure to end the rebellion in Southern Rhodesia.

SOCIETY

● **4 Jan**: President Johnson encourages trade with Eastern Europe in his State of the Union address.

● **11 Jan**: The 90-day detention clause is suspended in South Africa, but new powers are provided for the imprisonment of potential state witnesses for 180 days.

● **26 Jan**: Hindi replaces English as the official language in India, prompting disturbances in Tamil-speaking areas. On 24 Feb Sri Shastri announces that English will continue to be an associate official language.

● **1 Feb**: Ron Clarke (Aus) breaks the 5,000 m world record twice in three weeks.

● **8 Feb**: The British government announces plans to ban cigarette advertising on TV (›13 Jul).

● **21 Feb**: Malcolm X, the founder of the pro-violence Black Nationalist group, is assassinated (USA).

● **24 Feb**: In Madrid, 5,000 students clash with police in demonstrations for free student unions. On 1 Aug five professors are arrested for supporting the students.

● **27 Feb**: A referendum in Switzerland votes to continue with the government's anti-inflationary restrictions for another year.

● **Feb**: The West German company Krupp and the Polish government agree on industrial cooperation and on construction of manufacturing plants in Poland.

● **1 Mar**: East Germany agrees to provide the UAR with $100 million in economic aid.

● **2 Mar**: The Council of Ministers of the EEC decide to combine the executives of the EEC, ECSC and Euratom, and establish its future seat in Brussels. The merger treaty is signed on 8 Apr, to be effective from 1 Jan 1966.

● **4 Mar**: In Moscow, Afro-Asian students organize anti-American demonstrations which have to be broken up by police.

● **15 Mar**: The South African government orders stricter racial segregation policy for audiences at sports events and theaters.

● **24 Mar**: The West German Bundestag passes a bill to allow new murder prosecutions against Nazi war criminals until 31 Dec 1969.

● **15 Apr**: The FRG pays the final installment of reparations to Israel.

● **24 Apr**: Yugoslav participation in Comecon becomes effective, but Yugoslavia also makes application for full membership of GATT and associate membership of EFTA.

● **27 Apr**: The UK import surcharge, imposed in Oct 1964, is reduced from 15 to 10 percent after pressure from EFTA. On 12 May the IMF approve granting $1.4 billion in financial aid to help support the pound.

● **7 Jun**: The US Supreme Court invalidates the 1879 Connecticut law prohibiting birth control devices in a sweeping decision that establishes a new constitutional right of privacy.

● **21 Jun**: The UK, Canada and four Nordic states pledge $17,780,000 to help solve the UN's financial crisis. UN Secretary-General U Thant says that this voluntary contribution is only one-fifth of the total needed.

● **30 Jun**: EEC discussions in Brussels on farm policy financing break down due to French intransigence. On 2 Jul France announces a boycott of EEC meetings.

● **Jun**: British prime minister Harold Wilson puts forward a 10-point economic program for modernizing industry by promoting investment, research and exports.

● **13 Jul**: The US House of Representatives passes a bill requiring a health warning on cigarette packets and containers, to be effective from 1 Jan 1966.

● **30 Jul**: US economic aid to Nationalist China becomes effective by mutual agreement.

● **11 Aug**: Massive race riots break out in Watts, a Negro area of Los Angeles. By 17 Aug, when the curfew is lifted, 34 people have been killed, 800 injured and over 7,000 arrested (USA).

● **2 Sep**: The Chinese Cultural Revolution begins with a policy declaration issued in Beijing, urging revolutionaries in underdeveloped states to wage a people's war against the USA and other capitalist states.

● **21 Sep**: BP (British Petroleum Co) strike natural gas in the North Sea with the oil rig *Sea Gem*; but on 27 Dec the *Sea Gem* collapses, and 13 of the crew of 32 are lost.

● **2 Oct**: The Supreme Soviet adopts a plan to abolish the regional economic councils established by Khrushchev in 1957, and instead to establish central controls over the economy, and extend the use of the profit motive.

● **9 Nov**: The largest power failure in history blacks out all of New York City, parts of eight northeastern states and parts of Ontario and Quebec (USA/Can).

● **27 Nov**: Between 15,000 and 35,000 people take part in a march on Washington for peace in Vietnam (USA).

● A reform of the world monetary system, to create and distribute new reserves, is discussed and a report prepared by a team of experts for the "Group of 10", the 10 most industrialized states.

● Currency reforms and the introduction of new currencies take place in Brazil, Argentina and Albania.

● The millionth Mini car comes off the assembly line (UK).

● The Nobel Peace Prize is won by the United Nations Children's Fund.

CULTURE

●**8 Jan**: British singer Adam Faith cancels concerts in Johannesburg after being refused permission to play to multiracial audiences.

● **9 Feb**: First performance of a new ballet *Romeo and Juliet*, created for Margot Fonteyn and Rudolf Nureyev by Kenneth MacMillan.

● **15 Feb**: Death of American singer Nat King Cole, aged 45.

● Vaclav Havel: *The Memorandum*, play (Cze).

● Harold Pinter: *The Homecoming*, play (UK).

● Edward Bond: *Saved*, play (UK).

● Slawomir Mrozek: *Tango*, play (Pol).

● Tom Wolfe: *The Kandy-Kolored Tangerine-Flake Streamline Baby*, novel (USA).

● Wole Soyinka: *The Interpreters*, novel (Nig).

● Sylvia Plath: *Ariel*, poems published posthumously (UK).

● Norman Mailer: *An American Dream*, novel (USA).

● Nobel Prize for Literature is won by Mikhail Sholokhov (USSR).

● Igor Stravinsky: *Variations and Introitus: T.S. Eliot in Memoriam*. Eliot died on 4 Jan (USA).

● Paul Dessau: *Requiem for Lumumba*. Patrice Lumumba, the first prime minister of the independent Congo, was murdered in 1961 (GDR).

● Leonard Bernstein: *The Chichester Psalms*, for treble voice, chorus and orchestra (USA).

● Elliott Carter: Piano Concerto (USA).

● Release of hit song "The Sound of Silence" by Simon and Garfunkel.

● Petula Clark (UK) wins the US Grammy award for the best rock 'n' roll single record with "Downtown".

● Kenneth Noland: *Grave Light*, painting (USA).

● Anthony Caro: *Slow Movement*, painted steel (UK).

● Jesús Rafael Soto: *Vibration*, experimental sculpture (Venez).

● Peter Blake: *Doktor K Tortur*, painting (UK).

● Kenzo Tange: Roman Catholic Cathedral, Tokyo (Jap).

● Viljo Revell: Town Hall, Toronto (Can).

● The film of Boris Pasternak's novel *Dr Zhivago*, directed by David Lean and starring Julie Christie and Omar Sharif, is released (UK).

● *The Sound of Music*, directed by Robert Wise, stars Julie Andrews, with a score by Rodgers and Hammerstein.

● James Ivory: *Shakespeare Wallah* (USA).

● Kon Ichikawa: *Toyko Olympiad* (Jap).

● America's first Mod store, Paraphernalia, opens in New York.

SCIENCE

● **17 Feb**: US space probe *Ranger 8* is launched toward the Moon. On 20 Feb it relays TV pictures of the Moon's surface back to Earth.

● **18 Mar**: Aleksey Leonov, USSR cosmonaut, makes the first "space walk", leaving *Voskhod II* for 20 minutes in a spacesuit.

● **4 Apr**: The USA puts into orbit the first completely atomic-powered satellite, using the nuclear reactor SNAP 10 A.

● **Apr**: The British government grants £1,500,000 to the British Atomic Energy Authority for further research into desalination.

● **2 May**: The world's first commercial communications satellite, Early Bird, launched on 6 Apr, links the USA, Canada, UK and Europe, and begins the exchange of TV programs.

● **3 Jun**: US astronaut Edward White leaves *Gemini 4* for a 20-minute space walk.

● **15 Jul**: US spaceprobe *Mariner 4* sends back the first detailed photographs of Mars.

● **21 Aug**: A two-man spacecraft, *Gemini 5*, is launched with Gordon Cooper and Charles Conrad Jr aboard. On 29 Aug it lands after 120 orbits, the longest space flight so far.

● **26 Nov**: France launches its first satellite, A-1, in the Sahara.

● **4 Dec**: *Gemini 7* two-man craft is launched; on 15 Dec *Gemini 6* is launched, and meets *Gemini 7* in orbit, achieving the first rendezvous in space, an essential aspect of the Moon landing program (USA).

● H. Harlow demonstrates the negative emotional effect of rearing monkeys in total isolation (USA).

● A vaccine against measles is introduced.

● The Stanford Linear Accelerator Center (SLAC) is opened (USA).

● Soft contact lenses are invented.

● J. Ochsner uses Marlex, a plastic mesh, to bridge large defects in body tissue without risk of rejection.

● The Nobel Prize for Physiology or Medicine is won by F. Jacob, A. Lwoff and J. Monod (Fr) for their work on the regulatory activities of genes.

● R.P. Feynman (USA), S. Tomanaga (Jap) and J.S. Schwinger (USA) win the Nobel Prize for Physics for research into quantum electrodynamics.

● R.B. Woodward (USA) wins the Nobel Prize for Chemistry for the synthesis of organic compounds.

● R. Holley discovers the structure of a molecule of t-RNA, the space protein-building molecule (USA).

● F. Reines and J.P.F. Sellshop detect neutrinos from cosmic rays deep in a South African gold mine, the beginning of neutrino astronomy.

London became temporarily the fashion hub of the Western world as the Swinging Sixties really got into gear, typified by Andy Warhol's film "Chelsea Girls." But while the West concerned itself with Pop and Op art, Happenings and Flower Power, the Far East was suffering a very different kind of Cultural Revolution. A favorite European adjective for the Chinese is "inscrutable", but in 1966 it seemed that inscrutability had been overtaken by lunacy as the aging Mao Zedong let loose his Red Guards in an effort to purge the Communist state of revisionism and "bourgeois reactionary thinking". Even other Communist states protested, but to no avail. In Indonesia the Chinese suffered in the anti-Communist purges that followed the removal of General Sukarno. In Africa the frequently grim cycle of postcolonial readjustment continued: Kwame Nkrumah was overthrown in Ghana, while a coup toppled the government in Nigeria. In Vietnam, the bombs kept falling.

▲ Model girl Twiggy, the face of the Swinging Sixties.

● **1 Jan**: Pope Paul VI appeals for a settlement in Vietnam. (›24 Jan)

● **11 Jan**: India's prime minister Lal Bahadur Shastri dies after a heart attack. On 19 Jan Mrs Indira Gandhi, daughter of the late Jawaharlal Nehru, is elected to succeed him.

● **13 Jan**: Robert C. Weaver becomes the first Negro ever nominated to the US cabinet.

● **15 Jan**: The army seizes power in Nigeria. Prime minister Sir Abubakar Tafawa Balewa is killed. On 16 Jan Gen. Johnson T.U. Aguiyi-Ironsi takes over. (›29 Jul).

● **20 Jan**: Australian prime minister Robert Menzies announces his retirement after a record 17 years. He is succeeded on 25 Jan by Harold Holt.

● **24 Jan**: North Vietnamese premier Ho Chi Minh tells heads of state that if the USA wants peace, it must call a permanent halt to air attacks on North Vietnam and recognize the South Vietnamese Liberation Front.

● **31 Jan**: The USA resumes bombing of North Vietnam after a 37-day pause, a decision supported by the UK. (›8 Feb)

● **1 Feb**: China sends a protest note to the UK about the presence of US warships in Hong Kong.

● **8 Feb**: At talks in Honolulu, US president Johnson and South Vietnamese premier Ky issue a declaration outlining major US commitments in South Vietnam and stressing economic and social reform. (›8 Mar)

● **21 Feb**: French president de Gaulle calls for the dismantling of NATO. On 10 Mar he announces his intention to withdraw French troops from NATO and asks for removal of NATO HQ and bases from French territory. (›1 Jul)

● **22 Feb**: Prime minister Milton Obote of Uganda assumes all government power and arrests five ministers. The constitution is suspended on 24 Feb. (›10 Jun)

● **24 Feb**: President Kwame Nkrumah's government is overthrown in a military coup (Ghana).

● **1 Mar**: The GDR formally applies for UN membership.

● **5 Mar**: The OAU adopts a resolution urging the UK to use force in Rhodesia. (›17 Nov)

● **8 Mar**: Australia announces that it will triple its forces in Vietnam. (›26 Mar)

● **11 Mar**: After weeks of anti-Communist demonstrations, president Sukarno of Indonesia signs over political powers to army commander Lt-Gen. Suharto, though still retaining presidential powers. On 12 Mar the Indonesian Communist party is banned.

● **22 Mar**: Congolese president Joseph D. Mobutu abolishes parliament's functions and assumes all national legislative powers.

● **26 Mar**: Parades and rallies are held in several US and foreign cities as part of the International Days of Protest against US policy in Vietnam.

● **10 Apr**: In South Vietnam Buddhist leaders declare war on the military government. (›3 May)

● **16 Apr**: Major-Gen. Abdul Rahman Arif is elected president of Iraq to succeed his brother Abdas-Salām Arif.

● **3 May**: The USA acknowledges its first intentional shelling of Cambodia, claiming to have been subjected to heavy attack from the Cambodian side of the border. (›29 Jun)

● **7 May**: Romanian Communist party First Secretary Nicolae Ceauşescu declares Romania an independent country recognizing no supreme authority within the Communist movement.

● **26 May**: British Guiana becomes independent as Guyana.

● **27 May**: A Popular Front government forms in Finland under Rafael Paasia, which includes Communists for the first time in 18 years.

● **7 Jun**: Clashes take place between police and demonstrators wanting greater autonomy for east Pakistan.

● **10 Jun**: President Obote of Uganda dissolves the rebellious kingdom of Buganda into four smaller provinces administered by central government.

● **28 Jun**: Argentinian President Arturo Illia is deposed in a bloodless military coup.

● **29 Jun**: Mustafa al-Barzani, leader of the Kurds in northern Iraq, accepts the Iraqi government's plan for Kurdish autonomy, thus ending a five-year rebellion.

● **29 Jun**: North Vietnam's two major cities, Hanoi and Haiphong, are bombed by the USA for the first time. The UK government issues a statement dissociating itself from the bombing of populated areas. (›14 Jul)

● **Jun**: The Chinese leadership is purged in a campaign against "rightists". (›18 Aug)

● **1 Jul**: France withdraws all its forces assigned to NATO, and NATO HQ moves to Brussels.

● **6 Jul**: Malawi (previously Nyasaland) becomes a republic within the Commonwealth, with Dr Hastings Banda its first president.

● **14 Jul**: Israeli Air Force jets raid a water diversion project in Syria in retaliation for Syrian border incursions. (›13 Nov)

● **14 Jul**: President Marcos authorizes sending 2,000 Philippine troops to South Vietnam. A unit from Thailand also arrives later in Jul. (›30 Jul)

● **29 Jul**: Sections of the Nigerian army mutiny; Gen. Ironsi is overthrown and later reported killed.

● **30 Jul**: US planes bomb the demilitarized zone between North and South Vietnam for the first time. (›23 Sep)

SOCIETY

● **18 Aug**: Mao Zedong and his successor-presumptive Lin Piao appear at a rally in Beijing. In the following months, anything "bourgeois" is attacked in the name of the Cultural Revolution. Several nations, including the USSR, Cuba and East Germany, denounce Red Guard excesses (Chi).

● **6 Sep**: South African prime minister Hendrik Verwoerd, originator of apartheid, is assassinated on the front bench of parliament in Capetown. On 13 Sep he is succeeded by Balthazar J. Vorster.

● **23 Sep**: At a conference of non-aligned nations in New Delhi, India, the UAR and Yugoslavia call for immediate cessation of US air raids on North Vietnam without preconditions. (›24 Oct)

● **30 Sep**: Bechuanaland becomes independent as the Republic of Botswana, with Sir Seretse Khama its first president.

● **4 Oct**: The British colony of Basutoland becomes the independent state of Lesotho, with Moshoeshoe II as king, and Chief Leabua Jonathan as prime minister.

● **5 Oct**: Spain closes the land frontier with Gibraltar to all traffic except for pedestrians.

● **24–25 Oct**: At the Manila Conference, Australia, New Zealand, the Philippines, Thailand, South Korea and South Vietnam pledge political self-determination and aid to South Vietnam.

● **7 Nov**: Syria and Egypt sign a mutual defense agreement in Cairo establishing joint command over their armed forces.

● **13 Nov**: Israel attacks Jordan in the Hebron area. Jordan complains to the UN. On 23 Nov Jordan accepts a Saudi Arabian offer of 20,000 troops to help defend its border against Israel, and on 25 Nov the UN Security Council passes a resolution censuring Israel.

● **17 Nov**: The UN General Assembly adopts a resolution urging the UK to use force if necessary to overthrow the Rhodesian government. (›2 Dec)

● **22 Nov**: Gen. Franco introduces a new Spanish constitution providing for the appointment of a prime minister and making 100 seats in the Cortes elective.

● **30 Nov**: Barbados becomes an independent state within the Commonwealth.

● **2 Dec**: The UN General Assembly unanimously re-elects Secretary-General U Thant to a second term of office.

● **2–4 Dec**: British prime minister Harold Wilson and Ian Smith, leader of the rebel Rhodesian government, hold talks on the Rhodesian situation. On 5 Dec the Rhodesian cabinet rejects all British proposals. On 20 Dec the UK indicates that it would only offer legal independence under African majority rule. On 22 Dec, Smith declares Rhodesia a republic.

● **8 Jan**: Cardinal Wyszynski, Roman Catholic primate of Poland, is forbidden by the government to travel to the Vatican for the celebration of the 1,000th anniversary of Christianity in Poland.

● **12 Feb**: Cuba and the USSR sign a commercial agreement worth $913,000,000 providing for a 22 percent increase in trade between them.

● **Feb**: A new five-year plan in the USSR includes the transformation of the first 36 plants into a new centrally guided economic system.

● **15 Mar**: US president Lyndon B. Johnson signs a tax bill to help finance the Vietnam war and combat inflationary pressures in the economy.

● **14 Apr**: Sandoz Pharmaceuticals Inc., the only authorized distributor of the psychedelic drug LSD in the USA, recalls all its supplies and discontinues distribution due to growing controversy over allegedly widespread use of the drug.

● **27 Apr**: There are clashes between students and police at Barcelona University, followed on 2–5 May by clashes in Madrid (Sp).

● **24 Jun**: EEC countries agree on a common agricultural market, with free trade in agriculture to be effective by 1 Jul 1968.

● **26 Jun**: A civil rights rally in Jackson, Mississippi, attended by 15,000, marks the climax of the "Meredith March" from Memphis, Tennessee, marred by violence when James Meredith – the first black to break the color bar at the University of Mississippi – is shot and wounded (USA).

● **16 Jul**: Nigeria signs a treaty of association with the EEC, the first Commonwealth state to do so.

● **1 Aug**: The Inter-American Development Bank creates a $15,000,000 fund to promote the economic integration of Latin America.

● **9 Aug**: The Argentine government devalues the peso in the first of a series of measures to combat inflation.

● **27 Aug–12 Dec**: Francis Chichester (UK), in *Gipsy Moth IV*, becomes the first man to sail round the world singlehanded.

● **Aug**: The Indian government adopts a $31.6 billion five-year plan aimed at increasing agricultural production and promoting industrial growth. It also includes provision for a massive family planning program, in view of the rapidly increasing population and the lack of adequate food supplies.

● **4 Sep**: Racing driver Jack Brabham (Aus) wins the world championship in a car he built himself.

● **1 Oct**: Chittagong and the coastal areas of East Pakistan are devastated by a cyclone.

● **31 Dec**: Tariffs on industrial goods among EFTA members are completely abolished, thus establishing a complete industrial customs union.

CULTURE

● **May**: The Beach Boys' "Sloop John B" enters the pop music charts (USA).

● **6 Aug**: Hans Werner Henze's *The Bassarids*, an opera based on Euripedes' *The Bacchae*, is premiered in Salzburg.

● **16 Sep**: New York's Metropolitan Opera House opens with the world premiere of Samuel Barber's *Antony and Cleopatra*.

● Isaac Bashevis Singer: *In My Father's Court*, autobiography (USA).

● Bernard Malamud: *The Fixer*, novel (USA).

● Günter Grass: *The Plebeians Rehearse the Uprising*, play (FRG).

● Edward Albee: *A Delicate Balance*, play (USA).

● Truman Capote: *In Cold Blood*, a "non-fiction novel" about two murderers (USA).

● Johannes Bobrowski: *Wetterzeichen*, poems (posth.) (GDR).

● Italo Calvino: *Le cosmicomiche*, a collection of fables (It).

● Nobel Prize for Literature is won by S.Y Agnon (Isr) and Nelly Sachs (Swe).

● Harrison Birtwistle: *Punch and Judy*, chamber opera (UK).

● Harry Partch: *Delusion of the Fury*, an instance of the composer's use of invented instruments and his 43-note scale (USA).

● Iannis Xenakis establishes the School of Mathematical and Automatic Music (EMAMu) (Fr).

● Benjamin Britten: *The Burning Fiery Furnace*, opera (UK).

● The Beatles' successes this year include "Eleanor Rigby" and "Day Tripper".

● Roy Lichtenstein: *Yellow and Red Brushstrokes*.

● Claes Oldenburg: *Study for Giant Chocolate*, soft sculpture (USA).

● Yayoi Kusama: *Endless Love Room*, a "happening" – a mirror-lined room filled with red balloons (Jap).

● Experimental design studios Archizoom and Superstudio are founded in Florence (It).

● Release of *Who's Afraid of Virginia Woolf*, the screen version of Edward Albee's play, directed by Mike Nichols and starring Elizabeth Taylor and Richard Burton (USA).

● Nicholas Roeg: *Fahrenheit 451*, film taken from Ray Bradbury's science fiction novel (UK).

● Andy Warhol: *Chelsea Girls*, film (USA).

● Jean-Luc Godard: *Masculin-feminin* (Fr).

● Slender model Twiggy is the face of 1966, and the King's Road in London's Chelsea the center of fashion (UK).

● T.V. science fiction serial *Star Trek* begins (USA).

SCIENCE

● **3 Feb**: Unmanned Soviet spacecraft *Luna 9* makes the first successful soft landing on the Moon and begins relaying signals to Earth.

● **1 Mar**: *Venera 3*, launched by the USSR on 16 Nov 1965, crashes on Venus, the first manmade object to touch another planet.

● **16 Mar**: US *Gemini 8* two-man spacecraft docks in space with the Agena rocket, the first successful docking operation in space.

● **3 Apr**: Soviet spaceprobe *Luna 10* becomes the first manmade object to achieve a lunar orbit.

● **3 Jun**: Thomas Stafford and Eugene Cernan are launched in their *Gemini 9* spacecraft; they land safely on 6 Jun, after a record 2 hour 9 minute spacewalk by Cernan (USA).

● **18 Jul**: *Gemini 10* is launched, with John Young and Michael Collins aboard. On 21 Jul they land safely, having achieved rendezvous with two Agena rockets, docked with one, and used its engine to propel the craft 475 miles into space. *Gemini 11* and *Gemini 12* also make flights in 1966, completing the Gemini program (USA).

● **10 Aug**: *Lunar Orbiter 1* is launched, followed in Nov by *Lunar Orbiter 2*, which begins transmitting pictures of possible landing sites.

● H. Friedman, E.T. Byram and T.A. Chubb discover a powerful source of X-rays in the constellation Cygnus, coming from the galaxy Cygnus-A.

● The first radio immunoassay kit, to test for minute quantities of hormones, is devised (UK).

● H.M. Meyer and P.D. Parman develop a live virus vaccine against rubella (German measles).

● France is the first country to adopt brain inactivity, instead of heart stoppage, as the clinical definition of death.

● S. Spiegelman and I. Haruna discover an enzyme allowing RNA molecules to duplicate themselves.

● The Nobel Prize for Chemistry is won by R.S. Mulliken (USA) for his work on atomic bonds in molecules.

● A. Kastler (Fr) wins the Nobel Prize for Physics for his study of atomic structure by optical pumping.

● The Nobel Prize for Physiology or Medicine is won by Charles B. Huggins and Francis Peyton Rous (USA) for their work on cancer.

● Konrad Lorenz's study *On Aggression* is published (Aut).

● Fuel injection for automobile engines is developed (UK).

● Two US doctors develop a method of determining whether a fetus suffers from genetic defects.

● Laser radar is developed in Japan.

The simmering unrest between Israel and its Arab neighbors erupted into fullscale warfare in the Six-Day War of June 1967. By the time it chose to observe the ceasefire called by the UN, Israel had more than doubled its territory after devastating preemptive strikes on the air forces of the UAR, Syria, Jordan, Iraq and Lebanon had virtually crippled its opponents. The fragile truce established by the UN was repeatedly broken throughout the year. In Greece the barbaric regime of the "Greek Colonels" exiled the king and enforced its wishes by recourse to the torture chamber. Yet another military man, Colonel Ojukwu, led Biafra's secession from Nigeria, provoking a long and bitter civil war; while the world's most famous general, French president de Gaulle, soured relations with Canadian prime minister Lester Pearson by encouraging French separatism during a visit to Quebec.

▲ **A victorious moment for General Moshe Dayan's Israeli forces as they take the Dome of the Rock in formerly Arab-held Jerusalem during the Six-Day War.**

- **1 Jan**: The number of US troops in Vietnam reaches 380,000.

- **9 Jan**: Israeli forces use tanks for the first time in the worsening border conflict with Syria. (›22 May)

- **21 Jan**: US intelligence sources are quoted as saying aerial reconnaissance photographs confirm that civilian as well as military structures are being damaged by US bombing of North Vietnam. (›22 Mar)

- **27 Jan**: A UN treaty limiting the use of outer space for military purposes is signed by 62 nations including the USA and USSR.

- **Jan**: In China the People's Liberation Army is mobilized to support worker-peasants against the Red Guards. On 11 Feb Beijing is put under military rule.

- **22 Feb**: President Sukarno of Indonesia surrenders all powers to Gen. Suharto. On 12 Mar Suharto becomes acting president.

- **19 Mar**: In a referendum on independence, French Somaliland votes to remain under French rule, but with "increased autonomy".

- **22 Mar**: The USA announces that Thailand has allowed US bomber bases on its territory for closer access to Communist targets.

- **28 Mar**: U Thant announces that he has submitted a three-point peace plan recommending a standstill truce in Vietnam, preliminary talks between the USA and North Vietnam, and the reconvening of the 1954 Geneva Conference; the USA accepted the proposals but North Vietnam rejected them.

- **1 Apr**: A new constitution is promulgated in South Vietnam, and elections held in Sep and Oct for the office of president and for the Senate and House of Representatives, in an attempt, encouraged by the USA, to establish a more democratic administration. (›15 Apr)

- **10 Apr**: A Bolivian army patrol finds a fortified base of the Communist guerrillas, allegedly influenced by Cuban leader Fidel Castro, in the southeastern jungle, and on 12 Apr declares the jungle area a military zone. (›8 Oct)

- **15 Apr**: Over 100,000 people march through New York and assemble before the UN headquarters in protest against the Vietnam war.

- **20 Apr**: The USA bombs the major port city of Haiphong. (›11 Aug)

- **21 Apr**: A military coup in Greece imposes the regime of the "Greek Colonels". The king is put under house arrest and later exiled, and the Colonels take control of the Greek Orthodox Church and impose strict censorship.

- **22 May**: UAR closes the Strait of Tiran, at the mouth of the Gulf of Aqaba, to Israeli ships; Israel protests, calling the closure "an act of aggression". (›5 Jun)

- **30 May**: The Ibo eastern region of Nigeria secedes as Biafra, under Col. Odumegwu Ojukwu. The Nigerian federal government orders mobilization and imposes economic sanctions, beginning civil war.

- **5 Jun**: The growing tension between Israel and the Arab states erupts into the Six-Day War between the UAR (with Syria, Jordan, Iraq and Lebanon) and Israel. The Israeli air force destroys almost the entire Arab air forces on the ground in preemptive strikes.

- **10 Jun**: Israel finally observes the ceasefire called by the UN on 6 Jun. By this time Israel has captured territory at least four times its own size, and also has control of the Old City of Jerusalem. (›17 Jul).

- **5 Jul**: Fighting breaks out in the eastern Congo between the Congolese army and white rebel mercenaries. On 4 Nov the revolt ends and its leaders flee to neighboring Rwanda.

- **11 Jul**: UK officials impose a curfew in Hong Kong after pro-Communist riots.

- **17 Jul**: UN truce observers take up positions on both sides of the Suez Canal to supervise the UAR–Israeli truce, which has been repeatedly violated. (›21 Oct)

- **23 Jul**: Puerto Ricans vote to remain in the US commonwealth rather than become federated or independent.

- **24 Jul**: During a visit to Canada, French president de Gaulle shouts "Vive le Québec libre" ("Long live free Quebec") before a crowd in Montreal. Canadian prime minister Lester Pearson rebukes him, and the visit is cut short.

- **11 Aug**: US planes launch intensified attacks on North Vietnamese targets, coming within 10 miles of the Chinese border, an area formerly regarded as off-limits.

- **10 Sep**: A referendum in Gibraltar produces a massive vote for remaining under UK sovereignty.

- **11–14 Sep**: Border clashes erupt between Chinese and Indian troops on the Tibet-Sikkim border.

- **8 Oct**: Argentinian-born Cuban guerrilla hero Che Guevara is shot dead after his capture following a clash between guerrillas and the Bolivian army.

- **21 Oct**: The Israeli destroyer *Eilat* is sunk by Egyptian naval units off Sinai. On 24 Oct Israeli artillery destroys the Suez oil refineries.

- **3 Nov**: The start of five days of celebration marking the 50th anniversary of the Bolshevik Revolution. A sweeping amnesty reduces sentences and releases thousands of prisoners (USSR).

- **16 Nov**: Clashes between Greek and Turkish Cypriots break out. On 23 Nov US, UN and NATO representatives begin a coordinated effort to avert war, agreeing on 3 Dec on a peace formula.

SOCIETY

- **4 Jan**: Donald Campbell dies in an attempt on the world water speed record on Coniston Water in his boat *Bluebird* (UK).

- **6 Jan**: Opening of the Angostura Bridge over the Orinoco River, the longest suspension bridge in Latin America.

- **10 Jan**: President Johnson proposes a 6 percent surcharge to help finance the Vietnam war, which on 3 Aug is increased to 10 percent (USA).

- **Jan**: Complete tariff freedom among the EFTA countries comes into force.

- **4 Feb**: The US government orders further controls on the amount of hydrocarbons automobiles may emit into the atmosphere.

- **8 Feb**: The Brazilian government announces devaluation of the cruzeiro and a new cruzeiro worth 1,000 of the old units.

- **Feb**: US president Johnson announces the immediate allocation of 2,000,000 tonnes of food grains to India and recommends the dispatch of an additional 3,000,000 tonnes, since drought in India for the second successive year is bringing the danger of starvation.

- **18 Mar**: The Liberian tanker *Torrey Canyon* runs aground off Land's End, creating an oil slick extending over 260 sq km (100 sq miles) (UK).

- **12 Apr**: The USSR announces it will contribute funds to help the UN deficit.

- **12–14 Apr**: At a summit meeting of 18 OAS member states at Punta del Este, Uruguay, it is agreed to create a common market.

- **27 Apr**: Expo '67 opens in Montreal (Can).

- **30 Apr**: Muhammad Ali (Cassius Clay) is stripped of his world boxing title for refusing to be drafted into the US army. On 20 Jun he is sentenced to five years in prison and fined $10,000.

- **Apr**: National aid is given to the French computer industry.

- **2 May**: West Germany agrees to spend about $150,000,000 in the UK to offset maintenance costs for the UK Army of the Rhine.

- **11 May**: The UK, Ireland and Denmark make formal application for EEC membership. On 16 May UK membership is blocked by French president de Gaulle.

- **15 May**: Conclusion of the Kennedy Round of GATT talks. It is agreed to reduce overall tariff levels, liberalize trade in agricultural products, and establish a food aid program for hungry nations.

- **May–Jul**: Outbreaks of racial violence continue in many US cities. After fierce riots in Detroit (27 Jul) president Johnson appoints a commission to look into the causes of the riots.

- **6 Jun**: Kenya, Tanzania and Uganda sign a 15-year agreement establishing the East African Community, backed by the East African Development Bank, to come into force on 1 Dec.

- **Jun**: The Monnet Commission of the EEC proposes economic cooperation between the EEC, Comecon and the USA.

- **25 Jul**: Pope Paul VI pays a two-day visit to Turkey, and meets the ecumenical patriarch of Constantinople. The visit is seen as a step toward reconciliation of the Roman Catholic and Eastern Orthodox churches.

- **Jul**: Belgian Eddy Merckx becomes world cycling champion.

- **8 Aug**: ASEAN (Association of Southeast Asian Nations) is established by Thailand, Indonesia, Singapore, the Philippines and Malaysia to promote regional growth, social progress and cultural development, and also to provide security in face of the Chinese threat.

- **15 Aug**: Martin Luther King calls for a campaign of massive civil disobedience in northern US cities to pressure the administration and Congress into responding to Negro demands.

- **3 Sep**: Sweden changes to right-hand driving to conform with the rest of the continent. The move costs $120,000,000 and has taken four years of planning.

- **29 Sep**: The IMF and the International Bank for Reconstruction and Development (World Bank) approve a plan to increase the world's money supply by creating new permanent international monetary reserve assets to be used when needed by members. These assets are to be known as Special Drawing Rights (SDRs).

- **2 Oct**: French farmers demonstrate in Quimper and other parts of western France against the government's agricultural policy.

- **10 Oct**: The UK Road Safety Act comes into force, including provision for breath tests to determine the amount of alcohol consumed.

- **25 Oct**: An epidemic of foot-and-mouth disease begins in Shropshire (UK), becoming the worst epidemic of the disease to date in the 20th century. By the end of 1967, 346,500 animals have been slaughtered.

- **Nov**: Currencies in Israel, New Zealand, Spain, Denmark and Uruguay are devalued.

- The International Commercial Bank and the Société Financière Européenne are established.

- The world's largest hydroelectric power station, the Krasnoyarsk Dam on the Yenisei River in Siberia, is completed.

- Desmond Morris publishes *The Naked Ape*, which portrays man as a mammal.

CULTURE

- **8 Apr**: Sandie Shaw (UK) wins a runaway victory at the Eurovision Song Contest in Vienna with "Puppet on a String".

- **1 Jun**: The Beatles release their album *Sergeant Pepper's Lonely Hearts Club Band* (UK).

- **18 Jun**: The first large pop festival is held at Monterey, featuring Jimi Hendrix, Janis Joplin and The Who (USA).

- George Steiner: *Language and Silence*, essays (UK).

- Rolf Hochhuth: *Soldaten* (Soldiers), play about Churchill's decision to bomb Dresden in World War II (FRG).

- V.S. Naipaul: *The Mimic Men*, novel (UK).

- R.K. Narayan: *The Vendor of Sweets*, novel (Ind).

- William Styron: *The Confessions of Nat Turner*, based on the 1831 slave rebellion in Virginia (USA).

- William Golding: *The Pyramid*, novel (UK).

- Milan Kundera: *The Joke*, novel (Cze).

- Ibuse Masuji: *Black Rain*, novel (Jap).

- Gabriel García Márquez: *One Hundred Years of Solitude*, novel (Col).

- Nobel Prize for Literature is won by Miguel Asturias (Guatemala).

- Karlheinz Stockhausen: *Hymnen*, electronic work (FRG).

- Hans Werner Henze: Concerto for Double Bass and Orchestra (It).

- Aaron Copland: *Inscape*, for orchestra (USA).

- Toru Takemitsu: *November Steps* (Jap).

- György Ligeti: Cello Concerto (FRG).

- Herbert von Karajan founds the Salzburg Easter Festival (Aut).

- David Hockney: *A Bigger Splash*, painting (USA).

- Michelangelo Pistoletto: *Self-portrait with Soutzka*, sculpture (USA).

- Luis Tomasello: *Atmosphère é bromo-plastique no.180*, relief with wood cubes and paint (Arg).

- Robert Morris: *Untitled Felt Piece*, minimal art (USA).

- Buckminster Fuller: The US Pavilion at Expo '67, Montreal, a geodesic hemisphere.

- Sachio Otani: Conference Hall, Kyoto (Jap).

- Milos Forman: *The Fireman's Ball*, film (Cze).

- Release of *Elvira Madigan*, directed by Bo Widerberg (Swe).

- *Bonnie and Clyde*, film based on the real-life story of two American criminals in the early 1930s.

- Catherine Deneuve stars in Luis Buñuel's *Belle de jour* (Sp).

SCIENCE

- **27 Jan**: Three US astronauts die in a fire in an *Apollo* spacecraft during ground tests at Cape Kennedy. The Moon program is halted when the report reveals dangerous deficiencies in the design of the capsule.

- **29 Mar**: France's first nuclear-powered submarine, *Le Redoutable*, is launched.

- **19 Apr**: *Surveyor 3*, a US lunar probe, makes a perfect touchdown on the Moon. It sends back pictures and carries a mechanical shovel to find out more about the nature of the surface.

- **24 Apr**: Soviet cosmonaut Vladimir Komarov dies in the last stages of return to earth when the parachute of his spacecraft does not work properly.

- **17 Jun**: Communist China announces that it has exploded its first hydrogen bomb.

- **Jul**: North Sea Gas is first used commercially (UK).

- **18 Oct**: The Soviet spaceprobe *Venera 4* soft-lands on Venus. On 19 Oct the US probe *Mariner V* sails past Venus without landing.

- **3 Dec**: The world's first heart transplant is performed by Christian Barnard (SA) on Louis Washkansky, who dies on 21 Dec.

- The Nobel Prize for Physics is won by H.A. Bethe (USA) for his study of the energy production of stars.

- M. Eigen (FRG), R.G.W. Norrish and G. Porter (UK) share the Nobel Prize for Chemistry for their study of highspeed chemical reactions.

- The Nobel Prize for Physiology or Medicine goes to R.A. Granit (Swe), H.K. Hartline and G. Wald (USA) for their discoveries in the physiology and chemistry of the human eye.

- The Dolby noise-reduction system is invented (USA).

- The first pulsar is discovered by A. Hewish and J. Bell (UK).

- I.S. Cooper introduces cryosurgery as a treatment for Parkinson's disease (USA).

- H. Green forms hybrid cells containing both mouse and human chromosomes to study the possibility of genetic engineering (USA).

- BP announces its intention to build a plant to manufacture protein food, first for animals and later for humans, using yeast microrganisms grown on crude oil. This is seen as a possible solution to food shortage.

- The theory of plate tectonics is introduced by D.P. McKenzie, R.L. Parker (UK) and W.J. Morgan (USA).

- S. Weinberg, A. Salam and S.L. Glashow propose the electroweak unification theory (USA).

- A. Kornberg announces his synthesis of biologically active DNA (USA).

Revolution was in the air during the spring of 1968, both on student campuses and more seriously in Czechoslovakia, where the new First Secretary Alexander Dubcek attempted to introduce his policy of "Communism with a human face". Demands for reforms by students throughout Western Europe climaxed in violent clashes in Paris between protesting workers and students on the one hand and police on the other. President de Gaulle clamped down hard on the extremists and was rewarded with a surprise landslide victory at the general election, but it was to be less than a year before he was finally forced to resign. Dubcek's moves toward reform lasted even less long; the Prague Spring was followed only too rapidly by a Soviet winter, as Warsaw Pact tanks rolled in to reimpose hardline Communism. Meanwhile the Tet offensive revealed the bankruptcy of US strategy in Vietnam, and the My Lai massacre gave an indication of the degradation of the US troops. Protests at home against the war in Vietnam and the arbitrary assassinations of Martin Luther King and Bobby Kennedy raised the spectre of civil violence on a scale not seen since the civil war and decided Lyndon B. Johnson not to run again for the presidency.

▲ **US Marines and helicopters in action in Vietnam. On 31 October president Johnson ordered an unconditional end to all bombing to facilitate peace talks.**

● **4 Jan**: The number of US troops in South Vietnam now stands at 486,000.

● **5 Jan**: Alexander Dubcek succeeds Antonin Novotny as First Secretary of the Czech Communist party. (›5 Apr)

● **12 Jan**: Fidel Castro of Cuba calls for world unification against "Yankee imperialism".

● **15 Jan**: The Laotian garrison at Nambac is taken by the Pathet Lao Communist guerrillas in the worst defeat suffered by Laos government forces so far.

● **21 Jan**: North Korean raiders invade Seoul and attempt to kill the South Korean president Park Chung Hee. On 30 Jan the USA promises to increase military support to South Korea.

● **Jan**: The Vietcong's Tet (New Year) Offensive gains much ground, taking both South Vietnamese and US troops completely by surprise.

● **16 Mar**: US troops massacre the hamlet of My Lai, South Vietnam. On 17 Mar demonstrators against the Vietnam war attempt to storm the American Embassy in London. (›13 May).

● **4 Apr**: Dr Martin Luther King is assassinated at Memphis, Tennessee, triggering violence in cities throughout the USA. More than 150,000 people follow his funeral procession on 9 Apr.

● **5 Apr**: Czech premier Alexander Dubcek begins his Action Program, allowing freedom of the press and expression of minority views within the Czech Communist party – the process of liberalization known as the "Prague Spring". (›27 Jun)

● **6 Apr**: Pierre Elliott Trudeau succeeds Lester Pearson as leader of the Liberal party and prime minister (Can).

● **13 May**: Vietnam peace talks begin in Paris between USA and North Vietnam. (›18 Aug)

● **29 May**: The controversial Emergency Powers Bill is approved by the West German Bundestag. It safeguards the state in times of emergency but does not give the executive uncontrolled authority. The Western Allies now relinquish reserve powers in West Germany.

● **5 Jun**: Senator Robert Kennedy, brother of the late president J.F. Kennedy and himself a contender in the current presidential elections, is shot and dies the next day (USA).

● **11 Jun**: The East German government announces that West Germans and West Berliners will need visas to travel across East Germany. The Western powers protest.

● **26 Jun**: The Bonin Islands, including Iwo Jima, are returned to Japan by the USA.

● **27 Jun**: Czech intellectuals produce their "2,000 words", an appeal to speed up democratization. (›15 Jul)

● **1 Jul**: 62 nations, including the UK, USSR and USA, sign a nuclear non-proliferation treaty.

● **15 Jul**: Czech army leaders demand revision of Warsaw Pact to give the USSR's partners an equal say. On 16 Jul the USSR, East Germany, Hungary, Bulgaria and Poland send a joint letter to Czechoslovakia saying that its liberalization policy is unacceptable.

● **18 Jul**: Yugoslavia declares unconditional support for Czechoslovakia's liberalization policies. (›16 Aug)

● **2 Aug**: The Spanish secret police chief is killed in Guipuzcoa, allegedly by Basque nationalists.

● **16 Aug**: Romania and Czechoslovakia sign a 20-year treaty of friendship. (›20 Aug)

● **18 Aug**: North Vietnamese and Vietcong troops stage 19 separate attacks throughout South Vietnam. (›31 Oct)

● **20–21 Aug**: Czechoslovakia is invaded by Soviet tanks and troops, together with East German, Polish, Hungarian and Bulgarian forces, to restore strict Communism. Dubcek's reform movement is suppressed, and several government leaders arrested, including Dubcek himself.

● **23 Aug**: A draft resolution of the UN Security Council, condemning the invasion of Czechoslovakia and calling for the removal of forces, is vetoed by the USSR. (›4 Oct)

● **6 Sep**: Swaziland becomes independent within the Commonwealth, bringing to an end the UK's colonial links with Africa.

● **12 Sep**: The Albanian People's Assembly approves its formal withdrawal from the Warsaw Pact.

● **15 Sep**: At a summit meeting of the OAU in Algiers, heads of state appeal to Biafra to abandon its struggle for independence from Nigeria.

● **18 Sep**: After persistent incidents in the Middle East, the UN Security Council passes a resolution asking Israel and the Arab states to observe the ceasefire and cooperate with UN envoy Jarring.

● **4 Oct**: Czech leaders accede to Soviet demands that they dismantle the remnants of liberal policies, and agree to indefinite stationing of foreign troops in Czechoslovakia.

● **9–13 Oct**: Rebel Rhodesian leader Ian Smith and UK prime minister Harold Wilson hold talks on HMS *Fearless* off Gibraltar but reach no agreement. On 25 Oct the UN General Assembly adopts a resolution calling on the UK not to grant independence to Rhodesia before free elections and majority rule are established.

● **31 Oct**: President Johnson announces a halt to US bombing of North Vietnam, but the Paris peace talks are postponed indefinitely due to South Vietnam's refusal to participate if the National Liberation Front are present.

● **5 Nov**: Republican Richard Nixon is elected US president after Johnson decides not to run again.

SOCIETY

- **2 Jan**: President Johnson signs a social security bill that will raise the benefits of 24 million people by at least 13 percent (USA).

- **16 Jan**: In the UK, Wilson announces a series of cutbacks in home and defense spending, including withdrawal of forces from the Far East and Persian Gulf by 1971.

- **1 Feb–29 Mar**: The UN Conference on Trade and Development (UNCTAD) in New Delhi, India, discusses development assistance and East–West trade.

- **7 Feb**: All 10 provincial premiers approve prime minister Pearson's proposal to give the French language equal status with English in Canada.

- **7 Feb**: Colombia, Venezuela, Chile, Peru, Ecuador and Bolivia form the Andean Development Corporation.

- **16 Feb**: The US National Security Council abolishes draft deferments for most graduate students and suspends occupational deferments.

- **27 Feb**: As the number of Asian immigrants arriving from East Africa increases, the UK curtails the right of Asians with British nationality to emigrate to the UK.

- **11 Mar**: Major civil rights legislation in the USA prohibits racial discrimination in sale or rental of about 80 percent of US housing.

- **11 Mar**: Demonstrators in Warsaw, protesting about government interference in cultural affairs, fight with police and armed militia men.

- **16 Mar**: Over 200 are injured in a clash between left and rightwing students at Rome University, the latest in a series of student disturbances in Italy.

- **27 Mar**: Soviet cosmonaut Yuri Gagarin is killed when a special aircraft he is testing crashes.

- **28 Mar**: In Spain, Madrid University closes indefinitely following campus violence.

- **23 Apr**: Students stage a sit-in strike in Columbia University. On 30 Apr New York City police move in and make 628 arrests.

- **24 Apr**: Nine West African nations form the West African Regional Group to promote economic unification in the area.

- **24 Apr**: The IOC announces that South Africa will be excluded from the next Olympic Games, in Mexico.

- **30 Apr**: In the USA a "Poor People's Campaign" is officially opened by Martin Luther King's widow, Coretta King. On 19 Jun over 50,000 people, many of them white, take part in a Solidarity Day March in Washington.

- **2 May**: Violent protests by militant leftwing students in the Sorbonne University in Paris spread to the civilian population. Throughout the month students combine with workers in strikes and protest marches in Paris and other cities; factories are occupied, transport at a standstill. (›7 Jun)

- **3 May**: The South African House of Assembly votes to abolish parliamentary representation for the country's Cape Coloreds.

- **29 May**: The UN Security Council unanimously adopts a resolution urging all UN members to impose a total embargo on all trade and financial relations with Rhodesia.

- **2 Jun**: Belgrade University students, calling for more jobs for graduates and guaranteed freedom of public assembly, clash with police. On 9 Jun Tito promises university reforms (Yug).

- **7 Jun**: Violent clashes occur between French workers and police at the nationalized Renault motor plant at Flins. On 12 Jun the French government bans all protest demonstrations during the current election campaign and dissolves 11 extremist student organizations.

- **20 Jun**: Brazilian students clash with police during antigovernment demonstrations in Rio de Janeiro, one of many demonstrations during the year in various cities in Brazil.

- **15 Jul**: The first direct airline service between the USSR and USA is opened by Aeroflot and Pan-American World Airways.

- **29 Jul**: Pope Paul VI issues an encyclical, "Humanae Vitae", upholding the Roman Catholic prohibition against all artificial means of contraception.

- **15 Aug**: Nigeria rejects an International Red Cross plan to aid starving Biafrans, victims of the civil war, after peace talks break down.

- **Aug**: Romania rejects the proposal to transform Comecon into a supranational organization.

- **9 Sep**: Arthur Ashe wins the US Open tennis title in the first tournament open to professionals and amateurs.

- **18 Sep**: Mexican federal troops occupy the National University in Mexico City after seven weeks of student unrest. Clashes between students and troops begin.

- **27 Sep**: France vetoes interim commercial arrangements proposed by West Germany that would eventually lead to UK admission to the EEC.

- **5 and 6 Oct**: In Northern Ireland Roman Catholics clash with police while demonstrating against discrimination by the Protestant majority.

- **19 Nov**: A wave of major strikes in Italy prompts the resignation of prime minister Giovanni Leone and his minority government.

- **Dec**: The Barre plan for the introduction of a European Monetary Union is published (Fr).

- Nobel Peace Prize is won by René Cassin (Fr).

CULTURE

- **Apr**: Hit hippy musical *Hair* opens on Broadway (USA).

- Max Frisch: *Biographie*, metaphysical play (Swi).

- Janet Frame: *The Rainbirds*, novel (NZ).

- René Char: *Dans la pluie giboyeuse*, poems (Fr).

- Alexander Solzhenitsyn: *Cancer Ward*, novel (USSR).

- Marguerite Duras: *L'Amante anglaise*, play (Fr).

- Luciano Berio: *Sinfonia*, orchestral montage (It).

- Luigi Dallapiccola: *Ulisse*, opera (It).

- Formation of the London Sinfonietta, an orchestra dedicated to the performance of new music. (UK).

- Italian ensemble Musica Elettronica Viva create a "Sound Pool" in which both musicians and audience may take part.

- Joni Mitchell's first album *Song for a Seagull* is released (USA).

- Tom Wesselmann: *Great American Nude no 99*, painting (USA).

- Tomio Miki: *Ears*, bas-relief in cast aluminum (Jap).

- Tetsuya Noda begins his series of diary prints, using mimeograph, woodblock and silk screen (Jap).

- Ed Kienholz: *The Portable War Memorial*, assemblage (USA).

- Shoji Hamada is awarded the Order of Culture medal for reviving the art of ceramics (Jap).

- Ludwig Mies van der Rohe: National Gallery, Berlin.

- Denys Lasdun: University of East Anglia, Norwich (UK).

- Foundation of the Art Farm group of architects, specializing in inflatable architecture (USA).

- Release of *2001 – a Space Odyssey*, directed by Stanley Kubrick (USA).

- Release of the Beatles' cartoon film, *Yellow Submarine* (UK).

- Roman Polanski: *Rosemary's Baby*, starring Mia Farrow (USA).

- The film *Loin du Vietnam* is collectively directed, edited by Chris Marker. It includes sections by Jean-Luc Godard, Alain Resnais, William Klein.

- *Funny Girl*, directed by William Wyler, gives Barbra Streisand her first starring role (USA).

- The Beatles form Apple Corporation, including shops, a film company, a recording company and a boutique which is psychedelically decorated by the Dutch group Fool (UK).

- Calvin Klein starts his own fashion business (USA).

- Zandra Rhodes forms her own fashion house (UK).

- Nobel Prize for Literature is won by Yasunari Kawabata (Jap).

SCIENCE

- **9 Jan**: The fifth, and last, US *Surveyor* spacecraft softlands on the Moon to investigate its surface.

- **19 Jan**: The USA and USSR sign an agreement to cooperate in the fields of applied science and technology.

- **May**: After the effects of the drug thalidomide on unborn children is discovered, thalidomide trials open in Alsdorf, West Germany.

- **24 Aug**: France explodes its first hydrogen bomb in the South Pacific.

- **15 Sep**: The Soviet unmanned spacecraft *Zond 5* is put into orbit round the Moon, and successfully splashes down on 21 Sep in the Indian Ocean.

- **16 Nov**: The Soviet space station Proton 4 goes into orbit.

- **10 Dec**: The EEC countries and the UK agree upon cooperation in scientific research.

- **18 Dec**: Intelsat 3A, the first in a new series of communications satellites, is launched from Cape Kennedy (USA).

- **21 Dec**: US astronauts J.A. Lovell, W. Anders and F. Borman complete the first flight around the Moon in *Apollo 8*, completing 10 orbits.

- **31 Dec**: First commercial flight of a supersonic passenger aircraft, Tu-144 (USSR).

- The Nobel Prize for Physiology or Medicine is won by R.W. Holley, H.G. Khorana and M.W. Nirenberg (USA) for their work on the genetic code that determines cell function.

- L. Onsager (USA) wins the Nobel Prize for Chemistry for his study of the theoretical basis of diffusion of isotopes.

- The Nobel Prize for Physics goes to L.W. Alvarez (USA) for his discovery of resonance particles.

- A tidal power station opens in France.

- The US government move back the people of Bikini Atoll, claiming that the radioactive contamination from the 1956 hydrogen bomb explosion has diminished to a tolerable level.

- M. Arnstein develops a vaccine against meningitis (USA).

- A mother gives birth to sextuplets as a result of new fertility drugs (UK).

- Soviet physicist A.D. Sakharov campaigns in favor of nuclear arms reductions, thus coming into conflict with the Soviet government.

- The smallest ever time measurement is made at Bell Laboratories – pulses from a laser measure the picosecond (USA).

- Publication of *The Double Helix* by James Watson, explaining how he and Francis Crick discovered the structure of DNA (USA).

- Max Perutz announces the structure of hemoglobin (UK).

"The Eagle has landed," came the crackly American voice … at last, there was a man on the Moon: Neil Armstrong, the very model of a cleancut US astronaut, who was shortly joined by his companion Buzz Aldrin. The mission was a total success, and though in scientific terms it accomplished little that could not have been done more cheaply by an unmanned flight, it was a great propaganda success for a Great Power sorely in need of one. It gave a fillip to Richard Nixon, the "forgotten man" of US politics who had nevertheless been elected president, and who in the previous week had begun at last to withdraw US troops from Vietnam. Britain became embroiled in its own trauma when troops were sent to Northern Ireland, initially to protect the Catholic minority from rioting Protestants but eventually to conduct a protracted and increasingly bitter defensive war against terrorist groups associated with both sides. The IRA gained a potential benefactor in Colonel Muammar Qadhafi when he overthrew the monarchy in Libya to establish his idiosyncratic Socialist Arab Republic.

▲ "One small step for a man, one giant leap for mankind": Buzz Aldrin, one of the first two men to set foot on the Moon, contemplates the Stars and Stripes. The astronauts returned safely to Earth on 24 July, carrying samples of Moon rock for analysis.

● **16 Jan**: Czech student Jan Palach burns himself to death in Wenceslas Square, Prague, in protest against Soviet occupation. (›17 Apr)

● **18 Jan**: South Vietnam and National Liberation Front delegations join US and North Vietnamese teams at the peace talks in Paris. (›22 Feb)

● **20 Jan**: Richard Nixon is inaugurated as the 37th US president.

● **24 Jan**: Following disturbances, the Spanish government declares martial law until 25 Mar. Madrid University is closed and around 300 students arrested.

● **1 Feb**: A joint declaration by Romania and Yugoslavia refutes the Brezhnev doctrine that international Communist interests should override national interests.

● **3 Feb**: Al-Fatah (Palestine Liberation Movement) leader Yasir Arafat is elected chairman of the PLO.

● **22 Feb**: North Vietnam and the Vietcong launch a new series of attacks on South Vietnam. On 6 Mar US Ambassador Lodge protests at the Paris peace talks. (›8 Jul)

● **26 Feb**: Israeli prime minister Levi Eshkol dies of a heart attack, and is succeeded on 17 Mar by Mrs Golda Meir.

● **2 and 16 Mar**: Military clashes take place between Chinese and Soviet troops on disputed borderland at Ussuri River. (›11 Jun)

● **11 Mar**: North Korean and US forces exchange fire in the Korean demilitarized zone.

● **25 Mar**: President Ayub Khan of Pakistan resigns and hands over power to Gen. Yahya Khan, commander-in-chief of the army.

● **16–18 Apr**: East and central African states hold a summit conference at Lusaka, and adopt a manifesto condemning white-ruled regimes in southern Africa.

● **17 Apr**: Alexander Dubcek is deposed as Czech leader, and replaced by party hardliner Dr Gustav Husak. (›22 Aug)

● **22 Apr**: UN Secretary-General U Thant reports that a virtual state of war exists between Israel and Egypt along the Suez Canal. (›3 Jul)

● **27 Apr**: Defeat for president de Gaulle in a French referendum on regional and other reforms prompts his resignation. On 15 Jun Georges Pompidou is elected president.

● **8 Jun**: The Spanish government closes the land frontier with Gibraltar, and on 27 Jun suspends the ferry service from Spain to Gibraltar. (›4 Jul)

● **11 Jun**: China claims that Soviet tanks and armored cars crossed the border into Xinjiang on 10 Jun.On 8 Jul China complains that Soviet gunboats, troops and planes have crossed the Amur River into Manchuria. (›13 Aug)

● **20 Jun**: A referendum in Rhodesia approves a constitution which would perpetuate white rule and establish a separate republic.

● **24 Jun**: Undeclared war starts between El Salvador and Honduras after Salvadoreans settling in Honduras are expelled. (›29 Jul)

● **3 Jul**: The UN Security Council censures all measures taken to change the status of the City of Jerusalem. (›3 Aug)

● **4 Jul**: Gen. Franco offers Spanish citizenship to all Gibraltarians. (›1 Oct)

● **8 Jul**: Start of "Vietnamization" with gradual withdrawal of American troops from Vietnam, handing combat role to South Vietnam. (›16 Sep)

● **12 Jul**: A fresh outbreak of violence in Northern Ireland results from Protestant celebrations of the anniversary of the Battle of the Boyne. (›12 Aug)

● **23 Jul**: Prince Juan Carlos is selected to succeed Gen. Franco as ruler of Spain on Franco's retirement.

● **29 Jul**: El Salvador agrees to remove troops from Honduras in face of a threatened OAS embargo.

● **3 Aug**: Israel announces its intention to retain parts of the terrritory captured during the 1967 war. (›25 Aug)

● **3 Aug**: The Japanese Diet passes legislation increasing the authority of government to deal with campus disorders.

● **8 Aug**: The USA and West Germany announce the establishment of a "hot line" between Washington and Bonn.

● **12 Aug**: Roman Catholic/Protestant riots break out in Belfast and Londonderry. On 14 Aug the British government authorizes the use of troops, and on 19 Aug the British army is given control of Ulster security. (›11 Oct)

● **13 Aug**: Soviet troops cross the Xinjiang border into China; heavy casualties are reported.

● **22 Aug**: The Czech government issues tighter controls and emergency laws increasing penalties for rioters after demonstrations throughout Czechoslovakia to mark the first anniversary of the Soviet invasion. (›27 Sep)

● **25 Aug**: Zambian president Kenneth Kaunda declares a state of emergency due to a political crisis arising from tribal rivalries.

● **25 Aug**: Arab states foreign ministers meet in Cairo to discuss plans for a "holy war" against Israel to regain the Holy Places. (›20 Dec)

● **29 Aug**: Dr Kofia Busia's Progress party wins the first free elections in Ghana since 1956, and military rule comes to an end on 30 Sep.

● **31 Aug**: The Brazilian armed forces commanders-in-chief take over presidential powers while president Costa e Silva recovers from a stroke.

SOCIETY   CULTURE   SCIENCE

- **1 Sep**: A military revolt in Libya led by Col. Muammar Qadhafi overthrows King Idris I, and the Socialist Libyan Arab Republic is proclaimed.

- **3 Sep**: North Vietnamese president Ho Chi Minh dies, aged 79.

- **16 Sep**: President Nixon announces the withdrawal of an additional 35,000 men from South Vietnam by 15 Dec. On 20 Sep the foreign ministers of Australia, New Zealand, the Philippines, South Korea and Thailand announce that their combined force in South Vietnam will not be reduced.

- **27 Sep**: A new, more conservative cabinet takes over in Czechoslovakia. Alexander Dubcek and Joseph Smrkovsky are removed from the Communist party praesidium.

- **1 Oct**: Spain severs all telephone and cable services with Gibraltar.

- **3 Oct**: The Greek government announces the restoration of press freedom, abolition of arbitrary arrest and limitation of jurisdiction of special military courts, but with some qualifications.

- **11 Oct**: Fresh rioting breaks out in Belfast, and the British army sends 600 troops in next day.

- **21 Oct**: Syria closes the border with Lebanon in retaliation for Lebanese attacks on Arab guerrillas.

- **21 Oct**: Willy Brandt, previously mayor of West Berlin, becomes chancellor of West Germany.

- **27 Oct**: Nine opposition leaders, including Oginga Odinga, are arrested on charges of organizing the anti-government demonstration of 25 Oct. On 30 Oct Jomo Kenyatta bans the Kenya Peoples' Union (KPU), the leftwing opposition party.

- **6 Nov**: Al-Fatah guerrillas begin to withdraw bases from Lebanon to Syria after an agreement is reached in Cairo on 2 Nov.

- **11 Nov**: The UN General Assembly rejects for the 20th time a motion to seat Communist China.

- **17 Nov**: The USA and USSR start SALT (Strategic Arms Limitation Talks) talks in Helsinki. On 24 Nov the Nuclear Nonproliferation Treaty is ratified in ceremonies in Washington and Moscow.

- **21 Nov**: The USA agrees to return Okinawa and other US-held Ryuku Islands to Japan in 1972.

- **25 Nov**: President Nixon orders the destruction of US germ warfare stocks.

- **28 Nov**: West Germany signs a nuclear nonproliferation treaty.

- **2 Dec**: The US army board of inquiry begins closed hearings in Washington on the alleged massacre of South Vietnamese civilians in My Lai in May 1968.

- **20 Dec**: Arab states summit conference opens in Rabat, but ends on 23 Dec with a failure to agree on a united front against Israel.

- **1 Jan**: A second round of tariff cuts as stipulated by the GATT Kennedy Round agreement goes into effect.

- **12 Jan**: A demonstration against British immigration policies is held in London to coincide with the Commonwealth Heads of State Conference.

- **15 Jan**: Denmark, Finland, Norway and Sweden announce plans for a Nordic Economic Union.

- **24 Jan–19 Feb**: The London School of Economics is closed due to student disorders.

- **Jan**: A report on the economic situation by the US government shows the balance of trade positive for the first time since 1957.

- **18 Feb**: An Israeli El Al Boeing 720B is attacked by Arab terrorists at Zürich airport.

- **23–26 Apr**: Romania demands the opening of Comecon to non-Communist countries. In Oct the East German government demands a greater integration of the economies within Comecon.

- **Jun**: Negotiations are completed for an association agreement between the EEC and 18 African countries.

- **14 Jul**: The US Justice Dept calls for accelerated desegregation in 25 Alabama school districts.

- **25 Jul**: The International Red Cross turns over coordination of Nigerian relief flights to the federal government.

- **8 Aug**: France unexpectedly devalues the franc by 11.11 percent. Credits from the IMF and some central banks are made to support it. On 10 Aug the currencies of 14 African nations, all former French colonies, realign with the devalued franc.

- **3 Sep**: The French government announces a series of austerity measures to protect the devalued franc against inflation.

- **10 Sep**: Oil leases to a site on Alaska's North Slope sell in Anchorage for a record total of over $900 million.

- **15 Oct**: Mass national antiwar demonstrations take place in the USA, followed by further demonstrations on 15 Nov.

- **7 Nov**: EFTA reaffirms its readiness to negotiate integration with the EEC.

- **20 Nov**: The US government orders an end to the use of DDT in residential areas within 30 days.

- **1 Dec**: At a conference of EEC countries it is agreed to begin negotiation for UK entry in Jun 1970.

- **12 Dec**: A bomb explodes in a Milan bank, killing 14 and injuring about 100; three bombs also explode in Rome (It).

- Nobel Prize for Peace won by the International Labor Organization.

- The first Nobel Prize for Economic Sciences is won by Ragner Frisch (Nor) and Jan Tinbergen (Neth).

- **7 Jun**: Olivier Messiaen's oratorio *The Transfiguration of our Lord Jesus Christ* is first performed at the Gulbenkian Festival, Lisbon (Port).

- **2 Jul**: Brian Jones, guitarist with the Rolling Stones, dies aged 24.

- **2 Sep**: The Isle of Wight festival attracts around 250,000 spectators. Bob Dylan plays a two-hour set including "Tambourine Man" and "Subterranean Homesick Blues" (UK).

- Samuel Beckett (Ire) is awarded the Nobel Prize for Literature.

- Philip Roth: *Portnoy's Complaint*, novel (USA).

- Christa Wolf: *Nachdenken über Christa T*, novel (GDR).

- Miguel Angel Asturias: *Maladron*, novel (Guatemala).

- Luigi Nono: *Musiche per Manzù*, electronic music (It).

- Peter Maxwell Davies: *Eight Songs for a Mad King*, for voice and chamber ensemble (UK).

- Dmitri Shostakovich: Symphony No. 14 (USSR).

- Karlheinz Stockhausen: *Spiral*, for any soloist with shortwave receiver (FRG).

- John Cage: *HPSCHD*, mixed media piece for seven amplified harpsichords, multiple tapes and lighting effects (USA).

- Cornelius Cardew founds his Scratch Orchestra, of amateur and untrained musicians as well as professionals (UK).

- Gilbert and George: *Underneath the Arches*, a "singing sculpture" in which the two artists mime to the Flanagan and Allen song of the same name (UK).

- R.B. Kitaj: *Synchrony with F.B. – General of Hot Desire*, diptych painting (UK).

- Mark Rothko: *Orange Yellow Orange*, painting (USA).

- Niki de Saint Phalle: *Black Nana*, one of a series of three-dimensional female figures (Fr).

- Christo: *Wrapped Coast*, Little Bay, area of coastline wrapped in plastic and rope (Aus).

- I.M. Pei, H. Cobb and others: Hancock Tower, Boston (USA).

- Paul Newman and Robert Redford star in the film *Butch Cassidy and the Sundance Kid*, directed by George Roy Hill (USA).

- John Wayne wins his only Oscar for *True Grit*, directed by Henry Hathaway (USA).

- Franco Zeffirelli: *Romeo and Juliet* (It).

- The American film *Easy Rider*, directed by and starring Dennis Hopper, epitomizes the "acid culture".

- *Midnight Cowboy*, directed by John Schlesinger, stars Dustin Hoffman and Jon Voigt (USA).

- Premiere of *Monty Python's Flying Circus* on BBC TV (UK).

- **14 Jan**: Soviet spacecrafts *Soyuz 4* and *5* link up in space and transfer crews – the first linkup of two manned spacecraft.

- **Jan**: The USSR launches space probes *Venera 5* and *6*, which reach Venus in May.

- **15 Feb**: The first *in vitro* fertilization of human egg cells is carried out by Dr R.G. Edwards of the Cambridge Physiological Laboratory (UK).

- **25 Jun**: Dutch chemists identify the chemical that has been polluting the River Rhine as an insecticide used to dust vineyards and fruit trees.

- **Jun**: A report commissioned by the UN, *Problems of the Human Environment*, shows that two-thirds of the world's original forest has been lost for timber; and that increased reliance on fossil fuel has brought a 10 percent increase in atmospheric CO_2.

- **16 Jul**: US astronauts Neil Armstrong, Michael Collins and Edwin "Buzz" Aldrin head toward the moon in *Apollo 11*. On 20 Jul Neil Armstrong becomes the first man to set foot on the Moon, and Aldrin the second, while Collins waits in lunar orbit. On 24 Jul they return to Earth.

- **Aug**: US twin probes *Mariner 6* and *7* fly past Mars, sending back close-up pictures of the surface.

- **Aug**: Dorothy Hodgkin announces the structure of insulin (UK).

- **14 Nov**: *Apollo 12* carries Charles Conrad and Al Bean to the moon, where they make two moonwalks.

- **Nov**: Canada eliminates DDT completely from outside agriculture as a result of UN reports of dangers of its residues in soil and water.

- E. Hoff constructs the first silicon microprocessor (USA).

- The scanning electron micrograph is perfected for practical use.

- G.M. Edelman finds the amino acid sequence of immunoglobin G (USA).

- D. Cooley and D. Liotta make the first implant of an artificial heart.

- The Nobel Prize for Physiology or Medicine is shared by M. Delbruck, A.D. Hershey and S.E. Luna of the USA for their studies of the workings and reproduction of viruses.

- The Nobel Prize for Chemistry is won by D.H.B. Barton (UK) and O. Hassel (Nor) for determining the three-dimensional shape of organic compounds.

- Murray Gell-Mann (USA) wins the Nobel Prize for Physics for his classification of elementary particles.

- "Bubble memory" devices are invented for computers; they retain information even when the computer is turned off.

- The US government limits the use of monosodium glutamate after experiments linking food additives to cancer.

1970-1979

In Cambodia the moderate government of Prince Norodom Sihanouk was overthrown and the sinister Khmer Rouge extended its control. US president Nixon sent troops into Cambodia, provoking renewed antiwar demonstrations which moved into a shocking new dimension when National Guardsmen in Ohio shot dead four students, two of them girls, at Kent State University. More violent protests broke out in Jordan, where the PLO blew up three hijacked airliners at Dawson's Field. Although the hijackers gained some of their demands, including the release of terrorists, this was "Black September" for the PLO who were ejected from their bases in Jordan by King Hussain's emergency military government. Riots burst out in Poland too, with the Gdansk dockers in the forefront, and resulted in the downfall of Wladislaw Gomulka, demonstrating that even a Communist party boss was not invulnerable to popular discontent. In Chile, however, an avowed Marxist, Salvador Allende, came to power – uniquely – through a democratic election. The first Chinese satellite was launched into space, while far below in the North Sea large reserves of precious oil were discovered.

▲ Mick Jagger and the Rolling Stones in concert. 1970 was, sadly, a year in which rock lost two of its finest artists: the death of Jimi Hendrix in September was followed by that of Janis Joplin only a few weeks later.

● **3 Jan**: A new constitution in the Congo (Brazzaville) establishes the Congolese Workers Party, whose chairman automatically becomes head of state, and changes the country's name to People's Republic of the Congo.

● **12 Jan**: Gen. Ojukwu's flight to the Ivory Coast ends the Biafran secession from Nigeria and the civil war.

● **16 Jan**: Col. Muammar Qadhafi becomes premier of Libya.

● **7 Feb**: A five-nation Arab summit conference meets in Cairo to discuss military action against Israel.

● **23 Feb**: Guyana becomes a republic within the Commonwealth.

● **25 Feb**: Reported expansion of the US military role in Laos is criticized in the US Senate, but denied by the US Defense Secretary. (›24 May)

● **2 Mar**: Rhodesia declares itself a republic, dissolving its last ties with Britain. (›10 Apr)

● **5 Mar**: The Nuclear Nonproliferation Treaty of 24 Nov 1969 goes into effect, by now ratified by 45 countries.

● **7 Mar**: Malaysia and Thailand sign an agreement permitting their troops to combat Communist guerrillas in each other's territory.

● **11 Mar**: The Iraqi government reaches settlement with the Kurds, ending over eight years of war.

● **18 Mar**: Cambodian chief of state Prince Norodom Sihanouk is overthrown in a bloodless coup. On 9 Oct Cambodia becomes the Khmer Republic under Lon Nol. (›19 Apr)

● **19 Mar**: Heads of West and East Germany, Willy Brandt and Willi Stoph, meet in Erfurt, East Germany – the first meeting of heads of the two governments since the division of Germany. (›26 Mar)

● **21 Mar**: Alexander Dubcek, First Secretary of the Czech Communist party during the 1968 reform movement, is suspended from party membership, and on 26 Jun expelled from the party.

● **26 Mar**: Representatives of the USA, UK, France and the USSR meet in West Berlin to discuss the problems of Berlin for the first time in 11 years.

● **7 Apr**: British prime minister Wilson pledges to keep troops in Northern Ireland for as long as necessary.

● **10 Apr**: The general election in Rhodesia proves a landslide for the Rhodesian Front, and on 14 Apr Clifford Dupont is sworn in as the republic's first president.

● **16 Apr**: The USA and USSR reopen SALT talks in Vienna (until 14 Aug). The talks continue between 2 Nov and 18 Dec in Helsinki.

● **19 Apr**: Communist forces capture the town of Saang in Cambodia, 30 km (20 miles) south of Phnom Penh. Cambodian premier Lon Nol sends a personal appeal to US president Nixon for military assistance. (›30 Apr)

● **20 Apr**: Nixon announces the planned withdrawal of 150,000 troops from South Vietnam by spring 1971.

● **24 Apr**: Gambia becomes a republic within the Commonwealth.

● **30 Apr**: US and South Vietnamese troops attack Communist areas in Cambodia. On 2 May US aircraft bomb North Vietnam in the first raids since Nov 1968. (›24 May)

● **16 May**: French president Georges Pompidou calls for public calm after a series of bomb and arson attacks against police stations, public buildings and the homes of politicians.

● **20 May**: Soviet premier Kosygin acknowledges that the USSR is providing "extensive aid" to Arab nations to help them defend "legitimate national rights".

● **24 May**: Laotian troops are reported to have begun a counterattack against recent advances by the North Vietnamese and Pathet Lao. (›21 Nov)

● **4 Jun**: Tonga becomes an independent kingdom within the Commonwealth.

● **4 Jun**: The demilitarized zone between El Salvador and Honduras is policed by an OAS advisory force along the agreed border.

● **7 Jun**: Fighting breaks out between Palestinian guerrillas and the army in Jordan. On 10 Jun King Hussain and Al-Fatah leader Yasir Arafat agree on a ceasefire, but fighting continues. (›25 Jun)

● **18 Jun**: In the UK general election the Conservatives return to power, with a majority of 30; Edward Heath is the new prime minister.

● **25 Jun**: The USA presents a new Middle East peace proposal. On 23 Jul Egypt accepts the proposal, followed by Jordan on 26 Jul. Syria, Iraq and the Arab guerrilla organizations do not. On 4 Aug Israel accepts. (›7 Aug)

● **30 Jun**: The OAS General Assembly adopts a resolution condemning terrorism and political kidnapping.

● **24 Jul**: Moroccan voters approve a new constitution, ending a five-year state of emergency.

● **27 Jul**: Death of Antonio Salazar, Portugese premier, 1932-68, aged 81.

● **7 Aug**: The 90-day truce goes into effect on the Egyptian-Israeli front, but the Palestine guerrillas ignore it. On 25 Aug peace talks begin in New York, and on 5 Nov the ceasefire is renewed for a further 90 days.

● **16 Sep**: King Hussein of Jordan announces the establishment of a military government in an attempt to end the guerrilla anarchy, but the PLO rejects it. On 19 Sep Syrian tanks invade Jordan. On 27 Sep Hussein, eight other Arab heads of state and Palestinian leader Yasir Arafat sign an agreement to end the civil war.

● **28 Sep**: President Nasser of Egypt dies of a heart attack. Anwar Sadat is elected president on 15 Oct.

SOCIETY

● **6 Oct**: President Ovando Candia of Bolivia resigns after a revolt led by rightwing general Rogelio Miranda. Leftwing mineworkers, peasants and students back Gen. Juan José Torres Gonzales, who ousts Miranda and names himself president.

● **10 Oct**: Fiji becomes independent within the Commonwealth.

● **10 Oct**: Quebec minister of Labor Pierre Laporte is kidnapped by the Front de Libération du Québec, and on 17 Oct is found murdered.

● **24 Oct**: The Chilean congress chooses Dr Salvador Allende as president of Chile – the first Marxist head of state to be elected in the Western world.

● **6 Nov**: Italy and China establish diplomatic relations; ties are severed between Taiwan and Italy.

● **8 Nov**: After a five-day summit in Cairo, Egypt, Libya and Sudan agree to establish a federation; on 27 Nov Syria also joins.

● **9 Nov**: Death of French wartime Resistance leader and later president Charles de Gaulle, aged 80.

● **20 Nov**: UN General Assembly approves UN membership of China for the first time, but are 16 votes short of the two-thirds majority required.

● **21 Nov**: US planes carry out heavy bombing of military targets in North Vietnam, Laos and Cambodia. On 25 Nov the Vietcong and North Vietnam boycott the Paris peace talks in protest.

● **3 Dec**: In Spain, the trial by court martial in Burgos of 16 alleged Basque separatists accused of crimes against the state leads to strikes and demonstrations, and the Spanish government declares a state of emergency. (›28 Dec)

● **7 Dec**: West Germany and Poland agree a border along the Oder-Neisse line.

● **8 Dec**: In the Pakistan general elections the People's party under Zulfikar Ali Bhutto win a majority in West Pakistan, while in East Pakistan Sheikh Mujibu Rahman's pro-independence Awami League emerges with 167 out of 169 seats. (›25 Mar 1971)

● **16 Dec**: An international convention calling for "severe punishment" for hijacking of civilian aircraft is signed by 50 nations at The Hague.

● **20 Dec**: Polish Communist party First Secretary Wladislaw Gomulka and other key members of the government resign after a dockers' demonstration in Gdansk against food price rises turns into massive riots in which many civilians are killed. Edward Gierek replaces him.

● **28 Dec**: Death sentences are passed on six alleged Basque separatists in Spain. On 30 Dec Gen. Franco commutes the sentences to 30 years' imprisonment after appeals for clemency by various governments and private organizations.

● **1 Feb**: Contracts are signed between the USSR and the West German company Mannesmann for the supply of Soviet natural gas to West Germany in exchange for a West German pipeline.

● **6 Feb**: The EEC and Yugoslavia sign a fullscale trade pact, the first such agreement between the EEC and an East European nation.

● **16 Feb**: EEC finance ministers conclude an agreement on broad plans for the introduction of European Monetary Union by 1980.

● **14 Mar**: Expo 70 opens in Osaka, Japan, the first world's fair on the Asian continent.

● **22 Apr**: "Earth Day" observances focus attention on environmental problems throughout the USA.

● **4 May**: At an antiwar demonstration in Kent State University, Ohio, four students are shot dead by National Guardsmen.

● **21 Jun**: After winning the soccer World Cup trophy for the third time, beating Italy 4–1, Brazil is awarded the trophy in perpetuity.

● **30 Jun**: The UK, Denmark, Norway and Ireland open formal negotiations in Luxembourg for EEC membership.

● **4 Jul**: Libya nationalizes all its oil companies.

● **17 Jul**: At a UN Security Council meeting, African bloc countries demand mandatory enforcement of the 1963 embargo on arms sales to South Africa, which is approved.

● **10 Aug**: US House of Representatives approves a constitutional amendment to prohibit discrimination on grounds of sex.

● **6 Sep**: Palestinian guerrillas hijack a four passenger aircraft and obtain the release of Palestinians held in Israel, Switzerland, West Germany and the UK.

● **12 Oct**: The US Commission on Civil Rights reports that there has been a "major breakdown" in the enforcement of civil rights legislation.

● **Oct**: The UNCTAD conference agrees on a program of trade preferences in favor of developing countries.

● **12–13 Nov**: Cyclone and tidal waves hit East Pakistan. The official death toll is almost 20,000 with another 100,000 missing.

● **27 Nov**: The first demonstration in the UK by the Gay Liberation Front, already a powerful lobby in the USA, takes place in London to combat prejudice and discrimination against homosexuals.

● **1 Dec**: The Italian parliament approves a law legalizing divorce in certain circumstances.

● The Nobel Peace Prize is won by Dr Norman Borlang (USA), who produced new varieties of wheat giving higher yield.

● Nobel Prize for Economic Sciences is won by Paul Samuelson (USA).

CULTURE

● **10 Apr**: Paul McCartney quits the Beatles (UK).

● **7 Jun**: The Who perform their rock opera *Tommy* at New York's Metropolitan Opera House.

● **15 Jun**: Laurence Olivier is awarded a life peerage for his services to the theater (UK).

● **18 Sep**: Rock star Jimi Hendrix dies of a drug overdose aged 27 (USA).

● **Sep**: On the last but one day of the Kirov Ballet's season in London, dancer Natalia Makarova defects, and is granted asylum in Britain.

● **4 Oct**: Rock singer Janis Joplin dies of a drug overdose aged 27 (USA).

● **2 Dec**: Premiere of Michael Tippett's opera *The Knot Garden* (UK).

● Derek Walcott: *The Dream on Monkey Mountain and other Plays* (Trin).

● Saul Bellow: *Mr Sammler's Planet*, novel (USA).

● Peter Handke: *The Goalie's Anxiety at the Penalty Kick*, novel (FRG).

● Dario Fo: *The Accidental Death of an Anarchist*, play based on a real incident (It).

● Jorge Luis Borges: *Dr Brodie's Report*, stories (Arg).

● José Donoso: *The Obscene Bird of Night*, magic realist novel (Chile).

● Nobel Prize for Literature is won by Alexander Solzhenitsyn (USSR).

● Robert Crumb: *Ancient Voices of Children*, for orchestra and voices (USA).

● Elliott Carter: *Concerto for Orchestra* (USA).

● The spherical auditorium built for Karlheinz Stockhausen at Expo 70 in Osaka is the first hall built exclusively for the performance of electronic music.

● Colin McCahon: *Victory Over Death*, painting (NZ).

● Ralph Goings: *Airstream*, Superrealist painting (USA).

● Klaus Rinke: *Primary Demonstrations*, in which geometric configurations are mapped out slowly by bodily movements (Fr).

● Robert Smithson: *Spiral Jetty*, outdoor sculpture on a huge scale, made of rubble (USA).

● Hassan Fathy and the citizens of Gourma: New Gourma, a new town, near Luxor (since 1947) (Egy).

● The Ergonomi design group is founded (Scan).

● Jean Renoir: *The Little Theatre of Jean Renoir*, film (Fr).

● Michelangelo Antonioni: *Zabriskie Point*, his first American film.

● Release of *Days and Nights in the Forest*, directed by Satyajit Ray (Ind).

● Robert Altman: *M.A.S.H.*, film about the attitudes of young people to the Vietnam war (USA).

SCIENCE

● **14 Jan**: A US Senate subcommittee opens hearings on potential dangers of the contraceptive pill.

● **22 Jan**: The first "jumbo jet", the Boeing 747, enters transatlantic service.

● **24 Apr**: China launches its first satellite.

● **1–19 Jun**: Two Soviet cosmonauts set the record for the longest manned space flight. The effects on their bodies show that more research is needed before space stations, manned by scientists, could be safely set up.

● **2 Jun**: H.G. Khorana announces the manmade gene (analine-transfer RNA) assembled directly from chemical components (USA).

● **Jun**: Rich oilfields are discovered in the North Sea.

● **Jul**: Traces of PCBs (polychlorinated biphenyls) are found in the bodies of many British birds, raising alarm about possible damage to humans.

● **20 Sep**: The USSR lands the robot spacecraft *Luna 16* on the Moon.

● **26 Oct**: NASA engineers join Soviet scientists for discussions in Moscow on standardized docking systems.

● H.M. Temin and D. Baltimore discover reverse transcriptase, an enzyme causing RNA to be transcribed on to DNA, in viruses.

● Copper-wired IUD contraceptive devices are developed in Chile.

● Lasers are developed for use in eye operations.

● The Nobel Prize for Physics is won by L.E. Néel (Fr) and H.O. Alfvén (Swe), the former for his work in plasma physics and the latter for his in antiferromagnetism.

● The Nobel Prize for Chemistry is won by L.F. Leloir (Arg) for his work with sugar nucleotides.

● Bernard Katz (UK), Ulf von Euler (Swe) and Julius Axelrod (USA) share the Nobel Prize for Physiology or Medicine for discoveries in the chemical transmission of nerve impulses.

● The Anglo-French supersonic passenger aircraft Concorde reaches Mach 2 (twice the speed of sound).

● Heart pacemakers using nuclear-powered batteries, which only need to be replaced every 10 years, are implanted in three patients to correct "heart block" (Fr/UK).

● Mass vaccination is introduced for children in Western countries.

● The first successful nerve transplant is made in the FRG.

● G. Cotzias pioneers L-dopa therapy as a relief to patients with Parkinson's disease.

● Choh Hao Li synthesises the growth hormone somatotrophin (USA).

● The "floppy disk" is developed by IBM for storing computer data.

After an overwhelming victory in the polls the preceding December, Sheikh Mujibur Rahman and his Awami League proclaimed the independence of East Pakistan as Bangladesh. He was immediately arrested and president Yahya Khan's troops, sent in from West Pakistan, acted swiftly to prevent the secession. Guerrilla fighters of the Awami League maintained their resistance, and clashes between India and Pakistan increased as millions of refugees, especially Hindus, fled across the border into India. War broke out between India and Pakistan. An Indian invasion forced Pakistan's surrender and acceptance of an independent Bangladesh, and Sheikh Mujibur Rahman was released from jail to become its first president. One of the world's most ruthless dictators, "Papa Doc" Duvalier of Haiti, died at 64, leaving his poverty-stricken country to his teenage son. But the horrors perpetrated by the Duvalier regime would soon be surpassed by the new government of Uganda, led by Idi Amin. During the following months he progressed from one atrocity to another, culminating in 1972 in the wholesale expulsion of the Ugandan Asian community.

▲ Just one month after leading the military coup that ousted president Milton Obote, Major-General Idi Amin promoted himself to full general and appointed himself president of Uganda. The reign of terror that followed lasted until he was finally overthrown in 1979.

● **5 Jan**: Israel, Egypt and Jordan resume indirect talks in New York on the Middle East with UN mediator Gunnar Jarring. (›13 Jul)

● **22 Jan**: Vietcong raiders bomb the Cambodian capital Phnom Penh for the first time. (›8 Feb)

● **25 Jan**: Army officers led by Major-Gen. Idi Amin oust president Milton Obote in a military coup in Uganda. On 20 Feb Amin proclaims himself president.

● **8 Feb**: South Vietnamese troops supported by US aircraft invade Laos in an attempt to cut North Vietnamese supply routes to South Vietnam. Troops are withdrawn on 24 Mar. (›7 Apr)

● **10 Mar**: Three British soldiers are murdered in an ambush near Belfast. Northern Ireland prime minister Major Chichester Clark resigns under pressure from Protestants demanding stronger action against Catholics. On 23 Mar he is succeeded by Brian Faulkner. (›Jul)

● **12 Mar**: After mounting urban terrorism led by the extreme left Turkish People's Liberation Army, a bloodless military coup is carried out to restore order. On 26 Mar Nihat Erim forms a new government.

● **16 Mar–28 May**: Fourth round of SALT talks takes place in Vienna, followed by a fifth round in Helsinki and a sixth round in Vienna.

● **25 Mar**: Sheikh Mujibur Rahman, leader of the Awami League which is seeking independence for East Pakistan, is arrested after declaring East Pakistan the independent republic of Bangladesh. Civil war breaks out after Gen. Yahya Khan's military government orders troops to East Pakistan to restore order. (›6 Dec)

● **7 Apr**: US president Nixon announces a further 100,000 reduction in US troops in South Vietnam by 1 Dec. (›23 Apr)

● **19 Apr**: Sierra Leone becomes a republic within the Commonwealth.

● **21 Apr**: Death of François (Papa Doc) Duvalier of Haiti; he is succeeded by his son Jean-Claude, aged 19 and known as "Baby Doc".

● **23 Apr**: A week of anti-war demonstrations takes place in Washington. (›2 Jun)

● **27 May**: The USSR and Egypt sign a 15-year treaty of cooperation and friendship. On 9 Jun Israeli prime minister Golda Meir calls on the USA to provide Israel with armaments to match the increasing strength Egypt will have because of the treaty.

● **2 Jun**: US aircraft attack North Vietnamese troops in Cambodia in response to South Vietnam's call for help in preventing an invasion of South Vietnam. (›18 Aug)

● **8 Jun**: President Allende of Chile imposes a state of emergency on Santiago province following civilian unrest.

● **13 Jul**: The Jordanian army begins a campaign to remove Palestinian guerrillas from bases in north Jordan. On 23 Jul Syria closes its border with Jordan in protest. (›28 Nov)

● **Jul**: The UK government refuses to inquire into the killing of two civilians in Londonderry by UK troops, provoking the withdrawal of the Northern Ireland opposition party from the Stormont parliament; rioting and violence break out. (›9 Aug)

● **5 Aug**: The USA and USSR send a joint draft treaty to ban biological weapons to the Geneva disarmament conference.

● **9 Aug**: Northern Ireland prime minister Faulkner invokes emergency powers of preventative detention without trial and begins arrests of suspected leaders of the outlawed Irish Republican Army (IRA).

● **18 Aug**: New Zealand and Australia announce the withdrawal of their combat forces from Vietnam by Dec. (›12 Nov)

● **20 Aug**: Chiefs of state of Syria, Egypt and Libya sign a constitution for a federal union.

● **Aug**: NATO moves its naval HQ from Malta to Naples, in accordance with Maltese wishes.

● **3 Sep**: The "Big Four" sign an agreement on the status of Berlin. Western traffic will be able to cross Eastern territory to West Berlin, but the Berlin Wall is to remain, and the border will remain closed.

● **10 Oct**: In the general election, chancellor Bruno Kreisky receives the first majority to be held by an Austrian government since World War I.

● **25 Oct**: The UN General Assembly approve the admission of China and the expulsion of Taiwan.

● **27 Oct**: The Democratic Republic of Congo (Kinshasa) is renamed the Republic of Zaire.

● **12 Nov**: Nixon announces the withdrawal of 45,000 men from Vietnam by Feb 1972 and proclaims the end of the US offensive role in the war.

● **17 Nov**: In Thailand, armed forces and the Revolutionary party stage a bloodless coup and seize full power.

● **24 Nov**: UK Foreign Secretary Sir Alec Douglas-Home and Rhodesian rebel premier Ian Smith sign a draft agreement on Rhodesian independence.

● **28 Nov**: The Jordanian prime minister is assassinated by Palestinian guerrillas. On 1 Dec King Hussein rules out further talks with guerrillas.

● **6 Dec**: India recognizes the rebel government of Bangladesh.

● **19 Dec**: President Yahya Khan of Pakistan resigns, and is succeeded by Zulfikar Ali Bhutto. On 22 Dec Sheikh Mujibur Rahman, nominated president of Bangladesh, is released from prison.

● **21 Dec**: Kurt Waldheim (Aut) is appointed UN Secretary-General.

SOCIETY

● **8 Jan**: UK ambassador to Uruguay Geoffrey Jackson is kidnapped by leftwing guerrillas (Tupamaros), and not released until 9 Sep.

● **16 Jan**: The Swiss ambassador to Brazil, Giovanni Enrico Bucher, is released after being kidnapped by Brazilian terrorists on 7 Dec 1970.

● **31 Jan**: A telephone service between East and West Berlin is established for the first time in 19 years.

● **4 Feb**: Major UK company Rolls-Royce goes bankrupt; the government announces a partial takeover. Later in Feb the US aircraft manufacturer Lockheed gets into financial difficulties due to the Rolls-Royce failure. The US government passes a controversial $250,000,000 loan to save it.

● **7 Feb**: Men in Switzerland vote to give women the right to vote in federal elections and hold federal office.

● **11 Feb**: A treaty is signed by 63 nations banning nuclear weapon installations on the seabed in international waters.

● **14 Feb**: An agreement is signed in Tehran between Western oil companies and six oil-producing Gulf states settling a dispute over prices.

● **15 Feb**: The UK introduces decimal currency.

● **25 Mar**: EEC nations agree on a program of higher farm prices and modernization in response to protests by farmers.

● **Mar**: After the occupation of East Pakistan by Pakistani forces, refugees – especially Hindus – begin to crowd into India. In Jun Indian prime minister Mrs Gandhi seals the border.

● **6 Apr**: Announcement of a a new five-year plan in the USSR. Prime minister Kosygin calls for closer economic ties with Western Europe and increased living and cultural standards.

● **10 Apr**: The US table tennis team arrives in China to play a series of matches. US newsmen are admitted for the first time since 1949.

● **5 May**: European currency markets close after a rush of funds from $ into DM. On 9 May West Germany and Holland float their currencies; Austria and Switzerland carry out upward revaluation to stem monetary crisis.

● **28 May**: Residents of Filicundi Island, Sicily, begin leaving after Mafia leaders are exiled there by the Italian government.

● **1–8 Jun**: First special conference of UN Industrial Development Organization (UNIDO) is convened in Vienna. Developing countries demand that the organization is more independent from the industrial countries.

● **13 Jun**: The *New York Times* begins publishing papers from a leaked Pentagon study of US involvement in Vietnam 1945-67.

● **17 Jun**: President Nixon requests funds to combat drug abuse and names Jerome H. Jaffe to head the campaign (USA).

● **21 Jun**: The International Court of Justice at The Hague rules that South Africa's administration of Southwest Africa (Namibia) is illegal and should be surrendered to the UN. South African prime minister Vorster rejects the ruling.

● **30 Jun**: The USA extends full voting rights to 18-year-olds.

● **Jun**: Austria is admitted to membership of the OECD.

● **Jun**: A conference of EEC countries discusses a reorganization of the European monetary system and closer economic cooperation.

● **14 Jul**: In Zambia, militant students seize control of Lusaka University, accusing president Kaunda of "inconsistency" in his dealings with South Africa. From 15–30 Jun the university is closed down.

● **26 Jul**: The Belgian parliament approves two constitutional reform bills recognizing the two national language communities.

● **27–29 Jul**: The 25th session of the Comecon Council, in Bucharest, agrees on a 20-year plan for economic integration and a convertible currency.

● **6 Aug**: Scottish yachtsman Chay Blyth arrives in Hamble, after a 292-day nonstop voyage round the world in reverse (east to west).

● **15 Aug**: Nixon announces the suspension of conversion of the $ into gold, a 90-day wage and price freeze and a 10 percent import surcharge. US monetary experts and an EEC commission meet to discuss the international financial crisis.

● **16 Aug**: The US balance of trade shows a deficit for the first time since 1894. European governments close their foreign exchanges; US financial markets experience record trading and price rises; Japanese stocks record the worst decline in their history.

● **24 Aug**: An emergency meeting of the GATT Council opens to decide whether the US import surcharge is a violation of GATT's fair trade rules. (›18 Dec)

● **15 Oct**: The UK parliament passes legislation curbing nonwhite immigration into Britain.

● **Nov**: The 26th GATT session defines special rights for developing countries.

● **18 Dec**: The USA devalues the $ by 7.9 percent and lifts the 10 percent import surcharge. Values of other major currencies are realigned.

● **Dec**: 77 developing countries sign a declaration demanding participation in decisions on a new world monetary system.

● The Nobel Peace Prize is awarded to West German chancellor Willy Brandt.

● Nobel Prize for Economic Sciences is won by Simon Kuznets (USA).

CULTURE

● **6 Apr**: Death aged 88 of Russian composer Igor Stravinsky.

● **3 Jul**: Cult rock musician Jim Morrison dies in Paris aged 27 (USA).

● **6 Jul**: Death of jazz musician Louis Armstrong, aged 71.

● **1 Aug**: A concert in New York's Madison Square Gardens to raise money for victims of floods and civil war in Bangladesh is organized by ex-Beatle George Harrison and friends.

● **8 Sep**: The Kennedy Arts Center in Washington DC opens with the first performance of Leonard Bernstein's *Mass* for the late president.

● V.S. Naipaul's *In a Free State*, part fiction and part reportage, wins the Booker Prize (Trin).

● Samuel Beckett: *Breath and Other Short Plays* (Fr).

● Miroslav Holub: *Although*, poems (Cze).

● Alexander Solzhenitsyn: *August 1914*, novel (USA).

● Doris Lessing: *Briefing for a Descent into Hell*, novel (UK).

● Harold Pinter: *Old Times*, play (UK).

● Germaine Greer: *The Female Eunuch*, a feminist analysis of sexual stereotypes (Aus).

● Argentinian composer Mauricio Kagel's *Staatstheater*, for opera personnel, is first performed in Hamburg.

● Karlheinz Stockhausen: *Trans*, for orchestra, tape and light (FRG).

● Steve Reich: *Drumming*, for percussion, voices and piccolo (USA).

● Cornelius Cardew: *The Great Learning*, for organ.

● Iannis Xenakis: *Persepolis*, a *son et lumière* work involving laser torches with an eight-track electronic tape (Fr).

● *Jesus Christ Superstar*, written by Tim Rice and Andrew Lloyd Webber (UK).

● Malcolm Morley: *St John's Yellow Pages*, painting (USA).

● David Hockney: *Mr and Mrs Ossie Clark and Percy*, painting (UK).

● Oyvind Fahlstrom: *Exercise (Nixon)*, in which magnetized pieces have to be moved about by the spectator (USA).

● Pier Luigi Nervi: The Audience Hall, Vatican City.

● Kisho Kurokawa: Capsule offices and apartments, Tokyo (Jap).

● Andrei Tarkovsky: *Solaris*, film (USSR).

● Werner Herzog: *Land des Schweigens und der Dunkelheit* (Land of Silence and Darkness), film using a cast of deaf-and-dumb performers (FRG).

● Joseph Losey: *The Go-Between*, film (USA).

● Dirk Bogarde stars in Luchino Visconti's film of *Death in Venice* (It).

● Nobel Prize for Literature is won by Pablo Neruda (Chile).

SCIENCE

● **31 Jan**: *Apollo 14* is launched with three crew. On 5 Feb it lands on the Moon; two moonwalks are made and samples taken. It returns safely on 9 Feb (USA).

● **May**: Soviet *Mars 2* and *Mars 3* and US *Mariner 9* are launched; in Nov they all go into orbit round Mars.

● **26 Jul**: Three-man *Apollo 15* is launched, landing on the Moon on 30 Jul. The astronauts make three trips, using a "Moon car". They splash down on 7 Aug.

● **Nov**: London's Middlesex Hospital opens a new sterile nursing unit, the first of its kind. Lightweight panels form a bacteria-free room within the ward, supplied by filtered air at higher pressure than normal.

● **18 Dec**: The world's largest hydroelectric power station is completed in Krsnoyarsk (USSR).

● The Nobel Prize for Chemistry is won by Gerhard Herzbeg (Can) for his work on electronic structures and the geometry of molecules.

● The Nobel Prize for Physics is won by Dennis Gabor (UK) for his development of holography.

● Earl W. Sutherland (USA) wins the Nobel Prize for Physiology or Medicine for his work on the action of adrenalin in the body.

● The US Food and Drug Administration bans the prescription of diethylstilbestrol (DES) to control morning sickness in pregnant women due to evidence that the drug renders their daughters susceptible to cancers of the reproductive tract.

● The herpes virus is isolated from the lymph cell cancer Burkitt's lymphoma (USA).

● The newly formed British Microsurgical Instrumentation Reasearch Association develops the diamond-bladed scalpel.

● R.B. Woodward synthesizes vitamin B12 (USA).

● Intel Co. introduce the microprocessor (USA).

● Publication of *Design for the Real World*, the book by Victor Papanek that inspired design for the handicapped and the Third World.

● US astronomers identify two objects, discovered in 1968, as "new" galaxies adjacent to the Milky Way, about three million light years from Earth.

● ASH (Action on Smoking and Health) is formed by doctors and others to change public outlook on cigarette smoking.

● US scientists begin to use laser light to separate different isotopes.

● Texas Instruments introduces the first pocket calculator; it weighs more than 1 kg (2.5 lb) and costs around $150 (USA).

● Niklaus Wirth develops PASCAL, a popular language for home computers.

In another small step toward European unity, Britain, Ireland and Denmark joined the EEC. International rapprochement was in the air. Richard Nixon became the first US president to visit China and, three months later, the first to visit the USSR (he had been to Moscow before, as vice-president), but détente between the major powers did nothing to halt political terrorism, the bane of the 1970s. British troops, overreacting against rioters, shot 13 people dead on Bloody Sunday in Londonderry, and the IRA responded by killing seven men at Aldershot barracks with a bomb. A month later the British government imposed direct rule on the troubled province of Northern Ireland. In September, Arab guerrillas marked the anniversary of Black September by striking during the Olympic Games, an event supposedly devoted to international friendship (and from which white-dominated rebel Rhodesia was banned). Eleven Israeli athletes died in the Olympic Village.

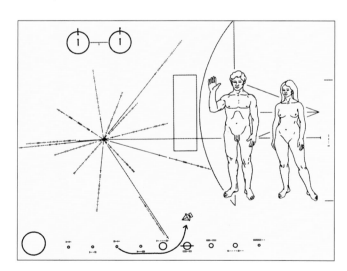

▲ In the same year that US president Nixon ordered NASA to start work on a manned space shuttle, two Pioneer spaceprobes were launched toward Jupiter. Each carried a pictorial plaque, indicating its origin in case it should be found by a member of another intelligent species. A plan of the solar system shows the route taken by the Pioneer craft in the early stages of the journey from Earth.

● **13 Jan**: President Nixon announces that 70,000 US troops will be withdrawn from Vietnam. On 25 Jan the USA makes public an 8-point peace plan to end the deadlock over Vietnam. (26 Apr)

● **30 Jan**: "Bloody Sunday" in Londonderry, Northern Ireland, when 13 civilians are killed by UK troops during riots against the 1971 internment laws. (›30 Mar)

● **30 Jan**: Pakistan withdraws from the Commonwealth in protest against the imminent recognition of Bangladesh by the UK (4 Feb), Australia and New Zealand (31 Jan).

● **4 Feb**: The sixth round of SALT talks ends in Vienna; talks reopen in Helsinki on 28 Mar. (›22 May)

● **21–28 Feb**: Nixon visits Beijing, the first visit of a US president to China.

● **25 Feb**: Zambia becomes a one-party state.

● **25 Feb**: Israel attacks South Lebanon in reprisal for Arab guerrilla raids. (›5 Sep)

● **10 Mar**: Cambodian prime minister Lon Nol takes over as head of state and dissolves the National Assembly.

● **13 Mar**: The UK and China resume diplomatic relations after 22 years.

● **27 Mar**: An agreement ends 16 years of civil war in Sudan.

● **30 Mar**: The UK imposes direct rule on Northern Ireland after 51 years' semi-autonomous rule and suspends its parliament. (›21 Jul)

● **10 Apr**: A convention outlawing biological weapons is signed in ceremonies in Washington, London and Moscow by numerous nations.

● **26 Apr**: Nixon announces his intention to withdraw 20,000 more troops from Vietnam in two months, despite the continuing North Vietnamese offensive. (›29 Aug)

● **22 May**: Nixon arrives in Moscow on a week's visit, the first US president to visit the USSR. On 26 May Soviet premier Brezhnev and Nixon sign a treaty on the limitation of strategic arms. (›3 Oct)

● **22 May**: Ceylon becomes the independent republic of Sri Lanka within the Commonwealth.

● **23 May**: The UK's Pearce Commission finds that the Rhodesian people view the 1971 agreement on independence as unacceptable; economic sanctions are therefore to remain in effect.

● **17 Jun**: Five men are seized while apparently trying to install eavesdropping equipment in the Democratic National Committee's HQ in Washington – the Watergate break-in. (›30 Jan 1973)

● **25 Jun**: France begins nuclear tests on Mururoa Atoll in the Pacific, despite protests.

● **3 Jul**: Indian prime minister Gandhi and Pakistani president Bhutto agree to renounce force in settlement of their disputes and improve economic/cultural relations.

● **21 Jul**: 22 bombs explode in 80 minutes in Belfast, killing at least 13 and wounding 130.

● **2 Aug**: Egypt and Libya announce an agreement to establish "unified political leadership" by 1 Sep 1973.

● **9 Aug**: Ugandan military dictator Idi Amin gives Asians of non-Ugandan citizenship 90 days to leave Uganda. Many with British passports flee to the UK. (›17 Sep)

● **29 Aug**: The USA announces a further reduction in troops in Vietnam. (›18 Dec)

● **5 Sep**: Arab guerrillas attack the Israeli building at the Olympic Village near Munich where the athletes are staying. 11 of the team are killed, along with a policeman and 5 terrorists. On 8 Sep Israeli planes attack Arab guerrilla bases in Lebanon and Syria in retaliation. (›21 Nov)

● **17 Sep**: Forces loyal to Uganda's former president, Milton Obote, unsuccessfully invade Uganda from Tanzania.

● **29 Sep**: An accord is signed that ends the technical state of war between China and Japan since 1937, and establishes diplomatic relations. Taiwan severs relations with Japan.

● **3 Oct**: The USSR and USA sign the last papers implementing SALT accords limiting submarine-carried and land-based missiles. (›21 Nov)

● **7 Nov**: Richard Nixon is reelected US president.

● **17 Nov**: Juan Perón, ex-president of Argentina, arrives in Buenos Aires from Spain after 17 years of exile. He rejects the presidential nomination offered by his party. (›11 Mar 1973)

● **21 Nov**: SALT II, the second round of US–USSR strategic arms limitations talks, begins in Geneva.

● **21 Nov**: Israeli and Syrian troops fight air/artillery/tank battles on the frontier in their most serious clash for two years.

● **24 Nov**: The UN grants East Germany permanent observer status, the same status as West Germany.

● **24 Nov**: Finland becomes the first Western nation to formally recognize East Germany and the first to establish ties with both Germanies.

● **25 Nov**: The New Zealand Labor party wins an unexpected landslide victory in the general election. On 2 Dec, in the first Labor party election win in 23 years, Gough Whitlam becomes prime minister of Australia.

● **18 Dec**: Nixon orders full-scale heavy bombing and mining of North Vietnam "until such time as a settlement is arrived at". His decision is criticized by both West and East.

SOCIETY

- **9 Jan**: A national coal strike begins in the UK, crippling industry and causing large-scale power cuts.

- **20 Jan**: Six Persian Gulf states sign an agreement with Western oil companies compensating them for the devaluation of the US $.

- **22 Jan**: The Treaty of Accession to the EEC is signed in Brussels by the UK, Ireland and Denmark, who will become part of the Community from 1 Jan 1973.

- **25 Jan**: The USA announces a trade deficit of $2,047 million in 1971, the first since 1888.

- **2 Feb**: The Winter Olympics open in Tokyo (Jap), the first winter games to be held in Asia.

- **17 Feb**: The Volkswagen "Beetle" overtakes the sales record of the Model T Ford (FRG).

- **23 Feb**: Argentina devalues the peso in an effort to ease its economic crisis.

- **2 Mar**: French customs agents in Marseille seize over 400 kg (900 lb) of pure heroin in the largest seizure to date. On 25 Mar an agreement to coordinate efforts to control trade in narcotic drugs is signed by 36 states.

- **15 Apr**: The USA and Canada sign an agreement on joint efforts to combat the pollution of the Great Lakes.

- **May**: West German finance minister Schiller demands drastic reduction of public deficit spending (FRG).

- **22 Jul**: An agreement is signed in Brussels between the EEC and EFTA members not planning to join the EEC, establishing a new free trade area to come into force 1 Jan 1973.

- **22 Jul**: Austria signs a special relations agreement with the EEC after nearly 10 years of discussion.

- **28 Jul**: Mexican president Echeveria decrees the expropriation of around 200,000 ha (500,000 acres) of private estates and distributes the land to peasants.

- **26 Aug**: The 20th Olympic Games open in Munich. US swimmer Mark Spitz wins seven gold medals. Rhodesia is barred from competing.

- **1 Sep**: Bobby Fischer becomes the first US world chess champion, beating Boris Spassky of the USSR.

- **25 Sep**: A referendum in Norway rejects entry to the EEC.

- **6 Nov**: UK prime minister Edward Heath announces an immediate 90-day freeze on wages, prices, rents and dividends in an attempt to curb inflation.

- **7 Dec**: France announces emergency anti-inflation measures.

- **23 Dec**: An earthquake in Nicaragua devastates the capital, Managua.

- Nobel Prize for Economic Sciences is won by Kenneth Arrow (USA) and John Hicks (UK).

CULTURE

- **29 Mar–30 Dec**: The British Museum exhibits the treasures of the tomb of the Egyptian pharaoh Tutankhamun.

- **17 Jun**: The musical *Fiddler on the Roof* hits a record 3,225 performances in a single run (USA).

- **12 Jul**: Premiere of Peter Maxwell Davies's opera *Taverner* at the Royal Opera House, Covent Garden (UK).

- **30 Aug**: John Lennon and Yoko Ono play Madison Square Gardens (USA).

- Allen Curnow: *Trees, Effigies, Moving Objects*, poems (NZ).

- Hans Magnus Enzensberger: *Der Kurze Sommer der Anarchie*, an investigation of the life and death of an anarchist (FRG).

- Tom Stoppard: *Jumpers*, play (UK).

- Seamus Heaney: *Wintering Out*, poems (Ire).

- Nobel Prize for Literature is won by Heinrich Böll (FDR).

- Frederic Rzewski: *Coming Together*, for ensemble and voices, a setting of. the words of prison rioters (USA).

- Dmitri Shostakovich: Fifteenth Symphony (USSR).

- Harrison Birtwistle: *The Triumph of Time*, for orchestra (UK).

- Luciano Berio: *Recital I (For Cathy)*, written for singer Cathy Berberian (It).

- Alvin Ailey: *The Lark Ascending*, ballet to music by Ralph Vaughan Williams (USA).

- Reg Butler: *Girl on a Long Base*, Superrealist sculpture (UK).

- American artist Carl André's collection of prefabricated bricks is bought by the Tate Gallery in London, and provokes a storm of protest.

- Richard Long: *Walking a Line in Peru*, long line inscribed in the earth (Peru).

- Bruce McLean, Ron Carra and Paul Richards form the satiric performance art group Nice Style (UK).

- Alvar Aalto: Finlandia Hall, Helsinki.

- Kisho Kurokawa: Nakagin Apartment Tower, Tokyo (Jap).

- New York's MoMA (Museum of Modern Art) presents an exhibition of Italian avant-garde designers.

- Rainer Werner Fassbinder: *Die bitteren Tränen der Petra von Kant* (The Bitter Tears of Petra von Kant), film (FRG).

- Liza Minnelli and Joel Gray star in *Cabaret*, a musical film based on Christopher Isherwood's stories of prewar Berlin (USA).

- Release of Francis Ford Coppola's blockbuster about the Mafia, *The Godfather*, starring Marlon Brando (USA).

- Bernardo Bertolucci: *Last Tango in Paris*, starring Marlon Brando (It).

- Two feminist magazines first appear, *MS* in the USA and *Spare Rib* in the UK.

SCIENCE

- **5 Jan**: President Nixon orders the National Aeronautics and Space Administration (NASA) to begin work on a manned space shuttle (USA).

- **2 Mar**: Launch of *Pioneer 10*, the first probe to Jupiter, and the first to have an atomic-powered battery (USA).

- **16 Apr**: *Apollo 16* is launched toward the Moon, carrying three astronauts – the fifth Apollo crew to land on the Moon. The first astronomical observatory is set up on the Moon.

- **Apr**: The inaugural meeting takes place of a commission for economic and scientific cooperation between the USSR and West Germany.

- **16 May**: The first stage of the Iron Gate Dam on the River Danube, Europe's largest hydroelectric power plant, is opened at a ceremony attended by president Tito of Yugoslavia and president Ceauşescu of Romania.

- **Jun**: John Prineas confirms that multiple sclerosis is caused by a virus similar to the measles virus.

- **Jun**: The US government announces that by the end of the year DDT will be banned for all but a few relatively small-scale and carefully controlled uses, because of its effect on the environment. However, legislation still permits export of DDT to Third World countries for malaria control.

- **Jul**: Soviet spaceprobe *Venera 8* soft-lands on Venus and sends back radio signals for twice as long as *Venera 7*. It confirms that the surface temperature is 7,500 degrees C and the pressure 90 times that of the atmosphere on Earth, making life unlikely.

- **3 Jul**: Launch of Landsat 1, the first of a series of Earth resources technology satellites that will send back pictures of Earth to discover whether such surveys could be of use for agricultural and forest management, urban planning and environmental protection (USA).

- **17 Oct**: The world's most powerful radio telescope officially opens at Mullard Observatory near Cambridge, UK. It is able to focus on objects only one-third the size of those visible to any other existing radio telescope.

- **7 Dec**: *Apollo 17* is launched, the last of the series (USA). Its crew spends 44 hours on the moon's surface and brings back 110 kg (243 lb) of materials.

- The Nobel Prize for Physics is shared by Americans John Bardeen (his second prize), Leon Cooper and John Robert Schrieffer for their work on superconductivity.

- The Nobel Prize for Chemistry is won by Christian Anfinsen (USA) for his work on the secondary structure of proteins, and Stanford Moore and William Stein (USA) for their development of a technique to work out the sequence of amino acids in proteins.

- Rodney Porter (UK) and Gerald Edelman (USA) win the Nobel Prize for Physiology or Medicine for their work on understanding the body's defenses against disease.

- An experimental power station is built in West Germany, in an attempt to increase the efficiency of generating electricity by gasifying coal.

- M. Calvin and M. Tributsch obtain minute quantities of electricity from a solar cell containing chlorophyll, the principle agent of photosynthesis (USA).

- I. Cooper develops a "brain pacemaker" for epileptics. Platinum electrodes are implanted in the cerebellum to receive radio signals which relieve spasticity, paralysis or seizures (USA).

- Robert Moog patents his electronic synthesizer, intended to make available any sound by electronic synthesis (USA).

- Computerized axial tomography (CAT or CT scanning) is introduced to give cross-sectional X-rays of the human body (UK).

- Murray Gell-Mann initiates quantum chromodynamics, the theory linking quarks and color forces in particle physics (USA).

- R.N. Manchester calculates the galactic magnetic field strength by measuring the Faraday rotation for different wavelengths of the polarization of radio waves emitted by pulsars.

- A team led by Professor John Postgate of Sussex University (UK) announces that they have successfully transferred the ability to fix nitrogen from the bacteria of leguminous root nodules to bacteria which do not naturally fix nitrogen at all.

- The large particle accelerator at Fermi National Accelerator Laboratory in Illinois begins operation (USA).

The last US troops finally pulled out of Vietnam in March, leaving the conflict in which the USA had suffered its first ever military defeat to revert to the status of a civil war. President Nixon, recently reelected, spoke of "peace with honor", but few signs of either were evident. Soon his conduct of domestic affairs was shown to be blatantly dishonorable. As the Watergate affair unfolded, his denials of personal involvement became steadily less convincing, and the revelation that tapes existed of conversations between Nixon and his aides promised to make the hearings of the Senate Investigating Committee a considerable embarrassment. Nixon's position was not improved when fullscale war erupted again between Israel and its Arab neighbors. The Arab oil-producing states employed a new tactic in their running battle with Israel and its supporters, raising the price of oil by 70 percent and at the same time reducing production. Some Arab states cut off oil supplies to the United States entirely, and the effects were rapidly felt worldwide. In Britain, the oil cuts exacerbated an already existing energy crisis and a state of emergency was declared.

▲ While the Watergate scandal threatened to topple US president Richard Nixon, in South America the Marxist president of Chile, Dr Salvador Allende, was killed in a CIA-backed bloody military takeover that put rightwing General Pinochet into power for the foreseeable future.

● **8 Jan**: Serious clashes occur between Israeli and Syrian forces. On 21 Feb Israeli fighter planes shoot down a Libyan Boeing 727 with 113 aboard over Israeli-held territory. (›10 Apr)

● **9 Jan**: Rhodesia closes its border with Zambia because of terrorist attacks.

● **17 Jan**: President Marcos proclaims a new constitution in the Philippines under which he rules indefinitely, and permanently reinstates martial law.

● **27 Jan**: The USA, North and South Vietnam and the Vietcong sign an agreement to end the war in Vietnam. (›29 Mar)

● **30 Jan**: Two former officials of US president Richard Nixon's reelection campaign are found guilty of attempting to spy on the Democratic National Committee HQ in the Watergate building complex. (›30 Apr)

● **21 Feb**: A ceasefire between the government and the Pathet Lao ends 20 years of war in Laos. A coalition government is established on 14 Sep.

● **7 Mar**: In the first general election in Bangladesh, Sheikh Mujibur Rahman's Awami League wins 292 out of 300 National Assembly seats.

● **8 Mar**: A referendum in Northern Ireland votes to remain part of the UK, though most Catholics boycott the polls. (›31 Jul)

● **11 Mar**: In the first elections in Argentina since 1965, the Peronista presidential candidate Hector J. Campora wins 49 percent of the votes. On 13 Jul he resigns to make way for the return of Juan Perón. (›23 Sep)

● **20 Mar**: Kuwait closes its border with Iraq following a border clash.

● **26 Mar**: President Sadat of Egypt takes on the office of prime minister.

● **27 Mar**: The White House says the USA will continue bombing raids on Cambodia until Communist forces stop offensive operations and agree to a ceasefire. (›6 Aug)

● **29 Mar**: The last US troops leave Vietnam, leaving 8,500 civilian technicians behind. Fighting continues between North and South Vietnam.

● **10 Apr**: In Lebanon, Israeli strike forces land on the outskirts of Beirut in a nighttime raid and shoot dead three Palestine guerrilla leaders. (›20 Jul)

● **30 Apr**: President Nixon makes a TV statement on the Watergate affair, accepting "responsibility" for the bugging, but saying he was not personally involved. (›16 Jul)

● **27 May**: In Syria's first parliamentary elections for over 10 years, the Baath party wins 122 out of 186 seats.

● **1 Jun**: The military regime in Greece proclaims the abolition of the monarchy and establishment of a republic. The new constitution is approved by 78.4 percent of the electorate in a referendum on 29 Jul. Georgios Papadopoulos becomes president on 19 Aug.

● **9 Jun**: Admiral Luis Carrero Blanco takes over from Gen. Franco as prime minister of Spain, though the latter remains chief of state and commander-in-chief of the armed forces. (›2 Jan 1974)

● **22 Jun**: Soviet prime minister Leonid Brezhnev, in the USA for a summit conference, signs a pact aimed at avoiding confrontations that could lead to nuclear war.

● **10 Jul**: The Bahamas become independent of the UK.

● **16 Jul**: In the Watergate hearings, former presidential aide Alexander Butterfield testifies that US president Nixon recorded his conversations and phone calls in the White House without the participants' knowledge. (›4 Jan 1974)

● **20 Jul**: A Japan Air Lines Boeing 747 is hijacked over the Netherlands by pro-Palestinian guerrillas. (›6 Oct)

● **31 Jul**: The first session of the new Northern Ireland legislature in Belfast ends in uproar when the Rev. Ian Paisley and 26 Ulster Loyalists take over the debating chamber. (›21 Nov)

● **6 Aug**: US planes accidentally bomb a friendly village in Cambodia, killing or wounding over 400. On 15 Aug the US Congress forces an end to the bombing of Cambodia.

● **11 Sep**: Marxist Chilean president Salvador Allende and at least 2,700 others are killed in a bloody coup led by Gen. Pinochet and a military junta.

● **18 Sep**: Both East and West Germany are accepted as UN members.

● **23 Sep**: Juan Perón is elected president, with his wife Isabel ("Isabelita") as vice-president (Arg).

● **6 Oct**: The Yom Kippur War, the fourth Arab-Israeli conflict, leads to a worldwide oil crisis and is the worst in 25 years. On 24 Oct Syria accepts the UN ceasefire and fighting on the Syrian front virtually ceases.

● **25 Oct**: US forces are placed on alert for fear of the USSR joining the conflict in the Middle East. The crisis eases when the USSR joins in approving the UN Security Council resolution establishing a peacekeeping force in the Middle East but barring major powers from the force.

● **7 Nov**: The USA and Egypt restore diplomatic relations, broken six years before. On 11 Nov Egypt and Israel sign a US-sponsored six-point ceasefire agreement. (›17 Dec)

● **21 Nov**: Political leaders in Northern Ireland agree on a compromise plan for the establishment of an 11-member executive that would share government between Catholics and Protestants.

● **9 Dec**: The UK, Northern Ireland and the Irish Republic agree to establish a Council of Ireland to deal with the mutual problems of Northern Ireland and the Republic of Ireland.

● **17 Dec**: Arab guerrillas kill over 30 at Rome airport and hijack a West German airliner to Athens.

SOCIETY

- **1 Jan**: The UK, Denmark and Ireland become members of the EEC.

- **17 Jan**: UK prime minister Edward Heath publishes the second phase of his anti-inflation program. On 27 Feb the first full-scale strike by UK civil servants opens a series of strikes opposing the program. (›13 Nov)

- **Jan**: The Italian government establishes a two-tier foreign exchange system in an effort to stop speculation against the lira.

- **2 Feb**: The West German government imposes a series of exchange controls following a massive flight from the $ and buying of DM. On 12 Feb the USA devalues the $ by 10 percent and allows it to float.

- **7 Feb**: A general strike by Northern Ireland Protestants, prompted by the internment of two Protestants in connection with a grenade attack, paralyzes Belfast.

- **13 Feb**: Japan permits the yen to float.

- **18 Feb**: The West German government announces a series of tax increases and a sharply trimmed budget to try to curb inflation.

- **27 Feb**: Red Indians occupy Wounded Knee, South Dakota, demanding investigation of federal treatment of Indians. The siege lasts until 6 May (USA).

- **2 Mar**: Representatives of 80 countries agree in Washington to a treaty outlawing trade in 375 endangered wildlife species.

- **2 Mar**: Exchange markets in London, Brussels, Frankfurt, Amsterdam, Vienna and Tokyo close temporarily in face of a new international monetary crisis. (›19 Mar)

- **16 Mar**: After a meeting in Paris of the finance ministers of 14 countries and the heads of the IMF, OECD and BIS, a new system of floating exchange rates comes into being.

- **19 Mar**: EEC countries decide to introduce a joint float against the $, and the foreign exchange markets are reopened.

- **31 Mar**: Red Rum wins the Grand National in record time (UK).

- **6 Apr**: The finance ministers of the EEC countries decide to establish a European fund for monetary cooperation.

- **15 Apr**: Libyan leader Muammar Qadhafi announces a five-point reform program including purging of political deviationists and implementation of Islamic thought – the Libyan "cultural revolution".

- **19 May**: The USSR and West Germany sign a 10-year pact for economic, industrial and technical cooperation.

- **22 May**: In the UN Security Council, the UK and USA veto a resolution to extend sanctions to South Africa and the Portugese African Territories.

- **29 Jun**: West Germany revalues the DM 5.5 percent.

- **4 Jul**: Barbados, Guyana, Jamaica and Trinidad sign the Chaguaramas Treaty establishing the Caribbean Economic Community, to come into operation on 1 Aug.

- **21 Jul**: France begins a series of nuclear tests in the South Pacific, despite international protests.

- **30 Aug**: Kenya bans the hunting of elephants and dealings in ivory.

- **30 Aug**: In Italy, bathing is banned at beaches near Naples following an outbreak of cholera.

- **17 Sep**: The Netherlands revalues the guilder by 5 percent.

- **Sep**: 11 black miners are killed by police in the Western Deep Levels gold mine during a riot over wages (SA).

- **1 Oct**: A natural gas pipeline is opened from the Ukraine to West Germany.

- **5 Oct**: Finland signs an industrial free trade pact with the EEC.

- **17 Oct**: The Organization of Arab Petroleum Exporting Countries (OAPEC) agrees to cut oil production to force the USA to change its policy in the Middle East. On 19 Oct Libya cuts off oil shipments to the USA, followed on 20 Oct by Saudi Arabia, and on 21 Oct by Kuwait, Bahrain, Qatar and Dubai.

- **Oct**: Iraq nationalizes US oil companies Exxon and Mobil Oil.

- **Oct**: The Nobel Peace Prize is awarded to Henry Kissinger (USA) and Le Duc Tho (N Viet) for their work in bringing about the ceasefire in Vietnam in Jan. Widespread protest follows since the truce was ineffective and fighting has cost around 50,000 lives by the time the prize is announced. Le Duc Tho declines to accept.

- **13 Nov**: The UK government declares a state of emergency, regulates fuel distribution and takes over public and private transport due to the energy crisis created by shortage of oil supplies and overtime bans by mineworkers and electricians. A three-day week for most industries in the New Year, to conserve energy, is announced on 13 Dec.

- **15 Dec**: J. Paul Getty III, teenage grandson of the US oil magnate, is found in Italy over five months after his disappearance, with one ear cut off, after payment of a ransom reported to be $2,800,000.

- There is serious famine in Ethiopia after the failure of the annual rains, causing unprecedented distress. The UN estimates 50,000–100,000 deaths.

- Economist E.F.Schumacher (UK) publishes an unexpected bestseller – *Small is Beautiful, a Study of Economics as if People Mattered*, putting forward suggestions to save the planet from human destruction.

- Nobel Prize for Economic Sciences is won by Wassily Leontief (USA).

CULTURE

- **8 Apr**: Death of artist Pablo Picasso, aged 91. His collection of modern paintings is to go to the Musée du Louvre in Paris.

- **16 Jun**: Premiere of Benjamin Britten's opera *Death in Venice*, based on the novella by Thomas Mann (UK).

- **Jul**: First performance of Polish composer Krzysztof Penderecki's First Symphony, in the UK.

- **20 Oct**: Australia's Sydney Opera House is opened.

- **5 Dec**: At Sotheby's, Picasso's *Femme assise* sells for £340,000, a record for a 20th-century painting.

- Erica Jong: *Fear of Flying*, novel (USA).

- Henri Michaux: *Moments: Traversées du temps*, poems (Fr).

- Thomas Pynchon: *Gravity's Rainbow*, novel (USA).

- Wole Soyinka: *Season of Anomy*, novel (Nig).

- Robert Lowell: *The Dolphin*, poems (USA).

- Patrick White: *The Eye of the Storm*, novel (Aus).

- Nobel Prize for Literature is won by Patrick White (Aus).

- Peter Shaffer: *Equus*, play (UK).

- Derek Walcott: *Another Life*, autobiographical poem (Trin), concerned with the resolution of the conflict between the West Indian and European cultural heritage.

- Dmitri Shostakovich: String Quartet No.14 (USSR).

- Pierre Boulez: *… explosante-fixe…*, for eight instruments and electronics (Fr).

- Thea Musgrave: Viola Concerto (UK).

- Peter Maxwell Davies: *Stone Litany*, for mezzo-soprano and orchestra (UK).

- Steve Reich: *Music for Mallet Instruments, Voice and Organ* and *Music for Pieces of Wood* (USA).

- Richard Estes: *Paris Street-scene*, Superrealist painting (USA).

- Duane Hanson: *Florida Shopper*, Superrealist sculpture (USA).

- Richard Serra: *Different and Different Again*, minimal art (USA).

- Robert Smithson: *Amarillo Ramp*, outdoor construction, finished posthumously (USA).

- François Truffaut: *La Nuit Americaine* ("Day for Night"), film (Fr).

- Release of *The Exorcist*, film directed by William Friedkin (USA).

- Rainer Werner Fassbinder: *Angst Essen Seele Auf* (Fear Eats the Soul), film (FRG).

- Werner Herzog: *Aguirre, Wrath of God*, film about the *conquistadores* in Mexico (FRG).

- Lindsay Anderson: *Oh Lucky Man!*, film (UK).

SCIENCE

- **8 Jan**: *Luna 21* unmanned spacecraft launched by the USSR; on 16 Jan the *Lunokhod II* ground-controlled Moon-rover lands on the Moon.

- **3 Apr**: Launch of the Soviet space laboratory Salyut 2.

- **14 May**: Space station Skylab is launched by the USA. On 25 May three astronauts are sent to rendezvous with Skylab, and they remain for 28 days.

- **30 Jun**: The longest eclipse of the sun for 1,500 years occurs in some parts of the Earth, lasting 195 minutes.

- **4 Dec**: *Pioneer 10* passes close by Jupiter, sending back close-up pictures of its red spot.

- The Nobel Prize for Chemistry goes to Ernst Otto Fischer (FRG) and Geoffrey Wilkinson (UK) for work on the combination of organic substances with metals.

- The Nobel Prize for Physiology or Medicine is won by Konrad Lorenz (Aut), Nikolaas Tinbergen (Neth) and Karl von Frisch (Aut) for their work on individual and social behavior patterns.

- The Nobel Prize for Physics is shared by Leo Eskai (Jap), Ivar Giaever (Nor) and Brian Josephson (UK) for their work on transistors.

- Uri Geller (Isr) arouses interest by his apparent ability to bend metal objects without physical force, as well as other feats inexplicable by conventional science.

- P. Musset and colleagues at CERN discover neutral currents in neutrino reactions, a partial confirmation of the electroweak theory.

- The nuclear magnetic resonator (NMR) is introduced to form images of soft body tissues (UK).

- The first demonstration is given of Oracle and Ceefax information to home TV receivers (UK).

- S.H. Cohen and H.W. Boyer demonstrate that molecules of DNA can be cut with restriction enzymes, joined with other enzymes and reproduced by inserting them into the bacterium *Escherichia coli*.

- The image intensifier, a TV camera tube for use in low light conditions, is developed (FRG)

- A calf is produced from a frozen embryo for the first time.

- It is discovered that communications through the *corpus collosum* – which links the two hemispheres of the brain – are defective in schizophrenics (UK).

- Radio immunoassay is used to test for spina bifida in the unborn fetus (Fin).

- Computer-coded labels are introduced in supermarkets.

- Drinks cans with push-through tabs are first manufactured.

The running drama of Watergate culminated in the resignation of US president Nixon, in preference to facing impeachment. Nixon was the most notable casualty among a large number of world leaders whose political careers ended more or less abruptly in 1974. In Japan, prime minister Tanaka resigned under suspicion of corruption; Israeli prime minister Golda Meir, in poor health, also resigned. Edward Heath was replaced by Labour leader Wilson as prime minister of Britain, while Hailee Selassie, the "Lion of Judah", was deposed by a clique of military Marxists in Ethiopia. German chancellor Willy Brandt ended his distinguished career over a minor spy scandal. Archbishop Makarios was overthrown by ultra-nationalist Greeks in Cyprus, while in Greece the colonels themselves resigned. Increasingly, though, people were becoming concerned about environmental as well as political problems, such as the effect on the ozone layer of hairsprays and other aerosols discharging CFCs.

▲ Russian author Alexander Solzhenitsyn, for long a thorn in the side of the Soviet authorities, was finally deported after the publication in the West of his epic work on the Soviet labor camps, *The Gulag Archipelago*.

● **1 Jan**: An executive governing body takes office in Northern Ireland, comprising both Protestants and Catholics and ending 21 months of direct rule by the UK government. (›28 May)

● **2 Jan**: Carlos Arias Navarra is sworn in as prime minister of Spain, after the assassination of Luis Carrera Blanco by members of the Basque separatist group ETA on 20 Dec 1973.

● **4 Jan**: US president Nixon refuses to comply with subpoenas calling for him to surrender hundreds of White House documents, claiming it would "destroy any vestiges of confidentiality of presidential communications". (›6 Feb)

● **18 Jan**: Egypt and Israel sign an agreement to separate their forces along the Suez Canal, ending a conflict which began on 6 Oct 1973. Fighting continues between Israel and Syria. (›31 May)

● **25 Jan**: The Argentine Chamber of Deputies passes a strong antiterrorism bill. On 26 Jan there are 19 bombing attacks against leftist organizations in various Argentine cities.

● **2 Feb**: China launches a new Cultural Revolution in a campaign aimed against the teachings of Confucius and the policies of the late defense minister Lin Piao.

● **6 Feb**: The US House of Representatives approves an impeachment investigation on president Nixon. On 27–30 Jul the House Judiciary Committee recommend that the House of Representatives impeach Nixon. (›3 Apr)

● **7 Feb**: Grenada becomes independent within the Commonwealth.

● **22 Feb**: A conference of Islamic heads of state and government begins at Lahore. The PLO is recognized as the sole representative of Palestinians, and demands that the Old City of Jerusalem be returned to Arab control. Pakistan officially recognizes Bangladesh. (›14 Oct)

● **27 Feb**: Sweden approves a new constitution to come into force on 1 Jan 1975; the king's assent to legislation is no longer needed.

● **28 Feb**: As a result of the all-out miners' strike, a general election is called in the UK, but no party gains a majority. Edward Heath resigns as prime minister and Labour leader Harold Wilson takes office on 4 Mar. (›10 Oct)

● **2 Mar**: Military rule in Burma, which began in 1962, ends. Gen. Ne Win becomes president and under a new constitution Burma becomes a socialist republic with one-party rule.

● **28 Mar**: Romanian Communist party leader Nicolae Ceauşescu is elected to the newly created post of president.

● **Mar**: Serious fighting takes place in South Vietnam, the worst since the ceasefire agreement of Jan 1973.

● **1 Apr**: Colombia holds its first free presidential election for 16 years. Alfonso Lopez Michelson is elected president.

● **2 Apr**: President Georges Pompidou of France dies in office. On 27 May Valéry Giscard d'Estaing is sworn in as president after narrowly defeating the leftist candidate François Mitterand.

● **3 Apr**: Nixon agrees to pay $432,787 in back taxes after reports show that he owes nearly $500,000. (›9 Aug)

● **9 Apr**: India, Pakistan and Bangladesh restore diplomatic relations.

● **10 Apr**: Israeli prime minister Golda Meir resigns, prompted by a report laying the blame for Israel's military unpreparedness at the start of the Oct 1973 war on the top military command. Itzhak Rabin replaces her on 4 Jun.

● **11 Apr**: 18 people, mostly women and children, die in an attack by Palestinian terrorists on the Israeli village of Kiryat Shemona. On 12 Apr Israeli troops raid six villages in Lebanon in retaliation. (›15 May)

● **24 Apr**: In elections in South Africa, premier Vorster's Nationalist party increases its majority, giving him a virtual mandate for apartheid policies.

● **25 Apr**: An almost bloodless military coup in Portugal overthrows Dr Caetano. A junta led by Gen. Antonio de Spinolo assumes power. On 30 Sep he resigns and is succeeded by Gen. Francisco Gomes.

● **6 May**: Willy Brandt, chancellor of the FRG, submits his resignation, taking full responsibility for the Guillaume spy affair, in which one of his aides was found to be an East German spy. Helmut Schmidt is sworn in as chancellor on 16 May.

● **15 May**: 190 Israeli village schoolchildren are taken hostage by three Palestinian guerrillas. Confusion leads to Israeli troops storming the school and the death of 20 children and the guerrillas. On 16 May Israeli fighter bombers carry out heavy raids on Palestinian refugee camps in Lebanon.

● **28 May**: The Northern Ireland Executive coalition collapses after only five months as a result of a general strike, begun on 15 May by a group of Protestant extremists. On 29 May the UK resumes direct rule of Ulster.

● **31 May**: An agreement is signed by Israel and Syria for disengagement of forces on the Golan Heights, after months of intensive negotiation by US Secretary of State Kissinger.

● **17 Jun**: An IRA bomb explodes in the Houses of Parliament, injuring 11.

● **1 Jul**: Death of Juan Perón. His widow Isabel succeeds him as the first woman head of state in the Americas. (›6 Nov)

● **15 Jul**: President Makarios of Cyprus is overthrown in a coup led by the Greek-officered National Guard. Greek Cypriot and former guerrilla leader Nikos Sampson is sworn in to succeed him.

SOCIETY   CULTURE   SCIENCE

- **20 Jul**: Turkey invades Cyprus, claiming the right to protect Turkish communities on the island. Both sides accept a UN ceasefire proposal, but fighting continues. (›30 Jul)

- **23 Jul**: The Greek military junta resigns; Constantine Karamanlis is invited to return from exile and form a government. (›17 Nov)

- **30 Jul**: Turkey, Greece and the UK sign an agreement providing for a ceasefire in Cyprus. It includes an expanded role for the UN peace keeping force and provisions for new talks to "reestablish constitutional government". However, fighting still continues.

- **9 Aug**: Richard Nixon becomes the first US president to resign, following the Watergate scandal. Vice-president Gerald Ford is sworn in as president. On 8 Sep he gives Nixon an unconditional pardon.

- **4 Sep**: The USA establishes diplomatic relations with East Germany.

- **12 Sep**: Emperor Haile Selassie of Ethiopia is deposed in a bloodless coup by military leaders. On 20 Dec Ethiopia is declared a socialist state.

- **10 Oct**: The second general election of the year takes place in the UK; Labour wins a majority of three seats.

- **14 Oct**: The UN General Assembly recognizes the PLO as "the representative of the Palestinian people". On 22 Nov the UN grants observer status to the PLO, and declares that the Palestinian people have a right to independence.

- **28 Oct**: 20 Arab nations call for an independent Palestinian state and recognize PLO leader Yasir Arafat.

- **6 Nov**: Argentine president Isabel Perón places the nation under a state of siege as political assassinations and terrorist attacks continue.

- **12 Nov**: The UN General Assembly votes 91-22 to suspend South African participation in its current session, though this does not exclude South Africa from membership.

- **15 Nov**: The Brazilian Democratic Movement, the only officially tolerated opposition group, defeats the government party in federal and state elections.

- **17 Nov**: The first democratic general election to be held in Greece since 1964 gives a decisive victory to prime minister Karamanlis and his newly founded New Democracy party. On 8 Dec a referendum rejects restoration of monarchy.

- **23 Nov**: Soviet premier Brezhnev and Ford begin two days of talks at Vladivostok. They reach tentative agreement to limit offensive strategic nuclear weapons over a 10-year period.

- **26 Nov**: Japanese prime minister Tanaka resigns after allegations that he has used his high political office to amass a personal fortune.

- **18 Jan**: The IMF Committee of 20 in Rome ends in disagreement over how to deal with the monetary effects of the oil crisis.

- **10 Feb**: Coalminers in the UK begin a full-scale strike, demanding 30–40 percent pay increases. On 11 Mar new prime minister Harold Wilson ends the state of emergency declared on 13 Nov 1973, and the miners return to work after accepting a pay deal.

- **14 Jun**: 10,000–30,000 are reported to have died in India, mainly in Bihar state, in a serious smallpox epidemic.

- **26 Jun**: West German Bankhaus I.D. Herstatt KG, one of the country's largest private banks, is the first bank to collapse due to heavy losses incurred in foreign exchange trading.

- **30 Jun**: Mrs Alberta King, mother of the murdered civil rights champion Martin Luther King, is assassinated during a church service (USA).

- **Jul**: At the Conference of Kingston held by 44 African, Caribbean and Pacific countries, association with the EEC is discussed.

- **31 Aug**: West Germany agrees to lend $2 billion to Italy to ease its serious economic crisis.

- **Sep**: 17 oil companies build a pipeline from the North Sea to the UK.

- **Sep**: Comecon takes up informal contacts with the EEC.

- **3 Oct**: EEC council of aid ministers agree to contribute $150,000,000 to help the 25 less developed nations worst hit by quadrupled oil prices.

- **4 Oct**: The IMF announces that it is drawing up plans for a major new lending operation. It will be funded mainly by oil-producing nations, and will benefit states in financial difficulty due to problems in paying higher prices for oil imports.

- **Oct**: US president Ford publishes his economic program to counter inflation and the energy crisis.

- **10 Nov**: Israel devalues the pound by 43 percent and imposes drastic austerity measures in an attempt to curb inflation.

- **29 Nov**: The British government passes legislation outlawing the IRA and giving police unprecedented powers to search and detain suspected terrorists and impose restrictions on travel between Ireland and England.

- **Nov**: Introduction of the currency unit Arcru by Arab countries to recycle income from the sale of oil.

- **25 Dec**: A cyclone strikes Darwin in northern Australia, destroying 90 percent of the city.

- **Dec**: US citizens are permitted to buy, sell and own gold for the first time since 1963.

- Nobel Prize for Economic Sciences is won by Friedrich von Hayek (UK) and Gunnar Myrdal (Swe).

- Nobel Peace Prize is won by Sean MacBride (UK) and Eisaku Sato (Jap).

- **13 Feb**: Author Alexander Solzhenitsyn is deported from the USSR and stripped of his citizenship after the publication in the West of *The Gulag Archipelago*, about his experiences in a Soviet labor camp.

- **Jun**: First performance of Iannis Xenakis's *Cendrées*, for chorus and orchestra, at the Lisbon Festival (Port).

- **20 Oct**: Premiere of Karlheinz Stockhausen's *Inori* (Japanese for "adorations"), for one or two mimes with orchestra (FRG).

- Philip Larkin: *High Windows*, poems (UK).

- Alejo Carpentier: *Reasons of State*, a "dictator-novel" concerned with the nature of power (Cuba).

- Athol Fugard: *Sizwe Bansi is Dead*, play (SA).

- Tom Stoppard: *Travesties*, play (UK).

- Alan Ayckbourn: *The Norman Conquests*, trilogy of English domestic comedies.

- Nobel Prize for Literature is won by Eyvind Johnson (Swe) and Harry Mastinson (Swe).

- György Ligeti: *San Francisco Polyphony*, for orchestra (FRG).

- Dmitri Shostakovich: String Quartet No. 15 (USSR).

- Richard Rodney Bennett: Concerto for Orchestra (UK).

- Olivier Messiaen: *Des canyons aux étoiles...*, for orchestra (Fr).

- Merce Cunningham: *Events*, a reconstruction of his 1952 ballet *Suite by Chance*.

- The Swedish group Abba shoot to international stardom after winning the Eurovision Song Contest with "Waterloo".

- Ed Paschke: *Minnie*, painting (USA).

- Richard Estes: *The Canadian Club*, Superrealist painting (USA).

- Vuminkosi Zulu: *Awaiting Trial*, painting (SA).

- John de Andrea: *Freckled Woman*, Superrealist sculpture (USA).

- Joseph Beuys: *Coyote: I Like America and America Likes Me*, performance work: the "performer" (Beuys) shares a space in a New York gallery with a wild coyote, conversing with it and introducing it to various objects upon which it urinates (USA).

- *Cadillac Ranch*, by Ant Farm (Chip Lord, Hudson Marquez, Doug Michels), places nosediving Cadillacs in the landscape (USA).

- Richard Long: *A Line in Ireland*, earth sculpture.

- Norman Foster: Willis, Faber and Dumas Building, Ipswich (UK).

- Louis I. Kahn: Parliament Building, Dacca (Bangladesh).

- *Chinatown*, directed by Roman Polanski and starring Jack Nicholson and Faye Dunaway (USA).

- **5 Feb**: US spaceprobe *Mariner 10* sends back pictures of Venus from as close as 42,000 km (26,000 miles); they show Venus to be wound round with a spiral of cloud. On 29 Mar it passes within 400 miles of Mercury.

- **18 May**: India becomes the sixth nation with a nuclear bomb. An underground explosion is carried out and provokes criticism abroad.

- **1 Sep**: A US Lockheed SR 71 Blackbird jet crosses the Atlantic in 1 hour 55 mins.

- **Nov**: A new subatomic particle, later known as the J/psi particle, is observed independently by Burton Richter and S. Chao Chung Ting (USA).

- **Dec**: US probe *Pioneer 11* passes within 42,000 km (26,000 miles) of Jupiter, providing a close-up of the red spot and Jupiter's moon Callisto. It then moves on toward Saturn.

- The Nobel Prize for Physiology or Medicine is shared by Albert Claude (Bel), George E. Palade (USA) and C.R. de Duve (Bel) for their work on intracellular structures and their functions.

- The Nobel Prize for Chemistry goes to Paul J. Florey (USA) for his work on the development of synthetic materials.

- Sir Martin Ryle (UK) and Anthony Hewish (UK) share the Nobel Prize for Physics for pioneering work on use of radiotelescopes.

- F.S. Rowland and M. Molina warn of the effects of CFCs (chlorofluoro-carbons) on the ozone layer.

- The US National Academy of Sciences, in consultation with other nations, calls a halt to research in genetic engineering until safer techniques are developed, in case of risks of starting new epidemics.

- It is discovered that certain "anti antibodies" can be purified to prevent reactions against skin grafts (UK).

- The holographic electron microscope, which is able to see the shapes of atoms, is developed (USA).

- Microbes are used to synthesize hormones for contraceptive pills (Jap).

- H.M. Georgi and S.L. Glashow develop the first of the "grand unified theories" (GUTs), an attempt to describe all known forces and the relationships between elementary particles in terms of a single unifying concept.

- The ATS-6, a direct-broadcast TV satellite capable of linking remote communities, is launched (USA).

- It is found that X-ray irradiation of children can lead to the development of tumors (Isr).

- Indian astronomer J.V. Narlikar suggests the existence of white holes to explain the mystery of qasars and the powerful X-rays that come from the center of ordinary galaxies.

1975

POLITICS

A memorable "first" in space exploration was the meeting between spacecraft of the USA and USSR 140 miles above the Earth's surface. The crews, three men in each, moved between the craft and shared meals and gossip in an operation that had taken three years to plan. Down on the surface, construction was under way on an artifact that would eventually be visible from Earth orbit – the pipeline designed to carry 2 million barrels of oil a day from Alaska's North Slope to the ice-free port of Valdez. A different sort of union took place in Southeast Asia, as the Communists took over in South Vietnam. Scenes of panic preceded the fall of Saigon (now to become known as Ho Chi Minh City) as the North Vietnamese tanks rolled in virtually unopposed. The Communists were successful in Laos, too, proclaiming in December the establishment of the Democratic Republic of Laos. 1975 was International Women's Year, and saw the scaling of Mount Everest by Japanese climber Mrs Junko Tobei as well as the election of Mrs Margaret Thatcher as the first female leader of Britain's Conservative party.

▲ As the Communist armies took power in Vietnam and Laos, Chinese archeologists unearthed a different kind of army altogether near the ancient Chinese capital of Xian – a 2,000-year-old terracotta army of 6,000 life-sized and lifelike warriors, drawn up in battle formation with their horses, spears and chariots, guarding the tomb of the first Ch'in emperor.

● **1 Jan**: A jury in Washington convicts four aides of ex-president Richard Nixon in the Watergate trial (USA).

● **19 Jan**: China publishes a new state constitution. It embodies the basic ideas of Mao Zedong, such as "He who does not work, neither shall he eat", and abolishes the post of president.

● **26 Jan**: Prime minister Sheikh Mujibur Rahman becomes president of Bangladesh. On 15 Aug he is assassinated in an army coup.

● **11 Feb**: Mrs Margaret Thatcher is elected leader of the Conservative party (UK).

● **12 Feb**: The USA increases its airlift of arms and ammunition to Pnom Penh, but on 17 Apr the Cambodian government surrenders to the Khmer Rouge.

● **13 Feb**: Turkish Cypriots proclaim the northern part of Cyprus a separate state and offer to join with the Greek Cypriot community in federation. The Turkish government expresses support, but Greek Cypriots and the Greek government denounce the action.

● **15 Feb**: The Ethiopian government declares a state of emergency in the province of Eritrea as fighting continues in the 13th year of conflict between the Ethiopian government and Eritrean secessionists.

● **25 Mar**: King Faisal of Saudi Arabia is assassinated by his nephew and succeeded by his brother, crown prince Khalid ibn Abdul Aziz.

● **30 Mar**: North Vietnamese troops, sweeping south, take the city of Da Nang in South Vietnam after the collapse of South Vietnamese resistance. Thousands of South Vietnamese panic and flee. (›30 Apr)

● **5 Apr**: Death of Jiang Jieshi, thought to be 87 years old (Taiwan).

● **13 Apr**: Fighting erupts between Muslims and Christians in Lebanon.

● **24 Apr**: Six West German terrorists blow up the West German embassy in Stockholm (Swe), killing two hostages, after the West German government refuses to release the Baader-Meinhof group of anarchists from jail.

● **25 Apr**: In Portugal, in the first free elections for the Constitutional Assembly for 50 years, the Socialist party led by Dr Mario Soares has a clear lead; it is identified as a strong opponent of both Communists and military dictatorship. (›11 Jul)

● **30 Apr**: South Vietnam surrenders to the North Vietnamese Communists. Saigon is to be popularly known as Ho Chi Minh City.

● **5 Jun**: In the first ever national referendum in the UK, the people vote overwhelmingly to stay in the EEC.

● **7 Jun**: The Greek parliament adopts a new constitution establishing parliamentary responsibility with executive and legislative authority for the president. On 20 Jun Constantinos Tstsos is sworn in as president.

● **9 Jun**: China and the Philippines establish diplomatic relations; Taiwan breaks off relations with the Philippines. Taiwan now has diplomatic ties with only 26 nations, whereas Beijing is recognized by 100.

● **12 Jun**: Indian prime minister Mrs Indira Gandhi is found guilty of corrupt election practices in the 1971 election and told to give up her seat in parliament. Opposition parties demand that she resign as prime minister, but she refuses. (›26 Jun)

● **25 Jun**: Mozambique gains independence from Portugal.

● **26 Jun**: The Indian president declares a state of emergency and several hundred political opponents are arrested. Press censorship is imposed and the government is authorized to conduct military operations to maintain public order.

● **4 Jul**: A bomb explodes in Jerusalem, killing 14 Israelis and wounding nearly 80 people.

● **11 Jul**: The Socialists withdraw from the Portugese government, followed on 17 Jul by the Popular Democratic party, thus further widening the breach between the ruling Armed Forces Movement and the exponents of parliamentary democracy. On 31 Jul a three-man military junta is established.

● **29 Jul**: Gen. Gowan, head of Nigeria's provisional government since 1966, is deposed in a bloodless coup while in Uganda. Brig. Murtala Muhammad becomes head of state.

● **30 Jul**: Leaders of 33 European nations and the USA and Canada sign the Final Act of the Conference on Security and Cooperation in Europe, which declares post-World War II boundaries "inviolable", renounces force and aid to terrorists, and promises to respect human rights.

● **23 Aug**: The Communist takeover of Laos is completed. The Pathet Lao begin efforts to force rightists out of government. On 3 Dec the People's Democratic Republic of Laos is established.

● **4 Sep**: Representatives of Israel and Egypt sign a US-mediated agreement providing for Israeli withdrawal in Sinai and the establishment of a new UN buffer zone.

● **5 Sep**: An assassination attempt is made on US president Gerald Ford, followed by a second on 22 Sep.

● **16 Sep**: Papua New Guinea achieves independence within the Commonwealth.

● **30 Oct**: Prince Juan Carlos assumes the powers of chief of state in Spain, taking over from 82-year-old Gen. Franco, who is critically ill. Franco dies on 20 Nov, and on 22 Nov Juan Carlos is proclaimed king and succeeds him.

● **10 Nov**: Angola achieves independence from Portugal but no international recognition of government, due to factional fighting.

● **6 Jan**: A strike begins in South Africa's largest gold mine, Vaal Reefs mine, to protest against a government ruling that 60 percent of all the earnings of Lesotho nationals must be deposited in a Lesotho bank and paid to workers only when contracts expire.

● **14 Jan**: The USSR rejects a trading agreement with the USA because of the latter's insistence on linking it with relaxation of emigration requirements for Soviet Jews.

● **20 Jan**: General Motors Corporation, following the lead of Chrysler and Ford, offers cash rebates to purchasers of new cars in an attempt to lift the automobile industry out of one of the worst slumps since the 1940s (USA).

● **Jan**: Air pollution in Madrid gets so bad that citizens are advised to breathe only through their noses in heavily contaminated areas, to take no physical exercise and to speak only at home.

● **5–6 Feb**: Police in Lima, Peru, go on strike demanding wage increases. The strike is put down by troops and tanks, but this sparks off rioting by civilians.

● **21 Feb**: The UN Human Rights Commission censures Israel for actions in the occupied Arab territories.

● **28 Feb**: Agreement is reached between EEC and ACP (African, Caribbean, Pacific) countries to regulate trade, financial and industrial cooperation (Lomé agreement).

● **4 Mar**: A meeting of OPEC heads of state in Algiers proposes a $10,000 million fund to help the Third World and some developed countries.

● **9 Mar**: Work begins on a 1,270 km (789 mile) Alaskan oil pipeline, the largest private construction project to date in the USA.

● **24 Apr**: The UK government announces its decision to take a majority shareholding in British Leyland motor company and plans investment of £1,500 million over the next few years.

● **Apr**: South Vietnamese orphans are airlifted to the USA and UK for adoption.

● **16 May**: Mrs Junko Tobei, a member of a 15-woman Japanese expedition, becomes the first woman to reach the top of Mount Everest, in 1975 which is International Women's Year.

● **May**: Peru nationalizes Gulf Oil de Peru.

● **5 Jun**: The Suez Canal reopens after eight years to all but Israeli traffic.

● **Jun**: Strikes and protests break out in Argentina in response to the high cost of living and the austerity measures imposed by the government to deal with an estimated 100 percent annual inflation rate.

● **Jun**: Brazilian soccer star Pele signs a three-year $7 million contract with the New York Cosmos (USA).

● **5 Jul**: Arthur Ashe (USA) becomes the first black player to win the men's singles at Wimbledon, beating Jimmy Connors (USA), the 25–1 favorite.

● **29 Jul**: The OAS ends its embargo on Cuba, in force since 1964 for fostering Communist guerrilla activities.

● **15 Aug**: Six men – who become known as the "Birmingham Six" – are sentenced to life imprisonment for murder when convicted of planting bombs that killed 21 people in Birmingham on 21 Nov 1974 (UK).

● **15 Aug**: Joanne Little, a 21-year-old black woman, is acquitted in a trial that had become a *cause célèbre* among feminists and civil rights activists. She had been accused of murdering her jailer, while she maintained that she was defending herself from rape (USA).

● **31 Aug**: The IMF announces its decision to dispose gradually of its holdings of around 4,250 million gm (150 million oz) of gold and remove all references to the status of gold in world monetary affairs from its articles.

● **9 Sep**: Czech star tennis player Martina Navratilova requests political asylum in the USA.

● **22 Sep**: South Africa devalues the rand 17.9 percent against the US$ in an attempt to counteract the falling price of gold and a worsening domestic recession.

● **27 Sep**: In Spain, five political prisoners convicted of acts of terrorism are executed by firing squad, despite protests throughout Europe.

● **27 Sep**: After four days of talks, OPEC countries announce a 10 percent increase in the price of oil from 1 Oct.

● **Sep**: The US government begins a $100 billion program to become self-sufficient in energy.

● **5 Oct**: Austrian racing driver Niki Lauda becomes world motor racing champion.

● **9 Oct**: Physicist Andrei Sakharov, who worked on the Soviet hydrogen bomb and became an outspoken advocate of civil liberties, is the first Soviet citizen to win the Nobel Peace Prize.

● **5 Nov**: After talks between the government, TUC and CBI, prime minister Wilson announces a common effort to reverse two decades of industrial decline, and give priority to aiding industry rather than subsidizing housing and health care (UK).

● **14 Dec**: The USSR outlines a new five-year plan, to start Jan 1976, emphasizing a return to traditional reliance on heavy industry. Previous efforts to establish an economy more favourable to the consumer are apparently abandoned.

● **16–19 Dec**: Conference on International Economic Cooperation takes place in Paris; 27 industrialized, developing and oil-producing countries are represented.

● Nobel Prize for Economic Sciences is won by Leonid Kantovovich (USSR) and Tjalling C. Koopmans (USA).

● **23 Apr**: First performance of Harold Pinter's play *No Man's Land* with John Gielgud and Ralph Richardson (UK).

● **9 Aug**: Death of Russian composer Dmitri Shostakovich.

● Vaclav Havel: *Audience*, the first of the "Vanek" plays (Cze).

● Saul Bellow: *Humboldt's Gift*, novel (USA).

● Gabriel García Márquez: *The Autumn of the Patriarch*, dictator-novel (Col).

● Wole Soyinka: *Death and the King's Horseman*, play (Nig).

● Ruth Prawer Jhabvala wins the Booker Prize for her novel about India, *Heat and Dust* (Ind).

● Paul Scott completes the final volume of the Raj Quartet, about India's transition to independence, with *A Division of the Spoils* (UK).

● Régis Debray: *L'Indésirable*, account of the life of a guerrilla fighter (Fr).

● Seamus Heaney: *North*, poems (UK).

● Carlos Fuentes: *Terra Nostra*, novel (Mex).

● Nobel Prize for Literature is won by Eugenio Montale (It).

● Dmitri Shostakovich: Viola Sonata (USSR).

● Karlheinz Stockhausen: *Tierkreis* (Zodiac), a set of 12 melodies, one for each sign of the zodiac, later published in various vocal and instrumental arrangements (FRG).

● Pierre Boulez: *Rituel*, for orchestra (Fr).

● Witold Lutostawski: *Les Espaces du sommeil*, for baritone and orchestra (Pol).

● Bruce Springsteen emerges as a star with "Born to Run" (USA).

● Disco music becomes popular (USA).

● Jamaican reggae star Bob Marley comes to fame with his "Natty Dread" album.

● Frank Stella: *Jardim Botanico I*, lacquer and oil on aluminum (USA).

● Dennis Oppenheim: *Theme for a Major Hit*, in which a puppet in a dimly lit room dances endlessly to its own theme song (USA).

● Foundation of OMA (Office for Metropolitan Architecture) in New York.

● *Murder on the Orient Express*, directed by Sidney Lumet (UK).

● Claude Chabrol: *Une partie de plaisir*, film (Fr).

● Volker Schlondorff: *The Lost Honor of Katherina Blum*, based on the novel by Heinrich Böll (FRG).

● Audiences scream at *Jaws*, Steven Spielberg's blockbuster about man-eating sharks (USA).

● Release of *Picnic At Hanging Rock*, directed by Peter Weir (Aus).

● Woody Allen writes, directs and acts in *Love and Death* (USA).

● **17 Jul**: First ever joint venture between USA and USSR when *Apollo 18* and *Soyuz 19* couple in space for over 40 hours, and the crews visit each other's capsules.

● **20 Aug**: US *Viking 1* spacecraft is launched toward Mars. On 9 Sep it is followed by *Viking 2*.

● **1 Oct**: US scientists warn of the environmental dangers of chlorofluorocarbons (CFCs), refrigerant and aerosol propellant gases.

● **Oct**: Two Soviet spaceprobes land on Venus and send back the first pictures of the planet's surface.

● The Nobel Prize for Physics is won by Aage Bohr (Den), Ben Roy Mottelson (Den) and L. James Rainwater (USA) for work on atomic physics.

● The Nobel prize for Chemistry is shared by John Warcup Cornforth (UK) and Vladimir Prelog (Swi) for work on the three-dimensional arrangement of atoms in molecules.

● The Nobel Prize for Physiology or Medicine is won by Renato Dulbecco (USA), Howard Temin (USA) and David Baltimore (USA) for their work on tumor viruses and their interaction with genetic material of the cell.

● A team from Glasgow University finds strong links between high levels of lead in drinking water, dissolved out of old lead piping, and numbers of births of mentally retarded children (UK).

● Whole-body X-ray scanners, invented in the UK, begin to be used in hospitals. They produce clear three-dimensional pictures of organs and other internal structures.

● V.C. Rubin and W. Kent discover the proper motion of the Milky Way, about 500 km (310 miles) per second (USA).

● The tau lepton or tauon is discovered: it is like an electron but with about 3,500 times the mass.

● A thermonuclear power station, Tokamak 10, begins operation to see if power generated from nuclear fusion could become commercially viable (USSR).

● Rhizobium is adapted to "fix" nitrogen in the laboratory in order to increase the protein content of crops (Aus/Can).

● LCDs (liquid crystal displays) for calculators and digital timepieces are marketed for the first time by BDH (UK).

● C. Milstein announces the results of his work in genetic engineering to create identical microorganisms or monoclonal antibodies (UK).

● Successful treatment of infertile women is achieved with Bromocriptine, a fertility drug (UK).

● J. Hughes discovers morphine-like chemicals, named endorphins, in the brain (UK).

The focus of world concern began to shift toward India, Africa and the Middle East. In India, the state of emergency imposed in 1975 after Indira Gandhi's refusal to resign from office was followed in 1976 by the suspension of basic constitutional rights, and the postponement of parliamentary elections for the first time since independence. The bitter conflict centred on Israel and its neighbors continued, seemingly insoluble. The Israelis scored a remarkable success over Palestinian terrorists when they flew three planeloads of commandos into Uganda, under the nose of Idi Amin, to release 100 hostages from a hijacked airliner at Entebbe airport with only four civilian casualties. The struggle against apartheid in South Africa filled the front pages when nearly 200 died and many more were injured in Soweto in clashes with police. Two young sportspeople caught the imagination of the public: 14-year-old Nadia Comaneci scored maximum marks in gymnastics at the Olympic Games, while Swedish tennis ace Bjorn Borg, aged 20, became the youngest player to win the men's singles at Wimbledon for 45 years.

▲ In Britain's capital a new form of youth protest manifested itself in the music, fashions and lifestyle of the punk movement, deliberately setting out to shock and disgust. The Sex Pistols' concerts were later banned from TV for their use of foul language.

● **5 Jan**: A new constitution comes into force in Cambodia, now Democratic Kampuchea.

● **5 Jan**: Ten Protestants are massacred in South Armagh where five Catholics were killed the previous night. The British government orders more troops to Ireland.

● **6 Jan**: In Italy, the resignation of prime minister Aldo Moro and his cabinet is provoked by an newspaper article in which the Socialist party secretary complains about the government's failure to consult his party over reflationary measures. (›13 Jul)

● **8 Jan**: The Indian government suspends basic rights guaranteed by constitution, agrees to continue indefinitely the state of emergency proclaimed in 1975, and amends the constitution to give prime minister Indira Gandhi more power in relation to the judiciary. Parliamentary elections are postponed for the first time since independence.

● **8 Jan**: The death of Zhou Enlai, Chinese prime minister, aged 78, is followed on 9 Sep by the death of Mao Zedong, aged 82. Hua Gofeng succeeds Mao as chairman of the Communist party and as prime minister.

● **11 Feb**: The OAU recognizes the Angolan People's Republic under the government of the Soviet-backed MPLA (Popular Movement for the Liberation of Angola) and it becomes the OAU's 47th member.

● **24 Feb–5 Mar**: 25th Soviet Communist party Congress. Soviet premier Leonid Brezhnev says the USSR will continue to favor détente with the USA, but will not abandon the struggle against capitalism.

● **25 Feb**: Rhodesian forces cross into Mozambique in pursuit of guerrillas. On 3 Mar Mozambique closes its borders with Rhodesia and mobilizes the armed forces. (›Aug)

● **26 Feb**: Spain hands over the Western Sahara to Morocco and Mauritania, as agreed in Nov 1974; but on 27 Feb the Polisario Front, an independence movement supported by Algeria, proclaims the Saharan Arab Democratic Republic. In Mar Algeria breaks off diplomatic relations with Morocco and Mauritania.

● **26 Feb**: Portuguese military and political leaders sign an agreement to end military rule and establish a freely elected government in Portugal. (›2 Apr)

● **14 Mar**: Egypt formally abrogates its 1971 treaty of friendship and cooperation with the USSR. (›11 Nov)

● **16 Mar**: UK prime minister Harold Wilson resigns, after leading the Labour party for 13 years. He is succeeded by James Callaghan.

● **24 Mar**: A bloodless military coup under Gen. Jorge Rafael Videla deposes president Isabel Perón of Argentina. On 25 Oct she is found guilty of embezzlement.

● **2 Apr**: Portugal receives a new constitution. On 25 Apr the Socialists gain enough seats to form a government, and Dr Mario Soares becomes prime minister.

● **11 Apr**: In Laos, hundreds are detained in a "Cultural Revolution".

● **13–19 May**: Fighting goes on between Muslim and Christian forces as civil war in Lebanon intensifies. On 31 May Syria sends troops to Lebanon in an effort to end the war, but Palestinian forces in Lebanon oppose the move. (›12 Aug)

● **28 May**: The USA and USSR sign a five-year treaty limiting the size of underground nuclear test explosions and allowing the USA to inspect USSR tests on-site.

● **9 Jun**: The Spanish parliament approves the lifting of the ban imposed by Franco in 1939 on all political parties (except for that on Communists and separatists). (›15 Dec)

● **10 Jun**: The USA agrees to sell 12 jet fighter planes to Kenya and other military equipment to Zaire to offset Soviet military aid to neighboring Uganda, Somalia and Angola.

● **23 Jun**: The USA vetoes Angola's application to join the UN because of the continued presence of Cuban troops in the country.

● **25 Jun**: President Idi Amin of Uganda is made president for life.

● **27 Jun**: An Air France plane hijacked by Palestinian extremists near Athens lands at Entebbe, Uganda. On 30 Jun and 1 Jul all the hostages are freed except 98 Israelis and Jews and the crew. On 3–4 Jul Israeli commandos fly in and storm the airport, freeing all but four of the hostages, who die in the raid.

● **29 Jun**: Communist party leaders from 29 European states meet in East Berlin. They endorse the independence of each national Communist party in seeking its own road to socialism – a break with the former dominance of the Soviet party.

● **2 Jul**: North and South Vietnam are reunited as one nation, and a socialist republic proclaimed.

● **2 Jul**: Sudan breaks off relations with Libya, and later with the USSR.

● **12 Jul**: In Brussels, the European Council reaches agreement on membership of the European parliament.

● **13 Jul**: After elections on 20–21 Jun produce a clear advance for the left, Giulio Andreotti forms a government (It).

● **1 Aug**: Trinidad and Tobago becomes an independent republic within the Commonwealth.

● **12 Aug**: Rightwing Christian forces capture the Palestinian refugee camp of Tall Zaafar, the last Muslim enclave in the Christian-dominated area of Beirut, after a 52-day siege (Leb). (›10 Nov)

SOCIETY   CULTURE   SCIENCE

SOCIETY

- **18 Aug**: North Korean soldiers attack a group of US and South Korean soldiers in the village of Panmunjon in the demilitarized zone, killing two US officers with axes and clubs.

- **25 Aug**: Jacques Chirac resigns as prime minister of France, due to disagreements with president Valéry Giscard d'Estaing over political strategy. He is replaced by Raymond Barre. (›5 Dec)

- **Aug**: Rhodesia organizes air strikes and ground operations against what it claims to be a black nationalist guerrilla camp in Mozambique, killing over 300.

- **20 Sep**: Sweden's Social Democratic party is defeated in parliamentary elections after 44 years in power.

- **24 Sep**: Rhodesian rebel leader Ian Smith accepts US Secretary of State Kissinger's proposal for the establishment of immediate biracial government and black majority rule in two years. However, a conference in Geneva on how to achieve majority rule ends in deadlock on 14 Dec.

- **6 Oct**: The army seizes power in Thailand in a bloody coup.

- **10 Oct**: In Cuba, elections are held for the first time since Fidel Castro came to power in 1959.

- **26 Oct**: South Africa grants independence to the Transkei within South Africa, the first of the black homelands to gain independence. Because of general disapproval of South Africa's policy of separate development for blacks and whites, the UN General Assembly declares its independence invalid.

- **2 Nov**: Governor of Georgia Jimmy Carter (Democrat) is elected the next US president, defeating Gerald Ford.

- **10 Nov**: Syrian military forces enter Beirut as part of a multinational Arab peacekeeping force. They encounter no resistance.

- **11 Nov**: The UN Security Council unanimously deplores the establishment of Israeli settlements in occupied Arab territories and Israel's annexation of East Jerusalem.

- **11 Nov**: In Egypt, president Sadat abolishes the single-party system.

- **15 Nov**: The USA vetoes Vietnam's application for UN membership.

- **19 Nov**: Algerians vote in a referendum for a new constitution with a national assembly and an elected president with increased powers.

- **5 Dec**: The Central African Republic proclaims itself an empire with president Sallah Bokassa as its first emperor.

- **9 Dec**: NATO rejects a Warsaw Pact proposal that the two alliances agree not to initiate use of nuclear weapons.

- **15 Dec**: A referendum in Spain gives approval to free parliamentary elections in spring. The new Cortes will have the power to rewrite the laws of the Franco era.

- **15 Jan**: The Roman Catholic church reiterates its condemnation of sex outside marriage and states that homosexuality cannot be condoned under any circumstances.

- **26 Feb**: The British government signs a contract with oil companies Shell and Esso regarding North Sea oil.

- **Feb**: Comecon publishes a plan for economic cooperation with the EEC; but the EEC rejects the proposals.

- **16 Apr**: In a measure to curb population growth in India, the minimum marriage ages are raised to 21 (from 18) for men and 18 (from 15) for women.

- **May**: An $800 million fund for developing countries is established by the OEEC.

- **16 Jun**: Race riots start in the black township of Soweto (SA) in protest against legislation to force the use of Afrikaans in some teaching. The police open fire on demonstrating black students, killing six and injuring 60. By 25 Jun, the death toll is 176 and over 1,000 have been injured.

- **3 Jul**: Swedish tennis player Bjorn Borg, aged 20, becomes the youngest Wimbledon men's singles champion for 45 years.

- **10 Jul**: The town of Seveso near Milan in northern Italy is evacuated after an accident at the chemical plant Givaudan-La Roche Icmesa, when a cloud of poisonous gas is released which spreads dioxins over an area of 730 ha (1800 sq miles).

- **17 Jul**: The Olympic Games open in Montreal (Can). 14-year-old Romanian Nadia Comaneci scores the first 10 out of 10 in gymnastics ever awarded.

- **2 Sep**: The European Commission on Human Rights finds the UK guilty of torture of internees in Northern Ireland in 1971, but not of discrimination against Catholics.

- **4 Sep**: In Londonderry, 25,000 Protestants and Catholics take part in a peace movement march. On 27 Nov 15,000 gather in London's Trafalgar Square in support of the peace movement (UK).

- **16 Sep**: The Episcopal church approves ordination of women to be priests and bishops.

- **Sep**: French prime minister Raymond Barre publishes a plan to counter inflation: a three-month freeze of all prices, income tax increases and credit restrictions.

- **15 Dec**: The UK government announces a series of measures designed to overcome its financial crisis.

- **17 Dec**: OPEC members Saudi Arabia and the UAE raise prices by 5 percent while the other 11 members decide on a rise of 10 percent.

- Nobel Peace Prize is won by Mairead Corrigan (UK) and Betty Williams (UK).

- Nobel Prize for Economic Sciences is won by Milton Friedman (USA).

CULTURE

- **12 Jan**: Death of the doyenne of detective novelists, Dame Agatha Christie, aged 85 (UK).

- **21 Jan**: Western newspapers including the *New York Times* and the British *Financial Times* go on sale in the USSR.

- **Mar**: Opening of the National Theatre in London (architect Denys Lasdun).

- **12 Jul**: World premiere in London of German composer Hans Werner Henze's opera *We Come to the River*.

- Manuel Puig: *The Kiss of the Spider Woman*, novel (Arg).

- Nobel Prize for Literature is won by Saul Bellow (USA).

- Alfred Shnitke: Piano Quintet (USSR).

- Luciano Berio: *Coro*, for a chorus of 40 singers, each positioned next to an instrument of corresponding range (It).

- Benjamin Britten: Third String Quartet, which receives its first performance just a few days before his death on 4 Dec (UK).

- Philip Glass and Robert Wilson: *Einstein on the Beach*, opera (USA).

- Formation of the Ensemble InterContemporain by Pierre Boulez at the Institut de Recherche et Coordination Acoustique/Musique (IRCAM) in Paris, specializing in 20th-century music (Fr).

- "Punk" music and style emerges on the streets of London. The first punk rock single is released in Dec (UK).

- Balthus: *La Japonaise a la table rouge*, painting (since 1967) (Fr).

- Jake Berthot: *Walken's Ridge*, painting (USA).

- Nam June Paik: *Fish Flew in the Sky*, a video installation (Kor).

- Daniel Buren: *On Two Levels With Two Colors*, a vertically striped band running at floor level through a gallery (USA).

- Julia Heyward: *Shake! Daddy! Shake!*, performance piece for solo arm (USA).

- Scot Burton: *Pair Behaviour Tableaux*, in which two figures strike a total of 80 poses over the period of an hour (USA).

- Kisho Kurokawa: Sony Tower, Osaka (Jap).

- Release of *Rocky*, the first film vehicle for Sylvester Stallone, directed by John V. Avildsen (USA).

- *All the President's Men*, directed by Alan J. Pakula, reconstructs the initial exposure of the Watergate scandal (USA).

- *One Flew over the Cuckoo's Nest*, an adaptation of Ken Kesey's novel directed by Milos Foreman, and starring Jack Nicholson, wins five Oscars.

- Werner Herzog: *Herz aus Glas* (Heart of Glass) (FRG).

SCIENCE

- **8 Mar**: Over a hundred stony meteorites fall in northeast China, the largest fragment weighing 1,766 kg (3,900 lb).

- **8 Jul**: Palapa I, the first of two geostationary satellites, provides the inhabitants of Indonesia's islands with TV, radio and telegraph communications.

- **20 Jul and 3 Sep**: US spaceprobes *Viking 1* and *Viking 2* land on Mars and send back pictures of the landscape.

- **Nov**: Professor Ted Cocking (UK) announces the development of a technique for creating artificial hybrids of two different plant species, marking a step toward the establishment of new species.

- The Nobel Prize for Chemistry is won by William Nunn Lipscomb ((USA) for work on how molecules are bonded.

- The Nobel Prize for Physics is won by Burton Richter and Samuel Ting (USA) for their independent discovery of the psi particle in 1974.

- The Nobel Prize for Physiology or Medicine is shared by Baruch Blumberg (USA), for the discovery of Australia antigen, a means of identifying carriers of hepatitis B so that they can be kept out of blood transfusion and dialysis units; and Carleton Gajdusek (USA) for showing that an infective agent is responsible for the brain disease kuru, leading to theories of so-called slow viruses.

- Doctors at the Pain Relief Unit near Oxford (UK) introduce a new treatment to reduce pain by blocking short sections of nerves by freezing.

- The value of fiber in diet becomes the subject of a growing amount of research.

- Europe's Big Machine, the 400 million giga-electron-volt particle accelerator, built for CERN (the 11-nation research organization near Geneva), is brought up to full power.

- The blood-clot preventing characteristics of prostaglandin are discovered (UK).

- Genetech, the first commercial company for developing products via genetic engineering, is established in San Francisco (USA).

- It is discovered that the drug Nootropyl enhances memory and learning performance by improving communications between the two hemispheres of the brain.

- Theories employing supergravity are introduced into physics.

- The Canon AE-1 is the first camera with micro-processor controlled exposure (Jap).

- Glass fiber cable is developed for use in telecommunications.

- T. Kibble proposes the idea of "cosmic strings", threads of energy surviving from the Big Bang.

The role of the United States took a new turn with the inauguration of Democrat Jimmy Carter as president. He promptly began on reforms at home – not always to popular support – and was outspoken on matters of human rights, denouncing Idi Amin's reign of terror in Uganda and the treatment of Soviet dissident Andrei Sakharov. He approved the admission to the USA of thousands of refugees from Southeast Asia. He also worked toward a settlement in the Middle East, and in this was aided by the decision of Egyptian president Sadat to shift his foreign policy away from the USSR in favor of the USA, and to announce his readiness to consider a peace settlement with Israel despite huge opposition from the other Arab states. The election of rightwing former terrorist leader Menachem Begin as Israeli prime minister did not seem promising, but by the end of the year a conference was under way that would result in the Camp David Accords of 1978. Another shift in world affairs came with the disgrace of the "Gang of Four" in China following Mao Zedong's death in 1976, widely regarded as a forecast of more moderate policies.

▲ **Richard Rogers's and Renzo Piano's controversial Centre Georges Pompidou brought High-Tech Postmodernist architecture to the very heart of Paris. The siting of all services outside the building frees the exhibition areas, and gives stunning views of Paris from the escalators.**

● **20 Jan**: Jimmy Carter, Democrat, is inaugurated as 39th US president.

● **24 Jan**: Rebel Rhodesian leader Ian Smith rejects British proposals for transition to black majority rule in 14 months. (›31 Aug)

● **3 Feb**: Brig.-Gen. Teferi Benti, Ethiopian chief of state and chairman of the Military Council, is shot dead and Lt-Col. Mengistu Haile Mariam takes over.

● **8 Mar**: 5,000 mercenaries march into Zaire from Angola and seize three cities. On 10 Apr France supplies aircraft to fly 1,500 Moroccan troops to Zaire to help fight the rebels.

● **8 Mar**: King Hussain of Jordan and PLO leader Yasir Arafat meet to discuss the possibility of establishing an independent Palestinian state.

● **14 Mar**: Violent student riots in Italy follow the death of a student shot by police; some of the participants are left-wing extremists disenchanted by Italian Communist party collaboration with the government.

● **18 Mar**: President Mgoubi of the Congo is shot and killed. An 11-man military committee takes control under Col. Joachim Yhomby Opango.

● **24 Mar**: Moraji Desai replaces Indira Gandhi as prime minister of India after the Congress party is heavily defeated in the general election.

● **6 Apr**: President Carter signs legislation giving the White House wide authority to change the structure of the executive branch of the US government.

● **7 Apr**: Israeli prime minister Itzhak Rabin resigns after revelations that he has violated the Israeli currency laws by holding illegal US bank accounts. Shimon Peres takes over. (›17 May)

● **9 Apr**: The Spanish Communist party is legalized after a 38-year ban.

● **28 Apr**: The first formal negotiations take place between the USA and Cuba when a fishing rights pact is approved after a month of talks.

● **Apr**: Martial law is imposed in three Pakistani cities after six weeks of strikes costing over 230 lives in protest against allegedly rigged elections. The opposition leaders are arrested, but on 14 Jun prime minister Zulfikar Ali Bhutto's government agrees to hold new elections before the end of the year. (›5 Jul)

● **4 May**: The draft of a new USSR constitution is published. It states the dominant role of the Communist party in ruling the USSR.

● **6 May**: The USSR and Ethiopia sign accords drawing them closer economically and politically, and reversing the latter's previous dependence on the USA. (›8 Aug)

● **17 May**: The Labor party is defeated in the Israeli elections for the first time in 29 years. On 21 Jun Menachem Begin, leader of the right-wing Likud party, takes office as prime minister at the head of a coalition government.

● **8–15 Jun**: At the Commonwealth Conference in London, 33 heads of government condemn the regime of Idi Amin in Uganda for "massive violation of human rights".

● **15 Jun**: Adolfo Suarez becomes prime minister after the first free parliamentary elections in Spain for 41 years.

● **16 Jun**: Leonid Brezhnev is named USSR president as well as Communist party leader.

● **27 Jun**: Former French Somaliland becomes independent as the Republic of Djibouti.

● **5 Jul**: In Pakistan, Gen. Zia ul-Huq ousts prime minister Bhutto.

● **22 Jul**: The "Gang of Four" – Jiang Qing, widow of Mao Zedong, and three fellow radicals – are expelled from the Chinese Communist party and Deng Xiaoping is rehabilitated.

● **8 Aug**: Ethiopia's conflict with Somalia over ethnic Somalis in Ogaden becomes full-scale war.

● **31 Aug**: Ian Smith's Rhodesian Front wins an overwhelming victory in the whites-only general election. This is seen as giving him a mandate to negotiate a direct political settlement with the black majority, rather than accept the proposals of UK and US negotiatiors.

● **7 Sep**: Two Panama Canal treaties are signed by the USA and Panama. The canal is to come under the full control of Panama from 1999 and to be permanently neutral.

● **28 Sep**: Cambodian leader Pol Pot arrives in Beijing, and is for the first time publicly identified as the secretary of the Cambodian Communist party.

● **20 Oct**: The civilian government of Thailand is ousted in a bloodless coup by the same military officers who installed it one year earlier.

● **31 Oct**: In the UN Security Council, the UK, USA and France veto motions to impose economic sanctions on South Africa. On 4 Nov, all 15 members of the Security Council approve a resolution calling for an immediate mandatory ban on military aid to South Africa.

● **9 Nov**: President Sadat of Egypt unexpectedly announces that he is ready to overcome obstacles standing in the way of permament peace in the Middle East. On 11 Nov Israel welcomes the move. (›5 Dec)

● **9 Nov**: After the shelling of a north Israeli town by the PLO, Israeli jets attack areas in south Lebanon, the first such raids for nearly two years.

● **5 Dec**: President Sadat breaks off diplomatic ties with Syria, Iraq, Libya, Algeria and South Yemen in retaliation for Arab criticism of his peace move toward Israel.

● **14 Dec**: A conference on the Middle East opens in Cairo with representatives from Israel and Egypt and US and UN observers.

SOCIETY

- **3 Jan:** The IMF approves a loan of $3,900,000 to the UK – the largest loan in the IMF's history.
- **17 Jan:** Convicted murderer Gary Mark Gilmore is executed at his own request by a firing squad, the first execution in the USA for 10 years.
- **17 Jan:** Catholic schools in South Africa begin admitting black and mixed-race students into previously all-white schools, breaching the government's policy of racial segregation.
- **27 Jan:** President Carter proposes a plan to stimulate the US economy, including tax cuts and public service jobs.
- **27 Jan:** The European Convention on the Repression of Terrorism is signed by the 17 member countries of the Council of Europe.
- **31 Jan:** The Czech government declares Charter 77, a human rights document signed by prominent intellectuals and others, which demands the implementation of human rights as provided for in the 1975 Helsinki agreement, to be illegal.
- **Jan:** An agreement on financial cooperation between the EEC and Egypt, Syria and Jordan is signed.
- **17 Feb:** US president Carter sends a personal letter to the Soviet dissident Andrei Sakharov in which he declares human rights to be a "central concern" of his administration. The Soviet government expresses displeasure at attempts to interfere in its internal affairs.
- **21 Feb:** Representatives of the Argentine Commission for Human Rights declare that under the 11-month regime of Gen. Videla, 2,300 people have been killed and 20,000–30,000 have disappeared.
- **23 Feb:** After President Carter denounces him for "horrible murders", Idi Amin forbids around 200 Americans to leave Uganda; the ban is lifted on 1 Mar. On the same day, mass killings are reported by refugees who have fled to Tanzania.
- **11 Mar:** Brazil cancels its 1952 military aid treaty with the USA after the US State Department criticizes Brazil's violations of human rights.
- **28 Mar:** Portugal applies for EEC membership, followed by Spain on 28 Jul.
- **4 Apr:** Sweden withdraws from the European currency linkage, known as the "snake".
- **20 Apr:** President Carter announces a national energy plan for the USA but it is strenuously opposed.
- **22 Apr:** A major blowout of oil and gas occurs on the production platform in the Ecofisk field, equidistant from the British, Danish and Norwegian coasts.
- **1–2 May:** Protesters are arrested in the first mass civil disobedience campaign against the construction of nuclear plant (USA).

- **10 May:** SALT II talks resume in Geneva. On 18 May a convention banning "weather warfare" is signed by 33 nations.
- **19 May:** The Kenyan government imposes an immediate ban on big-game hunting to preserve diminishing wildlife.
- **23 May:** South Moluccan extremists hold 105 schoolchildren and 50 adults hostages in a hijacked train in the Netherlands to draw attention to their demand for Moluccan independence.
- **24 May:** A 24-hour general strike takes place in France in protest against government austerity policies.
- **24 Jun:** OECD ministerial meeting ends in Paris with a commitment by the major non-Communist industrial nations to take measures to achieve a higher average rate of economic growth as a means of stemming rising European unemployment.
- **15 Jul:** President Carter approves the admission to the USA of around 15,000 refugees from Laos, Cambodia and Vietnam, many of whom are living on boats since they have been refused admission by other states.
- **6 Aug:** At a meeting in Paris, 14 nations agree to contribute $10 billion to a loan fund for countries suffering financial difficulties. It will be administered by the IMF.
- **25 Aug:** A rally and protest march is held in the Philippines in defiance of the 1972 martial law decree, to denounce alleged violations of human rights there.
- **12 Sep:** Black South African leader Steve Biko, aged 30, is found unconscious in his police cell and dies in hospital from brain injuries. Police later deny using violence against him.
- **15 Sep:** South African police arrest 1,200 black students who had gathered to mourn Biko's death. (›19 Oct)
- **19 Oct:** 18 anti-apartheid organizations are banned, two newspapers closed and many political activists arrested in South Africa. (›2 Dec)
- **1 Nov:** The USA leaves the ILO and withdraws its financial contribution, disagreeing with its political bias.
- **4 Nov:** In Belgrade, 14 Western countries call on the USSR and its allies to recognize human rights.
- **19 Nov:** A cyclone and tidal wave strike the southern states of India, killing an estimated 20,000, leaving 200,000 homeless and washing away 21 villages.
- **2 Dec:** After a three-week inquest, it is declared that no-one is to blame for the death of black South African Steve Biko. The US State Department is "shocked" by the ruling.
- Nobel Peace Prize is won by Amnesty International.
- Nobel Prize for Economic Sciences is won by James Meade (USA) and Bertil Ohlin (Swe).

CULTURE

- **26 Mar:** In China, Beethoven is rehabilitated; the ban on Shakespeare is lifted on 25 May.
- **16 Aug:** Elvis Presley, the king of Rock and Roll, dies at 42 (USA).
- **17 Sep:** Opera *diva* Maria Callas dies in Paris, aged 53.
- **14 Oct:** Death of US singer Bing Crosby, whose record "White Christmas" sold over 30 million copies, aged 75.
- Gunter Grass: *Der Butt* (The Flounder), novel (FRG).
- R.K. Narayan: *The Painter of Signs*, novel (Ind).
- Paul Scott wins the Booker Prize for his novel *Staying On* (UK).
- Toni Morrison: *Song of Solomon*, novel (USA).
- Tom Stoppard: *Every Good Boy Deserves Favour*, play (UK).
- Nobel Prize for Literature is won by Vicente Aleixandre (Sp).
- Greek composer Iannis Xenakis's UPIC system is realized: graphic composition onto a drawing board connected to a computer converts the "score" into sound (Fr).
- Karlheinz Stockhausen: *Sirius*, a semi-theatrical work for soprano, bass, basset horn, trumpet and tape (Fr).
- Harrison Birtwistle: *Pulse Field*, ballet (UK).
- Elliott Carter: *A Symphony of Three Orchestras* (USA).
- Peter Maxwell Davies's *The Martyrdom of St Magnus*, chamber opera, is performed at the first St Magnus Festival in Orkney (UK).
- Premiere of Michael Tippett's opera *The Ice Break* (UK).
- The Sex Pistols hit the headlines for their use of foul language, and their concerts are banned from TV (UK).
- Pina Bausch: *Bluebeard*, ballet choreographed for the Wuppertal Opera Ballet (FRG).
- Stephen Benton: *Crystal Beginnings*, holograph.
- Richard Rogers and Renzo Piano: Centre National d'Art et de la Culture Georges Pompidou, Paris.
- Rainer Werner Fassbinder: *Eine Reise ins Licht*, based on Vladimir Nabokov's novel *Despair*, starring Dirk Bogarde as Hermann Hermann (FRG).
- Steven Spielberg: *Close Encounters of the Third Kind*, a science fantasy with music by John Williams (USA).
- The soundtrack album from the film *Saturday Night Fever*, starring disco-dancing John Travolta, becomes a worldwide bestseller (USA).
- Blockbuster *Star Wars*, written and directed by George Lucas, is released (USA).
- Diane Keaton stars in *Annie Hall*, directed by and costarring Woody Allen (USA).

SCIENCE

- **8 Feb:** *Soyuz 24* links with orbiting Salyut 5 space lab followed by *Soyuz 26* on 11 Dec (USSR).
- **24 Feb:** L.F. Sanger describes the full sequence of bases in a viral DNA (UK).
- **11 May:** The US government announces that CFCs (chlorofluorocarbons) will be outlawed as propellants in spray cans in two years' time, after studies show an increased risk of cancers if the ozone layer – which the CFCs erode – is depleted.
- **20 Aug:** Launch of the spaceprobe *Voyager 1*, followed by that of *Voyager 2* on 5 Sep, toward Jupiter and the outer planets (USA).
- The Nobel Prize for Chemistry is won by Russian chemist Ilya Prigogine for his work on thermodynamics (Bel).
- The Nobel Prize for Physiology or Medicine is won by Rosalyn S. Yalow (USA) for the development of the radioimunnoassay, and Roger Guillemin (USA) and Andrew Schally (USA) for their work on hormones secreted by the brain.
- The Nobel Prize for Physics is won by John H. Van Vleck (USA), Sir Neville F. Mott (UK) and Philip W. Anderson (USA) for their independent contributions to the understanding of the behavior of electrons in magnetic, noncrystalline solid materials.
- EEC nations set up JET (Joint European Torus) in Oxfordshire, England. It will research the possiblities of harvesting power from nuclear fusion, as opposed to atomic fission.
- Praziauantal is developed to treat the debilitating parasitic disease bilharzia.
- The virus that causes lassa fever is discovered.
- Post-mortem studies of the brains of schizophrenics reveal chemical differences between them and normal brains, a disorder which leads to the discovery of dopamine.
- The neutron bomb – a weapon that can do more damage to troops in its vicinity and less to buildings and other civilian property – is developed.
- L. Lederman discovers the upsilon particle, confirming the quark theory of baryons.
- The Bell Telephone Company use optical fibers to transmit TV signals (USA).
- The Apple II is the first personal computer available in assembled form and the first to be really successful.
- Dutch scientists find that incinerated waste is contaminated by dioxins, potentially cancer-inducing chemicals.
- In New York, two homosexual men are diagnosed as having the rare cancer Karposi's sarcoma; although AIDS (Acquired Immune Deficiency Syndrome) is not officially recognized until 1981, they are probably New York's first AIDS victims.

The agreement reached between Egypt and Israel at Camp David caused an even wider split among Egypt and the Arab League nations, and although Egyptian president Sadat and Israeli prime minister Begin shared the Nobel Peace Prize for their efforts, the peace treaty was not ratified until 1979. The Middle East as a whole remained unstable, with widespread popular opposition to the oppressive, pro-Western government of the shah of Iran paralysing the country, while the Ayatollah Khomeini waited in the wings. In other areas of the world human rights, along with environmental concerns, became a focus for public attention. The record of several countries was severely criticized at the OAS General Assembly. In South America the Amazon Pact excluded other than member nations from taking part in the development of the Amazon Basin. Such development had frightening consequences for the rainforest area, but the worst environmental disaster of the year was the grounding of the supertanker "Amoco Cadiz".

▲ The 220,000 tonnes of oil poured out by the supertanker *Amoco Cadiz* fouled beaches the length of the Brittany coast – the worst spill ever known.

● **4 Jan:** Right-wing president Pinochet of Chile holds a national referendum to endorse his policies. He gains 75 percent support, and declares that no elections will be necessary for at least 10 years.

● **Jan:** The border conflict between Vietnam and Cambodia continues as Vietnamese troops advance to within 56 km (35 miles) of Phnom Penh. (›3 Dec)

● **2 Feb:** Leaders of Algeria, Libya, Yemen (Aden), Syria and the PLO meet in Algiers to coordinate plans to frustrate Egyptian president Sadat's peace initiative in the Middle East. (›18 Jul)

● **3 Mar:** An agreement between Rhodesian leader Ian Smith and moderate black leaders to transfer power to blacks by 31 Dec is denounced by Joshua Nkomo and Robert Mugabe, leaders of the Patriotic Front, and rejected by the UN Security Council as "illegal and unacceptable". Guerrilla warfare is stepped up. (›10 Sep)

● **14 Mar:** Israeli forces launch major assaults against PLO bases in South Lebanon in response to a PLO guerrilla attack on 11 Mar in which over 30 Israeli civilians were killed. On 19 Mar the UN Security Council votes to send an interim force to Lebanon.

● **15 Mar:** Somalia withdraws the last of its troops from the Ogaden region, ending its support for ethnic Ethiopian Somalis there who wanted to establish an autonomous region. On 24 Mar Ethiopia announces that it has wiped out all remaining guerrilla resistance in the area.

● **16 Mar:** Former Italian prime minister Aldo Moro is kidnapped by the Red Brigade, who demand release of Red Brigade prisoners. The Christian Democrat party refuse to make any deal, and on 9 May Moro is discovered dead.

● **18 Mar:** In Pakistan, former prime minister Zulfikar Ali Bhutto is sentenced to death by the High Court on charges of attempted murder.

● **25 Apr:** South Africa accepts a formula worked out in the UN Security Council for the independence of Namibia (Southwest Africa) by 31 Dec, though it gains only partial approval from guerrilla independence movement SWAPO (Southwest Africa People's Organization).

● **27 Apr:** In a military coup in Afghanistan, a Revolutionary Council seizes power and establishes a new government based on Islamic principles.

● **11 May:** Violent riots erupt in Tehran when thousands of Muslim extremists call for the removal of Shah Muhammad Reza Pahlavi. (›8 Sep)

● **15 Jun:** Italian president Giovanni Leone resigns after allegations of fiscal misconduct. Alessandro Pertini is sworn in as president on 8 Jul – Italy's first Socialist president.

● **18 Jun:** In Peru, the first polls (for a constitutional assembly, to draw up a new constitution in 12 months) in 15 years are held, and won by the Popular Revolutionary Alliance, led by Victor Haya de la Torre.

● **23 Jun:** The military government of Brazil introduces some constitutional reforms which promise greater, but still limited, freedoms.

● **7 Jul:** The Solomon Islands gain independence from British rule.

● **18–19 Jul:** Representatives of Egypt and Israel meet at US-sponsored talks at Leeds Castle, Kent (UK), though no agreement is reached on the future of the West Bank and the Gaza Strip. (›5 Sep)

● **18–22 Jul:** The OAU annual summit meeting in Khartoum is dominated by the issue of the presence of foreign troops in Africa. More radical African nations welcome Soviet and Cuban involvement, while moderate states urge strict non-alignment.

● **27 Jul:** In Portugal, prime minister Soares is dismissed. On 29 Aug industrialist Alfredo Nobre da Costa becomes prime minister, but is replaced by Carlos Alberto da Mota Pinto on 25 Oct.

● **22 Aug:** Kenyan president, veteran statesman Jomo Kenyatta, known as the "Old One", dies aged about 80. On 10 Oct Daniel Arap Moi succeeds him.

● **22 Aug:** In Nicaragua, the National Palace and 1,500 hostages are seized by Sandinista guerrillas, but president Somoza refuses to step down. (›9 Sep)

● **5–17 Sep:** US president Jimmy Carter hosts talks between Egypt and Israel at Camp David (USA), resulting in the Camp David Accords, which fix a schedule for peace negotiations. A formal treaty is to be signed within three months. The agreement also covers military disengagement. (›5 Nov)

● **8 Sep:** In Tehran demonstrations demand the removal of the shah and the establishment of an Islamic state headed by Ayatollah Ruhollah Khomeini, a religious leader in exile. (›6 Nov)

● **9 Sep:** Several Nicaraguan cities are seized by left-wing guerrillas and local residents as part of an attempt to force president Somoza to resign. National Guards eventually regain control.

● **10 Sep:** Martial law is declared in some areas of Rhodesia as a step toward controlling guerrilla activity. Ian Smith also warns Zambia and Mozambique to expect reprisals if they continue to provide sanctuary for guerrillas. On 20 Sep Rhodesia launches a four-day series of raids against 25 suspected guerrilla bases inside Mozambique. (›Oct)

● **20 Sep:** South African prime minister Vorster resigns, and is succeeded on 28 Sep by P.W. Botha, who announces that he would not even consider abandoning apartheid. On 29 Sep Vorster accepts the largely ceremonial post of president.

SOCIETY   CULTURE   SCIENCE

- **21 Sep**: Nigeria lifts a 12-year ban on political activity and ends the state of emergency in effect since 1966.

- **27 Sep**: France decides to join the UN disarmament committee after a 17-year absence.

- **5 Oct**: Swedish prime minister Thorbjorn Falldin resigns over limiting the use of nuclear power. On 18 Oct Ola Ullsten becomes prime minister.

- **11 Oct**: In Belgium, prime minister Tindemans resigns, and Paul Vanden Boeynants is sworn in as interim prime minister on 27 Oct.

- **27 Oct**: The UN military command in South Korea discover an invasion tunnel beginning in North Korea, passing under the demilitarized zone and penetrating 435 km (270 miles) into South Korea – large enough to allow 30,000 armed troops per hour to enter South Korea in a surprise attack. North Korea denies all knowledge of the tunnel, declaring it to be a fabrication of US imperialists.

- **31 Oct**: Ugandan forces invade Tanzania. On 27 Nov counterattacking Tanzanian forces penetrate 35 km (20 miles) into Ugandan territory.

- **Oct**: Ian Smith announces that the transfer of majority rule set for 31 Dec will have to be delayed due to unexpected problems in writing a new constitution.

- **3 Nov**: A 25-year treaty of friendship and cooperation in economic, scientific and technical endeavors is signed between the USA and Vietnam.

- **3 Nov**: Dominica gains its independence within the Commonwealth.

- **5 Nov**: The Camp David Accords are denounced by 20 Arab League nations at a Baghdad summit. The Arab leaders offer $50 billion in aid to Egypt if it will discontinue peace negotiations, but president Sadat refuses. (›17 Dec)

- **6 Nov**: The shah of Iran appoints a military government after the worst violence so far. On 27 Dec a civilian government is formed as economic and social chaos continues.

- **3 Dec**: Vietnam announces a new Vietcong to fight Pol Pot's regime in Cambodia, as Vietnamese troops continue to advance into Cambodia.

- **6 Dec**: A national referendum in Spain gives approval to a new constitution providing for a parliamentary system of government, constitutional monarchy and generous individual liberties.

- **17 Dec**: Israel and Egypt fail to sign the peace treaty within the three-month period agreed at the Camp David talks. Neither is willing to compromise on certain issues.

- **19 Dec**: Ex-prime minister of India Indira Gandhi is imprisoned for a week for breach of privilege and contempt of the house. A motion calls for her expulsion from parliament and detention in prison for the rest of the session.

- **13 Jan**: The USA and Japan reach a major trade agreement designed to reduce Japan's huge trade surplus and balance of payments accounts.

- **Jan**: Measures are taken by the US government to strengthen the dollar and to counter inflation.

- **2 Mar**: A new Chinese constitution puts unprecedented emphasis on economic development and the need to make rapid progress in science and technology, even at the expense of revolutionary ideology.

- **16 Mar**: The supertanker *Amoco Cadiz* runs aground off Brittany, spilling over 220,000 tonnes of oil.

- **Mar**: Vietnam joins Comecon.

- **1 Jul**: At the General Assembly of the OAS, several member nations, especially Uruguay and Paraguay, are severely criticized for persistently violating human rights.

- **3 Jul**: China cuts all aid to Vietnam in view of its treatment of ethnic Chinese and because it is "leaning toward the USSR". On 26 Sep China breaks off talks with Vietnam after failure of discussions about the treatment and future of ethnic Chinese living there.

- **4 Jul**: Brazil, Bolivia, Colombia, Ecuador, Guyana, Peru, Surinam and Venezuela sign the Amazon Pact, providing for the exclusive occupation and development of the Amazon River Valley by the signatories.

- **7 Jul**: EEC members agree to study a proposal that would stabilize exchange rates by linking together EEC currencies. In Dec they adopt a new European Monetary System (EMS) to go into effect on 2 Jan 1979.

- **14 Jul**: Anatoly Scharansky, Soviet dissident and a member of the Helsinki human rights group, is sentenced to three years in prison followed by 10 years in a labor camp on charges of espionage (USSR).

- **6 Aug**: Death of Pope Paul VI. On 26 Aug Albino Luciani is elected to succeed him as John Paul I. On 28 Sep he dies suddenly, and on 16 Oct Cardinal Karol Wojtyla of Poland becomes the first non-Italian Pope since 1523.

- **Aug**: The French motor company Peugeot-Citroen takes over Chrysler Europe, becoming Europe's largest car producer.

- **29 Sep**: The USA and Colombia sign an agreement in Bogotá to coordinate their efforts to combat illegal production and export of cocaine and marijuana into the USA.

- **12 Oct**: The air link between China and Hong Kong reopens after nearly 30 years.

- **17 Dec**: OPEC increases the price of oil by 14.5 percent.

- Egyptian premier Anwar Sadat and Israeli prime minister Menachem Begin share the Nobel Peace Prize.

- Nobel Prize for Economic Sciences is won by Herbert Simon (USA).

- **7 Apr**: A copy of the Gutenberg Bible is sold at Christie's auction rooms in New York for $2 million.

- **12 Apr**: Premiere of György Ligeti's opera *Le Grand Macabre*, a surrealist comedy about the end of the world, in Stockholm (Swe).

- **Sep**: First showing of the TV soap opera *Dallas* (USA).

- Dario Fo: *Mistero Buffo* (Mystery Farce), a satirical and hilarious one-man re-creation of the medieval mystery plays (It).

- Czeslaw Milosz: *Bells in Winter*, poems (USA).

- Toni Morrison: *The Bluest Eye*, novel (USA).

- Iris Murdoch's novel *The Sea, The Sea* wins the Booker Prize (UK).

- Alexander Solzhenitsyn completes *The Gulag Archipelago* (3 vols, since 1974) (USA).

- Polish-born Isaac Bashevis Singer (USA) wins the Nobel Prize for Literature.

- Elliott Carter: *Syringa*, for voices and small orchestra, with words simultaneously in Greek and English (USA).

- Peter Maxwell Davies: *Salome*, ballet (UK).

- A curvilinear structure of steel and vinyl called a "Diatrope" is constructed at the Place Beaubourg, Paris, for the performance of Iannis Xenakis's *son et lumière* electronic tape piece, *La Légende d'Eer* (Fr).

- Flautist James Galway's recordings reach the top of the pop charts.

- Pina Bausch: *Kontakthof*, ballet (FRG).

- David Hockney designs the Glyndebourne production of Mozart's *The Magic Flute* (UK).

- Opening of *Evita*, a musical by Tim Rice and Andrew Lloyd Webber about Eva Perón (UK).

- The Police's first album is released (UK).

- "Wuthering Heights" brings fame to Kate Bush (UK).

- Jorg Immendorf: *BrrrD-DDrrr (Café Deutschland – Winter)*, painting with a punning title using the acronyms for East and West Germany (FRG).

- Philip Guston: *The Ladder*, painting (USA).

- Release of *Grease*, directed by Randal Kleiser and starring John Travolta (USA).

- *The Deerhunter*, directed by Michael Cimino, wins five Oscars (USA).

- Rainer Werner Fassbinder's *The Marriage of Maria Braun* brilliantly reflects the first decade of postwar German life (FRG).

- Werner Herzog: *Nosferatu the Vampyre*, a reworking of Murnau's classic 1922 film, starring Klaus Kinski (FRG).

- **Jan**: Sweden becomes the first country to ban aerosol sprays, as from 1 Jan 1979.

- **Mar**: The patenting of hybrid bacterium produced artificially for breaking down oil slicks at sea and producing protein food from waste oil is allowed in the USA.

- **22 Jun**: James W. Christy and R.S. Harrington (USA) discover the existence of Charon, the only known satellite of Pluto.

- **Jun**: Professor Walter Gibson and colleagues at Harvard University succeed in making bacteria manufacture insulin to the instructions of synthetic DNA (USA).

- **25 Jul**: Birth of the first "test-tube" baby, Louise Brown, in Manchester (UK).

- **26 Aug**: *Soyuz 31* is launched with the first East German cosmonauts aboard, to link with Salyut 6 in orbit.

- **2 Nov**: Two Soviet cosmonauts return to earth after setting a new record for space endurance of 139 days, which they spent on board Salyut 6.

- **4 Dec**: US spaceprobe *Venus 1* enters orbit round Venus. On 9 Dec *Venus 2* lands on the surface of Venus. In the same month Soviet probes *Venera 11* and *Venera 12* also land on Venus.

- The Nobel Prize for Physiology or Medicine is won by Daniel Nathans (USA), Hamilton Smith (USA) and Werner Arber (Swi) for their discovery of restriction enzymes, important for genetic engineering.

- The Nobel Prize for Physics is won by Arno A. Penzias (USA) and Robert Wilson (USA) for their discovery of "black body" radiation, which provides evidence for the Big Bang theory: and Pyotr Kapitza (USSR) for work on low temperature physics.

- The Nobel Prize for Chemistry is won by Peter Mitchell (UK) for work on photosynthesis.

- It is found that Legionnaire's disease is caused by the bacterium *Legionella pneumophila*.

- EMI produce the first brain scans using NMR (nuclear magnetic resonance) scanning.

- S.C. Harrison announces the first high-resolution structure of an intact virus, the tomato bushy stunt virus.

- A form of natural rubber that can be molded and recycled is developed (UK).

- W. Pauli succeeds in measuring the life of a neutron, about 15 minutes (USA).

- Laser cooling of trapped positive ions is demonstrated for the first time.

- Compact discs are first demonstrated (FRG).

- Seasat I satellite is launched to measure sea surface temperatures, wind and wave movement, icebergs and ocean currents (USA).

In an eventful year, Iran dominated the news. The shah was forced into exile and the grim figure of the Ayatollah Khomeini returned to gain power. By the end of the year he was in total constitutional control of the country and instituting trials and executions of alleged opponents of his uncompromising brand of Islamic fundamentalism, which rapidly spread to other Muslim countries. Anti-Americanism was a keynote: in Tehran, the staff of the US embassy were seized as hostages for the return of the shah to stand trial, and much of the Islamic world became a no-go area for Americans. The United States were forced to recognize the success of other opponents, most notably the Sandinistas in Nicaragua, but could take comfort in the emergence of a stalwart ally in the new British prime minister, Margaret Thatcher (the first woman to hold that post), and in the ultimately ill-advised invasion of Afghanistan by the USSR. In Africa two appalling dictators were overthrown – Idi Amin in Uganda and the "Emperor" Bokassa in the Central African Republic – and Rhodesia's rebellion against Britain ended, preparing the way for majority rule and independence.

▲ Television journalism ensured that the features of religious leaders such as the Ayatollah Khomeini quickly became as well known as those of politicians and pop stars. Perhaps best known of all was the newly elected Pope John-Paul II, Polish-born Karol Wojtyla, here seen on a visit to his native country.

● **1 Jan**: Diplomatic relations are formally established between China and the USA for the first time since the establishment of the People's Republic. The USA breaks off relations with Taiwan. (›29 Jan)

● **7 Jan**: Vietnamese troops and Cambodian rebels capture Phnom Penh and overthrow the Pol Pot regime.

● **16 Jan**: After months of demonstrations and riots, Shah Muhammad Reza Pahlavi is finally forced to leave Iran. On 1 Feb religious leader Ayatollah Ruhollah Khomeini returns after a 15-year exile. Islamic law is imposed on 11 Feb, and in Mar, the people vote overwhelmingly in favor of the establishment of an Islamic Republic. (›4 Nov)

● **29 Jan**: China's deputy prime minister Deng Xiaoping visits the USA.

● **10 Feb**: The Islamic legal code is instituted in Pakistan.

● **14 Feb**: The US ambassador to Afghanistan is abducted by Muslim extremists and killed when security forces attempt to free him.

● **17 Feb**: China invades Vietnam, avowedly in response to Vietnamese "aggression" over the previous six months. The withdrawal of forces is announced on 16 Mar.

● **22 Feb**: St Lucia achieves independence within the Commonwealth.

● **16 Mar**: End of civil war in Chad as the government agrees to coalition with Muslim rebels.

● **26 Mar**: President Sadat (Egy) and prime minister Begin (Isr) sign a peace treaty, ending nearly 31 years of war. Egypt is censured by the Arab League, and on 31 Mar diplomatic ties are broken and an economic boycott approved by ministers of 18 Arab League states and the PLO. (›25 May)

● **30 Mar**: Airey Neave, MP, opposition spokesman on Northern Ireland, dies when an IRA bomb explodes in his car (UK). (›27 Aug)

● **31 Mar**: The military relationship between Malta and the UK ends after 181 years.

● **4 Apr**: In Pakistan, former president Zulfikar Ali Bhutto is executed after being convicted of conspiracy to murder.

● **11 Apr**: Idi Amin is deposed after eight years by a Ugandan exile force and Tanzanian soldiers.

● **17 Apr**: The first one-man one-vote elections take place in Rhodesia under the internal settlement. On 1 Jun Bishop Abel T. Muzorewa becomes the first black prime minister of the new state of Zimbabwe Rhodesia. (›20 Nov)

● **18 Apr**: The Lebanese Christian Militia Group secedes, declaring a strip of land 10 km (6 miles) wide along Israeli border independent as "Free Lebanon".

● **3 May**: After the UK general election, Conservative party leader Mrs Margaret Thatcher becomes the first female prime minister in Europe.

● **9 May**: Italy mobilizes its army to curb terrorism by the Red Brigades and other extreme left-wing organizations, which have become an almost daily occurrence (› 3 Jun).

● **22 May**: The Progressive Conservative party wins the general election in Canada and its leader, Joseph Clark, becomes Canada's youngest ever prime minister, ending Pierre Trudeau's 11-year tenure.

● **25 May**: Israeli troops pull out of the Sinai town of Al-Arish, which they have occupied for 12 years, following the peace treaty with Egypt.

● **3 Jun**: In the general election in Italy, the Communist party suffers its biggest setback since World War II and no party achieves an overall majority. On 5 Aug Francesco Cossiga is sworn in as prime minister, heading a three-party coalition.

● **4 Jun**: South African president Vorster resigns after a financial scandal.

● **4 Jun**: Flt-Lt. Jerry Rawlings leads a successful coup in Ghana. On 18 Jun the first general election for nine years takes place, and on 24 Sep Dr Hilla Limann becomes president.

● **6 Jun**: A state of siege is declared in Nicaragua in response to a general strike and guerrilla fighting. (›17 Jul)

● **7 and 10 Jun**: Voters in EEC countries elect the first MEPs (Members of the European Parliament). Simone Weil of France is elected president of the European Parliament at its first meeting.

● **18 Jun**: SALT II treaty is signed by US president Carter and Soviet premier Brezhnev in Vienna.

● **15 Jul**: Indian prime minister Moraji Desai resigns after over 100 MPs leave his Janata party. Charan Singh becomes prime minister on 28 Jul.

● **17 Jul**: The resignation and flight of president Somoza of Nicaragua ends 43 years of autocratic rule by members of the Somoza family. On 19 Jul Sandinista rebels capture the capital and a five-man junta takes power.

● **11 Aug**: Voting ends in Nigeria's first general election for 15 years, and on 1 Oct Alhaji Shehu Shagari becomes head of state and Nigeria returns to civilian rule after 13 years of military leadership.

● **27 Aug**: Earl Mountbatten of Burma, the last British viceroy of India, is killed in an IRA bomb explosion on his boat at Mullaghmore, Co. Sligo.

● **20 Sep**: Emperor Bokassa I of the Central African Empire, who seized power from David Dacko in 1966, is himself overthrown by Dacko.

● **1 Oct**: Panama takes control of the American Canal Zone after 70 years of US control.

SOCIETY   CULTURE   SCIENCE

SOCIETY

● **16 Oct**: President Carlos Humberto Romero of El Salvador is overthrown in a military coup. A new junta with a civilian majority succeeds, promising free elections.

● **16 Oct**: Gen. Zia ul-Haq of Pakistan postpones elections indefinitely and bans all political activities.

● **25 Oct**: In referendums in the Basque country and Catalonia, voters approve statutes granting home rule in these areas.

● **26 Oct**: President Park Chung Hee of South Korea is assassinated by his head of intelligence after 18 years in power. Prime minister Kyu Ha Choi is elected president on 6 Dec.

● **27 Oct**: St Kitts and the Grenadines achieve independence from the UK.

● **4 Nov**: Iranian militants storm the US embassy in Tehran, taking staff hostage, and demand that the USA return the exiled shah, now in a US hospital, to Iran. Despite demands from the UN Security Council and the International Court of Justice for their release, many of the hostages are not freed until 20 Jan 1981. (> Society, 12 Nov)

● **6 Nov**: Nehdi Bazargan resigns as Iran's prime minister, and Ayatollah Khomeini orders the Revolutionary Council to run the country. (>2 Dec)

● **16 Nov**: Bolivia's Congress elects Lydia Gueiler Tejada, who becomes Bolivia's first female president.

● **20 Nov**: President Kaunda of Zambia puts his country on war alert as tension mounts on the border with Zimbabwe Rhodesia. (> 12 Dec)

● **21 Nov**: Islamic anti-American riots erupt in Pakistan after it is rumored that an attack on the holy mosque at Mecca was US-backed. The USA evacuates all nonessential personnel from embassies in 10 Islamic nations, and warns Americans to avoid travelling to Islamic countries in the Gulf and the Middle East.

● **2 Dec**: In Iran, electors ratify a new constitution that makes Ayatollah Khomeini absolute leader for life.

● **12 Dec**: NATO agrees to install 572 medium-range missiles in Europe by 1983.

● **12 Dec**: Zimbabwe Rhodesia reverts temporarily to its former status as a British colony as governor Lord Soames takes control, ending a 14-year rebellion against the crown. The UK lifts sanctions imposed against Rhodesia since 1965.

● **21 Dec**: Peace pacts are signed in London to end the Rhodesian conflict, seven years to the day after the start of the guerrilla war. Cross-border raids are to end immediately.

● **23 Dec**: In Czechoslovakia, six leading dissidents including playwright Vaclav Havel are convicted of subversion.

● **25 Dec**: The USSR begins an invasion of Afghanistan in support of a Marxist regime following a coup.

● **1 Jan**: Introduction of the European Monetary System (EMS) by the EEC.

● **1 Jan**: China adopts the Pinyin phonetic alphabet. Under the new system, Peking becomes Beijing.

● **27 Mar**: OPEC increase the price of oil by 9 percent, with a further increase of 23.7 percent to come in Jun.

● **28 May**: The UK government agrees to take in 982 Vietnamese "boat people" picked up by the freighter *Sibonga* in the South China sea.

● **May**: The OECD demands a greater use of coal from its members in order to reduce consumption of oil.

● **2 Jun**: Pope John Paul II begins a visit to his native Poland.

● **3 Jun**: In the Gulf of Mexico, the blowout of the IXTOC exploration wellhead causes massive oil slicks.

● **26 Jun**: The 33rd session of Comecon opens in Moscow. New methods of economic cooperation are proposed.

● **28 Jun**: The number of Indochinese refugees being admitted into the USA each month is reported to have increased from 7,000 to 14,000.

● **28–29 Jun**: Fifth economic summit in Tokyo of the seven major Western industrial nations. A secret agreement on trade is made with China, and it is agreed to limit oil imports to 1978 levels until 1985.

● **11 Jul**: The International Whaling Commission bans factory ships indefinitely from hunting sperm whales.

● **15 Jul**: US president Carter announces anti-inflationary measures in a major TV speech on energy and economic policy, including a $140 billion energy program to curb US oil imports. (>12 Nov)

● **Jul**: OPEC increases its fund for supporting developing countries.

● **15 Aug**: Sebastian Coe becomes the first man to hold the 800m, 1500m and mile world records simultaneously (UK).

● **10 Sep**: In the UK, British Leyland announce plans to close 13 plants and axe 25,000 jobs.

● **24 Sep**: The EMS revalues the Deutschmark upward against the other currencies.

● **12 Nov**: President Carter announces an immediate halt to the import of Iranian oil. On 14 Nov he freezes $500 million of Iranian government assets in US banks.

● **26 Nov**: The IOC votes in favor of readmitting the People's Republic of China after a 21-year absence.

● The Nobel Peace Prize is awarded to Albanian-born Mother Teresa for her work among the deprived people in the slums of Calcutta.

● Nobel Prize for Economic Sciences is won by W. Arthur Lewis (W Ind) and Theodore Schultz (USA).

CULTURE

● **2 Feb**: Ex-Sex Pistols member Sid Vicious dies of a heroin overdose (UK).

● **23 Aug**: Russian ballet dancer Alexander Godunov defects to the USA during a Bolshoi ballet tour.

● Samuel Beckett: *Company*, prose piece (Fr.).

● Peter Hall directs Peter Shaffer's play *Amadeus*, about Mozart and his jealous rival Salieri, at London's National Theatre.

● Arthur Kopit: *Wings*, play concerned with mental illness (USA).

● V.S. Naipaul: *A Bend in the River*, novel about emergent Africa (UK).

● Ted Hughes: *Moortown*, poems (UK).

● Nobel Prize for Literature is won by Odysseus Elytis (Gre).

● The Gay Men's Press is founded in London specifically to publish works by and about male and female homosexuality.

● John Cage: *Roaratorio, an Irish Circus on Finnegan's Wake*, for orchestra and voices (USA).

● John Adams: *Shaker Loops*, for string septet (USA).

● Harrison Birtwistle: *...agm...*, for chorus and small orchestra (UK).

● Michael Tippett: Triple Concerto (UK).

● Release of Dire Straits' first single (UK).

● Elvis Costello becomes internationally famous with his third album.

● Philip Guston: *The Rug*, painting (USA).

● Jim Dine: *Jerusalem Nights*, painting (Isr).

● Shusaku Arakawa: *Study for the I*, painting (USA).

● Judy Chicago: *The Dinner Party*, painting (1974-79) a celebration of 1,038 women, all historical figures (USA).

● Jean Tinguely: *Klamauk*, automobile sculpture (Swi).

● Richard Meier: The Atheneum, Indiana (USA).

● Denys Lasdun: European Investment Bank (Lux).

● Francis Ford Coppola: *Apocalypse Now*, film that sets Joseph Conrad's novel *Heart of Darkness* in 1970s Vietnam (USA).

● Woody Allen: *Manhattan*, with Diane Keaton (USA).

● Andrei Tarkovsky: *Stalker*, fantasy film (USSR).

● Canada becomes the first country to operate a satellite TV broadcasting service.

SCIENCE

● **1 Jan**: The first digital recording in the UK is released by Decca.

● **28 Mar**: An accident at the Three Mile Island nuclear power station, due to a defect in the cooling system, causes the greatest crisis in the nuclear industry to date (USA).

● **19 Aug**: Soviet cosmonauts Vladimir Lyakhov and Valery Ryumin return to earth after 175 days in space, breaking the 139-day record set in 1978. They had lived and worked on Salyut 6.

● **Aug**: US spaceprobe *Pioneer 11* sends back the first close-up picturers of Saturn and its rings, including evidence of a previously unknown 11th moon and two other possible moons, and two rings invisible from Earth.

● **Oct**: Smallpox is declared "eradicated" by the WHO, after a campaign lasting 22 years and costing $100 million.

● The Nobel Prize for Chemistry is won by Herbert Brown (USA) and George Wittig (FRG) for their discovery of new synthetic pathways, enabling chemists to produce new pesticides and simplify vitamin A manufacture.

● The Nobel Prize for Physiology or Medicine is won by Godfrey Hounsfield (UK) and Allan Cormack (USA) for pioneering the body scanning technique of computerized axial tomography (CAT), which enables pictures of the body to be produced electronically.

● The Nobel Prize for Physics is won by Steven Weinberg (USA), Sheldon Glashow (USA) and Abdus Salam (Pak) for their work on unifying two of the fundamental forces of nature – the "weak" force and the "electromagnetic" force.

● The hepatitis virus is cultured by P. Provost and M. Hilleman.

● Dick Rees develops a leprosy vaccine.

● The gluon (a fundamental particle of matter) is observed at the Deutsches Elektronen Synchotron (DESY) in Hamburg (FRG).

● French and German scientists discover fossil remains of living cells in rocks firmly dated as 3,800 million years old, thus lengthening the known history of life by several hundred million years.

● *Voyager 1* and *Voyager 2* explore the moons of Jupiter, and also discover that it has a ring, invisible from Earth.

● The Sony Walkman personal stereo is launched (Jap).

● George Dodd produces evidence to show that humans, like other animals, produce pheromones (smell signals which help to control behavior at the unconscious level) (UK).

● Jean Ichbiah and coworkers develop ADA, a computer language intended for use by the US armed services.

1980-1989

In an unprecedented manifestation of popular power, Polish shipyard worker Lech Walesa and his colleagues secured the right to establish an independent trade union, Solidarity, defiantly proclaiming to their fellow workers that "we are co-masters of this land". Political compromise was certainly unexpected in Eastern European countries, but the even more instransigent government in Iran finally agreed to release the US hostages held in Tehran since November 1979. The Iranian change of heart was possibly induced by a different crisis; the opportunistic attack on the country by its neighbor, Iraq, hoping to take advantage of reputed low morale in the Iranian army after the flight of the shah. As so often happens, some of the most peaceable people, in the Middle East and elsewhere, died by violence. John Lennon, pop star and peacenik, was shot dead in New York, and in San Salvador Archbishop Romero was killed while celebrating mass.

▲ On 18–19 May, the long-dormant volcano on Mount St Helens (USA) erupted, causing havoc over a wide area.

● **6 Jan**: Indira Gandhi is reelected as prime minister of India. (›17 Feb)

● **8 Jan**: Soviet troops are reported to be in control of most parts of Afghanistan. On 14 Jan, the UN General Assembly votes by 104 to 18 to call for immediate withdrawal of foreign troops from Afghanistan.

● **25 Jan**: In Iran's first presidential election, Abolhassan Bani Sadr gains 70 percent of the vote. The first Islamic parliament (*mahjlis*) opens on 28 May.

● **5 Feb**: China attends the disarmament conference in Geneva for the first time.

● **14 Feb**: Polling begins in Rhodesia for 20 white seats in the new parliament of independent Zimbabwe, followed on 27 Feb by polling for 80 black seats. On 5 Mar Robert Mugabe and Joshua Nkomo agree to form a coalition government, and Mugabe becomes Zimbabwe's first black prime minister.

● **17 Feb**: Mrs Gandhi dismisses legislative assemblies in nine states and brings them under direct rule. She later orders elections and wins sweeping victories in eight of the states, though disorder and violence persist.

● **18 Feb**: Pierre Trudeau is returned to power in the Canadian general election.

● **22 Feb**: In Afghanistan, martial law is imposed in the capital Kabul in response to a general strike protesting against the Soviet invasion.

● **9 Mar**: Voters in the Basque region of Spain elect the first regional parliament, ending 40 years of direct rule from Madrid. On 21 Mar voters in Catalonia elect their first regional parliament since 1932.

● **7 Apr**: President Carter breaks diplomatic relations with Iran and announces a ban on all trade with Iran because of continued detention of US hostages (since 4 Nov 1979).

● **25 Apr**: A US commando mission to rescue the embassy hostages in Iran has to be abandoned. Eight US crewmen die when a helicopter hits a transport plane, and Secretary of State Cyrus Vance resigns. (›2 Nov)

● **30 Apr**: Princess Beatrix becomes queen of the Netherlands on the abdication of her mother, Queen Juliana.

● **4 May**: Death of Josip Broz Tito, ruler of Yugoslavia for 35 years, aged 87. A collective rotating presidency takes over.

● **18 May**: The first general election in Peru since 1963 gives a landslide victory to former president Fernando Belaunde Terry. On 28 Jul 12 years of military dictatorship end.

● **20 May**: In French-speaking Quebec voters reject a proposal to allow the provincial government to negotiate independence from Canada.

● **12 Jun**: Japanese prime minister Masayoshi Ohira dies of a heart attack.

● **12–13 Jun**: EEC heads of government issue a communiqué recognizing the "right of self-determination of the Palestinian people".

● **23 Jun**: Vietnam invades Thailand by way of Cambodia.

● **23 Jun**: Indira Gandhi's son and political heir-apparent Sanjay dies in an air crash (Ind).

● **30 Jun**: Vigdis Finnbogadottir (Ice) becomes Europe's first democratically elected female head of state.

● **27 Jul**: Muhammad Reza Pahlavi, shah of Iran 1941–79, dies in exile in Cairo.

● **29 Jul**: The UN General Assembly calls for the establishment of a Palestinian state and Israeli withdrawal from all occupied lands.

● **30 Jul**: The Israeli Knesset approves a bill proclaiming united Jerusalem as capital of Israel.

● **11 Aug**: China orders the removal of most public portraits, poems and slogans of Mao Zedong. (›7 Sep)

● **24 Aug**: In a major political shake-up in Poland, Josef Pinkowski replaces Edward Babiuch as prime minister, and 14 other top officials are replaced. Communist party leader Edward Gierek announces major economic reforms and secret trade union ballots in response to worker demands. (›1 Dec)

● **7 Sep**: Hua Guofeng and Deng Xiaoping resign from the state council in China. On 10 Sep Zhao Ziyang replaces Hua as prime minister.

● **12 Sep**: After months of political violence in which at least 15,000 die, there is a military coup in Turkey. Gen. Kenan Evren becomes head of state, and on 21 Sep Bulent Ulusu is appointed civilian prime minister.

● **22 Sep**: War breaks out in the Persian Gulf as Iraq invades Iran to gain control of the strategic Shatt-al-Arab waterway.

● **20 Oct**: Greece rejoins the military wing of NATO after a six-year absence.

● **2 Nov**: The Iranian parliament votes to release the US embassy hostages, subject to certain conditions.

● **4 Nov**: Republican Ronald Reagan is elected as US president. Republicans also take control of the Senate.

● **20 Nov**: China's "Gang of Four" and six others go on trial on treason charges. On 29 Dec the prosecutor demands the death penalty for Jiang Qing (Mao's widow).

● **1 Dec**: EEC heads of government warn the USSR not to intervene in Poland after labor strikes bring down Communist party leader Gierek. On 2 Dec the USA backs up this stance. On 5 Dec, Warsaw Pact leaders agree to renounce the use of force, but vow that Poland will remain a socialist state.

● **13 Dec**: José Napoleon Duarte becomes the first civilian president of El Salvador in 49 years.

SOCIETY

● **Jan:** President Carter imposes restrictions on trade with the USSR as a consequence of its invasion of Afghanistan.

● **22 Jan:** Dissident physicist Andrei Sakharov is stripped of honors and exiled from Moscow.

● **4 Feb:** US dietary guidelines recommend avoiding excessive fats, cholesterol, sugar, salt and alcohol.

● **12 Feb:** Winter Olympics open at Lake Placid, New York State. US ice-speed skater Eric Heiden wins all five gold medals for his sport, establishing a Winter Olympic record.

● **27 Feb:** In Colombia, left-wing terrorists storm the Dominican embassy and take 80 hostages. The siege ends on 27 Apr when the guerrillas fly to Cuba.

● **23 Mar:** In a national referendum, Swedish voters approve the use of nuclear power.

● **24 Mar:** Catholic archbishop Oscar Romero is shot dead while celebrating mass in San Salvador, capital of El Salvador. At his funeral on 30 Mar, bombs and gunfire cause a stampede, and 39 die.

● **27 Mar:** Nearly 150 UK and Norwegian workers are killed when the offshore oil rig *Alexander Keilland* capsizes in the North Sea.

● **4 Apr:** 25 Cubans seek political asylum in the Peruvian embassy in Havana, hoping for exit visas after relaxation of emigration rules. By the end of the year about 125,000 Cubans have left their homeland.

● **30 Apr:** Armed gunmen seize the Iranian embassy in London, demanding the release of political prisoners in Iran. On 5 May SAS troops storm the embassy, rescue 19 hostages and kill five terrorists.

● **17–19 May:** Race riots begin in Miami after an all-white jury acquits four white policemen charged with the fatal beating of a black man (USA).

● **18 May:** The EEC votes for limited economic sanctions against Iran.

● **May:** 115 bankers and governors of central banks from 23 countries meet to discuss the financing of oil imports.

● **18 Jun:** In South Africa, over 40 are reported dead in three days of violence in colored townships around Capetown.

● **22–23 Jun:** The sixth economic summit of the major Western industrial nations issues declarations on the world economy and the Afghanistan war. They vow to develop alternatives to oil and fight inflation.

● **30 Jun:** The Sioux Indian nation wins $122.5 million in compensation and interest for the federal government's illegal seizure of their Black Hill land in 1877.

● **Jun:** Crop failures due to prolonged drought and local wars produces widespread famine throughout East Africa.

● **5 Jul:** Bjorn Borg (Swe) becomes the first to win five successive men's singles tennis titles at Wimbledon.

● **19 Jul–3 Aug:** The Olympic Games are held in Moscow, but are boycotted by over 45 nations over the Soviet invasion of Afghanistan.

● **2 Aug:** 84 die, 200 are injured in a terrorist bomb explosion in Bologna station (It).

● **5 Aug:** The USA and Canada sign a pact to curb acid rain.

● **13 Aug:** French fishermen seeking government aid begin two weeks of blockades at Channel ports, causing widespread disruption.

● **13–17 Aug:** Hindu-Muslim riots in the Indian state of Uttar Pradesh leave 142 dead. On 22 Sep the Indian government assumes wide powers of arrest and detention to maintain security and public order.

● **14 Aug:** Strikes spread among Baltic shipyard and other workers demanding free trade unions and other reforms. On 22 Aug a Polish strike committee, chaired by Lech Walesa and representing 120,000 workers, presents a list of demands to the government. (›Politics, 24 Aug)

● **31 Aug:** After further labor unrest, workers at Gdansk's Lenin shipyards are allowed to form an independent trade union, Solidarnosc (Solidarity), led by Lech Walesa, unprecedented in the Soviet bloc. (Pol). (›10 Nov)

● **Sep:** Discussions take place between France and the UK on a joint agricultural policy.

● **Sep–Oct:** Annual meeting of the IMF and World Bank discusses the external debts of the developing countries.

● **3 Oct:** A bomb explodes outside a synagogue in Paris, killing four and injuring 12, following a wave of attacks on Jewish targets.

● **25 Oct:** A month-long world synod of Roman Catholic bishops in Vatican City ends after reaffirming traditional teachings on abortion, birth control and other family issues.

● **10 Nov:** Poland's supreme court upholds an appeal by the trade union Solidarity against recognizing the supremacy of the Communist party in its charter, thus averting the threat of a major strike.

● **14 Nov:** Poland stops almost all food exports to counteract shortages at home.

● **1 Dec:** The USSR announces a new five-year plan. Agriculture is the only major sector planned to increase appreciably faster than in the previous five-year period.

● China becomes a member of the World Bank, IFC and IDA instead of Taiwan.

● Nobel Peace Prize is won by Adolfo Pérez Esquivel (Arg).

● Nobel Prize for Economic Sciences is won by Lawrence Klein (USA).

CULTURE

● **9 Apr:** ITV feature *Death of a Princess*, concerning the execution of a Saudi Arabian princess and her lover for adultery, provokes a political storm (UK).

● **15 Apr:** Death of French writer and philosopher Jean-Paul Sartre, aged 74.

● **24 Jul:** Death of Peter Sellers, film actor, aged 54, two weeks after the premiere of his latest film, *Being There*.

● **21 Nov:** The episode of *Dallas* in which it is revealed who shot JR breaks viewing records.

● **8 Dec:** John Lennon is shot dead in New York by a deranged fan; hundreds gather there in a candlelight vigil (USA).

● Joseph Brodsky: *A Part of Speech*, poems (USA).

● William Golding's novel *Rites of Passage* wins the Booker Prize (UK).

● John Le Carré : *Smiley's People*, spy thriller (UK).

● Howard Brenton's play *The Romans in Britain* so shocks the National Theater's backers that they threaten to withdraw its funding, but the Director of Public Prosecutions refuses to take it to court for obscenity (UK).

● Ngugi Wa Thiong'o (James T. Ngugi): *Devil on the Cross*, his first novel written in Gikuyu (Ken).

● Nobel Prize for Literature is won by Czeslaw Milosz (Pol/USA).

● Elliott Carter: *Night Fantasies*, for piano (USA).

● Jonathan Harvey: *Mortuos plango, vivos voco*, a work for tape, realized at IRCAM in Paris (UK).

● Laurie Anderson: *United States Parts 1 and 2*, an eight-hour combination of electronic music and film (USA).

● Douglas Lilburn: *Soundscape with Lake and River*, for tape (NZ).

● Philip Glass: *Satyagraha*, opera (USA), premiered in Rotterdam (Neth).

● New York's Museum of Modern Art puts on a huge exhibition of Pablo Picasso's works.

● Balthus: *Sleeping Nude*, painting (Fr).

● Jack Beal: *The Harvest*, painting (USA).

● Richard Diebenkorn: *Ocean Park No. 122*, painting (USA).

● Herbert George: *Visit and the Apparition*, sculpture (USA).

● Frank Gehry: Spiller House, Venice, California (USA).

● Judith Chafee: Ramdada House, Arizona (USA).

● *The Elephant Man*, directed by David Lynch, stars John Hurt and Anthony Hopkins (UK).

● Volker Schlondorff's film of Gunter Grass's novel *The Tin Drum* (FRG, 1979) becomes the first German work to win an Oscar for best foreign film.

● Release of *Kagemusha*, directed by Akira Kurosawa (Jap).

SCIENCE

● **16 Jan:** Scientists announce laboratory production of interferon, a disease-fighting protein (USA).

● **Mar:** Publication of world conservation strategy, product of three years' research and discussion by 450 government agencies. It reveals that at least 20,000 km sq (8,000 sq miles) of tropical rainforest is being destroyed each year, threatening wildlife and also reducing the forests' capacity to absorb CO_2, thus contributing to dangerous global warming.

● **11 Oct:** Two Soviet cosmonauts return to Earth after setting a new endurance record of 185 days, spent in the Salyut space station.

● **12 Nov:** US spaceprobe *Voyager I* passes within 77,000 miles of Saturn.

● The Nobel Prize for Physics is won by James Cronin and Val Flitch (USA) for their discovery that the universe is unexpectedly asymmetrical in space and time, one consequence being the evolution of life, which could not have occurred in a symmetrical universe.

● The Nobel Prize for Physiology or Medicine is won by Baruj Benacerraf (Ven), Jean Dausset (Fr) and George Snell (USA) for their discoveries concerning the genetic and chemical factors which govern the acceptance or rejection of grafted tissues and organs.

● The Nobel Prize for Chemistry is won by Paul Berg (USA), Walter Gilbert (USA) and Fred Sanger (UK) for their discoveries of the techniques for decoding genetic codes and transplanting genes into new hosts.

● A.H. Guth proposes a modification to the Big Bang, known as the inflationary universe theory.

● The first of the Intelsat V series of communications satellites funded by a consortium of 18 nations is launched by NASA.

● Several research groups announce that neutrinos may possess a tiny mass, and this mass may represent the "missing mass" unaccounted for in the context of the Big Bang theory.

● The US Supreme Court rules that a microbe developed by General Electric Co for use in cleaning up oil spills can be patented.

● Dornier Medical Systems of Munich develops the lithotripter, using sound waves to break up kidney stones (FRG).

● H. Rohrer (Switz) and G. Binnig (FDR) develop the scanning tunnelling microscope.

● Insulin produced by genetically engineered bacteria is first tested in diabetic human patients.

● Microorganisms are developed to ferment organic waste to produce alcohol for use as a fuel to replace oil, and as a means of carrying out vital synthetic steps in chemical industries without the need for energy-expensive high temperatures and pressures needed in conventional syntheses.

The temperature of the political conflict in Poland continued to rise, culminating in the banning of Solidarity and the imposition of martial law by the new prime minister, General Jaruzelski, in December. The guns of assassins were again in operation, the victims including President Sadat of Egypt, killed by Islamic fundamentalists. The new US president, Ronald Reagan, and the Pope both survived similar attacks. A certain confusion surrounded the attempt on the Pope's life, but the greatest mystery of the year was a small plastic cube, made up of smaller, interlocking cubes of different colors, invented by Hungarian mathematician Erno Rubik, who was suspected by some frustrated would-be solvers of the cube of harboring a secret grudge against the human race. On Earth the sinister and inappropriate acronym AIDS first became familiar, and in space a "Voyager" probe demonstrated that the rings of Saturn are more complex than had been suspected. The USA launched the first space shuttle, "Columbia," as part of its space research program, and IBM launched the personal computer, beginning a new phase of the communications revolution.

▲ As the first space shuttle is launched and *Voyager 2* sends back pictures of Saturn, space-age technology makes itself felt on the ground with France's new highspeed trains, one of a number of new designs for ever faster express trains.

- **7–14 Jan**: A UN-sponsored conference on Namibia fails to agree a ceasefire and implementation of UN plan for Namibia's independence.

- **20 Jan**: Iran releases all 52 US embassy hostages (held since 4 Nov 1979) following the signing of an agreement in Algiers and the transfer of frozen Iranian assets from the USA to a Bank of England account.

- **20 Jan**: Ronald Reagan is inaugurated as US president. (›30 Mar)

- **25 Jan**: Jiang Qing (Mao Zedong's widow) and Zhang Chunqiao receive death sentences suspended for two years; the other two of the "Gang of Four" receive long jail sentences for treason and other antistate activities (Chi). (›29 Jun)

- **29 Jan**: Adolfo Suarez resigns as prime minister of Spain in face of growing opposition from the right wing of his party. On 10 Feb Leopoldo Calvo Sotelo y Bustelo becomes prime minister, and on 26 Feb a cabinet is named – the first since 1939 with no generals. (›23 Feb)

- **4 Feb**: Gro Harlem Brundtland becomes Norway's first woman prime minister.

- **9 Feb**: Polish prime minister Josef Pinkowski is forced to resign after five months of unrest. His place is taken by the defense minister, Gen. Wojciech Jaruzelski. (›5 Jun; Society ›18 Feb)

- **23 Feb**: In Spain, 200 civil guards led by Col. Tejero Molina storm the Cortes and hold 350 MPs at gunpoint in an attempted coup. The civil guards surrender on 24 Feb after King Juan Carlos denounces them.

- **30 Mar**: President Reagan and three aides are shot in an assassination attempt in Washington (USA).

- **1 Apr**: The heaviest fighting since the 1976 civil war breaks out in Beirut and Zahlé when clashes occur between Lebanese rightwing Christian militia and Syrian peacekeeping troops. On 29–30 Apr Syria installs Soviet-made surface-to-air missiles in Lebanon.

- **7 Apr**: In the Philippines, voters overwhelmingly approve a new constitution giving sweeping powers to president Marcos.

- **6 May**: The USA expels all Libyan diplomats because of the Libyan government's support for international terrorism. (›19 Aug)

- **10 May**: François Mitterand is elected the first Socialist president of France since the foundation of the Fifth Republic in 1958, replacing Giscard d'Estaing.

- **24 May**: President Jaime Roldos Aguilera of Ecuador is killed in a terrorist-directed air crash.

- **26 May**: In Italy, Arnaldo Frolani's government resigns after revelations of links between top officials and an illegal secret Masonic lodge, "P2". On 28 Jun Giovanni Spadolini becomes prime minister.

- **30 May**: President Ziaur Rahman of Bangladesh is shot dead in an attempted military coup.

- **5 Jun**: The USSR Communist party Central Committee sends a letter to its Polish counterpart expressing concern about the Polish government's loss of control and its "endless concessions to anti-socialist forces". In Sep the USSR sets up the biggest naval exercise since World War II in the Baltic. (›12 Jun)

- **8 Jun**: Israeli planes bomb a nuclear power plant being built for Iraq by France near Baghdad. On 19 Jun the UN Security Council condemns the strike.

- **12 Jun**: Polish prime minister Jaruzelski removes five cabinet ministers and proposes a major reconstruction of government to tackle the severe economic crisis. On 3 Jul eight further ministers are dismissed. (›15 Dec)

- **29 Jun**: Hu Yaobang succeeds Hua Guofeng as Communist party chairman. Mao Zedong is discredited for mistakes in leadership.

- **24 Jul**: Israel and the PLO endorse ceasefire agreements, ending two weeks of hostilities on the borders.

- **4 Aug**: A military junta takes over government in Bolivia.

- **19 Aug**: US fighter aircraft shoot down two Libyan jets attempting to intercept US fighters participating in naval exercises in the Gulf of Sirte. On 1 Sep Libyan president Col. Qadhafi threatens to create an "international catastrophe" by attacking US nuclear bases in the Mediterranean if the USA enters the Gulf of Sirte again.

- **30 Aug**: In Iran, prime minister Bahomar and president Rajaj are among some 15 killed in a terrorist bomb explosion.

- **1–2 Sep**: President David Dacko of the Central African Republic is overthrown in a military coup.

- **20 Sep**: British Honduras becomes independent Belize.

- **6 Oct**: President Anwar Sadat of Egypt is assassinated by extremist Muslim soldiers. He is succeeded by Hosni Mubarak on 13 Oct.

- **18 Oct**: The first socialist government in Greece is elected under Andreas Papandreou.

- **14 Nov**: Gambia and Senegal announce a decision to form a confederation to be known as Senegambia.

- **30 Nov**: US and Soviet negotiators in Geneva begin talks on nuclear arms limitations.

- **15 Dec**: Gen. Jaruzelski imposes martial law on Poland in a clampdown on strikes and demonstrations. Lech Walesa, leader of the trade union Solidarity, is now under arrest. (›Society)

- The USA grants $161 million in military and economic aid to El Salvador to help combat leftwing guerrillas.

SOCIETY

- **1 Jan**: Greece becomes the tenth member of the EEC.
- **11 Jan**: A three-man British team led by Sir Ranulph Fiennes completes the longest and fastest crossing of Antarctica yet, reaching Scott Base in 75 days after traveling 4,000 km (2,500 miles).
- **26 Jan**: The UK announces £900 million pounds in government aid for British Leyland motor company.
- **Jan**: The European Monetary Fund (EMF) is established and the European Currency Unit (ECU) introduced.
- **18 Feb**: US president Reagan presents his economic program to reduce the budget deficit by $41.4 billion and increase the defense budget by $90 billion in the next four years, the largest package of tax cuts and spending curbs ever proposed by a US administration.
- **18 Feb**: The Independent Students Association in Poland registers as Eastern Europe's only student group that is not directly under Communist party control. (▷1 Apr)
- **2 Mar**: Terrorists of the militant Al-Zulfiqar organization hijack a Pakistani plane with 148 aboard. All hostages are released on 15 Mar after Pakistan frees over 50 political prisoners.
- **29 Mar**: 6,700 runners compete in the first London marathon. It is won by Dick Beardsley (USA) and Inge Simonson (Swe).
- **1 Apr**: Western banks and governments assemble a massive package of food and financial aid for Poland. (▷17 Apr)
- **11 Apr**: In the UK, 114 police and 192 civilians are injured in violent rioting in Brixton, south London, an area with a large black population and much unemployment. (▷3 Jul)
- **17 Apr**: In Poland, 3.7 million private farmers win the legal right to form an independent union, Rural Solidarity. (▷7 Aug)
- **20 Apr**: Snooker player Steve Davis (UK) wins the world championship at the age of 23.
- **5 May**: Robert Sands is the first of 10 IRA hunger strikers to die in the Maze prison in Hillsborough. Riots erupt in Northern Ireland after his death.
- **13 May**: Pope John-Paul II is seriously wounded by a gunman in St Peter's Square in Rome.
- **24 May**: In Spain, police storm a Barcelona bank and release hostages held for nearly two days by terrorists.
- **3 Jun**: The Aga Khan's horse Shergar wins the Derby (UK).
- **16–17 Jun**: A meeting of the Minister Council of the OECD calls for liberalization of trade and economic cooperation with developing countries.
- **3–13 Jul**: Riots break out between police and black and white youths in areas of London, Liverpool, and over 30 other towns in the UK.

- **17 Jul**: Opening of the Humber Bridge, the longest singlespan bridge in the world, 1,410 m (4,646 ft) across (UK).
- **25 Jul**: Rugby fans clash with demonstrators in New Zealand, preventing a match with South Africa's Springboks team. Antiapartheid disturbances continue through the rest of the Springboks' controversial eight-week tour.
- **Jul**: A flood in China's Sichuan and Hubei provinces kills over 700 and injures over 28,000; it leaves 1.5 million homeless.
- **7 Aug**: Around 1 million members of the trade union Solidarity go on strike against food shortages and economic crises in Poland. (▷12 Dec)
- **28 Aug**: Sebastian Coe (UK) regains the world mile record (broken two days earlier by Steve Ovett, also of the UK) in Koblenz (FRG), in 3 min 48.4 secs.
- **Aug**: Declaration of Tegucigalpa: Middle American countries demand to be better integrated into the world economy.
- **3–4 Sep**: Over 1,500 opponents of government are arrested in Egypt. Muslim fundamentalists stage massive demonstrations in Cairo in protest.
- **9 Sep**: Nicaragua declares a state of economic emergency and bans strikes.
- **14 Sep**: Sweden devalues its currency by 10 percent in an attempt to increase Swedish industry's export competitiveness, and freezes prices until the end of the year.
- **10 Oct**: Around 250,000 demonstrate in Bonn against NATO's plan to install new nuclear missiles in Europe. On 24 Oct massive demonstrations follow in many European cities.
- **22–23 Oct**: A North-South summit, attended by leaders of 14 developing nations and 8 industrial countries, meets in Cancún, Mexico, but fails to reach agreement on ideas for reducing poverty in the Third World.
- **9 Nov**: The IMF approves its largest loan ever, $5.8 billion for India in SDRs.
- **12 Dec**: Polish trade union Solidarity calls for a day of protest on 17 Dec and a referendum on replacing the government. On 13 Dec martial law is declared and Solidarity banned. Gen. Jaruzelski announces the formation of a Military Council of National Salvation to run the country.
- **29 Dec**: President Reagan announces a program of limited economic sanctions against the USSR because of its support for martial law in Poland.
- Hungarian architect Erno Rubik introduces his Rubik Cube, with 42.3 quintillion possible configurations.
- Nobel Peace Prize is won by the office of the United Nations High Commissioner for Refugees.
- Nobel Prize for Economic Sciences is won by James Tobin (USA).

CULTURE

- **Jan–Mar**: "A New Spirit in Painting", large-scale exhibition of Postmodernist painting, is held at the Royal Academy, London.
- **15 Mar**: Premiere of Karlheinz Stockhausen's opera *Donnerstag aus Licht* (Thursday from Light) in Milan (It), the first of his proposed seven-evening cycle *Licht*.
- **11 May**: Death of Jamaican exponent of reggae music and black rights activist Bob Marley, aged 36.
- **29 Jul**: A worldwide TV audience estimated at over 700 million watches the wedding of the Prince of Wales and Lady Diana Spencer. (UK).
- Elias Canetti (UK) is awarded the Nobel Prize for Literature.
- Janet Frame: *Living in the Maniototo*, novel (NZ).
- John Updike: *Rabbit is Rich*, the last novel in the trilogy begun in 1960 with *Rabbit, Run* and continued with *Rabbit Redux* in 1971 (USA).
- Claude Simon: *Les Georgiques*, novel (Fr).
- Mario Vargas Llosa: *War of the End of the World*, novel (Peru).
- Salman Rushdie: *Midnight's Children*, novel (UK).
- Toni Morrison: *Tar Baby*, novel (USA).
- Debut of the 4X music computer in Pierre Boulez's *Répons* (Fr).
- Arvo Pärt: *Passio domini nostri Jesu Christi secundum Joannem*, for voices and chamber ensemble (FRG).
- Peter Maxwell Davies: Organ Sonata (UK).
- Opening of *Cats*, a musical by Tim Rice and Andrew Lloyd Webber based on the poems in T.S.Eliot's *Old Possum's Book of Practical Cats* (UK).
- Bruce Springsteen (USA) emerges as a major rock star with his UK tour.
- Francesco Clemente: *Toothache*, painting (It).
- Jake Berthot: *Belfast*, painting (USA).
- Jon Borofsky: *Hammering Man at 2,772,489 (JB27 sculp)*, aluminum and steel sculpture (Swi).
- Georg Baselitz: *Model for a Sculpture*, limewood (FRG).
- Denys Lasdun: Hurva Synagogue, Jerusalem (Isr).
- Mario Botta: Casa Rotonda, Ticino (Swi).
- Balkrishna V. Doshi: "Sangath" Studio, Ahmedabad (Ind).
- Release of *Raiders of the Lost Ark*, directed by Steven Spielberg and starring Harrison Ford (USA).
- Release of *Reds*, directed by and starring Warren Beatty, set against the background of the Russian Revolution (USA).
- Andrzej Wajda: *Man of Iron*, centred on the 1980 riots in Gdansk (Pol).
- Hugh Hudson: *Chariots of Fire* (UK).

SCIENCE

- **12 Apr**: Launch of the first space shuttle *Columbia*, a reusable manned space vehicle. It returns on 14 Apr.
- **25 Aug**: US spaceprobe *Voyager 2* sends back the most detailed pictures of Saturn yet available, passing within 101,000 km (63,000 miles) of the planet.
- The Nobel Prize for Physics is won by Nicholas Bloembergen (USA) and Arthur Schawlow (USA) for their work on the development of laser spectroscopy, and Kai Siegbahn (Swe) for the development of high resolution electron spectroscopy.
- The Nobel Prize for Chemistry is won by Kenichi Fukui (Jap) and Roald Hoffman (USA) for independent development of a theory for predicting whether hypothetical chemical reactions could occur in practise.
- The Nobel Prize for Physiology or Medicine is won by Robert Sperry (USA) for work on "split brain" patients and David Hubel (USA) and Torsten Wiesel (Swe) for work in analyzing the cell structure of the visual cortex of the brain.
- Biotechnologically grown insulin is marketed (USA).
- AIDS (Acquired Immune Deficiency Syndrome) is officially recognized for the first time (USA).
- First transfer of genes from one animal to another is achieved by scientists at Ohio University (USA).
- First successful cloning of a fish, a golden carp, is achieved (Chi).
- A. Heller, B. Miller and F.A. Thiel announce a liquid junction cell that converts 11.5 percent of solar energy into electricity.
- SODAR (sonic detection and ranging) is installed at Frankfurt and other large West German airports to measure air currents.
- J.P. Cassinelli and colleagues discover the most massive star known, R136a, with a mass 2,500 times greater than the Sun (USA).
- Launch of IBM personal computer (PC) (USA).
- A vaccine against foot-and-mouth disease, made by inserting viral genes into bacteria, is made commercially available (USA).
- Introduction of diaphragm pacing technique – regular electrical stimulation of the nerves supplying the diaphragm – which replaces the use of iron lungs and other ventilators for people paralysed from the neck down.
- Doctors in the UK successfully treat children suffering from normally progressive and fatal disease caused by genetic defects by implanting bone marrow grafts taken from close relatives.
- Researchers in ICI's corporate laboratory succeed in artificially synthesizing the complete gene for a form of interferon.

The British people were surprised to find their country engaged in a colonial war, an everyday occurrence 80 years ago but in 1982 an unexpected phenomenon, when the Argentineans invaded the remote Falkland Islands. But the Argentinian dictator General Galtieri had chosen a bad moment. Britain's "Iron Lady", prime minister Margaret Thatcher, was not the sort to stand by while someone snatched her possessions, and a British "task force" was promptly despatched to throw out the Argentineans. The UN took an equally strong line against another invader, Israel, which in angry desperation at continuing Palestinian terrorism invaded the Lebanon. The highest Palestinian casualties, however, were caused not by the invading Israelis but by the Christian Falangists, who carried out a massacre in the Beirut camps following the death of president-elect Gemayel in a bomb attack. In November the last old-style Stalinist leader of the Soviet Union died unlamented. Gray-faced and doddery, Leonid Brezhnev had apparently been overtaken by senility years earlier. He was succeeded by another "gray man", Yuri Andropov.

▲ After 12 years of intermittent warfare, Israeli forces finally drove the PLO terrorists from their power base in Beirut; but the multinational peacekeeping force that supervised the PLO withdrawal soon found itself having to contend with a further confused and bitter struggle between the Muslims Druse militia and Christian Falangists, in which the Lebanese president-elect Bashir Gemayel was an early casualty.

● **1 Jan**: Javier Perez de Cuellar becomes Secretary-General of the UN.

● **17 Feb**: Zimbabwean opposition leader Joshua Nkomo is dismissed by prime minister Robert Mugabe for allegedly plotting a coup. On 16 Aug he retakes his seat in government after exile in Botswana and the UK.

● **11 Mar**: In the UK, the government announces its decision to buy the US Trident 2 system to replace Polaris.

● **24 Mar**: In Bangladesh a military coup removes president Abdus Sattar. Lt-Gen. Muhammad Hossain Ershad declares himself martial law leader.

● **28 Mar**: First free elections for 50 years in El Salvador are monitored by a team of international observers. Five right-wing parties agree to form a government of National Unity.

● **2 Apr**: Argentinean forces invade the Falkland Islands (Malvinas), a British colony for the last 150 years, and overthrow the British administration. On 3 Apr the UN Security Council votes in favor of a resolution demanding that Argentina withdraw. On 4 Apr the first ships of a Royal Navy task force leave Britain. (›2 May)

● **17 Apr**: A new constitution severs Canada's last colonial link with the UK and makes it completely independent.

● **21 Apr**: Israeli planes attack Palestinian strongholds in Lebanon after an Israeli soldier is killed by a land mine in Lebanon. The violence ends a nine-month-long ceasefire.

● **25 Apr**: Israel completes withdrawal from Sinai as pledged in the Egyptian-Israeli peace treaty of 1979. (›6 Jun).

● **2 May**: The Argentinean cruiser *General Belgrano* is sunk by a British submarine, killing about 368. (›14 Jun)

● **18 May**: Soviet premier Leonid Brezhnev calls for an immediate freeze by the USA and USSR on strategic arms, and new talks on arms limitation which begin on 29 Jun.

● **24 May**: In the war between Iran and Iraq, Iranian troops recapture the city of Khorramshahr, occupied by Iraq since Oct 1980.

● **30 May**: Spain becomes the 16th member of NATO.

● **6 Jun**: An attack on the Israeli ambassador to the UK by Palestinian terrorists on 3 Jun is countered with the invasion of southern Lebanon. The UN Security Council demands Israeli withdrawal, but Israel rejects the demand and fighting continues. On 21 Aug PLO evacuation of Beirut begins. (›28 Aug)

● **13 Jun**: King Khalid Ibn Abdul Aziz of Saudi Arabia dies of a heart attack, and is succeeded by his half-brother Fahd Ibn Abdul Aziz al-Saud.

● **14 Jun**: The Argentinean military commander signs surrender documents in Port Stanley. On 17 Jun Gen. Galtieri resigns as president of Argentina. On 23 Jun the army assumes total control. (›4 Nov)

● **13 Jul**: Iran invades Iraq for the first time in their 22-month-old conflict. On 16 Jul Iraqi president Saddam Hussein claims to have defeated Iranian forces.

● **15 Aug**: Somalia declares a state of emergency in areas bordering Ethiopia after six weeks' fierce fighting.

● **28–30 Aug**: War breaks out between the Druse Muslim militia and the Lebanese army. (›14 Sep)

● **1–12 Sep**: At the 12th Congress of the Chinese Communist party, a new party constitution restructures the leadership. Deng Xiaoping is elected chairman of new Central Advisory Commission to the party.

● **10 Sep**: Poul Schluter becomes prime minister of Denmark, heading a center-right coalition.

● **14 Sep**: President-elect of Lebanon, Bashir Gemayel, is killed in a bomb explosion in Beirut. On 23 Sep his brother Amin becomes president.

● **15 Sep**: Israeli troops push into West Beirut. On 16–18 Sep Christian Falangist militia men enter refugee camps in West Beirut and massacre over 800 Palestinian civilians in retaliation for Gemayel's death.

● **17 Sep**: The coalition government of Social Democrat chancellor Helmut Schmidt collapses after 13 years. On 1 Oct Christian Democrat Helmut Kohl is elected chancellor and forms a new coalition government with the Free Democrats (FRG).

● **10 Oct**: Bolivia returns to civilian rule under Hernan Siles Zuazo.

● **28 Oct**: Socialist Felipe Gonzalez leads his party to victory in the Spanish general elections. On 2 Dec he is sworn in as the first Socialist prime minister of Spain.

● **30 Oct**: In Portugal, a new constitution comes into effect, ending eight years of military influence on the country's politics.

● **4 Nov**: The UN General Assembly calls on the UK and Argentina to resume negotiations on the sovereignty of the Falklands.

● **7 Nov**: Turkish voters endorse a new draft constitution giving a seven-year presidential term to Gen. Kenan Evran.

● **10 Nov**: Soviet president Leonid Brezhnev dies of a heart attack, aged 75. On 12 Nov Yuri Andropov succeeds him as General Secretary of the Central Committee of the Communist party.

● **22 Nov**: President Reagan announces a decision to deploy 100 MX intercontinental nuclear missiles in Wyoming (USA).

● **1 Dec**: The 43rd government since World War II, led by Amintore Fanfani, is sworn in in Italy.

● **14 Dec**: Garret Fitzgerald replaces Charles Haughey as prime minister after the Irish general election.

● **15 Dec**: Spain reopens its border with Gibraltar to allow pedestrian travel for the first time since 1969.

SOCIETY

• **16 Jan:** The Vatican and UK reestablish full diplomatic relations, broken in 1532. On 28 May Pope John-Paul II begins the first papal visit to the UK.

• **19 Jan:** In Poland, food price rises from 1 Feb of 200–400 percent are announced. (›5 Feb)

• **4 Feb:** Laker Airways, a company providing a cut-rate transatlantic passenger service since 1977, collapses with debts of £276 million (UK).

• **5 Feb:** Following the USA's move in Dec 1981, the UK imposes economic sanctions against Poland and the USSR in protest against martial law in Poland. On 22–24 Feb Belgium, Japan and Canada follow suit. (›4 May)

• **5 Feb:** Bolivia devalues the peso and announces other measures to alleviate economic problems.

• **11 Feb:** France, under Socialist president Mitterand, nationalizes five groups of major industries and 39 banks, and in Jun begins a four-month price and wage freeze as part of an economic package following devaluation of the franc.

• **23 Feb:** In a national referendum, Greenlanders vote to leave the EEC, after joining as part of Denmark.

• **19 Mar:** 15 UK cricket players who made an unofficial tour to South Africa are banned from international cricket for three years.

• **Apr:** The EEC imposes economic sanctions on Argentina, supporting the UK in the Falkland Islands crisis.

• **4 May:** Poland reinstates harsh security measures in several cities after three days of anti-government demonstrations. (›31 Aug)

• **22 Jun:** New Zealand announces a 12-month freeze on prices and wages.

• **20 Jul:** IRA bombs explode in London's Regent's Park and Hyde Park, killing 11 soldiers and injuring 59 soldiers and civilians.

• **31 Aug:** Riot police clash with demonstrators in major Polish cities, and over 4,000 are arrested on the second anniversary of the establishment of the trade union Solidarity. (›8 Oct)

• **1 Sep:** Mexico nationalizes private banks. Inflation is at 70 percent and around eight million are out of work.

• **8 Oct:** The Polish parliament passes a new law banning Solidarity and the establishment of new trade unions. The USA imposes further trade sanctions on 10 Oct. Martial law is lifted on 30 Dec, but many repressive features remain.

• **12 Dec:** Over 20,000 women encircle the Greenham Common airbase in a peaceful protest against the installation of US cruise missiles (UK).

• Nobel Peace Prize is won by Alfonso García Robles (Mex) and Alva Myrdal (Swe).

• Nobel Prize for Economic Sciences is won by George Stigler (USA).

CULTURE

• **9 Mar:** Luciano Berio's opera *La vera storia*, to a text by Italo Calvino, is first performed at La Scala, Milan (It).

• **14 Sep:** Princess Grace of Monaco (film star Grace Kelly) dies after a car crash, aged 52.

• Thomas Keneally's novel *Schindler's Ark* (Aus) wins the Booker Prize.

• R. K. Narayan: *Malgudi Days*, short stories (Ind).

• Derek Walcott: *The Unfortunate Traveller*, poems (Trin).

• Edward Brathwaite: *Sun Poem* (Bar).

• Bruce Chatwin: *On the Black Hill*, novel (UK).

• Gabriel García Márquez: *Chronicle of a Death Foretold* (Col). Márquez is awarded the Nobel Prize for Literature.

• György Ligeti: *Horn Trio* (FRG).

• Peter Maxwell Davies: *Into the Labyrinth*, for tenor and chamber orchestra (UK).

• Jonathan Harvey: *Bhakti*, for ensemble and tape, realized at IRCAM in Paris (UK).

• "Rap" music becomes popular and increases in sophistication in the USA and UK.

• Frank Auerbach: *Primrose Hill, Early Summer*, painting (UK).

• Sandro Chia: *Crocodile Tears*, painting (It).

• Julian Schnabel: *Humanity Asleep*, painted ceramic relief on wood (FRG).

• Joseph Beuys: *Dernier espace avec introspecteur*, installation (FRG).

• Robert Arneson: *Californian Artist*, sculpture (USA).

• Andy Goldsworthy: *Arch*, earth art (UK).

• Jean-Michel Basquiat, who started as a graffiti artist in the 1970s, holds eight one-man shows during 1982 (USA).

• Raj Rewal: Asian Games housing, New Delhi (Ind).

• Philip Johnson and John Burgee: AT&T Building, New York City, Postmodern architecture (USA).

• Charles Correa: Cidade de Goa, hotel (Goa).

• Release of *On Golden Pond*, directed by Mark Rydell and starring Katherine Hepburn and Henry Fonda (US).

• Werner Herzog (FRG) directs *Fitzcarraldo*, filmed in the South American jungle; at the same time a documentary film, *Burden of Dreams*, charts the making of the film.

• Andrzej Wajda: *The Danton Affair*, film about contemporary oppression (Fr).

• *ET – the Extra Terrestrial*, directed by Steven Spielberg (USA), becomes a smash hit with children and adults on both sides of the Atlantic.

• *Gandhi*, directed by Richard Attenborough, stars Ben Kingsley (UK).

SCIENCE

• **1 Mar:** Soviet spaceprobe *Venera 13* softlands on Venus, sending back the first color TV pictures of the planet's surface. It also analyzes rock samples in its minilab, despite a temperature of 460 degrees C. On 5 Mar *Venera 14* lands on a different part of the planet.

• **30 Apr and 4 Jul:** US space shuttle *Columbia* completes its third and fourth trial flights, thus completing its test program. In Nov it becomes operational on its fifth flight, putting its first commercial payload, two satellites, into orbit.

• **29 Aug:** A single atom of element 109 is created (FRG).

• **5 Sep:** The presidents of Brazil and Paraguay inaugurate the Itaipu Dam, part of the world's largest hydroelectric scheme.

• **10 Sep:** *Ariane*, a rocket built by several European companies, plunges into the Atlantic Ocean 14 minutes into its first operational mission.

• **15 Oct:** Halley's Comet is sighted for first time since 1911.

• **2 Dec:** Surgeons at Utah University (USA) replace the diseased heart of a 61-year-old man and replace it with an artificial substitute designed as a permanent, not just temporary, replacement. He survives until 24 Mar 1983.

• **10 Dec:** Two Soviet cosmonauts return after a record 211 days in orbit in the space station Salyut 7.

• The Nobel Prize for Chemistry is won by Aaron Klug (SA) for work in analyzing 3-D structures of viruses and the way in which DNA is coiled within genes in chromosomes.

• The Nobel Prize for Physics is won by Kenneth G. Wilson (USA) for his work on phase transitions.

• The Nobel Prize for Physiology or Medicine is won by Sune Bergstrom (Swe) and Bengt Samuelsson (Swe) and John Vane (USA) for their work on prostaglandins.

• Blas Cabrera (USA) claims to have detected a single magnetic monopole (that is, a single magnetic pole, north or south, without an equivalent opposite pole to balance it), predicted in theory; but this is not corroborated by further experiments.

• Innovative fashion designer Gianni Versace uses lasers to seam rubber and leather (It).

• Introduction of the supercomputer Cray I, which can perform 100 million arithmetical operations per second (USA).

• The first compact disc players are commercially available in Japan (and in Europe and the USA in 1983).

• Ground boring in the USA and USSR reaches a depth of 11 km (7 miles).

• The XA Olympus camera is given Japan's G-mark award.

• Successful treatment of severe infectious hepatitis is achieved with interferon (Isr).

• M. Epstein identifies the first virus implicated in human cancer, the Epstein-Barr virus (UK).

• The gene for rat growth hormone is transferred to mice, the first time a gene from one mammal has functioned in another mammal.

• Karl Setter (FRG) discovers a primitive bacterium able to live in sea water heated by the escape of volcanic material to 105 degrees C. He theorizes that they have remained unchanged for 4,000 million years because they faced no competition from other species.

• Jerrold Petrovsky develops a system which enables a girl paralyzed from the waist down to walk again by using a computer that controls electrical stimulation of her leg muscles in sequence, producing the movements needed for walking.

• Scientists carrying out transplants of brain tissue between rats show that a transplant could restore the ability to learn and remember to rats who had lost it through experimental injury. The issue gives rise to discussion of the ethical problems that would arise if a demand began to grow for brain tissue for human transplants.

• Robert Weinberg and Mariano Barbacid pinpoint a small chemical change in one single base (subunit of DNA) in one gene, which alone causes the transformation of normal human bladder epithelial cells into malignant cells. When the abnormal gene is transplanted into healthy animals, it could cause cancer (USA).

• An Italian boy is successfully treated for thalassemia by eliminating his own defective bone marrow with cytotoxic drugs and then giving him a transplant of healthy bone marrow from his sister.

• The first computerized heart pacemaker is fitted to a 49-year-old man (UK).

The sufferings of the Lebanon continued to dominate the news. The Israelis took steps to extract themselves from the maelstrom into which their precipitate invasion had flung them. A peace conference attended by all involved parties met in Geneva, but within a month Shi'ite suicide bombers killed almost 300 US and French soldiers of the international peacekeeping force, while dissident members of the PLO, supported by Syria, attempted to oust their long-time leader, Yasir Arafat. A new trouble spot appeared in the Caribbean when the government of Grenada was overthrown and the prime minister assassinated. US Marines promptly landed and defeated the rebels with their Cuban allies. The US action was widely and hypocritically deplored, but not by the majority of Grenadans. Besides policing the Caribbean, the USA revealed plans for policing outer space, when president Reagan proposed his Strategic Defence Initiative, a new type of missile shield based on short wavelength lasers and promptly nicknamed "Star Wars."

▲ Star of the Eighties Madonna storms her way to success in the charts with a heady mixture of sex, self-confidence and business acumen.

• **18 Jan**: Namibia's interim National Assembly is dissolved by South Africa. Direct rule from Pretoria is reimposed after five years of semiautonomous government.

• **6 Feb**: In the presidential election in Paraguay, Gen. Stroessner is returned for his seventh five-year term of office.

• **11 Feb**: Israeli defense minister Ariel Sharon resigns after an inquiry into the massacre of Palestinian refugees in West Beirut on 16–18 Sep 1982.

• **15 Feb**: The Lebanese army takes complete control of Beirut for the first time since 1975. (›18 Apr)

• **5 Mar**: In Australia the election is won by the Labor party under Robert Hawke, defeating the ruling coalition of Malcolm Fraser.

• **22 Mar**: The 44-member French cabinet resigns and prime minister Pierre Mauroy names a new cabinet of only 15 members.

• **5 Apr**: France expels 47 Soviet diplomats and nationals on charges of spying, unprecedented in French-Soviet relations.

• **18 Apr**: The US Embassy in Beirut is bombed, killing over 30 (›17 May).

• **24 Apr**: Austrian chancellor Bruno Kreisky resigns after 13 years in office when the Socialist party fails to win an overall majority in the general election.

• **25 Apr**: In Portugal, Socialist Mario Soares becomes prime minister in a coalition government.

• **17 May**: Israel and Lebanon sign an agreement on withdrawal of Israeli troops from Lebanon, despite Syrian rejection of the agreement, after negotiations during US Secretary of State George Schultz's tour of the Middle East in Apr. (›24 Jun)

• **30 May**: A 60-day state of emergency and suspension of civil rights is declared in Peru due to political crisis and bombings by left-wing rebels.

• **9 Jun**: The Conservative party under Margaret Thatcher is reelected in the UK with an overall majority of 144.

• **16 Jun**: Yuri Andropov is elected president of the Soviet Presidium.

• **19 Jun**: Li Viannian becomes China's first president since 1968.

• **24 Jun**: Syria expels PLO leader Yasir Arafat and Syrian tanks lay siege to his guerrilla bases in Lebanon. (›3 Sep)

• **10 Jul**: In the Western Sahara, war flares up again after an 18-month lull, when Polisario guerrillas attack Moroccan defensive positions.

• **21 Jul**: Martial law in Poland is lifted after 19 months, and amnesty for political prisoners declared.

• **4 Aug**: Bettino Craxi becomes Italy's first Socialist prime minister, at the head of a coalition government.

• **6 Aug**: The USA sends aircraft to support Chad against Libyan-backed rebels. On 19 Aug 3,500 French troops leave for Chad to reinforce some 3,000 already there.

• **21 Aug**: Philippine opposition leader Benigno Aquino is assassinated at Manila airport on his return from a three-year exile in the USA to fight an election. Violent demonstrations follow, calling for the resignation of president Marcos.

• **1 Sep**: A South Korean passenger plane is shot down by a Soviet war plane after it flies into Soviet territory. All 269 on board are killed. The USSR claims it was spying, but widespread international protests follow.

• **3–4 Sep**: Civil war in central Lebanon between Christian and Druse militias breaks out again after Israel withdraws to a new front line along the Awali River. (›26 Sep)

• **15 Sep**: Israeli prime minister Menachem Begin resigns, and is succeeded by Yitzhak Shamir on 10 Oct.

• **19 Sep**: The Caribbean islands of St Kitts-Nevis become independent.

• **26 Sep**: A ceasefire comes into effect in Lebanon when the government agrees to a conference of national reconciliation. On 31 Oct the conference opens in Geneva, attended by leaders of the principal Lebanese militias and political parties, Syrian delegates and Israeli observers. (›23 Oct)

• **2 Oct**: Neil Kinnock becomes the new leader of the UK Labour party.

• **23 Oct**: Suicide terrorists set off explosives at US and French barracks in Beirut, killing over 240 US and around 60 French members of the peacekeeping force (Leb). (›3 Nov)

• **25 Oct**: After a Marxist coup in Grenada US troops land to "protect US citizens", and discover a Cuban and Soviet presence. On 27 Oct organized resistance by Cubans and Grenadian rebels ends. On 31 Oct the governor of Grenada confirms that he had requested assistance from eastern Caribbean forces and indirectly from the USA.

• **2 Nov**: In an all-white referendum in South Africa, a new constitution giving limited political rights to Coloreds and Asians is approved.

• **3 Nov**: In north Lebanon, fighting breaks out between PLO loyalists and dissidents demanding the overthrow of Yasir Arafat. On 15 Nov Syrian forces and Palestinian dissidents launch a final assault on the last refuge of the PLO leader in north Lebanon.

• **15 Nov**: The Turkish Cypriot legislative assembly issues a unilateral declaration of independence of the Turkish section of the island. On 18 Nov the UN Security Council declares the action legally invalid.

• **22–23 Nov**: Breakdown of USA–USSR arms reduction talks. NATO and the USSR announce an increase in nuclear forces.

• **10 Dec**: Raul Alfonsin is inaugurated as president of Argentina, the first civil president for eight years.

SOCIETY

● **14 Jan**: Soviet dissident Anatoly Shcharansky ends the hunger strike he began in Sep 1982.

● **17 Jan**: Nigeria orders the immediate eviction of around 2 million illegal immigrants. On 30 Jan Ghana reopens its border with Nigeria (closed since Sep 1982) to speed the exodus of refugees.

● **25 Jan**: EEC countries agree on new fishing quotas on all fish except herring, though the policy is not implemented until 14 Dec.

● **Jan**: Prime minister Thatcher publishes her economic policy aimed at curbing inflation and reducing the budget deficit (UK).

● **Jan**: Switzerland becomes a member of the "Group of 10" of the IMF.

● **5 Feb**: Nazi war criminal Klaus Barbie (alias Klaus Altmann) is imprisoned in Lyon (Fr) after his deportation from Bolivia.

● **16-19 Feb**: Bush fires in South Australia burn 6,700 km sq (2,590 sq miles) and kill 70 people.

● **Feb**: Soviet leader Andropov announces economic measures to counter the lack of economic discipline in the USSR.

● **8 Mar**: The Australian $ is devalued by 10 percent.

● **14 Mar**: OPEC agrees to cut crude oil prices in view of world glut. The price is reduced from $34 to $29 per barrel, the first price cut since OPEC was founded.

● **14 Mar**: A hunger strike in Israel by 2,000 doctors in pursuit of a pay claim brings the medical system almost to collapse. On 26 Jun the government agrees to independent arbitration.

● **21-22 Mar**: At the EEC summit conference in Brussels, the EMS exchange rates are revised with a revaluation of the DM, the Dutch guilder, the Danish crown and the Belgian and Luxembourg francs, and a devaluation of the French franc, the Italian lira and the Irish pound.

● **25 Mar**: In France, the cabinet approves a tough package of economic measures, including severe restrictions on private spending abroad. On 5 May riot police are involved in serious clashes with protestors demonstrating against the austerity measures.

● **Mar**: The USA introduces a plan to leave farmland fallow because of production surplus and sale problems.

● **Mar**: US president Reagan announces his intention to procure $5 billion for the creation of work.

● **1-4 Apr**: Over 200,000 anti-nuclear protestors hold demonstrations in the UK, Italy, the Netherlands and West Germany. (›22 Oct)

● **20 May**: A car bomb explosion kills 18 and injures around 200 near the air force HQ in Pretoria (SA). The ANC (African National Congress) claims responsibility. On 23 May South African jets attack ANC bases in Mozambique in retaliation.

● **28-30 May**: An economic summit of the seven major industrial nations discusses measures for the recovery of the world economy.

● **Jun**: The Argentinean currency unit is changed from the Peso Ley to the Peso Argentino. The new unit is worth 10,000 of the old.

● **18 Jul**: Seven members of the environmental protection group Greenpeace are seized when their ship *Rainbow Warrior* is caught by a Soviet gunboat, after they landed illegally at a Soviet whaling station in Siberia.

● **23 Jul**: Rebels from Sri Lanka's Tamil minority kill 13 government soldiers, sparking off ethnic riots. The eventual death toll reaches 350.

● **7-14 Aug**: The first official World Athletics championships are held in Helsinki. Daley Thompson (UK) adds the World Athletics title to his Olympic and Commonwealth titles.

● **25 Sep**: 38 prisoners, members of the IRA, escape in a mass breakout from the Maze prison in Northern Ireland.

● **26 Sep**: *Australia II* (skipper John Bertrand) becomes the first boat to take the Americas Cup from the New York Yacht Club.

● **5 Oct**: Richard Noble (UK) takes the world land-speed record, reaching 633.6 mph in a jet-powered car in Nevada, USA.

● **22 Oct**: Vast crowds in cities throughout Europe, including over 600,000 demonstrators in West Germany, gather to protest against the planned installation of US medium-range nuclear missiles in Europe.

● **14 Nov**: The first cruise missiles arrive in the UK from the USA. On 15 Nov 141 peace campaigners, mostly women, are arrested during violent demonstrations outside the Greenham Common air base, while more protest at the House of Commons.

● **25 Nov**: Thieves steal £26 million worth of gold bullion and diamonds from a warehouse near Heathrow Airport, London.

● **12 Dec**: The terrorist group Islamic Jihad carries out six bombings in Kuwait, two at the US and French embassies.

● **17 Dec**: A car bomb planted by the IRA explodes outside Harrods department store in London, killing six and wounding 90 more (UK).

● **Dec**: The US $ reaches a new peak in Europe.

● Large areas of Ethiopia are reported to be in the grip of the worst drought since 1973, bringing famine to at least a million. Disruptions caused by civil war compound the effects of drought.

● Lech Walesa, leader of the Polish trade union Solidarity, is awarded the Nobel Peace Prize.

● Nobel Prize for Economic Sciences is won by Gerard Debreu (Fr/USA).

CULTURE

● **15 Apr**: King Juan Carlos opens the largest ever exhibition of the work of artist Salvador Dali, in Madrid (Sp).

● **25 May**: The film *Return of the Jedi*, a sequel to *Star Wars*, grosses a record $6.2 million on its opening day (USA).

● **20 Nov**: Nearly 100 million in the USA watch the TV film *The Day After* on the effects of nuclear attack.

● **28 Nov**: Premiere of Olivier Messiaen's opera *Saint François d'Assise* in Paris.

● **6 Dec**: A record £8,140,000 is paid at Sotheby's auction rooms for a 12th-century manuscript, the most ever paid at auction for a single object.

● Salman Rushdie: *Shame*, novel (UK).

● Peter Handke: *Der Chinese des Schmerzes*, novella (Aut).

● Alice Walker's novel *The Color Purple* wins the Pulitzer Prize (USA).

● Nobel Prize for Literature is won by William Golding (UK).

● Harrison Birtwistle: *The Mask of Orpheus*, opera (first performed London, 1986) (UK).

● Steve Reich: *The Desert Music*, for ensemble (first performed Cologne, 1984) (USA).

● Hans Werner Henze: *The English Cat*, opera (FRG).

● Merce Cunningham: *Quartets*, dance pieces (USA).

● Singer Madonna shows her navel and wears underwear as outerwear (USA).

● Jorg Immendorf: *Café Deutschland Hörerwunsch*, painting (FRG).

● Mimmo Paladino: *Noa Noa*, painting (It).

● Brad Davis: *Evening Shore*, painting (USA).

● Bridget Riley: *Midi*, painting (UK).

● Nancy Graves: *Triped*, sculpture (USA).

● Bulgarian-born artist Christo wraps 11 islands in Biscayne Bay, Miami, Florida (USA) with 600,000 m sq (6.5 million sq ft) of pink polypropylene fabric.

● Ricardo Bofill: Les Espaces d'Abraxas, Marne-la-Vallée (Fr).

● Arata Isozaki: Tsukuba Civic Center (Jap).

● Former architect Rifat Ozbek (Tur) shows his first fashion collection in London.

● Chanel's new design director Karl Lagerfeld begins to modernize the Chanel style (Fr).

● Release of *Terms of Endearment*, directed by James Brooks and starring Shirley MacLaine, Debra Winger and Jack Nicholson (USA).

● Release of *The Year of Living Dangerously*, directed by Peter Weir, which is set in Indonesia in 1965 (Aus).

● Andrei Tarkovsky: *Nostalgia* (USSR).

SCIENCE

● **23 Mar**: President Reagan announces the beginning of the so-called "Star Wars" (Strategic Defence Initiative or SDI) program. The principal anti-missile weapons are to be short wavelength lasers (USA).

● **23 Mar**: Artificial heart recipient Barney Clark dies after 112 days (USA).

● **13 Jun**: US *Pioneer 10* crosses the orbit of Neptune, becoming the first spacecraft to travel beyond the known planets.

● **16 Jun**: First flight of European satellite-launching rocket *Ariane*, on its sixth attempt.

● **18 Jun**: Sally Ride, mission specialist aboard *Challenger* on its second flight (first launched 4 Apr), becomes the first US woman in space.

● **Jun**: Work begins on construction of new "millimeter" telescope on Mauna Kea mountain in Hawaii. It will be the world's largest radio telescope (USA).

● **Aug**: IBM introduces the first personal computer with a hard disk memory device, PC-XT.

● **17 Oct**: Reports published by the Environment Protection Agency and National Academy of Sciences (USA) predict serious problems may arise due to global warming, the warming-up of the earth through the "greenhouse effect" caused by the build-up of CO_2 through burning of fossil fuels.

● **Oct**: Soviet spaceprobes *Venera 15* and *Venera 16* arrive in orbit round Venus, mapping the surface of the planet.

● **28 Nov**: The first flight of Skylab, an orbiting laboratory, launched by the reserviced shuttle *Columbia* (USA).

● The Nobel Prize for Chemistry is won by Henry Taube (USA) for his discovery of the basic mechanism of chemical reactions.

● The Nobel Prize for Physics is won by W. Fowler and S. Chandrasekhar (USA) for their work on nuclear "burning" in stars and on processes which take place when stars burn out and collapse into white dwarfs.

● The Nobel Prize for Physiology or Medicine is won by Barbara McClintock (USA) for her work on mobile genetic elements, revealing the significance of translocated genes.

● A microchip with 1 billion bits per qcm is developed in Japan.

● A method is developed for dating ancient objects based on chemical changes in obsidian.

● The HIV retrovirus, from which AIDS can result, is identified.

● A.W. Murray and J.W. Szostak create the first artificial chromosome.

● First observation of W and Z particles by C. Rubbia and colleagues at CERN confirms the electroweak theory.

The horrors of starvation in Ethiopia, dramatically presented to the world by television, prompted a variety of plans to raise money for famine relief. In Brighton IRA terrorists bombed the Grand Hotel in hope of killing prime minister Thatcher and most of her cabinet, while in Delhi Sikh extremists suborned members of prime minister Indira Gandhi's bodyguard into assassinating her. Her son Rajiv succeeded her, but was unable to prevent hundreds of deaths in attacks on innocent Sikhs throughout India. Within weeks India suffered another man-made disaster: many thousands were killed or blinded by toxic methyl isocyanate gas escaping from a storage tank in a chemical plant in Bhopal owned by a US-based company. The rise of racial conflict in South Asia exemplified by Hindu-Sikh riots extended to Sri Lanka, where Tamil separatists resorted to increasing violence and government forces responded in kind.

▲ **The IRA explode a bomb at the Grand Hotel, Brighton (UK) during the Conservative party conference.**

- **1 Jan**: Brunei achieves independence after 95 years as a British protectorate.

- **3 Jan**: In Nigeria, a 19-member Supreme Military Council under Gen. Muhammad Buhari takes office.

- **9 Jan**: In Jordan, parliament is reconvened for the first time in 10 years. On 12 Mar voters go to the polls for the first time in 17 years. For the first time in national elections, women are allowed to vote.

- **10 Jan**: Opposition leader Benazir Bhutto, daughter of the late premier Zulfikar Ali Bhutto, is released from house arrest in Karachi (Pak).

- **17 Jan**: 35-nation East/West conference on disarmament in Europe opens in Stockholm.

- **6–7 Feb**: Shi'ite Muslim and Druse militias take control of most of West Beirut. The deterioration of the situation prompts withdrawal of the international peacekeeping force. (›5 Mar)

- **9 Feb**: Death of Soviet premier Yuri Andropov, aged 69, of kidney failure. On 13 Feb he is succeeded by Konstantin Chernenko, aged 72, as General Secretary of the Communist party, who on 11 Apr becomes president of the Supreme Soviet.

- **16 Feb**: South Africa and Zambia announce joint steps to establish an effective ceasefire in the border war.

- **29 Feb**: Pierre Trudeau, prime minister of Canada and leader of the Canadian Liberal party for 15 years, resigns. He is succeeded by the Conservative leader John Mulroney in the general election in Sep.

- **1 Mar**: A joint South African-Angolan monitoring commission begins supervision of withdrawal of South African troops from Angola.

- **5 Mar**: President Gemayel of Lebanon declares that the 1983 troop withdrawal agreement with Israel will now be considered null and void.

- **16 Mar**: South Africa and Mozambique sign an anti-guerrilla accord.

- **3 Apr**: A military coup in Guinea follows the death on 26 Mar of president Sekou Touré.

- **17 Apr**: Policewoman Yvonne Fletcher is killed and 11 injured when a gunman fires from the Libyan embassy on demonstrators in St James's Square in London. On 22 Apr the UK severs relations with Libya.

- **20 Apr**: Following talks in Beijing, UK Foreign Secretary Geoffrey Howe confirms that the UK will withdraw from administration of Hong Kong in 1997. The treaty returning Hong Kong to China is signed on 19 Dec.

- **5–7 Jun**: Hundreds die when Indian troops storm the holiest Sikh shrine, the Golden Temple at Amritsar, which militant Sikh separatists had been occupying in a bid for their own state. On 11 Jun Sikh soldiers mutiny at eight army bases in protest. (›31 Oct)

- **3 Aug**: Upper Volta is renamed Burkina Faso.

- **12 Aug**: In Northern Ireland, one person dies and 20 are injured in clashes between Republicans and police at a rally in Belfast. (›12 Oct)

- **13 Aug**: At the request of the Egyptian government, British, US and French warships go to the Suez Canal to clear mines laid by unknown terrorists. (›Aug)

- **13 Aug**: A federation between Libya and Morocco is established.

- **21 Aug**: Thousands of Filipinos gather in Manila to mark the anniversary of the death of opposition leader Benigno Aquino and to protest against the US-backed dictatorship of president Marcos.

- **Aug**: Equipment and experts are sent by several countries to clear the Red Sea of mines placed by a group of Shi'ite Muslim fanatics, the Islamic Jihad. (›20 Sep)

- **3 Sep**: In South Africa, at least 14 are killed in rioting in Sharpeville and other black townships around Johannesburg after a new constitution, which gives limited concessions to Asians and those of mixed race, but none to blacks, comes into force.

- **17 Sep**: France announces an agreement with Libya for withdrawal of all French and Libyan forces from Chad by mid-Nov.

- **17 Sep**: In South Africa, the first 19-member multiracial cabinet is sworn in.

- **20 Sep**: In Lebanon, a bomb explosion set off by an Islamic Jihad suicide bomber at the US embassy in Beirut kills 20.

- **12 Oct**: The IRA launch a bomb attack on the Grand Hotel in Brighton (UK), where most of the British cabinet are staying during the Conservative party annual conference. Prime minister Thatcher is unhurt, but 5 die and 32 are injured.

- **31 Oct**: Indian prime minister Indira Gandhi is assassinated by two Sikhs from her security guard. Her son Rajiv Gandhi is immediately sworn in as her successor. Over 1,000 die in the violence that follows as Hindu mobs seek revenge on the Sikh community. (›19 Dec)

- **6 Nov**: Ronald Reagan is reelected as US president in a landslide victory.

- **6 Nov**: President Pinochet of Chile declares a state of siege in response to terrorist violence and popular unrest.

- **14–15 Nov**: South African police round up 2,300 black workers in raids on a black township.

- **25 Nov**: Uruguay holds its first elections since 1971. A civilian government is to take over from the military in Mar 1985.

- **19 Dec**: Rajiv Gandhi wins the Indian general election by a huge majority.

SOCIETY

• **3 Jan**: Tunisia declares a state of emergency after widespread riots over food price rises.

• **25 Jan**: Staff at Government Communications HQ (GCHQ) are deprived of the right to belong to a trade union, in the interests of national security. Despite appeals the ban is unanimously upheld by the House of Lords on 22 Nov (UK).

• **7–19 Feb**: At the Winter Olympics in Sarajevo (Yug), British skaters Jayne Torvill and Christopher Dean take the gold medal for ice dancing with their exciting interpretation of Ravel's *Bolero*.

• **17–24 Feb**: French lorry drivers blockade roads on French/Italian borders to protest a variety of grievances, including delays by customs officials.

• **Feb**: New legislation is passed regarding the control of banks and the credit system (FRG).

• **12 Mar**: Mineworkers stage a coal strike in over 100 pits throughout the UK, in a protest against layoffs and mine closures scheduled by the Coal Board. Police and mineworkers, under their militant union leader Arthur Scargill, clash violently throughout the next months. Miners start to return to work in Nov.

• **24 Mar**: Red Brigade terrorists rob a Rome security company of $21.8 million.

• **24 Mar**: Civil servant Sarah Tisdall is jailed for six months for passing on classified information about the arrival in the UK of US cruise missiles to a daily newspaper (UK).

• **30 Mar**: The USA and several South American nations agree to a package of loans totaling $5 billion to aid Argentina with international debts.

• **Apr**: White South African runner Zola Budd joins the British Olympic team, after a controversial campaign to provide her with a British passport as a way of avoiding the ban on South African athletes.

• **14 May**: West German metalworkers strike for a shorter week. The strike lasts until 2 Jul and involves 440,000 workers.

• **May**: Stock markets all round the world see billions of dollars wiped off the value of shares, following a big fall on Wall St caused by fears of a global interest rates war.

• **7–9 Jun**: At an economic summit of the seven major industrial nations to discuss the world economic situation, a new package of proposals to meet the problem of international debt is agreed.

• **12–14 Jun**: Third summit of Comecon in Moscow, the first for 15 years, issues a declaration on intensified economic cooperation.

• **7 Jul**: Czech-born tennis star Martina Navratilova, now a US citizen, wins the women's singles title at Wimbledon for the fifth time.

• **18 Jul**: 21 die when a gunman opens fire at McDonalds hamburger restaurant in San Ysidro near San Diego (USA).

• **28 Jul–12 Aug**: The Los Angeles Olympic Games is boycotted by the USSR and all Eastern European countries except Romania, on the pretext of security fears and revulsion at commercialism, in fact as retaliation for US boycott of the Moscow Olympics in 1980.

• **25 Aug**: Fears of nuclear pollution grow when the French freighter *Mont Louis*, carrying radioactive cargo, collides with a ferry and sinks in the North Sea. All cargo is later recovered.

• **Sep**: President Reagan refuses governmental support for the troubled US steel industry.

• **24 Oct**: The Ethiopian government appeals for massive help to save an estimated 6.4 million facing starvation, but Western aid is hampered by bureaucracy and internal feuding in Ethiopia. By the end of the year, the death toll is around 900,000.

• **31 Oct**: OPEC cuts oil production in an effort to keep prices at the official level of $29 per barrel.

• **3 Nov**: Over 200,000 attend the funeral of "workers' priest" Father Jerzy Popieluszko, a supporter of the union Solidarity, who was kidnapped by the police and found murdered on 30 Oct. On 16 Dec the worst clash of the year takes place between police and Solidarity supporters in Gdansk (Pol). (>7 Feb 1985)

• **20 Nov**: British Telecom shares go on sale as part of the Conservative government's privatization plans in the UK – the largest share issue in the world, four times oversubscribed.

• **4 Dec**: In Sri Lanka, several hundred die in two weeks of violence precipitated by Tamil separatists.

• **4 Dec**: Bolivian unions end a week-long general strike that crippled most of Bolivia, ending a year of high prices and strikes.

• **8 Dec**: The third Lomé "trade and aid" pact links the EEC with 65 African, Caribbean and Pacific countries.

• **Dec**: A toxic gas leakage at the US chemical company Union Carbide in Bhopal, India, causes at least 2,500 deaths and affects a further 200,000 with blindness, and liver and kidney problems.

• There are now 18 "special economic zones" in China where foreign investors may operate with Chinese labor outside of normal customs duties and other regulations. (The first four opened in 1979).

• The Nobel Peace Prize is awarded to Bishop Desmond Tutu, general secretary of the South African National Council of Churches, for his nonviolent struggle against apartheid.

• Nobel Prize for Economic Sciences is won by Richard Stone (UK).

CULTURE

• **24 Mar**: Premiere of Philip Glass's opera *Akhnaten* in Stuttgart.

• **23–29 May**: Steven Spielberg's film *Indiana Jones and the Temple of Doom* grosses a record $45.7 million in its opening week (USA).

• **5 Aug**: Welsh-born actor Richard Burton dies in Geneva, aged 58.

• **Dec**: Top names in pop music are brought together by singer Bob Geldof to form Band Aid and produce a chart-topping single called "Do They Know it's Christmas?" for famine relief in Ethiopia.

• Keri Hulme's novel *The Bone People* (NZ) wins the Booker Prize.

• Milan Kundera: *The Unbearable Lightness of Being*, novel (Fr).

• Seamus Heaney: *Station Island*, poems (Ire).

• Sarah Kirsch: *Katzenleben*, poems (FRG).

• Joseph Heller: *God Knows*, novel in the form of a monologue by King David of Israel (USA).

• Nobel Prize for Literature is won by Jaroslav Seifert (Cze).

• Actor Anthony Sher causes a sensation in the Royal Shakespeare Company's new production of *Richard III* (UK).

• Michael Tippett: *The Mask of Time*, choral work (UK).

• Luciano Berio: *Un re in ascolto* (A King Listens) opera (It).

• Karlheinz Stockhausen's *Samstag aus Licht* (FRG) is first performed in Milan.

• Prince's album *Purple Rain* is a bestseller (USA).

• Michael Jackson's album *Thriller* sells over 37 million copies, breaking all records, and makes a profit of over $75 million (USA).

• Sandro Chia: *I am a Fisherman*, painting (It).

• James Stirling and Michael Wilford: Neue Staatsgalerie, Stuttgart (FRG).

• Norman Foster and Associates: Hong Kong and Shanghai Bank, Hong Kong.

• Release of *The Killing Fields*, directed by Roland Joffe (UK).

• Wim Wenders: *Paris, Texas* (USA).

• Krzysztof Kieslowski: *No End*, film (Pol).

• Release of the film of E.M. Forster's novel *A Passage to India*, directed and scripted by Sir David Lean.

• Woody Allen: *Broadway Danny Rose* (USA).

• Katherine Hamnett's fashion collection is inspired by women's antinuclear protests at Greenham Common air base (UK).

• The TV dramatization of Paul Scott's Raj Quartet of novels about India on the eve of independence, *The Jewel in the Crown*, with Dame Peggy Ashcroft and Tim Pigott-Smith, is a runaway success (UK).

SCIENCE

• **2 Feb**: The first successful embryo transplant is performed when a sterile woman has an embryo taken from another woman implanted in her womb (USA).

• **7 Feb**: US astronaut Bruce McCandless becomes the first man to fly in space with the aid of back pack, without a safety line.

• **11 Apr**: The crew of US space shuttle *Challenger* complete the first repair of a satellite in orbit.

• **1 Aug**: Peatcutter Andy Mould discovers the body of "Lindow Man", a body preserved in a peat bog for over 2,000 years (Ire).

• A. Wilson and R. Higuchi are the first to clone genes from an extinct species; they extract genes from the preserved skin of a quagga, a kind of zebra (USA).

• S.A. Willadsen successfully clones sheep.

• The American Heart Association lists smoking as a risk factor for strokes.

• The World Congress of *In Vitro* Fertilization and Embryo Transfer is held in Helsinki (Fin).

• Birth of a "chimaera", a cross between a sheep and a goat, made by wrapping embryonic cells from a goat in cells from a sheep embryo and implanting the mix into a sheep (UK).

• First successful surgery on a fetus before birth is carried out by W.H. Clewall (USA).

• Two further rings of Saturn are discovered by J.C. Bhattacharya and colleagues (Ind).

• D. Shechtman, I. Blech, D. Gratias and J.W. Cahn discover the first quasicrystal (USA).

• IBM introduce a megabit RAM memory chip with four times the memory of previous chips.

• Genetic "fingerprinting" – the identification of certain core sequences of DNA unique to an individual – is developed by Alec Jeffreys (UK).

• Optical disks for data storage are introduced.

• C. Rubbia and colleagues at CERN announce their evidence for the top quark and for monojets, particles predicted by super symmetry theories.

• The Nobel Prize for Physics is won by Simon van der Meer (Neth) and Carlo Rubbia (It) for their joint discovery of W and Z bosons, particles which carry "weak force".

• The Nobel Prize for Chemistry is won by Bruce Merrifield (USA) for the development of a technique for synthesizing sections of protein molecules.

• The Nobel Prize for Physiology or Medicine is won by Georg Kohler (FRG) and César Milstein (UK) for work on the making of monoclonal antibodies, and Niels Jerne (Den) for his studies of the immune system.

Anxiety concerning the natural environment was rising throughout the 1980s and, in September 1985 British scientists in Antarctica discovered a hole in the ozone layer, which protects the Earth from excessive ultraviolet radiation. Damage to the ozone layer had been predicted earlier, but this dramatic proof engaged the concern of ordinary people. At the sharp end of the environmental movement, Greenpeace members, operating from their ship "Rainbow Warrior", demonstrated considerable courage in attempting to impede Japanese whaling and French nuclear tests. The ship was about to sail for the French Pacific test site when she blew up in Auckland harbor, killing one person. New Zealand investigators later charged two people, who turned out to be agents of the French government. The activities of other hooligans, running amok in the Heysel stadium in Brussels, resulted in the deaths of 41 – mainly Italian – soccer fans and the banning of English teams from European football competitions. In June, new Russian premier Mikhail Gorbachev announced a policy of "perestroika" and set in motion the momentous events of the late 1980s and early 1990s in Eastern Europe.

▲ The horrific scale of the famine in Ethiopia brought a massive response from the Western public, who alone gave over £50 million through Bob Geldof's Live Aid concerts in 1985. But relief efforts were hampered by bureaucracy and mistrust in Ethiopia, exacerbated by ongoing civil warfare.

● **2 Jan**: The USA officially withdraws from UNESCO. The UK follows on 31 Dec.

● **7 Jan**: Vietnamese in occupied Kampuchea launch an attack against the non-Communist Khmer People's National Liberation Front (KPNLF) causing thousands of civilians and resistance fighters to seek refuge in Thailand.

● **14 Jan**: The Israeli cabinet decides on a three-stage withdrawal from occupied Lebanon, beginning in Feb.

● **20 Jan**: President Ronald Reagan is sworn in for a second term of office (USA).

● **25 Jan**: In South Africa, president Botha opens a new three-chamber parliament for whites, Indians and coloreds.(›15 Aug)

● **5 Feb**: In Gibraltar, the frontier with Spain is reopened after 16 years. Talks begin in Geneva between British and Spanish foreign ministers on the future of "The Rock".

● **25 Feb**: In Pakistan, 38 former members of the banned Pakistan People's party win seats in elections to the National Assembly, despite a ban by president Zia on political parties in the contest. On 2 Mar Zia announces major constitutional changes increasing presidential power. On 30 Dec he ends martial law.

● **28 Feb**: Eight police and a civilian die in an IRA bomb attack on Newry police station in Co. Down, Northern Ireland. (›27 Nov)

● **1 Mar**: Julio Sanguinetti takes office as Uruguay's first elected president for 12 years.

● **10 Mar**: President Karamanlis of Greece resigns after prime minister Papandreou puts forward proposals to curb the powers of the presidency.

● **10 Mar**: Death of Soviet premier Konstantin Chernenko, aged 73. On 11 Mar Mikhail Gorbachev succeeds him as General Secretary of the Communist party; on 2 Jul Andrei Gromyko becomes president.

● **12 Mar–23 Apr**: A new round of arms limitation talks takes place between the USSR and USA in Geneva. (›19 Nov)

● **21 Mar**: In South Africa 19 die and 36 are injured when police fire on a crowd of blacks in Uitnhage on the 25th anniversary of the Sharpeville Massacre. On 22 Mar president Botha announces a judicial commission of inquiry after international condemnation. (›20 Jul)

● **6 Apr**: In Sudan, president Gaafar Nimeiri is overthrown in a bloodless coup led by Gen. Abdul-Rahman Suwar al-Dahab.

● **11 Apr**: Death of Enver Hoxha, Albanian head of state for over 40 years. He is succeeded by Ramiz Alia.

● **22 Apr**: José Sarney becomes Brazil's first civilian president for 21 years.

● **14 May**: In Sri Lanka, 146 die during Tamil separatist attacks in the holy city of Anuradhapura.

● **13 Jun**: The coalition government of Mario Soares of Portugal collapses. On 6 Oct, the Social Democrats form a new government.

● **17 Jun**: South Africa names a new multiracial administration in Southwest Africa/Namibia but retains the right to defend the country and dictate foreign policy. SWAPO insurgency continues.

● **20 Jul**: The South African government declares a state of emergency in 36 districts. On 29 Jul it is reported that 1,215 have been arrested and 18 killed since the start of the state of emergency. (›15 Aug)

● **24 Jul**: After Sikh extremist attacks in India, prime minister Rajiv Gandhi reaches agreement with moderate Sikh leaders designed to lessen their hostility toward central government, but on 20 Aug moderate Sikh leader Sant Harchand Singh Longowol is assassinated by Sikh extremists.

● **27 Jul**: Ugandan president Milton Obote is ousted in a bloodless coup led by Brig. Basilio Olara Okello.

● **15 Aug**: President Botha reaffirms South African commitment to apartheid and rules out the possibility of parliamentary representation for blacks. On 30 Aug 28 are reported dead in three days of violence in townships around Cape Town. (›18 Oct)

● **17 Aug**: 60 die and 100 are injured in a car bomb explosion in Christian East Beirut. On 19 Aug a Christian revenge car bomb explosion in the Muslim quarter of Beirut kills and injures 89.

● **13 Sep**: The UK government expels 25 Soviet diplomats and officials named as KGB officers. On 14 Sep the USSR expels 25 British diplomats from Moscow. Further expulsions follow.

● **1 Oct**: Israeli bombers attack the PLO HQ in Tunis, killing 60, in retaliation for the murder of three Israelis by the PLO in Cyprus. On 7 Oct Palestinian guerrillas hijack the Italian liner *Achille Lauro* in the Mediterranean, and murder a US hostage.

● **18 Oct**: Benjamin Moloise, black activist and poet, is hanged for the murder of a policeman despite worldwide protests and riots in Johannesburg (SA).

● **25 Oct**: The Argentinean government imposes a 60-day state of siege to facilitate government efforts to combat right-wing violence.

● **27 Oct**: Julius Nyerere retires as president of Tanzania and is succeeded by Ali Hassan Mwinyi.

● **19–21 Nov**: President Reagan and Mikhail Gorbachev meet in Geneva. They issue a joint statement that nuclear war could not be won and must never be fought, and that neither will seek military superiority.

● **27 Nov**: Anglo-Irish accord is passed, giving Eire consultatative rights in the running of Northern Ireland. In the UK, Ulster Unionist MPs stage a mass resignation from the House of Commons.

SOCIETY

- **Jan**: Jacques Delors, chairman of the EC Commission, publishes a plan for the realization of European integration by the establishment of a European market.

- **5 Feb**: Libya releases four detained UK nationals after negotiations by the archbishop of Canterbury's envoy Terry Waite.

- **7 Feb**: In Poland, four secret police officers are convicted of the murder of Father Jerzy Popieluszko, an outspoken supporter of Solidarity whose death in Oct 1984 provoked considerable unrest. (›1 May)

- **9 Apr**: The Japanese prime minister urges his countrymen to buy foreign goods to resolve Japan's foreign trade surplus.

- **15 Apr**: South Africa announces an end to the ban on mixed marriages. The move is criticized by conservatives and anti-apartheid activists alike.

- **1 May**: 10,000 Solidarity supporters clash with police during a May Day parade (Pol).

- **1 May**: The USA imposes a total trade and financial embargo on the Sandinista regime in Nicaragua. On 12 Jun the House of Representatives votes to allocate $27 million in nonmilitary aid to the Contra rebels fighting to overthrow the government.

- **2–4 May**: Economic summit of the seven major industrial nations in Bonn agrees measures against inflation and a reduction of budget deficits. There is disagreement over a possible program to curtail drug abuse.

- **28 May**: The UK is found guilty of sex discrimination in immigration policy by the European Parliament.

- **29 May**: 41 die at Heysel Stadium, Brussels (Bel), as a result of British soccer hooliganism against Italian and Belgian fans. On 2 Jun the UEFA bans UK soccer clubs from Europe indefinitely.

- **3 Jun**: The Vatican and Italy ratify a concordat that reduces the privileges of the church. Roman Catholicism is no longer the state religion, and compulsory Roman Catholic instruction in schools ends.

- **8 Jun**: Barry McGuigan (UK) beats Panamanian Eusebio Pedroza to win the WBA featherweight boxing championship.

- **11 Jun**: 25 Western agents, jailed in East Germany and Poland, are handed over in West Berlin in exchange for four Eastern Europeans convicted of espionage.

- **14 Jun**: In efforts to beat inflation, currently running at 1,000 percent, Argentina introduces the new austral to replace the peso; it is worth around 1,000 times more. Salaries and prices are to be frozen.

- **Jun**: In a key speech on the future economic development of the USSR, new Soviet leader Mikhail Gorbachev announces a policy of *perestroika* (reconstruction).

- **7 Jul**: West German Boris Becker, aged 17, becomes the youngest ever winner of the men's singles tennis title at Wimbledon.

- **10 Jul**: The *Rainbow Warrior*, a ship belonging to the environmental pressure group Greenpeace, is torn apart by explosions in Auckland harbor (NZ), just before leading a flotilla of vessels in a protest against French nuclear testing at Mururoa Atoll; one man dies. French agents later accept responsibility, causing a political row.

- **20 Jul**: The OAU ends a three-day meeting in Addis Ababa, Ethiopia, with a declaration that most African nations are on the brink of collapse.

- **6 Aug**: In Japan, 55,000 take part in ceremonies at Hiroshima marking the 40th anniversary of the atomic bombing of the city in World War II.

- **27 Aug**: President Botha announces that South Africa will impose a four-month freeze of repayment of foreign debt, following the refusal of international bankers to extend credit because of the worsening internal political situation and his refusal to consider immediate reforms. (›9 Sep)

- **30 Aug–1 Sep**: Salvage experts locate the wreck of the *Titanic*, which sank on the Atlantic seabed south of Newfoundland (Can) in 1912.

- **9 Sep**: Reagan announces selective US economic sanctions against South Africa. On 10 Sep the foreign ministers of the nine full members of EEC and two future members approve sanctions against South Africa.

- **19 Sep**: An estimated 20,000 die in a massive earthquake in Mexico City measuring 7.8 on the Richter Scale, followed by a further quake next day.

- **28 Sep**: Riots erupt in Brixton, south London, after a black woman, Cherry Groce, is shot during a police raid. On 6 Oct the death of a black woman in Tottenham, north London, during a police search sparks off violent clashes in which one policeman dies.

- **Sep**: The World Health Organization declares AIDS an epidemic.

- **Oct**: UNCTAD conference in Geneva publishes declaration on economic support for developing countries.

- **13 Nov**: In Colombia, at least 25,000 are believed dead when Nevado del Ruiz volcano erupts, swamping the town of Armero and surrounding a vast area with ash and mud.

- **8–9 Dec**: OPEC leaders meeting in Geneva agree to abolish oil production quotas so as to force non-OPEC members to restrain output.

- Sharp's QT50 pastel-colored radio cassette player is the first Japanese "lifestyle" product to reach the West.

- Nobel Peace Prize is won by the International Physicians for the Prevention of Nuclear War.

- Nobel Prize for Economic Sciences is won by Franco Modigliani (USA).

CULTURE

- **18 Apr**: A new world record is set for the sale of a painting when Mantegna's *Adoration of the Magi* is sold at Christie's auction rooms for £8.1 million ($10.4 million) (UK).

- **13 Jul**: Singer Bob Geldof brings together international stars including Mick Jagger, David Bowie, Dire Straits and Queen in two simultaneous Live Aid concerts staged at London's Wembley Stadium and JFK Stadium in Philadelphia, to raise money for famine victims in Ethiopia. Over 1.5 billion worldwide watch and donate over £50 million.

- **17 Sep**: Fashion designer Laura Ashley dies, aged 60. Her clothes and furnishings changed the style of a generation (UK).

- **2 Oct**: Film actor Rock Hudson dies aged 59 after a long struggle against AIDS (USA).

- **10 Oct**: Death of US film director Orson Welles, whose 1940 film *Citizen Kane* became a classic.

- Gabriel García Márquez: *Love in the Time of Cholera*, novel (Col).

- Amy Clampitt: *What the Light was Like*, novel (USA).

- Anita Brookner's novel *Hotel du Lac* wins the Booker Prize (UK).

- Vaclav Havel: *Temptation*, play (Cze).

- Alison Lurie's novel *Foreign Affairs* wins the Pulitzer Prize (USA).

- Nobel Prize for Literature is won by Claude Simon (Fr).

- Luigi Nono: *Prometeo-Tragedia dell'ascolto*, for orchestra and tape, in a performance environment specially designed by architect Renzo Piano (It).

- Iannis Xenakis: *Thallein*, for orchestra (Fr).

- Peter Maxwell Davies: Violin Concerto (UK).

- Don Driver: *Bushfire Installation*, a room-sized assemblage with sound tape of gongs and drums (Aus).

- Lucian Freud: *Self-Portrait*, painting (UK).

- Eileen Cooper: *Baby Talk*, painting (UK).

- Bulgarian-born artist Christo wraps the Pont Neuf in Paris with 33,000 sq m (40,000 sq yards) of canvas.

- Rafael Moneo: Museo de Arte Romano, Merida (Sp).

- Jørn Utzon: National Assembly Building (Kuwait).

- Akira Kurosawa: *Ran*, film (Jap).

- Release of *Out of Africa*, based on Karen Blixen's story of her experiences in Africa in the 1920s, starring Meryl Streep and Robert Redford, directed by Sydney Pollack (USA).

- Release of John Boorman's Brazilian rainforest movie *The Emerald Forest* (USA).

- Milos Forman's film *Amadeus* wins seven Oscars (USA).

SCIENCE

- **Sep**: The British Antarctic Survey discovers a hole in the ozone layer over Antarctica, as ozone levels reach an all-time low. Satellite records show that the hole has been forming for several years.

- The Nobel Prize for Chemistry is won by Herbert Hauptman (USA) and Jerome Karle (USA) for their development of a direct method of X-ray crystallography used in determining structures of organic and inorganic molecules and crystals.

- The Nobel Prize for Physics is won by Klaus von Klitzing (FRG) for his work on the behavior of electrons.

- The Nobel Prize for Physiology or Medicine is won by Michael Brown and Joseph Goldstein (USA) for their discovery of genetic mechanisms responsible for abnormal vulnerability to stroke and heart disease.

- Testing takes place of energy production by means of laser-fired nuclear fusion (USA/Jap).

- The Tevatron particle accelerator at Fermilab in Batavia, Illinois, begins operation (USA).

- J. Deisnhofer, R. Huber and H. Michel succeed in determining the exact arrangement of the more than 10,000 atoms composing the protein complex (FRG).

- AT&T Bell Laboratories succeed in sending the equivalent of 300,000 simultaneous phone conversations over a single optical fiber (USA).

- Information on lanxides – crosses between ceramics and metals – is released when the US Defense Dept declassifies this subject.

- The European Space Agency, USSR and Japan all launch spaceprobes to rendezvous with Halley's Comet in Mar 1986. The USA will observe it from a space shuttle orbiter.

- It is confirmed that there is a black hole at the centre of our galaxy, accelerating stars and dust towards itself, after a detailed radio map of the galaxy is made by US radio telescopes.

- B.L. Vallee and colleagues discover the tumor angiogenesis factor, which stimulates the growth of new blood vessels; it is renamed angiogenin.

- Lasers are used for the first time to clean out clogged arteries (USA).

- The gene markers for polycystic kidney disease and for cystic fibrosis are found.

- In the USA, the "synfuels" project, intended to develop new sources of energy from coal or oil shales, loses almost all its funding in reaction to the petroleum glut.

- Peter A. Rona discovers the first deep-sea ocean vents, or hot springs, on the Mid-Atlantic Ridge.

- C.G.Sibley and J.E. Ahlquist use DNA studies to revise the evolutionary history of Australian and New Guinean birds.

The explosion of the no.4 reactor at Chernobyl in the Ukraine confirmed the fears of many people concerning the safety of nuclear power. Human error appeared to have been chiefly responsible, but the structure of the plant itself was called into question. The effects of escaping radiation were felt as far away as Wales. The USA also experienced a devastating accident in a high-technology field when the space shuttle "Challenger" exploded soon after takeoff. The people of the Philippines finally lost patience with the excesses of their dictator-president Marcos. After declaring himself reelected in a transparently fraudulent election, Marcos was overthrown and his opponent Corazon Aquino, widow of the opposition leader assassinated by Marco's agents of 1983, became president. After Libyan harassment of admittedly provocative US naval exercises in the Gulf of Sirte, US warplanes launched raids on Tripoli and Benghazi. President Qadhafi, who was believed to have instigated acts of terrorism in the West, was apparently one of the intended targets.

▲ The US space shuttle *Challenger* exploded on lift-off, killing its seven astronauts, including schoolteacher Christa McAuliffe, who had been selected as the first "citizen in space". The tragedy dealt a devastating blow to the shuttle program, already in trouble because of escalating costs.

● **6 Jan**: Gen. Samuel K. Doe, Liberian head of state since he seized power in 1980, is sworn in as president of a new civilian government.

● **19 Jan**: Rebels seize power in South Yemen after a six-day battle in which thousands die.

● **26 Jan**: The Ugandan National Resistance Army, led by Yoweri Museveni, takes over the capital Kampala and dissolves the government.

● **7 Feb**: President-for-life Jean-Claude "Baby Doc" Duvalier of Haiti flees to France after widespread demonstrations against his regime. Gen. Henri Namphy forms a new National Government.

● **15 Feb**: President Marcos is declared the winner of the 7 Feb presidential election in the Philippines, despite widespread allegations of ballot-rigging. On 24 Feb, following massive defections from the army and civilian protest, he flees abroad with US assistance. His opponent Mrs Corazon Aquino is sworn in as president. (›25 Mar)

● **16 Feb**: Dr Mario Soares becomes the first civilian president of Portugal in 60 years.

● **24 Feb–6 Mar**: 27th Congress of the USSR Communist party in Moscow approves sweeping changes to membership of the Central Committee and Politburo. Prime minister Nikolay Ryzhkov declares that the economy is being undermined by red tape, unrealistic costing and outmoded thinking.

● **28 Feb**: Swedish prime minister Olof Palme is assassinated in Stockholm. Ingvar Carlson succeeds him.

● **2 Mar**: The Australia Bill formally severs Australia's constitutional ties with the UK.

● **3 Mar**: Widespread mob violence and intimidation occurs in Northern Ireland during a 24-hour loyalist strike against the Anglo-Irish agreement.

● **7 Mar**: In South Africa, the state of emergency imposed in 1985 is suspended. During that time 7,996 have been arrested and 757 have died in violent incidents. (›18 Apr)

● **12 Mar**: In a referendum in Spain, voters choose to stay in NATO, but not in its command structure, and to continue to ban nuclear weapons from its territory. It is the first such vote by any of NATO's 16 members.

● **16 Mar**: In the French general election, the two major opposition parties gain a narrow majority, ending five years of Socialist rule. On 20 Mar Jacques Chirac is named prime minister. The French coin the expression "cohabitation" for the subsequent enforced collaboration between Socialist president François Mitterand and the rightwing Chirac.

● **16 Mar**: Swiss voters reject a proposal that Switzerland become a full member of the UN.

● **24 Mar**: US aircraft attack targets in Libya after alleged Libyan missile attacks on US aircraft participating in exercises in the Gulf of Sirte. Libyan president Muammar Qadhafi calls for Arab reprisals and the USSR issues warnings about the threat to world security. Terrorist reprisals follow. (›15 Apr)

● **25 Mar**: In the Philippines, president Aquino dissolves parliament, declares a provisional government, gives herself emergency powers and announces an interim constitution.

● **15 Apr**: US bombers carry out air raids from US warships and from bases in the UK on targets around Tripoli and Benghazi in an attempt to wipe out terrorist bases. Libya retaliates with missiles directed at radar installations on the Italian island of Lampedusa.

● **18 Apr**: The South African government rescinds the pass laws, and announces that those imprisoned or awaiting trial for violations of the laws will be released immediately. (›12 Jun)

● **3 May**: An Air Lanka Tri-star is blown up at Colombo airport by a terrorist bomb thought to have been planted by Tamil separatist guerrillas; 16 are killed. On 18 May, 19 die as Sri Lankan forces attempt to restore government control over the Jaffna peninsula, held by Tamil insurgents for over a year.

● **9 May**: Mrs Gro Harlem Brundtland takes over again as prime minister of Norway and names an 18-person cabinet which includes eight women.

● **19 May**: China and Taiwan hold face to face talks for the first time since 1949.

● **19 May**: South African forces carry out raids on alleged ANC bases in Zambia, Zimbabwe and Botswana, frustrating efforts by the visiting Commonwealth Eminent Persons Group to find a peaceful solution to the race problem. (›12 Jun)

● **8 Jun**: Ex-UN Secretary-General Kurt Waldheim is elected president of Austria, despite allegations of wartime Nazi involvement.

● **12 Jun**: A new state of emergency is declared in anticipation of widespread unrest on the 10th anniversary of the uprising in Soweto on 16 Jun. At least 1,000 black activists are taken into custody under emergency powers, and restrictions imposed on media reporting. On 16 Jun millions of blacks defy the government by refusing to report to work (SA).

● **12 Jun**: The UK government dissolves the Northern Ireland Assembly, set up in 1982.

● **27 Jun**: As a result of New Zealand prime minister Lange's determination to ban visits to New Zealand by nuclear-armed naval vessels, the USA declares itself no longer bound to abide by the ANZUS Pact commitments of 1951 regarding the defence of New Zealand.

SOCIETY   CULTURE   SCIENCE

- **27 Jun**: The International Court of Justice at The Hague rules that US aid to Contra rebels in Nicaragua is illegal. (›13 Nov)

- **2–3 Jul**: In Chile, a strike leaves eight dead, and is accompanied by demands for an end to the almost 13-year-old regime of president Augusto Pinochet Ugarte. (›7 Sep)

- **3 Jul**: The emir of Kuwait dissolves the National Assembly – the only freely elected Arab representative body in the region – after an attempt is made to bomb Kuwait's oil pipelines.

- **14 Aug**: Riots erupt across Pakistan as supporters of Benazir Bhutto's Pakistan People's party demonstrate against the government of president Zia on Pakistan's independence day. Three are shot and Miss Bhutto is arrested by police.

- **7 Sep**: A state of siege is declared in Chile and new restrictions on civil liberties imposed after an assassination attempt on president Pinochet.

- **22 Sep**: 35-nation Stockholm Security conference ends with formal adoption of the first conventional arms agreement since World War II. Also, each side pledges to give the other advance notice of all significant military exercises and the right of inspection.

- **10 Oct**: Juan Pérez de Cuéllar (Peru) is reelected for a second term as UN Secretary-General, from 1 Jan 1987.

- **11–12 Oct**: US president Reagan and Soviet premier Mikhail Gorbachev hold a mini-summit in Reyjavik (Ice), but fail to reach agreement on arms control; the sticking point is Reagan's refusal to abandon the SDI ("Star Wars") program.

- **15 Oct**: Gen. Ershad gains an overwhelming victory in the presidential election in Bangladesh, but the opposition parties boycott the election and ballot-rigging is alleged.

- **20 Oct**: Yitzhak Shamir takes over from Shimon Peres as prime minister of Israel for a 25-month term under the rotation agreement signed in 1984. Peres takes on Shamir's post as foreign minister.

- **24 Oct**: The UK breaks off relations with Syria because of Syrian government complicity in a plot to blow up an El Al airliner on a flight from London.

- **13 Nov**: The Irangate affair: in a televised speech, Reagan admits secret arms deals with Iran. On 25 Nov US vice-admiral Poindexter (Reagan's National Security Advisor) and Lt Col Oliver North are dismissed from the National Security Council after it is revealed that money from arms sales to Iran has been channeled to Nicaraguan Contra rebels. (›26 Feb 1987)

- **21 Dec**: Chinese police break up demonstrations on the third day of mass protests in Shanghai by students demanding more democracy. On 23 Dec the demonstrations spread to Beijing.

- **1 Jan**: Spain and Portugal become the 11th and 12th members of the EEC.

- **8 Jan**: President Reagan freezes all Libyan government assets in the USA and in US banks overseas because of its role in promoting international terrorism.

- **11 Feb**: USSR dissident Anatoly Shcharansky and three others convicted of spying are released in return for five Eastern Europeans held in the West for spying.

- **12 Feb**: The Channel Tunnel Treaty between Britain and France is signed.

- **26 Apr**: Chernobyl nuclear reactor no.4, near Kiev (USSR), explodes, leading to a huge release of radioactivity that kills and contaminates unknown numbers of people and animals. Food has to be destroyed in many parts of Europe in the following months.

- **4–6 May**: At the economic summit meeting of seven Western leaders in Tokyo, five terrorist rockets explode near the conference center. The summit ends with a declaration on proposals to counter terrorism and a statement on the Chernobyl disaster.

- **25 May**: The "Race Against Time" raises £100 million for famine relief.

- **20 Jun**: A conference of 120 nations in Paris calls for sweeping sanctions against South Africa.

- **7 Jul**: In Malaysia, two Australians become the first foreigners to be hanged for drug trafficking.

- **24 Jul–7 Aug**: 32 out of 88 countries refuse to attend the Commonwealth Games in Edinburgh (UK) in protest against the British government's refusal to implement further sanctions against South Africa.

- **21–22 Aug**: At least 1,700 die in Cameroon after toxic gases erupt from volcanic Lake Nyos.

- **Aug**: After a sudden collapse in the price of crude oil in Jan, OPEC agrees to abide by previously established production quotas. Non-OPEC countries agree to cut production.

- **13–20 Sep**: The ministers of GATT countries meet in Uruguay. The USSR requests affiliation with GATT.

- **Oct**: At the annual meeting of the IMF and World Bank, consultations take place on the situations of the developing countries and their external debts.

- **10 Nov**: Environmental experts report that tonnes of chemicals have accidentally spilled into the River Rhine near Basel (Swi), threatening to destroy all life in the river.

- **19 Dec**: Dissident scientist and Nobel prize winner Andrey Sakharov and his wife Yelena Bonner are permitted to return to Moscow after seven years' internal exile (USSR).

- Nobel Peace Prize is won by Elie Wiesel (USA).

- Nobel Prize for Economic Sciences is won by James M. Buchanan (USA).

- **7 Aug**: Premiere of Harrison Birtwistle's opera *Yan Tan Tethera* in London.

- **31 Aug**: Henry Moore, a dominant influence in 20th-century sculpture, dies aged 88 (UK).

- The Nobel Prize for Literature is won by Wole Soyinka, Nigerian poet and playwright, the first black African to win it.

- In the USSR, Mikhail Gorbachev institutes his policy of *glasnost* (openness), in both the arts and the media, but especially in literature. Many previously banned works published only in the West start to become available to a Soviet readership.

- Kazuo Ishiguro: *An Artist of the Floating World*, novel (Jap).

- Paul Auster: *The New York Trilogy* (*City of Glass*, 1985, *Ghosts* and *The Locked Room*, 1986), novellas (USA).

- Patrick White: *Memoirs of Many in One*, novel (Aus).

- Kingsley Amis (UK) wins the Booker Prize for his novel *The Old Devils*.

- Paul Simon uses black South African musicians on his album *Graceland* (USA).

- Frank Auerbach: *Head of Catherine Lampert*, painting (UK).

- Gilbert and George: *Class War, Militant, Gateway*, photomontage triptych (UK).

- Jeff Koons: *Rabbit*, cast stainless steel sculpture (USA).

- Miranda Payne: *Saint Gargoyle*, in which the artist stands on a wall-mounted pedestal against a poster background of a landscape, playing the part of a figure in the landscape (UK).

- John Jesurun: *Deep Sleep*, in which three characters are imprisoned in a film projected on the walls of the stage, leaving a fourth to man the projector (USA).

- Richard Rogers: Lloyds Headquarters, London (UK).

- Sydney Pollack's film *Out of Africa* wins seven Oscars (USA).

- *The Mission* by Roland Joffe, with Robert De Niro and Jeremy Irons (UK), wins the Grand Prix at the Cannes Film Festival.

- Paul Hogan stars in *Crocodile Dundee*, directed by Peter Faiman (Aus).

- Woody Allen: *Hannah and her Sisters*, with Mia Farrow, Barbara Hershey, Dianne West and Michael Caine (USA).

- *Top Gun* is directed by Tony Scott, with Tom Cruise and Kelly McGillis (USA).

- Andrei Tarkovsky's last film, *The Sacrifice*, made in Sweden, is released.

- **24 Jan**: *Voyager 2* flies within 82,100 km (50,000 miles) of the clouds of Uranus, showing that it has an outer atmosphere of gas, no real surface, and is partly shrouded in reddish-brown fog.

- **28 Jan**: Space shuttle *Challenger* explodes shortly after takeoff, killing its seven astronauts and calling a temporary halt to shuttle launches (USA).

- **14 Mar**: European *Giotto* spaceprobe transmits pictures of Halley's Comet taken at a range of 540 km (335 miles).

- **Dec**: Surgeons at Papworth Hospital, Cambridge (UK), perform the first triple transplant (heart, lung, liver) on a 35-year-old woman.

- The Nobel Prize for Physics is won by Ernst Ruska (FRG), Gerd Binnig (FRG) and Heinrich Rohrer (Swi) for their pioneering work in the development of the electronic microscope.

- The Nobel Prize for Chemistry is won by Dudley Hersbach, Yuan Lee (USA) and John Polanyi (Can) for their work on reaction dynamics.

- The Nobel Prize for Physiology or Medicine is won by Rita Levi-Montalcini and Stanley Cohen (USA) for their work on chemical growth factors controlling growth in animals and humans.

- L. Kunkel and colleagues discover the defective gene in Duchenne muscular dystrophy.

- An eye operation in which a laser is used to remove tissue from the cornea is tested on monkeys.

- Discovery of the homeobox, a sequence of DNA in virtually identical form in all living things, which is thought to control the ordered development of different parts of the body.

- R.A. Weinberg and colleagues discover the first known gene to inhibit growth, in this case of the cancer retinoblastoma (USA).

- The electronic microscope shows the AIDS virus for the first time (USA).

- Climatologists conclude that the "greenhouse effect" has already begun to happen, and will continue.

- There is growing concern over the holes in the ozone layer – that over Antarctica is growing larger annually, and in 1986 one also appears over Spitzbergen.

- First "high" temperature superconductors, at 30 degrees K, are discovered by K.A. Muller (FRG).

- Individual quantum jumps in individual atoms are observed for the first time (USA/FRG).

- It is discovered that the Milky Way and galaxies of the local group, as well as parts of the local supercluster of galaxies, are moving toward a point in the direction of the Southern Cross.

A remarkable solo flight took place in 1987, when German 19-year-old Mathias Rust, who had previously registered only 24 hours flying time, took off in a four-seater Cessna aircraft from Helsinki and, after buzzing the Kremlin landed in Moscow's Red Square, where he amiably signed autographs for bemused citizens. Soviet leaders were not amused; the young man was sentenced to jail (though soon released) and heads rolled among the air defense staff. Perhaps it was fortunate that the first agreement ever between the USA and the USSR on the reduction of their nuclear arsenals had been singed. It was a year of accidents, others far more serious than the failures of Soviet air defense. Nearly 200 died when a cross-Channel ferry capsized off Zeebrugge, and a far greater number when a ferry in the Philippines collided with a tanker. England seemed singled out for disasters, winds of hurricane force causing heavy damage (though surprisingly few human casualties) and a fire in the subway system killing 30 Londoners. Many thousands more died in a dreadful avalanche of mud in Colombia, in worse than usual floods in Bangladesh, and in a series of earthquakes in Ecuador.

▲ Soviet premier Mikhail Gorbachev and his wife Raisa during a visit to Czechoslovakia, which quickly began a process of political and economic reform similar to that set in motion by Gorbachev in the USSR. The Cold War began to crumble with the signature in December of the first ever agreement between the USA and USSR to reduce the size of their nuclear arsenals.

● **16 Jan**: China's Communist party general secretary Hu Yuobang resigns after accepting blame for policy mistakes in handling massive student demonstrations for more democracy.

● **2 Feb**: In a referendum in the Philippines, 81 percent approve a new US-style constitution. On 11 May the first democratic elections for 16 years are held for the Senate and House of Representatives. (›28 Aug)

● **22 Feb**: A force of around 7,000 Syrian troops enters West Beirut at the request of Lebanese leaders in an effort to end fighting between Shia Muslim and Druse forces.

● **26 Feb**: The report of the Tower Commission, appointed to investigate the activities of the National Security Council, says that president Reagan was not fully aware of the way in which the Iran arms sale policy was implemented or of its consequences, and criticizes senior White House staff for their role in the affair (USA).

● **27 Feb**: French-backed Chadian troops of president Habré move into Faya Largeau as Libyan troops retreat north, effectively ending Libya's ambitions in Chad.

● **28 Feb**: Soviet premier Gorbachev proposes an immediate separate agreement on abolition of medium-range nuclear missiles in Europe, dropping his insistence on curtailment of US SDI program. On 8 Dec, USSR and USA sign a treaty to end all intermediate-range nuclear weapons in Europe – the first agreement by the two superpowers to reduce the size of the nuclear arsenals.

● **1 Mar**: In Italy, the Socialist government of Bettino Craxi resigns after 3 ½ years, the longest serving government in Italy since World War II.

● **19 Mar**: In Czechoslovakia, Gustav Husak announces far-reaching political and economic reforms similar to those sought by Gorbachev in the USSR.

● **13 Apr**: China and Portugal sign an agreement for return to Chinese sovereignty in 1999 of Macao, a Portugese colony for 442 years.

● **6 May**: In the South African whites-only general election, the ruling National Party led by P.M. Botha wins an overwhelming victory; a million blacks stay away from work in protest.

● **11 May**: The Indian government imposes direct rule on the Punjab because of the failure of the state government to deal with the Sikh extremists' terror campaign for autonomy.

● **17 May**: 37 US crewmen die when Iraqi Exocet missiles hit USS *Stark* in the Gulf. Iraq apologizes for the attack and says it was a mistake.

● **28 May**: 19-year-old West German pilot Mathias Rust lands his small plane in Moscow's Red Square, having evaded detection by Soviet air defense surveillance on his flight from Helsinki (USSR).

● **1 Jun**: Lebanese prime minister Rashid Karami dies in a bomb explosion aboard his helicopter. Selim Hoss becomes acting prime minister.

● **11 Jun**: The Conservative party is returned with a majority of 101 in the UK general election. Thatcher becomes the first British prime minister for 160 years to be reelected for a third term.

● **21 Jun**: In the USSR, voters in some local government elections are able to select from multicandidate lists for the first time.

● **28 Jun**: In South Korea, government agrees to opposition demands for political change and direct presidential election after three weeks of rioting. 534 political prisoners are released and in the first direct presidential election for 16 years on 16 Dec, Roh Tae Woo wins a substantial majority.

● **19 Jul**: For the first time since the 1974 revolution a single party gains an overall majority in the Portuguese general elections. Anibal Cavaco Silva, leader of the Social Democrats, becomes prime minister.

● **20 Jul**: The UN Security Council unanimously adopts a resolution calling on Iran and Iraq to implement ceasefire in the Gulf.

● **22 Jul**: US navy warships begin escorting Kuwaiti tankers in the Persian Gulf after Iranian threats against shipping there. (›21 Sep)

● **29 Jul**: A peace accord is signed with India to end bloodshed in Sri Lanka between separatist Tamil guerrillas and mainly Sinhalese government. (›5 Oct)

● **7 Aug**: The presidents of Guatemala, El Salvador, Honduras, Nicaragua and Costa Rica sign a plan designed to bring peace to the region.

● **28–29 Aug**: Around 50 die and 275 are injured in the fifth coup attempt against president Aquino since she came to power in the Philippines.

● **10 Sep**: Under a new civilian constitution, Ethiopia is declared a republic, ending 13 years of military rule. Col. Mengistu Haile Mariam is elected president.

● **21 Sep**: US helicopters fire on an Iranian ship caught laying mines in the Persian Gulf, killing five Iranians.

● **5 Oct**: In Sri Lanka, 12 Tamil separatists commit suicide while in custody in Jaffna, sparking off fresh conflict between Tamils, Sinhalese and the Indian peacekeeping force.

● **6 Oct**: After two successive bloodless coups, Fiji is declared a republic. Ratu Sir Penaia Ganilau becomes president.

● **7 Nov**: Habib Bourguiba, president of Tunisia since independence in 1956, is deposed in a bloodless coup led by Zine al-Abidine Ben Ali.

● **29 Nov**: Presidential elections in Haiti are abandoned when at least 23 die in murderous attacks at polling stations by remnants of the Tonton Macoute, ousted dictator Duvalier's secret police.

SOCIETY

- **20 Jan**: In Lebanon, the Archbishop of Canterbury's envoy Terry Waite disappears in Beirut while seeking to negotiate the release of Western hostages.

- **24 Jan**: 162 police and 33 demonstrators are injured in violent riots outside Rupert Murdoch's News International printing plant at Wapping, London. On 5 Feb the print unions decide to end their year-long dispute with the company and stop mass picketing (UK).

- **2 Feb**: Steelworkers in America return to USX Corporation steel mills, ending a work stoppage that began in Aug 1986, the longest strike in US steel history.

- **15 Feb**: The EC commission publishes the Delors package, which includes reformation of agricultural policy, establishment of a structure fund and the introduction of new budget principles.

- **22 Feb**: Intensive economic cooperation and a reduction of differences in the balance of payments are agreed by the major Western industrial nations (Louvre accord).

- **Feb**: EC and the USA plan common measures against Japanese trade restrictions and trade policy.

- **5–6 Mar**: A series of earthquakes in Ecuador leave around 2,000 dead and 75,000 injured.

- **6 Mar**: Townsend Thoresen cross-Channel roll-on roll-off ferry *Herald of Free Enterprise* capsizes off Zeebrugge, Belgium, killing at least 188. The bow doors had been left open, letting water pour into the car deck.

- **10 Mar**: The Roman Catholic church bans conception by artificial methods, including embryo transfers, artificial insemination and surrogate motherhood.

- **Apr**: A conference on external debt among the developing countries discusses a possible suspension of those debts.

- **19 Jun**: In Spain, 17 die in an ETA (Basque separatist) car bomb attack in Barcelona.

- **Jun**: The New Zealand All Blacks win the first Rugby Union World Cup, beating Wales 49–6 – Wales's worst ever defeat.

- **4 Jul**: Nazi Klaus Barbie, known as "The Butcher of Lyon", is jailed for life for war crimes after an eight-week trial in Lyon (Fr).

- **14 Jul**: In Pakistan, 72 die and 250 are injured in two bomb blasts in central Karachi.

- **31 Jul**: Fighting erupts in Mecca, Saudi Arabia, between Saudi police and Iranian religious pilgrims when the Iranians gather for a political demonstration, forbidden under Saudi law. Around 400 die, 275 of them Iranians.

- **9–30 Aug**: South Africa's black National Union of Mineworkers strikes in pursuit of a 30 percent pay claim. Nine die and 300 are injured during the strike.

- **17 Aug**: Ex-Nazi leader Rudolf Hess commits suicide in Spandau prison, Berlin, after spending 40 years there.

- **19 Aug**: In the UK's worst ever mass shooting, 14 die when Michael Ryan runs amok in Hungerford, Berkshire, then shoots himself. Two others die later. On 21 Aug the government announces an urgent review of firearms laws.

- **Aug**: Canadian Ben Johnson breaks the 100m world record with 9.83 secs.

- **4 Sep**: In Bangladesh, over 20 million are reported homeless or facing starvation after the worst floods in the region for 40 years.

- **27 Sep**: In Colombia, at least 175 die in a mudslide in Medellin, and over 300 are buried in rubble.

- **10 Oct**: Poland announces sweeping economic changes, including less government control of wages and prices. On 29 Nov, in a referendum on reform, only 44 percent of voters endorse the government proposals; a third of the electors do not vote.

- **16 Oct**: A freak storm in southeast England sends winds of 149 kph (93 mph) across the country, felling an estimated 15 million trees in the worst storm in the UK for 300 years.

- **19 Oct**: Worldwide stock exchange crash, due to disturbances in the international financial markets.

- **28 Oct**: The US $ slumps on world markets in face of US failure to take action over its $23,000 million budget deficit. On 31 Dec the US $ hits an all-time low against leading currencies in spite of action by central banks.

- **8 Nov**: 11 die and over 60 are injured when an IRA bomb explodes at a Remembrance Day service in Enniskillen, Co. Fermanagh.

- **18 Nov**: In London, 30 die in a fire at Kings Cross underground station (UK).

- **26 Nov**: In Zimbabwe, rebel guerrillas massacre 16 whites at a mission near Bulawayo.

- **3 Dec**: The West German Bundesbank and other European central banks decide to reduce the head interest rates to avoid further financial disturbances.

- **16 Dec**: 338 people are convicted in Palermo in the biggest Mafia trial ever held (It).

- **21 Dec**: Nearly 3,000 die in a ferry disaster in the Philippines. The ferry collided with an oil tanker.

- Work begins on the Channel Tunnel between France and England.

- The Nobel Peace Prize is awarded to president Arias of Costa Rica in recognition of his efforts to bring peace to Central America.

- Nobel Prize for Economic Sciences is won by Robert Solow (USA).

CULTURE

- **30 Mar**: Christie's auction rooms in London sell Van Gogh's painting *Sunflowers* for £24,750,000 ($39.9 million) – a world record for a work of art of any kind. The record is broken on 11 Nov when Christie's in New York sell Van Gogh's *Irises* for £30 million ($53.9 million).

- **2 Apr**: At a sale in Geneva (Swi), jewelry owned by the late Duchess of Windsor sells for £31 million ($50 million) – five times their ordinary retail value as jewels. The proceeds go toward cancer research.

- Mario Vargas Llosa: *The Storyteller*, novel (Peru).

- Peter Redgrove: *The Apple Broadcast*, poems (UK).

- Tom Wolfe: *The Bonfire of the Vanities*, a savage satire on life in New York (USA).

- Nobel Prize for Literature is won by Joseph Brodsky (USA).

- Judith Weir's opera *A Night at the Chinese Opera*, has its first performance (UK).

- John Adams: *Nixon in China*, opera based on the visit of US president Richard Nixon to China in 1972, opens in Houston, Texas, directed by Peter Sellars and with choreography by Mark Morris.

- George Benjamin's *Antara* (UK), for two DX7 synthesizers (using sampled panpipes as sound source) and chamber orchestra, is realized at IRCAM in Paris, using the 4X computer.

- The popularity of Youssou n'Dour and others marks an upsurge of interest in pure African music.

- U2 release *The Joshua Tree* (Ire).

- Georg Baselitz: *Double Painter*, painting (FRG).

- Rainer Fetting: *Embrace at the Pier*, painting (FRG).

- Lucian Freud: *Painter and Model*, painting (UK).

- Jannis Kounellis: *Installation at Walcot Chapel*, Bath (UK).

- Quinlan Terry: Howard Building, Downing College, Cambridge (UK).

- Jean Nouvel: Institut du Monde Arabe, Paris.

- BOOR/A, ELS Design Group and Barton Myers Associates: Portland Centre for the Performing Arts, Portland, Oregan (USA).

- Norman Foster: Century Tower, Tokyo (Jap).

- Krzysztof Kieslowski: *A Short Film About Killing*, one of his "Decalogue" cycle of films based on the Ten Commandments (Pol).

- Godfrey Reggio: *Powaqqatsi*, film, with music by Philip Glass (USA).

- Jack Nicholson plays the devil in *The Witches of Eastwick*, directed by George Miller (USA).

- Wim Wenders: *Wings of Desire*, with Bruno Ganz (FRG).

SCIENCE

- **9 Mar**: The Numerical Aerodynamic Simulation Facility, a supercomputer capable of a top speed of 1,720,000,000 calculations per second, begins operation.

- **Dec**: USSR cosmonaut Yuri Romanenko returns to earth after spending a record 327 days in orbit in space station Mir.

- The Nobel Prize for Physiology or Medicine is won by Susumu Tonegawa (Jap) for his pioneering work on the mechanics of antibody production.

- The Nobel Prize for Chemistry is won by Charles Pedersen (USA), Donald Cram (USA) and Jean-Marie Lehn (Fr) for their work on molecular chemistry.

- The Nobel Prize for Physics is won by Karl Alex Muller (Swi) and Georg Bednorz (FRG) for joint discovery of high temperature superconductivity.

- B. Tully announces his discovery of the Pisces-Cetus Supercluster Complex.

- H. Naarman and N. Theophilou develop a form of polyacetylene that is doped with iodine to become a better conductor of electricity than copper.

- Ching Wu Chu and colleagues create a material superconducting at –196 degrees Celsius, the temperature of liquid nitrogen (USA).

- A South African grandmother gives birth to her own daughter's triplets, after the daughter's ova is fertilized outside her body and implanted into the mother, as she was unable to bear children herself.

- Discovery of a gene marker for cancer of the colon by W. Bodmer, E. Solomon, H.J.R. Bussey and A.J. Jeffreys.

- Discovery by K.P. Campbell and R. Coronado of the calcium release channel, a protein used to regulate the passage of calcium into and out of muscle cells.

- Genes for human growth are inserted into goldfish and loach, and result in much quicker growth (Chi).

- The gene for maleness is discovered by D.C. Page.

- H. Fricke uses a submersible to study coelacanths in the Indian Ocean.

- Introduction of digital audio tape cassettes (Jap).

- A glass fiber cable (TAT 8) is laid across the Atlantic Ocean.

- For the first time, a criminal suspect is convicted on the basis of genetic fingerprinting (UK).

- I.N. Madrazo conducts experiments into implanting cells from a person's adrenal gland into the brain to alleviate Parkinson's Disease.

- Fossilized dinosaur's eggs containing unhatched dinosaurs are discovered by Kevin Aulenback in Alberta (Can).

A number of persistent conflicts seemed on the way to settlement in 1988. The withdrawal of Cuban troops from Angola opened the way for the independence of Namibia (Southwest Africa). The USSR decided to withdraw from Afghanistan. The border disputes between Laos and Thailand, and Ethiopia and Somalia, were settled, the Vietnamese withdrew from Kampuchea (Cambodia), the Iran-Iraq war ended, and PLO leader Yasir Arafaat recognized the existence of Israel. In other respects, hostility between Muslims and Westerners was exacerbated. A US warship in the Gulf shot down an Iranian airliner on a scheduled flight. British author Salmon Rushdie incurred the wrath of Islam for his portrayal of the prophet Muhammad in "The Satanic Verses", and was later forced to go into hiding to evade potential assassins. Coincidentally, the 1988 Nobel Prize for literature was awarded to an Arab novelist. Terrorists also caused the crash of a Jumbo jet at Lockerbie in Scotland – the worst-ever air disaster in Britain.

▲ Florence Griffith-Joyner of the USA wins the 100 m at the Seoul Olympics in September. The success of the largest ever Olympic Games was marred by the discovery that Canadian sprinter Ben Johnson had been taking drugs, highlighting a growing problem in sport worldwide. He was disqualified from accepting his gold medal.

● **29 Jan**: Angolan-Cuban talks open in Luanda, with US participation. They conclude with agreement in principle on Cuban military withdrawal from Angola to pave the way for Namibian independence. On 22 Dec the independence agreement is formally signed at the UN by Angolan, South African and Cuban foreign ministers.

● **8 Feb**: USSR premier Mikhail Gorbachev announces that Soviet troops will begin withdrawal from Afghanistan on 15 May, subject to signature of a peace agreement between Pakistan and Afghanistan. The withdrawal is to be completed by 15 Feb 1989. (›14 Apr)

● **19 Feb**: A ceasefire in the border dispute between Laos and Thailand is signed. On 25 Jun Laos holds its first national elections in 13 years.

● **26 Feb**: In the USSR, Gorbachev makes an unprecedented TV appeal for calm after a week of nationalist demonstrations in Armenia. On 1 Mar 31 die after troops are called in to enforce curfew in Azerbaijan. (›21 Sep)

● **26 Feb**: President Delvalle of Panama is forced to resign after attempting to dismiss Gen. Manuel Noriega, who remains effective leader despite his earlier indictment in the USA for involvement in drugs traffic. On 16 Mar a US-backed coup to oust Noriega fails.

● **6 Mar**: In Gibraltar, three suspected IRA terrorists are shot dead by British SAS forces. On 7 Mar Foreign Secretary Geoffrey Howe states that a bomb plot, aimed at British forces on the Rock, had been uncovered.

● **16 Mar**: In Belgrade, Gorbachev proposes reciprocal US-USSR freeze on naval forces in the Mediterranean. USA responds by reaffirming commitments to NATO allies. (›7 Dec)

● **23 Mar**: In Nicaragua, a 60-day ceasefire agreement is signed by government officials and Contra rebel commanders, but on 9 Jun ceasefire talks end without agreement.

● **Mar**: The Bangladesh general election results in a major victory for the ruling Jatiya party, led by Gen. Ershad. The main opposition parties boycott the polls, which are marred by violence.

● **2 Apr**: Indian forces move to seal the border with Pakistan to stop infiltration of Sikh extremists.

● **3 Apr**: Ethiopia and Somalia conclude a provisional peace agreement, ending 11 years of border and other conflict.

● **14 Apr**: Afghan Accords resolve international aspects of the conflict in Afghanistan (Afg, Pak, USSR, USA).

● **18 Apr**: US planes and warships destroy two Iranian oil platforms, cripple two frigates and sink a patrol boat in the Persian Gulf in retaliation for damage to a US frigate on 14 Apr. In the land war, Iraqi forces recapture the Fao peninsula from Iranians in a major offensive. (›8 Aug)

● **21 Apr**: Israeli prime minister Shamir and US president Reagan agree a five-year continuation of the US-Israel "unique dialogue".

● **8 May**: François Mitterand is reelected as president of France. On 10 May Jacques Chirac resigns as prime minister and is succeeded by Michel Rocard.

● **26 May**: Vietnam announces withdrawal of 50,000 troops from Kampuchea by late 1988, the remainder being placed under Kampuchean control.

● **May**: Belize and Guatemala agree a permanent commission to formulate a treaty to end their territorial dispute.

● **20 Jun**: President Leslie Manigat of Haiti is deposed in a military coup by Gen. Henri Namphy but on 18 Sep Gen. Namphy is himself deposed and Brig.-Gen. Prosper Avril declares himself president.

● **28 Jun–1 Jul**: National conference of USSR Communist party in Moscow ends with approval of six resolutions for implementation of *perestroika*. (›30 Sep)

● **8 Aug**: After acceptance by Iran and Iraq of a UN peace plan, the Security Council orders an end to hostilities in the Gulf. On 25 Aug direct peace talks begin in Geneva.

● **17 Aug**: Pakistani premier Gen. Zia, the US ambassador and 33 others are killed when their plane explodes in mid-air. Zia is succeeded by the first woman leader of a Muslim country, Benazir Bhutto, sworn in on 2 Dec.

● **21 Sep**: The USSR declares a state of emergency in Nagorno-Karabakh in view of worsening ethnic clashes.

● **30 Sep**: Opponents to USSR reforms are voted out of office, and Mikhail Gorbachev is appointed president of the USSR, while retaining his position as General Secretary of the Communist party.

● **3 Oct**: Chad and Libya formally end their war and establish diplomatic relations.

● **5 Oct**: In a referendum in Chile, voters reject the proposal that Gen. Pinochet remain in power for a further eight years.

● **8 Nov**: In the US presidential elections, vice-president George Bush gains 54 percent of the vote and defeats his Democrat rival Michael Dukakis.

● **10 Nov**: Diplomatic ties are restored between the UK and Iran.

● **7 Dec**: President Gorbachev, addressing the UN General Assembly, announces plans to reduce USSR armed forces by 500,000 and cut conventional arms.

● **13 Dec**: PLO leader Yasir Arafat makes a speech at a special session of the UN in Geneva, renouncing terrorism and recognizing Israel. On 14 Dec the USA announces resumption of contacts with the PLO, ending a 13-year boycott.

- **17 Jan**: In Lebanon, Lt-Col. William Higgins, chief of the UN Truce Supervising Organization, is kidnapped by Muslim extremists, claiming he was a CIA agent.

- **26 Jan**: Health ministers and experts from 148 countries begin a three-day conference in London on AIDS. The London Declaration on AIDS urges governments to take urgent action on "a serious threat to humanity".

- **24 Feb**: The South African government announces sweeping new curbs on antiapartheid movements. On 29 Feb archbishop Desmond Tutu and 100 clergy are arrested in Cape Town while attempting to present a petition to parliament in protest.

- **Feb**: The Winter Olympics open at Calgary (Can).

- **8 Mar**: Five out of 11 hijackers of an Aeroflot airliner are killed when USSR security forces storm the plane at Leningrad.

- **31 Mar**: The US Senate approves a $47,900,000 package including $17,700,000 in humanitarian aid for the Nicaraguan Contras and the same amount for medical treatment of children injured in the war in Nicaragua.

- **5 Apr**: Shia Muslim extremists hijack a Kuwaiti Airways jumbo jet, forcing it to fly to Iran and later to Cyprus where two passengers are shot dead. On 20 Apr the hijack ends in Algiers, but the terrorists are given safe passage out of Algeria.

- **6 Apr**: At a summit meeting in Brasilia, the presidents of Argentina, Brazil and Uruguay sign the Act of Alvorada, providing for enhanced economic integration.

- **10 Apr**: In Pakistan, 100 are killed and 700 injured in a massive explosion at an army ammunition dump. Afghan agents are believed to be responsible.

- **22 Apr**: The FAO reports that sub-Saharan Africa faces a resurgence of famine because of vast swarms of locusts which are moving south from north Africa.

- **2 May**: In Poland, seven Solidarity union leaders are detained by police when thousands of shipyard workers go on strike in Gdansk. (›28 Aug)

- **2 Jun**: In Australia, Canberra High Court unanimously approves the sale in Australia of ex-MI5 officer Peter Wright's book *Spycatcher*, dismissing the UK government's final appeal after 18 months of legal proceedings.

- **14 Jun**: In West Germany, riot police attempt to restore order in Düsseldorf when violence occurs among British, Dutch and German supporters attending the European football championships.

- **19-21 Jun**: Economic summit of the seven major industrial nations in Toronto discusses rescheduling of poorest countries' debts and reduction of agricultural subsidy.

- **25 Jun**: Beginning of official relations between EC and Comecon.

- **27 Jun**: Two-day summit conference of EC heads of government opens in Hanover (FRG) and declares 1992 goal of a single European market "irreversible".

- **3 Jul**: US warship *Vincennes* shoots down an Iranian civilian airliner in the Gulf with loss of all 290 aboard. President Reagan tells Congress it was a justified act of self-defense.

- **6 Jul**: 166 people are killed by a gas explosion on the British oil rig *Piper Alpha* in the North Sea.

- **10 Aug**: In Burundi, tribal conflict flares up between the Hutu and dominant Tutsi, resulting in thousands of deaths in the following weeks.

- **26 Aug**: Soviet authorities announce plans for leasing of agricultural land by private individuals in a bid to increase agricultural efficiency.

- **28 Aug**: Polish premier Gen. Jaruzelski calls for new attempts at national reconciliation as a two-week wave of strikes continues. On 31 Aug union leader Lech Walesa holds talks with the Interior Minister – his first since the banning of Solidarity in 1981 – after which he urges workers to end the strikes.

- **31 Aug**: In Bangladesh, around 25 million are left homeless and hundreds die in widespread flooding.

- **Aug**: In Sudan, over 1 million are reported homeless and many dead after flooding in Khartoum and surrounding provinces.

- **17 Sep–2 Oct**: The Olympic Games in Seoul (S Kor) are the largest yet, but athletics are overshadowed by a drug scandal surrounding Canadian sprinter Ben Johnson.

- **8 Nov**: GATT concludes its annual meeting with the assertion that the Uruguay Round of multilateral trade negotiations can only succeed if the Third World's need for special treatment is acknowledged by the industrial states.

- **7 Dec**: 50,000 are killed and 500,000 are made homeless by a massive earthquake in Armenia. An unprecedented international relief operation is mounted.

- **14 Dec**: In Spain, trade unions stage a 24-hour general strike, the first general strike in Spain for 50 years.

- **21 Dec**: In the UK, a Pan Am Boeing 747 crashes at Lockerbie, Scotland, killing all 259 aboard and 11 on the ground in the worst ever air disaster in the UK. Investigators later confirm that the crash was caused by a terrorist bomb.

- By mid-1988 around 50 countries have ratified the Montreal Protocol, which targetted a global freeze in CFC production at 1986 levels, and a 50 percent production cut by 1999.

- Nobel Peace Prize is won by the United Nations Peacekeeping Forces.

- Nobel Prize for Economic Sciences is won by M. Allais (Fr).

- **8 Jul**: Premiere in Houston, Texas, of Philip Glass's opera *The Making of the Representative for Planet 8*, based on Doris Lessing's novel in the *Canopus in Argos* series.

- **18 Jul**: Many world-famous pop and rock stars play in a concert for jailed black South African leader Nelson Mandela's 70th birthday, and there are worldwide demands for his release.

- **28 Nov**: In the UK, Picasso's painting *Acrobate et jeune arléquin* sells at Christie's salerooms for £20.9 million ($38 million), a record for a 20th- century painting.

- Iris Murdoch: *The Book and the Brotherhood*, novel (UK).

- Salman Rushdie: *The Satanic Verses*, novel. The bitter controversy between the Islamic East and liberal West sparked off by the book resulted in its banning in India in Oct, and the issuing of a death threat against Rushdie by Ayatollah Khomeini of Iran on 14 Feb 1989 (UK).

- Umberto Eco: *Foucault's Pendulum* (It).

- Peter Carey's novel *Oscar and Lucinda* (Aus) wins the Booker Prize.

- Toni Morrison: *Beloved*, novel (USA).

- Nobel Prize for Literature is won by Naguib Mahfouz (Egy) for the first part of his *Cairo Trilogy*, which examines his country in the years between 1917 and 1945.

- Karlheinz Stockhausen: *Montag aus Licht*, third opera in the seven-day cycle *Licht* (FRG).

- Elliott Carter: Oboe Concerto (USA).

- First performance of Barry Cooper's "completed" version of Beethoven's Tenth Symphony (UK).

- Philippe Manoury: *Pluton (Creation)*, for piano and 4X computer (Fr).

- Ansel Krut: *The Student of Philosophies*, painting (UK).

- Roberto Marquez: *Mirrors Have No Mercy*, painting (Sp).

- Gilbert and George: *Force*, photomontage (UK).

- Anselm Kiefer: *The High Priestess*, photographs mounted on lead (since 1985) (FRG).

- Frank Gehry: California Aerospace Museum, Los Angeles (USA).

- Bernardo Bertolucci's film *The Last Emperor* wins nine Oscars (USA).

- Peter Brook: *Mahabharata*, film of the holy Hindu epic (UK).

- Animation and live actors mix in the film *Who Framed Roger Rabbit?*, starring Bob Hoskins (USA).

- **Apr**: A patent is issued to Harvard University for a strain of genetically engineered mice, developed to discover the causes of cancer (USA).

- **15 Nov**: Soviet space shuttle *Burian* makes its maiden flight, unmanned, under radio control from Earth.

- **22 Nov**: US Stealth bomber, the most expensive war plane ever built, invisible to radar and heat-seeking missiles, makes its first public appearance.

- **Nov**: Space technology cooperation agreement is reached between China and Australia.

- The Nobel Prize for Physiology or Medicine is won by Gertrude Elion (USA) and George Hitchins (USA) for work that had led to drugs to combat herpes, leukemia and malaria, and to the prevention of rejection of transplants; and by Sir James Black (UK), whose work had led to the development of drugs to treat heart disease and prevent recurrence of stomach ulcers.

- The Nobel Prize for Physics is won by Leon Lederman (USA), Melvin Schwartz (USA) and and Jack Steinberger (USA) for their discovery of the subatomic particle the mu-neutrino.

- The Nobel Prize for Chemistry is won by Johann Deisenhofer (FRG), Robert Huber (FRG) and Hartmut Michel (FRG) for their work on photosynthesis.

- R. Jaenisch and colleagues succeed in implanting the gene for a hereditary disease of humans in mice, in order to study the disease.

- New warm-temperature superconductors are developed based on bismuth (Jap) and thalium (USA).

- F.C. Moon and R. Raj build an almost frictionless high-speed bearing using a superconductor.

- The human-powered aircraft *Daedalus 88* sets a new record for human-powered flight (Gr).

- The first image is obtained from a positron transmission microscope.

- John Ellis (UK) discovers "molecular chaperones" – substances whose task is to ensure reactions proceed in a proper manner and at the right pace. Without them, vital enzymes cannot perform their tasks properly.

- Beginning of a major project by US scientists to map human genes.

- Embryo cloning of dairy cattle is developed (USA).

- The World Health Organization estimates the number of people infected by HIV to be between five and 10 million, with 120,000 cases of AIDS reported worldwide.

Domestic opposition to totalitarianism in Eastern Europe had been growing for many years, and the first cracks had appeared in the system with the introduction of "perestroika" and "glasnost" in the USSR. In 1989 the dam burst. A flood of East German refugees to the West culminated in the opening of the Berlin Wall. Within just a few weeks Communist rule was overthrown in Hungary, East Germany, Bulgaria and Czechoslovakia, on the whole with little violence. There were battles in Romania before dictator Nicolae Ceauşescu was overthrown and shot. "Glasnost" also came to South Africa with accession to office of F. W. de Klerk, who began a tentative movement toward reform. But popular revolution did not succeed everywhere. In China the occupation of Tianenmen Square by young people demonstrating peacefully for democratic rights was barbarously ended by tanks ordered in by the old and fearful powerbrokers of Beijing.

▲ The Berlin Wall was opened on 10 November 1989 after nearly thirty years.

- **1 Jan**: Namibia is granted independence from South Africa. Elections are held on 11 Nov. SWAPO gains a majority of seats in the Constituent Assembly, but not emough to give it complete control.

- **7 Jan**: Death of Hirohito, emperor of Japan since 1926.

- **11 Jan**: Start of Cuban troop withdrawal from Angola. (›22 Jun)

- **12 Jan**: In an effort to end ethnic violence in Nagorno-Karabakh, the Soviet government decides to place the region temporarily under direct rule from Moscow.

- **20 Jan**: George Bush is inaugurated as 41st president of the USA.

- **3 Feb**: Alfredo Stroessner, president of Paraguay for nearly 35 years, is overthrown in a military coup.

- **14 Feb**: Ayatollah Khomeini of Iran issues his *fatwa* (death sentence) against British author Salman Rushdie for offence to Muslims caused by the latter's novel *The Satanic Verses*. On 7 Mar Iran severs relations with UK.

- **23 Feb**: Algerians approve a new constitution that will pave the way for a multiparty system.

- **7 Mar**: The Chinese government imposes martial law on Tibet, after three days of violent clashes between Tibetans and Chinese police.

- **26 Mar**: The first democratic Soviet elections take place, to elect the Congress of People's Deputies (USSR).

- **7 Apr**: The Soviet government deploys troops to Tbilisi, capital of Georgia, to end strikes and demonstrations demanding greater political and economic independence from central government.

- **13 Apr**: US Congress votes aid to Nicaraguan Contra rebels, earmarked for food, clothes and medicine, to support them until the proposed elections in Feb 1990. (› 5 Aug)

- **18 Apr**: Students hold a rally in Beijing, demanding greater democratic freedom and the resignation of Deng Xiaoping and Li Peng and on 19 Apr a huge crowd of 10,000 gathers on Tiananmen Square. On 27 Apr at least 100,000 defy government troops by marching through the streets shouting slogans. By early May demonstrations have spread to other cities (Chi).

- **13 May**: 3,000 students begin a hunger strike in Tiananmen Square in Beijing. On 20 May the government imposes martial law on (Chi). (›4 Jun)

- **14 May**: Peronist Carlos Saul Menem is elected president in the first free elections in Argentina.

- **25 May**: Mikhail Gorbachev is elected president of the USSR by the newly constituted 2,250-member Congress of People's Deputies.

- **3 Jun**: Death of Ayatollah Khomeini of Iran after 10 years in power; he is succeeded by Hojatoleslam Ali Akbar Rafsanjani as prime minister (29 Jul), with extended powers under a new constitution.

- **4 Jun**: First partly democratic elections in Poland. On 24 Aug Tadeusz Mazowiecki, an advisor to Solidarity, is appointed as prime minister.

- **4 Jun**: The student revolt in China is brutally crushed. On 21 Jun the first public execution of demonstrators takes place.

- **22 Jun**: Marxist-led government of president José Eduardo dos Santos of Angola and the guerrilla forces of Jonas Savimbi agree to observe a ceasefire from 24 Jun.

- **30 Jun**: The Sudanese government of Sadiq al-Mahdi is overthrown in a military coup.

- **5–7 Aug**: Latin Accord is signed by presidents of Costa Rica, El Salvador, Guatemala, Honduras and Nicaragua, stating that by 8 Dec at latest, Nicaraguan Contra rebels operating from bases inside Honduras will be disbanded. The USA vigorously opposes this decision.

- **10 Aug**: Violence flares up in the civil war in Lebanon. Christian and Muslim strongholds are bombarded with reckless disregard for civilian populations. A ceasefire is declared on 22 Sep.

- **14 Aug**: P.W. Botha resigns as president of South Africa, and F.W. de Klerk becomes acting president.

- **22 Aug**: The Lithuanian parliament declares the 1940 occupation and annexation of Lithuania, Latvia and Estonia by the USSR invalid. On 23 Aug hundreds of thousands of citizens in the three Baltic republics link hands to symbolize their demand for independent states. (›27 Nov)

- **10 Sep**: The Hungarian government opens its border with Austria and announces that it has decided to permit thousands of East Germans to seek a new life elsewhere. Tens of thousands of East Germans have already made their way to West Germany, even though their travel documents are invalid. (›18 Oct)

- **20 Sep**: Gorbachev engineers the removal of five members of the Communist party hierarchy, replacing them with men expected to vigorously carry out his agenda and reassert the supremacy of the party, especially in those regions clamoring for "unacceptable change".

- **15 Oct**: The South African government releases eight prominent political prisoners, including Walter Sisulu, leading to speculation that Nelson Mandela may soon be released.

- **18 Oct**: The East German Communist party ousts Erich Honecker, hardline head of state and of the East German Communist party for 18 years. Egon Krenz becomes president. (›7 Nov)

- **19 Oct**: The Hungarian parliament votes to legalize opposition political parties, ending over 40 years of one-party Communist rule. New multiparty elections are expected to be held in 1990, after a new constitution has been drawn up.

SOCIETY

- **23 Oct:** A new Hungarian Republic is declared on the 33rd anniversary of the Hungarian Uprising.

- **25 Oct:** Yugoslavia's official press agency reports that the Central Committee of the Communist party has adopted a platform that supports the development of political pluralism, labor unions, individual rights and free and democratic elections.

- **7 Nov:** Faced with a massive exodus of East Germans to West Germany and demands for radical change, East German prime minister Willi Stoph and his government agree to step down. On 8 Nov most of the Politburo also resigns. On 9 Nov the government removes virtually all restrictions on travel to the West.

- **10 Nov:** The Berlin wall – in place since 1961 – is opened. (›3 Dec)

- **10 Nov:** Todor Zhivkov, long-time president of Bulgaria and leader of the Bulgarian Communist party, resigns both posts. He is later expelled from the party. On 17 Nov demonstrators demand democracy and freedom.

- **24 Nov:** Czechoslovak leaders resign, after a week of demonstrations demanding democracy. On 28 Nov the new leaders of the Communist party, yielding to intense pressure, agree to give up the party's monopoly of political power. (›7 Dec)

- **27 Nov:** The USSR condemns Lithuania's moves towards greater autonomy.

- **3 Dec:** Krenz and all the East German Politburo and central committee resign following revelations of widespread corruption. Huge crowds demand total dissolution of the Communist party and the reunification of Germany.

- **7 Dec:** Czech prime minister Ladislav Adamec resigns after Civic Forum (a coalition of anti-Communist party forces) demands his removal. Marian Calfa becomes prime minister and announces that he will form a multiparty government. Gustav Husak resigns as president on 10 Dec. (›28 Dec)

- **20 Dec:** US troops begin an all-out assault on preselected targets in Panama in an effort to capture Gen. Noriega, sought by the US authorities to face drugs charges, and accused by a report of 13 Nov of violating political rights by annulling the May election. Noriega flees, and Guillermo Endara becomes president.

- **22 Dec:** Dictator Nicolae Ceauşescu's brutal regime is overthrown in Romania after a fierce battle with security forces. On 23 Dec Ceauşescu is captured, and he and his wife are executed on 25 Dec, convicted of genocide and gross misuse of power.

- **28 Dec:** Alexander Dubcek, deposed after the failure of his liberalization campaign in 1968, is elected chairman of the Czech parliament, and on 29 Dec writer, philosopher and veteran anti-government protestor Vaclav Havel becomes president.

- **12 Jan:** At a chemical weapons conference in Paris, 149 nations sign a total ban on use of gas, toxins and bacteriological weapons.

- **20 Jan:** Israel orders indefinite closure of all Palestinian schools in occupied territories, claiming that students are partly responsible for the increase in violence that over the previous month has resulted in the deaths of 30 Palestinians at the hands of Israeli soldiers. Gradual reopening of schools begins in Jul.

- **Jan:** Estonian and Lithuanian legislatures pass laws making Estonian and Lithuanian the official languages of the republics. This underscores growing resentment against perceived efforts to impose the Russian language and culture on minority groups in the USSR.

- **12 Mar:** Around 200,000 Latvians stage a demonstration in the capital Riga, to demand that Latvian be the official language of the republic.

- **24 Mar:** A fully loaded oil tanker, the *Exxon Valdez*, ruptures on charted reefs in Prince William Sound, Alaska, spilling an estimated 11 million gallons of oil. The investigating team reports that the ship's captain was drunk at the time of the accident (USA).

- **17 Apr:** A court in Warsaw officially restores the legal status of the trade union Solidarity as part of an agreement between labor leaders and government officials (Pol). (›15 Nov)

- **10 Jul:** Miners' strikes begin in Siberia and spread to other areas, forcing concessions from the government over pay and conditions (USSR).

- **13 Jul:** France begins celebration of bicentennial of the French Revolution.

- **5 Sep:** Hundreds of thousands of blacks begin a two-day boycott of jobs and schools to protest against the exclusion of blacks from voting in the parliamentary elections on 6 Sep (SA).

- **27 Sep:** The British government announces its plans to give an unspecified number of Hong Kong citizens the right to immigrate into the UK after Hong Kong reverts to China in 1997. The announcement meets with opposition from Beijing.

- **29 Oct:** The US authorities seize 20 tonnes of cocaine in California, the largest single drugs seizure anywhere to date.

- **15 Nov:** Solidarity leader Lech Walesa asks the US Congress for help similar to the postwar Marshall Plan, since Poland's economic situation is desperate. Polish external debt stands at $39 billion.

- **Nov:** EC discussions on the new situation in Eastern Europe take place.

- **Dec:** The EC agrees a schedule for economic and monetary union.

- Nobel Peace Prize is won by the Dalai Lama of Tibet.

- Nobel Prize for Economic Sciences is won by Trygve Haavelino (Nor).

CULTURE

- **13 Jul:** Opening of the Opéra Bastille in Paris, formally inaugurated by French president François Mitterand.

- **7 Dec:** Premiere of Kenneth MacMillan's new ballet *The Prince of the Pagodas* (UK).

- Margaret Atwood: *Cat's Eye*, autobiographical novel (Can).

- George Steiner: *Real Presences*, essay on meaning in literature (UK).

- Vaclav Havel: *Redevelopment*, play, originally banned in Czechoslovakia (Cze).

- Kazuo Ishiguro's novel *The Remains of the Day* (Jap) wins the Booker Prize.

- Jim Sheridan: *My Left Foot*, a film on the life of disabled writer Christy Nolan (Ire).

- Thomas Pynchon: *Vineland*, novel (USA).

- Nobel Prize for Literature is won by the poet Camilo José Cela (Mex).

- Pierre Boulez: *Le Visage nuptial*, final revision of the original 1947 cantata on texts by René Char for voices and orchestra (Fr).

- Michael Tippett: *New Year*, opera (UK).

- Conductor Claudio Abbado assumes directorship of the Berlin Philharmonic Orchestra after the resignation of Herbert von Karajan from ill health. Karajan dies at his home near Salzburg on 16 Jul (FRG).

- Peter Sellars directs three Mozart-Da Ponte operas at the Pepsi Summerfare festival, all reset in contemporary New York (USA).

- Painter David Hockney sends a picture piece by piece via a fax machine from the USA to be assembled in the UK.

- Peter Halley: *Red Cell*, painting (USA).

- Roger Brown: *Chicago Taking a Beating*, painting (USA).

- HRH The Prince of Wales publishes his book *A Vision of Britain*, in which he voices his objection to "modernism" in architecture and calls for a return to classicism and the use of traditional materials in vernacular styles (UK).

- Bruce Beresford: *Driving Miss Daisy*, with Jessica Tandy (USA), wins four Oscars and the Academy Award for Best Picture.

SCIENCE

- **May–Jul:** Genetically engineered white blood cells are transfered into cancer patients for the first time, in order to attack tumors (UK).

- **15 Aug:** The first test is conducted with the new LEP particle accelerator in Geneva (Swi), producing Z particles.

- **25 Aug:** US *Voyager II* reaches within 4,800 km (3,000 miles) of Neptune, sending back pictures to earth, and then leaving the solar system for ever.

- **Aug:** Researchers in Canada and the USA confirm they have pinpointed the gene that is defective in the disease cystic fibrosis, the commonest fatal disease caused by a genetic defect.

- The Nobel Prize for Physics is won by Norman Ramsey (USA), Hans Dehmelt (USA) and Wolfgang Pauli (FRG) for the development of principles on which atomic clocks, accurate to within one second in 30,000 years, are based.

- The Nobel Prize for Chemistry is won by Sidney Altman (USA) amid Thomas Cech (USA) for their discovery of the catalytic properties of RNA.

- The Nobel Prize for Physiology or Medicine is won by Michael Bishop (USA) and Harold Varmus (USA) for their discovery of oncogenes, genes which can cause various cancers when they malfunction.

- West Germany hosts "Solarmobile 1989", an exhibition of solar-powered cars.

- The first successful operation is carried out by M. Harrison and colleagues on a fetus removed from the womb then returned after lung surgery (USA).

- Greg Winter and his team (UK) announce the success of a new technique for making antibodies and fragments of antibodies able to carry out some of the functions of complete antibodies, which avoids the use of animals, and which makes them more cheaply and quickly.

- Greg Winter produces new types of antibodies capable of being used as biodegradable pesticides (UK).

- Stanley Pons (USA) and Martin Fleischmann (UK) announce that they have succeeded in producing nuclear fusion in a bottle on a laboratory bench at room temperature. However, during the year, attempts by other laboratories to produce "cold fusion" fail.

1990-

The conflict between the power of the state and the rights of its citizens seemed to be turning the way of the people. As Communist rule faded in Eastern Europe, the Baltic countries moved towards independence. Soviet president Gorbachev seemed unlikely to stop them, though they set an unwelcome precedent inevitably followed by other states of the USSR. The brutal dictatorship of Pinochet in Chile also came to an end, and the movement in favor of democracy was evident in countries as remote as Burma (though the results of the election were soon suppressed), while in South Africa the long-awaited release of Nelson Mandela opened the way for constructive dialogue between the white government and its chief opponent, the ANC. Not all dictators were feeling the winds of change, however. Saddam Hussein of Iraq, having recently concluded a long, unjustified, savage and unsuccessful war against one neighbor (Iran), tried his luck again by invading a less formidable one, Kuwait, upon which Iraq had long-standing territorial claims. Saddam failed to realize that the Cold War was over, and the countries of the United Nations were almost all ranged against him.

▲ Nelson Mandela, symbol of hope and progress for South African blacks and for the oppressed worldwide, is released from jail. He was sentenced to life imprisonment in 1964 as organizer of the banned African National Congress.

● **1 Jan**: Cuba rejoins the UN Security Council after a 30-year break.

● **3 Jan**: Protesters riot in the Soviet republic of Azerbaijan, and KGB units are sent to restore order.

● **22 Jan**: Landslide vote at the congress of the Communist party of Yugoslavia to abandon the one-party system.

● **Jan**: Soviet president Mikhail Gorbachev visits the Lithuanian capital Vilnius to try to persuade the nationalists leaders of the rebellious republic to drop their plans for independence. (›24 Feb)

● **1 Feb**: Communist leaders in Bulgaria resign to make way for a broad-based coalition.

● **2 Feb**: President F.W. de Klerk lifts the 30-year ban on the ANC and the South African Communist party.

● **24 Feb**: The first genuine multiparty elections since 1917 are held in the USSR, for the new Lithuanian parliament. (›11 Mar)

● **26 Feb**: President Daniel Ortega of Nicaragua is defeated in the first truly free poll since his Sandinista movement took power in 1979.

● **26 Feb**: President Vaclav Havel announces that all Soviet troops will be withdrawn from Czechoslovakia by July 1991.

● **Feb**: In fighting in Beirut between rival Christian forces, some 200 are killed, mostly children.

● **10 Mar**: The military ruler of Haiti, Prosper Avril, is ousted from power.

● **11 Mar**: Augusto Pinochet, President of Chile, hands over power to Patricio Aylwin, ending his dictatorship.

● **11 Mar**: Lithuania declares independence, and Vytautas Landsbergis is elected as leader.

● **18 Mar**: East Germany holds its first genuinely democratic election. Right wing parties win a clear victory.

● **25 Mar**: Estonia's Communist party votes to break with the Soviet Communist party over a period of six months.

● **8 Apr**: King Birendra of Nepal agrees to demands to end Nepal's feudal-style monarchy and lift the 30-year ban on political parties.

● **9 Apr**: Troops enter Natal to end weeks of black factional fighting that has left around 400 dead (SA).

● **30 Apr**: Beijing lifts martial law in Tibet, 14 months after sending in troops to crush anti-Chinese demonstrations.

● **4 May**: The Latvian parliament votes for independence from the USSR.

● **28 May**: The National League for Democracy wins the first multiparty elections in Burma for 30 years.

● **Jun**: President Iliescu appeals to the miners to help deal with students' antigovernment demonstrations, provoking violence on the streets of Bucharest (Rom).

● **6 Jul**: The 16 NATO members agree to redefine their military strategy, and clear the way for a settlement with the USSR over a united Germany's defense role and closer European cooperation.

● **7 Jul**: Rioting breaks out in Nairobi after a rally to demand multiparty democracy (Ken).

● **27 Jul**: Arthur Robinson, prime minster of Trinidad, members of his cabinet, and 40 others are seized by Muslim extremists in a coup. The rebels surrender unconditionally on 1 Aug.

● **2 Aug**: Iraq invades Kuwait and on 8 Aug annexation is announced.

● **7 Aug**: Prime minister Benazir Bhutto is sacked by president Gulan Ishaq Khan, who accuses her government of "undermining the workings of the constitution" (Pak).

● **23 Aug**: The Republic of Armenia declares its independence from the USSR.

● **9 Sep**: Samuel Doe, President of Liberia, is beaten to death by rebel troops.

● **24 Sep**: The USSR parliament votes to give Gorbachev power to rule by decree, giving him authority to handle every aspect of reform. (›19 Oct)

● **3 Oct**: German reunification. The Volkskammer and Bundestag ratify the treaty of 20 Sep. (›4 Dec)

● **8 Oct**: Israeli border police shoot dead 21 Arabs during rioting around the Western Wall and the Dome of the Rock, Jerusalem. Irazi president Saddam Hussein attempts to use the shooting to break the fragile Arab/Western alliance.

● **19 Oct**: The Supreme Soviet endorses the introduction of the market economy and adopts Gorbachev's plan to introduce it over two years.

● **17 Nov**: USSR parliament agrees to change the constitution in an attempt to prevent collapse. Gorbachev wins increased powers, the republics are to have more say in central government, but so too are the police, KGB, and army.

● **19 Nov**: The Cold War officially ends when 22 heads of state sign the Treaty on Conventional Armed Forces in Europe (CFE Treaty), which drastically reduces the amount of conventional weapons held by NATO and Warsaw Pact countries.

● **22 Nov**: British prime minister Thatcher announces that she will not fight on for the Tory party leadership. On 27 November, John Major defeats Michael Heseltine and Douglas Hurd to become party leader and prime minister.

● **4 Dec**: Helmut Kohl's Christian Democrats win the first nationwide elections in Germany since 1933.

● **9 Dec**: Lech Walesa wins a landslide victory in the Polish presidential elections.

● **Dec**: Anti-Communist violence grows in Albania.

SOCIETY

- **4 Jan:** At least 225 are killed and 400 injured in a train crash in south Pakistan.

- **19 Jan:** Marion Barry, the black mayor of Washington, is secretly filmed smoking "crack" and faces a possible prison sentence.

- **28 Jan:** Around 150 are feared drowned in Bangladesh when an overcrowded river ferry collides with another vessel and sinks.

- **Jan:** In Sudan, at least 600 are reported killed in clashes between Muslim tribesmen and non-Muslim southerners.

- **Jan:** Hurricane-force winds in UK kill at least 46, and some 3 million trees are lost.

- **1 Feb:** Troops and tanks are sent in to Kosovo to quell ethnic violence (Yug).

- **4 Feb:** New Zealand cricketer Richard Hadlee becomes the first to take 400 Test wickets.

- **11 Feb:** Nelson Mandela is released from Victor Verster prison near Cape Town (SA).

- **14 Feb:** The Perrier company withdraws its entire stock of 160 million bottles of mineral water from the world market after traces of benzine are found in the water (Fr).

- **14 Feb:** An Indian Airlines Airbus bursts into flames as it comes in to land at Bangalore, killing 92.

- **23 Feb:** UK ambulance union leaders reach an agreement with the management to end the long-running dispute.

- **6 Mar:** The USSR parliament passes a law sanctioning the ownership of private property.

- **Mar:** Violent demonstrations take place across England and Wales as councils set their poll tax rates.

- **1 Apr:** A riot erupts in Strangeways prison, and prisoners take control of buildings. The unrest spreads to other prisons in UK. The siege finally ends on 25 Apr.

- **3 Apr:** At least 32 are killed in the Punjab by a bomb believed to have been planted by Sikh separatists.

- **17 Apr:** Moscow imposes an economic blockade on Lithuania.

- **Apr:** Floods swamp vast areas of Queensland, New South Wales and Victoria, prompting mass evacuations (Aus).

- **10 May:** 50,000 students battle with police on university campuses throughout South Korea, protesting against the inauguration of president Roh Tae Woo's "dictatorial and undemocratic" Liberal Democratic party.

- **14 May:** Hundreds protest in Manila against the presence of US military bases. 55 are injured in clashes with police.

- **30 May:** An earthquake in Peru buries four villages and kills over 115.

- **30 May:** France announces a ban on all imports of beef and cattle from the UK, joining USSR, Austria and West Germany, due to fears of the cattle disease BSE.

- **May:** 34 countries sign a declaration at the UN Environmental Conference at Bergen, Norway, agreeing to prevent and attack the causes of "environmental degradation".

- **May:** Ethnic violence between Mohajirs and Sindhis in south Pakistan claims over 200 lives.

- **May:** 688 die when a cyclone hits Andhra Pradesh, India.

- **22 June:** Earthquake in Northwest Iran kills 40,000 and injures at least 100,000.

- **1 July:** Germany reaches economic and monetary union.

- **7 Jul:** Martina Navratilova (USA) wins a record 9th Wimbledon singles tennis title.

- **27 Jul:** OPEC agrees to raise the official price of oil for the first time in 10 years. The deal is made to avert the threat of military action in the Gulf from Saddam Hussein, who wants to rescue Iraq's economy by boosting the price of oil, and who has forced the issue in recent weeks in a row with Kuwait, who openly flouts OPEC production quotas.

- **24 Aug:** A state of emergency is imposed on 27 townships in South Africa as the death toll from two weeks of violence reaches 500.

- **8 Oct:** UK formally joins the ERM.

- **Oct:** The Indian government faces opposition to its plans to improve the lot of the lower castes. Upper-caste Hindus take part in violent demonstrations, and dozens of students burn themselves to death.

- **29 Nov:** Germany begins to airlift food supplies to Moscow as USSR faces the threat of famine and rationing. One of the side effects of *perestroika* has been the collapse of the state agriculture and distribution system, and the problem has been made worse by hoarding and a flourishing black market.

- **1 Dec:** French and British workers shake hands, having dug through each other in the Channel Tunnel.

- **7 Dec:** Four years of negotiations between GATT countries collapse, heightening fears of an international trade war. The deadlock arose over farm subsidies, and a final breakdown is only averted by setting a new deadline.

- Australia faces the worst recession since World War II. Bankruptcy is rife, and stock exchange trading is slow.

- The Nobel Peace Prize is won by Mikhail Gorbachev (USSR).

- International relief effort is set up to aid Romania, after reports of the catastrophic health situation there. The country has the highest death rate among the under fives in Europe, and the highest maternal mortality rate.

CULTURE

- **14 May:** Japanese Ryoei Saito pays US$83 million for Van Gogh's *Portrait of Dr Gachet*, making it the world's most expensive painting.

- A.S. Byatt's novel *Possession*, wins the Booker Prize (UK).

- Octavio Paz, Mexican essayist and poet, wins the Nobel Prize for Literature.

- The "Three Tenors' World Cup Concert" in Rome, with Luciano Pavarotti, Placido Domingo and JoséCarreras, is seen on TV all over the world.

- Release of *Shirley Valentine*, starring Pauline Collins (USA).

- Release of *Dick Tracy*, starring and directed by Warren Beatty (USA).

- *Ghost*, starring Patrick Swayze and Demi Moore (USA).

- *Pretty Woman*, starring Richard Gere and Julia Roberts, is released (USA).

- Bernardo Bertolucci: *The Sheltering Sky* (UK).

- The cartoon characters Teenage Mutant Hero Turtles become a craze.

- World of Music and Dance (WOMAD) is founded by Peter Gabriel.

- Archeologists discover an additional 644 miles of the Great Wall of China in Liaoning province up to the Korean border.

SCIENCE

- **30 Jan:** Guy's Hospital (UK) performs the world's first successful heart surgery on a baby in its mother's womb.

- **Apr:** The Hubble space telescope launched from the shuttle *Discovery*.

- **Oct:** Launch of spacecraft *Ulysses* on a mission to oberve the poles of the Sun in 1994 and 1995. The craft is built jointly by ESA and Nasa.

- **20 Dec:** Pierre Chambon and colleagues report the discovery of the gene which may be crucial in the spread of breast cancer (Fr).

- Nobel Prize for Physics is won by Jerome Friedman, Henry Kendall (USA) and Richard Taylor, for their pioneering work in the discovery of the structure of protons and neutrons.

- Nobel Prize for Chemistry is won by Elias James Corey (USA) for finding new ways of producing and synthesising chemical compounds.

- WHO reports the development of an effective male contraceptive which is reversible and gives minimal side effects.

- US astronomers discover a new moon of Saturn, the smallest of the 18, and the first to be found orbiting within the rings.

- Canadian geologists find tiny rings and discs in sandstone 600 million years old, making them the oldest fossils of multicellular animals.

- A Japanese laboratory succeds in producing a plastic which exhibits magnetic properties at low temperatures. It can be pressed into thin films to make new types of magnetic sensors.

- Scientists in the USSR produce diamond powder from carbon soot using only a conventional laser.

- Studies in the USA on the survivors of Nagasaki and Hiroshima show the risks from exposure to low levels of radiation is 3 to 4 times higher than previously thought.

- Fred Gage and colleagues inject modified cells from rat skin into the brains of rats suffering the equivalent of the human condition Parkinson's disease, and find brain function is partially restored (USA).

- Astronomers in Canada report that the Pole Star is changing from a star which pulsates into one which is stable, a process which will take about 10 years. The star has been pulsating for 40,000 years.

- Pellets of fat and fishmeal with live viruses inside are distributed in the European countryside. The viruses immunise foxes against rabies and the process is helping to eradicate the disease and prevent it spreading to domestic animals.

- Canadian scientists discover that killer whales "speak" a number of different "dialects" and "languages".

Saddam Hussein's refusal to obey a UN resolution requiring the evacuation of occupied Kuwait brought about another war conducted by the USA, actively supported by a number of other countries, and regarded with benevolent neutrality by most of the remainder. In a short, hi-tech campaign, the Iraqis were swiftly driven from Kuwait; but the USA, fearful of arousing the hostility of the Arab world, forebore to carry the campaign to its logical conclusion – the overthrow of Saddam. The result was civil war in Iraq, death and destruction for the Kurds in the north and the Shi'ites in the south, and the continuance of Saddam's regime. The total collapse of the Communist system in Europe and the disintegration of the USSR, the most momentous political development since 1945 – fuelled by the refusal of the Russian Federation to accept an attempted coup – was welcomed by the majority of the people. It did cause some international concern, since the world would be left with only one superpower, the USA. It seemed probable too that some of the individual republics would experience problems like those of another fracturing federation, Yugoslavia, approaching the brink of full-scale civil war.

▲ **Oilwells blaze on the Kuwait-Iraqi border during the Gulf War. The deliberate destruction of wellheads led to widespread fears for the environmental consequences even after the cessation of hostilities permitted experts to begin to bring them under control.**

● **4 Jan**: President Siad Barre of Somalia announces he is ready for peace talks with rebels and opposition groups and will accept the outcome of negotiations. However, fighting continues. (›27 Jan)

● **16 Jan**: War breaks out in the Gulf when US-led allied forces launch an air strike on Baghdad. The UN deadline for withdrawal from Kuwait had expired at 5 pm GMT.

● **18 Jan**: Iraq fires Scud missiles on Israeli cities in an attempt to force Israel to enter the war, and therefore split the allies.

● **20 Jan**: Iraq fires 10 Scud missiles at Riyadh and Dhahran, in Saudi Arabia. US spokesmen say that one landed harmlessly and the rest were intercepted by Patriot missiles.

● **24 Jan**: The allies liberate the first piece of Kuwait, the island of Qaruh, after a 5-hour battle.

● **27 Jan**: Somali president Barre flees after rebels overrun his palace.

● **Jan**: Yugoslav government accuses Serbia of undermining the monetary system and jeopardizing the federal program of economic reforms when it emerges that the republic illegally printed currency to prop up its bankrupt economy.

● **1 Feb**: In a speech at the opening of parliament, president de Klerk announces that the Land Acts of 1913 and 1936 and the Group Areas Act of 1966, reserving most of the land for whites and segregating residential areas, will be abolished during the current parliamentary session (SA).

● **3 Feb**: The Italian Communist party disbands itself, abandons Marxism, and is renamed the Democratic Party of the Left.

● **5 Feb**: Sudan decrees a federal system in an attempt to end seven years of civil war.

● **10 Feb**: Referendum in Lithuania votes in favour of independence from Moscow.

● **20 Feb**: President Ramiz Alia takes over "all powers" in Albania, to bring about reform in the country. A student strike in Tiranë had threatened to become a nationwide protest. (›27 Apr)

● **20 Feb**: Slovenia votes to give local laws precedence over federal legislation, the first formal step toward independence. Croatia folows suit on 21 Feb.

● **23 Feb**: Military leaders seize power from the elected government in Thailand, with the support of King Bhumibol.

● **28 Feb**: Bangladesh is thrown into new political uncertainty after the first democratic election in its history leaves no party with an outright majority.

● **28 Feb**: US president George Bush announces that the war to liberate Kuwait has been won and that fighting is to stop at 5 am.

● **4 Mar**: The port of Basra in south Iraq falls to forces opposed to Saddam Hussein and fighting spreads to other cities. Kurdish rebels also begin fighting in the north of the country.

● **17 Mar**: The first ever referendum in the USSR is held, on whether the USSR should be preserved as a federation of equal sovereign republics. The result is a narrow majority in favor.

● **26 Mar**: The army seizes power in Mali after four days of pro-democratic rioting. President Moussa Traore and family are put under arrest.

● **29 Mar**: Giulio Andreotti resigns as Italy's prime minister, ending the 49th postwar government. He is forced to resign by demands from the Socialist party and president Cossiga.

● **Mar**: European states, USA and Canada urge nonessential embassy staff and families to leave Ethiopia after victories by northern rebels in their offensive launched on 23 Feb.

● **9 Apr**: Georgia proclaims formal independence from Moscow. On the following day, USSR troops move in to reassert control in the racially troubled South Ossetia region, causing the nationalist authorities to proclaim a general strike in protest.

● **10 Apr**: Students and youths in Togo fight riot police in the capital Lomé, demanding the resignation of president Eyadema, in power since 1963.

● **17 Apr**: US forces move into northern Iraq to start setting up safe havens for Kurdish refugees.

● **27 Apr**: The first US government aircraft since 1979 lands in Iran, delivering blankets for Kurdish refugees.

● **Apr**: For the first time since the end of the Vietnam war, the USA gives a symbolic amount of aid to Hanoi. The move is prompted by Hanoi's cooperation in acounting for 2,276 USA still missing from the war and in ending the Cambodian civil war.

● **Apr**: Rebel Kurds regroup for an attack on key cities, now that they are no longer hampered by their families, which are in refugee camps on the Iranian and Turkish borders.

● **Apr**: The ANC rules out any form of legislative veto for minority groups in a post-apartheid society, saying it would frustrate majority rule by universal suffrage (SA).

● **16 May**: General strike begins in Albania, bringing down the Communist government after 20 days.

● **21 May**: Rajiv Gandhi, former prime minister of India, is killed in a bomb attack.

● **3 Jun**: President Gorbachev and regional leaders decide to drop "socialist" from the country's name and call it the Union of Soviet Sovereign Republics, though official news agency Tass is told that the decision does not mean a rejection of socialist ideals.

● **15 Jun**: Sikh militants, demanding a separate homeland in the Punjab, kill over 100 passengers in attacks on two trains.

● **17 Jun**: The longest general election in India comes to an end, resulting in another hung parliament. P.V. Narasimha Roa becomes the new prime minister.

● **20 Jun**: The German parliament votes to move the country's seat of government from Bonn to Berlin.

● **24 Jun**: Unconditional and unlimited ceasefire comes into operation in Cambodia, ending the 12-year conflict.

● **27 Jun**: Open warfare breaks out in Slovenia as Yugoslav tanks move in to bring the rebel republic to heel. On 30 Jun, the Yugoslav army agrees to withdraw and a fragile peace ensues.

● **Jun**: USSR is forced to agree to new arms concessions when USA warns that future relations with Moscow and a superpower summit depend on the successful outcome of negotiations to resolve differences over the CFE treaty.

● **1 Jul**: Leaders of the six Warsaw Pact countries meet in Prague and sign a protocol terminating the alliance.

● **7 Jul**: Federal troops intervene in eastern Croatia to break up a day-long gun battle between Serbs and Croats.

● **8 Jul**: Yugoslavia takes a step back from civil war after the federal government accepts a peace agreement mediated by the EC.

● **9 Jul**: Tension grows in Croatia between Serbs and Croats, and Serbs set a Croatian village alight.

● **16 Jul**: President Bush, at the G7 summit in London, wins unanimous support for renewed use of military force if Iraq continues to defy the resolution demanding the destruction of all Iraqi nuclear weapons.

● **29 Jul**: US and USSR negotiators initial the most complicated arms control agreement ever, after nine years of talks, the first that requires the superpowers to reduce their stocks of long-range nuclear weapons, rather than regulating any increase.

● **Jul**: Reports are received that a ceasefire agreement has been reached between the Lebanese government and the PLO.

● **18 Aug**: President Gorbachev is imprisoned at his holiday villa by hardline Communist conspirators carrying out a coup. The coup crumbles on 21 Aug, and its leaders flee Moscow, as Boris Yeltsin, president of Russia, rallies the population. Gorbachev is restored as president.

● **25 Aug**: Gorbachev resigns as leader of the Communist party in the USSR, and the party prepares to dissolve, ending seven decades of Communist supremacy.

● **30 Oct**: Talks begin in Madrid between Israel, Syria, Jordan and Palestinian delegates.

● **1 Feb**: Earthquake in the Northwest Frontier Province in Pakistan, and in Afghanistan, kills 1,500.

● **1 Mar**: US expert "Red" Adair is called in to tackle blazes on all Kuwait's 950 producing oilwells, which have been set alight by Iraqi troops or allied bombing.

● **27 Mar**: The IOC readmits South Africa to the Olympics after a 30-year absence.

● **4 Apr**: The USSR parliament is told that the country faces imminent financial collapse as its 15 republics have either neglected to pay or frozen their agreed contributions to the central budget.

● **22 Apr**: The first UN relief supplies for Kurdish refugees reach Iraq. 20,000 per day are said to be returning to Iraq.

● **30 Apr**: Israel prepares to rescue around 20,000 Ethiopian Jews trapped in Addis Ababa before it falls to rebel forces, in one of the largest airlifts in history.

● **Apr**: The EC lifts most of the remaining sanctions on South Africa.

● **Apr**: A cholera outbreak in South America reaches epidemic proportions.

● **12 Jun**: Mount Pinatubo erupts, threatening to obliterate the US 13th Air Force at Clark Air Base (Phil).

● **Jun**: Referendum in Leningrad votes to change its name back to St Petersburg.

● **Jun**: After the worst race riots in its history, Belgium grants nationality to 40,000 immigrants and makes it easier to gain citizenship for those born in Belgium of foreign parents.

● **1 Jul**: Sweden applies formally for membership of the EC, after months of speculation over whether it would affect her policy of neutrality.

● **17 Jul**: G7 leaders promise USSR a special association with the IMF and World Bank, which would offer help and advice, as well as technical help from the OECD, though there are no offers of financial aid.

● **18 Jul**: Massive flooding affects half of China after torrential rains in the north and west – the worst since the 1930s.

● **8 Aug**: John McCarthy, UK hostage in Beirut for 1,943 days, is released.

● It is revealed that the trade in babies in Peru has risen dramatically since austerity measures aimed at controlling the economy plunged millions into abject poverty. Childless Western couples offer $10,000-$17,000 for a baby.

● Collapse of the Bank of Credit and Commerce International on the discovery of massive fraud, panics investors worldwide.

● Nobel Prize for Peace is awarded to human rights campaigner Aung San Suu Kyi (Burma)

● **21 Feb**: Death of ballerina Margot Fonteyn, aged 71 (UK).

● **3 April**: Death of writer Graham Greene, aged 86 (UK).

● Franco Zeffirelli's film of *Hamlet* starring Mel Gibson, Alan Bates and Glenn Close is released (USA).

● *Dances with Wolves*, starring and directed by Kevin Costner (USA).

● Jonathan Pryce and Lea Salonga, stars of the Broadway production *Miss Saigon* win Tony awards for the best musical acting.

● Pulitzer Prizes are won by Neil Simon for his play *Lost in Yonkers* and by John Updike for his novel *Rabbit at Rest* (USA).

● The film of *Cyrano de Bergerac*, stars Gérard Depardieu (Fr).

● Egyptian experts announce the discovery of a previously unknown Pharonic city hidden beneath a village on the outskirts of Cairo.

● Trevor Lloyd Davies, a physician, and his wife Margaret, a theologian, put forward the hypothesis that Jesus did not die on the cross, but that he lost conciousness because of diminished blood supply to the brain, was taken to have died, and was later resuscitated (UK).

● Nobel Prize for Literature awarded to Nadine Gordimer (South Africa)

● Experts from the International Atomic Energy Agency warn of the risks of a nuclear disaster in Bulgaria at the plant at Kozlodoy.

● UK researchers find a way of assessing how long people with HIV are likely to remain healthy before developing AIDS. The lower the levels of a certain type of white blood cell, the higher the risk.

● UK scientist Peter Jones works out how snowflakes form by discovering why some fall as stars and other as tiny plates of ice.

● The study of tiny beads of glass in Haiti by US scientists gives the clearest evidence yet that dinosaurs were extinguished by a cataclysmic event 65 million years ago.

● Japanese and US astronomers discover an erupting quasar, 2 billion light years away, which emitted as much emergy in three minunutes in 1989 as the sun does in 1 million years.

● Scientists develop heart operations that could make transplants largely unnecessary. The techniques involve rebuilding damaged areas of heart with muscles taken from the patient's body.

● Scientists produce an inhalent form of calcitonin, a drug that helps prevent the bone-loss disease osteoporosis. At present, the drug is expensive and only available through injection (UK)

● US scientists use genetic engineering to breed pigs that have hemoglobin in their blood, making an important step forward in the search for a substitute for human blood.

● Texas Instruments and South California Edison announce a new low-cost process for producing solar cells.

● US scientists suggest a high-fiber diet could help protect some women against breast cancer.

● Researchers extract a chemical from the leaves of the European Yew which has produced results in the treatment of ovarian cancer.

● US and European researchers announce that they have isolated the gene responsible for fragile-X syndrome, the most common cause of mental handicap.

● UK researchers discover a link between some cot death cases and a variety of microorganisms and fungi found in mattresses; babies lying face down are therefore able to inhale them.

● Irun Cohen and colleagues at the Weizmann Institute, Israel, report that they have found a naturally occurring peptide which cures diabetes in mice.

● AIDS has now attacked more than 170,000 Americans since 1981 and another 6,000 develop the disease every month. By the year 2000, 40 million people worldwide may be infected with HIV, according to WHO.

INDEX OF PEOPLE

References to the main listings contain both numbers and letters. The numbers refer to years, not to page numbers. The letters following the year refer to the strand. P = Politics; S = Society; C = Culture; Sc = Science. Figures in italics refer to the captions to the illustrations. Thus 60So = 1960, Society; *60* = 1960 illustration caption.

215

GENERAL INDEX

into nitric acid 02Sc; atomic bonds 61Sc; atomic weights 14Sc; Bakelite 09Sc; benzene ring, stability of 31Sc; berkelium 50Sc; biochemistry *see* biological sciences; californium 50Sc; carbon-14 40Sc, 45Sc, 46Sc; chemical bond 16Sc, 54Sc; chemical reactions 56Sc, 83Sc; chlorophyll synthesized 60Sc; colloid solutions 25Sc; cordite 11Sc; crystal structure, Bernal chart 26Sc; diamond powder produced from soot 90So; dienes 50Sc; dipoles 36Sc; disperse systems 26Sc; duralumin 10Sc; dyes 05Sc; einsteinium 52Sc; electrochemical analysis 22Sc; electron diffraction in gases 36Sc; electronic theory of dissociation 03Sc; electrostatic precipitator 10Sc; element 109 created 82Sc; elements, transmutation of 22Sc; transuranic 51Sc; fermentative enzymes 29Sc; Fischer-Tropsch reaction 25Sc; fluorine 06Sc; Grignard reagent of value 12Sc; Haber process 08Sc, 09Sc, 18Sc; heavy hydrogen 34Sc; helium liquefied 08Sc; high speed chemical reactions 67Sc; high-pressure 31Sc; hormones synthesized 54Sc, 55Sc, 74Sc; hydroaromatic compounds 05Sc; hydrogen manufacture 25Sc; hypothetical chemical reactions 81Sc; icosahedral symmetry 52Sc; immunochemistry 04Sc; insecticides 39Sc, 54Sc; isotopes 22Sc, 43Sc, 68Sc; lanxides 85Sc; low temperature 49Sc; LSD 43Sc, 66So; metallic glasses 52Sc; microanalysis of organic substances 23Sc; molecular chaperones 88Sc; molecule 13Sc, atomic bonding 61Sc, bonding 76Sc, electronic structures and geometry 71Sc, molecular chemistry 87Sc, three-dimensional arrangement of atoms 75Sc; myoglobin, structure determined 62Sc; napalm 42Sc; nitrogen, fixing 72Sc, 75Sc, production of 02Sc; nobelium 57Sc; noble gas compounds 62Sc; nucleotide coenzymes 57Sc; organic compounds combined with metals 65Sc, 73Sc; organic substances, microanalysis 23Sc; oxygen production 02Sc; paint manufacture 18Sc, 26Sc; paper chromatography 44Sc, 52Sc; pH meter 34Sc; pH scale 09Sc; photosynthesis 78Sc, 88Sc; plastics *see* plastics; plutonium 51Sc; polargraphic analysis 59Sc; polyamide 32Sc; polymers *see* plastics; radicals 00Sc; radio 28Sc; radiocarbon dating *see* archeology; Raschig process 20Sc; reaction dynamics 86Sc; resonance 31Sc; RNA, catalytic properties 89Sc; serum proteins 48Sc; silicones 04Sc, 43Sc; sterols 28Sc; sugar nucleotides 70Sc; sulfur compounds 55Sc; surface 32Sc; synthetic materials *see* synthetic materials; synthetic pathways 79Sc; thermal cracking technique 11Sc; thermochemistry 20Sc; titanium oxide 08Sc; TNT 02Sc; tryptophan discovered 00Sc; whole-number rule 22Sc; X-ray crystallography 85Sc; X-ray diffraction in gases 36Sc

Chernenkov effect 58Sc

Chile

Andean Development Corporation 68So; Argentina, economic unity with 53So; Chaco War mediating committee 35P; Ibanez, resignation of 31P; international conference on social issues 42So; nitrate trade 15So; handover of power 90P, referendum rejects 88P, state of siege declared 84P, 86P; socialist government 32P; Tacna-Arica, dispute over 29P; Valparaiso earthquake 06So; War of the Pacific 04P; workers' unrest 05So; World War II 45P

China

Anglo-Chinese bank 12So; atomic weapons 63P, 64Sc, 67Sc; banks 04So, 07So, 13So, 28So; Beijing placed under military rule 67P; Boxer indemnity 24P, 24So; Boxer Rebellion 00P, 01P, *01*; Burma Road closed 40P; Cambodia's "struggle against imperialism" supported by 63P; capital transferred to Nanjing 28P; Chang Jiang River floods 11So; child marriages outlawed 50So; Ch'in terracotta army *75*; China Foundation for the Promotion of Education and Culture 24So; Chinese Soviet Republic, Jianxsi province 31P; civil war 20P, 46P, 48P, 49P; Comecon 58So; Communists 24P, 27P, 35P, 45P, 46P, 48P, 49P; Communist party restructure 82P; Communists cooperate with Nationalists against Japan 37P; Confucian teachings attacked 74P; constitution 75P, 78So; Cultural Revolution 65So, 66P, 74P; earthquakes 22So, 32So; economy 08So, 53P, 55So, 56So, 78So; foreign investment 84So; special economic zones 84So; famines 07So, 20So; floods 24So, 31So, 35So, 81So, 91So; Franco-Japanese agreement 07P; Fujian declared independent 31P; Gang of Four 77P, 80P, 81P; Great Leap Forward 58So; Guangau period 08P; Guangdong declared independent 31P; Guangzhou government 31P; Guanxi declared independent 31P; Guizhou declared independent 31P; Guomindang (Kuomintang; KMT; Nationalists) 07P, 12P, 13P, 27P, 45P, 46P, Beijing occupied by 28P, Communists allowed to join 24P, defeat by Communists 50P, Japan, Communist alliance against 37P, northern campaign 26P, US backing 48P; Ho-Umezu Agreement 35P; Hong Kong air link reopened 78So, British agreement to return to Chinese rule 84P, 89So, illegal emigration to 62So; Hunan 31P; IFC 80So; India invaded 62P; Indian border clashes 59P, 67P; infanticide outlawed 50So; International Development Association (IDA) 80So; Japan 28P, 32P, 33P, 34P, 35P, invasion of China 36P, 38So, civilians killed 13P, goods boycotted 31P, property in Manchuria transferred to 51So, Manchuria and Mongolia, Japan demands rights in 15P, 16P, Russo-Japanese agreement 07P, Russo-Japanese convention 16P, Shanghai 32P, 35P, Sino-Japanese clashes 28P, Sino-Japanese crisis 31P, Sino-Japanese War *see* Sino-Japanese War; Jianxsi province, Chinese Soviet Republic 31P; Kiaochow returned 21P; Korean War *see* Korean War; leadership purged 66P; legal code revised 02So; Lin Piao attacked 74P; Long March 27P, 34P, *34*, 35P; Macao 87P; Manchu dynasty 05P, 06P, 09P, 11P, 17P; Manchuria 45P, Communists capture 48P, Japan demands rights in 15P, 16P, Japanese military action in 33P, Japanese property in transferred 51So, Russia offers deal over 01P, siege of Mukden 31P; Manzhouguo 32P, 34P; Mao Zedong 34P, 50P; meteorites fall in 76Sc; Mongolia, Japan demands rights in 15P, 16P, Outer, autonomy recognized 13P, placed under Chinese suzerainty 19P, Russia offers deal over 01P; Nanjing, capital transferred to 28P; Nanjing government 40P, challenged by Yen Hsi-shan 30P, provisional constitution 31P, recognition 28P, 28So; National Army 46P; Nationalist China *see* Taiwan; Nixon's visit 72P; nuclear test 64Sc; open door policy 00C, 07So, 21P; opium cultivation and consumption 06So; parliament 09P, 12P, 13P; People's Liberation Army 67P; People's National Convention 31P; People's Republic of 49P; Pinyin phonetic alphabet 79So; polygamy outlawed 50So; prodemocracy demonstrations 86P, 87P; Progress party 12P; Quemoy Islands bombarded 58P; Red Guards 66P, 67P; reforms 02So; revolution (1911) 11P; satellite launched 70Sc; "Second Revolution" 13P; Shandong Treaty 21P; Sino-Japanese War *see* Sino-Japanese War; slavery abolished 10So; South Africa, Chinese coolies imported by 03So; Soviet Union, mutual aid and friendship pact 50P; nuclear materials and scientific knowledge shared 55P; Soviet aid 59So; Soviet border clashes 69P; Soviet military advisors 24P; Soviet-Chinese talks concerning ideological differences 63P; space technology agreement with Australia 88Sc; Sun Yat-sen elected president 11P; Taiwan *see* Taiwan; Tiananmen Square demonstration 89P; Tibet *see* Tibet; trade, NATO countries announce trade relaxation 58So, secret trade agreement with Western nations 79So, tariff autonomy 29So, 30So; US agreement 04So, unification 28P; United Kingdom, Anglo-Chinese treaties 02So, 06P, Britain abandons Shanghai and Tianjin province 40P, British goods and shipping boycotted 25P, diplomatic relations resumed with 72P, Hong Kong, agreement to return to Chinese rule 84P, 89So, ministerial visit to 63P; United Nations bans shipment of strategic materials to 51P; United Nations membership 71P, approved 70p, rejected 50P, *50*, 62P, 65P, 69P; United States, boycott of US goods 05So, Chinese excluded from 05So, commercial and friendship treaty 46So, diplomatic relations established 79P, trade agreement 04So, US newsmen allowed in 71So, US table tennis team visit 71So; Vietnam, aid cut 78So, China protests over US involvement in 62P, Chinese invasion 79P; Vietnam War *see* Vietnam War; World Bank membership 80So

chlorofluorocarbons (CFCs) 74Sc, 75Sc; Montreal Protocol 88So; Swedish ban 78Sc; United States ban 77Sc

Chosen, Korea renamed 10P

Christmas Islands 57P

chromosomes *see* biological sciences

Civic Forum 89P

cloud chamber 11Sc, 12Sc, 48Sc

cocktails 22So

coelacanth 38Sc, 87Sc

coenzyme A 47Sc

Cold War *87*, official ending 90P

Colombia

Amazon Pact 78So; Andean Development Corporation 68So; Dominican Embassy hostages taken 80So; drugs, production and export of illegal 78So; Lopez 34P; Michelson elected president 74P; mudslide in Medellin 87So; Nevado del Ruiz erupts 85So; Pan-American Conference 48P; Panama Canal 03P, 21So; social reforms 34P; Venezuelan border dispute 22P *see also* Panama

Colombo Plan 51So

Colossus calculating device 43Sc

Colt .45 automatic pistol 11Sc

Comecon *see* Council for Economic Assistance

Comintern (Third International) 19P, 35P; Anti-Comintern Pact 36P, 37P, 39P; democratic nations supported against fascist states 35P; dissolved 43P; France 20P; rearmament, opposition to ceased 35P

Commonwealth Games 30So, 86So

Commonwealth of Nations 48P, 49P

Commonwealth Immigrants Act (UK) 62So

communism

Cominform (Communist Information Bureau) 47P; Comintern *see* Comintern; domino effect 53P; national parties' independence endorsed 76P; Roman Catholic supporters threatened with excommunication 49P; Second International 00P; Surrealists, alignment with 27C; Third International *see* Comintern; Truman doctrine 47P; United States 48P, commitment to resist Communist aggression in Middle East 57P, Communist party outlawed 54So

compact disc 78Sc, 82Sc

Compasso d'Oro awards 54C

computer

4X music computer 81C, 87C, 88C; ADA language 79Sc; analog 25Sc; differential analyzer 30Sc; Apple II 77Sc; Atanasoff-Berry Computer (ABC) 42Sc; Atlas 61Sc; automated banking 56So; automatic general-purpose 44Sc; Binary Automatic Computer (BINAC) 49Sc; bubble memory 69Sc; COBOL language 59Sc; computerized weather forecast 50Sc; Cray I supercomputer 82Sc; cryotron device 57Sc; digital 36Sc; electromagnetic relays 41Sc; electronic 39Sc, 42Sc, 45Sc; Electronic Delay Storage Automatic Computer (EDSAC) 49Sc; Electronic Discrete Variable Computer (EDVAC) 45Sc; Electronic Numerical Integrator and Computer (ENIAC) 45Sc, 46Sc, 50Sc; electronic stored program computer 49Sc; flip-flop electronic switching circuit 19Sc; floppy disc 70Sc; FORTRAN programming language 56Sc; IBM 44Sc, 60Sc, personal computer launched 81Sc, hard disk 83Sc; Lisp (List Processor) language 56Sc; magnetic tape data storage 51Sc; Mark 1 48Sc; microchip 61Sc, 69Sc, 83Sc, 84Sc; microprocessor 69Sc, 71Sc; Numerical Aerodynamic Simulation Facility 87Sc; PASCAL language 71Sc; personal 77Sc; punched data tape 41Sc; RAM memory chip 84Sc; UNIVAC 51Sc; UPIC music system 77C; word processor 64Sc; Z2 41Sc

concentration camps *45*;

Auschwitz 45P; Bergen-Belsen 45P; Boer War 00P; Buchenwald 33P, 45P; Dachau 45P

German 38P, 45P; Majdanek 44So; World War II 33P, 39So, 42So, 44So, 45P

Conference on Security and Cooperation in Europe 75P

Congo

army mutiny 60P; Belgian 08P, 09P, 21So, Congo Free State 04P, infrastructure developed 21So, Katanga Mining Union 06So, liberalizing reforms 09P, United Nations action 60P; civil war 60P, 61P; Congolese Workers Party 70P; constitution 70P; Free State, labor conditions; investigated 04P; French 10P, 60P; Katanga incorporation 62P, *62*, 63P; independence declared 60P, 61P; Mobuto 66P; parliament's functions abolished 66P; People's Republic of 70P; rebel strongholds captured 65P; renamed Zaire 71P; Tananarive Conference 61P; Tshombe sworn in as premier 64P; United Nations troops sent *62*; white rebel mercenaries 67P

Congo-Brazzaville, declared republic 58P

Congress of the International Association for the Legal Protection of Workers 01So

conservation *see* environment

Constantinople, Treaty of 13P

Constructivism 22C

contact lenses 58Sc, 65Sc

contraception *see* birth control

Conventional Armed Forces in Europe, Treaty on 90P

Cook Islands, annexation by New Zealand 00P

copyright

United Kingdom 11So; United States, film industry 08So; Universal Copyright Convention 55So

cordite 11Sc

Corsica 38P, 43P

cortisone 35Sc, 36Sc, 48Sc

cosmic rays 12Sc, 25Sc, 31Sc, 32Sc, 36Sc, 45Sc, 48Sc, 54Sc, 58Sc, 65Sc; examination with photographic plate 37Sc; *Explorer* satellite studies 58Sc; tracks discovered in bubble chamber 52Sc

Costa Rica

Bryan Chamorro Treaty 14So; Federation of Central America 21P; Latin Accord 89P; Pact of Union 21P; peace plan signed 87P

Council of Europe 49P; European Convention on the Repression of Terrorism 77So

Council for Mutual Economic Assistance (Comecon) 49So, 63So, 79So, 84So; 20-year plan approved 71So, Albania expelled 61P; China and North Korea join 58So; Comecon/US/EEC

238

240

Nationalist party 64P; Afrikaner Bond 10P; Afrikaner Nationalist party 51P; Anglo-Chinese labor Convention 04So; Anglo-Dutch equality 03P; Angola, withdrawal from 84P; apartheid *see* apartheid; arms sales to South Africa blocked 70So; Bantustans, self-governing 63P; Basutoland 63P; Bechuanaland 63P; Biko, death of 77So; black factional fighting 90P; black homelands 76P, 77P; Boer separatism 14So; Boer War 00P, 02P; Bophutswana 77P; British-imperialist Unionist party 10P; Bureau of Race Relations 47P; Chinese coolies, importation 03So, 04So; Chinese Labor Ordinance 04So; Citizenship Act 49P; Commonwealth Eminent Persons Group, visit by 86P; Commonwealth of Nations 60P, withdrawal from 61P; Communist party, ban on lifted 90P; constitution 10P, reform 83P; constitutional convention 08P; economy 32So, 49So, 75So; emergency powers introduced 53P, 55So; Ethiopia, boycott of South African goods 61So; franchise 30So, 54So, 68So, 89So; general strike 14So; German Southwest Africa 15P, 19P; Ghana 59So, 60So; Het Volk 05P, 07P, 10P; Immigration Act 14So; imperial trade tariffs 32So; imprisonment of potential state witnesses 65So; independence, request for 19P; Indian population 27P; International Labor Organization 61So, 64So, withdrawal from 64So; Italians driven out of Kenya 41P; Kissinger, visit by 76P; Labor party 54So; Ladysmith, relief of 00P; Land Acts, abolition 91P; Macmillan's "wind of change" speech 60P; Mandela, release 90P, 90So, *90*, trial and sentence 63P, 64P; military aid to banned by UN 77P; mining industry 13So, 14So, 73So, 75So, 87So; Moloise executed 85P; Mozambique, anti-guerrilla accord 84P; multiracial cabinet sworn in 84P; Namibia *see* Namibia; National Government 33P; National party 87P; Nationalist party 14So, 19P, 34P, 53P, 74P; native affairs commission 20So; native reservations 20So; newspapers, closure of 77So; Nigeria boycotts South African goods 61So; Orange River Colony 07P; Orangia Unie 05P, 10P; parliamentary system 08P; political activists, arrest of 77So; political prisoners 89P; Portugal, convention with 28So; Progressive party 59P; Public Safety Bill 53P; republic status, vote for 60P; sanctions against 59So, 60So, 61So, 62P, 77P, 85So, 86So, British refusal to implement 86So, European Community lifts 91So; Sharpeville 60So; South Africa party 10P, 34P; South African Government Bill 52P; South African Union Bill 09P; Southern Rhodesia, offer to join rejected by 22P; Southwest Africa, South Africa demands 46P, 47P; sports boycott 68So, 84So; Springboks, New Zealand tour 81So; state of emergency 85P, 86P; suffrage 06P, 09P, 51P, 83P, 84P; Swaziland 63P; three-chamber parliament for whites, Indians and coloreds 85P; Transkei 76P; Transvaal, local autonomy granted to 06P, 07P; Uitnhage shootings 85P; Union of South Africa 09P; United Kingdom cricket players tour 82So; United Nations 60So, 61So, 63P, 73So, 77P, South African membership 58P, 74P, withdrawal 55P; United party 34P; Vereeniging, Treaty of 02P; Zambian border war 84P

South Korea *see* Korea

South Yemen 77P

Southeast Asia Treaty Organization (SEATO) 54P, 55P

Southern Rhodesia

African nations' plan of action 66P; border closed 76P; British crown colony 23P, 79P; independence, British proposals rejected 77P, draft agreement on 71P, 72P, Kissinger's proposals 76P, transfer of power 78P; martial law declared 78P; Mozambique, attacks on 76P, 78P; Muzorewa, election as first black prime minister 79P; Olympic Games, barred 72So; one-man one-vote elections 79P; Patriotic Front 78P; peace pacts 79P; Pearce Commission 72P; referendum approving white rule 69P; republic declared 66P, 70P; Rhodesia and Nyasaland Federation Bill 53P; Rhodesian Front 77P; Unilateral Declaration of Independence (UDI) 64P, 65P, 66P; Union of South Africa, invitation to join 22P; United Kingdom withdraws support for Central African Federation 63P; United Nations 62P, 63P, 66P, 68P; United Nations and Britain impose economic sanctions 65P; white missionaries killed 77P; Zambia 73P, 78P; Zimbabwe African People's Union (ZAPU) 63P; *see also* Zimbabwe

Southwest Africa, South Africa demands to annex 46P, 47P

Southwest Africa People's Organization (SWAPO) 78P, 85P, 89P

Soviet Union *see* Union of Soviet Socialist Republics

space, outer

satellites *see* satellite; United Nations resolution promoting peaceful use of 59So; treaty limiting military use of 67P

space exploration

Ariane 82Sc, 83Sc; European Space Agency 85Sc, 86Sc; German Democratic Republic, cosmonauts 78Sc; *Giotto* spaceprobe 85Sc, 86Sc; Japanese 85Sc; Jupiter 73Sc; Mars 64Sc, 65Sc, 71Sc, 76Sc; monkeys, space trip survived by 59So; moon 59Sc, 62Sc, 64Sc, 65Sc, 66Sc, 67Sc, 68Sc, car 71Sc, lunar astronomical observatory 72Sc; moon landings 65Sc, 66Sc, 67Sc, 68Sc, 69Sc, *69*, 71Sc, 72Sc; moonwalk 69Sc; Neptune 83Sc, 88Sc; Uranus 86Sc; Venus 62Sc, 66Sc, 67Sc, 69Sc, 78Sc, 82Sc; *see also* space exploration, Soviet *and* space exploration, United States

space exploration, Soviet 59Sc, 67Sc, 75Sc, 78Sc, 82Sc; *Burian* space shuttle 88Sc; dogs sent into space 60Sc; earth orbited 61Sc, *61*, 62Sc, 63Sc, 64Sc; endurance records 78Sc, 79Sc, 80Sc, 82Sc, 87Sc; female cosmonaut 63Sc; Gagarin *61*, 68So; Halley's Comet, rendezvous with 85Sc; *Luna* probes 66Sc, 70Sc, 73Sc; lunar orbit 66Sc; *Lunik* space probes 59Sc, 63Sc; *Lunokhod II*, ground-controlled moon-rover 73Sc; *Mars 2* and *3* orbit Mars 71Sc; Mars photographed 64Sc; moon 59Sc, 66Sc, 68Sc; Proton 4 68Sc; Salyut space stations 73Sc, 77Sc, 78Sc, 79Sc, 80Sc, 82Sc; *Soyuz* program 69Sc, 75Sc, 77Sc; space walks 65Sc, 66Sc, 84Sc; US/Soviet cooperation 70Sc, 75Sc; *Venera* program 66Sc, 69Sc, 83Sc; Venus 67Sc, 75Sc, 78Sc, 82Sc; *Voskhod* 64Sc; *Vostok* program *61, 62Sc; Zond* program 64Sc, 65Sc, 68Sc

space exploration, United States 61Sc; Agena rocket 66Sc; *Apollo* program 68Sc, 72Sc; *Apollo 18* and *Soyuz 19* couple 75Sc; *Apollo* moon landings 69Sc, 71Sc, 72Sc, moonwalk 69Sc, spacecraft fire 67Sc; atomic-powered battery 72Sc; Cape Canaveral testing ground 49Sc; *Challenger* space shuttle 83Sc, 84Sc, 86Sc, *86; Columbia* space shuttle 81SC, 82Sc, 83Sc; *Discovery* shuttle 90Sc; docking operation 66Sc; earth orbited *61*, 62Sc, 63Sc; endurance record 70Sc; female astronaut 83Sc; *Gemini* program 65Sc, 66Sc; Halley's Comet 85Sc; Jupiter, photographed 74Sc; lunar astronomical observatory 72Sc; *Lunar Orbiter 1* and *2* 66Sc; manned space shuttle 72Sc; *Mariner* program 62Sc, 64Sc, 65Sc, 67Sc, 69Sc, 71Sc, 74Sc; Mars 64Sc 65Sc, 69Sc; moon 64Sc, 65Sc, 67Sc, 68Sc, landing program 65Sc, 66Sc, 67Sc, 68Sc, *69*; moon car 71Sc; National Aeronautics and Space Administration (NASA) 58So, 70Sc; *Pioneer* program 60Sc, 72Sc, *72*, 73Sc, 74Sc, 79Sc, 83Sc; *Ranger* program 62Sc, 64Sc, 65Sc; *Saturn 5* 67Sc; Saturn 79Sc, 81Sc, moons discovered 80Sc; Skylab 73Sc, 83Sc; space rendevous 65Sc; space walks 65Sc, 66Sc, 84Sc; *Surveyor* moon landings 67Sc, 68Sc; *Ulysses* 90Sc; Uranus studied 86Sc; US/Soviet cooperation 70Sc, 75Sc; Venus 67Sc, 74Sc; *Venus* spaceprobes 78Sc; *Viking 1* and *2* 75Sc, 76Sc; *Voyager 1* and *2* 77Sc, 79Sc, 80Sc, 81Sc, 86Sc, 88Sc

Spain

Algeciras Conference 06P; Anglo-Italian agreement on independence of 37P; Anti-Comintern Pact 39P; Argentina, commercial agreement 46So; Associations Law 33So; Azana's reforms 36P; Azcarraga, resignation 01So; Barcelona Universal Exhibition 29C; Basque region *see* Basque region; Blanco, assassination 74P; Canalejos, assassination 12P; Carlists 00P; Catalonia 01So, 09P, 19P, 34P, 39P, autonomy granted 32P, restored 36P, independence declared 34P, referendum approves home rule 79P, regional parliament elected 80P, separatists 26P, 76P; Civil War *see* Spanish Civil War; communism 34P, 35P, 39P, 76P; Communist party 77P; communist regime declared in Asturias 34P; communist uprising 32P; constituent assembly 31P; constitution 31P, 31So, 47P, 66P; Cortes 02P, 23P, 33P 76P; coups 23P, 39P, attempted 81P; economy 67So, 82So; eight-hour working day 19So; elections 31P, 76P, 77P; European Economic Community membership 77So, 86So; Franco regime 36P, 39P, 66P; general strikes 10So, 11So, 30P, 88So; Gibraltar 66P, 69P, 82P, 85P; Grimaldi, execution 63P; Italy, treaty of friendship 26P; Jaca mutiny 30P; Junta of National Defense 36P; League of Nations membership 26P; martial law 11So, 19So, 69P; military insurgence 29P; military service 09P; miners' strikes 03So, 10So; monarchy 31P, 47P, 69P, 75P; Morocco 04P, 06P, 12P; National Defense Council 39P; North Atlantic Treaty Organization (NATO) 82P, 86P; nuclear weapons banned from Spanish territory 86P; Pact of Cartagena 07P; political parties, ban lifted 76P; political prisoners, execution 75So; Popular Front 36P, 37P; religion 01So, 10So, 31So, religious establishment regulated 33So; Republican constitution 31P; Republican party 24P, 31P; Republican-Socialist coalition 31P; revolution, call to establish by force 30P; Revolutionary Marxist party (POUM) 35P; Riffians 21P, 25P; Rivera government 25P; Socialist party 33P, 37P, 82P; student disturbances 65So, 66So, 68So; Tangier Convention 24P; terrorism 81So; United States military bases 53P; Western Sahara 76P; Zamora government 31P

Spanish Civil War 36P, 38P, 39P; Barcelona and Catalonia captured 39P; Bilbao 37P; British-Italian agreement 38P; *For Whom the Bell Tolls* 40C; *Guernica* 37C; Guernica, destruction of 37P; *Homage to Catalonia* 38C; international brigades 36P; Italian legionaries defeated at Briheuga 37P; Italy 37P, 38P; naval blockade 37P; nonintervention protocol 36P; offensive in Catalonia 38 P; Santander 37P; siege of Madrid 36P

Spartakists 18P, 19P, 20P

sport

American football 02So; athletics 35So, 54So, *54*, 81So, 83So, 87So; baseball 03So, 20So, 21So, 27So, 45So; boxing 08So, 13So, 19So, 30So, 51So, 56So, 59So, 64So, 85So; chess 24So; cricket 09So, 26So, 30So, 32So, 38So, 47So, 82So; cycling 03So, 50So, 67So; drugs 60So; four-minute mile *54*; golf 27So, 34So; gymnastics 76So; horse racing 73So, 81So; ice skating 84So; International Amateur Athletic Federation 13So; judo 18So; London marathon 81So; motor racing 00C, 02So, 03So, 06So, 07So, 23So, 27So, 28So, 32So, 50So, 55So, 66So, 67So, 75So; motorcycle racing 07So; orienteering 18So; rugby union 06So, 30So, 81So, 87So; sailing 66So, 71So, 83So; snooker 81So; soccer 06So, 16So, 30So, 38So, 49So, 50So, 58So, 70So, 75So, 85So, 88So, Fédèration Internationale de Football Associations (FIFA) 04So; South Africa banned from international participation 68So, 84So; speedway racing 23So; swimming 08So, 11So, 22So, 23So, 24So, 26So, 50So, 62So, 72So; table tennis 21So, 71So; tennis 05So, 12So, 15So, 19So, 20So, 23So, 38So, 51So, 52So, 57So, 68So, 75So, 76So, 80So, 84So, 85So, Davis cup 00C; transfer fees 20So; women 22So, 26So; wrestling 00C; *see also* Asian Games, Commonwealth Games, Central American and Caribbean Games, Far Eastern Games, Olympic Games

Sri Lanka

Ceylon, name changed from 72P; Commonwealth of Nations 72P; independence 72P; Indian peace accord 87P; Indian peace-keeping force 87P; Tamil separatists 83So, 84So, 85P, 86P, 87P; *see also* Ceylon

St-Germain, Treaty of 19P

Stavisky fraud affair 34P

steady state theory 58Sc

steam turbine 10Sc

steel

continuous casting 43Sc; stainless 11Sc, 56So; steel industry 01So, 03So, 09So, 55So, 87So

stereo sound 31Sc, 57C, 79Sc

Stern Gang 48P

Stimson-Layton Agreement 40P

Stockholm Convention 59So

Stockholm Security Conference 86P

Strategic Arms Limitation Talks (SALT) 69P, 70P, 71P, 72P; II 72P, 77So, 79P

Strategic Defense Intitiative (SDI) (Star Wars program) 83Sc

Stresa Conference 35P

submachine gun 16So, 20Sc

submarine

Anti-Submarine Detection Investigation Committee (ASDIC) detectors 18Sc; atomic-powered 52Sc, 54Sc, 60Sc, 63Sc, 67Sc; echo sounder 22Sc; first British 01Sc; L-34 sunk 24So; *Nautilus* 54Sc; sound navigation and ranging (SONAR) 15Sc; undersea passage of North Pole 58Sc; underwater ultrasonic detection 16Sc

Sudan

Anglo-Egyptian agreement over 36P; Arab League membership 56P; calls for unification with Egypt 50P; civil war 72P, 89P, 90So, 91P; coups 76P, 85P, 89P; draft constitution 52P; Egyptian forces reenter 36P, withdraw 24P; Egyptian-Libyan-Sudanese-Syrian federation 70P; French 59P; independent democratic republic declared 56P; irrigation 26So; Libya, relations with broken 76P; limited self-rule offered by Britain 52P; Mali 59P; Soviet Union, relations with broken 76P; UAR signs agreement on sharing Nile waters 59So; United Nations membership 56P, supervised plebiscite proposed 51P

Sudetenland *see* Czechoslovakia

Suez Canal

Anglo-Egyptian agreement 54P; Canal Users' Association 56P; Egyptian seizure of 56P; Entente Cordiale 04P; Israel, canal reopened for Israeli use 75So, denied use of canal 57P, destroys Suez oil refineries 67P; mined 84P

Suez crisis 56So, 57So;

Anglo-Egyptian agreement 54P; Anglo-Egyptian settlement 59P; anti-British riots 52P; British forces in Canal Zone 36P, 51P, 56P; British/United States/French talks 56P; Egypt calls for British troop evacuation 50P; United Nations action 56P

suffrage *see* franchise

suffragette movement *see* franchise

sulfa drugs 32Sc, 35Sc, 36Sc, 37Sc

sun-spots 46Sc

superconductivity 11Sc, 62Sc, 86Sc, 87Sc, 88Sc

supergravity 76Sc

Superrealism 70C, 73C, 74C

Suprematism 15C, 18C

Numbers refer to years. P = Politics; So = Society; C = Culture; Sc = Science

surgery *see* medicine
Surinam 78So
Surrealism 17C, 24C, 26C, 27C, 29C, 30C, 36C; communism, Surrealists align themselves with 27C; Dali 38C, 41C; film 28C, 30C; International Surrealist Exhibition (London) 36C; International Surrealist Exhibition (Paris) 38C, theater 27C
surrogate motherhood 87Sc
Swaziland 63P; Commonwealth of Nations 68P; independence 68P
Sweden
  aerosol sprays, ban on 78Sc; capital punishment abolished 21So; constitution 74P; economy 31So, 77So, 81So; European Community membership application 91So; European Free Trade Association (EFTA) 59So; franchise 07P, 19So; German embassy blown up 75P; German nonaggression pact 39P; Kreuger match plant 13So, 32So; monarchy 74P; neutrality 39P; Nobel Institute of Physics 37Sc; Nordic Economic Union 69So; North Sea Convention 08P; Norway, union dissolved 05P; nuclear power 78P, 80So; Olympic Games 12So; Oslo Agreement 30So; Oslo Convention 32So; Palme, assassination 86P; parliamentary government 07P; Scandinavian common labor market 54So; Social Democratic party 52P, 76P; socialist government 32P; Stockholm Convention 59So; Stockholm Security Conference 86P; Swiss-Swedish-Danish defense league 14P; World War I 17So;
Switzerland
  Army Bill 07P; economy 31So, 34So, 65So; European Free Trade Association (EFTA) 59So; Eurovision 54C; Geneva Disarmament Conference 32P; German commercial treaty 04So; Great St Bernard Tunnel 62So; League of Nations 19P; neutrality 38P; Romansch, recocognition of 37So; St Gotthard railroad 10So; St Moritz Winter Olympics 28So; Simplon tunnel 06So; standing defense militia 07P; Stockholm Convention 59So; Swiss-Swedish-Danish defense league 14P; United Nations, full membership of rejected 86P; women's franchise 71So; *see also* banking
Sydney Harbor Bridge 32Sc
Sydney Opera House 56C, 73C
Symbolism 08C
synthetic materials 03Sc, 28Sc, 74Sc; acetate 20Sc; Acrilan 52Sc; artificial diamond 55Sc; Dacron 41Sc; Lycra 58Sc; nylon 30Sc, 38Sc, 42Sc; polyamide, synthesis 32Sc; polyester 41Sc; polyethylene 53Sc; polypropylene 53Sc; polystyrene 30Sc; polyvinyl chloride (PVC) 30Sc, 43Sc; Rayon 16So; rubber 09Sc, 27Sc, 33Sc; Spandex fibers 58Sc; Terylene 41Sc, 50Sc; viscose artificial silk 05Sc; *see also* plastics
Syria
  Arab guerrilla bases 72P; Arab League 45P; Arab-Israeli conflict 56P, 72P, 73P, 74P, 83P *and see* Arab-Israeli conflict; Baath party 73P; constitution 30P; coup d'état 61P; Druse uprising 25P; Egypt 55P, 66P, 77P; European Economic Community cooperation agreement 77So; Faisal 20P; France 20P, 33P, 36P, 45P; French mandate 20P, 36P; government overthrown 63P; Iraqi military union 63P; Israel *see* Arab-Israeli conflict *above*; Israeli border conflict 62P, 66P, 67P; Jordan 70P, 71P; Kurdish insurrection 37P; League of Nations membership 36P; Lebanon 56P, 69P, 81P; National Council of the Revolution 63P; Palestine Liberation Organization (PLO) 76P, 83P; Pan-Arab Conference 37P; parliament, prorogation 34P; republic 30P; Syrian Arab Republic 61P; Syrian-Egyptian economic union 57So; Syrian-Egyptian-Libyan federation 71P; Syrian-Egyptian-Libyan-Sudanese federation 70P; Turkey 37P, 57P; United Arab Republic (UAR) 58P, 67P, secession from 61P; United Kingdom, British occupation 45P, diplomatic relations broken 86P; World War II *see* World War II

T

Tahiti 06So
Taiwan (Formosa)
  Chinese belligerence 54P, 55P; Chinese Nationalist government 49P, 52P; diplomatic recognition 75P; diplomatic relations severed with France 64P, Italy 70P, Japan 72P, United States 79P; Quemoy Islands 58P; United Nations, expulsion 71P; United States, economic aid 65So, prevention of Chinese invasion, commitment to 54P, talks with China 86P
Tamil separatists *see* Sri Lanka
Tananarive Conference 61P
Tanganyika
  British rule 19P; closer union with Kenya and Uganda, demands for 35P; Commonwealth 61P; constitution 55P; independence 61P, 62P; Republic of Tanganyika and Zanzibar 64P; Tanzania 53P, 64P
Tangier Convention 24P
tank 15So, 16P, 17P, *17* tank warfare 43P
Tanzania 64P, 76P
  Britain, relations with broken 65P; East African Community 67So; Nyerere, retirement of 85P; Uganda 72P, 78P
tape recorder 30Sc, 37So; tapes 54C, 87Sc; Walkman personal stereo 79Sc
Tariff League (UK) 03So
tariffs *see* trade
Tartu, Treaty of 18P, 19P
Tassili rock paintings 33Sc
Tata iron and steel empire 03Sc
teddy bear 03C
Teddy Bears 58C
Teflon 38Sc, 58C
Tegucigalpa, Declaration of 81So
telegraph 02So, 06So, 07Sc, 09So
telephone 00Sc;
  answerphone 04Sc; automatic exchange 00Sc, 09Sc; British Telecom privatized 84So; dial 19Sc; hotline links, United States-Soviet Union 63P, United States-West Germany 69P; London-New York service 27Sc; optical fibers 85Sc; radio 02Sc; repeaters 43Sc; transatlantic cable 56Sc; transcontinental calls 15So; visual 56Sc
teleprinter 31Sc
telescope
  Hubble 90Sc; Mount Wilson 17Sc; radio 74Sc, directional 37Sc, Mauna Kea 83Sc, millimeter 83Sc, Mullard Observatory 72Sc
television 08Sc, 26Sc; ATS-6 satellite 74Sc; British Broadcasting Corporation (BBC) 36So, 46C, 69C; broadcasts 51C, 53So, 55C, 66C, 69C, 78C, 80C, 83C, 84C; Canadian satellite TV broadcasting service 79C; cathode-ray tube 08Sc, 11Sc, 32Sc; Ceefax 73Sc; color 25Sc, 28Sc, 49Sc, 50Sc, 54So; commercially available sets 28So; dissector tube 27Sc; Early Bird satellite 65Sc; Eurovision 54C, 56C; image intensifier 73Sc; international transmission 28Sc; news, mobile television unit records sequences for 34C; optical fibers, transmission of TV signals by 77Sc; Oracle 73Sc; portable transistorized 59Sc; Soviet Union 31C; Telstar satellite 62Sc; United States 28So, 41So; video 56Sc; Vidicon camera tube 50Sc
territorial waters
  Baltic Convention 08P; North Sea Convention 08P
terrorism
  Algerian terrorist campaign on French mainland 58P; Beirut 85P; Conference on Security and Cooperation in Europe 75P; ETA Barcelona car bomb attack 87So; European Convention on the Repression of Terrorism 77So; hijacks *see* hijacks; Iran 81P; Iranian Embassy in London, seizure of 80So; Irgun 46P, 47P, 48P; Irish Republican Army (IRA) *see* Irish Republican Army; Islamic Jihad 83So, 84P; Israeli ambassador to Britain attacked 82P; Israeli team members killed at Munich Olympics 72P; Italy 69So, 79P, 80So; kidnaps, Bucher 71So, Jackson 71So, McCarthy 91So, Moro 78P, Waite 87So; Libya, international terrorism supported by 81P, 86So; Lockerbie air crash 88So; Palestine Liberation Organization (PLO) *see* Palestine Liberation Organization; Red Brigade 78P, 79P, 84So; Sikh extremists 85P, 87P; South Africa 83So; Spain 81So; Suez Canal, mines laid in 84P; Tamil separatists *see* Sri Lanka
Teschen 19P, 38P
Texas Instruments 54Sc, 71Sc; silicon chip 61Sc; solar cells production 91Sc
Thailand
  Association of Southeast Asian Nations (ASEAN) 67So; Kampuchean refugees 85P; Laos, border dispute 88P; Malaysian agreement over communist guerrillas 70P; military coups 71P, 76P, 77P; military takeover 91P; Revolutionary party 71P; Siam renamed 49P; Southeast Asia Treaty Organization (SEATO) 54P; United Nations, complaint to over communist threat 54P; United States forces sent to 62P; Vietnam War 66P, 67P, 69P; Vietnamese invasion 80P; World War II 43P
thalidomide 58Sc, 61Sc, 68Sc
theater
  Abbey Theatre 04C, 07C, 23C, 29C; *Abraham Lincoln* 18C; *Accidental Death of an Anarchist, The* 70C; *L'Aigle a deux têtes* 46C; *All My Sons* 47C; *Amadeus* 79C; *L'Amante anglaise* 68C; *Andorra* 61C; *Anna Christie* 21C; *Antigone* 44C; *Armstrong's Last Goodnight* 64C; *Audience* 75C; *Balcony, The* 56C; Bauhaus stage 25C; *Bedbug, The* 29C; Berlin Proletarian Theater 24C; Berliner Ensemble 49C; *Biographie* 68C; *Birthday Party, The* 58C; *Blacks, The* 58C; *Blood Wedding* 33C; *Blues for Mr Charlie* 64C; *Blithe Spirit* 41C; *Les Bonnes* 48C; *Breath and Other Short Plays* 71C; *Die Buchse der Pandora* 04C; *Camino Real* 53C; *La Cantatrice chauve* 48C; *Caretaker, The* 60C; *Cathleen na Houlihan* 02C; *Caucasian Chalk Circle, The* 48C; *Chairs, The* 51C; *Cherry Orchard, The* 04C; *Chicken Soup with Barley* 58C, 60C; *Cocktail Party, The* 49C; *Confidential Clerk, The* 54C; *Cosi è se vi pare* 17C; *Crucible, The* 53C; *Cyrano de Bergerac* 46C; *Dark is Light Enough, The* 54C; *Death and the King's Horseman* 75C; *Death of a Salesman* 49C; *Delicate Balance, A* 66C; *Devils, The* 61C; *Deirdre* 07C; *Deirdre of the Sorrows* 09So, 11C; *Dream Play, A* 02C; *Dream on Monkey Mountain and other Plays, The* 70C; *Drums in the Night* 22C; *Dumb Waiter, The* 57C; Edinburgh Festival 47C; *Elder Statesman, The* 58C; *En attendant Godot* 52C, 53C, 55C; *Entertaining Mr Sloane* 64C; *Entertainer, The* 57C; *Equus* 73C; *Erdgeist* 04C; *Every Good Boy Deserves Favour* 77C; *Exiles* 18C; Expressionist 09C; *Family Reunion, The* 39C; *Fin de partie* 57C; *Fire-Raisers, The* 58C; *Five Finger Exercise* 58C; *Flood, The* 62C; Futurist 15C, 20C, 24C, New Futurist Theater 24C, Synthetic Theater manifesto 15C; *Ghost Sonata, The* 07C; *Glass Menagerie, The* 44C; *Good Person of Setzuan, The* 43C; *La Guerre de Troie n'aura pas lieu* 35C; *Happy Days* 61C; *Heartbreak House* 19C; *Homecoming, The* 65C; *Hostage, The* 14C, 58C; *Huis Clos* 44C, 46C; *Human Comedy, The* 43C; *I am a Camera* 54C; *Iceman Cometh, The* 46C; *I'm Talking About Jerusalem* 60C; *Inadmissible Evidence* 64C; *Insect Play, The* 21C; *L'Invitation au château* 47C; *Jedermann* 11C; *Le Jet de sang* 27C; *John Bull's Other Island* 04C; *Jumpers* 72C; *Juno and the Paycock* 24C; Kitchen Sink Drama 56C; *König Nicolò, oder So ist das Leben* 01C; La Mama Experimental Theater Club 61C; *Lady's not for Burning, The* 48C; *Last Days of Mankind, The* 21C; *Life of Galileo, The* 43C; *Long Day's Journey into Night* 56C; *Look Back in Anger* 56C; *Lost in Yonkers* 91C; *Luther* 61C; *La Machine infernale* 34C; *Les Mains sales* 48C; *Major Barbara* 05C; *Les Mamelles de Tiresias* 03C; *Man and Superman* 03C, 05C; *Marat/Sade, The* 64C; *Der Marquis von Keith* 00C; *Memorandum, The* 65C; *Mistero Buffo* 78C; *Mörder, Hoffnung der Frauen* 09C, 21C; *Mort sans sépulture* 46C; Moscow Arts Theater 00C; *Mother Courage and her Children* 41C; *Les Mouches* 43C; *Mourning Becomes Electra* 31C; *Mousetrap, The* 52C; *Murder in the Cathedral* 35C; *Night of the Iguana, The* 62C; *No Man's Land* 75C; *Norman Conquests, The* 74C; *Old Times* 71C; Old Vic (London) 50C; *On Baile's Strand* 04C; *Pauvre Bitos* 56C; Performing Rights Society 14C; *Peter Pan* 04C; *Phoenix Too Frequent, A* 46C; *Physicists, The* 62C; *Playboy of the Western World, The* 07C; *Plebeians Rehearse the Uprising, The* 66C; *Plough and the Stars, The* 26C; *Pygmalion* 13C; *Quare Fellow, The* 56C; *Queen Christina* 03C; *Red Roses for Me* 42C; *Redevelopment* 89C; *Reigen* 00C; *Requiem for a Nun* 51C; *Resistible Rise of Arturo Ui, The* 41C; *Rhinoceros* 59C; *Riders to the Sea* 04C; *Ring Round the Moon* 56C; *Romans in Britain, The* 80C; *Roots* 59C, 60C; *Royal Hunt of the Sun, The* 64C; *RUR* (Rossum's Universal Robots) 22C; *St Joan* 24C; *Salome* 05C; *Saved* 65C; *Les Sequestrés d'Altona* 59C; *Serjeant Musgrave's Dance* 59C; *Sex* 27C; Shakespeare Memorial Theatre (UK) 46C; *Silver Tassie, The* 29C; *Six Characters in Search of an Author* 21C; *Sizwe Bansi is Dead* 74C; *Skin of our Teeth, The* 42C; *Soldier's Tale, A* 18C; *Soldaten* 67C; *Der Stellvertreter* 63C; Stratford East Theater Workshop (UK) 59C; *Streetcar named Desire, A* 47C, 48C; Surrealist 27C; *Tango* 65C; *Taste of Honey, A* 59C; *Temptation* 85C; Theater of the Absurd 00C, 48C; Theater of Cruelty 27C; Théâtre Alfred Jarry 27C; *Three Sisters* 01C; *Travesties* 74C; *Ubu enchaîné* 00C; *Ubu roi* 00C; *Die Uhr schlagl eins* 61C; *Uncle Vanya* 00C; *Und Pippa Tanzt* 06C; *View from the Bridge, A* 55C; *Visit, The* 56C; *Waiting for Lefty* 35C; *Wings* 79C; *Winslow Boy, The* 46C; *Yerma* 34C; Ziegfeld Follies 07C; *Zoo Story* 59C
theology
  Bible, New English 61C; "Revised Standard Version" 46C; Dead Sea Scrolls, discovery of 47C; hypothesis that Jesus did not die on the cross 91C; St Paul's epistles, analysis 63Sc; *The quest for the Historical Jesus* 06C; *see also* religion
thermodynamics, third law of 06Sc
thermos flask 04Sc
Third World
  developing nations economic cooperation 81So; external debts 31So, 80So, 84So, 86So, 87So, 88So; participation in world monetary decisions demanded by 71So; poverty gap warning by World Bank 59So; General Agreement on Tariffs and Trade (GATT) 64So, 71So, 88So
Thrace 19P, 20P
Three Mile Island accident 79Sc
Tibet
  Anglo-Chinese treaty 06P; British control 06P, mission to 04P, trading posts 04P, treaty 04P; China grants religious freedom 51P; Chinese control 07P, invasion 50P, martial law, imposition of 89P, lifted 90P, occupation 56P, raid on Chinese troops 13So; revolt against Chinese 59P; Dalai Lama 40So, 56P, flees Tibet 50P, 59P, United Nations, appeals to 61P; integrity guaranteed 07P; Lhasa 04P, 51P; Russian advance 04P
Tiranë, Treaty of 26P
Tiranë, Treaty of (second) 27P
Titanic see ships
Tobago, independence 62P
Tobruk 41P, 42P
Togo 91P
Togoland
  Ghana 57P; independence 60P
Tokyo earthquake 23So
Tonga 00P, 70P; independence 70P
Tonkin, Gulf of 64P
Tours Congress 20P
trade
  ACP/EEC trade

245

ACKNOWLEDGEMENTS

Picture Credits

10–11 Scarborough Beach, HDC
11 Marconi and assistant Kemp, Marconi
32–33 German railroad battery, National Archive, Washington
33 Suffragette, Buckinham palace, 1914, HDC
54–55 LC
55 Charles Lindberg, HDC
76–77 Ziegfield girls, K
77 Family in tent, LC
98–99 Concentration Camp, Lee Miller Archives 1985
99 Frank Sinatra, Moss Hart and Ethel Merman, HDC
120–1 Supermarket, LC
121 Fidel Castro, Havana, 1959, Bettmann Archives, NY
142–3 Berlin Wall, M/Henri Cartier Bresson
143 Protest march, Beale Street, 1968 UPI/Bettmann Archives, NY
164–5 Hippies, California, M/Kubota
165 Richard Nixon's resignation speech, White House, 1974, UPI/Bettmann Archives, NY
186–7 Homeless, London, N/Laurie Sparham
187 Royal wedding, 1981, RF
208–9 Georgia becomes an independant state, M/Zachmann
209 Prince performing, Redferns/Mick Hutson

1 HDC **2–3** HDC **4** RF/Sipa Press **6** K **9** M/Cornell Capa **12** RHPL/Robert Cundy **14** MEPL **16** MOMA/Film Studios Archive **18** Smithsonian Institute **20** from "Die Erste photoreporter" by André Bonet **22** HDC **24** Bettmann Archive, NY **26** HDC **28** RHPL **30** MEPL **34** HDC **36** HDC **38** MEPL **40** PF **42** ILN **44** K **46** PF **48** HDC **50** MEPL **52** HDC **56** RV **58** K **60** RHPL/John G Ross **62** HDC **64** TPS **66** Andromeda Archive **68** TPS **70** K **72** HDC **74** HDC **78** RHPL **80** K **82** HDC **84** HDC **86** M/René Buri **88** PF **90** Suddeutscher Verlag **92** PF **94** HDC **96** K **100** M/Zucca **102** RF/Sipa Press **104** HDC **106** HDC **108** TPS **110** HDC **112** HDC **114** HDC **116** M/Robert Capa **118** HDC **122** Z **124** HDC **126** SPL/Los Alamos National Laboratory **128** HDC **130** PF **132** HDC **134** M/Erich Lessing **136** M/Burt Glinn **138** RF/Sipa Press **140** HDC **144** M/Cornell Capa **146** SPL/Novosti **148** M/Ian Berry **150** HDC **152** Andromeda Archive **154** HDC **156** HDC **158** M/Cornell Capa **160** HDC **162** SPL/NASA **166** RF **168** RF/Sipa Press **170** SPL/NASA **172** HDC **174** RF **176** RHPL **178** RF **180** RHPL **182** RF **184** RF **188** RF **190** RF **192** M/Giles Peress **1194** FSP/M. Hicks **196** FSP/Gaywood **198** RF/Tom Haley **200** SPL/NASA **202** FSP/P. Aventurier **204** FSP/Gamma **206** RF **210** RF/R. Young **212** FSP/L. Van der Stockt

Abbreviations used

FSP	Frank Spooner Pictures, London
HDC	Hulton Deutsch Collection, London
ILN	Illustrated London News
K	The Kobal Collection, London
LC	Library of Congress
M	Magnum Photos, London
MEPL	Mary Evans Picture Library, London
MOMA	Museum of Modern Art, NY
N	Network
PF	Popperfoto, London
RF	Rex Features
RHPL	Robert Harding Picture Library, London
RV	Roger-Viollet
TPS	Topham Picture Source, Kent, UK
UPI	Universal Press Information
Z	Zefa, London

Editorial and research assistance
Sue Phillips, Lin Thomas

Photographs
Thérèse Maitland, Joanne Rapley

Typesetting
Brian Blackmore, Niki Whale

Production
Stephen Elliott

Origination
Eray Scan Ltd, Singapore
Lithocraft, Coventry, UK